Joseph Strutt

A Biographical Dictionary

Vol. I

Joseph Strutt

A Biographical Dictionary
Vol. I

ISBN/EAN: 9783337093020

Printed in Europe, USA, Canada, Australia, Japan

Cover: Foto ©ninafisch / pixelio.de

More available books at **www.hansebooks.com**

A

BIOGRAPHICAL DICTIONARY;

CONTAINING AN HISTORICAL ACCOUNT OF ALL THE

ENGRAVERS,

FROM THE EARLIEST PERIOD OF THE ART OF
ENGRAVING TO THE PRESENT TIME;

AND

A SHORT LIST OF THEIR MOST ESTEEMED WORKS.

WITH

THE CYPHERS, MONOGRAMS, AND PARTICULAR MARKS, USED BY
EACH MASTER, ACCURATELY COPIED FROM THE ORIGINALS,
AND PROPERLY EXPLAINED.

TO WHICH IS PREFIXED,

AN ESSAY ON THE RISE AND PROGRESS OF THE ART
OF ENGRAVING, BOTH ON COPPER AND ON WOOD.
WITH SEVERAL CURIOUS SPECIMENS OF THE PERFORMANCES OF THE
MOST ANCIENT ARTISTS.

By *JOSEPH STRUTT.*

VOL. I.

LONDON:
PRINTED BY J. DAVIS,
FOR ROBERT FAULDER, NEW BOND STREET.
M,DCC,LXXXV.

PREFACE.

THE Art of Engraving was never more encouraged than in the prefent day, efpecially in England, where almoſt every man of taſte is in ſome degree a collector of prints. It is therefore rather extraordinary, that a work of this kind, which I need not ſay is greatly wanted, ſhould have been ſo long neglected; particularly when we recollect, that we have not any ſatisfactory account of the Engravers, or their works, in the Engliſh tongue.

In France the example has been ſet us by Baſan, who, with the aſſiſtance of the Notes of M. Mariette, has given us a regular account of upwards of a thouſand artiſts. It is a very ingenious compilation, and, as far as it goes, exceedingly uſeful. The deſcriptions which he gives of the prints belonging to each artiſt are very accurate, and the obſervations which occur, are no ſmall proofs of the ſolidity of his judgment; but he has generally omitted to inform us of the ſtyle or manner in which they worked: neither has he given us the marks or monograms, which they often fubſtituted inſtead of their names; and theſe omiſſions render his work much leſs valuable than it would otherwiſe have been, becauſe it affords us but little aſſiſtance in diſtinguiſhing the works of one maſter from thoſe of another of the ſame name, or who might uſe the ſame mark.

The other foreign publications upon the ſubject, though very multifarious, are, neverthelefs, exceedingly defective; few of them ſpeak of the Art of Engraving abſtractedly; and the greater part of them are little more than unſatisfactory catalogues of the names of the artiſts, or liſts of their works, without any proper deſcription. If Profeſſor Chriſt had paid ſufficient attention to this particular, his Dictionary of Monograms would have afforded infinitely more aſſiſtance in diſtinguiſhing the works of the old maſters, the one from the other; though it is confeſſedly, as it ſtands, a very deſirable performance. In Engliſh, we have Evelyn's *Sculptura*, a ſmall book entitled *Sculptura Hiſtorico-*

PREFACE.

Hiſtorico-Technica, compiled originally by the elder Faithorne; and *The Series of Engravers,* publiſhed at Cambridge: Theſe, excepting *Catalogues* of particular maſters works, are all the books I can recollect of any conſequence, in which the artiſts are generally ſpoken of (for Virtue's Catalogue of the Engravers, publiſhed by the Hon. Mr. Walpole, is confined to the Engliſh ſchool only); and that they are very defective, a ſmall degree of examination will abundantly prove. I need not ſay how expenſive it would be to purchaſe all the publications, which bear any reference to the Art of Engraving; but I fear, the information to be gained, from the far greater part of them, would be neither adequate to the coſt, nor the ſtudy which muſt neceſſarily be beſtowed upon them.

In the proſecution of the preſent work, I have followed Mr. Pilkington's plan, and arranged the names of the artiſts alphabetically, (in the manner of a dictionary) rather than chronologically; becauſe by this method they are much more eaſily referred to. But I thought it highly neceſſary to add, for the conveniency of the Reader, a Chronological Table of the ſame names, with a Liſt of the Diſciples of each Maſter; which will, of courſe, be placed at the end of the ſecond volume.

Nearly three thouſand names are included in the narrow limits of this work; the lives of the artiſts muſt, of courſe, be drawn up in as ſhort a compaſs as poſſible. I am well aware of the dryneſs of a mere Dictionary Hiſtory, as alſo of the frequent repetitions which muſt neceſſarily occur; and I have endeavoured to compenſate for theſe defects, by a diligent attention to truth: at the ſame time, whenever I could meet with an intereſting anecdote to enliven the performance, I have gladly inſerted it. But ſo many of the engravers lived and died in obſcurity, that little, very little matter of amuſement, excluſive of the arts, can be gathered from the barren ſoil. Theſe unfavourable circumſtances will not, I hope, be placed to my account, even when it appears, that I have choſen rather to leave the ſubject naked as it is, than to adorn it in a more pleaſing manner, at the expence of veracity.

With

PREFACE.

With respect to the general character of each artist, I have written as an Engraver, and endeavoured as clearly as possible, to point out the style in which he worked, and wherein his great excellence consisted; and upwards of twenty years experience, may, perhaps, plead a little in favour of my judgment. I have constantly, however, endeavoured to deliver my sentiments in the most impartial manner; and if I am in any instance thought to speak too highly in favour of the artist, I hope to claim some small share of indulgence, because I constantly speak as I feel, and never presume to give my opinion positively, without adding the reasons upon which it is grounded.

The prints contained in the several lists, are either such as are most generally esteemed, or such as best illustrate the criticisms I give of each master's works. I am too well convinced of the difficulty of deciding precisely upon the works of a great master; or saying positively which is his best print. I freely own, that looking over the battles of Alexander, engraved by Girard Audran from Le Brun, I have constantly considered that as best, which I last examined. Finding it so very hard a task to form a decisive opinion in my own mind, I could not reasonably presume to dictate to others; especially as I am certain that this book must fall into the hands of many, whose judgment is greatly superior to my own.

The work is preceded by an introductory Essay on the Origin and Progress of the Art of Engraving, with copies from the works of the oldest and scarcest masters; and at the end of each volume are given two tables, the first containing the initial letters used by the artists mentioned in it; and the other, an explanation of the monograms, cyphers, and other marks, with which they occasionally distinguished their engravings.

The Reader, by barely looking over the outlines of this work, will readily conceive the great labour and difficulty which must attend the prosecution of it, and on this account, I hope for indulgence. Many errors must necessarily have escaped my notice, not a few of them arising from the obscurity of a great number of the artists, and the

confusion

confufion their works are fubject to, from the want of proper diftinction; feveral of them ufing precifely the fame mark, and copying from each others engravings. Many omiffions doubtlefs will be found; but to compenfate in fome meafure for them, it muft be remembered, that I have made an addition of nearly two thoufand names, to the Catalogue of Bafan; and, I hope, at leaft, that the name of no artift of any great confequence will be found wanting in the work. To the candour of the Public I now fubmit it, and doubt not but that the judgment I fhall receive, will be given without partiality.

CHARLTON STREET,
AUGUST 1, 1785.

AN

ESSAY

ON THE

ART OF ENGRAVING,

WITH A FULL ACCOUNT

OF ITS

ORIGIN AND *PROGRESS.*

CHAPTER I.

The Excellency of the Art of Engraving; the Qualifications requisite for an Engraver; the different Modes of Engraving; and some Observations concerning the Criticisms upon Prints.

SECT. I. THE improvement of the Arts has ever been considered as an object of great importance, by the enlightened part of mankind; and there is no nation in the world, where the art of engraving is held in higher esteem, or more generously encouraged, than in England. Hence it is, that Great Britain, at this time, abounds with artists, equal in number, and superior in abilities, to those of any other country. A view then of the rise and progress of an art, of such national consequence, naturally becomes interesting, not only to the engravers themselves, but to all who profess the love of it. And if England can lay no claim to the invention of engraving, we shall prove at least hereafter, that her pretensions to the early exercise of it are as justly founded, as those of the Italians or the Germans.

With respect to the use and excellency of the art of engraving, I beg leave to subjoin the following observations. They were drawn up by a gentleman of great taste, and are the result of a critical examination of the works of the greatest masters; and will, I trust, be still more acceptable to the public, as they are not the remarks of an engraver, but of a gentleman, no otherways interested in the cause, than as a man of science, and a lover of the arts.

" Of all the imitative arts, painting itself not excepted, engraving is the most applicable
" to general use, and the most resorted to from the necessities of mankind. From its
" earliest infancy, it has been called in, as an assistant in almost every branch of know-
" ledge; and has, in a very high degree, facilitated the means of communicating our
" ideas, by representing to the sight whatever is capable of visible imitation; and thereby
" preventing that circumlocution, which would ill explain, in the end, what is immedi-
" ately conceived from the actual representation of the object.'

" From the facility of being multiplied, prints have derived an advantage over paint-
" ings, by no means inconsiderable. They are found to be more durable; which may,
" however,

"however, in some degree, be attributed to the different methods in which they are pre-
"served. Many of the best paintings of the early masters have generally had the mis-
"fortune to be either painted on walls, or deposited in large and unfrequented, and
"consequently damp and destructive buildings; whilst a print, passing, at distant inter-
"vals, from the *porte feuille* of one collector to that of another, is preserved without any
"great exertion of its owner: And hence it happens, that whilst the pictures of Raphael
"have mouldered from their walls, or deserted their canvass, the prints of his friend and
"contemporary, Mark Antonio Raimondi, continue in full perfection to this day, and give us
"a lively idea of the beauties of those paintings, which, without their assistance, had been
"lost to us for ever; or, at least, could have been only known to us, like those of Zeuxis
"and Apelles, by the descriptions which former writers on these subjects have left us.

"Perhaps there are no representations, which interest so strongly the curiosity of man-
"kind as portraits. A high degree of pleasure, of which almost every person is suscep-
"tible, is experienced from contemplating the looks and countenances of those men, who,
"by their genius or their virtues, have entitled themselves to the admiration and esteem
"of future ages. It is only in consequence of the facility, with which prints are multi-
"plied from the same engraving, that this laudable appetite is so frequently gratified.
"Whilst the original portrait is limited to the wall of a private chamber, or adorns some
"distant part of the world, a correct transcript of it, exhibiting the same features, and
"the same character, gives to the public at large the full representation of the object of
"their veneration or esteem.

"In this country, where the genuine paintings of the ancient masters are extremely
"scarce, we are much indebted to prints for the truth of our ideas, respecting the merits
"of such masters. And this is no bad criterion, especially when the painter, as is fre-
"quently the case, has left engravings or etchings of his own. With respect to the prin-
"cipal excellencies of a picture, a print is equally estimable with a painting. We have
"there every perfection of design, composition, and drawing; and the outline is marked
"with a degree of precision, which frequently excels the picture; so that where the merit
"of the master consists more particularly in the knowledge of these primary branches of
"the art, his prints may be better than his paintings; as was notoriously the case with
"Peter Testa, who, possessed of every excellence of a painter, except a knowledge in
"the art of colouring, acquired that reputation by his etchings, which his paintings
"never could have procured him.

"A knowledge of the style and manner of the different masters is only to be obtained by
"a frequent inspection, and comparison of their works. If we were to judge of Raphael
"himself from some of his pictures, we should be disposed to refuse our assent to that praise,
"which he has now for so many centuries enjoyed. Every master has at times painted
"below his usual standard, and consequently is not to be judged of by a single picture; and
"where is the collection, that affords sufficient specimens of any of the elder masters, to
"enable a person to become a complete judge of their merits?---Can we from a few pic-
"tures form an adequate idea of the invention and imagination of a painter,---of the
"inexhaustible variety of form and feature, which is the true characteristic of superior
"excellence? But let us look into a collection of prints after any eminent artist, engraved
"either by himself or others, and we shall then have an opportunity of judging of his
"merits, in the first and indispensable qualifications of a painter. If we find grandeur of
"design, united with elegant composition and accurate drawing, we have the strongest
"testimonies of superior abilities; and from a general comparison and accurate observa-
"tion of a number of such prints, we may venture to form to ourselves a decisive opinion,
"respecting the merit of such masters. On examining the prints after Raphael, we find,
"that his first manner was harsh, and Gothic; in short, a transcript of his master
"Perugino; but that from some fortunate circumstance, he afterwards adopted that sub-
"lime and graceful manner, which he ever retained.

"Wherever a painter has himself handled the graver, his prints are most generally
"impressed with the same character as his paintings; and are therefore likely to give us a
"very accurate idea of his style. The prints of Albert Durer, Rembrandt, and Sal-
' vator

" vator Rofa, are all fuch exact counterparts of their paintings, that at this time, when the
" colouring of their pictures is often fo far changed, as to anfwer little farther purpofe,
" than that of light and fhadow, they become in a manner their rivals; and, in the gene-
" ral acceptation of the world, the prints of fome of thefe artifts have been as highly
" valued, as their paintings.
" Independent of the advantages which prints afford us, when confidered as accurate re-
" prefentations of paintings, and imitations of fuperior productions, they are no lefs valuable
" for their pofitive merit, as immediate reprefentations of nature. For it muft be
" recollected, that the art of engraving has not always been confined to the copying other
" productions, but has frequently itfelf afpired to originality, and has, in this light, pro-
" duced more inftances of its excellence, than in the other. Albert Durer, Goltzius,
" and Rembrandt, amongft the Dutch and Germans; Parmigiano and Della Bella,
" amongft the Italians, and Callot amongft the French, have publifhed many prints,
" the fubjects of which, there is great reafon to fuppofe, were never painted. Thefe
" prints may therefore be confidered as original pictures of thofe mafters, deficient only in
" thofe particulars, in which a print muft neceffarily be inferior to a painting.
" The preceding diftinction may perhaps throw fome light on the proper method of
" arranging and claffing a collection of prints, which has been a matter of no fmall dif-
" ficulty. As an art imitating another, the principal fhould take the lead, and the defign,
" compofition, and drawing in a print, being previous requifites to the manner of execu-
" tion, and finifhing; prints engraved after paintings fhould be arranged under the name
" of the painter: and every perfon, who looks upon engraving only as auxiliary to
" painting, will confequently adopt this mode of arrangement. But when engraving is
" confidered as an original art, as imitating nature without the intervention of other
" methods, then it will certainly be proper to regulate the arrangement, according to the
" names of the engravers.
" The invention of printing, in the fifteenth century, was undoubtedly the greateft
" acquifition, which mankind ever made towards the advancement of general fcience.
" Before that event, the accumulated wifdom of ages was confined to the leaves of a
" few mouldering manufcripts, too expenfive to be generally obtained, and too highly
" valued to be often trufted out of the hands of the owner. Hiftory affords us many
" inftances of the difficulty, with which even the loan of a book was procured, and of fure-
" ties being required to be anfwerable for its return; but the difcovery of printing broke
" down the barriers, which had fo long obftructed the diffufion of learning; and the rapid
" progrefs in civilization, which immediately took place, is itfelf the happieft teftimony
" of the great utility of the invention. What printing has been, with refpect to general
" fcience, engraving has been to the arts; and the works of the old Italian mafters will
" be indebted to engraving for that perpetuity, which the invention of printing has
" fecured to the Jerufalem of Taffo, and the tragedies of Shakefpeare and Corneille."

SECT. II. Of all the fpecies of engraving, that of hiftorical fubjects is the moft noble, and requires the greateft exertions of genius and application to bring it to perfection. But before I enter into an enquiry concerning the neceffary qualifications to form a good hiftorical engraver, I wifh to make, what appears to me very neceffary, a proper diftinction between tafte and judgment, abftractedly confidered, as relative to the arts, particularly the executive part of them.

Judgment I conceive to be the refult of a uniform habit of thinking, founded upon fome given principle, received into the mind, as the ftandard of excellence, from which a comparifon is formed, and things are admitted as perfect or imperfect, in proportion as they approach to or recede from thofe ideas of beauty, by which the mind is prepoffeffed. Hence it appears, that a man of judgment only will be a mannerift, in a greater or lefs degree; and this proportion muft alfo depend upon the number of the objects the artift unites together, upon which he forms thofe decided ideas in his mind. If the object be fingle, of courfe his ideas will be unvaried; and the fame ftyle of execution will appear continually, and cannot fail of difgufting at laft, though excellent in itfelf to a fuperior degree.

This habit of thinking, and expressing the thoughts, may be acquired by practice, whether it relates to the speculative notion of prints, or the manual execution of them.

Taste, I should wish to define, as the effect of a natural genius, or propensity in the mind, by which it is led to assimilate to itself a diversity of such forms as are generally allowed to be beautiful, and place them in such points of view, as shall render them agreeable to the eye. And this propensity must exist in the mind, previous to the application of the foreign aids of instruction and study, which, though they may, and certainly do, cultivate and improve the genius, can never bestow it. A blind man might as soon reason concerning the beauty of colours, and a deaf man upon the harmony of sounds, as a superior artist be produced by dint of study only. A neat, stiff, laboured engraving he might accomplish; but a spirited, free, and unaffected performance, is far beyond the reach of simple industry. It is the union of genius and judgment, which completes the artist; and without them both he can never be superlatively great.

On this account, we frequently see a man possessed of great judgment in drawing, and every other requisite for the execution of a plate, excepting taste, produce a cold, formal work; and though we cannot help perhaps admiring the patience of the artist, and the precision, with which he has finished the engraving; yet this admiration is mixed with a sort of pity for him. We conceive a painful idea of drudgery, which still increases, in proportion as we examine the performance; and we are obliged to confess, that it is no more equal to the animated works of genius, than the motionless statue of the animal, to the living animal itself.---To be convinced of this, let us compare the works of Jerom Wierix, or any of the precise German masters, with those of Henry Goltzius, or Gerard Audran. Upon the same principle it is, that all the learning in the world, exclusive of an animated conception, could never make a Shakespeare or a Milton.

These observations naturally lead me to others equally important, by which I mean to prove a manifest difference between neatness and high finishing, which are too frequently confounded. The first of these consists in the precision and exactness of the mechanical execution of a plate; the second, in the harmony and powerfulness of the effect, and a judicious distribution of the light and shadow. It is true, some proportion of neatness is also requisite, in order to produce a highly finished effect; but a print, on the other hand, may be extremely neat, and yet, when held at a distance, have all the appearance of a slight sketch. To elucidate these observations, I must again have recourse to the old engravers, and more particularly Jerom Wierix and his followers with respect to neatness; and the Sadelers, Cornelius Cort, and Villamena, nay, we may add Henry Goltzius himself: in all the works of these artists, though executed in a masterly manner, we find the lights left clear and broad, not in masses, but frequent spots, equally powerful upon the distances, as upon the principal objects, which confuses the subject, and fatigues the eye. These, when compared with the more modern engravings of Drevet and Edelink in France, and of Woollett, with other great artists in our own country, (where the management of the claire-obscure has certainly been carried to a very superior pitch of excellence) will sufficiently manifest the difference.

From nature an historical engraver should possess strong mental faculties, a lively genius, and a just eye for proportion. To these he must add great application; the most excellent models of the art he ought constantly to have before him; and, above all things, he should acquire a thorough grounded knowledge of the human figure. Harmony of effect, and the management of the claire-obscure, are also to be considered as absolutely necessary. And having acquired a facility of managing the point, or graver, or rather of both, let him always bear in memory, that however he may suppose himself arrived at a superior degree of excellence, it will be greatly to his discredit, as an engraver, if he forgets to pay that attention to the picture he copies, which is due to its author; and, instead of giving us the style of the painter, exhibits one of his own. For though he should justly avoid the servile manner of a Chateau, he certainly ought not, on the other hand, to take the unwarrantable liberty of a Dorigny, who, engraving from Raphael, forgot the master, and transmitted to us his own mannered designs, under the sanction of that celebrated name. I need not, I hope, apologize for adding, that I consider

ON THE ORIGIN AND PROGRESS OF ENGRAVING. 5

fider Gerard Audran, without exception, as the greateſt hiſtorical engraver that ever exiſted; and I think his works will abundantly prove, that he poſſeſſed, in a ſuperior degree, every one of thoſe requiſites, which I have mentioned, in the character of an engraver, as drawn above.

The illiberal reflections, which, by ignorant pretenders to the art, have been caſt upon the engravers, hardly merit an anſwer, and particularly, when not mentioned under proper reſtrictions; namely, that they deſerve not the name of artiſts, but are to be conſidered as mere copyiſts. Now, not to mention the works of Albert Durer, Lucas Van Leyden, Goltzius, Parmigiano, Della Bella, Callot, and a variety of other maſters, which are perfectly original, we may examine thoſe only, which are profeſſedly copies from the pictures of other maſters. And then we muſt obſerve, that every tranſlator of a poem, however meritorious, falls preciſely under the ſame cenſure; but how little underſtanding muſt that man poſſeſs, who would tell us, that Hobbes diſplayed as great an exertion of genius, in his Homer *done into Engliſh*, as Pope, in the elegant tranſlation, which he has given us of that poet, and which is not more generally than juſtly admired. Admitting (which, I believe, is far from being true,) that the firſt has adhered to the preciſe and literal meaning of each word, compared with the original, can it be ſaid, he felt what he wrote, or that the leaſt ſpark of poetical animation can be found in the whole work? whilſt the other enters, as it were, into the ſoul of the poet, (if I may be allowed the expreſſion) and writes, as Homer might have been ſuppoſed to have done, had he been a native of England. What the poet has to do with reſpect to the idiom of the language, the engraver has alſo to perform in his tranſlation, for ſo it may be called, of the original picture upon the copper; with this manifeſt diſadvantage, that he has only one colour given him to expreſs the ſame harmony and powerfulneſs of effect, which the painter ſo happily produces with variety. Would Raphael have ſpoken ſo diſrepectfully of Marc Antonio, Rubens of Bolſwert, or Le Brun of Gerard Audran?---The reſpect which they paid to theſe admirable engravers, plainly evinces the contrary.

SECT. III. Prints may naturally be arranged under three general heads: I. Hiſtorical and Emblematical Subjects; II. Landſcapes; III. Portraits. And all theſe may eaſily be ſubdivided at pleaſure.

The different modes of engraving are the following:

In STROKES cut through a thin wax, laid upon the copper, with a *point*, and theſe ſtrokes bitten or corroded into the copper with *aqua fortis*. This is called *etching*.

In STROKES with the graver alone, unaſſiſted by *aqua fortis*. In this inſtance, the deſign is traced with a ſharp tool, called a *dry point*, upon the plate; and the ſtrokes are cut or ploughed upon the copper with an inſtrument, diſtinguiſhed by the name of a *graver*.

In STROKES, firſt etched, and afterwards finiſhed with the *graver:* by this expedient the two former methods are united.

In DOTS without ſtrokes, which are executed with the point upon the wax or ground, bitten in with the *aqua fortis*, and afterwards harmonized with the *graver*; by the means of which inſtrument ſmall dots are made; or with the graver alone, as in the fleſh and finer parts, unaſſiſted with the *point*.

In DOTS, firſt etched, and afterwards harmonized with the *dry point*, performed by a little *hammer*, called *opus mallei*, or *the work of the hammer*, as practiſed by Lutma and others.

In MEZZOTINTO, which is performed by a dark barb, or ground, being raiſed uniformly upon the plate, with a toothed tool. The deſign being traced upon the plate, the light parts are ſcraped off by inſtruments for that purpoſe, in proportion as the effect requires.

In AQUA TINTO, a newly invented method of engraving. The outline is firſt etched, and afterwards a ſort of waſh is laid by the *aqua fortis* upon the plate, reſembling drawings in Indian ink, biſter, &c.

On WOOD, performed with a ſingle block, on which the deſign is traced with a pen, and thoſe parts which ſhould be white carefully hollowed out; and this block is afterwards printed by the letter-preſs printers, in the ſame manner as they print a book.

On

On wood, performed with two, three, or more blocks; the firſt having the outlines cut upon it; the ſecond is reſerved for the darker ſhadows; and the third for the ſhadows, which terminate upon the lights; and theſe are ſubſtituted in their turn, each print receiving an impreſſion from every block. This mode of engraving is called chiaro-ſcuro, and was deſigned to repreſent the drawings of the old maſters.

On WOOD and on COPPER: in theſe the outline is engraved in a bold, dark ſtyle upon the copper; and two or more blocks of wood are ſubſtituted to produce the darker and lighter ſhadows, as before.

SECT. IV. In criticiſing upon prints, the following obſervations may not be unworthy of notice, ſo far, at leaſt, as they have any tendency to prevent an over-haſty deciſion with reſpect to their merit; for certainly no artiſt is ſo liable to accidents, which may lead the unwary to misjudge of his works, as the engraver. His plates may be badly printed: copies may be impoſed upon the collector for originals; and retouched impreſſions of no value may be ſold for genuine. Neither are theſe all the diſadvantageous circumſtances, which ſhould come under our conſideration. The works of the artiſt himſelf may be unequal, eſpecially when they are exceedingly numerous. In this caſe, it is abſolutely neceſſary for the collector to ſee all, or the greater part of the engravings by ſuch a maſter, or perhaps a prejudicial judgment may be formed from his worſt prints, whilſt the moſt excellent remain unſeen.

The works of all the old maſters lie under theſe manifeſt diſadvantages; but none more particularly ſo, than thoſe known by the name of little maſters, who are chiefly German artiſts, and diſtinguiſhed by the epithet of *little*, from the diminutiveneſs of their works. Their plates, whilſt in good condition, have often been badly printed; but the impreſſions moſt generally met with, are ſuch, as are ſpoiled by retouching, ſo as not to retain the leaſt ſhadow of that excellence, which diſtinguiſhes the print in its original ſtate.

For theſe cauſes I conceive, no decided opinion ought to be formed of the works of an engraver, in general, and of the old maſters, in particular, till a number of their prints, and thoſe too fine impreſſions, have been carefully examined. If theſe rules were candidly attended to, I am ſure the latter would ſtand much higher in the public eſtimation, than they do at preſent.

Prints, if they be original works, may be conſidered as beautiful, I. With reſpect to the drawing, the ſpirit of the compoſition, or the management of the claire-obſcure, excluſive of the mechanical part of the execution; and of this ſpecies are the painter's etchings; or II. Principally for the excellence of the mechanical part of the engraving, as in the works of Wierix, Beham, and others of the German ſchool eſpecially; or III. For the correctneſs of deſign, and freedom of execution, as in thoſe of Henry Goltzius and his contemporaries; or IV. For the beauty of the finiſhing; and V. When they are copies from the paintings of others, the more ſtriking reſemblance they bear to the originals, from which they are taken. And no prints ought abſolutely to be thrown aſide, if they excel in any one of theſe particular beauties, however they may be deficient in another. For want of this diſcrimination, we too frequently ſee many of the moſt valuable works of the old maſters, and etchings of the fineſt painters, paſſed over with contempt by the unſkilful, when nothing can be more certain, than that the etchings of Guido, and other great artiſts, are as excellent in their way, as the moſt highly finiſhed and ſtriking engravings of Edelink, Nanteuil, or Poilly.

Neither is it reaſonable entirely to condemn the works of an artiſt, becauſe he followed the eſtabliſhed taſte of his country. This was a fault too much authoriſed by cuſtom; but indeed originality of taſte is much confined; few, very few, have poſſeſſed it; and even of thoſe, all have not been ſucceſsful. If the ſtyle of drawing or compoſition is not agreeable to the ideas we have formed of excellence in our own mind, ſhall we entirely paſs over the beauties, which may be found either in correctneſs of drawing, neatneſs, or harmony of effect? The fertility of invention, and variety of character, which appear in the works of Albert Durer, make great amends for his want of that ſimplicity and correctneſs, which is the characteriſtic of the Italian ſchools; and his ſkill in the mechanical

part

part of the art deferves every poffible encomium. Upon this principle, a perfon, fond of a powerful effect, would throw afide the works of Henry Goltzius, becaufe they are not equal, in that refpect, to thofe of Rembrandt Gerretz, difregarding, at the fame time, the fuperior excellence, and correctnefs of drawing, which they poffefs, and the aftonifhing freedom of execution with the graver, by none out-done, if ever equalled by any.

CHAPTER II.

The Antiquity of the Art of Engraving, and by whom it appears to have been firft practifed.

THOSE productions of art, by which the mind is delighted or improved, naturally intereft our affections. We feel, as it were, an obligation incumbent on us, and are folicitous of tracing out the man, to whom we ftand indebted for the gratification we have received. And it appears to be a tribute juftly due to him, to refcue, if poffible, his name from oblivion, and place the laurel he deferves upon his brow. If we fail in this, the art itfelf becomes the object of our refearches. We wifh to know, at what period it was invented, and where it originated. If it fhould be faid, this knowledge does not contribute to the improvement of the art, or add to the merit of its author, yet the defire of attaining it proves, at leaft, the decided part we take in their favour, and is a convincing argument, that our hearts are fufficiently warmed with gratitude to repay the obligation we conceive ourfelves to lie under, if it were in our power.

But refearches of this kind, efpecially with refpect to an art, which has gone through fo many changes as that of engraving, and may be divided into fo many different branches, are by no means to be neglected; for they may not only be pleafing to thofe, who intereft themfelves in its caufe; but by fhowing the variety of modes, which have been practifed, in its gradual advancement from its infancy to its prefent maturity, may be ufefully confidered by the artifts themfelves, and prove perhaps productive of improvements hereafter, which at prefent are not thought of.

There is no art, but mufic excepted, which can pofitively claim a priority to that of engraving; and though its inventor cannot be difcovered, there is little doubt of its exiftence long before the flood. Tubal Cain, the fon of Lamech, according to Mofes, was the firft artificer in metals. It is faid of him, in the original, that he was,

לטש כל־חרש נחשת וברזל

The whetter or fharpner of all inftruments of copper and of iron. And thefe words imply great fkill in metallurgy; for the working of iron, and fetting an edge upon copper, fo as to make inftruments fit for ufe, are proofs, that Tubal Cain was no fmall proficient in that art. To what degree of perfection he carried the mechanical part of his profeffion, cannot be difcovered; but we may reafonably fuppofe, his performances were rude, and fimple in their forms, and that he confulted ufe, rather than elegance or beauty; and probably had no leifure to ornament them with unneceffary decorations. But as his defcendants increafed, and the number of workmen was multiplied, new inventions were naturally brought forward, and comparative merit, of confequence, would enhance the value of one man's performances, in preference to thofe of another. Hence neatnefs, and even elegance, progreffively became neceffary; and the love of finery, fo generally prevalent in the human mind, eafily led men to prefer thofe works, which were moft handfomely decorated. The ornamental parts of drefs, as clafps, buckles, rings and diadems; alfo cups, and other houfehold furniture, together with the arms of military chieftains, were probably enriched with the firft fpecimens of engraving. Thefe, in the remoteft periods, appear to have been ornamented in this ftyle, even among the moft barbarous nations: rude portraitures are mentioned, as carved and engraved upon the fhields, and other accoutrements of war.

The

ON THE ORIGIN AND PROGRESS OF ENGRAVING.

The immediate defcendants of Tubal Cain may lay a claim to the invention of the art of engraving, which appears to me to be well founded, and certainly prior to any exhibited in profane hiftory, unlefs the Grecian Vulcan really was, as fome have thought, no other perfon than Tubal Cain, diftinguifhed by another name. To what length the exercife of this art was carried by our Antediluvian progenitors, is totally unknown. Soon after the flood, if ancient records are to be credited, it had, as well as fculpture, made a confiderable progrefs. I fhall however pafs over the works of the old Greek and Roman writers, concerning the hiftory of thefe early periods; for the facts, as related by them, are not only exceedingly doubtful in themfelves; but convey no certain intelligence.

Terah, the father of Abraham, lived in the days of Nimrod, and he is faid to have been the firft man after the flood, who fabricated carved images; and the carving of that remote æra, in many inftances bore a great refemblance to engraving, and frequently is not diftinguifhed from it. Thefe poffibly might be the very images, which Rachel afterwards ftole from her father Laban, and are called תרפים *Teraphim* by the facred hiftorian; and by Laban himfelf diftinguifhed by the name of Gods; for he fays to Jacob,

למה גנבת את־אלהי

Why haft thou ftolen away my Gods? And thefe are fuppofed to have been perfonal reprefentations of the Deity.

Mofes, when he fpeaks particularly concerning the art of engraving, does not mention it by any means as a new invention, but feems to confider it as too well underftood among the Ifraelites, to need any previous defcription. For though Bezaleel and Aholiab are the firft names, mentioned profeffedly as engravers, and by way of commendation of their excellence, it is faid, that *God filled them with wifdom of heart to work all manner of work of the engraver, &c.* Yet this does not by any means apply the invention of the art to either of them; for indeed, prior to the commencement of the workmanfhip for the tabernacle, it is faid of Aaron, that he fafhioned the calf he had made *with the graving tool*. It is highly probable, that this art, among a variety of others, as, cafting of metals, forming of images, carving in wood and ftone, working embroidery, &c. was learned by the Ifraelites in Egypt. The Egyptians were certainly famous at that time for their knowledge; for which reafon St. Stephen, fpeaking in praife of Mofes, fays, *he was learned in all the wifdom of the Egyptians.*

There are feveral words, ufed by the facred hiftorian to exprefs the works of the engraver; among which the following are more particularly applicable to my purpofe. The firft occurs, Exodus xxviii. verfe 9. פתח fignifies *to make an opening or incifion*; and hence comes the noun פתח with its plural פתוחים *engravings*; in the Septuagint it is rendered by γλυψις.——In the 11th verfe of the fame chapter we have alfo, חרש the name of the engraver, one of the original fenfes of the root is *to plough up*; fo that he is called *the plougher*; and frequently the word אבן *a ftone*, is added for diftinction, and both together may be properly tranflated *the plougher* or *engraver in ftone*. No word can exprefs more perfectly the operations of the engraver on copper or other metals in the prefent day, when performed fimply with the graver, (which is of all modes the moft ancient,) than the verb *to plough*; though it is true, the word חרש is principally applied to the mechanic in general, but his way of working is ufually diftinguifhed. To thefe we may add, קלע which occurs in the 6th chapter of the firft book of Kings, and is ufed to exprefs the *hollowing out of the carved work upon the* cherubim, palm trees, and open flowering in the fanctuary, which were afterwards *filled up* with gold. This word in the Latin Vulgate is rendered *fculpfit*; by others *cælavit*: and by Junius *incidit*.

The tables which God delivered to Mofes are faid, Exodus xxxii. 16. to be *the work of God, and the writing was the writing of God* חרות engraved *upon the tables.* In the Chaldee and Syriac verfions the word is ufed in the fame fenfe. The Seventy render it κικολαμμενη, engraved; and the Latin Vulgate *fculpta*; and St. Paul, 11 Cor. ii. 7. εντετυπωμενη, engraved. Both פתח and קלע are expreffed in the Syriac verfion by the words גלף or גליף from whence evidently the Greek word γλυφω. I fhall only add the following remarkable paffage from the book of Job, ch. xix. ver. 23, 24. which Mr. Evelyn fays, comprehends and alludes to all the forts of ancient writing and engraving, both plates, ftone, and ftyle.

ON THE ORIGIN AND PROGRESS OF ENGRAVING.

מי־יתן אפו ויכתבון מלי מי־תן בספר ויחקו:
בעט ברזל ועפרת לעד בצור יחצבון:

which literally rendered in Englifh will read thus : *Who fhall give* (or ordain) *now, that my words fhall be drawn* (or written?) *who fhall give, that in a book* (or memorial) *they fhall be delineated. That with a pen* (or graver) *of iron and lead, they fhall be hewn out in the rock for ever?* In this paffage the word עט may fignify any fmall inftrument of iron, ufed either as a ftylus or pen to mark upon wax or other ductile fubftances ; and alfo as a graver to cut out and engrave upon metals, in the fame manner as Mofes, Exodus xxxii. verfe 4, ufes the word חרט adding the affix ב, that is, *with a flender inftrument of iron*, Aaron fafhioned the brazen calf, which the Seventy tranflate ἐν τῇ γραφίδι ; and in the Chaldee we have the word עפצא *ftylus fculptorius*, or the *engraving tool*, as it is properly tranflated in our Englifh bible. In the Syriac verfion it is rendered ܡܣܦܐ *Typa* ; and the Samaritan gives it a larger fignification, calling it only a *marking tool*.

A fufficient number of words, befides thefe already quoted, might be produced from the above languages, equally applicable to the art of engraving. But after all, it is, doubtlefs, very difficult to determine how far the work of the ancient engraver may bear a refemblance to that of the artift of the prefent day ; becaufe the words above-mentioned are equally applicable to carving and chafing. The beft mode of explaining them, will therefore be, to have recourfe to the reliques of antiquity, and learn from them, if poffible, how far thefe arts may have been blended together, and with what propriety we can fuppofe them, in many cafes, to refer to the works of the engraver only.

CHAPTER III.

The Remains of Antiquity confidered.—The military Accoutrements of the barbarous Nations ornamented with Engravings.—An Egyptian Figure of Ifis defcribed.—The Defcription of an Etrufcan Patera and Parazonium.—The Style of Engraving among the Anglo-Saxons.—The Brafs Plates on Tomb-ftones of ancient Date—Variety of Religious and Domeftic Ornaments executed by the Engraver.

The firft engravings, profeffedly mentioned as fuch, are thofe which we have already fpoken of, executed by Aholiab and Bezaleel, for the decoration of the Tabernacle, and the ornaments for the drefs of Aaron. It is particularly faid, that upon the plate of gold, which he wore upon his tiara or mitre, the words קדש ליהוה *holinefs to the Lord*, were engraved. But thefe productions of the art, as has been before obferved, are by no means to be confidered as of original invention. The art itfelf certainly exifted long before, to whatever degree of perfection it might be advanced by them.

The firft fpecimens of engraving, we may reafonably conclude, were nothing more than rude portraitures, expreffed by fimple outlines, fuch as are defcribed by Herodotus to have been traced upon the fhields of the Carians, who ornamented their arms in this manner, long before the cuftom was adopted by the Grecians. The ancient Celtic and Gothic nations, even in their moft barbarous ftates, are faid, in like manner, to have engraved, upon their military accoutrements, rude delineations expreffive of their valour.

The hieroglyphical figures of the Egyptians afford us perhaps the moft ancient remains of engraving on metal ; and I mean now to confine myfelf entirely to that branch of the art. They are not uncommonly met with ; and many of them were immured as a fort of talifmans, in the coffins of the mummies. We have feveral very beautiful fpecimens of thefe figures at the Britifh Mufeum ; and one in particlar, in brafs, which bears every mark of great antiquity. It reprefents *Ifis*, and is carved in alto relievo. The goddefs appears ftanding upon two crocodiles ; holding in each hand two ferpents, a creature like a fcorpion, and a four-footed animal. From the tails of the crocodiles arife two ornaments. Upon the top of one is a bird ; but the reprefentation on the top of the other is fo obliterated by time, that it cannot eafily be afcertained. The flat part or ground of the relief, together

VOL. I.   C   with

with the bottom edges, and back part of it, are ornamented with figures and fymbolical characters, executed entirely with the graver, without any other affiftance; the backs of the
crocodiles, and the heads of the four footed animals, are alfo finifhed with the fame inftrument, in a very careful manner. This valuable curiofity was purchafed from the collection of Matthew Duane, Efq. It is four inches high, and three inches four tenths broad
at the bottom, from which it gradually decreafes to the the breadth of three inches at the
top.

The Phœnicians probably learned the art of engraving from the Egyptians; and their
coins, which are faid to be the moft ancient extant, prove they were by no means indifferent artifts. From Phœnicia it reached Greece, where, in Homer's time, it was carried
to a confiderable degree of perfection. But it is generally believed, that neither Egypt, Phœnicia, nor Greece, can produce any remains of fculpture, painting, and engraving,
prior to thofe of Etrufcan original. The beautiful vafes and other curious reliques of the
antiquities of that people, collected by Sir William Hamilton, and at prefent depofited
in the Britifh Mufeum are fufficient proofs of this affertion. In this noble collection,
among other valuable fpecimens of the art of engraving, are the two, reprefented upon
the frontifpiece of this volume. That at the bottom is fuppofed to be part of the fheath
of a *parazonium* or dagger. It is more than three inches and three quarters wide at the
top, and decreafes gradually to an inch and quarter at the bottom. Its prefent length is
eight inches and an half. The ftory engraved upon it, appears to be taken from Homer.
The trophy at the bottom, is fymbolical of war. Above the trophy, two warriors are
delineated with a woman, who feems to accompany them with great reluctance, which, I
conceive, may reprefent Paris, with his accomplice, conducting Helen to the fhip, in order
to make their efcape to Troy; and at the top, the meffenger, a fervant of Menelaus,
is relating to his lord the ungrateful behaviour of his Trojan gueft. The figures are
exceedingly rude, and feem to indicate the very infancy of the art of engraving: for
they are executed with the graver only, upon a flat furface, and need only to be filled
with ink, and run through a printing prefs (provided the plate could endure the operation)
to produce a fair and perfect impreffion. " The print fo produced," fays Monfieur
D' Ankerville (who has drawn up a defcriptive catalogue of the antiquities collected
by Sir William Hamilton), " would certainly be the moft ancient of all, that are pre-
" ferved in the collections of the curious; and demonftrate to us, how near the ancients
" approached to the difcovery of this admirable art, which in the prefent day forms fo
" confiderable a branch of commerce. We may indeed fay that they did difcover it;
" for it is evident, from the valuable relique of antiquity before us, that they only wanted
" the idea of multiplying reprefentations of the fame engraving. After having con-
" quered every principal difficulty, a ftop was put to their progrefs by an obftacle, which,
" in appearance, a child might have furmounted. But in the courfe of the arts, it is
" much eafier for the workman to conceive, what he can do himfelf, than forefee to what
" lengths the labours, which he executes, fhall be carried in futurity, or to what unknown
" ufes they may be properly applied. For it happens very rarely indeed, that the firft
" inventors of an art have conceived all the fubfequent confequences, which may be
" derived from it. It is thofe rather who follow, and know how to profit from the exer-
" tions of others, who generally pafs for the inventors."

Upon the fame plate is the reprefentation of another valuable fpecimen of ancient
engraving, greatly fuperior to the former in workmanfhip. It is a *patera*, or inftrument
ufed by the priefts in their facrifices: and is fuppofed, with great reafon, to have belonged
to an altar, dedicated to Hercules, who is reprefented upon it combating, as it appears to
me, with Hippolite the queen of the Amazons, whofe girdle he was enjoined by Euryf-
theus to unloofe, and take from her. But M. D' Ankerville, the gentleman mentioned
above, conceives it to reprefent Minerva, leaning upon the head of that hero, and
preffing him forward in the arduous paths of glory. His bow and quiver are behind him.
It is precifely feven inches in diameter, and about half an inch thick, and apparently
made of brafs; but the ornaments and borders are inlaid with filver. " It is," fays the
above author, " without contradiction, the richeft and moft remarkable remnant of anti-
" quity,

"quity, and of all the Etrufcan bronzes the beft executed, and moft happily preferved." Under each figure is an infcription in the Etrufcan character, which probably is the name of the perfonage reprefented above it. Part of that under Hercules is obliterated; what remains may be read HERECEL. The fecond and laft letters under the female figure are uncommon; and their power has never been properly afcertained. The others are M.*ACV*. The reader will eafily perceive, that the letters which compofe thefe infcriptions muft be read from the right hand to the left, which is a ftrong proof of their great antiquity. The figures and ornaments upon this valuable antiquity are carved in low relief; but the hair of the woman, the ornamental parts of the drapery, and the fmaller folds, are evidently the work of the graver only.

It is impoffible to fay, which of the two fpecimens, given upon this plate, is the moft ancient. Judging from the rudenefs and fimplicity of the Dagger Sheath, one would be inclined to decide in its favour. But the Patera has alfo every external mark of great antiquity; and the mixed manner of workmanfhip, which appears upon it, confifting of carving and engraving, Homer and Hefiod feem to have been well acquainted with, and, I think, it is clearly alluded to, by the firft, in his elaborate defcription of the fhield of Achilles; and by the laft (if the poem be by him) in that of Hercules. That thofe fhields were fuppofed to have been ornamented with engraving, has been conftantly underftood by the generality of authors, both ancient and modern. Quintilian, fpeaking of the former, fays exprefsly, *in cælaturâ clypei Achilles*, " the engraved fhield of Achil-
" les." That the figures were partly carved, and protuberated more or lefs, both the defcriptions fufficiently indicate. The fhields are exprefsly faid to have been inlaid with different metals, in order to vary the colour and appearance of the feveral objects; and this is in fome meafure the cafe with the Patera. The fhields of the feven chieftans, who fought againft the Thebans, are defcribed by Æfchylus as ornamented with emblematical figures, ιοχματιται, expreffed upon them, which feems to refer to the fame kind of workmanfhip. They were alfo inlaid with different metals, for the fake of ornament and diftinction.

It is extraordinary enough, that both Homer and Hefiod, who have fo minutely defcribed the fhields of Achilles and Hercules, with all the ornaments belonging to them, and the metals with which they were inlaid, have neither of them ufed any decifive words, expreffive of *engraving, carving, or inlaying*. The tranflators of Homer, however, many of them, have not fcrupled to fubftitute the word *engrave*, without any other authority, than the reafonablenefs of the fuppofition, that they might have been the work of the engraver. And if they confine themfelves to fuch parts, as are evidently engraved upon the Patera, and other ancient reliques of antiquity, they are, I believe, certainly right. But if they conceive the whole to have been executed in that manner, exclufive of carving, I am not of their opinion. Granting, however, the argument either way, I cannot think that they are perfectly juftifiable, in ufing fo determined a word, without explaining the fenfe in which they would have it underftood.

The two fpecimens I have given in the frontifpiece, are fufficient to explain the manner in which the ancients engraved. But the curious reader may meet with many others, if he pleafes to confult the works of antiquity, publifhed by Montfaucon, Francifcus Gori, and a variety of other excellent writers upon the fubject of antiquity.

It is impoffible to fay, how early the art of engraving exifted among our Britifh and Saxon anceftors. In the earlieft account of them we find, that they traced rude delineations upon their fhields, and other military accoutrements of war. And fuch remains, as are found in the ancient tumuli, and places of fepulture belonging to them, frequently bear the marks of the graver. But if other proofs were wanting, their coins would be abundantly fufficient, which are evidently no other than impreffions from engravings, cut upon iron, or fteel. Thefe indeed are exceedingly rude; and if a judgment were to be formed from them, concerning the ftate of the arts in England, even after the conqueft, the fentence would be very unfavourable, with refpect to the abilities of the artifts. But thefe are by no means proper examples of the engravers fkill, any more than they are of the fculptors.

Under the protection of that good and excellent monarch, Ælfred the Great, the arts began to manifeft themfelves in a fuperior degree, notwithftanding the load of inteftine troubles, which deftroyed the nation. He not only encouraged fuch artifts, as were in England at that time, but invited others from abroad to affift them. And the works of the Anglo-Saxon goldfmiths, who were the principal engravers of that day, were held in the higheft efteem, not only in England, but alfo upon the continent. The fhrines and cafkets, which they made for the prefervation of the reliques of faints, and other pious purpofes, are faid to have been curioufly wrought in gold, filver, and other metals, adorned with engravings, and ornamented with precious ftones, in fo excellent a ftyle, as to excite the admiration of all who faw them.

It is greatly to be defired, that a fufficient number of fpecimens of the works of the artifts of this early period, could be produced, by which a complete judgment might be formed of the perfection, to which they arrived. There is, however, yet preferved, in the Mufeum at Oxford, a very valuable jewel, made of gold, richly adorned with a kind of work refembling filligree, in the midft of which is feen the half figure of a man, fuppofed to be Saint Cuthbert. The back of this curious remnant of antiquity is ornamented with foliage, very fkilfully engraved. I have given a more particular defcription of this jewel, which was made at the command of Ælfred, with a faithful reprefentation of it, in the fecond volume of the Chronicle of England, publifhed fome few years ago.

Dunftan, archbifhop of Canterbury, who died, A. D. 988, is in particular mentioned by the hiftorians as an artift. He was a defigner and a painter, and practifed the working of metals, whether of gold, filver, iron, or brafs, in the greateft perfection. He alfo frequently ornamented his works with images and letters, which he engraved thereon. Ofborn, his biographer, fays of him, *prætcrea manu aptus ad omnia, poffe facere picturam, literas formare, fculpello imprimere, ex auro, argento, ære, et ferro, quicquid liberet operam.* But we muft confider, that thefe are the inflated praifes of a monkifh bigot; for he, who could add the title of faint to the name of Dunftan, would not hefitate to call him a Raphael in painting, or an Audran in engraving. We have indeed a fpecimen of his drawing, in an ancient manufcript, preferved in the Bodleian library at Oxford, which I copied for my firft volume of the Manners and Cuftoms of the Englifh; but if his engravings were not fuperior to his drawing, we have little to regret in the entire lofs of them.

Soon after the conqueft, a new fpecies of engraving was introduced into England, much more perfect in itfelf, than any which had preceded it; and, in every refpect, diftinct from the work of the carver or the chafer. In the former ages, the engraver feems to have united both thofe profeffions to his own; but, in the prefent inftance, he feems to have depended upon the graver only. I am now fpeaking of the brafs plates, fo frequently found in our churches, upon the tomb-ftones, which are ufually embellifhed with the effigies of the perfon, to whofe memory they are dedicated; and were probably invented to fupply the place of fculpture, being, without doubt, confiderably cheaper than carved images, whether in high or low relief; and for this reafon I fuppofe they came into fuch general ufe. I cannot pretend to fay, at what period they were firft introduced into this kingdom; but they are certainly of a very early date. In the fourteenth, fifteenth, and fixteenth centuries efpecially, they were fo generally adopted, that there is fcarcely an old church, of any confequence in England, which cannot produce fome fpecimen of this kind. The Englifh, indeed, appear to have been famous for thefe engravings, and, I believe, no nation in Europe can produce a greater variety of them.

They are executed entirely with the graver, the outlines being firft made; and the fhadows are expreffed by ftrokes, ftrengthened in proportion as they require more force, and occafionally croffed with other ftrokes, a fecond or third time, precifely in the fame manner, as a copper-plate is engraved for printing. They were ufually laid flat upon the ftones, to which they belonged, and expofed to the feet of the congregation, conftantly paffing over them. They were, of neceffity, executed in a coarfe manner, and the ftrokes very deeply cut into the metal, efpecially if the engraver was defirous that his works fhould endure for any confiderable time. Very neat or exquifite workmanfhip cannot therefore be expected. But however, fome few of them may be found, which bear no fmall evidence of the abilities of the workmen, by whom they were performed.

By thofe very artifts, who executed the monumental effigies, we may reafonably fuppofe, were engraved the boffes and clafps for the monaftic books, boxes, fhrines, and ornaments for t e altars of churches; alfo cups; and a variety of other furniture of metal, as well

for

for religious as fecular purpofes. Hence we fee the art of engraving was not only dif-covered, but practifed, ages before it entered into the idea of man to conceive, to what great and noble ufes it might be applied.

CHAPTER IV.

The firſt Diſcovery of producing Impreſſions from Engraved Plates conſidered; and the Claim of the Germans and Italians to this Invention, examined; with an Account of the moſt ancient Engravings of each Country, and a curious Specimen of the Workmanſhip of an Artiſt ſuppoſed to be a Native of England.

HAVING proved, in the preceding part of this Eſſay, the great antiquity of engraving, it remains now to conſider the art in a far more extenſive point of view, and to examine, when it was profeſſedly executed for the purpoſe of producing ſpecimens on paper; which happy invention increaſed its reputation, and rendered it more generally uſeful. The conſequence it now acquired with the public, occaſioned its ſeparation from the ſhop of the goldſmith, and worker in metals, with whom it ſeems to have remained for many ages, as a branch of their profeſſion; and the engraver by himſelf was properly conſidered, as an artiſt of the firſt rank.

The Germans and the Italians both lay claim to the invention of the art of taking impreſſions, from engraved plates, on paper. The former place their dependance upon the antiquity of the works which they produce; as the engravings of the old maſters of that country; the latter upon the poſitive aſſertion of Georgio Vaſari, who attributes it to Maſo Finiguerra, a Florentine artiſt; and declares, that it was accidentally diſcovered by him about the year 1460.

Profeſſor Chriſt mentions ſeveral old engravings, evidently the production of ſome German artiſt; one of them dated as early as 1465; the reſt 1466 and 1467; which account, reſpecting the two latter dates, is confirmed by M. Heineken, an excellent and able writer upon this ſubject, whoſe publications are frequently referred to in the courſe of this work. Theſe, it ſeems, were the earlieſt German prints they could produce with dates; whereas the firſt dated engravings in Italy, are ſaid to be the geographical charts for an edition of Ptolemy, publiſhed at Rome, A. D. 1478. The plates for the large edition of the Poems of Dante, invented by Boticelli, and engraved by him, or Baldini, did not appear till 1481. Hence we find the difference of twelve years, between the date of the Italian engravings, and thoſe produced in Germany.

It is indeed remarkable, that no print has hitherto been produced by the Italians, which can with the leaſt degree of certainty be attributed to Finiguerra. Neither has there been found in the foreign collections any engravings of a prior date to thoſe mentioned above; but others rudely executed, and without dates, are mentioned however as proofs of the exerciſe of the art, as well in Italy, as in Germany, before the publication of thoſe prints which were dated. But it would be highly improper to place an implicit faith upon an evidence ſo doubtful; for if there be no date to a print, it is totally impoſſible to aſcertain the time preciſely, in which it was executed; for its rudeneſs, and the indifference of its workmanſhip, are by no means to be conſidered, as certain proofs of its antiquity; though in ſome caſes they may have their weight, eſpecially when ſtrengthened by other corroborating circumſtances: yet even then a poſitive deciſion in their favour ought to be very cautiouſly made.

From the ſimplicity of Andrea Mantegna's ſtyle, I wonder not, that he has been often conſidered, as one of the moſt early engravers. For I own, before I was convinced by experience of the contrary, I concluded, that his manner of engraving was, of all others, the moſt ancient. One of the earlieſt ſpecimens of this kind of workmanſhip, which I have ſeen, is faithfully copied, plate V. of this volume. If the F. which appears upon the pedeſtal cloſe to the hand of the ſeated figure, be granted to ſtand for Finiguerra, the print muſt be conſidered as a very valuable acquiſition; for it would inconteſtibly prove, that this ſpecies of engraving, which was practiſed in Italy only, was more ancient than any other adopted in that country, and

in

14   ON THE ORIGIN AND PROGRESS OF ENGRAVING.

in some measure exculpate Vasari for attributing the invention to Finiguerra, even if it should hereafter be proved, that the Germans practised the art of taking impressions, from engravings prior to the Italians. But this interpretation of the letter F. is not without some difficulty. It is expresly said by Vasari, that Baldini was instructed by Finiguerra, and Boticelli again by Baldini. Yet if we look at the plates, executed by one or both the last artists for the great edition of Dante, dated 1481, we shall find the strokes, which constitute the shadows, laid this way or that indiscriminately, as the engraver thought proper, and crossed with second strokes almost continually, and sometimes with thirds, as the reader may see upon plate VII. which is a faithful copy of one of the engravings for Dante. The style of the engraving, plate V. is precisely the same as was afterwards adopted by Andrea Mantegna, see plate VI. which is taken from a print executed by him. The outline is first cut upon the copper in a very powerful manner, and the shadows are expressed by simple strokes, running from one corner of the plate to the other, without any crossing, or considerable variation, precisely in imitation of drawings made with a pen. Now, if Finiguerra worked in this style, it is not reasonable to suppose that his immediate disciple, Baldini, or Boticelli, instructed by Baldini, should have so totally differed from it.

It is as confidently reported, on the other hand, that Andrea Mantegna learned the art of engraving from the works, if not from the instructions, of Finiguerra, or his scholars. If this be true, it will also appear incredible, that he should not in some measure have followed the style of his instructors. The print, plate V. has every external appearance of being executed prior to the works of Mantegna; the mechanical part of whose engravings is far superior, firmer, and more decided. It is therefore highly probable, that from this master, whoever he might be, Mantegna received his first instructions. This species of engraving was carried to a still further degree of perfection by John Antonio Brixianus, and other artists of that time. After which period it died away, and we hear no more of it. And that this style of workmanship was not the most ancient, we need only to refer to the oldest dated prints, and beyond them to the brass plates on tombs, and other specimens of the art, for centuries past, and the strokes, promiscuously laid upon them, forming the shadows, and crossed or recrossed without the least restraint.

According to what has been said, it appears, that 1465 is the earliest date affixed to any print, produced by the Germans, except indeed one mentioned by Sandrart, in his Academy of Painting, which he says he had seen bearing date ten years earlier, and marked with a cypher, composed of an H. and an S. joined to the cross-bar of the H. precisely in the same manner, as that used by Hans Schauflein. But even the most sanguine of his own countrymen, cannot help allowing their suspicion of a mistake in the date; and some have said, it should have been written 1477, which others think is still too early. It is readily allowed that an older master than Schauflein did exist, who used the same monogram; but his prints in general bear the evident marks of being copies from others, and by no means, from the manner of their execution, justify the supposition of their being the works of a master, greatly anterior to the year 1500. The subject of the print mentioned by Sandrart, is a *girl caressing an old man while she steals his purse from him*. This subject, it is well known, was frequently engraved, both on copper and on wood, by a variety of ancient masters; but, except Sandrart, I never heard of any one, who had seen the print alluded to. A fuller account of this artist, with his works, may be seen in the second volume, under the article Schauflein. The story, that Peter Schoffer invented the art of engraving on copper, and taking impressions from plates of that metal, does not bear any similitude to the truth; neither have we the least plausible reason given, in support of such an assertion.

With respect to the edition of the Ptolemy, printed at Rome in the year 1478, we must take notice, that the plates were not engraved by Italian artists, but by Conrad Sweynheym, and Arnold Buckinck, both of them Germans. The former, as appears from the dedication, first brought, not only the art of taking impressions from engraved plates, but that of printing also, to Rome, where he died, three years after the commencement of the work; which was at length completed by the latter; and the plates for this book are supposed to have been begun, about the year 1472. It will doubtless seem very extraordinary, that the art of engraving should have been discovered at Florence, so early as 1460, and yet unknown twelve years afterwards at Rome, where it was first introduced by foreign artists. It

appears

appears from this circumstance, that though Finiguerra, Boticelli, and Baldini, all of them Florentines, possessed the secret, they did not divulge it speedily; and hence, as a good presumptious proof, it may be urged, that such Italian engravings, as are to be found prior to the year 1472, are by the hand of one or other of these artists. If this be granted, and great plausibility, at least, is on its side, it will follow that the originals, from whence the plates II. and III. are taken, are so. These curious and valuable specimens of ancient engravings, which, I believe, are unique, must have been executed as early as the year 1464; a very short interval, from the time, which Vasara gives us for the invention of the art; and are considerably more early, than any hitherto produced, though all the great foreign libraries have been repeatedly searched for that purpose. Two of them, I thought, were sufficient, to shew the style in which they are executed; but the set consists of eight plates, namely, the seven planets, and an almanack by way of frontispiece, on which are directions for finding Easter from the year 1465 to 1517 inclusive; and the dates regularly follow each other, which plainly proves, that there can be no mistake with respect to the first; and we may be well assured, in this case, the engravings were not antedated; for the almanack of course became less and less valuable, every year. A full description of all these engravings will be given in the seventh chapter of this Essay.

If we are inclined to refer these plates to either of the three Italian artists before mentioned, we shall naturally suppose them to be the work of Finiguerra, or Baldini; for they are not equal, either in drawing or composition, to those ascribed to Boticelli; which we know at least were designed by him; and as Baldini is expressly said to have worked from the designs of Boticelli, it will appear most probable, if they are to be attributed to any one of these three artists, they belong to the former. The reader must be left to judge for himself, whether he conceives them to be sufficiently well executed; for he is to remember, that Finiguerra is spoken of by Vasari, as a man of no small ability. I own, after all, if I could but tell to whom one might reasonably ascribe these curious plates, I should yet be tempted to suppose the original of the plate No. V. was really the production of Finiguerra's graver.

We have now seen what pretensions the Italians have laid to the invention of the art of engraving, and have proved, by producing undoubted specimens, that it did exist nearly about the time stated by Vasari. With respect to what he has said, concerning the art of taking impressions, from engraved plates being invented by Finiguerra, the ingenious observations of M. Heineken are well deserving of notice. "According to Vasari," says he, "and " others, his countrymen, it was the goldsmith Finiguerra, who invented this art about " the year 1460; and perhaps he was not mistaken, if he speaks of Italy only. It is very " possible, that the art of engraving should have been long practised in Germany, and " unknown in Italy. The Italians, those of Venice excepted, had very little correspon- " dence with the Germans. For this reason, Finiguerra might discover this art, without " knowing, that it had been already invented in Germany. All the merchandizes of this " country were sent from Antwerp to the Italians, who were much better acquainted with " the people of the Low Countries, than those of the other provinces. For this cause, " Vasari supposed that Martin Schoen, who was born at Culmback, and resided at Colmar, " was a Fleming, and constantly calls him Martin of Antwerp."

We shall now proceed to examine, what claim the Germans can bring, prior to that of the Italians; and in that case we shall have recourse to their works. The earliest dated print I ever saw produced by this school, is copied, plate I. and the date is evidently 1461. And we shall see, however faulty it may be with respect to the drawing, or defective in point of taste, the mechanical part of the execution of it has by no means the appearance of being one of the first productions of the graver. We have also several other engravings, evidently the works of the same master, and concerning which the same observations may be justly made. Besides, the impressions are so neatly taken from the plates, and the engravings so clearly printed in every part, that, according to all appearance, they could not be executed in a much better manner, in the present day, with all the conveniencies, which the copper-plate printers now possess, and the additional knowledge they must necessarily have acquired, in the course of more than three centuries. Hence we may fairly conclude

clude, that, if they were not the firſt ſpecimens of the engraver's workmanſhip, they were much leſs the firſt efforts of the copper-plate printer's ability. Not that plates being badly printed is any certain proof of their antiquity; but we can hardly imagine, that the firſt attempts to take impreſſions from engravings ſhould immediately have arrived at perfection; and that at a time, when we cannot ſuppoſe them to have been aware of every circumſtance, neceſſary to inſure ſucceſs; eſpecially when we find it no eaſy matter, in the preſent day, at all times, to procure good impreſſions from our plates.

The artiſt to whom we owe this ſingular curioſity was, without doubt, a goldſmith. And indeed, it is certain, that the art of engraving plates, for the purpoſe of printing, firſt originated with thoſe ingenious mechanics, or elſe with the engravers, who executed the braſs plates for the monuments; but as I have ſaid before, I do by no means ſuppoſe, that this print is the firſt ſpecimen of engraving, even if we ſhould allow its author to have been the inventor of the art. There are other plates, ſome of which I ſhall ſpecify hereafter, that, I think, bear evident marks of priority, particularly thoſe of the maſter, who uſed the Gothic initials F. and S. ſeparated by a very ſingular mark, and who is called by Abbé Marolles, Francois Stofs, or Stoltzhirs; but upon what authority does not appear.

Martin Schoen, a painter, engraver, and goldſmith, who was born at Culmback, and reſided chiefly at Colmar, is ſaid, with great appearance of truth, to have worked from 1460 to 1486, in which year he died. This artiſt was apparently the diſciple of Stoltzhirs; for he followed his ſtyle of engraving, and copied from him a ſet of prints, repreſenting the *paſſion of our Saviour*. So that, allowing Stoltzhirs to have preceded his diſciple only ten years, this carries the æra of the art back to 1450, without having any recourſe to the fabulous relation of ſome authors upon this ſubject, who ſpeak of one Luprecht Ruſt, as the maſter of Martin Schoen, abſurdly declaring, that he was an engraver on wood. Admitting therefore, that ſuch an artiſt really did exiſt; it is by no means reaſonable to ſuppoſe, that he ſhould teach the art of engraving on copper to another, when he was not, according to their own account, acquainted with it himſelf. Martin Schoen never engraved on wood, as far as I have heard; but his works on copper, it is well known, are very conſiderable.

Iſrael van Mechelen, or Meckenen, whoſe engravings are as multifarious, as thoſe of Martin Schoen's, was born at Mecheln, a ſmall village near Bocholt, where he chiefly reſided. The latter is a town ſituated upon the banks of the Aa, in the biſhoprick of Munſter, in Weſtphalia. He died, A. D. 1523. According to the tradition of the inhabitants of Bocholt, the father of this artiſt was a goldſmith, and his baptiſmal name was Iſrael. Hence M. Heineken concludes, that he alſo was an engraver, and that a great part of the prints, attributed to the ſon, belong to him. "An attentive examination," concludes that author, "will make it appear, that all theſe prints are not by the ſame hand. I " am almoſt certain, that Iſrael the father engraved ſeveral, thoſe eſpecially, which have the " greateſt marks of antiquity, and are executed in a rude ſtyle, approaching neareſt to the " work of the goldſmith. " Nor (adds he) will I deny, but that the ſon may have com- " menced originally as a goldſmith, by armorial bearings, foliages, croſſes, and other " ornamental works. But as he was a painter, as well as an engraver, and a man of " tolerable abilities in the art of deſign, conſidering the time in which he lived, it is not " at all aſtoniſhing, that among the prints produced by his graver, we ſhould " find ſome by no means wanting in merit." How far theſe obſervations may be conſidered as juſt by the experienced collector, I cannot pretend to ſay: For my own part, I ſee no reaſon to divide the works of this artiſt; nor can I find, upon ſtrict examination, any other difference in the prints, which I have ſeen attributed to him, than what one might reaſonably expect to find in the works of any one man, who with his own hand performed ſo great a number of engravings. Of courſe, his moſt early productions are the rudeſt, and maniſeſt the leaſt ſkill; but all of them are equally defective in point of drawing, eſpecially when he attempted to expreſs the naked parts of the figure.

It is certainly true, that the manner of engraving, adopted by Martin Schoen, differed exceedingly from that of Iſrael van Mechelen. The works of the former are more

firm

firm and determined, and, upon the whole, greatly superior. Let any one take the trouble of examining the print, representing St. Anthony carried into the air by the demons, which was first engraved by Martin Schoen, and afterwards copied by Israel, and the question will be readily decided in favour of the former, without adding the anecdote, recorded by Vasari, that Michael Angelo was so pleased with this engraving, which is truly a master-piece of Schoen's, that he copied it in colours. The inferiority of Israel van Mecheln, when compared to Martin Schoen, as an artist, is by no means any proof of his priority in point of time. The only advantage, which M. Heineken gains by making the father of Van Mecheln an artist, as well as himself, is a greater length of time for the execution of those works, attributed to him; and upon this supposition he says, "I place the engravings of "the two Israels between the years 1450 and 1503." The son was certainly a more modern artist than Martin Schoen; and we have a print by him, which bears so late a date as 1502. He was contemporary with Albert Durer; and some have supposed, that he visited that artist at Nuremberg. Sandrart attributes to Israel Van Mecheln, the invention of engraving, and tells us, that his first prints were executed about the year 1450. If this account indeed be true, it must make much in favour of M. Heineken's conjecture, concerning the engravings of the father; but the argument at present unfortunately wants sufficient proof, to be admitted as absolutely conclusive; and, until some more satisfactory account shall be produced, I cannot help declaring, that I am of a different opinion. The earliest dated print, which I have seen by Israel van Mecheln, is in the collection of Dr. Monro. It represents the Virgin and Child, with four angels. The engraving is rude, and coarser than the works of that artist are in general; and the date is 1480. He engraved however, I believe, something earlier than this period. In the same collection, is preserved a circular print, where the Deity appears surrounded by an ornamental border, in which the symbolical representations of the four Evangelists are depicted with St. Jerom, and three other saints. Upon the desk of St. Jerom, who is seated and writing, is the date 1466. There are several copies of this plate, and one of them by Israel Van Mecheln, apparently not greatly posterior to the original, which probably was executed by the same master as the print, dated 1461, mentioned already in the present chapter.

What has been said will, I doubt not, sufficiently prove, that there is the greatest reason to believe, that the art of taking impressions from engraved plates was practised in Germany, before it reached Italy; especially if we agree with Vasari, who expressly declares, it did not appear in that country before the year 1460; when, on the other hand, we may, I think, with the greatest justice, place it at least ten years earlier among the Germans.

Before I conclude this chapter, I beg leave to recommend to the attention of my readers a very curious specimen of English engraving, as ancient, according to all external appearance, as any of those produced in the course of this Essay, the Patera and Parazonium sheath, represented in the frontispiece, excepted. (See plate No. 4.) And it is to be observed, that this print is not a copy, as the others are, but an impression from the original plate, which is in my possession, and was purchased, in the course of last winter, in a sale, consisting of coins, medals, prints, and a variety of other curiosities, at the auction rooms belonging to Mr. Hutchins. A particular description of this plate, and of all the others already referred to, will be found in the seventh chapter of the Essay, to which they are annexed.

England has constantly been omitted in the list of those countries, which have produced ancient engravers. Our own authors had nothing to offer upon the subject in the least satisfactory. Evelyn indeed says, "the art of engraving, and working from plates of cop-"per, which we call *prints*, was not yet appearing or born with us, till about the year "1490." By the word *us* he evidently means the moderns collectively in contradistinction to the ancients, whose works he had, in the preceding chapters, been speaking of, and not the English alone; nor indeed does it refer to them at all, as any one will be convinced, who peruses the context, but to the æra of the first invention of engraving, which he himself soon afterwards clearly explains. M. Heineken however has mistaken this paffage, and, in fact, one cannot much wonder that he fhould, where he fays, according to Evelyn, "the art of engraving on copper was exercifed in England about "the year 1490." But, according to our own authors, the firft book, which appeared with copper cuts in England, was the *Birth of Mankind*, otherwife called the Woman's Book, dedicated to queen Catherine, and publifhed by J. Raynalde, A. D. 1540. Yet it is by no means certain, that thefe plates were engraved in England, or the work of Englifh artifts. Chambers muft have given himfelf very little trouble to examine the ftate of the arts in England, when he ignorantly afferted, in his dictionary, that engraving was firft introduced here by John Speed, being brought by him from Antwerp in the reign of James the Firft.

Indeed no one feems to have fuppofed, that we could lay even the moft diftant claim to a rivalfhip (much lefs to a priority) with refpect to the early practice of engraving, with any of the continental nations, famous for the arts. But when we confider, how many engravers we had in England, about the time in which the difcovery of taking impreffions from copper-plates was made, as the many monumental engravings, remaining in our churches to this day, fufficiently teftify (and a little examination of thefe early fpecimens of the art will prove how well they are adapted to the purpofe of printing), we fhall readily conceive, that, if they did not themfelves difcover this mode of multiplying their works, they would at leaft have inftantly adopted it, as foon as the knowledge of fuch an invention had reached them.

There can be little doubt of the antiquity of the engraving here produced; and that it was made for the purpofe of printing, the letters being reverfed upon the plate fufficiently prove. So that if it fhould be urged, though I fee no kind of reafon for fuch a fuppofition, that the plate itfelf was executed abroad, at the command of fome Englifh devotee, it muft at leaft be granted, that the mode of taking impreffions from it, was underftood in England, or the plate could not have been of any ufe to the owner of it; and that the engraving was the work of fome Englifh artift, or executed at the defire of fome Englifh perfonage, no one, I conceive, will doubt, on examining the contents of the infcriptions. They confift of particular invocations to all faints, comprehended in feven compartments, the initial letters of each invocation or prayer being ornamented with the reprefentation of the perfonages to whom it is addreffed. The firft is to the Virgin Mary; the fecond, to the Archangels, Angels, and Celeftial Powers; the third, to the Patriarchs and Prophets; the fourth, to the Apoftles Peter and Paul, &c. the fifth, to the Martyrs and Confeffors of the Faith. This prayer is firft addreffed to Thomas Beckett, whofe murder is reprefented in the midft of the initial letter; then to Edward the Confeffor, or Edward the Martyr; and the name of Stephen, mentioned in the laft line, refers alfo, without doubt, to fome other favourite Englifh faint. The fixth petition is to the Popes and Prelates of the church; and the laft to the Virgins, and holy Women diftinguifhed for their piety. The whole is concluded with a general prayer, including an addrefs to all of them, and a petition to God, that their merit and example may tend to the falvation of the perfon, who is reprefented as offering it up to Heaven, in behalf of himfelf, and the church of which he was a member. The addrefs to the Englifh Saints, in the fifth petition, plainly, I think, determines the country to which it belonged; and the names of more Englifh perfonages may eafily be traced out in the fixth and feventh prayers. If the perfon at the bottom could be difcovered, I have little doubt, but the date of this fingular curiofity might be nearly afcertained. The ftyle of the drawing, and the manner in which the little figures are compofed, being placed in the initial letters, bear an exact refemblance to the illuminated delineations, which we meet with in manufcripts of the fifteenth century, efpecially towards the commencement of it; and the writing alfo has every appearance of an equal antiquity. It is evidently ftamped upon the plate with fmall punches, and retouched afterwards with the graver. The figures are executed entirely with the graver, in a very flight and unfkilful manner; which feems evidently to prove the inability of the artift, who, perhaps being ufed to the execution of large figures on monumental brafs plates, met with no little difficulty in contracting his defign, and expreffing it in fo fmall a compafs. Yet though this print is fo very indifferently executed,

ON THE ORIGIN AND PROGRESS OF ENGRAVING. 19

executed, it has been considered as not sufficiently rude for a first attempt. To this objection I answer: First, with respect to the drawing and composition, many designs much superior may be seen, delineated in manuscripts, as early as the thirteenth and fourteenth centuries; consequently greatly prior to this. And secondly, with respect to the mechanical part of the execution of the engraving, many specimens of ancient workmanship with the graver may be produced, considerably more early, and much more skilfully performed.

M. Heineken observes, that, prior to the commencement of printing, the images and portraitures of saints were impressed on slips of paper, resembling playing cards, and put into the hands of the ignorant, to amuse them, whilst, at the same time, they reminded them of their religious duties, and the benefit they might receive from the prayers of those holy personages, agreeably to the superstitious opinions of the time. And this very print seems to prove, that the most early impressions from copper-plates were devoted to the same pious purposes. In this point of view, the present engraving may justly be considered as one of the most early specimens of the art, which has as yet been produced. With these observations, I shall conclude this long, and I fear tedious chapter, leaving them entirely to the determination of my readers, how far they are to be considered as worthy of their attention.

CHAPTER V.

The peculiar Style of the German School, and an Examination of the Works of the Artists belonging to that School; especially with respect to the Mechanical Part of the Execution of their Engravings, from the Year 1461 to 1500.

BEFORE I enter upon the subject of this chapter, it will, I conceive, be very necessary for me to explain, as clearly as possible, my own ideas of *beauty* and *elegance*, and the acceptation, in which I wish the expressions *stiff* and *Gothic*, which occur so frequently in the course of this work, should be received, as applicable to historical compositions in general.

Beauty, I conceive, consists not only in a variety of forms, but in a variety of elegant forms. Streight lines convey the idea of solidity and strength, without motion, and are therefore very improper for any figure, which in itself is supposed to be capable of motion. For this cause it is, that a figure standing upright, with both the legs, and both the arms, precisely in the same position, and the head neither inclining to the right nor to the left, will be called a stiff figure, without requiring the examination of the artist's eye.

A variety of forms, judiciously contrasted with each other, naturally convey the idea of motion; and though the figure be represented as standing still, the same idea still subsists in the mind; and we conceive it could move, if it pleased: the reason is easily given. For, as all our ideas of external objects are acquired from the objects themselves, it follows, that, as we see no animal motion without variety of form, the same variety of form, represented in a picture, should produce the same idea of motion, or of the possibility of motion; so that, strictly speaking, *stiffness* is a something we conceive to be improperly formed for motion. And the more or less this idea is prevalent in the mind, the more or less we consider the object of our contemplation as censurable.

Hence it is we call those draperies *stiff*, or *Gothic*, in which the folds do not fall into such forms, as we naturally expect they should. Every appearance of studied exactness, in the disposition of them, is a constraint upon the easy flow of motion; and the more or less we discover it, we praise or condemn it in the same proportion. The common eye is no mean judge in this particular; for the common eye cannot help observing the ordinary appearances of simple nature, and judges accordingly, without any previous bias.

Much has been said with respect to elegance in the general form of the human figure. I have observed, that in the most estimable antique statues, the outlines of all the parts are expressed by large convex and small concave lines. I am not singular in this observation; from an artist of the first rank in this kingdom, whose friendship I am honoured with, I first received it; and repeated examination has abundantly confirmed the fact. It is evident, at least to me, that exact lines of any kind, even if they be drawn in the ser-

D 2   pentine

pentine form, cannot give the perfect expreſſion of beauty and elegance; for theſe, if traced preciſely, will have a formal appearance; and if they convey the idea of motion at all, it is the conſtrained motion of the jack-worm, rather than that of an animal, which can freely move itſelf at its own pleaſure.

Such forms therefore, as convey the cleareſt idea of thoſe flowing lines, which motion naturally gives, or ſeem diſpoſed in the fitteſt order to move, appear to me moſt elegant and graceful; whilſt, on the contrary, thoſe forms, which are apparently unfit for motion, and leaſt varied from one another, I conſider as proportionably *ſtiff* and *Gothic*.

The reaſon why we have ſo few great artiſts amongſt the number, which in all ages are purſuing the arts, is, becauſe ſo few have the eye to ſee, and the faculty to retain, the beautiful variety of forms, which nature continually produces. Thoſe, not poſſeſſed of theſe abilities, ſubſtitute in their own minds, a ſet of forms, which they themſelves approve; and which they uſe on all occaſions. The continual repetition becomes tireſome and diſguſting; for variety alone can delight the mind. Thoſe who, by painful attempts at neatneſs and laboured execution, endeavour to compenſate for the want of genius, often fail ſtill more than the manneriſt. Nature ſets the compaſſes at defiance; and no rule can be ſufficient to inſtruct that man to draw her correctly, who has not the eye to ſee her naked as ſhe is, and the idea, firſt ſtrongly impreſſed upon his own mind, of what he means to expreſs: For if he feels not the effects of beauty in himſelf, how can he poſſibly communicate them to another?

The want of natural ſimplicity, diſtinguiſhed by the appellation *Gothic*, was a ſtrong characteriſtic of the German ſchool, eſpecially at that early period, which we now are proceeding to ſpeak of.

All the ancient German maſters were exceedingly defective in drawing, eſpecially when they attempted to execute the naked parts of the human figure. Martin Schoen ſucceeded the beſt; and a ſmall upright print by him, repreſenting St. Sebaſtian tied to a tree, may be produced as a ſpecimen, by no means unfavourable. The body of the figure poſſeſſes great merit, and the head is not devoid of expreſſion; but the other extremities are by no means equally well drawn. Drawing from nature ſeems to have been no part of an artiſt's education at this time; and as they had not the admirable remains of antiquity to direct their taſte, no wonder they fell into a manner, which, however diſguſting it may appear to us, was probably conſidered as excellent by them, who had not the opportunity of examining any works ſuperior to their own.

From the old maſter, whoſe prints are marked with an F. and an S. named by Marolles Francois Stofs, or Stoltzhirs, I am greatly inclined to believe, that Martin Schoen learned the art of engraving. It is certain, however, that he not only copied the prints of Stoltzhirs, but imitated his ſtyle of engraving alſo; which indeed he improved to a very great degree. Schoen appears to have had a conſiderable number of ſcholars, who followed his manner; but none of them ever equalled him. Among theſe may be reckoned, Bartholomew Schoen, the elder Schaufflein, Francois van Bocholt, Bofche, Wenceſlaus of Olmutz in Bohemia, Adam Gamperlin, Pleydenwurff of Nuremberg, Michael Wolgemuth, Mathew Zagel, and Mair, whoſe works are mentioned under their reſpective names. To theſe may be added the following, known by their marks only; who, as they certainly worked during this period, may very properly be mentioned here: as, I. C. and S. and P. P. Theſe letters are ſeparated by a ſort of croſs. W. H. Theſe letters are ſeparated by a mark, ſomething reſembling that of Martin Schoen's. B. M. Theſe initials are ſeparated by a ſort of croſs. W. h. F. and W. with a ſort of croſs. T. W. and L. with a flouriſh, reſembling a Gothic Z. All theſe artiſts were diſciples or imitators of Martin Schoen.

I have given it as my opinion, in the former chapter, that the artiſt, to whom we owe the curious print copied in this volume, and dated 1461, (See plate I.) was the maſter, from whom Iſrael van Mecheln received his inſtructions in the art of engraving. The manner of Iſrael van Mecheln differed exceedingly from that of Martin Schoen, eſpecially in the management of the fleſh and draperies, which are executed in a neater and

more

more laboured ſtyle. The ſtrokes are much finer, in general, and often aſſiſted in the finiſhing with a tender interline; by which they may be conſtantly diſtinguiſhed. All the imitators of Iſrael adopted the ſame method; particularly the engraver, who ſub‑ſcribed his prints, Z. Wott, or Z. Woll. He executed many of his plates in a very neat, careful ſtyle; but they are ſo miſerably defective in point of drawing, and ſo totally devoid of taſte, that few collectors, I fear, will take the trouble of examining them.

We have ſeveral engravings by the ancient artiſt, mentioned above as the maſter of Iſrael van Mecheln; but one of them is too ſingular to be omitted. It repreſents the Sibyl, ſhowing to the emperor Auguſtus, the Virgin Mary, with the infant Chriſt, in the clouds. The figures are loaded with drapery; and the crown, with other parts of the habit of the emperor, is richly ornamented with jewels. In the back-ground is repre‑ſented a town at a diſtance; which, M. Heineken informs us, is a view of the town of Culm‑bach, with the caſtle of Bleſſenberg: from which circumſtance he conjectures, that the artiſt was a native of that place; at leaſt, adds he, I am perſuaded, that the inventors of the art of engraving did live at Culmbach, or at Nuremberg, or at Augſbourg. He ſpeaks of this as a very ancient print, and declares, " that every part of it proves it to " have been the work of ſome goldſmith, which perfectly demonſtrates the immediate com‑" mencement of the art." This print is ſeven inches and a half wide, by ten inches and a half high. The mechanical part of the execution is preciſely the ſame, as in that which is dated 1461: and the ſtyle of drawing, with every other mark of diſtinction, correſponds ſo exactly, that I am perfectly perſuaded, they were both performed by the ſame hand. So alſo are thoſe, I verily believe, marked with an E. and an E. with an S. or elſe by a diſciple, who imitated this maſter's ſtyle of engraving in a moſt admirable manner. The print mentioned by profeſſor Chriſt, dated 1465, which, he ſays, is marked with a C. and an E. joined together, is by the ſame hand. And though I have never met with a print, ſo dated, with that mark, yet I have ſeen the ſame mark upon another print, with the date 1466; and, I conceive it is an E. and S. joined together in the Gothic ſtyle. This print repreſents the Deity, with Chriſt and the Holy Spirit, ſurrounded by many angels, in a ſort of gallery; whilſt beneath an arch the Virgin appears ſeated, holding the infant Jeſus; and an angel, with other figures, accompanying her; a man and woman are alſo repreſented kneeling at her feet. Upon the arch is an inſcription in honour of the Virgin. This print is eight inches and a quarter high, by four inches and three quarters wide. I have alſo ſeen a St. Sebaſtian, marked E. S. dated 1467. The Virgin and Child with angels; alſo a ſingle figure of the Virgin; the Virgin and Child appearing to St. John; and a ſuderium ſupported by St. Peter and St. Paul; all marked with the ſame letters, and bearing the ſame date. Theſe are in the collection of Dr. Monro; and all appa‑rently by the ſame hand, though the latter are finiſhed the moſt. But to return to Iſrael van Mecheln. Beſides Zwoll, he had ſeveral diſciples, or profeſſed imitators, who lived in this century; after which his ſtyle of engraving was nearly loſt; and the works of Albert Durer were conſidered as moſt worthy of imitation. Among them is Michael Bogner, and the artiſt who uſes the Gothic initials I. A. another, who marks his prints B. M. every way different from him, mentioned before, who uſed theſe letters divided by a ſort of croſs; he alſo who ſigned the initials B. R. the letters being divided by a mark bearing ſome ſmall reſemblance to an anchor; and another, who ſubſcribes his prints S. A. but above all, that great artiſt, Lucas Jacobs, better known by the name of Lucas van Leyden, of whoſe works we ſhall give an account hereafter. The engraver, who uſed the W. diſtinguiſhed by a ſort of croſs, worked occaſionally in the ſtyle of Martin Schoen, and of Iſrael van Mecheln; and ſo alſo did Francois van Bocholt, and ſome others.

The German engravings therefore, prior to the ſixteenth century, may be divided into two claſſes: Thoſe of Upper Germany, which reſemble the ſtyle of Martin Schoen; and thoſe of the Low Countries are imitations in, a greater or leſs degree, of the works of the old maſter, upon which Iſrael van Mecheln founded his ſtyle of engraving.

C H A P.

CHAPTER VI.

The general Style and Character of Design among the Italian Engravers, and the Extent of their Knowledge, in the Execution of the Mechanical Part of their Plates, examined, from 1464 to 1500.

AS we divided the engravings of the old German school into two distinct classes, we shall do the same, and with still more propriety, with respect to those of the ancient Italian school. As first those which bear the nearest resemblance to drawings with a pen, in which the strokes, that express the shadows, are laid from the one corner of the plate to the other; and this style of engraving was adopted by the artist who executed plate V. also by Andrea Mantegna, Pollaioli, and their followers. Secondly, The engravings in which the strokes are laid to form the shadows, without the least constraint; and crossed with other strokes, as often as the artist pleased, unconfined by any particular rule. In this style the Planets, dated 1461, are executed; one of which is copied plate III. together with the frontispiece belonging to the set, plate II; and are particularly described in the seventh chapter of this Essay. The same method was adopted by Boticelli, and apparently by Baldini; also by an artist, who uses the intitals, L. A. F. and by another, who marks his plates with an N. Several others, as will be noticed presently, engraved in both these manners, and that sometimes upon the same plate.

The prints belonging to the Italian school, from the very commencement of the art, are easily distinguished from those engraved in Germany; not only by the visible difference which appears in the execution of the mechanical part of the workmanship, but also by the simplicity of style, with which the former designed the human figure; and this simplicity in some degree is constantly found in the slightest Italian compositions: being professedly acquired by the study of the works of antiquity. But perhaps the distinction between the German and Italian engravings is no where more strikingly evident, than in the drawing of the draperies, and the disposition of the folds. In the one, it is plain and unaffected; the folds are long and flowing, and the turn of the figures has always more or less of that grace, which is so powerfully demonstrated in the statues, bass reliefs, and other remains of the ancients: whilst the Germans, forsaking nature, or contenting themselves with viewing her in disguise, and having no assistance to correct their taste, degenerated into what is called manner, and drew the human figure, not as it really did, but as they conceived it should appear to them.

And the manifest difference in the drawing and composition, as well as in the style of engraving, which appears in the prints, belonging to these schools, may be considered as an argument of some force, in favour of the ingenious opinion of M. Heineken, who conceives, that Finiguerra might have discovered the art of engraving in Italy, without being conscious that it was practised at the same time in Germany, and consequently could not be a new invention. For had one nation taken it from the other, it is reasonable to suppose, that some resemblance would have been easily traced, with respect to the mechanical execution of the work; and when the Germans copied the works of the Italians, we constantly find that it was so. For Boticelli engraved several plates of the Prophets, and Sibyls, soon after the discovery of engraving by Finiguerra, which were imitated soon after by the Germans, in a style much resembling the originals; though the copies have all the appearance of labour, and are executed with much servility. The imitations are also in some circumstances to be distinguished from the originals, by the orthography: as for example, No. XIV. instead of *David*, the name is written *Davit*. These Prophets and Sibyls are single figures, five inches and a half high, by four inches one-eighth in width. The originals are very rudely executed, and bear every mark of priority, when compared with the plates for the Dante. They are also very badly printed, and, without doubt, the first efforts of Boticelli in the exercise of engraving.

The Prophets and Sibyls of Boticelli were also copied by an Italian artist, in a style superior to the originals, and by no means resembling them in the mechanical part; being

being executed very neatly, in the manner adopted by Mantegna. Thefe prints have feveral Italian verfes underneath them; and were apparently the works of Giov. Ant. Brixianus, or fome other engraver, contemporary with him, and his equal in point of merit.

Boticelli is fpoken of as a man of genius, in the hiftory of the painters. He certainly did not draw incorrectly upon the whole; though the outlines of the figures are frequently overcharged, which gives them too great an appearance of fhortnefs. The limbs and extremities, in particular, are heavy, and often very indifferently marked. It muft be remembered, that I fpeak of him now as an engraver; and thefe obfervations refer to him in that character only. His friend Baldini, who worked conjointly with him, or from his defigns, is generally allowed to have been deficient in the art of drawing, but fuperior to him in the management of the graver. There are a fet of upright plates, more than fixty of which I have feen, on which are depicted the Seven Planets, the Nine Mufes, the Four Ages, the Liberal Arts and Sciences, together with the Trades, and Mechanical Employments of Mankind. They are reprefented chiefly by fingle figures, enclofed in a twifted border, and bear every mark of great antiquity. They are little more than outlines, but very neatly engraved, and printed in fuch a manner, as proves, that the artift knew much better how to engrave, than to take impreffions from his plates. I never met with the fet compleat. Dr. Monro has near forty; and Mr. Thane lent me twenty-one. The names of the planets, mufes, arts, trades, &c. are written at the bottom in capitals; and an alphabetical letter is put at the left-hand corner, and the number of the print at the oppofite corner, in a line with the name. Thefe prints are feven inches high, by three inches three-eighths in width; and, I verily believe, they are fome of the firft productions of the graver in Italy, and probably the works of Baldini, affifted perhaps in the defigns by his friend Boticelli. An artift, who figned his plates with an L. and an A. joined together, with an F. ftanding, I prefume, for *fecit*, engraved in the fame ftyle; fo alfo did another artift, whofe fignature is a fpecies of N. And both are very ancient. From thefe mafters, it is probable, Giovanna Mariae Brixienfis, the Carmelite of Brefcia, learned the art of engraving; for he did not entirely follow his brother, who imitated the manner of Mantegna; but fometimes connected both ftyles together. And this is the fource from which Marc Antonio Raimondi acquired that knowledge, which has rendered him fo juftly famous, and ftamped fo high a value upon his excellent performances.

The print, plate V. is executed in that flight, fimple ftyle, which Mantegna afterwards improved. The outline is engraved very powerfully, and the fhadows are expreffed by ftrokes, running from one corner to the other of the plate, which are rarely, if ever, croffed. The fubject of this print is certainly emblematical. It reprefents the engraver at work; and Hercules is ftanding before him, fupporting the univerfe upon his fhoulders, to fhow, that all vifible beings are the objects of the artift's imitation. By the figure of Hercules is teftified that labour and ftrength of mind, which are neceffary to arrive at perfection. The book, the fphere, and other emblems of learning, are to fhew us, that the artift ought to be a man of fcience; and he is reprefented as an old man, becaufe a confiderable length of time is neceffary for ftudy and practice, before he can be fuppofed to arrive at any very high degree of excellence. The foregoing ingenious interpretation of this print, I owe to a worthy friend; as alfo feveral other important obfervations, which occur in the courfe of the Effay. By this very artift, we have another print, of nearly the fame fize, and executed in a manner exactly fimilar. The fubject is alfo allegorical, and reprefents Cupid binding the God of War, and claiming his laurels. Probably both might belong to a fet of emblems. Thefe two, however, are all I have feen. The laft has no infcription, letter, or mark to diftinguifh it. It is, at this time, in the poffeffion of Mr. Thane.

There is a large print, length-ways, by an engraver, who lived at this period; but ufed no mark of any kind. It reprefents the laft judgment. Chrift, with a multitude of faints and angels, appears above, feated in the air; other angels, on one fide, are conveying the fpirits of the juft men into Paradife; whilft, on the other fide, the devils are

are thrusting the wicked into separate pits of fire, where they are punished according to the nature of their crimes, which are written on labels above them: as, LUSSURIA, IRA, GOLA, AVARITIA, INVIDIA. It is very rudely executed, and, without doubt, very ancient; yet some of the figures, and most of the heads, are by no means destitute of merit. The maps or geographical charts, mentioned in the fourth chapter of this Essay, as engraved by Conrad Sweynheym and Arnold Buckinck, for the edition of Ptolemy, published at Rome, 1478, are also very rudely engraved, according to Heineken, in this style, which he distinguished by the appellation of *traits de zigzag*, or zigzag lines; and in this manner, says he, the goldsmiths usually ornamented their work. The letters, continued he, are executed with much labour, being stamped upon the plate with punches, by the assistance of the hammer. The zigzag mode of workmanship adopted by these artists, seems to prove, in my judgment, that though they were natives of Germany, they learned, however, the art of engraving in Italy, where only it was practised in this style, and never in Germany, or indeed in any other country, that I can recollect. Pollaioli and Andrea Mantegna imitated the foregoing masters; and a fine specimen of the work of the latter is copied on the plate No. VI. subjoined to this Essay. These were followed by Giovanna Ant. Brixianus; an artist, who signs his name I. F. T. and was probably a disciple of Brixianus; together with several others, whose names are totally unknown and undistinguished by any mark.

The two following prints are, without doubt, very ancient, and prior to the sixteenth century. And because of their singularity, I have thought it necessary to describe them, though they have no mark, by which they can be properly distinguished. They are executed in a mixed style, formed in part upon that of Boticelli, and in part upon that of Mantegna. The one represents Judith putting the head of Holophernes into the bag, which her maid holds for her. It is a large print, one foot high, by eight inches and three quarters wide. It is rudely engraved; and the drawing is very defective, especially with respect to the extremities of the figures. The other is seventeen inches and a half long, by twelve in height, still more rudely executed than the former, and by no means more correctly drawn. In the front, we see a woman sleeping upon a bench, whilst a satyr is lifting up the drapery, with which she is covered. Near him is another satyr, apparently frighted by a young man, who is clothed and lying down, presenting to him two flutes, which he holds in his right hand. Towards the left we see a large bason, with water issuing from it; and fishes, ducks, and frogs, are depicted swimming in the stream below. Among the rushes is an inscription upon a scroll, which is perfectly unintelligible to me.

I have a small print, seven inches high, by nearly four inches and an half wide. It represents St. Sebastian, a standing figure, bound to a column. From the manner in which it is executed, I take it to be the work of Boticelli; and if so, it is certainly the finest specimen of this style of engraving, that I ever saw. The figure is carefully drawn, and possesses great merit. Marc Antonio improved upon this style of engraving, and by it acquired such great reputation, that it was presently adopted by nearly all the Italian engravers; whilst that of Mantegna and his followers was totally neglected, soon after the commencement of the sixteenth century.

ON THE ORIGIN AND PROGRESS OF ENGRAVING. 25

CHAPTER VII.

A Description of the Eight first Plates referred to in the foregoing Essay.

AS the engravings which accompany this Essay are occasionally referred to in more places than one, it was judged most eligible to put them all together, (the frontispiece excepted) with such a description as was necessary for their explanation, and a reference to the collections from whence they are taken.

THE FRONTISPIECE.

On this plate is represented an ancient Etrurian *patera* or *sacrificing instrument*, and part of a *sheath* for a sword or dagger; these are particularly described page 10 of the Essay; the originals are preserved in the British Museum, and were brought from Italy by Sir William Hamilton.

PLATE I.

The Virgin and Child, a very ancient German engraving; the date which appears under the tree is 1461; the four is very commonly written in this manner in the old manuscripts, and it seems to have continued longer in use among the Germans than the other European nations. The original print from whence this engraving is taken, is in the collection of Dr. Monro, who kindly permitted me to copy it.

PLATES II. AND III.

The original prints from which these two plates are engraved, belong to a set which consists of eight; seven of them represent the seven planets, and the influence those heavenly bodies are supposed to have upon the human constitution. The plate marked with the No. II. served as the frontispiece; it is a sort of almanack, exhibiting a calender of the saints days, and a calculation of the day on which Easter would fall, from 1465 to 1517 inclusive. Upon twelve small circles in the middle of the plate, are represented the employments for the twelve months of the year, with the zodiacal sign belonging to each month; and the gradual increase and decrease of the days, is expressed by the extent of the shadow upon the border, within which these delineations are inclosed. They are as follows:

January. An elderly gentleman seated at a table, spread with provisions, near the fire, holding a glass with liquor in his hand.
February. The gardener digging his ground.
March. The employment of the two figures represented in this compartment is rather obscure; probably the man is planting shrubs or herbs in the garden, according to the direction of the lady who is standing by him.
April. Hawking and hunting the hare.
May. Running at the ring.
June. Mowing.
July. Gathering in corn and thrashing.
August. Sickness; the doctor is examining the urinal.
September. Gathering grapes.
October. Making wine.
November. Ploughing.
December. Killing of Swine, and providing the good fare for Christmas.

The

The following directions are written in Italian at the bottom of the plate: *If you will know when Easter shall be, find the date of the year in this engraving, the letter A. standing for April, and the letter M. for March.*

PLATE III. represents the planet Venus, she appears in the clouds riding in her chariot drawn by doves, accompanied by Cupid, who has just discharged an arrow at one of the ladies standing in the balcony; at a distance we see an unfortunate lover upon his knees, invoking the assistance of the deity; the rest of the figures appear to be immediately under the direction of her powerful influence. On the wheels of her chariot are represented the Bull and the Balance, with these inscriptions: TORO and BILANCE, the signs of the zodiac over which this planet was supposed to preside.

At the bottom of this and six other plates, are inscriptions importing the properties of the planets represented upon them. I shall give the following entirely as a specimen for the whole; one line of it only being copied upon the plate No. III.

VENERE. E SEGNO. FEMININO. POSTA. NEL. TERZO. CIELO. FREDDA. E VMIDA. TENPERATA LA QVALE. AQVESTE. PROPRIETA. EAMA BELLI. VESTIMENTI. ORNATI. DORO. E DARGENTO. E CHANZONE. E GAVDII. E GVOCHI. ET. E LACIVA. ET HA DOLCE PARLARE. EBELLA NELLIOCHI. E NELLA. FRONTE. E DI. CORPO. LEGGIERI. PIENA. DI CARNE. E DI. MEZZANA. STATVRA. DATA. A. TVTTI. OPERE. CIRCA. ALLA. BELIZZA. ET. E SOTTO POSTO. ALLEI. LOTTONE E. IL. SVO. GIORNO. EVENERDI. E LA. PRIMA. HORA. 8. 15. ET 22. E. LA. NOTTE. SVA. E MARTE. DI. E IL. SVO-AMICO. E GIOVE. EL NIMICO. MERCVRIO. ET. HA. DVE HABI-TATIONNI. EL. TORO. DI. GIORNO. E LIBRA. DI. NOTTE. E PER-CONSIGLIERE. EL. SOLE. E LAVITE. SVA. EX ALTATIONE. EIL PESCE. ELA MORTE EDVMILIAZIONE. E VIRGO. E. VA. IN IOMESI. IZSENGI. INCOMIN CANDO. DA. LIBERA. E IN 25. GIORNO. VA VNO. SENGNO. E IN. VN GIORNO. VA VNO GRADO. E IZ. MINVTI. E. IN VNA ORA. 30 MINVTI.

I thought two specimens sufficient to be engraved, in order to shew the style in which these curious plates were executed. However, I doubt not but that a short description of the rest, will be also very acceptable to many of my readers.

GIOVA, *Jupiter.* He is seated in his chariot in the clouds, with a crown upon his head, and a dart in his left hand; before him is represented Ganymede kneeling, with a small vase in one hand, and a cup in the other. The chariot is drawn by two eagles, and on the wheels are the two signs Sagittarus and the Fishes, with the words SAGITARIO and PISCE. The distance is a mountainous country, with figures on horseback and on foot, hunting and hawking; in the foreground towards the right we see an emperor upon his throne with figures doing him homage; and to the left, three figures representing (as it is supposed) Boccace, Dante, and Petrarch seated in an alcove, &c. with the inscription underneath, beginning thus:

GIOVE. EPIANETA. MASCVLINO. POSTO. NEL SESTO. CIELO. CALDO. E HVMIDO. TEMPERATO. DI NATURA. DARIA. DOLCE. SANGVIGNO. SPERANTE. &c.

SOLE, *the Sun.* He is represented splendidly armed, with a crown upon his head, and seated in his chariot, drawn by four horses; upon the chariot wheel is the zodiacal sign of the Lion, inscribed beneath LEO. In the back-ground we see a castle upon an hill, and some figures shooting at a mark with cross-bows; near them are two men praying to a crucifix; others are diverting themselves with mock fights, and a laughable figure of a dwarf is standing by them with a sword under his arm; others again are throwing stones and wrestling, whilst in the front an emperor is seated, and three tumblers are depicted before him, exhibiting their feats of activity. The inscription begins in this manner:

SOLE. E. PIANETA. MASCVLINO. POSTO. NEL QVARTO. CIELO. CALDO. E. SECHO. INFOCATO. CHOLERICO. DI. COLORE. DORO. &c.

MARTE

MARTE, *Mars*. He is feated in his chariot, drawn by two horfes, and reprefented compleatly armed, with wings upon his head, and a fword in his right hand; upon the wheels of the chariot are expreffed the Ram and the Scorpion, two figns of the zodiac, and under them is written ARIETE and SCARPIONE. At a fmall diftance is a caftle, with figures fighting before it, and a man is reprefented ringing the alarm bell; in the fore-ground, a foraging party of foldiers are feen falling upon a company of herdfmen, and feizing their cattle, the infcription begins in the following manner:

MARTE. ESENGNO. MASCULINI. POSTO. NEL QUARTO. CEILO, MOLTO. CALDO. FOCOSO. ET HA QUESTE. PROPRIETE. DAMARE. MILIZIA. BATTAGLE. ET UCCISIONI. MALIGNO. DISCORDINATO, &c.

SATVRNO, *Saturn*. He is feated in his chariot, drawn by two dragons, in his right-hand he holds a fcythe, and upon the wheels of the chariot are two figns, the Goat and the Water-Bearer, infcribed CAPRICORNO and AQUARIO; the diftant country is bounded with mountains, and with caftles, and a figure is reprefented hanging upon a gallows holding a crofs in his hands; near to the fpectator is feen a man ploughing with two oxen, in a large fpace, overflowed with water, and other men are thrafhing corn in the open field. Towards the left appears an hermitage furmounted with a crofs, and the hermit is feated at the door, near which is a man cutting wood, and two other labourers with their tools; in the fore-ground, to the right, is a prifon, and before it a man feated with his legs and arms in the ftocks, and two grotefque figures are ftanding in the front; towards the left are men killing hogs, one of which is hanged upon a tree. The infcription at bottom begins as follow:

SATVRNO. E PIANETA. MASCVLINO. POSTO, NEL SETIMO. CIELO. FRIDDO. E SECHO. MA. ACCIDEITAL MENTE. HVMIDO. DI NATVRA. DI TERRA, &c.

MERCVRIO, *Mercury*. He is reprefented in his chariot, holding his caduceus and drawn by two birds like hawks; on the wheels of his chariot are two zodiacal figns, the Virgin and the Twins, infcribed VIRGO and GEMINI; we are here prefented with the infide of a city; in the back-ground is a view of a ftreet, and in the front, towards the right, a large building, which the workmen are decorating with ornaments; below appears the potter with a variety of fmall veffels, and in the front the fculptor carving a head in ftone; above him are two philofophers holding a celeftial fphere, and near them a table covered with viands; in the buildings towards the left, we fee a mufician playing upon an organ; it is fingular enough that the bellows, by means of which the inftrument is fupplied with wind, refembles the common bellows which we have in our houfes at this day; in a compartment below, are two figures at a table writing, and a third is regulating a clock. The perfpective, in which fcience the artift had here an opportunity of fhewing his abilities, is moft dreadfully defective. The infcription at the bottom begins in this manner:

MERCURIO. E PIANETA. MASEVLINO. POSTO NEL SECONDO. CIELO. ET SECHO. MA PERCHE. LA SUA. SICCITA. E MOLTO PASSIVA LVI. E FREDO. &c.

LVNA, the *Moon*. She is feated in her chariot, drawn by two females, holding a bow in her left-hand, and a dart in her right; upon the wheel of the chariot is the zodiacal fign of the Crab, with the Latin name CANCER, written underneath it. The diftance reprefents a mountainous country, with a caftle and a town, very rudely executed. Nearer to the eye is a fowler fetting his nets, figures fifhing in a boat, and a man fhooting at a flock of birds with a bow and arrow; near him, fome people are feated, at a table playing at dice; in the fore-ground, towards the left, is a water-mill, part of the wheel of which appears, and a bridge over the river upon which we fee a man on horfe-back

back, and an afs fallen down under his load; beneath the bridge are naked figures in the water fifhing with a net. The infcription at the bottom of the plate begins as follows:
LA LVNA. E PIANETA. FEMININO. POSTO. NEL PRIMO. CIELO. FREDA. E. VMIDA. FLEMATICHA. MEZANA TRA EL MONDO. SVPERIORE ET LO. INFERIORE. AMA. LA GEOMETRIA, &c.

Thefe curious and valuable fpecimens of ancient engravings are in the collection of Dr. Monro, with whofe permiffion I copied the two above defcribed.

PLATE IV.

This fingular curiofity is already fpoken of in the fourth chapter of this Effay; there is the greateft reafon to believe that it was engraved in England, and the plate itfelf bears every mark of great antiquity. It had a hole at the top quite through it, by which it appears to have been faftened with a nail to the wall, perhaps of fome religious place, and to this circumftance, it is not improbable, we owe its prefervation. The fcratches and other defacements which it has fuftained from the hand of time, could not be removed without danger of deftroying the originality of the engraved work, and for that reafon, it was conceived to be much better to let them remain as they are, than run any hazard that was not abfolutely neceffary. This plate is in my own poffeffion.

The prayers contained upon the plate are, as my readers will readily fee, in Latin; but as this work may fall into the hands of fome perfons unacquainted with the old manufcript form of letters, which are here clofely imitated, I have tranfcribed them (fome few words excepted, which are by no means intelligible to me.)

ORATIO DE OMNIBUS SANCTIS.

Gaude mater falvatoris
Felix fide flos decoris
   Mundique folatium
Nunc letare celi choris
Ju hoc fefto et langoris
   Noftri fis remedium.

Gaude Petre cum fodali
Paulo Chrifto fpeciali
   Luceus orbis climata
Et caterva generali
Veftri fita loco tali
   Nos cum iis adjuva.

Gaude Michael in hac die
Gabriel Raphaelque Meffie
   Augelorum ordines
Nos precamur nobis pie
Sitis caufa melodie
   Supra celi cardines

Gaude Thoma fpes auglorum
Et Georgi tutor horum
   Cum Edwardo nobili
Tu *Laurenti* rege lorum
Ut *tuamur poli* chorum
   Cum favore Stephani.

Gaude ventre confervatus
O Baptifta mire natus
   Sacer degens feculo
Patriarchis fociatus
Et prophetis viæ flatus
   Fac finire jubilo

Gaude preful O martine
Nicholae hugo lini
   Poffe nobis gratiam
Erkenwalde que Birine
Jam cum tuis auguftine
   Da fupremo gloriam.

Gaude virgo Katerina
Margaretta Magdalena
  Cum   Brigida
Auna fides & Chriftina
Nos fervando divina
Geus celorum jubila
Amen letamini in Domino &c.
Et Gloria omnes.

Concede

Concede quibus omnipotens Deus ut interceſſio ſanctæ Dei genetricis Mariæ ſanctarum que omnium celeſtium virtutum & beatorum patriarcham prophetarum apoſtolorum evangeliſtarum martyrorum confeſſorum atque virginum & omnium electorum tuorum nos ubique letificet ut dum eorum merita recolemus prœmia ſeutiamus
per eundem Chriſtum dominum noſtrum amen.

The words printed in Italics, are ſuch as are very difficult to decypher; and I am by no means certain, that the true meaning is given to them. In the ſeventh prayer, there are two words which I cannot explain.

PLATE V.

An emblematical ſubject in which an engraver is repreſented at work. This print is faithfully copied from a very ancient engraving of the ſame ſize, in the collection of Dr. Monro. The letter F. which appears upon the ſtone near the hand of the artiſt, gives ſome plauſibility for ſuppoſing the plate to have been the work of Finiguerra. See a more particular account of it in the fourth chapter of this Eſſay.

PLATE VI.

The Virgin and Child, from a print of the ſame ſize, engraved by Andrea Mantegna. The original is in my own poſſeſſion.

ADI P S IACOPO E FILIPPO +
ADI III LA T VENEIONE DI S CROX
DI VI S COVANNI PORTA LATINA
DI VIII LAPARICION E D S MICAEL
DI XIII S BONIFACIO MARTIRE
DI XXV S URBANO MARTIRE
DI OETO S EA NOBI PISHOPE ECOFOR
DI XXXI S PETRONILLA VIRGINIS

GVONO DI XXX LVNA XXVIII
ADI DVA S ERASMO
ADI XI S BARNABE APLI
ADI XIII S ANTONIO DA PADVA
ADI XVIII STORV SERVASI
ADI XXIII VIGILIA
ADI XXIIII S GOVANI BATISTA +
ADI XXVI STORV IOHA III S EPAVL
ADI XXVIII S PIERO ET S PAVLO

LVGLO ADI XXXI LVNA TRENTA
ADI XV S CVIRICI E IVLITE
ADI XX S MALGHARITA
ADI XXII S MARIA MADALENA
ADI XXIII S APLINARO ES B OIDA
ADI XXIIII S CRESTINA E VIGILIA
ADI XXV S IACOPO APLO I S XPFANO
ADI XXVII S PANTALEONE MARTIRE
ADI XXX S ABOON ET SENE

AGHOSTO DI XXXI LVNA XXVIII
ADI P S PIERO T VINCVLA
ADI TRE LA VENEIO DI S STEFANO
ADI X S LAVRENCIO +
ADI XII S CIARA
A DI XV S MARIA +
ADI +XXIII S BARTOLOMEO APLO
ADI XXVIII S GOVANI DICOLATO

SETENBRE ADI XXX LVNA XXX
ADI VIII LA NATIVITA D S MARIA +
ADI XIIII LA ESVLTACIONE D S CROCE
ADI XX VIGILIA
ADI XXI S MATEO APLO E VANGELISTA
ADI XXII S MARICIO MRE
ADI XXV S IVSTINA
ADI XXVII S S COSMA E DAMIANE
ADI +XXVIII S MICHELE +

OTOBRE ADI XXXI LVNA XXVIII
ADI P S REMIGIO
ADI IIII S FRANCESHO
ADI VIIII S DIONISIO MARTIRE
ADI XVI S GHALLO ABATE VANGELIST
ADI XVIII S LVCA VANGELISTA +
ADI XXI S VRSOLA CO S VA CO PAGNIA
ADI XXVII VIGILIA
ADI XXVIII S SIMON E S IVDA +

ESEGNO·FEMININO·POSTA·NEL·TERSO·CIELO·FREDDA·E·VMIDA·TENPERATA·LAQVALE·A·QVESTE·PRO

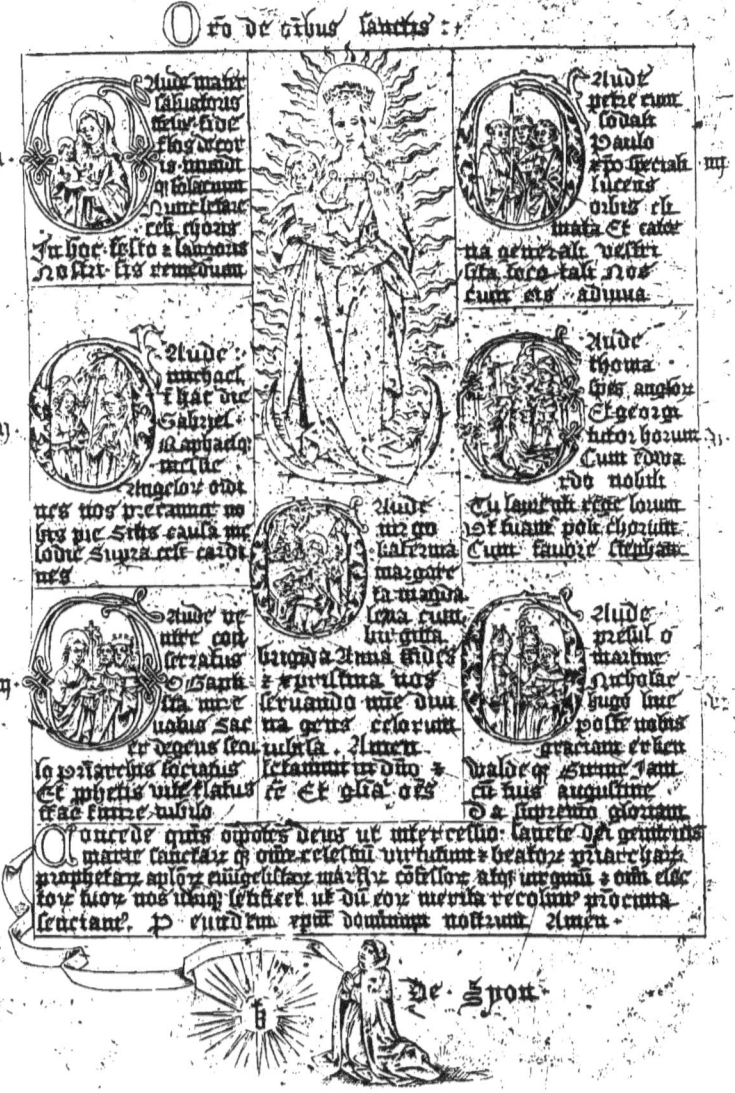

A DICTIONARY

OF

ENGRAVERS.

H. VANDER AA.
Flourished, 1701.

HE was nearly related to Peter Vander Aa, the great publisher of Leyden. I find no account of his life; and, as an artist, he merits little notice. His works were chiefly for books; and as they are very indifferent, he seldom subjoined his name; but in the multifarious collections of Peter Vander Aa, by whom he seems to have been greatly employed, some few prints occur, to which it is affixed.

The style in which they are engraved is coarse and heavy, all executed with the graver; and the strokes are crossed stiffly one over the other, in a square manner, without any harmony; the drawing and effect in these prints are still more deficient:—I shall only mention the following.

The title for the book of Adrian Pars, named *Index Batavicus*, printed at Leyden in 1701, 4to.

The portrait of Otho Archiep. et Vice-Comes Medicolan H. V. der Aa del. et sculpsit, in the collection entitled *Principium et illustrium Virorum Imaginis, Lugd. Batav.* folio. In this book is also a statue of Erasmus, drawn by this artist, and engraved by Stoopendael.

ANTONIO.

ANTONIO ABACCO.
Flouriſhed, 1558.

This artiſt is alſo ſometimes called La Bacco.—He was the diſciple of Antonio da ſan Gallo, and followed the profeſſion of an architect at Rome, where he publiſhed a great work, ornamented with fine prints, engraved by himſelf, in the year 1558, entitled *Libro d' Antonio Abacco, apartenente a l'architettura, nal quale ſi figurano alcuone nobili Antichita de Roma*, folio.

He alſo engraved the plans for the church of St. Peter at Rome, from he deſigns of Antonio da ſan Gallo, his maſter.

H. ABBE.
Flouriſhed, 1670.

This artiſt was of Antwerp, at which place, according to M. Chriſt, ſome prints engraved by him were publiſhed, A. D. 1670. M. Heineken mentions him as a deſigner only; and, beſides a portrait drawn by him, takes notice of ſeveral deſigns made by him for Ovid's Metamorphoſis, publiſhed by Banièr.

J. ABERRY.
Flouriſhed, 1753.

Known only, I believe, by an etching of Sir Watkin Williams Wynne, from T. Hudſon, half length. This artiſt, who probably worked only for his own amuſement, has adopted the ſtile of Worlidge; and his performance is by no means devoid of merit, eſpecially, if it be conſidered as a firſt attempt in the art.—He has put his name to it, and it is dated 1753.

GIUSEPPE ABBIATI.
Flouriſhed, 1700.

A deſigner, who, according to M. Heineken, lived at Milan, in the beginning of this century. He engraved ſome few things; amongſt the reſt, an emblematical ſubject, from a deſign of his own, with his name: alſo ſeveral ſmall battles.

P. M. ABBIATIS.
Flouriſhed

An artiſt of no kind of note, who ſeems only to be known by a portrait, engraved by him, of Jerom Cornaro, procurator of St. Mark, without date, or the name of the painter.

LEONARD ABENTS.
Flouriſhed

According to M. Chriſt, this artiſt was a native of Paſſau. He engraved

A C C   [3]   A D A

engraved for the topography of Braun the plan of the town of Paſſau, to which he put his monogram, which may be found in the table, at the end of this volume.

CÆSAR ANTONIUS ACCIUS.
Flouriſhed, 1609.

According to M. Heinekin (who is the only author I have met with, that mentions this artiſt as an engraver) there is a landſcape length-ways, in which are three figures, one of which holds a drum,—mark'd at the left upon a tablet, Cæſar Ant. Accius fecit et im. A. D. 1609.

ARNOLD VAN ACHEN.
Flouriſhed, 1700.

Lived in the beginning of this century, and was brother to a famous drapery painter of the ſame name, who reſided at London, and was called the Taylor Van Achen, from the facility with which he clothed his figures. Arnold etched ſome frontiſpieces to plays, and other ſmall works for the bookſellers.

ADAM of FRANCKFORT, ſee ELSHEIMER.

ADAM of MANTUA, ſee GHISSI.

P. ADAM.
Flouriſhed,

An artiſt of little merit, and of whom we have no account. His works are only a few landſcapes, etched in a ſtiff, taſteleſs ſtile. The mechanical part is poorly executed, and his foregrounds are fatigued with little dots, without any mark of the maſter.—I have ſeen ſix of theſe landſcapes, in one of which is repreſented a figure ſeated on a bank, engraved in the ſtile of Melan, without any croſs hatching upon the firſt ſtroke. They are marked with his name at length, the P and the A joined together in a cypher.

CHARLES ADAMS.
Flouriſhed,

M. Heineken, who mentions this engraver, tells us, that he engraved a portrait of *Charles Stuart, King of England,* on horſeback.—But he has neglected to inform us, whether it is the portrait of Charles the Firſt or Second.—The Hon. Mr. Walpole and Mr. Grainger are both ſilent with reſpect to this print; and I have not been able to meet with it in any collection, for which reaſon, was I not well aſſured of the accuracy of my author, I ſhould be led to ſuſpect ſome miſtake in the name. But I have often met with ſingle prints of little note, bearing the names of obſcure artiſts, which have repeatedly eſcaped the eye of the moſt accurate writers.

writers. This man was probably a foreigner, and his works of no value, as this seems to be the only print remaining of them.

ROBERT ADAMS.
Flourished, 1589.

An English artist. He was surveyor of the buildings to Queen Elizabeth, and died in London. Besides some large plans, he engraved the representations of the several actions between the English fleet and the Spanish armada, on the British coasts, which plates were published by Augustus Ryther, A. D. 1589.

PHILIP ADLER, PATRICIUS.
Flourished, 1518.

This extraordinary artist was doubtless a German, though we have no account of his life; nor is it easy to discover, from whom he learned the art of engraving, or rather etching; for he made but little use of the graver in his works.—At a time when etching was hardly discovered, and, even in the hands of the greatest artists of the day, carried to no perfection, we find this ingenious man taking up the point, and producing such plates, as not only far excelled all that went before him in that way, but laid the foundation of a fine style, which his imitators have, even to the present time, scarcely improved. His point is firm and determined, and the shadows broad and powerful. It is true, his drawing is by no means correct, or his faces fine; and his draperies are in the German gusto, without much freedom. But notwithstanding all these blemishes (for which great allowance must be made, when we consider, that he only followed the prevailing taste of his country) his prints will always be estimable to the curious; not only as greatly meritorious in themselves, but because to them we doubtless owe the Hopfers, who followed his style, and after them, that truly excellent artist Hollar himself.

If it can be said, that this master borrowed his style from another, I should suspect his making great use of those prints, which we find marked with a W, having an O on the top of it, and which are generally ascribed to Michael Wolgemuth, the master of Albert Durer; a remarkably fine print of this artist in the collection of Dr. Monro, on which this observation is founded, will be considered in the next volume: where see Wolgemuth.

Florent le Comte mentions a print by Adler, whom he calls Adler Paticina, of St. Christopher carrying the infant Jesus, dated 1518. But the best print I have seen of his, is of a midling size, nearly square; where, beneath an arch richly decorated with foliage, are several figures of both sexes. In the middle of them appears the Virgin Mary crowned, and near her is a female saint, holding the infant Christ, who is distinguished by the glory round his head. On a tablet in the middle of the arch is written OCH OPVS FECIT. PHILIPUS ADLER PATRICIUS MDXVIII.

MDXVIII. The mark, which Florent le Comte and others atribute to this master, may be seen in the table at the end of this volume.

ADMIRAL, see LADMIRAL.

J. A. CEPH. ADORF.
Flourished,
Who calls himself a student in philosophy, says M. Heineken, engraved for his amusement the portrait of *Andre Ebrig Med. Cultor.* A. 59, in 8vo.

—— AELS.
Flourished,
Seems only to be known by a print marked with his name, where Joseph appears in a landscape, leading the infant Christ by the hand.

NICHOLAS VAN AELST.
Flourished, 1550 to 1600.
A native of Brussels, but established at Rome, where he lived from 1550 to 1600, and carried on a very considerable commerce in prints, It was very common with him to omit the name, both of the engraver and the painter, to such plates as were engraved for his collection, and insert his own with the word *Formis*, to denote his being the publisher. And indeed, so indifferent, in general, were the works he published, that this omission leaves us little to regret. However, as M. Heineken informs us, there are some plates with the word *fecit*, and others with the word *sculpsit*, added to his name, which proves, that he sometimes took up the graver. Hence it seems very reasonable to suppose, that he might retouch his plates as occasion required, though the manner, in which they were repaired, will certainly be no credit to him.—My author mentions a set of birds on twelve plates, as engraved by him.

M. Christ and others atribute to Nicholas Van Aelst such prints, as are marked with the letters N. V. A. But this, at best, is a very doubtful matter.

P. VAN AELST, see COECK.

P. AENEAS.
Flourished,
A printseller and engraver in Mezzotinto, and, as it seems, chiefly of portraits; amongst others, according to M. Heinekin, is that of Nicholas. Blankard, profess. a Fran. aged 68 years, in folio. P. Aenea' fecit et excud.

AFFNER, see HAFFNER.

COUNT D'AFFRY.
Flourished,

Lieutenant general to the king of France, and ambassador in Holland, according to M. Heineken, etched for his amusement a landscape, the fore-ground of which he has embellished with a rotundo, and the distance with a steeple.

RALPH AGGAS.
Flourished, 1578 to 1589.

He was, according to the Hon. Mr. Walpole, a surveyor, and related to Edward Aggas the printer. He published the plan of Oxford and Cambridge, in the year 1578. And also a map of Dunwich, 1589. He engraved also on wooden blocks, the large plan and view of London, afterwards engraved on copper by Geo. Vertue.

FREDERIC AGNELLI.
Flourished, 1600.

An engraver who lived at Milan, in the beginning of the seventeenth century. His chief employment seems to have been portraits, though he sometimes engraved architecture and emblematical subjects.

Amongst his portraits is that of Simplicien, bishop of Milan. The dome of Milan was engraved by him on several large plates, to which he has put his name and *Carolus Butius Architect. Ædific:*

AGOSTINO DE SAN AGOSTINO.
Flourished,

An Italian engraver, of whom we have no account. Amongst other prints of this artist is the Zingara of Corregio; that is, the Virgin Mary, habited in the Bohemian manner, seated in the midst of a landscape, with the infant Jesus; also, St. John seated writing, from a picture of Corregio in the church of St. John at Palma.

CHRISTOPHER LUDWIG AGRICOLA.
Born 1667. Died 1719.

A landscape and portrait painter; was born, according to M. Heineken, at Ratisbon; and, after having travelled into several countries, died in his own, aged 52. He amused himself but little with the graver, as the only print my author notices of his is a landscape, in which is represented the fable of Diana and Acteon, marked Agricola fec.

GIOVANNA

GIOVANNA AGUCCHIA.
Flourished,

He was an ancient engraver of Milan, and lived, says M. Heineken, in the sixteenth century. According to the Abecedario and M. Christ, his mark was G. A. Initials of Giovanna Agucchia. The large design for the dome or cathedral of Milan has his name at length.

To a portal of a large building he has placed the initials, as above only.

JOHN VAN AKEN.
Flourished,

This artist has been mistaken for John Van Achen or Aken, who was a painter, born at Cologne, 1556, but never engraved. John Van Aken, of whom we now speak, has left no memorial behind him of the time or place of his birth. By the style of his etchings I should conclude, that he lived in the sixteenth century. All the works I have seen of his, are a few small landscapes, length-ways. The set consists of six; of which some are from his own designs; and the others from the designs of an artist, whose mark is a sort of monogram, which appears to be an H an E and an L; which, according to M. Heineken, signifies Lingelback or Saftleben; but this I leave entirely to the judgment of the curious. These etchings are very slight, but have something masterly in the style, and appear to be the work of a painter; because they are more free and less determined, than might have been expected from the point of an engraver only.

Besides these six, there is a small landscape length-ways, where a horse saddled appears in the fore-ground, and a man seated behind it, with only his back seen; and, towards the left, another man with a hat on. This, which is said to be very scarce, is marked with his name, J. V. Aken inv. et fec.

WILLIAM AKERSLOOT.
Flourished, 1624.

He was, according to M. Heineken, a painter as well as an engraver, and lived at Harlem. I have never seen any specimens of his painting; nor do I recollect any engraving from his designs. He engraved not only portraits, but historical subjects, amongst the latter is Peter denying Christ, from P. Molyn; and another of Christ loaded with chains, from the same. He engraved also from A. Van der Velde and other masters.

FRANCESCO ALBANI.
Born 1578. Died 1660.

It is almost needless to inform the reader, that this eminent artist was an historical painter, born at at Bologne, and that he was the disciple of Lodov. Carracci and of Guido. His works, so justly esteemed, are the best eulogium, that can be produced in his praise. As an engraver, he has by no means added to the fame his other works have eftablifhed. Confcious, no doubt, that the time and pains he muft beftow upon this branch of the arts, to arrive at any great degree of perfection, would too much engage him from his other purfuits, he quitted the point, after having made but one fmall folio etching of Dido killing herfelf; in which he has by no means well fucceeded.

CHERUBINO ALBERTI BORGHEGIANO.
Born 1552. Died 1615.

The laft name was given to him becaufe he was born at Borgo S. Sepolcro.—From his father Michele Alberti, he learned the firft rudiments of hiftorical painting, in which art he made very confiderable progrefs. His greateft works are in Frefco at Rome. He alfo painted in oil; but his fuperior merit as an engraver is no lefs remarkable. From whofe inftructions he learned the ufe of the graver, is quite uncertain; but his beft ftyle of execution feems evidently to have been founded on the prints of C. Cort and Agoftino Carracci; though without doubt, in his friezes and other flighter plates, he owed much to the works of Francefco Villemena, whofe freedom of handling the graver is juftly admired.

Like all thefe artifts, he worked entirely with the graver, and feems never to have called in the affiftance of the point.—His engravings, which are very numerous, are not all in the fame ftyle, but thofe are the moft excellent, which approach the neareft to that of Agoft. Carracci. Some times he is very neat, and at other times, as in his friezes, and fmaller fubjects, he runs into a loofe open manner, very flight and frequently quite unequal to himfelf. This manner, however, Henry Goltzius improved upon, and carried to the greateft perfection.

The engravings of Alberti, are never very highly finifhed, or powerful in effect. The great fault of this time was, the little attention paid to the Chiaro-Scuro. The lights are fcattered and left untinted, as well upon the diftances, as upon the principal figures, of the fore-ground; which deftroys the harmony and prevents the proper gradation of the objects. The drawing of the naked parts of the figure in the works of this artift, is rarely incorrect; the extremities are well marked; and the characters of the heads generally very expreffive; but his draperies are apt to be rather ftiff and hard. His prints may be confidered as very extraordinary efforts of a great genius; whilft the art was as yet at fome confiderable diftance from perfection. According to the *Lettere Pittoriche*, Lattantio Pichi, brother-in-law to Alberti, formed the defign of publifhing fuch of his prints, as had not appeared in his life time; and though this project was never entirely executed, it is certain however, that fome of his plates were publifhed after his death, by his heirs: and for this reafon the year, dated on his prints, does not always fignify the year, in which they were engraved; but frequently the year of their publication. His ufual mark may be feen on the plate at the end of the volume.

The number of plates, great and fmall, engraved by this artift, amounts to to nearly 180; of which 75 are from his own compofitions; the reft from Michael Angelo Buonaroti, Raphael, Polidoro, Andrea del Sarto, &c. The limits of my work being fo confined, I can only take notice of a few:—and the rather becaufe the works of Alberti are far from being uncommon.

A large nativity, with his cypher, from his own defign.
A dead Chrift, fupported by an angel, oval.—ibid.
Several *figures* from the laft judgment of M. Angelo.
St. Jerom feated in a landfcape, meditating upon the crofs, a large upright plate from the fame.
The refurrection of our Saviour, from Raphael, a large plate length-ways, dated 1628, publifhed by his heirs.
A holy family, where the Virgin holds the infant Chrift upon her knees, and St. John prefents him with a bird; Elizabeth is kneeling by the fide of the Virgin, and the back ground is a landfcape, dated 1582, a large upright plate from the fame.
Creation of Adam and Eve,—Adam and Eve driven out of Paradife,—and Adam and Eve fubjected to work: three fmall plates length-ways, from Polidoro.
Great part of the *friezes*, which were painted by the fame mafter, in the houfes of feveral noblemen at Rome; in thefe are reprefented the ftories of *Niobe, the rape of the Sabines*, &c.—long narrow prints, engraved on feveral plates each.
The miracle of St. Philip Benizzo, where the men, who defpifed the exhortations of the faint, are ftruck dead with lightning: a large upright plate, engraved from the picture of A. Del Sarto, which is in the convent of the Servites at Rome. This I always efteemed, as one of the moft excellent prints of the mafter.

DURANTE ALBERTI.
Flourifhed, 1590.

With his two brothers Cofmio and Giorgio, painters and engravers, mentioned by Gandallini; according to him they were natives of Borgo S. Sepolcro. The two firft engraved upon copper and wood; the laft upon copper only, and he died young, 1597. Durante lived to the age of 75, and died at Rome, 1613.—M. Heineken very reafonably concludes, that they were artifts of no great note, and worked for the bookfellers only, as their prints are not to be found at prefent. Perhaps indeed the *portrait* of Henry the Fourth of France, with emblematical figures round it, marked C. Albert, and dated 1585, is by Cofmio.

PIETRO FRANCESCO ALBERTI.
Born, 1584. Died, 1638.

An hiftorical painter, fon to Durante Alberti, mentioned in the preceding article. By this artift we have a print, called the *Academia de Pitori*, a large plate length-ways, containing many figures flightly etched, but with fpirit, and in a style that indicates much of the master: it is signed at bottom, Petrus Francifcus Albertus inventor et fecit.

H. C. ALBERTUS.
Flourished,

Painter of Saxony. He painted and engraved the portrait of John Seckendorff, rector and profeffor at Zwickau.

C. ALBRECHT.
Flourished,

An engraver and architect at Berlin.

M. Heineken mentions this artist, and adds: " I cite him, becaufe I would not omit the name of any one I have knowledge of. But his engravings were only for the bookfellers, and of fo little value, as not to merit a feparate lift."

H. VAN ALDE.
Flourished, 1650.

He was a painter, and excelled in portraits. We have by him an etching, from a picture of his own, of Gafper de Charpentier, an ecclefiaftic of Amfterdam, which *portrait* is dated 1650.

HENRY ALDEGREVER.
Born, 1502. Died,

Many of the ancient engravers, particularly thofe of Germany, applied themfelves chiefly to the engraving of fmall plates; and for that reafon the French authors, by way of diftinction, firft called them *little mafters*; which appellation is now generally ufed. In this clafs we muft place Aldegrever; and in this clafs he doubtlefs claims the firft rank.

This celebrated artift was born at Zouft in Weftphalia, in the year 1502; but we have no certain account of his family. Both his names have been miftaken; for by fome authors he is called Aldergraft; and others tell us, his chriftian name was Albert. But, where his fir name is written at full length, as upon his own portrait, it is Aldegrever; and M. Chrift affures us, that his chriftian name was Henry, and not Albert. It is reported, and with great appearance of truth, that he went to Nuremberg, and ftudied under Albert Durer; for he certainly copied the ftyle of that mafter. The time of his deceafe is by no means known; but the laft date, which appears upon his prints, is faid to be 1558; and the number of his plates is extraordinarily great: according to Abbé de Marolles, no lefs than 350.

The criticifms, which have been made upon the works of this mafter, are much to his honour; and the efteem his pieces are juftly held in, is no fmall proof of their value. It is univerfally fuppofed, that if he had made his

his refidence in Italy, where he might have had the opportunity of examining the beautiful remains of antiquity there preferved, and the pictures of the greateft mafters of the age,—the genius and ability, which fo confpicuoufly difplayed itfelf in his own country, would have fhone with double luftre, affifted by fuch manifeft advantages. However, whilft we lament in his works the want of that elegance and fimplicity which mark the Italian fchool, let us not lofe fight of the expreffion, and propriety of compofition, with a variety of other beauties, which we find in them at prefent.

The mechanical part of the engraving is extremely neat, executed entirely with the graver, and in a ftyle (as before obferved) evidently founded upon that of Albert Durer. The light parts upon his flefh he has often rendered very foft and clear, by the addition of fmall long dots, which he has judicioufly interfperfed occafionally. His drawing of the naked figure, which he feems very fond of introducing, is much correcter, than is ufually found amongft the old German mafters; and much lefs of that ftiff tafte, fo common to them, appears in his beft works. But Florent le Comte's obfervation is certainly very juft, that his men figures are far more correct, than his women. His heads are very expreffive, in general; and his other extremities well marked; but fometimes rather heavy. As a painter alfo, he is fpoken of very highly, and confidered as nearly, if not entirely, equal to his mafter Albert Durer.

As this artift's works are fo very numerous, they cannot be fuppofed to be all equal; it is, therefore, neceffary to fee many of his prints, before any adequate judgment can be formed; and it is juft as neceffary to be careful, that they are good impreffions. For thofe retouched, or ill printed (which is often the cafe) are unworthy of prefervation; whilft the good impreffions of the fame plates are highly eftimable. His monogram may be feen in the plate at the end of the volume.

I fhall only notice the following:

His own *portrait* twice, and feveral other *portraits*; as thofe of Knipperdolling, Philip Melancthon, &c.

The hiftory of Sufannah and the two Elders, on four fmall plates lengthways, dated 1558.

Dives and Lazarus, in five fmall plates length-ways, 1554.

The Paffion of Chrift, in thirteen fmall upright plates.

The Labours of Hercules, thirteen fmall plates length-ways.

Several *madonas,* &c. many *hiftorical fubjects,* as well facred as prophane; a variety of *goldfmith ornaments* very beautifully engraved; and fome few nudities; amongft which is *the fociety of Anabaptifts,* a fmall plate length-ways. This laft was copied in the fame fize, by Virgil folis, with the mark of Aldegrever; but he has added his own.

Alfo three proceffions; and many fingle figures, &c.

There is only one etching attributed to this mafter, which is very free, but flight, reprefenting *Orpheus* playing on a violin, *and Eurydice* feated at the foot of a tree, a fmall upright plate, dated 1528.

JOHN ALEXANDER.
Flourished, 1718.

A Scotſman by birth, and, according to M. Heineken, eſtabliſhed at Rome about the year 1718; but whether as an engraver or printſeller, we are not informed. His works are ſlight, looſe, incorrect etchings; and ſo very indifferent, that the latter ſeems more probable than the former. They are (or at leaſt all thoſe I have ſeen) from pictures of Raphael in the Vatican; and, as he himſelf informs us, both drawn and engraved from the originals: but certainly they do him no kind of credit. There are ſix of them with a title, dedicated to Coſmio III. great duke of Tuſcany, middling ſize plates length-ways, as follows:

The benediction of Abraham, which I ſhould rather call, the Deity appearing to Noah, and commanding him to build the ark, dated 1717.
The ſacrifice of Abraham, 1718. *The three Angels appearing to Abraham. The departure of Lot from Sodom. Jacob's ladder,* 1718. *The Deity appearing to Moſes in the burning buſh,* 1717.

ALEMANNA.
Flouriſhed,

This artiſt is mentioned by Papillon (in his uſual ſlight way, quoting from the Abbé Marolles) as an eminent engraver in wood; and ſome excellent figures are attributed to him. But we have no account of his country, or the time in which he flouriſhed.

DON EPIFANIO D'ALFIANO.
Flouriſhed, 1600.

To which name M. Heineken adds, *Monaco Valembroſo*; but gives no further account of him, than that he was a lover of the arts, who for his amuſement engraved
A ſet of feſtivals and decorations, A. D. 1592, and a book of writing, A. D. 1607, in which he ſtyles himſelf, *Priori dello Spirito Santo di Firenze.*

NICHOLAS WILLIAM ALFORÆ.
Flouriſhed,

An Italian artiſt of Lorrain, as himſelf ſeems to teſtify, and ſettled at Rome. By him we have a book of flowers, conſiſting of twelve ſmall upright plates, not very neatly engraved, but with great ſpirit, and in a maſterly ſtyle. To theſe he has ſubſcribed, *Nicolaus Guilielmus Alforæ Lotharingus fecit Romæ.*

ALESSANDRO ALGARDI.
Born, 1598. Died, 1654.

This excellent artiſt was both a ſculptor and an architect, born at Bologna. He was the diſciple of Julius Cæſar Conventi; and the reputation he acquired
in

in sculpture nearly equalled that of Michael Angelo Buonaroti. It is said, that he much frequented the school of the Carraccii, where perhaps he learned the art of engraving; for the style he adopted (if those plates be the work of his hand, which are attributed to him) was very like that of Augostino Carracci: all executed with the graver in a bold open manner,—slight and free. Two plates supposed to be his, are

Christ upon the cross, a large plate upright, and *the deliverance of the souls from Purgatory*, in a small oval.

His mark is given on the plate at the end.

COUNT ALGAROTTI.
Died, 1763.

This gentleman, says M. Heineken, is known by his writings, which are highly esteemed. They were published in eight volumes at Livourne, A. D. 1763; of which some treat upon the fine arts. He died at Pisa, the same year, and was buried in the church of Campo Santo, where a magnificent monument was erected to his memory. He designed and engraved, for his amusement, several plates of *heads* in groupes; one of which, containing thirteen in the antique style, is dated February 15, 1744. This article is entirely from M. Heineken; for I do not recollect to have ever seen any of this gentleman's performances. See his mark on the plate at the end of the volume.

JOHN ALIX.
Flourished, 1672.

This artist was a painter, the disciple of Philip Champagne, and for his amusement took up the point. The only print noticed of his, is an *holy family* from Raphael; which he has executed in a very pleasing style, and marked with these letters, R. V. P. that is, Raphael Urbin pinxt.

HUYCH ALLARD.
Flourished,

What relationship there was between this man, and the two following of the same name, I cannot learn; but from the great sameness in the style of engraving, which appears in almost all their works, one may be led to conclude, that they lived nearly at the same time. Their prints, in general, are confounded together without distinction; for they usually marked them with the name of Allard only. It is, however, a matter of little signification; for their plates, which are exceedingly numerous, are all of them very indifferent; and by no means worthy the trouble of a particular description, in order to ascertain, how many of them each of these three artists might separately claim as his own; I shall therefore content myself with mentioning such only, as are distinguished in the marking by themselves.

The *portrait* of David Gloxin, I. V. D. *Huych Alaerd, scu.* Also the portrait of Adrianus Paw, Legat. Holland, marked in the same manner.

ABRAHAM ALLARD was established at Leyden; where, besides
engraving,

engraving, he traded in prints. M. Heineken mentions twelve plates, *views of towns*; to which he adds, exactly drawn and engraved by Abraham Allard at Leyden.

Amongst some miscellaneous prints at the British Museum, is a very large plate length-ways, entitled, *Het. Lust-Hof van flora*; where, in a garden, is represented a fountain and a variety of figures, partly etched, and finished in a stiff, bad style, with the graver; very poorly drawn, and totally devoid of taste: *A. Allard cecinit—C. Allard edit.*

CHARLES ALLARD was a printseller, as well as an engraver. He also scraped some mezzotintos, according to M. Heineken. These I do not recollect to have seen. But of his engravings there are, amongst the loose prints at the British Museum, four plates representing *the seasons*, half figures, exceedingly bad, and engraved in a coarse, heavy style, devoid of all taste. He also engraved some portraits; but they are in little or no estimation.

ANTONIO ALLEGRI, called CORREGGIO.
Born, 1494. Died, 1534.

This extraordinary artist, one of the greatest painters Italy ever produced, is said by Abbé Marolles to have engraved several plates, from his own compositions. But the truth of this assertion is exceedingly doubtful; nay indeed, positively denied by M. Heineken, in his *Idèá generale d'une collection d'Estempes.*" Certainly there is no mark, that ever I heard of, to ascertain these etchings, if any such there be. The mistake, I doubt not, lies with the Abbé, who, in several other places of his catalogues, for want of sufficient examination, has hastily attributed to one master what evidently belongs to another.

GUISEPPE ALLEGINI.
Flourished, 1746.

An Italian engraver, by whom we have the following plates:

A Virgin Mary, half figure, with the infant Christ with this inscription: *Egreditur virga de radice, &c.*

The circumcision, inscribed, *Guis. Allegrini Stamp. in rame delle croce rosa.* a middle sized plate length-ways.

The stoning of St. Stephen, the same.

A small print of *Rinaldo and Armida.*

A large *architectal opera-scene* length-ways, from Joseph Chamont.

FRANCESCO ALLEGRINI.
Flourished, 1760.

This artist designed, as well as engraved, and, according to M. Heineken, lived at Florence. By him we have a vast number of *portraits*, from different masters.

The *frontispiece* to the collection, entitled, *Cento Ritratti della Real Famiglia de Medici*, for the new edition published 1762. Several of the plates for the collection, entitled, *Dei grand duchi di Toscana della a reale casa de Medici, Protettori delle lettere e delle belle Arti*, &c.

The image of St. Francis d'Assise, which is held in high estimation at Sienna, in the church named, L'Alberino.

G. L. ALLEMAND, see L'ALLEMAND.

FLOPERT VAN ALLEN.
Flourished, 1686.

He is also named Van Alten Allen, as we find upon the view of the town of Vienna, which he drew, A. D. 1686. This was engraved on two plates by J. Mulder, at Amsterdam. But he himself engraved *the town of Prague* a large, slight print, with many figures; and marked with his name,—Van Allen.

FRANCIS ALLEN.
Flourished, 1652.

I found the name of this obscure engraver, at the bottom of an octavo *frontispiece*, to a book, entitled, *Dialogus D. Urbani Regi. Lubeck* 1652. On each side of the inscription stands a figure, one representing Moses, and the other our Saviour, and a view of Lubeck is seen at the bottom; all slightly etched, in imitation of the stile of Callot; but the figures are exceedingly incorrect, and the whole but very indifferent.

JOHN CHARLES ALLET, or ALET.
Flourished, from 1690 to 1732.

This engraver, according to M. Heineken, was a Frenchman, and worked a long time in Italy, and is supposed to have died at Rome. Owing to his not having always put his two baptismal names, (or the initials,) to his plates, but signing some few of them with Charles only, some have been led to imagine, that there were two *Allets*. But my author with great reason supposes, from the sameness of style, as well with respect to the drawing as the engraving, which appears on the plates, with both signatures, they were done by the same person. In the Abcedario he is called Carlo Alet only.

He drew and engraved several *portraits* of eminent persons; and, amongst them, Cardinal Alvisio Amodei, from a picture painted by J. M. Morandi, in folio, dated 1690. Also that of Carol. Eman. 1. to which he has put, J. C. Allet ad vivam: dated 1732.

Also a variety of other subjects, saints, and sacred history, from different masters: amongst them,

Ananius restoring sight to St. Paul, a large upright plate, from Peter Beretin de Cortona; which picture is over the altar in the church of the Capuchins at Rome.

The vision of St. Paul, from a picture of the same artist, in the same church.

These

These two prints, which appear to me to be his best in the historical line, are executed entirely with the graver, in a cold silvery manner. They show that he had great command of hand, though very little taste. His style is evidently formed upon the finer prints of F. Spierre, and Corn. Bloemart. But he has greatly failed in his imitation. The lights are harsh and unharmonized; and the shadows thin and feeble. The drawing, though not incorrect, is often stiff; and the heads in general, want character. His hands and feet, however, are by no means devoid of merit: they are usually well proportioned, and not badly marked.

JOHN ALMELOVEN.
Flourished,

This artist, who was a Dutchman, professed painting, as well as engraving. The latter he did chiefly for the booksellers; and as M. Heineken observes, his works prove him to have been a man of ability. Besides the *portrait* of Gisbert Voetius, to which he puts, J. Almeloven inv. et fec. we have six small *landscapes*, length-ways, from his own drawings.

Also, twelve *views* of towns and villages, the same; and four *landscapes*, representing the four seasons of the year, after Saftleven; all these are small plates length-ways.

BALDASSARE ALOISI, called GALANINO.
Born, 1577. Died, 1621.

A painter of great eminence in portrait and history, born at Florence. He learned from his father Alessandro Aloisi the first principles of painting; but finished his studies from the works of other masters. As an engraver, little can be said of him; for I know of but one print by him, which is a copy of that beautiful etching of Guido's, from Annib Carracci, where *St. Rock is giving charity to the poor:* but the copy is far inferior to the original.

ALBERT ALTDORFER.
Flourished, 1511.

Authors, in general, have agreed, that this remarkable artist was a native of Altdorff, in Switzerland. But Mr. Wild, a senator of Ratisbon, who is, according to M. Heineken, a very learned connoisseur, with great reason, imagines him to have been born at a town named Altdorff, in Bavaria. And he is confirmed in this opinion, by several documents, discovered at Ratisbon; where this family was known in the fifteenth century, being then established in that town, or its environs. And the name of our Albert is found in the registers, amongst the citizens of Ratisbon, in the year 1511; where his artist, having passed through all the civil offices, was at last made a member of the interior senate, and architect to the town. He died A. D. 1538, without issue. Some of his pictures are at Ratisbon; and at the town-house is preserved a complete collection of his engravings. The French call him *Le petit Albert*: that is, the little Albert, because he engraved

engraved ſmall prints only; and for this reaſon, he is ranked amongſt thoſe artiſts, diſtinguiſhed by the name of little maſters.

His merit, as a painter, muſt have been very conſiderable, if the obſervation of M. Heineken be juſt, where he ſays: " *He applied himſelf more to engraving than painting.* But however, being the diſciple of Albert Durer, and a man of genius, his pictures may be placed in the ſame rank with thoſe of his maſter, being executed in the ſame taſte." From the few pictures I have ſeen of this artiſt, it would not be fair to form a decided judgment. It is true, they ſeemed by no means to merit ſo high an eulogium. But ſurely the prints of thoſe two maſters ought not to be ſet in competition with each other; for whatever merit we may allow to Altdorfer, it certainly cannot be ſaid to equal that of A. Durer. Neither does it ſo clearly appear, that he was the diſciple of A. Durer. His engravings, eſpecially thoſe on copper, have much leſs the ſtyle of that maſter in the mechanical part of their execution, than might have been expected, if he had really been his ſcholar. But this I ſhall not inſiſt upon. It is certain, that his beſt prints are thoſe, which he has cut in wood. He appears to have had a lively fancy, and facility of invention. He deſigned with freedom, in the German ſtyle, and executed his deſigns with great preciſion. I ſpeak now of his wooden cuts; and their flight, ſketchy appearance hides, in a great meaſure, thoſe defects, which appear more viſibly, as he approaches nearer to neatneſs, and high finiſhing, becauſe a more determined outline is then required. For, in his engravings on copper, we find the drawing, though ſpirited, very incorrect; the heads neither beautiful nor expreſſive, and the outlines of the other extremities exceedingly defective. He marked his plates with two ſorts of monograms, though little different from each other: ſee both upon the plate at the end of the volume. The ſecond has been falſely attributed by ſome to Aldegrever, notwithſtanding the monogram of that maſter is ſo very different: but the ſtyle of the plates themſelves would be ſufficient evidence to detect the miſtake; for Aldegrever, as an artiſt, doubtleſs was greatly ſuperior to Altdorfer.

From the ſpirited wooden cuts of this maſter, Hans or John Holbein is ſaid to have drawn great aſſiſtance. And this opinion ſeems to me to be well grounded. For evident traces of the ſtyle of Altdorfer, appear in the prints of that inimitable artiſt, prodigiouſly improved indeed, as well with reſpect to the ſpirit and taſte of the deſign, as to the excellency of the execution.

The number of his engravings on wood and copper amount at leaſt to 170; of courſe they cannot be all ſuppoſed to be equal in merit: it is requiſite therefore to ſee many of them, before a juſt judgment can be formed of his ability.

I ſhall only mention ſome few of the engravings of this artiſt of both ſorts: and firſt thoſe on wood.

The fall and redemption of man,—forty very ſmall upright prints. A certain perſon, the initials of whoſe name are G. L. F. having found ſome of theſe blocks, cauſed what was deficient to be copied, to the number of 38, and publiſhed them at Zuric, A. D. 1604, with a deſcription of each print in verſe, and this title, *Alberti Dureri Noriberg. German. Icones ſacræ nunc primum è tenebris in lucem editæ;* which proves, in the firſt place, the ignorance of the man, in attributing theſe prints to Albert Durer, notwithſtanding they

they have the mark of Altdorfer, and his difingenuity, in declaring that time to be the firſt publication of them.

The *reſurrection of Chriſt*, a ſmall upright plate dated 1512, generally eſteemed one of his moſt ſpirited and beſt prints.

The *beautiful virgin of Ratiſbon*, from the image of the virgin, which was in the cathedral of that town, a ſmall plate upright. This is printed in two tints, or chiaro-ſcuro, though there are ſome few impreſſions from the ſingle block, on which were engraved the outlines, without the half tint.

St. Jerom, kneeling before the crucifix, in a cavern, a ſmall upright plate.

Another *St. Jerom*, a ſmall upright plate: Theſe are two ſpirited prints; the back ground of the latter is very romantic, and executed with great ſpirit.

All theſe have his monogram.

On copper: one of the earlieſt I have ſeen, is the *head of an infant* dated 1507.

An *Adam and Eve*, a very ſmall upright plate.

Several *virgins*, with the *infant Chriſt*, all ſmall.

A *crucifixion*, with ſeveral figures, a ſmall upright plate.

Another, with the Virgin Mary and St. John, the ſame.

St. Jerom in his grotto, with an altar, in which ſtands a croſs; a book is open before it, and a tablet over it, on which is the monogram of Altdorfer.

Venus leaving the bath, a ſmall upright plate.

A *crouching Venus*, the ſame. Theſe two are copied from prints of M. Antonio Ramondi, in a very neat ſtyle, and the figures not badly proportioned, except the extremities, which are rather heavy.

A variety of other ſubjects and *figures of heroes* and *heroines*, and many *ornamental* plates for goldſmiths, &c.

To theſe may be added two etchings:

A ſmall *landſcape*, length-ways, executed with great freedom, eſpecially the trees in the fore-ground, which are touched in a maſterly manner.

A *cup* or *chalice*, adorned with ornaments.

ANDRE ALTOMONTE.
Flouriſhed, 1728.

What countryman this engraver was, I cannot learn; but I find that he reſided at Vienna, and was employed there by Prenner, to aſſiſt him in engraving certain plates from the pictures in the Imperial gallery, publiſhed 1728.

WILLIAM ALTZENBACK.
Flouriſhed,

This engraver, with William his ſon, according to M. Heineken, lived in the ſeventeenth century, and worked at Paris, amongſt other places, with Landry. After this, they reſided at Straſburgh, where many of their plates were publiſhed by Gerard Altzenback, a printſeller, and probably a relation. Amongſt others they engraved,

Twenty plates of *bible ſubjects*, conjointly with other maſters.

St.

St. Bridget kneeling before our Saviour, and the martyrdom of St. Margaretta, both upright prints, from Touffaint.

The *marriage of St. Catherine*. Wilhelm. Altzenback le june, Gerard Altz. ex.

A fet of *flower pieces* from Touffaint and others, by W. Altz. and Fr. Brun.

FRANCISCO AMATO.
Flourifhed,

An Italian painter. Some flight, fpirited etchings are attributed to him, which are executed in the ftyle of Bifcanio: amongft others we have the following:

St. Jofeph, feated, reading a book, accompanied by the infant Chrift, a fmall upright plate, marked, Francifcus Amatus in.

St. Jerom, the fame.

The *prodigal fon*, an upright plate, but no name.

CHRISTOPHER AMBERGER.
Born,   Died, 1550.

A native of Nuremberg, but he refided at Augfburg, where he died, 1550. He was difciple to the famous Hans or John Holbein; and he fucceeded fo well in imitating the ftyle of his mafter, that many of his pictures have been taken for Holbein's. He painted both hiftory and portraits; in the latter of which he is faid chiefly to have excelled.

Abbé Marolles, and, after him, Florent le Comte mention Amberger, as an engraver, without fpecifying his works; and Bafan tells us, that he engraved in wood feveral prints, from his own compofitions.

DOMENICO AMBROGI.
Flourifhed, 1653.

An Italian artift, who painted both hiftory and landfcape. He was the difciple of Brizio; and for that reafon called *Minghino del Brizio*. In the Abecedario he is fpoken of with great praife, and mentioned as an engraver; and Malvafia fays, that in the year 1653, he executed on wood fome prints in chiaro-fcuro. Amongft others, engraved by him, is

A woman feated in a triumphal car, holding two flambeaux and a ferpent; conducted by Neptune.

FRANCESCO AMICI.
Flourifhed,

A modern engraver at Florence, who, according to M. Heineken, employed himfelf in engraving fmall plates of devout fubjects: fuch as, *Chrift praying in the garden*; *Chrift before Pilate*; *the carrying the crofs*; and the *entombing of Chrift*, &c.

JACOPO AMICONI.
Born, 1675. Died, 1758.

According to the beſt accounts, this artiſt was a native of Venice, where he ſtudied for ſome years the art of painting, and afterwards went to Rome to complete himſelf in his profeſſion. He travelled into ſeveral countries of Europe, and was much encouraged, eſpecially at London, where he reſided ſome time. He died at Madrid, A. D. 1758, being then employed by the king of Spain.

His works, as an engraver, are very inconſiderable, becauſe he only followed that art as an amuſement; but he is more remarkable for teaching it to Joſeph Wagner, to whom it is no ſmall credit, that Mr. Bartolozzi was formerly his pupil.

By Amiconi there is a ſmall upright plate, repreſenting *our Saviour*, half figure, inſcribed, *Salvator mundi*.

Jupiter and Califta, a ſmall plate length-ways *Gi Giove di Cinthia, &c*.

And *Zephyrus and Flora*, the ſame, *a Zefiro de cui, &c*.

CARL GUSTAV. AB AMLING.
Born, 1651. Died, 1702.

This artiſt, who was a German, born at Nuremberg, A. D. 1651, was a painter and deſigner, as well as an engraver. He learned the art of engraving from Francis de Poilly, whoſe ſtyle he followed. But never nearly equalled his maſter. He chiefly excelled in portraits, (in which line he was much employed) many of which have great merit. He failed moſt in hiſtorical ſubjects. His drawing of the naked figure was not correct, neither are his heads in theſe plates ſufficiently expreſſive, or the other extremities well marked. The effect of the whole is cold and ſilvery, the draperies heavy, and the lights much fatigued. However upon the whole, his works, which are very numerous, are held in no ſmall eſteem by many collectors. He was, according to Baſan, engraver to the duke of Bavaria, and died, A. D. 1702.

Amongſt his portraits are,

Maximilian Emanuel, prince electorial, from Thomas Macolinus, dated 1670, an oval, this is ſaid to be very ſcarce.

Maximilian Emanuel, elector of Bavaria, from J. B. Champagne, a large upright plate, this is eſteemed as one of his beſt.

Amongſt his hiſtorical, I ſhall mention only the following:

The *hiſtory of the Emperor Otho*, from the tapeſtries at the palace at Munich, which were made after the paintings of Peter Candido; engraved on thirteen plates of different ſizes.

The *four ſeaſons*, from the ſame tapeſtries, by the ſame maſter, &c.

JOST or JODOCUS AMMAN or AMMON.
Born, 1539. Died, 1591.

M. Papillon obſerving, that this artiſt had ſigned his name two different ways, and that he ſometimes added to it, *of Zurick*, where he was born; at other times, *of Nuremberg*, where he reſided, has taken upon him confidently

to

to affert, that there were two artifts of this name, the one of *Zurick*, and the other of *Nuremberg*; pretending, that this opinion is perfectly eftablifhed by the confiderable difference, which may be found between the works of the one mafter and the other. But this argument is by no means decifive. For fuppofe, we fhould take thofe prints alone, where the artift has figned, *of Zurick*, we fhall find on examination, that they differ full as much from one another, as thofe do, which are figned, *of Nuremberg*, from fuch as bear the fignature *of Zurick*. And the fame obfervation will hold equally good, if we examine thofe figned, *of Nuremberg*, alfo by themfelves. For this reafon I am readily inclined to agree with fuch other authors, as have fuppofed, that the prints figned both ways belong to the fame perfon.

Joft Amman was born at Zurick in Switzerland, A. D. 1539, and died at Nuremberg, where he refided, A. D. 1591, aged 52. He was a defigner, as well as an engraver; for many of his compofitions were engraved by other artifts. He is ranked amongft the *little mafters*, fo called from the diminutivenefs of their works.

If patience and affiduity of themfelves could complete an artift, I know of no one more likely to have attained to a fuperior degree of excellence than Joft Amman. The multitude of defigns which he made, and the number of plates which he engraved, are almoft incredible. But though a great genius may be much improved by cultivation, yet it is equally certain, that neither pains nor ftudy can create a great genius. I mean not, that this obfervation fhould detract from the merit of our artift. Much merit he certainly poffeffed as an engraver; but not equal to what one might have expected from the labour he evidently muft have beftowed upon his profeffion. He lived at a time, when almoft every book, which made its appearance, was ornamented with prints; and he was employed by moft of the great bookfellers; efpecially by the celebrated Feyeraband.

The engravings by Joft Amman, are chiefly upon wood. We have fome alfo by him on copper; but the laft are much inferior to the former. His prints do not difcover any very great variety of invention. His figures are well proportioned; and in general not incorrect in the drawing. The hand of the mafter appears in his defigns; and animals, in particular, he touched with great fpirit. His manner of engraving is neat and decided; but if his ftrokes are more regular than was ufual with the engravers on wood of his time, it is to be feared, that as much as he gained, by the pains he took with this part of his execution, he loft in freedom and fpirit.

I fhall mention only the following of our artift's performance:

Πανοπλια, *omnium liberalium mechanicarum et fedentarium artium genera continens &c.—Edit per Hoftman Schoperum, Francof.* 1564. This work confifts of the different tradefmen and artifts, reprefented in their refpective employments: and there are fome excellent figures amongft them. The collection amounts to 115 prints; and it is faid, that Amman has given his own portrait in that which reprefents the art of engraving.

The above edition is very fcarce. It was re-printed, A. D. 1574, and again 1588, in large octavo.

Neuive

A M M   [22]   A N K

Neuive Biblifchi Figuren, Franckfurt, per Jo. Amman von Zurych, 1564, ibid.
He alfo engraved on wood fome detached pieces; and on copper, the *illuftrious women*, begining at Eve, with this title, *Eva die Gebererinn*, on twelve plates, fmall upright, figned, *Joft Amman fec. Stefan Herman, exc.* Thefe are chiefly etched, and in a flight incorrect ftyle.
A fet of *figures of warriors*, 1590, fmall upright plates. The *four feafons*, and the *four elements*, fmall long plates, 1569; and two *portraits*, one of *Cafparis de Colignon*, marked, *Fecit Norimbergæ, Joft Ammon Tigurinis*, 1573. See his marks on the plate at the end of the volume.

JOHN AMMAN.
Flourifhed, 1623.

According to M. Chrift, John Ammon was not only an artift, but a bookfeller. He lived at Hanau in Germany, about the year 1640; and marked his engraving in this manner, I. A. The fame letters, we are well affured, were alfo frequently ufed by Joft Amman. To this artift, amongft other things, is attributed a fet of fmall wooden cuts, reprefenting the *paffion of our Bleffed Saviour*, executed greatly in the ftyle of Joft Amman. They are very neat and fpirited, and poffefs a confiderable fhare of merit. Thefe prints were publifhed at Amfterdam with Latin verfes, A. D. 1623.

CLEMENT AMMON.
Flourifhed, 1651.

He was fon-in-law to the famous Theodore de Bry; and followed the bufinefs of a bookfeller, as well as the profeffion of an engraver; induced thereto perhaps from the confcioufnefs of a want of fufficient abilities to fupport himfelf by the latter, independent of the former; for his engravings in general, are very poor and ftiff, executed indeed in a laborious ftyle, copied from the works of his father-in-law, but without tafte, and vaftly inferior to them. His greateft work was the continuation of the collection of *portraits*, firft publifhed by Theodore de Bry, and afterwards by his fons, entitled, *Bibliotheca Calcographica*, in fix volumes, quarto. To thefe Clement added a feventh, and an eighth volume; the firft of which was publifhed at Frankfort, A. D. 1650, to which he puts, *Sculptore Clemen. Ammon junior, Calcograp.* and to the laft, publifhed in the year 1652, *Sculptore Clemente Ammonio chalcogr: Franc.* to both is added, *Imp. Joh. Ammon.*

JOHANN AMMON.
Flourifhed,

This artift, according to M. Heineken, was a native of Schaffhoufen. His engravings, of which my author cites half a dozen, are *portraits* only; amongft which is one of John Locke, Phil. without any name of the painter.

ANKER VON ZWOLL. See Zwoll.

                                  SIMON

SIMON RENARD DE ST. ANDRE. See RENARD.

NICOLO DI ANDREA.
Flourished, 1578.
Of the life of this engraver I can find no account. M. Heineken informs us, that in the year 1578, he engraved at Constantinople, the *portrait* of the ambaffador, Giles de Noailles, Abbé de St. Amand.

ALESSANDRO DE ANDREA.
Born,   Died, 1711.
A native of Abriozzo, and the difciple of Solimene, who engraved a few things for his amufement only. This article I have from M. Heineken; but have never feen any of his works. According to this author, he died in 1711.

JEROME ANDREAE. See APSCH.

T. ANDREAE.
Flourished,
An artift of no great merit, whofe name, to the beft of my recollection, is not mentioned by any author. There is a fmall upright etching by him; it is a fort of *emblematical subject*, in which is reprefented a woman fallen down in the front, and another woman ftanding over her, who holds a book in her hand, on which is written, *Guilio Cefare opera*. The defign is not amifs; but the execution is fo flight, that much of the original intention is loft. The heads are but indifferent, and the other extremities very badly drawn. He figns his name, T. Andreae inv. et fec.

ANDREA ANDREANI.
Born,   Died, 1623.
This juftly celebrated artift was a native of Mantua; for which reafon he has frequently added to his name or monogram, INTAGLIAT. MANTUANO; or elfe, IN MANTOUA; which it feems has led fome haftily to miftake him for Andrea Mantegna, an artift who lived nearly an hundred years before Andreani. Others again call him Andreaffi; whilft others have run into a ftill groffer error, and confounded him with Altdorfer, a native of Switzerland, under the name of the *Petit*, or little Albert: which appellation was given to Altdorfer, on account of the fmallnefs of his engravings in general. This laft miftake, it is likely, was occafioned by the great refemblance there is between the monograms of the one and the other.

When our artift was born does not appear fo clearly; but he died, A. D. 1623, at a very advanced age. Befides the prints which he performed himfelf, he procured a great many other engravings, the works of different mafters, and fold the impreffions, with his own name, often effacing the name of the true artift, to fubftitute his own with more fecurity. Thus, amongft others, we
find

find the death of Ajax, a small plate length-ways, from Polydore, has his cypher with the date 1608, whereas the first impressions of that print bear the name of IO. NIC. VICENT, who was really the engraver, without the cypher of Andreani, or the date. In the same manner he has adopted some of the engravings of Hugo da Carpi and Antonio da Trento, &c. This disingenious artifice, altogether unworthy of him, renders it very difficult to distinguish his works precisely; for, after all, it is most likely, that many prints are attributed to him, in which he had no concern.

Andreani engraved on wood only, in a peculiar style, distinguished by the name of *chiaro-scuro*; which is performed with two, three, or more blocks of wood, according to the number of tints required, these are stamped upon the paper one after another, so as to produce the effect of a washed drawing. The invention of this species of engraving was greatly prior to the æra of our artist. Among his countrymen he had Hugo da Carpi and Antonio da Trento for models; and, in the early part of his time, he seems to have followed them very closely. But at length he carried the mechanical part of the work to a far greater degree of perfection; and we often find in his prints a correct and determined outline. At times, he used only two blocks (as for some of his slighter performances) but oftner three: one for the outline, and very dark shadows, the other two for two different tints. This number, I believe, he never exceeded. His great merit, as an artist, is acknowledged by all who are conversant in prints. His drawing is excellent, executed with great spirit, and in a very masterly style. The heads of his figures, though slight, are characteristic and expressive; and he has displayed great judgment in the management of his various tints. In short, his works are justly considered as admirable transcripts from the sketches of many of the greatest painters.

Amongst his most finished prints may be reckoned, *Christ departing from Pilate*, who is washing his hands: a large print, lengthways, on two blocks, engraved from a bass relief of Giovan. Bologna. On the shield of one of the soldiers is written, *Gian. Bologna sculps. Andrea Andriano Iontagliatore.* Dedicated to *Giovan. Baptista Deti*, a gentleman of Florence: without date.

An emblematical print, representing the Christian, after his spiritual warfare in the present-life, received as victorious into Heaven, and crowned by Christ. At the left corner is this mark, B. F. which signifies the name of the painter, Baptista Franca of Venice. It has also the cypher of Andreani; and the date 1610, with this inscription: *Bonum certamen certavi, cursum consummavi, Fidem servavi, reposita est mihi Corono Justitiæ.* Pauli Epist. ad Timo. cap. IV. This print is of a middling size, upright. Some of the impressions are with a dedication to Louis Gonzago.

To these may be added,

The Triumph of Julius Cæsar, from Andrea Mantegna, the original of which is at Hampton-Court. It is cut on ten blocks of wood, including the title, dated 1598. But it is very difficult to find all these pieces of the same colour or equally good impressions.

The

AND [25] ANG

The *entombing of Chrift*, from Raphael da Reggio, a fmall upright plate, half figures.

The *rape of the Sabines*, from a group, by the fculptor, Giovan. Bologna; three feveral views, dated 1583 and 1584.

Another print of the *fame fubject* from a bafs-relief of the fame mafter, on three blocks, dated 1585.

Variety of other prints equally excellent, from Raphael Urbin, Polidoro, Permigiano, &c. &c. The fcarceft of all his works is faid to be *the pavement of Sienna*, after a drawing of Francefco Vanni, from Domenico Beccafuni Sanefe. See the cyphers or monograms which Andriani often put to his engravings, inftead of his name, on the plate at the end of the volume.

FRANCOIS ANDRIOT.
Flourifhed, 1672.

A French engraver, who worked both in France and Italy. We have feveral prints hiftorical and others, from fome of the greateft painters, by this artift. He worked chiefly with the graver, in the ftyle of Francois de Poilly, but without any powerful effect. His drawing is ftiff, and the extremities of his figures in general, are rather heavy.

I fhall only notice the following:

The good Samaritan, a large print, length-ways, from Nicholas Poufin.

The incredulity of Thomas, the fame, from Nicholas Le Sueur.

The portrait of John Everhard, Card. Nidard, from Jonas de la Bonde, dated 1672.

And fome of the *anatomical ftatues*, publifhed at Rome by Rofli, 1691.

JAMES ANDROUET DU CERCEAU.
Flourifhed, 1576.

This artift was a Frenchman, and fome fay a native of Orleans. I have feen a book in folio, entitled, *Premier Volume de plus excellent Baftiments de France, par Jacques Androuet du Cerceau, Architecte a Paris*, 1576. That is, The firft volume of the moft excellent Buildings in France, by James Androuet du Cerceau, Architect at Paris. The plates, which are faid to be done by himfelf, are etched in a very flight coarfe ftyle, without any tafte; yet fufficiently correct perhaps for his purpofe.

MARCO ANGELI.
Flourifhed,

According to Gandellini, this Angeli engraved fome grotefque figures and ornaments; if, fays M. Heincken, the author has not, as I fear, miftaken the name of fculptor for that of engraver. I have never feen any print by this artift.

NICOLO ANGELI.
Flourifhed, 1635.

The difciple of Remigius Canta Gallina. He engraved, conjointly with his

his mafter, the feftivals which were publifhed at Florence in the year 1635, from the drawings of Giulio Parigi.

FILIPPO DI ANGELI, called NAPOLITANO.
Born, 1640. Died, 1680.

According to moft authors, this artift was born at Rome, A. D. 1640; and the name of Napolitano was given him becaufe he was carried to Naples by his father, whilft he was very young. To fome prints, engraved by himfelf, he figns his name, Theodor. Filippo de Liagnio Napol. from whence fome have doubted whether he was not really a Neapolitan. But leaving this matter, which we have not fufficient light to clear up, we find he purfued his ftudies as a painter with great fuccefs, and returned to Rome, where he was employed, and died in 1680, aged 40 years. As an engraver he is not fo well known. However, we have etched by him a fet of thirteen fmall prints of military habiliments, &c. which are marked with his name in the manner fpecified above.

GIOVANNA BATISTA DE ANGELIS.
Flourifhed,

An Italian artift, who, according to Pafcoli, engraved fome plates in Italy; but we have no particular account of him or his works.

ANGELO ALBANASI.
Flourifhed,

An artift by whom we have fome very pretty, fpirited etchings of ruins, chiefly in and about Rome. From the appearance of the ftyle of thefe little prints, I fhould fuppofe he flourifhed at the begining of the prefent century.

PETER ANGELUS.
Flourifhed, 1611.

An obfcure engraver, of whom I have met with no account. Amongft the collections of Mr. Bagford for a hiftory of printing, which are in the Harlenian library at the Britifh Mufeum, I found an *ornamental frontifpiece* to a folio volume of Lud. Tena's commentaries upon St. Paul's epift. to the Hebrews, by this engraver. It confifts of feveral figures, with the Trinity reprefented at the top; all rudely defigned and executed, entirely with the graver, in a bad ftyle, without the leaft mark of tafte or judgment: the drawing and effect are equally indifferent.

PAUL ANGIERS.
Flourifhed, 1749.

What countryman this young artift was, I have not been able to learn. The beft information I could meet with is, that he refided in London, and
was

was inftructed in the art of engraving by John Tinney. He never arrived at any great excellence. It feems he was chiefly employed in engraving landfcapes, and alfo fmall plates for bookfellers. His landfcapes are etched in a flight ftyle fufficiently neat, and with no great tafte. M. Heineken informs us that he was only thirty years old when he died; which was within thefe few years. His beft print is faid to be landfcape entitled, *Vue de Tivoli*, after Moucheron. I have before me *a view of Roman ruins*, from Paul Panini, a middling fized plate, length-ways, with figures. This print is very neatly engraved, but the figures are very indifferent. It is dated November 4, 1749.

ANGLOIS. See LANGLOIS.

BENJAMIN ANGLUS.
Flourifhed,

M. Heineken mentions this engraver, but without any account of him, or the time when he lived; and cites two *emblematical fubjects* engraved by him, one from Antonio Tempefta, the fecond moft probably from his own defign, as he adds the word *fecit* to his own name.

PIETRO ANICHINI.
Flourifhed, 1655.

This was an Italian artift; but we have no account of his life. Amongft other plates, engraved by him, are the following: A fmall *holy family* in a landfcape, length-ways, dated 1655. The Virgin is feated holding the infant Chrift upon her knees, he is reading a fcroll, which St. John, who is kneeling, prefents him. The *good Samaritan*, alfo a fmall plate, length-ways; and the *portrait* of Cofmus P. Etruriæ, P. Anichinus fec.

ANSELME or ANSHELME.
Flourifhed, 1590.

Among thofe prints, the engravers of which are unknown, is a very fine one of a middling fize upright, reprefenting *Hercules and Omphale*, from B. Spranger. The ftyle of this engraving, feems to me to be a ftrong evidence, that its author received his inftructions in the fchool of Henry Goltzius; and the manner of John Muller, a difciple of this mafter, the moft refembles it. There is a fine impreffion of this curious print in the Britifh Mufeum, which I examined very carefully. It is not equal to Muller, either in freedom or correctnefs. Omphale is a back figure, entirely naked, excepting her right fhoulder, over which is thrown a part of her robe. Her hand is too large: excufing this fault, the drawing and general proportion of the figures are not amifs. The draperies are very neat; yet the whole is flight, and the lights are too much fcattered, which deftroys the effect. But harmony was by no means the characteriftic of this æra of engraving. Inftead of a name fubjoined to this print, we have a fingular fort of rebus: a capital A; and, between

ANT [28] ANT

tween it and the word *fecit*, a cafque or helmet, which is copied on the plate at the end of this volume. It is dated 1590. Profeffor Chrift gives us the following ingenious folution of this extraordinary mark: " *C'eft vraifemblablement un nommé* Anfelme, *qui a voulu fe cacher fous ce rebus; comme* Michel Ange Anfelme, *peintre de Sienna, fort connu en ce temps, & dont Vafari parle avec éloge.*" To this M. Sellius the tranflator adds the following explanatory note : " *Cafque fignifie en Allemand* Helme, *dont la figure, jointe au reft, peut former un* Rebus, *pour exprimer* Anfelme *ou* Anfhelme." In Englifh thus: " This artift very probably was named *Anfelme*, and chofe to conceal his name under this *rebus*, like *Michael Angelo Anfelme*, a painter of Sienna, well known at that time, and of whom *Vafari* speaks with praife. In the note is added, " cafque fignifies in German *helme*, the figure of which, joined with the reft, may form the *rebus*, to exprefs the name *Anfelme* or *Anfhelme*." I have thought that the firft letter may be the initial of the artifts baptifmal name, and then it may be read *A. Helme.*

Whatever appearance of truth this conjecture may be allowed to bear, I hope it will be remembered, that I give it as a conjecture only; and, I truft, I fhall ftand excufed for adding to my lift fuch names, as plaufibility at leaft will admit, until fuch time as the true name fhall be difcovered, or a more reafonable conjecture propofed : efpecially, as, on all occafions of this fort, I fhall be fcrupuloufly careful not to miflead the reader by giving that for fact, which is built on fuppofition only.

SEBASTIAN ANTOINE.
Flourifhed, 1729.

Native, as it feems, of Nancy, the capital of Lorrain. But whether he refided there entirely or not, I cannot difcover. It was there he engraved the *portrait* of R. P. Auguftin Calmet, in a large oval, A. D. 1729. The *enterprife of Prometheus*, from the cielings of Verfailles, painted by Mignard, was alfo engraved by him; and the *crown of precious ftones*; with which Louis XV. was crowned, Oct. 25, 1722. He worked chiefly with the graver in a thin feeble ftyle, without effect ;—he was alfo very deficient in the other requifites of the art.

SILVIUS ANTONIANUS.
Flourifhed, 1567.

An engraver on wood, who, according to Papillon, ornamented with cuts, a fmall book of fables by Gabriel Faerno, publifhed at Antwerp, entitled, *Centum Fabulæ ex antiquis Auctoribus delectæ, & a Gabriele Faerno Cremonenfi, Carminibus explicitæ. Antuerpia exofficina Chriftoph. Plantini*, 1567. To each fable he has given a print, the whole of courfe amounting to an hundred; all which, two or three excepted, are marked with a fort of cypher, compofed of an A and an S; which is copied on the plate of monograms, at the end of the volume: thefe are the initials, adds my author, of the name of *Silvius Antonianus*, the engraver of this work, which was dedicated to Cardinal Charles Borromee who was canonized after his death.

Upon

Upon what foundation Papillon inferted this name, I cannot difcover. M. Chrift takes notice of the fame cypher, and informs us, that it is to be found on the prints of the emblems of Sambucus alfo; and attributes it very falfely, in my opinion, to Abraham de Bruin of Antwerp.

PIETRO ANTONIO DE PITRI.
Flourifhed,

This artift feems to have been an Italian, and perhaps refided at Rome: but I have not met with any account of his life. He engraved a *frontifpiece* to a collection of *altar-pieces* by Mariotti, which Gio. Giacomi de Roffi, publifhed at Rome: it is from Ciro Ferri, a flight, fpirited etching, in a ftyle fomething bordering upon that of Pietro Aquila. The drawing is good; the extremities are touched in a mafterly ftyle: it is infcribed Pietro Antonio de Pitri, fculp.

MARC ANTONIO. See RAIMONDI.

ANTONIO DA TRENTO. See TRENTO.

CORNELIUS ANTONISZE.
Flourifhed, 1536.

This artift was a painter, and lived at Amfterdam; where, about the year 1536, he engraved a fet of twelve prints on blocks of wood, reprefenting ancient Amfterdam, with the convents, churches, and other buildings.

G. APPELMANS.
Flourifhed, 1671.

The bookfellers appear to have been the chief, if not the only employers of Applemans. We find the *portrait* of T. Bartholinus to the octavo edition of his book of anatomy engraved by this artift, as were many of the anatomical plates in the edition of 1674. They are all executed with the graver in a neat, ftiff ftyle, the effect of labour without genius. The portrait, which is the beft, has little to recommend it: however, it was again repeated by him for Hondius's collection of eminent men.

C. APENS.
Flourifhed, 1673.

He refided at Groningen in the Netherlands, about the year 1670, where he engraved the *portrait* of Samuel Marefius, Theol. in quarto, A. D. 1673.

JEROME ANDREAE APSCH.
Born,   Died, 1556.

According to M. Heineken, this artift was a native of Nuremberg. He engraved

engraved on wood, and affifted Burckmayer in the works which the emperor of Germany defigned to publifh. He died, it is faid. A. D. 1556.

CRISTAFANO DELL' AQUA, or ACQUA.
Flourifhed, 1760.

His employment feems to have been chiefly for the bookfellers, as far as I can judge from the prints I have feen of his. Many of them are in the architectal line; all executed with the graver, in a poor feeble ftyle, without effect. he engraved, befides, the *portrait* of the prefent king of Pruffia. There is alfo a large upright plate by him, reprefenting *merit crowned by Apollo*, from Andrea Sacchi, and fome other portraits and vignettes, &c.

FRANCESCO FARAONE AQUILA.
Flourifhed, 1691 to 1722.

An engraver of fome eminence, born at Palerma; but he appears to have refided chiefly at Rome, where it is likely he died. His engravings are numerous, and many of them efteemed. We find from the fignatures upon his plates, that he ufually made the drawings himfelf, from the pictures he intended to engrave. How far he fucceeded in them, the prints will in fome meafure fhow. In merit he certainly never equalled Pietro Aquila, who refided at Rome at the fame time, and very probably was not only of the fame family, but alfo a near relation. His ftyle of engraving in general is rather neater than that of Pietro; but in drawing and expreffion he fell far fhort of him. Thofe plates, which he executed with the graver only, are cold and filvery, without effect, and by no means fo meritorious as thofe, where he called in the affiftance of the point. Some of the ftatues, which he engraved for Roffi, are of this ftamp.

Among the fets of prints, which he publifhed, I fhall notice the following:

Le Camere Sepolcbrali di Livia Augufta, confifting of forty plates, after the defigns of P. Ghezzi.

Picturæ Raphaelis Urbinatis, &c. or the pictures of Raphael Urbin, which are in the hall and chambers of the Vatican, engraved on twenty-two large plates, including the title, dated 1722.

Amongft his fingle prints,

A *Repofe*, where the Virgin, with the infant Chrift, is reprefented feated under a tree, and Jofeph appears working in the back-ground, a large upright plate, engraved at Rome, A. D. 1691, from Correggio.

The *firft Mofaic Arch* in the church of St. Peter of the Vatican, a large plate, engraved A. D. 1696, from Ciro Ferri.

The *rape of Europa*, a large plate, length-ways, dated February 1, 1699; from Paolo de Mattei.

He alfo engraved from Albano, Pietro de Cortona, Bernini, Annib. Carracci, Giovanni Lanfranchi, Carlo Maratti, Nicholas Poufin, and feveral other mafters.

PIETRO AQUILA.
Flouriſhed, 1696.

The prevalence of genius in this artiſt was ſuch, that even the gloomy retirements of an eccleſiaſtic life could not overcome it. He was born at Palerma, and in his youth applied himſelf to ſuch ſtudies, as might capacitate him for the reception of orders, which he actually took upon him, and ſupported his character in a very reſpectable manner. His ſtudies and retirements, however, prevented not his following the dictates of his natural inclination, with reſpect to the arts. How much he loved them may be eaſily conceived, by the rapid progreſs he made in them. As a deſigner and a painter, he ſtands high in the eſtimation of the curious. But as an engraver, he is more generally, and perhaps more deſervedly known. He drew admirably, and etched in a bold, free manner, finiſhing his lights, and harmoniſing his ſhadows with ſmall dots. His greateſt faults are want of effect from ſcattering his lights, and what by the artiſt is called *manner* in his drawing. The firſt gives a confuſed, flat appearance to his prints; and the laſt preſents us with a ſtyle of his own, inſtead of that of the painter from which he copied; and theſe faults ſeem never more glaring, than in his prints from Raphael; where the chaſte ſimplicity of outline, the great characteriſtic of that wonderful maſter, is loſt in the *manner* of Pietro Aquila. It is from Annib. Carracci, that he has beſt ſucceeded; and his prints from that artiſt will, I truſt, be always held in great eſtimation. In all his works he diſcovers much ſcientific knowledge. The extremities of his figures, in general, are well proportioned, the heads expreſſive, and the characters finely preſerved; but his outlines are often too hard upon the lights; and the folds of the drapery too ſtrongly marked. It appears from his prints, the drawings of which he made from the original pictures, that he reſided chiefly, if not entirely, at Rome, where perhaps he alſo died.

He engraved ſeveral plates from his own compoſition: amongſt the reſt,

An adoration of the wiſe men, a large, upright plate.

Two of *the flight into Egypt* : the one a ſmall, the other a large plate, both length-ways.

Diana and Acteon, a ſmall plate, length-ways.

Many from other maſters : amongſt the reſt,

Imagines veteris ac novi Teſtamenti, commonly called *Raphael's Bible*, from the pictures of that maſter in the Vatican. This work conſiſts of fifty-five plates, of which Cæſar Fantetti drew and engraved the firſt thirty-ſix plates, and the fortieth.

The battle of Conſtantine, on four large plates, from the picture of Julio Romano, which he painted from the deſigns of Raphael.

Concilium Deorum, commonly called *Lanfranc's Gallery*, repreſenting the aſſembly of the Gods, on nine plates, including the title, a large folio, from Giovan. Lanfranchi.

The battle of Arbella, where Alexander overcame Darius king of Perſia, from Pietro de Cortona, a large print on two plates.

The rape of the Sabines, a large plate, length-ways, from the ſame.

The ſacrifice of Polyxana, the ſame, from the ſame.

The triumph of Bacchus, the same, from the same.
Sacrifice to Diana, by Xenophon, on four large plates, from the same.
Moses striking the Rock, from Ciro Ferri, a large plate, length-ways.
The triumphs of the Christian religion, an emblematical print, from Carlo Maratti, a large plate.
The death of the Virgin, a large plate, length-ways, from Giovan. Morandi.

AQUILA. See ARENT VAN HALEN.

TOBIAS AQUILANUS.
Flourished, 1570.

I find no account of this artist. He engraved an upright plate of the Crucifixion, dated 1570.

HORATIUS DE SANCTIS AQUILANUS. See SANCTIS.

POMPEO AQUILANO, or DELL'AQUILA.
Flourished, 1550, to 1570.

A Neapolitan painter, born in the town of Abruzzo. He is spoken of in the Abecedario as an artist of great merit. It is also said, that he engraved; and to him is attributed, the lower part of a *descent from the cross*, from a composition of his own; the whole of which was afterwards engraved by Horatius de Sanctis, A. D. 1572. Florent Le Comte mentions seven prints, of this artist, without specifying, whether they were engraved by him or not.

LEONARDO DELL' ARCA.
Flourished,

Engraved, according to the Abbé de Marolles, some plates of ornaments and grotesque figures.

JAMES MAC ARDELL.
Born,   Died, 1765.

The works of this excellent artist are too well known, and too much esteemed, to need any eulogium here. Basan calls him " *one of the best engravers in mezzotinto, that England ever produced.*" Whether he has been surpassed or not by our more modern artists, I shall leave entirely to the judgment of my readers. It is generally said, that he was an Irishman by birth. I have heard indeed (though not by sufficient warrant to assert it for fact) that he was born in England, but of Irish parents. However this may be, he resided chiefly in London, and died June 2, 1765.

The far greater part of his works are portraits, and many of them from the most celebrated painters of his time. I think it is generally remarked, that he succeeded best in his engravings from Vandyke. Two most beautiful prints from this master are,

Time

Time clipping the wings of Love, an upright plate; and *Moses in the ark of bulrushes*, found by Pharoah's daughter, the same.

Add the following portraits also from Vandyke:

George duke of Buckingham and his brother, whole lengths, from the picture at Kensington, dated 1752.

Rachel, countess of Southampton, seated in the clouds, whole length, upright, dated 1758,

I shall also take notice of the following: namely,

St. Francis, a most beautiful print, whole length, from Morillis.

St. Jerom, the same.

The portrait of Rubens with his wife and child, from a picture painted by Rubens himself.

The tribute money, from Rembrandt, a very fine print.

Daniel Lock, from Hogarth.

Mr. Garrick and Mrs. Cibber, in the characters of Jaffier and Belvidera, in Venice Preserved, a large plate, length-ways, from Zoffany.

The countess of Waldegrave, from Sir Joshua Reynolds.

SANTES DE ARDUINIS.
Flourished, 1515.

He is also called Arduino de Bologna; and, according to Gandellini, was both a painter, and an engraver on wood; but his prints are not specified.

ANT. JOSEPH D'ARGENVILLE. See DEZAILLIER.

JONAS ARNOLD, or ARNOUL.
Flourished,

A painter and engraver of history and portraits. He worked, amongst other places, at Nuremberg, at Ulm, and at Paris. He drew the *portraits* and *figures* for Sigismond Van Bircken, Spiegel der Ehren, or *Mirrour of Honour*, which were engraved by Philip Kilian. Among his own engravings are,

Louis le Grand, seated upon his throne, whole length, a large upright plate, from Antoine Dieu.

Louis Dauphin, whole length, the same, and from the same painter.

JOHN ARNOLD.
Flourished,

An engraver of no great merit, by whom, among other things, is a small plate of *Daniel in the lion's den*, from Fr. Xav. Palco.

N. ARNOULT.
Flourished, 1684.

A French engraver, who resided at Paris, and acquired some reputation by his portraits *a la mode*, of the perſonages at court. Of this kind are a ſet of *ſix figures* in folio, publiſhed in the years 1673 and 1674; alſo the portrait of *Madame la marquis d'Angeau* at her toilet, with many others, all engraved in a poor, coarſe manner, without any taſte.

BALTHASAR ARNOULLET.
Flouriſhed,

Papillon informs us, that there is in the collection of the King of France, a large print, length-ways, of the *town of Poitiers*, engraved, as it ſhould ſeem, on wood, by Balthaſar Arnoullet of Lions, with the privilege of his *royal majeſty* for ſix years.

ARRE.
Flouriſhed,

A Swediſh artiſt, by whom we have the *portrait* of Thorſtan Ruden, Epis. de Linkoping, in the form of a medallion.

COSMAS DAMAN ASAM.
Born,   Died, 1739.

A native of Bavaria; he went to Rome to purſue his ſtudies as a painter, and ſucceeded both in hiſtory and portraits. After which he reſided at Munich, where he died, A. D. 1739. On the plates, to which he engraved his name, it is inſcribed *Coſmus* Aſam; he is alſo called *Coſme Damien* Aſam, and *Goſmond Daniel* Aſam. We have by him,

An *altar-piece*, repreſenting a Franciſcan before the Virgin Mary, who appears in the air, ſurrounded by Angels: a large, upright plate.

Another large *altar-piece*, like the former in ſize, where Joſeph is preſenting a book to a biſhop: both from his own deſigns.

ASNE, See MICHAEL LASNE.

JOHN ASNER.
Born,   Died, 1748.

He was born at Vienna, and inſtructed in the art of Engraving by Dietel. However, he never produced any very meritorious work, being chiefly employed on devotional ſubjects. He died at Vienna, where he reſided, A. D. 1748.

AMICO ASPERTINI.
Born, 1474. Died, 1552.

Native of Bologna, and the diſciple of Franceſco Francia. Maſini pretends, that he alſo engraved on copper, without ſpecifying his works. The invention, if not the engraving, of a large upright plate, repreſenting the *ſacriſice of Cain*, is attributed to him: a ſtrange groteſque deſign. Above we ſee the Angel driving our firſt parents out of Paradiſe: whilſt nearer to the front

front is an altar with an offering. Below, on the left side of the print, is Adam lying upon the ground, with an axe by his side; and opposite to him Eve seated holding a scepter. In the middle Cain appears holding a mirror and near to him a tree, at the foot of which is represented the serpent. The engraving is very indifferent, and the drawing worse. I should much rather suppose it to have been done by one of the inferior scholars of Marc Antonio.

FRANTZ ASPRUCK.
Flourished,

Was born at Bruffels. From a great resemblance, discovered in the works of this artist, with those of Spranger, some have been led to conclude, that he was the disciple of that master. He seems chiefly to have employed himself in painting figures: many of which have been engraved by different masters. He also sometimes amused himself with the graver; and his usual mark was F. A. the initials of his name. By him we have,

Four archangels, half figures, on four small plates: namely, Michael, Gabriel, Raphael, and Uriel.

Love and Anteros, half figures, a small plate, marked with his name, Frantz Aspruck, B. fecit.

JOHN WALTHER VAN ASSEN.
Flourished, 1514.

Among the early prints on wood, we find few superior to those attributed to this master. They are very boldly cut, with great spirit, and show a vast fertility of invention. However, when he has attempted to express the naked parts of the figure, he has by no means succeeded so well, as in the expression of his heads, and the variety of characters he has given them. His mark, which is very singular, is copied on the plate of monograms, at the end of the volume, The reader will readily see the difficulty, which attends the explication of it. However, as it is thus decyphered by M. Christ, and I can by no means find a better solution, I have therefore willingly avoided all unnecessary dispute, by giving it as I found it. A small upright print by this artist, representing *an armed figure on horseback,* inscribed St. Hadrianum, has also written upon it, 'Amstelodamus, in Ædibus Donardi Petri ad signe Castri Angelici:' from which we may reasonably conclude, he resided at that time at Amsterdam; but whether he was a native of that city or not, I cannot take upon me to say. We have besides by him, a set of prints on wood, in circles about nine inches diameter, representing *the life and passion of our blessed Redeemer,* dated 1514. That which represents *Christ praying in the garden* is particularly excellent.

Some very spirited *processions,* &c.

ADRIAN ASSCHOONEBECK.
Flourished,

A Dutch engraver, by whom we have some slight, incorrect etchings, published lifhed in Holland the latter end of the laft century, reprefenting the flight of king James of England: with a defcription of each plate. Thefe etchings are of a middling fize, length-ways.

JOHN AUBERT.
Flourifhed, 1700.

This engraver was a native of France, and mentioned by M. Heineken as an architect. As an engraver he is much better known, at leaft, I believe in England. His prints in general, are little more than etchings, very flight, and without effect. Befides *academy figures* from Edme. Boucherdon, he engraved, among a variety of other things, a *book of ftudies for drawing*, from Raphael and other great mafters, after the drawings of Boucherdon. Add to thefe the *portrait* of Gillot, an upright oval.

MICHAEL AUBERT.
Born,   Died, 1740.

This artift, as well as the former, was a Frenchman, and perhaps of the fame family. He refided at Paris, and died, A. D. 1740. He was much employed in engraving portraits; but we have many other fubjects by his hand. His manner was flight and free; and in his beft hiftorical fubjects, he feems to have had an eye to the prints of G. Audran.

Amongft his portraits I fhall only notice the following:

Louis the Dauphin of France on horfeback, an upright plate from Le Sueur.

Louis XV. alfo on horfeback, the fame.

Mars and Venus, bound by Love, middling fize, upright plate, from Paolo Veronefe, for the Crozat collection.

Mars difarmed by Venus, of the fame fize, from the fame mafter and for the fame collection.

Laban feeking for his gods, and the *reconciliation between Jacob and Efau,* two middling fized upright prints, from Stephen Jeaurat.

The brazen ferpent; from Rubens; and many others from various mafters.

AUBRIER.
Flourifhed,

A name, as M. Heineken informs us, found upon the portrait of Cæfar Bargio, duke of Valentinois.

ABRAHAM AUBRY.
Flourifhed, 1650.

A native of Oppenheim; about the year 1650, he refided at Strafbourg, where he followed the employment of a printfeller. As an engraver, he poffeffed fo little merit, that his works are not worth recording.

The *twelve months,* from Sandrart, eleven of which are engraved by Abraham Aubry, are among his beft plates: the twelfth, the month of May, is by F. Brun.

PETER

PETER AUBRY.
Flourished,

An engraver and printseller, a native of Oppenheim, and probably of the same family with the preceding artist, was also established at Strasburgh, where he traded very largely; especially in portraits, of which we have a great number engraved by him, or under his direction. But they are so very indifferent, as not to merit a separate list. Professor Christ attributes to this engraver, those prints, marked P. A. but I must differ from him in this instance; for all the prints I have seen thus marked, are in a style as much superior as it is different from that of Peter Aubry.

JOHN PHILIP AUBRY.
Flourished,

An Engraver and printseller at Franckfort, of the same family with the preceding, who also engraved a prodigious number of prints, some of them being portraits, as well for the booksellers as for his own collections; but by no means superior to the former in merit.

ROBERT VAN AUDEN-AERD.
Born, 1663. Died, 1743.

From the town of Oudenord, or, as the French often write it, Audenaerde, of which his father was a native, our artist is said to have taken his name. He himself was born at Ghent, A. D. 1663, and very early in life applied himself to painting. He studied under Mierhop Van Cleef, and several other masters; and going to Rome, was received by Carlo Maratti, into his academy. As a painter he is spoken of with great praise. It is sufficient, in the present work, to consider him as an engraver only. But his studies in the art of engraving were interrupted in their beginning, by the following unexpected incident. He frequently used to amuse himself at his leisure, with the point; and being pleased, as it should seem, with a sketch of his master, representing the *marriage of the Virgin*, he etched a plate from it. The impressions being circulated abroad, Carlo Maratti accidentally saw one of them in a print shop; and by enquiry soon discovered its author. Auden-aerd felt severely the effects of his resentment, which he carried to such an height, that he forbid him to approach his school, declaring he would never see his face again. However, after some time had passed, his friends made known to Maratti, how very sorrowful the young man was for his offence; and by their intercession, and his promising never to publish any thing again from his pictures without his consent, the fault was excused; and the pupil was again received by his master, who encouraged him to pursue the art of engraving with assiduity; which he accordingly did, and made such great progress, that Maratti was extremely pleased with his performances, and employed him afterwards to engrave many of his best pictures.

After residing a long time at Rome, he returned to his own country, where he died, A. D. 1743. His prints have not always the name at full length; but after an R he substituted a cypher, compoſed of an A and a V, adding the word *Gaudenfis*, that is, of Ghent, the name of the town where he was born. See the cypher on the plate, at the end of the volume.

The plates, which were done by this artiſt, entirely with the graver are not equal, in my opinion, to thoſe, where he alſo uſed the point : they are cold, and deſtitute of effect, and often, from his great ſolicitude to avoid an outline, his draperies appear heavy, and want ſharpneſs in the folds. The ſame heavineſs appears alſo in his heads and other extremities, and all the naked parts of the figure in general; as I think, will readily be allowed on examination of that print, which repreſents the *aſſumption of the Virgin*, from Carlo Maratti, a middling ſized, upright plate, with this inſcription, *Quaſi aurora conſurgens*; which, if compared with the ſlight etching of *Hagar and Iſhmael*, from the ſame maſter, I think the ſpirit of the latter will well repay the want of that neatneſs, which is found in the former. He certainly poſſeſſed great knowledge of the human figure; and his drawing is ſeldom incorrect, unleſs it may be thought, that the extremities are ſometimes rather large.

Among his beſt prints are generally ranked the few which follow :

The birth of the Virgin, a large upright plate, arched at the top, from Annibal Carracci.

The death of the Virgin, a large plate, length-ways, from Carlo Maratti.

The martyrdom of St. Blaze, a large upright plate, from the ſame maſter.

Saint Phillippe Neri, a middling ſized upright plate, from the ſame.

Apollo and Daphne, a large print, length-ways, on two plates, from the ſame.

Among his other works, which are from a variety of maſters, there are ſome *portraits*, and alſo three etchings from Domenichino, which are very ſlight and indifferent.

CLAUDE AUDRAN.
Born, 1592. Died, 1677.

The firſt of the celebrated family of the Audrans, mentioned as an artiſt. He was the ſon of Louis Audran, an officer belonging to the wolf-hunters, in the reign of Henry the Fourth of France. Claude Audran was born at Paris, A. D. 1592, but I think he did not take up the graver till rather late in life; and we have very few things done by him. He never made any great progreſs in the art; ſo that his prints are held in little or no eſtimation. Yet though he acquired no great reputation by his own works, it was no ſmall honor to him to be the father of three great artiſts, Germain, Claude, and Girard; the laſt of which has immortalized the name of the family for ever. Claude Audran retired from Paris to Lyons, where he reſided, and died A. D. 1677.

CARL or KARL AUDRAN.
Born, 1594. Died, 1674.

It is generally believed, that this eminent artiſt was the brother of Claude Audran, mentioned in the preceding article; but others have aſſerted, that he was coufin-german to him only. It is, however, univerfally agreed, that he was born at Paris, A. D. 1594. In his infancy he difcovered much tafte, and a great difpofition for the arts; and to perfect himfelf in engraving, which he appears to have been chiefly fond of, he went to Rome, where he produced feveral prints, that did him great honour; at his return, he adopted that fpecies of engraving, which is performed with the graver only.

What mafter he ftudied under at Rome, cannot eafily be determined. The ftyle he adopted is very like that of Cornelius Bloemart, but ftill neater; perhaps the prints of Lucas Kilian and of the Sadelers may have laid the firft foundation which he built upon. A print I have now before me by him, namely, an *emblematical fubject*, wherein is reprefented a prince, feated upon a throne, furrounded by a variety of figures, from Alex Vajanus, has much of Kilian's manner.

On his return to his own country, he fettled at Paris, where he died. A. D. 1674, without having ever been married. The Abbé Marolles, who always fpeaks of this artift with great praife, attributes 130 prints to him: amongft which, the *annunciation*, a middling fized plate, upright, from Annabale Carracci; and the *affumption*, in a circle, from Domenichino, are the moft efteemed.

In the early part of his life he marked his prints with C, or the name of Carl, till his brother Claude publifhed fome plates with the initial only of his baptifmal name; when, for diftinction fake, he ufed the letter K, or wrote his name Karl, with the K inftead of the C. Befides thofe prints already mentioned, I fhall notice the following:

A large emblematical print, length-ways, from Pietro de Cortona.

A holy family, with St. Catherine, accompanied by many Angels, a middling fized plate, length-ways, from James Stella.

Another *holy family*, where the Virgin is taking an apple, which St. John prefents to her; and St. Catherine, who is reprefented kneeling before her, is raifing the infant Chrift, with this infcription beneath: *Ofculetur me, &c.*

A dead Chrift, with two Angels, from J. ab Ach. This print is evidently copied after that, which Raphael Sadeler engraved from the fame painter. It has much of the manner of Sadeler, and is of the fame fize.

Several *portraits*, and a vaft variety of other fubjects, from the greateft mafters.

GERMAIN AUDRAN.
Born, 1631. Died, 1710.

This artift was the eldeft fon of Claude, mentioned in the preceding article but one, and was born at Lyons, where his parents then refided. Not content with the inftructions of his father, he went to Paris, and perfected himfelf under his uncle Carl; fo that, upon his return to Lyons, he publifhed feveral prints, which did great honour to his graver. His merit was in fuch eftimation, that he was made a member of the academy eftablifhed in that town, and chofen a profeffor. He died at Lyons, A. D. 1710, and left behind him four fons, all artifts: namely, Claude, Benoift, John, and Louis.

Among his works are some *portraits*, and a variety of other subjects, as *ornaments, vases, cielings*, &c. &c.
A large book of *views in Italy.*
A book of six *landscapes* from Gaspre.

CLAUDE AUDRAN.
Born, 1639. Died, 1684.

The second of this name, and second son to Claude, of whom we have spoken in a former page. He was born at Lyons, A. D. 1639, and went to Rome to study painting, he succeeded so well, that, at his return, he was employed by Le Brun, to assist him in the battles of Alexander, which he was then painting for the king of France. He was received into the Royal Academy in the year 1675, and died unmarried at Paris, A. D. 1684. His virtues, says Abbé Fontenai, were as praise-worthy as his talents were great. M. Heineken mentions this artist as an engraver, without specifying any of his works in this line. I own I have never seen any.

GIRARD, or GERARD AUDRAN.
Born, 1640. Died, 1703.

The most celebrated artist of the whole family of the Audrans. He was the third son of Claude Audran, mentioned in a preceding article, and born at Lyons, A. D. 1640. He learned from his father the first principles of design and engraving: following the example of his brother, he left Lyons, and went to Paris, where his genius soon began to manifest itself; and his reputation brought him to the knowledge of Le Brun, who employed him to engrave the *battle of Constantine*, and the *triumph* of that emperor; and for these works he obtained apartments at the *Gobelins.* At Rome, where he went for improvement, he is said to have studied under Carlo Maratti, in order to perfect himself in drawing; and in that city, where he resided three years, he engraved several fine plates; among the rest, the *portrait* of pope Clement the Ninth. M. Colbert, a great encourager of the arts, was so struck with the beauty of Audran's works, whilst he resided at Rome, that he persuaded Louis XIV. to recall him. On his return, he applied himself assiduously to engraving; and was appointed engraver to the king, from whom he received great encouragement. In the year 1681, he was named counsellor of the Royal Academy; and died at Paris, A. D. 1703. He had been married; but left no male issue behind him.

I own my great partiality for this master; and that partiality may by some of my readers be thought to lead me too far, when I say, that I consider him as the greatest engraver, without any exception, that ever existed in the historical line. However, I am not singular in this opinion; and, I believe, a careful examination of the *battles of Alexander* alone, engraved by this artist (which are said to be equal, if not superior to the pictures) will justify the assertion. His great excellency, above that of any other engraver, was, that though he drew admirably himself, yet he contracted no *manner* of his own; but transcribed (if I may be allowed the expression) on copper simply,

simply, with great truth and spirit, the style of the master, whose pictures he copied. On viewing his prints you lose sight of the engraver, and naturally say, it is Le Brun, it is Poussin, it is Mignard, or it is Le Sueur, &c. as you turn to the prints, which he engraved from those masters. Let any one examine the *battles* above-mentioned from Le Brun, the *preservation of the young Pyrrhus* from Nicholas Poussin, the *Pest* from Mignard, and the *martyrdom of St. Laurence* from Le Sueur, and then judge candidly of the truth of this observation. Thus much, I hope, the reader will excuse my saying; and I thought it the more indispensably necessary in this place, because a modern writer on prints has professed to give, in one of the chapters of his *essay*, the characters of the " *most noted masters*" in the art of engraving; and begins that chapter with the " *masters in history*." But neither in it, nor in any other part of the book, has he once mentioned the name of Girard Audran. Indeed Francois de Poilly, Girard Edelink, Robert Nanteuil, Lucas Vosterman, and very many other great artists, are in the same predicament. From what cause so unwarranted an omission could proceed, I am at a loss to account. The engravings of all the artists above-mentioned are too well known, one would think, to escape the observation of an author, pretending to criticise on the works of the " *most noted masters* ;" and if they were known to him, and he has not thought them worthy a place in his list, it must argue, that his want of judgment on the one side must be as great as his carelessness on the other. It is a harsh unpleasing task to censure others; for me especially, because I am thoroughly sensible of the numberless errors, which must unavoidably be found in the course of a work, like this of mine, and for which I shall stand in great need of the excuse, and indulgence of my readers. Yet in justice to the public in general, and this excellent artist in particular, I thought it a duty incumbent on me to speak as I have done. To what has been said, I beg leave to add the following judicious observations, on the works of Girard Audran, by the Abbé Fontenai, taken chiefly from M. Basan, with some small variation and additions. " This sublime artist, far from conceiving,
" that a servile arrangement of strokes, and the too frequently cold and
" affected clearness of the graver, were the great essentials of historical
" engraving, gave worth to his works by a bold mixture of free hatchings
" and dots, placed together apparently without order, but with an inimitable
" degree of taste; and has left to posterity most admirable examples of the
" style, in which grand compositions ought to be treated. His greatest works,
" which have not a very flattering appearance to the ignorant eye, are the
" admiration of true connoisseurs, and persons of fine taste. He acquired
" the most profound knowledge of the art by the constant attention and
" study, which he bestowed upon the science of design, and the frequent
" use he made of painting from nature. This great man always knew how
" to penetrate into the genius of the painter he copied from; often improved
" upon, and sometimes even surpassed him." Thus far my author, who then adds the following assertion : " without exception, he was the most cele-
" brated engraver, that ever existed in the historical line. We have, says he,
" several subjects, which he engraved from his own designs, that manifested

" as much taſte, as character and facility. But, in the battles of Alexander,
" he ſurpaſſed even the expectations of Le Brun himſelf."

One may, I think, very properly divide the works of Girard Audran into four claſſes, without mentioning his portraits.

First, his ſlight prints or etchings; to which very little or nothing was done with the graver. Among theſe I ſhall rank the following:

The *deluge*, a large plate, lengthways, from La Fage.

The *paſſage through the Red Sea*, the ſame, from the ſame.

The *combat of Joſhua againſt the Amalekites:* with other plates, from the ſame.

The *empire of Flora*, from Pouſin, a middling ſized plate, length-ways.

An admirable large print on two plates, length-ways, from the ſame maſter, repreſenting *the preſervation of Pyrrhus.*

A *cieling* from Le Brun, wherein is repreſented the *four ſeaſons* of the year, dedicated to Louis XIV. engraved on five plates, which being paſted together form an oval, &c.

Secondly, thoſe more finiſhed, but in a rough, bold manner. For example:

Paul and Barnabas at Lyſtra, from the tapeſtries in the Vatican, a large print, length-ways.

Coriolanus appeaſed by his family, on two plates, a large print, length-ways, from Pouſin.

Time ſupporting Truth, from the ſame, an admirable print. The impreſſions, without the piece of drapery over the figure of truth, are very rare.

The cieling of the chapel *de Saulx*, repreſenting the *accompliſhment of the old law by the new one:* engraved 1681, from Le Brun, on ſix large plates, which join together. Great ſpirit, character, expreſſion, and beautiful drawing, are wonderfully united in this print.

The *death of St. Francis*, from Annibale Carracci, a large upright plate.

Thirdly, thoſe in his moſt finiſhed manner: as,

The battles of Alexander, three very large prints, length-ways, each conſiſting of four plates, which join together, from Le Brun : namely,

The paſſage of the Granicus.

The battle of Arbela.

Porus brought to Alexander, after his defeat.

To this ſet are added two more large prints, length-ways, on two plates each, from Le Brun; as follow:

Alexander entering the tent of Darius,

And *the triumphal entry of Alexander into Babylon.* The former was engraved by Girard Edelink, and the latter by Girard Audran. It is to be remarked of all theſe plates, that thoſe impreſſions are generally moſt eſteemed, which have the name of Goyton, the printer, marked upon them.

The *Peſt,* from Peter Mignard, a large plate, lengthways. In the firſt impreſſions, the figure in the clouds is Juno with her peacock behind her; in the latter, the peacock is obliterated, and the wings of an Angel are added to the figure.

The *baptiſm of the Phariſees,* on two large plates, length-ways, from N. Pouſin.

The *martyrdom of St. Laurence,* from Euſtache le Sueur, a large plate, upright, arched at the top.

The

The *martyrdom of St. Agnes*, from Dominichino, of the same size, and usually made a companion for the former.

And FOURTHLY, such as he did with the graver only: these are but few and by no means equal in merit, as I think, with the former. I shall only mention,

Æneas saving his father Anchises from the plunder of Troy, after Dominichino.

A small folio *frontispiece* to the effigies of the popes and cardinals, published at Rome, from Cyro Ferri.

His works, of which these are only a few, are very numerous, from Raphael Stella, Ant. Coypel, and many other masters.

BENOIT AUDRAN.
Born, 1661. Died, 1721.

He was the second son of Germain Audran, born at Lyons, A. D. 1661, where he learned the first principles of design and engraving, under the instruction of his father. But soon after going to Paris, his uncle Girard Audran took him under his tuition, and Benoit so greatly profited by his instructions, that though he never equalled the sublime style of his tutor, yet he acquired, and deservedly too, great reputation. Nay, the Abbé Fontenai adds this eulogium: " we admire in his works a share of those beauties, " which we find in the engravings of the illustrious Girard." He was honoured with the appellation of the king's engraver, and received the royal pension. He was made an academician, and admitted into the council, A. D. 1715. he died unmarried at Louzouer, where he had an estate, A. D. 1721.

His manner was founded upon the bold, clear style of his uncle. His outlines were firm and determined; his drawing correct; the heads, of his figures, are in general, very expressive; and the other extremities well marked. His works, when compared with those of his uncle, appear to want that mellowness and harmony, which are so conspicuous in the latter; they are more dry; and the round dots, with which he finishes his flesh upon the lights, are often too predominant. In his most finished plates, we find the mechanical part of the engraving extremely neat, and managed with great taste and judgment. Among his neatest prints may be reckoned that, which represents

Alexander sick, drinking from the cup, which his physician presents him: a circular plate, from Le Sueur.

I shall also notice the following:

Moses defending the daughters of Jethro, engraved by him, conjointly with his brother John; a large plate, length-ways, from Le Brun.

The espousals of Moses, companion to the former, from the same.

The brazen serpent, a large plate length-ways, from the same.

The elevation of the cross, the same, from the same.

The seven sacraments, copied from those of Pesne, seven large plates, length-ways, from N. Pousin.

Two fine plates from Rubens, engraved for the collection, from the Luxembourg gallery.

Christ with Martha and Mary, a large plate, length-ways, from Eustache Le Sueur.

St. Paul preaching at Athens, the same, from the same.
Several excellent *portraits*, and a variety of other fine plates, from different masters.

JOHN AUDRAN.
Born, 1667. Died, 1756.

The third son of Germain Audran; was also born at Lyons, A. D. 1667; and, after having received instructions from his father, went to Paris, to perfect himself in the art of engraving, under his uncle Girard Audran. At the age of twenty years, the genius of this great artist begun to display itself in a surprising manner; and his future success was such, that, A. D. 1707, he obtained the title of engraver to the king, and had a pension allowed him by his majesty, with apartments in the Gobelins; and the following year he was made a member of the Royal Academy. He was eighty years of age, before he quitted the graver; and near ninety, when he died at his apartments, assigned him by the king. He left three sons behind him; one of which was also an engraver, as we shall see below.

The most masterly and best prints of this artist, in my opinion, are those, which are not so pleasing to the eye at first sight. In these the etching constitutes a great part; and he has finished them in a bold, rough style. The scientific hand of the master appears in them on examination. The drawing of the human figure, where it is shown, is correct. The heads are expressive, and finely finished; the other extremities well marked. He has not, however, equalled his uncle. He wants that harmony in the effect; his lights are too much and too equally covered; and there is not sufficient difference between the style, in which he has engraved his back grounds, and his draperies. This observation refers to a fine print by him of *Athaliah*, and such as he engraved in that style.

At other times he seems almost to have quitted the point, and substituted the graver. But here, I think he has not so well succeeded. The effect is cold and silvery. See, for example, the *Andromache* from Silvestre. One of his best finished prints, in this neat style, seems to me to be *Cupid and Psyche*, from Ant. Coypel.

The following prints, among a large number of others by this master, are usually much esteemed:

Moses saved by Pharoah's daughter a large plate length-ways, from Ant. Coypel.

Athaliah rending her cloaths, on discovering the king in the Temple; a large plate, length-ways, from the same master.

Esther before Ahasuerus, a large plate length-ways, from the same master.

Cupid and Psyche, a middling sized print, length-ways, from the same.

The presentation of Christ in the Temple; a large plate, length-ways, from Mich. Corneille, a masterly performance.

The *miraculous draught of fishes*, from Jouvenet, and its companion, the *resurrection of Lazarus*, from the same master, both large plates, length-ways.

Duchange added to these plates two more: The *merchandisers driven from the Temple by our Saviour*, and *Christ's repast with Simon the Pharisee*: both of the same size as the former, and from the same master.

Three plates from Rubens, in the collection engraved from the Luxembourg gallery, painted by that master.

The *battles of Alexander*, copied smaller from the large prints, engraved by Girard Audran from the pictures of Le Brun.

Moses defending the daughters of Jethro, from the same master, engraved conjointly with his brother Benoit. This plate and its companion, *Moses espousing the daughter of Jethro*, were copied smaller by this artist, assisted by Bernard Picart, the Roman.

The miracle of the five loaves, a large plate, length-ways, from Claude Audran.

Christ healing the sick and lame, a large plate length-ways, from Ant. Dieu.

Christ carrying the cross, a very large plate, length-ways, from the same.

Andromache interceding for her son, a large plate, length-ways, from Louis Silvestre.

St. Scholastic, a large plate, upright, arched at top, from John Restout.

St. Benoit, the same, from the same.

Many good *portraits*, and other *fine prints*, from various masters.

LOUIS AUDRAN.
Born, 1670. Died, 1712.

The last son of Germain Audran, born at Lyons, A. D. 1670; from whence he went to Paris, after the example of his brothers, to complete his studies in the school of his uncle Girard. He died suddenly at Paris, A. D. 1712, aged 42, before he had produced any great number of prints by his own hand. He assisted, it is presumed, his brothers in their more extensive works. Among the most esteemed prints by this artist, are the following:

The *seven acts of mercy*, on seven middling sized plates, length-ways, from Sebastian Bourdon.

The *cadavre* or *corps*, from R. A. Houasse, a middling sized plate, length-ways.

BENOIT AUDRAN.
Flourished, 1735.

This Benoit, the second of that name, an engraver, was the son of John Audran, and nephew to the former Benoit; and was also established at Paris. He engraved but a few plates. It is necessary, however, to be careful not to confound him with his uncle. But a little attention will easily prevent this mistake; for the second Benoit is vastly inferior to the first, in point of merit.

We have some few *portraits* by this artist; and among other plates, the *descent from the cross*, from a picture of Poussin.

The *ages and elements*, from Lancret, engraved conjointly with Desplaces and Nicholas Tardieu.

J. VAN

J. VAN DER AVEELE.
Flourished, 1698.

The name of an obscure artist, affixed to the *frontispiece* of the nineteenth volume, in folio, of the work, entitled, *Thesaurus Antiq. Rom.* published by Peter Vander Aa, 1698. It is executed entirely with the graver, in a style, that reflects but little honour on the artist.

JOHN VAN DER AVELEN.
Flourished, 1696.

A Dutch engraver, who lived in the latter part of the last, and the beginning of the present century. He was chiefly employed by the booksellers. He made a large etching of *shipping*. He also etched a large *view*, length-ways, of the *Orangerie de Sorguliet*; and several of the *plates* for *Lilii Giraldi opera, Lugd. Bat.* 1696, in folio, are by this engraver. Also the *cabinet of the fine arts*, copied from that which was published at Paris by Perault.

JOSEPH AVELINE.
Born, 1638. Died, 1690.

An obscure engraver, who seems to have worked for the booksellers only. His name is cited by M. Heineken, without any reference to his works.

ANTONY AVELINE.
Born, 1662. Died, 1712.

A Frenchman by birth, and settled at Paris, where he died, A. D. 1712, aged 50. His engravings are chiefly landscapes and views; which he also designed himself, or drew from nature, and executed in a neat pleasing style. I shall notice,

A set of twelve *landscapes*, middling sized plates, length-ways, from his own designs.

Another set of six *landscapes*, the same.

A set of *views of Paris*, the same.

A set of *views of different towns in France*.

A set of *views of different towns in Europe*, &c.

PETER AVELINE.
Born, 1711. Died, 1762.

This artist was a Frenchman; but the place of his birth has not been noticed by any author I have met with. Perhaps he was born at Paris; and most likely was of the same family with Antony Aveline, mentioned in the preceding article. According to M. Heineken, he was instructed in the art of engraving in the school of the Poillys, and died at Paris, A. D. 1762, aged 51. He designed, as well as engraved; and his general style appears to have been founded upon the neater manner of John Baptista de Poilly. His drawing of the human figure was rather mannered than correct; and his extremities often appear to be much neglected. His prints, for the most part,

A V E [47] A V I

part, are not highly finished; but we frequently find in them a clearness of effect, which is very agreeable.

We have a prodigious number of plates, engraved by this artist, which one does not so much wonder at, seeing how slightly they are finished in general.

He engraved a few plates from his own designs; the rest are from a variety of masters, as well ancient as modern. I shall mention the following:

The *death of Seneca*, from Luca Giordano, a large plate, length-ways, after a picture by that master in the gallery at Dresden.

Noah preparing to enter the ark, and its companion, the *departure of Jacob*, two large plates, length-ways, from the pictures of J. Ben. Castiglione, which are in the Dresden gallery.

A large landscape, length-ways, with figures and cattle, from Berghem.

The birth of Bacchus, and *the rape of Europa*, its companion, two large plates, length-ways, from Francois Boucher.

Folly, a middling sized plate, length-ways, from a design of Cornelius Visscher; in which he has attempted, and not unhappily, the style of that master's engraving.

A set of *Academy figures*, from Boucherdon. *A set of boys* in groups, from Boucher. *Some portraits*, &c.

LEON AVEN. See DAVEN.

JOHN GOTTFRIED AVERBACH.
Born, 1687. Died, 1743.

This artist was painter to the emperor Charles the Sixth, and was born at Mulhausen, A. D. 1687. He resided at Vienna, where he died 1743, aged 56. As an engraver, he is cited by M. Heineken, who mentions a print wherein he has introduced his own portrait, and in which he is represented painting that of his wife, which is engraved by himself.

AUGUSTIN VENETIAN. See MUSIS.

GASPER AB AVIBUS.
Flourished, 1560 to 1580,

This engraver appears to have been a native of Padua; because he sometimes subscribes his prints, *Gasper Patavinus*. When he was born does not appear; but I am inclined to think, he studied under George Ghissi Mantuanus, many of whose prints he professedly copied, and whose manner in them he entirely adopted. But though he possessed some degree of merit, he never nearly equalled that excellent artist. He often signed his prints with a curious monogram, composed of the letters, which form the word *Gaspar*. It is given on the plate at the end of the volume. At other times, he put *Gaspar* only, or G. A. P. F. and sometimes Gasper Ossello Padovano; and his prints are dated from 1560 to 1580.

I shall

I shall first take notice of a few of his prints, copied from George Ghisi. The *last supper*, which that artist engraved from Lamb. Lombard; of the same size, or nearly, with the original print, marked GAS. P. F. 1564.

Venus and Adonis, and its companion, *a youth carrying his mistress upon his shoulders*; two middling sized upright plates, with the cypher above mentioned, dated 1563, from Lucas Pennis.

Venus bathing, from the same painter, marked on a tablet, GASP. F. dated 1564.

The Mount Parnassus, a large plate, length-ways, from the same painter. These are chiefly the contrary way, from the originals. Other prints of his are,

The woman taken in adultry, a middling sized plate, length-ways, marked Gaspero Osello Padovano *f.* from an uncertain master.

The scourging of our blessed Saviour, a large upright plate, Gaspar ab Avibus Citadelensis fecit.

But his chief work appears to have been the large folio volume, in five parts, containing the portraits of the emperors, archdukes, princes, &c. of the Austrian family. Each portrait is a whole length figure; and the plates are embellished with ornamental borders. Here he has changed his manner; and something more of the style of the Sadelers appears in it. The figures are very neat, but stiff, yet well proportioned, and possess much merit. He signs himself Gaspar Patavinus incisor, 1569, and at the bottom he has also added the word *Citadelensis* to his name.

CÆSAR AB AVIBUS.

Is cited by M. Heineken, as an engraver and a native of Padua; and it is said, that he also signed himself Cæsar Patavinus. But, I own, I must doubt the existence of such an artist, and those very portraits of the Austrian family, which Florent Le Comte has attributed to this engraver, belong evidently to Gasper ab Avibus, mentioned in the preceding article. Others, depending upon the assertion of Le Comte, have been led into the same error.

The CHEVALIER AVICE.
Flourished, 1655.

A lover of the arts, who lived at Paris, and, for his amusement, made some slight, spirited, but incorrect etchings, from Nicholas Poussin and others. Among these the *adoration of the Magi*, a middling sized plate length-ways, from Poussin, is much esteemed.

PETER VANDEN AVONT.
Flourished, 1645.

He was a native of Antwerp, and a painter of figures and landscapes. He engraved some few plates, and sold the engravings of other artists whom he employed. Among those, which he performed himself, are the following: three *Madonas*, and a *Magdalen* ascending to Heaven; but from his pictures a great many plates were engraved by various masters.

NICHOLAS AUROUX.
Flourished, 1650.

According to M. Heineken, this engraver was a native of Lyons; but he worked also at Turin, chiefly, I suppose, for the bookfellers. The plates I have seen by him are executed with the graver, and in a very indifferent manner. The above-mentioned author speaks of four *portraits* by him, and a *Virgin*, seated, holding the infant Christ, and St. John kissing his feet, in folio, inscribed Sancta Maria Mater, &c. published at Lyons; and the *frontispiece* to the second volume of Daniel Sennertus is by him, dated 1650.

C. AUTGUERS.
Flourished, 1623.

An obscure engraver, who seems only to have worked for the bookfellers, and probably resided at Lyons; for I have seen some few *frontispieces* engraved by him for books, which were there published, and one of them is dated 1623. His works are by no means estimable.

AUTREAU.
Flourished,

An engraver of *portraits*, as it should seem, by whom we have the princefs Hesse Homberg.

AUVRAY.
Flourished, 1760.

An engraver of little eminence; according to M. Heineken, he was instructed in the art of engraving at Paris, and resided at Basile, and produced some few *portraits* of French comedians.

JOHN AZELT.
Flourished,

He also signed his name Azeld or Atzueld, and according to M. Heineken, resided at Nuremberg. He seems to have confined himself entirely to portraits; and in that line he never rose higher than mediocrity. Amongst his works are the following.

The *emperor Joseph*, from A. Hanneman.
George Frederick prince of Waldeck.
A set of *portraits*, of the kings of Spain, of Hungary, of Bohemia, and of Denmark.
And many of those plates in *Freheri Theatrum Virorum Eruditione clarorum.*

B.

FRANCIS DE BABYLONE.
Flourished,

This name, according to M. Chrift, has by some authors been attributed to an artift called the *mafter of the caduceus*, becaufe he conftantly marked his engravings with a *caduceus*, without any name or initial letters. He doubts however, the authority upon which this affertion is grounded. And indeed, in a variety of other cafes, where we have not only marks, but even initials, I fear juft as much muft be given upon conjecture, as in the prefent. With this caution, I have ventured to place the engravings of this mafter, which are too fingular to be omitted, under this name. Thofe authors muft certainly be very greatly deceived, who have called him Ifrael Martin, and confidered him as a very ancient engraver; adding further, that Albert Durer, Lucas Van Leyden, and Aldergrever, were his difciples. Judging, from a careful examination of the ftyle of his prints, I fuppofe that he flourifhed about the middle of the fixteenth century. His manner of engraving appears to be quite original. He executed all his plates (at leaft all thofe that I have feen) with the graver, in a flight manner, with fine ftrokes, and not much croffed. His drawing of the naked figure is generally very defective, efpecially the extremities, which are continually too large, and very poorly marked. His heads are neither characteriftic nor expreffive; and his drapery is divided into a prodigious number of fmall folds, like cords, which have a difagreeable effect. But the fingularity of his prints gives them a confequence, they would never otherwife have obtained. Among others are the following:

A fmall upright plate, reprefenting *Apollo and Diana*.

Another fmall upright plate, reprefenting *three men bound*.

A *holy family*, on a fmall fquare plate, half figures: the Virgin is leaning on the ftump of a tree, and the head of Jofeph is feen towards the right hand of the print.

Another *holy family*, a fmall plate, length-ways, where the Virgin is reprefented feated at the foot of a tree; the child is ftanding by her fide; Elizabeth is feated near him; an angel is playing upon a mufical inftrument; and Jofeph appears at the right hand of the print.

The *wife mens' offering*, a fmall upright plate.

St. Jerom writing, and a crucifix before him, a fmall plate, length-ways.

Two fmall upright plates: one reprefenting a *man carrying a boat* and the other, a *woman with a child in her arms*. Jerom Hopfer has engraved both thefe figures on one plate, much larger, and decorated the head of the woman with ftars and a glory.

A

BAC [51] BAD

A *facrifice to Priapus* (which is attributed to M. Antonio, becaufe it has his tablet) is copied fmaller by this artift, and the indecency, which appears in the former plate, is here removed. It reprefents a woman ftanding by the altar, and another oppofite to her, holding an infant; and an old woman's head appears in the back ground.

The mark, which he conftantly puts to his engravings, is given on the plate of monograms, at the end of the volume.

BACCIARELLI.
Flourifhed,

A modern engraver, chiefly, I believe, of portraits. There is by him a portrait of Auguft. Staniflaus Poniatowfki, king of Poland.

E. BACH.
Flourifhed,

I have never feen any of this artift's performances: he is, however, cited for fome hiftorical pieces.

J. BACHELEY.
Flourifhed, 1760.

According to M. Bafan, this artift refided at Roan. He engraved feveral landfcapes from different mafters.

LUDOLPH BACKHUYSEN.
Born, 1631. Died, 1709.

This great artift was born at Embden, A. D. 1631. His firft inftructions in painting he is faid to have received from Albert Van Everdingen; but he perfected himfelf chiefly by his own obfervation of other mafters. His great excellency confifted in painting fhipping, fea-pieces, and fea-ports; and his merit, in this line, is too generally known to require any repetition. He died at Amfterdam, A. D. 1709, aged 78. As an engraver, we have a few little etchings by him, *views of the Y*, a fmall arm of the fea near Amfterdam.

SISTO BADALOCCHIO.
Flourifhed, 1607.

This artift was born at Parma, A. D. 1581, according to Bafan; and died at Rome A. D. 1647, aged 66. But what authority that writer had for his affertion, I do not know. Other authors tell us, that he died young. He was the difciple of Annibale Carracci, and made a very confiderable progrefs in his profeffion as a painter. He alfo amufed himfelf with the point; and we have many etchings by him, in a flight, free, mafterly ftyle. They are generally more finifhed, than thofe of Guido; but the extremities are by no means fo finely drawn.

H 2 Amongft

Amongst others are the following:

Raphael's bible, from the pictures of Raphael in the Vatican: small plates, lengthways, engraved conjointly with Lanfranchi.

The *Gallery*, which Annibale Carracci painted for cardinal Fernase, engraved also conjointly with Lanfranchi, and dedicated to his master, A. D. 1607.

A *holy family*, with St. John, a small upright plate, half figures only.

Several spirited etchings from his own designs, and some from Correggio.

He usually marked his etchings, Sisto. B. F.

ALESSANDRO BADIALI.
Born, 1626. Died, 1671.

This artist was a painter of confiderable eminence, born at Bologna, A. D. 1626. He was the disciple of Flaminio Toro, and died A. D. 1671, aged 45. He amused himself with etching, which he performed in a very slight style. Among others, there are by him the following pieces:

Christ taken down from the cross, a small upright plate, from his master Flaminio Toro.

A *holy family*, the same, from the same.

A *Virgin* seated, with the infant Christ upon her lap; a bishop and an ecclesiastic are kneeling before her: a middling sized, upright plate, from a composition of his own.

J. BAECK.
Flourished,

A modern engraver at Augsbourg, who, according to professor Christ, engraved several small plates, which he marked with B. fc. and *J. B. fe.* The mark I. B. F. I have seen affixed to some very masterly etchings of the cardinal virtues, from a painter whose name I know not; but these initials are substituted for it, A. C. I. which perhaps may mean Agostino Carracci, inv.

J. A. BAENER.
Flourished,

I have seen a large folio plate by this obscure artist, representing an emblematical subject, in which we see a man kneeling at the feet of another man, with a book before him; and an hand, holding a sword, is striking from the clouds at the latter: a very indifferent print, executed entirely with the graver, in a heavy, coarse, and bad style.

M. BAES.
Flourished,

An engraver of very little note, whose labours, I suppose, were chiefly confined to the libraries. I have seen a small scratchy etching by him, on an upright oval plate. The portrait of F. Paulus, a jesuit, who was put to death.

Emble-

Emblematical of his suffering, the designer, according to the usual method, has represented a sword thrust into his breast.

ALEXANDER BAILLE.
Flourished, 1764.

What countryman this obscure engraver was, I cannot tell. His works however, are but little known. I have seen a print by him of St. Cecilia, engraved on a middling sized upright plate, representing only half of the figure, from Francis Fernando, dated 1764. To his own name he added del. et. sculp.

F. BAILLEUL.
Flourished, 1722.

A modern French engraver, who was employed, among a variety of other artists, upon the plates, which were engraved at Paris, representing the coronation of Louis XV.

PETER BAILLU or BALLIU.
Flourished, 1643.

This engraver is said to have been a native of Antwerp. He learned the first principles of the art of engraving in his own country; after which he went to Italy, to perfect himself in drawing; where he engraved some few plates. On his return to Antwerp, he was much employed; and his engravings, by many collectors, are held in no small estimation. To me his drawing appears exceedingly defective. His heads are seldom expressive or beautiful; and his extremities are constantly heavy, and not well marked. His general style, particularly in his best prints, seems to have been founded on that of Paul Pontius. He executed also his plates, like that artist, entirely with the graver. But, in point of merit, I conceive Baillu falls infinitely short, when compared with Pontius.

Among his most esteemed prints are reckoned the following:

A *dead Christ*, lying upon the knees of the Virgin Mary, a large upright plate, from Annibale Carracci.

St. Michael overcoming the Demon, from Guido; a middling sized upright plate.

The *reconciliation between Jacob and Laban*, from Rubens, a large upright plate.

Christ praying in the garden, a small upright plate, from the same.

The *combat of the Lapithæ*, a large plate, length-ways, from the same.

A *crucifixion*, from Ant. Vandyck, a middling sized, upright plate, dated 1643.

A *Virgin* in the clouds, a middling sized plate, upright, from the same.

Rinaldo sleeping with Armida, a large upright plate from the same. The companion of this print is engraved by Peter de Jode.

A *holy family*, from Theodore Rombout.

Susanna

Susanna and the Elders, a middling sized upright plate, from Martin Pepyn.

Christ scourged, a large upright plate, from Abraham Diepenbeck.

The *crowning with thorns*, the same, from the same.

Several esteemed portraits, and other plates, from Pietro de Cortona, Rembrandt, John Thomas, and others.

BENARD BAILLU or BALLIU.
Flourished, 1672.

His name is also written Baleu. He appears to have been much employed in engraving portraits, which with his other works were chiefly published at Rome: from whence it seems reasonable to conclude, that his principal residence was at this city. But whether he was a native of Flanders, or of the same family with the preceding artist, I cannot discover. He worked entirely with the graver. His style is heavy, and his portraits have no great share of merit, either with respect to the drawing, or the execution of the mechanical part of the engraving. He certainly flourished towards the latter end of the last century. The time of his birth, and of his decease, are to me equally as uncertain, as the place of his nativity.

Among his other works I note the following:

The portrait of *Cardinal Ursini*, afterwards pope Benedict III. 1672.

Some of the plates for the book, entitled, *Effigies Cardinal. nunc viventium*, published at Rome by Jacobo di Rubeis.

Part of the *cornishes* and *cielings*, in a large folio volume, containing engravings from the pictures of Pietro de Cortona, painted in the palace of the great duke of Tuscany.

I. BAILLY.
Flourished,

I found the name of this artist to some very spirited etchings from Callot, in which the style of that master was exceedingly well imitated; but without a date.

JAMES BAKKER.
Born, 1608. Died,

Basan tells us, that this artist was a native of Haerlem; that he etched at Amsterdam several pieces of his own composition, and that he died in the year 1638 or 1641. I wish the author had specified these pieces: I never saw them; nor can I tell, what subjects employed his point. There was a Jacob Bakker or Backer, painter of portraits and history, born, according to Pilkington, at Harlingen 1609, who died 1651. James Bakker, the same author informs us, was a native of Antwerp, and was dead before the above Jacob was born.

BALDASSARE. See PERUZZI.

BACCIO BALDINI.
Flourifhed, 1480.

A goldfmith, born at Florence, to whom, according to Vafari, Mafo Finiguerri communicated the invention of engraving, which he had lately difcovered. Baldini, not being able to make the defigns for his engravings, revealed the fecret to Aleffandro Boticelli, and they worked conjointly. At this diftance of time it is impoffible to fay, with any degree of certainty, what part of the ancient reliques of engraving belong to this mafter. There are none of his works fpecified by any of the early writers; nor is any mark, by which they may be diftinguifhed, put upon them. Some curious prints, without doubt coeval with this artift, and which, I am much inclined to think, are the productions of his graver, are defcribed in the fixth chapter of the effay at the begining of this volume, to which the reader is referred.

They reprefent the *mufes*, the *planets*, the *arts*, and *fciences*; with various *trades*, and *handicraft-occupations*, &c. chiefly by fingle figures inclofed in a narrow border, engraved on fmall upright plates, one for each figure, to the amount of fixty or upwards. Twenty-one were lent me by Mr. Thane; the reft I found in the collection of Dr. Monro.

VITTORIO BALDINI.
Flourifhed, 1599.

According to M. Papillon, there was a printer of this name, who alfo engraved. He cites the *frontifpieces* to the acts of the play called Aminthe, written by Taffo; which are rudely cut; and one of them is marked B. F. for *Baldini fecit*. This play was publifhed by him, A. D. 1599.

JOHANNSSEN BALDUNG.
Flourifhed, 1534.

An artift of the German fchool. Johannffen, the firft name, fignifies the fon of John. According to M. Heineken, he was alfo called Baldung-Grien; or, as M. Chrift reads it, Grun. M. Papillon makes another artift of this Grien, and reads the name Hans or John Bald Green, mentioning Baldung by himfelf in another place. But, for want of proper attention to the fubject, this laft author has been betrayed into fuch a multitude of miftakes, that it is dangerous to follow him. I know of no fufficient authority, that he could have for the above affertion; therefore I fhall follow the opinion of the two firft mentioned authors. If the monogram, compofed of an H. a B. and a G. be attributed to him, as from the ftyle I think it fafely may with great appearance of certainty, then it will appear, that he worked from A. D. 1510, to 1534. He alfo frequently ufed the H. and the B. joined together, without the G. All thefe marks the reader will find faithfully copied on the plate at the end of the volume. He worked only on wood; and his engravings are

executed

executed in a bold style, with great freedom of hand; and possess (his latter prints especially) an uncommon share of merit. His figures are rather expressive than correct; the naked parts of them are poorly drawn; and the extremities, though free and spirited, are often heavy, and not well marked.

Among the variety of prints attributed to this master, are the following:

An *incantation*, a middling sized print, upright, dated 1510.

A *man with a horse*, a large upright in folio, no date.

Christ and the *twelve Apostles*, on separate blocks, small upright prints, dated 1519.

All these are marked with the H. B. and G. joined together.

Add the following:

Four small upright prints, representing the effects of love:
I. *Solomon's Idolatry*; II. *Samson betrayed by Dalilah*; III. *David and Bathsheba*; IV. *Aristotle and his mistress*. These are very spirited, fine prints, and all I have seen belonging to this set; though originally there might be more of them: they are all inclosed in ornamental borders.

A *holy family*, with Elizabeth and St. Catherine, half figures, a middling sized upright print, dated 1512.

A *singular print*, representing a fore-shortened figure of a man, lying on his back in the fore-ground. Above appears an horse, and an old woman holding a light; exceedingly spirited, and well. These have the H. and the B. without the G.

Two middling sized prints, length-ways, very finely cut, and exactly in the style of that last mentioned. They represent *horses in a forest*, and have the name BALDVNG written at length, and the date 1534, on each of them.

JOHN JOSEPH BALECHOU.
Flourished, 1750.

A very celebrated and well known French engraver. He died, according to Basan, some few years since at Avignon. This extraordinary artist worked entirely with the graver; and he was perfectly master of that instrument. The clearness of his strokes, and the depth of colour which he produced, are far beyond any production prior to his own. But he did not draw well; on this account his prints want that freedom, correctness and harmony, which a perfect knowledge of drawing generally produces. With all their beauty they appear heavy; and the flesh is not sufficiently distinguished, by the style of engraving, from the other parts of the figure; but has a cold silvery effect. This observation must be supposed to refer only to his figures. The two large plates, which he did from Vernet, one representing a *storm*, the other a *calm*, must ever be considered as very astonishing exertions of the artist. They are too well known, and too much admired, to need any further eulogium; and were never equalled, until they were surpassed by a countryman of our own. Let any one look at the Niobe, the Ceyx and Alcyone, &c. from Wilson, and, I believe a very moderate share of judgment will be necessary to turn the balance in favour of the latter.

His most esteemed prints are,

The portrait of the *king of Poland*, whole length, from Rigaud, a large
upright

BAL [57] BAN

upright plate, which is placed at the head of the collection of prints, engraved from the gallery at Drefden.

The portrait of *Crebillon*, from Aved, twice engraved, large and fmall.

Saint Genevieve, the patronefs of France, a large upright plate, from Vanloo.

The *ftorm*, a large plate, length-ways, from Vernet.

The *calm*, its companion, from the fame painter.

A large print, length-ways, from the fame, in which is reprefented feveral *women bathing*. Thefe four laft prints are ufually feen with thick ftrokes engraved over the writing; but in the firft impreffions, thofe ftrokes are wanting.

ANTONIO BALLESTRA.
Born, 1666. Died, 1740.

A painter of great eminence, born at Verona. After having fpent fome time in learning the firft principles of the art of painting from Antonio Belucci, he vifited Bologna and Rome, ftudying from the works of the greateft mafters; and, at laft, entered the fchool of Carlo Maratti. The progrefs he made under that mafter is fuch, that he is faid to have nearly equalled him. He died A. D. 1740, aged 74. We have fome few etchings by him, in a bold, mafterly ftyle, but very flight. Among the reft, a fmall upright print, reprefenting the *Virgin, with the infant Jefus and St. John*. The heads of three cherubs appear at the top: marked Antonius Baleftra inv. et fecit, 1702.

F. BALTESYS.
Flourifhed,

An obfcure artift, who engraved the portrait of *Sir William Brog*, an officer of one of the Scotch regiments. 1600, ætat 37.

J. BALZER.
Flourifhed,

An engraver I believe, but little known: by him we have the portrait of *Joann. Amos Comenius*.

BAMBOCCIO. See PETER VAN LAER.

PETER VANDER BANCK.
Born, Died, 1697.

This artift, apparently of Dutch extraction, was born at Paris, and received his inftructions in the art of engraving from the celebrated Francois de Poilly. He came over into England with Gafcar the painter, about the year 1674, and married the fifter of a gentleman of eftate in Hertfordfhire, named Forefter. He was a laborious artift; but the pay he received for his plates, being by no means adequate to the time he beftowed upon them, he was reduced to want; and, retiring from bufinefs, fought an afylum in the houfe of his brother in law. He died at Bradfield, and was buried in the church there,

there, A. D. 1674; leaving his widow in poffeffion of the chief part of his plates, which fhe difpofed of to Brown, a printfeller, to great advantage, and left an eafy fortune.

His chief employment was engraving of portraits; and, according to Virtue's account of this artift, publifhed by the Hon. Mr. Walpole, he was the firft in England, who engraved them on fo large a fcale. But even the novelty, it feems, added to their merit, could not fufficiently recommend them to fupport the artift. Like many of Poilly's difciples, his great merit confifts in the laboured neatnefs, and management of the mechanical part of the art. Freedom, harmony, and chaftenefs of outline, are by no means the characteriftic of his prints. However, though they cannot rank with the fuperior productions of Edelink or Nantueil, &c. they have their fhare of merit, and doubtlefs will be always efteemed in England, as preferving the beft refemblance of many eminent perfons, who were living at that time.

Among his portraits, the following are much efteemed:

Sir Thomas Allen, a very large whole fheet print.
Thomas Lamplugh, archbifhop of York, a large half fheet print.
Frederick duke of Schomberg, the fame.
George lord Dartmouth, the fame.
James Smith, writing-mafter, from Faithorn, half fheet print.
Sir William Temple, after Lely, the fame.
Richard Lord Maitland, 1683, the fame.

A portrait of *Wood*, the miller, whofe arm was torn off by the mill-wheel, has the name of P. Vanderbank, fubfcribed to it. " This could not," fays the Hon. Mr. Walpole, " be done by P. Vanderbank the elder; for Wood's arm was torn off in 1737. As I find no account of his fecond fon (for he left three behind him) his name, (continues the fame author) was probably Peter, and he might be an engraver." This plate was certainly executed by Vanderbank the painter, from whofe defigns we have a fet of prints for Don Quixot, &c. Whether he was a fon of Peter Vanderbank mentioned above, or not, I cannot difcover.

BANE.
Flourifhed,

A name found at the bottom of a portrait of *Ann Scott*, duchefs of Monmouth.

ALEXANDER BANNERMAN.
Flourifhed,

A modern Englifh artift, by whom we have feveral etchings; among others the *death of Jofeph*, a middling fized plate, length-ways, from Velafco; and feveral other plates from the fame mafter.

BANNOIS.
Flourifhed,

A name fubfcribed to a print of *queen Elizabeth*.

J. BAPTIST.
Flourished, 1720.

The name of an obscure and very indifferent engraver which I found subscribed to some of the plates belonging to a collection in folio, entitled *Figures de la Bible*, published at Amsterdam, 1720. These plates are engraved from the designs of Picart and others.

JOHN BAPTISTA. See MONNOYER.

JACOB BAPTISTA.
Flourished,

An obscure engraver, whose name is affixed to some *portraits*; among the rest, to one of *Martinus Geterus*, Dr. Theol. Sax.

MAURICE BAQUOY.
Flourished, 1720.

An engraver of this century, says Basan, by whom we have several etchings; amongst the rest,

A *naval combat*, from Martin. This is one of the four plates executed for the Czar.

A set of very neat vignettes, for the history of France by Daniel, from drawings by Boucher.

He also engraved some of the large views of Versailles.

JOHN and CHARLES BAQUOY. I believe, these were both sons to the above artist. The first, Basan assures us, was; and I have met with the latter name on very modern prints: perhaps they may be both living.

ANTONIO BARATTI.
Flourished, 1759.

This artist engraved some of the plates for a collection of prints from the pictures of the marquis Gerini, entitled, *Raccolt di Stampe, reprefentanti i quadri piu fcelti dei Signori Marchefi Gerini. Tomo I.* in large folio, published at Florence.

LE BARAUDIE.
Flourished, 1638.

An artist mentioned by Florent le Comte, who engraved several plates of *defigns and ornaments for gardens*, which were printed at Paris, and published by Michael Van Lochon, 1638.

LOUIS BARBASAN.
Flourished,

An ecclesiastic of Premontre, who engraved the *plan and perfpective view of the abbey of Premontre*, where he refided, from a drawing executed by Francois Bayette, another ecclefiaftic belonging to the fame abbey.

BARBAULT.
Flourifhed,

A modern artift, who refided at Rome, where he died, according to Bafan, not many years fince. He was a painter ; but, I believe, of no extraordinary eminence. As an engraver, we have by him a collection of prints, in folio, of the *antiquities of Rome*; alfo a few etchings; amongft the reft, the *martyrdom of St. Peter*, from Peter Subleyras.

JOHN BAPTISTA BARBE.
Flourifhed, 1638.

A Flemifh artift, born at Antwerp, and apparently inftructed in the art of engraving by the Wierixes, whofe ftyle he imitated with great fuccefs. Not content, fays M. Bafan, with what he learned from the mafters of his own country, he went to Italy for improvement, particularly in the art of drawing, a requifite though pofitively neceffary, yet frequently neglected by engravers in general. He never indeed loft fight of that ftiff, laboured ftyle, which was the characteriftic of the time in which he flourifhed. His prints, though prodigioufly neat, (being performed with the graver only) are however flat and wanting in effect. But his drawing is generally correct, and the extremities of his figures well marked.

He engraved fome of the plates for *vita, paffio, et refurrectio Jefu Chrifti*, the life, paffion, and refurrection of Jefus Chrift, publifhed by the Collaerts, 1638, confifting of fifty middling fized prints, length-ways, from Martin de Vos.

Some *devotional fubjects*, of various fizes, exactly in the ftyle of the Wierixes.

A *holy family*, where the infant Chrift is reprefented turning and kiffing Jofeph, a fmall upright plate, from P. P. Rubens: the firft impreffions are without the name of Rubens.

He alfo engraved from J. Bap. Paggi, Francifco Franck, Theodore Van Loon, &c.

BARBERI.
Flourifhed,

A French artift, mentioned by Florent le Comte, as the engraver of a print, reprefenting *Paul and Silas* in prifon, with the convertion of the goaler, from Montagne: to him is alfo attributed the portrait of *Madam de Miramion*.

ANTONY BARBEY.
Flourifhed, 1697.

I found the name of this engraver upon a large whole fheet *map of Rome*, very neatly executed, and dated 1697.

GIOVANNI FRANCESCO BARBIERI.

Born, 1590. Died, 1666.

GUERCINO DA CENTO is the appellation, by which this juftly celebrated painter is moft commonly known. He was called Guercino, from a caft in his eyes: and Cento, from the village named Cento, where he was born. The pictures and drawings of this artift are univerfally held in the greateft eftimation. As an engraver, he has left only two memorials behind him, which are executed with great freedom and fpirit, in a manner much refembling thofe admirable drawings of his with a pen; fome of which were poorly imitated by Jo. Bap. Pafqualianus on copper; and fince that time, in a very fuperior ftyle, by an excellent, and well known, modern artift, from the original drawings in the collection of his prefent majefty.

The etchings by Guercino, are,

St. John, a fmall upright plate, and

St. Antony of Padua, a half figure reading, nearly of the fame fize with the preceding print.

DOMENICO DEL BARBIERE.

Flourifhed,

This artift is better known by the name of Diomenico Fiorentino. He has often been confounded with Dominique Barriere; but the difference fo eafily to be difcovered in the works of thefe two artifts, will on examination, evidently prove the miftake. Domenico del Barbiere was born at Florence. Bafan fpeaks very highly of him as a painter, and greatly commends his works in ftucco, which he performed under the infpection of Roffo in France. As an engraver, he certainly does not merit equal commendation. The prints, which I have feen of his, are chiefly groups, and fometimes fingle figures, from Michael Angelo, and other great mafters. They are often executed entirely with the graver, in a very ftiff incorrect ftyle. His etchings are by no means more meritorious. Confidering him as a painter the drawing and the effect of his prints ought to have been greatly fuperior to what we find they are: for in thefe he is as defective, as in the mechanical part of engraving. Among the reft of his engravings is,

An *Angel*, ftanding on a globe, holding two trumpets; and the artift's name is fubfcribed Domenico del Barbiere Fiorentino.

To the *groups* and *fingle figures*, from the laft judgment of Michael Angelo, he ufually writes his name Domenico Fiorentino.

V. BARDUCCI.

Flourifhed, 1768.

By this engraver we have a portrait of *Pafcal Paoli*, the Corfican general.

M. BARGAS.
Flourished,

According to Bafan, this artist lived at the beginning of the prefent century, and etched feveral plates from the pictures of Peter Bout; amongft the reft, from that mafter, are two large *hiftorical landfcapes*.

A. F. BARGAS.
Flourished,

I have feen a fet of fmall *landfcapes*, length-ways, with cattle and figures, flightly etched; but in a free mafterly ftyle, fubfcribed, A. F. Bargas, inv. et fec.

THOMAS BARLACCHIUS.
Flourished,

A name inferted in the catalogue of the engravers, at the end of the Abecedario; but none of his works are fpecified. I never faw any engravings by this artift.

FRANCIS BARLOW.
Born,   Died, 1702.

This artift was born in Lincolnfhire, and received his firft inftructions in painting from Shepherd, a portrait painter. His chief excellency lay in defigning birds, fifhes, and animals of all kinds, which he drew with great fpirit, and in a very mafterly ftyle. His drawings are generally flight; and the colouring of his pictures is by no means equal to the defigns. The figures, which he often introduced into his compofitions, are well executed, and difpofed with great judgment. And the diftances and admirable landfcapes, with which he alfo ufually embellifhed them, prove the fertility of his invention, as well as the excellence of his tafte. I have now before me a fet of twelve prints, engraved from him by Hollar, reprefenting feveral ways of *hunting, hawking*, and *fifhing*, publifhed by John Overton; which prove, in every inftance, in my opinion, the truth of thefe obfervations. According to Mr. Symonds, he refided in Drury-lane, near the Drum. Mention is alfo made of his felling a picture of fifhes for eight pounds. But whether this was a price adequate or inadequate to its merit, cannot be afcertained; unlefs the fize of the picture, and the labour beftowed in finifhing it, had been fpecified. I fhould fear he was not well paid for his performances, unlefs he lived extravagantly; for notwithftanding all his excellency in defign, the multitude of pictures and drawings he appears to have made, and the affiftance alfo of a confiderable fum of money, faid to have been left him by a friend, he died in indigent circumftances, A. D. 1702.

He defigned the cuts for Ogilby's tranflation of *Æfop's Fables*, and etched feveral of the plates himfelf.

Part of the plates for Edward Benlow's Divine Poems, called *Theophila*, in folio, publifhed A. D. 1652, were alfo engraved by him.

A print

A print reprefenting an *eagle flying in the air, with a cat in its talons*. This event the artift himfelf was witnefs of in Scotland, whilft he was drawing views there. The eagle was overpowered by the ftruggling of the cat, and both fell to the ground, where he took them up.

He frequently ufed the initials of his name, inftead of inferting it at full length, as F. B. and thofe he fometimes inclofed in a fmall circle.

FREDERICO BAROCCIO.
Born, 1528. Died, 1612.

This admirable artift is better known as a painter, than as an engraver. He was born at Urbino, A. D. 1528, and died at the fame city, in the year 1612, aged 84. His genius for the arts difcovered itfelf in the very early part of his life; and according to De Piles, while yet a young man, he was employed at Rome by Pope Paul III. for whom he painted feveral things in frefco. His great reputation as a painter need not be recited here; fuffice it to fay, that he engraved feveral plates from his own compofitions; which though flight, and not well managed, with refpect to the mechanical part of the workmanfhip, are neverthelefs moft admirable, on account of the expreffion, and excellent drawing, which is difcovered in them. His heads are very beautiful and characteriftic; and the other extremities of his figures finely marked. Amidft all the difficulties he appears to have met with, in biting his plates with the aquafortis, after he had etched them, and his unfkilfulnefs in handling the graver, to harmonize and finifh them, the hand of the mafter appears fo evident, that the beauties we difcover in them far overbalance the defects.

The following are by him, and from his own compofitions.

An *annunciation*, a large upright plate.

A fmall print in which the *Virgin* is reprefented holding the infant Chrift. This plate was never compleatly finifhed at the bottom.

St. Francis receiving the ftigmata, or pretended marks upon his hands, feet, and fide, a fmall upright plate.

The *extatic vifion of St. Francis*, in which our Saviour and the Virgin appear to him, a large plate upright, arched at the top.

JOHN BARON, or BARONIUS.
Flourifhed,

He is alfo called *Tolofano*, becaufe he was native of Touloufe. He refided chiefly at Rome, as it feems from his works; the greater part of which were publifhed there. He executed his plates entirely with the graver, in a fervile, dry manner, very neatly, but exceedingly defective in drawing, expreffion, and effect. Judging from the ftyle and appearance of his prints, I fhould imagine he flourifhed towards the latter end of the laft century.

We have by him,

The *Peft*, a large plate length-ways, from Nicholas Poufin.

A middling fized plate upright, reprefenting an *emblematical fubject*, from
Andrea

Andrea Sacchi; where several ecclesiastics, clothed in white, are represented ascending to heaven; which was also engraved by Giacomo Freii.

A *Madona*, a small plate, from Bernini.

A variety of other subjects from different masters.

BERNARD BARON.
Born,   Died, 1762.

This artist was a native of France, and in his own country received the first instructions in the art of engraving. He was brought into England by Du Bosc; but they disagreeing about the plates of the history of Ulysses, engraved from Rubens, went to law with each other. Being afterwards reconciled, Baron accompanied Du Bosc to Paris, where he engraved some plates for the Crozat collection. How soon afterwards he returned to England, I know not: but he died in Panton-square, Piccadilly, January 24, 1762. His manner of engraving seems to have been founded on that of Nicholas Dorigny. It is slight and coarse, without any great effect; and his drawing is frequently very defective. Among his best plates may be reckoned, the *Jupiter and Antiope*, from Titian, a large plate, length-ways, from the Crozat collection.

The *Conaro family*, from the pictures of Titian at Northumberland-house.

Charles the First on horseback, from Vandyck, a large upright plate.

The *Pembroke family*, from a picture of the same master at Wilton, a large plate length-ways.

Belisarius, the same, from the same.

The *Nassau family*, the same, from the same: the picture is in possession of earl Cowper.

Henry the Eighth granting the charter to the barber surgeons, from John Holbein, a large plate, length-ways, &c.

JOSEPH BARON.
Flourished, 1720.

I have seen but few prints by this engraver; and those are very indifferently executed. If he was not a native of Venice, it seems by his prints, (which were, I believe, chiefly engraved for the booksellers) that he resided there. His manner is coarse and unpleasing; and his drawing exceedingly defective. I shall only remark,

A large upright plate, arched, representing the *crucifixion of our Saviour*, with angels in the air, and Mary Magdalen and Saint John at the foot of the cross; which was engraved by him for a large folio book, thus entitled, *Il gran Teatro delle Pitture di Venezia*, 1720, with his name Iseppo Baroni Incid.

JOHN BARRA.
Flourished, 1624.

An engraver of the last century, of whom we have no account. He resided however at London, as we find by some of his prints. Of what country
he

he was a native, or when he died, are equally uncertain. He executed his plates entirely with the graver, and without any etching. At leaſt, all that I have ſeen are in this ſtyle. He ſeems to have formed his taſte upon the prints of the Sadelers. But though he imitated, in ſome degree, their manner of engraving, yet he by no means equalled them, either in correctneſs of the drawing or expreſſion. His prints are cold and ſilvery. We ſee in them a painful, laborious exertion, without genius. He engraved the portrait of *Lodowick*, duke of Richmond and Lenox, A. D. 1624.

Time and Truth, a ſmall upright plate, from Paulus ab Eſtatis.

Bathſheba at the bath, a ſmall upright plate, from a painter whoſe initials are G. W.

Some *groteſque ornaments*, from Nicaſius Rouſſeel, inſcribed John Barra ſculp. Londini.

SEBASTIAN BARRAS.
Flouriſhed, 1700.

An engraver in mezzotinto, who was employed by M. de Boyer, counſellor of the parliament at Aix, conjointly with James Coelmans, to engrave the pictures of the great maſters, which were in the poſſeſſion of that connoiſſeur. The plates of this artiſt are all ſcraped in a very indifferent ſtyle; the lights are too ſudden upon the ſhadows, and the grounds appear to have been very badly laid; ſo that the effect is coarſe and harſh. His drawing is alſo very defective.

GEORGE BARRET.
Died, 1784.

An excellent landſcape painter, by whom we have ſome ſlight, but ſpirited etchings of landſcapes. He was a member of the Royal Academy, and died at London, A. D. 1784.

GIACOMO BARRI.
Flouriſhed, 1650.

This artiſt was a painter, born at Venice, but he alſo amuſed himſelf with the point; and we have ſeveral etchings by him, as well from his own compoſitions, as thoſe of other maſters. In the year 1651, he publiſhed at Venice a book greatly eſteemed, entitled *Viaggio Pittoreſco d'Italia*, octavo.

I ſhall only notice the following etching by him, which I have now before me: A *nativity*, from Paolo Veroneſe, with angels in the clouds above: a middling ſized upright plate, very ſlight and free, but by no means correct.

DOMINIQUE BARRIERE.
Flouriſhed, 1650.

This artiſt (who is often confounded with Domineco del Barbiere, of whom we have ſpoken above) was a native of Marſeilles, and flouriſhed according to Baſan, about the middle of the laſt century. His etchings greatly reſembled thoſe

those of Stephen de la Bella; and we have by him many pretty *landscapes* and *sea-views*, from his own compositions; and others from Claud Lorrain. Also the *history of Apollo*, consisting of several plates, from the pictures of Dominichino and Viola.

A. BARRODUCCEO.
Flourished,

A name I found inscribed to some small upright plates, representing the *liberal arts and sciences*, executed in a stiff, dry style, entirely with the graver. The heads and other extremities of the figures are very incorrectly drawn. These plates were published by the artist himself.

BARTOLOMEO. See BREENBERGH.

GOTFRID BARTASH or BARTASCH.
Flourished,

I find no account of this artist, Basan indeed tells us, that he was a native of England; but without assigning any reason for such an assertion. I find his name to the small collection of prints, from the gallery at Berlin. It is possible he may have been a Prussian; but however, as an engraver, he possessed very little merit. All the prints I have seen by him, are executed in a poor, dark style, without taste; and greatly defective in the drawing.

I shall only notice,

A *holy family*, from Vandyke, a small plate, length-ways.

And the portrait of *Catherine de Bohra*, wife of Martin Luther.

Basan attributes to him a print from Rubens, representing *Meleager presenting the head of the boar to Atalanta*, a middling sized upright plate: but I do not recollect to have seen it.

PIETRO SANTE BARTOLI, called PERUGINO.
Born, 1635. Died, 1700.

This celebrated artist was a native of Perugia, and appears to have been born about the year 1635. He resided chiefly at Rome, where he is said to have died A. D. 1700. He is mentioned, as a painter; but his reputation is certainly much better established, as an engraver. He drew in a correct, agreeable style; and his plates, which are chiefly etched, are executed in a free, masterly manner. His great excellency lay in copying the bass-relief, and other works of the ancients. Though he has not always marked his name at full length upon his plates, yet to a person, the least acquainted with his works, they are easily distinguished, as his manner is original; and the freedom and lightness of his point, cannot easily be counterfeited.

He did many of the plates, and certainly the best of them, for the *Admirandi Antiq. Romanorum*. The following also are sets of prints:

The *Trajan*, and *Antonine columns*.

The *tomb of the Nafonian family*, and the ancient pictures, &c. found therein.
The *actions of Leo the Tenth*, from Raphael.
The *friezes* painted in the Vatican, in imitation of the antique, by the same master.
Julii Romani Picturæ in Mufeo Mantuano, dated 1680.
The *hiftory of St. Peter*, from Lanfranchi, &c.
Among his detached prints I shall notice the following:
A large upright plate, reprefenting *St. Charles kneeling, accompanied by an Angel*, from Antonio Carracci, the natural fon of Agoftino Carracci. This is the only print we have from this mafter, of whom the greateft expectations were formed; but he died young.
The *adoration of the shepherds*, from Annibale Carracci, a large upright plate.
He alfo engraved from Pietro Perugino, Polidore Caravaggio, Albano, Pietro di Cortona, Pietro Tefta, F. Mola, and other mafters. He fometimes, though not frequently, put only the initials of his name to his plates, with the letter F, for *fecit*: as P. B. F. But ufually he abreviated it in the following manner: Petr. Ss. Barts fc. Romæ.

H. BARY.
Flourifhed, 1659.

I fufpect, that this artift was a native of Holland; at leaft I think, it appears from the portraits which he engraved, that he refided there. His ftyle of engraving feems to have been formed upon the prints of Cornelius Viffcher; and the imitation appears moft evident in his portraits, efpecially thofe which he has executed in his neateft manner. However, it is but a feeble attempt. In drawing, tafte, and harmony, he is, I think, greatly deficient. Yet fometimes he has difcovered much mechanical knowledge, and feems to have handled the graver with great facility. One of his beft and moft finifhed prints, I believe, is *Summer and Autumn*, reprefented by two children; one of which holds a handful of corn: a fmall upright plate, from Vandyke, companion to the Spring and Winter, which Munichuyfen engraved from Girard Laireffe. This plate is executed entirely with the graver (which, I believe, was his conftant cuftom) in a neat clear ftyle, and fhows his management of that inftrument in the moft ftriking light.

Among his portraits are noticed,

Hugo Grotius, a middling fized upright plate, from Michael Janfon Mireveldt.

Van Tromp, the Dutch admiral, from F. Bol. a large upright plate.

Admiral Ruyter, the fame, from the fame.

Ketels the painter, engraved from a picture, which that artift painted himfelf, and dated 1659, a fmall upright plate.

Arnold Geefterfun, a fmall upright plate.

A variety of other fubjects, from different mafters.

BAS [68] BAS

MARTIN BAS, or BASSE.
Flourished, 1591 to 1622.

An artist who flourished at the beginning of the last century; and his style of engraving is in that neat, stiff manner, which characterised the small portraits of that time. It seems very likely to me, that he studied in the school of the Wierexes; at least, he certainly imitated them. His chief employment appears to have been the engraving of portraits. Among them are the following:

The portrait of *Edmund Genings*, the jesuit, prefixed to his memoirs, published 1591.

The portrait of *Philip Bosquieri*. To this he signs his name, Mart. Basse.

A small frontispiece representing *St. Peter* and *St. Paul*, dated 1622.

JAMES PHILIP LE BAS.
Flourished, 1754.

A modern French artist, by whom we have some excellent prints. His great force seems to lie in landscapes and small figures, which he executed in a superior manner. His style of engraving is extremely neat; but yet he proves the freedom of the etching, and harmonizes the whole with the graver and dry point. We have also a variety of pretty vignettes by this artist. Among the rest, the chief part of those, which adorn the octavo edition of Rollin's Ancient History in English, published by the Knaptons, A. D. 1754.

Among his most esteemed works are the following plates:

The *works of mercy*, a large plate, length-ways, from Tenier.

A set of several *Dutch merry-makings, fairs*, &c. from the same master, all large plates, length-ways.

The *Italian chase*, and the *milk-pot*, two large plates, length-ways, from Philip Wouvermans.

The *wild boar*, from the same master, a large plate, length-ways.

Several large plates of *hunting*, &c. from Van Falens.

The *seaports of France*, after Vernet, very large plates, length-ways: the etchings of these plates were by Cochin.

The *environs de Groningue*, a large plate, length-ways, from Ruysdaal.

The *environs de Guelders*, its companion, the same.

He also engraved from Bergham, Vander Velde, Watteau, Oudry, Parocel, Lancret, Gravelot, &c.

BASIRE.
Flourished,

An engraver of maps, and father of the present Mr. John Basire, engraver to the Antiquarian Society.

J. BASS.
Flourished.

A name subscribed to the portrait of *Uladislaus VII*. Sigis. Rex.

CÆSAR

CÆSAR BASSANUS.
Flourished, 1622.

This artist was a painter, as well as an engraver, and according to Florent le Comte, there are three prints engraved by him, from J. Battista Lampus, Joan. Ant. Lœlius, and Jacobus Lodus; and from him nine prints have been engraved; but he has not specified any of them. I have seen in a small upright oval, the portrait of *Gasper Asselius*, executed with the graver, in a style something resembling that of Cornelius Cort, and inscribed *Bassanus fec.* Also an *architectal frontispiece* with figures, &c. dated 1622.

DANIEL BASSELLI.
Flourished,

I have seen by this engraver a large upright plate, arched at the top, from P. Caton, representing *Daniel in the lion's den*, etched, and retouched with the graver, in a very slight style. The effect is not well managed, nor is the drawing correct.

BASSEPORTE.
Flourished, 1729.

This ingenious lady engraved, among other things, some of the plates for the Crozat collection, which was published at Paris, A. D. 1729.

T. BASTON.
Flourished, 1721.

An English artist, though of no great eminence. His chief employment was painting sea-pieces and shipping; many of which were engraved in mezzotinto, and other ways, by Kirkall, Harris, &c. He himself etched some few plates from his own designs; among the rest, a large print length-ways, representing the *Royal Anne*, surrounded with other ships, dated 1721.

BATHON.
Flourished,

A name subscribed to the portrait of *Fran. Mieris*, the painter, a middling sized upright print.

STEPHEN BAUDET.
Flourished, 1672 to 1700.

By what master this artist was instructed in the art of engraving does not appear. From a careful examination of his prints, I have been led to suppose, that he frequented the school of the Poillys: unless he was educated at Rome, where his most early works seem to have been done; and then perhaps the works of Cornelius Bloemart may have laid the foundation of his first style, which was all with the graver. These prints are in general, exceeding

ing neat; but the effect of them is cold and silvery; and the extremities of the figures are heavy, and not well marked. But at times he called in the assistance of the point, and produced much bolder engravings, in a manner greatly resembling that of John Baptista de Poilly; and these prints, in my opinion, are far superior to the former in freedom, drawing, and effect.

Among those in the first style is,

The *tribute money*, a middling sized plate, nearly square, from Valentino, which, I think, is the most masterly of all he executed in that manner.

Add to this,

Four large *landscapes*, length-ways, with figures from Albano, published at Rome, 1672.

The *four elements*, large circular prints, from the same, dated 1695.

The *martyrdom of St. Stephen*, a large plate, length-ways, from Annibale Carracci.

Among those in the second style, are the following:

Moses trampling upon the crown of Pharoah, a large plate length-ways, from Nicholas Poussin.

Moses striking the rock, the same, from the same master.

The *Israelites dancing round the golden calf*, a spirited print, the same, from the same.

Several large *landscapes*, length-ways, from the same.

Some of the *statues*, in the garden at Versailles, were engraved by Baudet. These he has executed with a single stroke, without any hatching, in imitation of Melan, who performed the greater part of those statues.

Baudet engraved also, from different masters, a variety of other plates, both at Rome and at Paris, at which last place I think, it is likely that he died.

S. R. BAUDOUIN.
Flourished,

According to Basan, this gentleman was an officer in the French guards, and a lover of the arts. He etched for his amusement a set of prints, from his own compositions, consisting of sixty-three plates, representing the *military exercise of the French infantry*.

Several *battles*, from Charles Parocel.

Several little *landscapes*, from Michaut, and others.

ANTONY FRANCIS BAUDUINS, or BAUDOUINS.
Flourished, 1660.

This artist was, I believe, a native of France, and, according to M. Heineken, the disciple of Vander Meulen. He etched in a bold, free style; not unlike that adopted afterwards by Chatelain, a well known artist, who died in England some years since. Bauduins' best engravings are from the pictures of Vander Meulen, consisting of many plates; some of them large, and others of various sizes, which may be found in the works of that painter, in three large folio volumes.

R. BAUDOUX.
Flourished,

The name of an artist who according to Florent le Comte, engraved some plates from the designs of Lucas Van Leyden. I do not recollect to have seen any of them.

J. BAUGIN.
Flourished,

The name of an obscure engraver, affixed to the portrait of *H. de la Mothe*.

JOHN WILLIAM BAUR.
Born, 1610. Died, 1640.

A painter of no small eminence, born at Strasburgh, A. D. 1610. He was the disciple of Frederic Brendel, and is universally considered as a man of great genius and fertile imagination. His landscapes, in which species of painting he chiefly excelled, he usually enriched with architecture, and a variety of figures. But his paintings in water colours on vellum, are held in the highest estimation. He resided a considerable time in Italy, and died at Vienna, A. D. 1640, aged 30. This artist engraved a vast number of plates from his own designs; and his works were completed by Meichior Kussel, to the amount of 500 prints, including those by his own hand. As his engravings from the metamorphoses of Ovid, are generally preferred to the rest, I shall only mention those, with the following short observations. They are slightly etched, and retouched with the graver. The figures, which are introduced, are generally small, and very incorrect in the drawing; the backgrounds are dark and heavy, and the trees want that lightness and freedom which are necessary to render the effect agreeable. The pieces of architecture, which he is very fond of introducing into his designs, appear to be well executed; and the perspective is finely preserved. In his manner of engraving he seems in some degree, to have imitated Callot; and the nearer he approaches to the style of that master, the better are his productions. These designs manifest great marks of a superior genius, but without cultivation, or the advantage of a refined judgment to make a proper choice of the most beautiful objects.

The *metamorphoses* consist of 150 middling sized plates, length-was.

PETER BAUT.
Flourished,

By this artist, who appears to have been a painter, I have seen a slight etching of a *Dutch market*, executed in a style, that does little honour to him.

HERCULES BAZICALVA.
Flourished, 1641.

The name of an engraver, mentioned in the index, at the end of the Abecedario; but none of his works are specified. I do not recollect, that I have seen any prints by this master.

NICHOLAS BAZIN.
Flourished, 1692.

This engraver never arrived at any great excellency; he was chiefly employed upon devotional subjects, which he executed in a stiff, dry manner, entirely with the graver. Among others, we have by this artist *Saint Marguerite*, after Raphael, from a picture of that master, in the king of France's collection, a small upright plate.

And the portrait of *Jean Craffet*, à jesuit, dated 1692.

THOMAS BEARD.
Flourished, 1728.

A modern engraver in mezzotinto, of no great eminence; a native, I believe of Ireland. Among other prints of his, we have the portrait of the *archbishop of Armagh*, a whole length, from P. Ashton, dated 1728. Also the *countess of Clarendon*, from Kneller; and *John Sterne*, bishop of Clogher, from Carlton, &c.

NICCOLO BEATRICI.
Flourished, 1550.

This artist was a native of Lorrain; but the chief part of his works were executed at Rome. I will not take upon me to say, that he was a disciple of Marc Antonio Ramondi; but, I think, there is some foundation for such an opinion. And the manner of engraving, which he usually adopted, seems to me to have been founded on a beautiful print by that master, after Raphael, representing the tempest described by Virgil, in the opening of the Æneid, where *Neptune is rising from the sea, and speaking to the winds*. The frame or border consists of several compartments, in which are designed the continuation of the story of Æneas. How far he fell short in the imitation, granting it to have been such, his prints, compared with the beautiful original, will too evidently declare. I know no reason why his works are valuable, but as they are, in several instances the only copies we have from the designs of some of the greatest masters. I own, to me they seem to want every requisite, that a fine engraving ought to possess, namely, drawing, character, effect, and mechanical execution.

There is a considerable number of prints, attributed to Beatrici, which certainly, in my opinion, do not belong to him. They are by an artist every way superior to him; an artist, who does honour to the school of Marc Antonio, and whose manner he imitated. These prints are variously marked; sometimes

sometimes with a plain dye; then it has figures upon it, and often, instead of the figures, the letter B. However, on examining carefully the separate engravings thus marked, they appear evidently to belong to the same master. And those, in particular, with the B. have been falsely attributed to Beatrici. I shall defer what I have further to say upon this matter for the present, and speak more fully upon it under the name of Bartolomeo Beham. A curious cypher, attributed to Beatrici, is copied on the plate at the end of the volume. His usual marks were N. B. joined together, or separate, or N. B. L. F. and, when he wrote his name at length, in the following manner: Nicolaus Beatricius Lotheringus fecit.

I shall notice the following prints, which are certainly by this engraver:

The *conversion of St. Paul*, a large print, length-ways, from M. Angelo Buonaroti.

The *prophet Jeremiah*, a large upright plate, dated 1547, after a picture by the same master, in the chapel of the Vatican.

The *annunciation*, a large plate, length-ways, from the same master.

An *emblematical subject*, representing boys carrying a dead ox, whilst others are seething flesh in a caldron. Towards the left, is a female satyr with two children; one of which is at her breast: a middling sized plate, length-ways. The same subject was also engraved by Marc da Ravenna.

The *sacrifice of Iphigenia*, a middling sized plate, length-ways, from Perino del Vaga.

St. Elizabeth, queen of Hungary, relieving the distressed, a large upright plate, from Jerom Musciano.

A *river god*, dated 1560.

There is a beautiful middling sized upright print, representing the *fall of Phaeton*; and at the bottom appear his three sisters, and a river god. From Michael Angelo; but who the engraver originally was is uncertain, it not having any name or mark, by which it might be distinguished. This plate fell into the hands of Beatrici, and he retouched it, adding his own name, *Beatrix Lotaring. restitut.* I apprehend, Beatrici was a printseller, as well as an engraver; for we frequently find by the inscriptions upon his plates, that he published them himself.

He engraved a great variety of other plates from different masters.

ROBERT BEAUDOUX.
Flourished, 1628.

A native of Brussels; but an artist of no great eminence. He worked chiefly, if not entirely, with the graver; and his style resembles that of De Ghyen. Among others, by this engraver, are some of those large plates, length-ways, which were published in a book entitled, *Academie de L'espée de Girard Thibault d'Anvers*, dated 1628.

BEAUMONT.
Flourished,

A modern French engraver, by whom we have several prints, from different

ferent masters: among the rest, eight middling sized plates, length-ways, from Wouvermans; and two upright plates, from the same master.

NICHOLAS DAUPHIN DE BEAUVAIS.
Flourished, 1722.

A French engraver of some eminence. It is uncertain under what master he studied; but, I think, something of the style of Girard Edelink is often found in his best works, though his manner is much varied. Among his most esteemed prints may be placed the following:

The *Virgin with the infant Jesus upon a pedestal*, and several saints below, from a picture of Corregio in the Dresden gallery, a large upright plate.

St Jerom, after Vandyke, from a picture in the same gallery, a middling sized plate, length-ways.

Mary Magdalen in the desert, a middling sized upright plate, from Bennedatto Lutti, for the Crozat collection.

The *triumph of Bacchus and Ariadne*, from Nicholas Poussin, a middling sized plate, length-ways.

Love stealing Jupiter's thunder, from Le Sueur, a middling sized circular plate.

He also engraved from Le Brun, and other masters.

DOMENICO BECCAFUMI. See MICARINO.

ISAAC BECKET.
Born, 1653. Died,

An engraver in mezzotinto of some eminence. He was born in Kent, A. D. 1653; and was first an apprentice to a callico printer; but becoming acquainted with Lutterel, an engraver in mezzotinto, he was desirous of learning that art. Some time after, being obliged to leave his business, in consequence of an intrigue, he had recourse to one Loyd, a printseller, who was acquainted with the secret of scraping mezzotinto, but unable to practise it himself; and from him Becket obtained it. They entered into articles together, and Becket engaged to work for Loyd; but falling into trouble again, he was assisted by Lutterel; and from that time an intimacy commenced between them. Becket, not long after, married a woman of some fortune, and entered into business upon his own account, being still assisted by Lutterel, who drew better, and was more expeditious.

Becket's mezzotintos possess some degree of merit. They are often clear and well scraped; but it has been remarked, that his middle tints are not sufficiently distinguished, which makes his shadows appear flat and heavy. One of his best prints, in my opinion, is engraved on a middling sized upright plate, representing *Adrain Beverland* drawing from a statue. In the background are monuments, pyramids, and several other relics of antiquity.

Add the following,

Lady Williams, whole length, a large upright plate.

John duke of Lauderdale, a middling sized upright plate, oval.

His royal highness, *George prince of Denmark*, &c.

CORNELIUS BEGA, or BEGEYN.
Born, 1620. Died, 1664.

This artist, a native of Haerlem, was disciple to Adrain Oftade; and under that master he made such improvement, as to be esteemed his best scholar. Happy had it been for him, if his assiduity had been equal to his natural abilities. But running into a licentious way of living, his father disowned him; and he, in return, despising his family name, which was *Begeyn*, assumed that of *Bega*.

He died of the plague, A. D. 1664, aged 44 years. His death was occasioned by his excessive attachment to a favorite female, whom, though she had caught that dreadful disorder, he could not be prevailed upon to quit; and from her he received the infection, and outlived her only a few days.

He etched several drolleries, and a set of thirty-four prints, representing ale-house scenes, &c.

LAURENTIUS BEGER.
Flourished, 1700.

Laurentus Beger, says professor Christ, was nephew to the famous antiquary of the same name. According to this author, he engraved at Berlin, about the year 1700, twelve anatomical plates, taken from the designs in *Vesalius*; and it is likely, adds he, that the greater part of the plates of antiquities, published by his uncle, under the title of *Thesaurus Brandenburgicus*, were engraved by this artist.

HANS or JOHN SEBALD BEHAM.
Flourished, 1540.

The works of this eminent artist, being chiefly very small, he is ranked in that class of engravers, distinguished by the name of *little masters*. By the Abbé Marolles, Le Comte, and other authors, he is falsely called Hisbens. How such an unaccountable mistake should happen I know not; for he has more than once written part of his name at length thus, Sebald or Sebaldus Beham; and his monogram is composed of an H. an S. and a B. all joined together. Because he has omitted the word Hans or John, where his other names are written, professor Christ supposes, that it did not belong to him. But, I think with Sandrart, that it is not reasonable to imagine he would have added the H. to his cypher, without sufficient reason. It is necessary to caution my readers, not to confound this master with a more early engraver, who used a monogram much like his, but substituted a P. instead of the B. Beham styles himself of Nuremberg; and most likely he was a native of that city. To what master he owed his instructions in the art of engraving, is very uncertain. It might be Henry Aldegrever; at least, it is certain, that the works of that artist, and his tutor Albert Durer, were the sources, from which Beham drew his greatest improvement. Like them he engraved on wood, as well as on copper, and also etched some few plates; but these last are by far the most indifferent, as they are the smallest part of his works.

If Beham's style of engraving be not original, it is at least, an excellent and a spirited imitation of that which was adopted by the best preceding masters of the country in which he resided. His pictures (for he was a painter) as well as his engravings, were held in such high estimation, that the poets of that age celebrated him in their poems, calling him in Latin Bohemus.

He was certainly a man of much genius, and possessed great fertility of invention. But the Gothic taste, which so generally prevailed in Germany at this time, is much too prevalent in his works. His draperies are stiff, and loaded with a multiplicity of short, inelegant folds. His drawing of the naked figure, which he is fond of introducing, though mannered, is often very correct, and sometimes masterly. His heads, and the other extremities of his figures, are carefully determined, and often possess much merit. The mechanical part of the engraving, on his copper-plates, is executed with the graver only, in so clear and delicate a manner, that his great facility and judgment in handling that instrument is abundantly evident. Those prints, which he has cut in wood, are slight, but very spirited and free. Of these last I shall only mention

A set of prints for a small octavo book, entitled, *Biblicæ Historiæ artificiosissimè depictæ. Francfort*, 1537, with his mark.

On copper, his works are so numerous, and the subjects so different, that even a general list would far exceed the limits of this book. I shall therefore only notice the following:

History of the creation and fall of man, very small upright plates, with his mark.

The *labours of Hercules*, twelve very small plates, length-ways, with his mark, dated from 1542, to 1548.

The *virtues and vices*, small upright plates.

Several very small plates, length-ways, representing *rustics fighting*, &c.

The *marriage at Cana in Galilee*, a small plate, length-ways; where, on a tablet, is his cypher, and part of his name, SEBOLT BEHAM.

Several small upright plates, representing *melancholy, faith, fortune*, &c. dated from 1539 to 1549.

Patience, a small upright plate, on which is written, *Sebaldus Beham pictor Noricus Faciebat*, with his cypher.

BARTOLOMEO BEHAM.
Flourished, 1540.

This artist is generally allowed to have been the brother of John Sebald Beham, mentioned in the preceding article. But his residence was chiefly at Rome, where perhaps he died.

Sandrart and other authors inform us, that he was the disciple of Marc Antonio Raimondi. If it be true, that he studied under Marc Antonio (and I see no reason to doubt it) we may naturally suppose, that, in his drawing and engraving, he contracted something of the manner of that eminent master. This will evidently appear, if those prints really belong to Beham, which are marked B. B. and they have always been attributed to him without any dispute. From a strong resemblance between those prints, and

some

some others too excellent to be omitted, marked with a die (which in some few cases is plain, but more generally diftinguifhed by the numbers upon it, or the letter B. when the numbers are wanting) I have been led to confider the latter, as productions of the same hand with the former. I am aware, that the generality of authors are againft me; following Maroiles, they have attributed thefe prints, marked with the B. upon the die, to Beatrici. And fome, for want of better information, have placed thofe marked with the die, without the B. to an engraver, named *Dado*; which word in Italian fignifies a die. However, the exiftence of fuch an artift as Dado is very doubtful; but granting that he did exift, and that the prints attributed to him are really the productions of his graver, it will follow, that thofe prints, having the B. upon the die, muft belong to him alfo; for the ftyle of the drawing and engraving is fo precifely alike in both, that it is next to an impoffibility, that they fhould be the works of different artifts. My reafon for fuppofing that they did not belong to Beatrici, I have already mentioned, in the account of that artift, they being greatly fuperior, in every refpect, to his engravings. The B. may refer to both the names of Beham; and if it be objected, that the die can have no reference to either of his names, I have only to anfwer, that the fame may be faid of the tablet ufed by Marc Antonio, with which he frequently marked his engravings, without his monogram, or any other means of diftinction. In imitation of Marc Antonio, his mafter; Beham may have adopted the dies, and ufed them occafionally without any letter, as he did his tablet.

If we confider all thefe plates as engraved by Beham, he will appear to have been a very excellent artift, and one of the fuperior fcholars of Marc Antonio, whofe ftyle of engraving he imitated with great fuccefs. His drawing is correct and mafterly; his heads are characteriftic, and the other extremities of his figures well marked.

I fhall, however, diftinguifh the feveral plates, mentioning only a few under each mark.

And FIRST, thofe marked B. B. F. The *four Evangelifts*, middling fized upright plates. Hieronimus Cock excud. 1551. Fine impreffions of thefe plates are rarely feen.

SECONDLY, thofe marked with the letter B. upon the die: *Apollo caufing the fatyr Martias to be flead*, a middling fized plate, length-ways, from Raphael.

Chrift giving his charge to Peter, a fmall plate, length-ways, from the fame.

A *naval combat*, a large plate, length-ways.

A *landfcape*, with many animals lying round a tree; at the top of which appears a phœnix, fetting fire to her neft; with eight Italian verfes underneath; a fmall plate, length-ways.

Four middling fized *friezes*, length-ways, ornamented with feftoons of flowers, and boys playing. RAPH. VRB. IN. Ant. Laferii formis.

THIRDLY, thofe with the die, without the letter:

Apollo and the Python, a middling fized upright plate.

Apollo and Daphne, the fame.

I do not in the leaft hefitate in my own opinion, to attribute to this engraver,

graver, whoever he might be, all those prints for the Cupid and Psyche of Apuleius, which are usually said to be by Marc Antonio, but without any solid foundation. It is also, according to M. Heineken, exceedingly doubtful, whether they were designed by Raphael or not. He himself, however, seems to think they were not; but has not given his reasons, they being reserved for a future volume of his valuable work.

FRANCOIS JOACHIM BEICH or BEISCH.
Born, 1665. Died, 1748.

An excellent painter of landscapes and battles, who was born at Ravensburg in Swabia, and died at Munich, A. D. 1748, aged 83 years. He etched some few landscapes from his own compositions.

MATHIAS BEITLER.
Flourished, 1616.

This artist appears to have resided at Augsburg; and it is possible he may have been a native of that place. He is cited by professor Christ for several small engravings of *foliage*, published at that city, A. D. 1616, which he mentions with some degree of approbation. See his cypher on the plate at the end of the volume.

BEK.
Flourished,

An engraver little known in England, by whom we have, among other things, the portrait of *Peter Malmberg*, almoner to Charles XII. king of Sweden.

T. BELBRULE.
Flourished,

" I have seen," says Papillon, " by this artist some *ornamental flowers*, " engraved very delicately on wood; and I have a book, containing the *figures* " *of the Sibyls*, engraved on copper, by John Rabel, in which is a small wood " cut, exceedingly well executed, by T. Belbrule. This book is dedicated " to Louisa de Lorrain, wife to Henry the Third, king of France. Opposite " to the portrait of this Queen are some Latin verses, composed by *John* " *Belbrulii Lemovicensis Advocatus*, the brother of the present artist, in honor " of J. Rabel."

STEFANO DE LA BELLA.
Born, 1610. Died, 1664.

This excellent artist was born at Florence, A. D. 1610. His father was a goldsmith; and he himself began to work at his father's business. But whilst he was learning to draw, in order to perfect himself in that profession,

some

some of the prints of Callot fell by accident into his hands; with which he was so delighted, that he prevailed upon his father to permit him to apply himself to engraving; and he became the disciple of Canta Gallina, who was also the instructer of Callot. De la Bella, at first imitated the manner of Callot. His abilities soon began to manifest themselves; and as, by degrees, he acquired a facility in the handling of the point, he quitted the style in which he only shone as an imitator, and adopted one entirely his own, which in freedom and spirit is said even to have surpassed that of his fellow disciple.

He went to Paris, A. D. 1642, where he formed an acquaintance with Israel Silvestre, then newly returned from Rome; and he was much employed by Henriete, the uncle of Silvestre. Some time after, Cardinal Richelieu engaged him to go to Arras, and make drawings of the siege and taking of that town by the royal army; which drawings he engraved at his return. He also went to Holland, where, it is reported, he saw some of the prints of Rembrant Gerretsz, and attempted to imitate them; but finding he did not succeed to his expectations, he dropped that design, and continued to pursue his own manner, as most suitable to his genius.

After abiding some considerable time at Paris, his family affairs obliged him to return to Florence; where he obtained a pension from the great duke, and was appointed to instruct the prince Cosmus, his son, in the art of design. Being subject to violent pains in the head; his life was rendered very uncomfortable by this cruel disorder, which at last put an end to it, A. D. 1664, when he was only 54 years of age.

The free and masterly etchings of this excellent artist are well known; and the high estimation they are generally held in, by the best judges of their merit, renders it unnecessary for me to say much in praise of them; and it would be still more foreign from my purpose, to enter into that fruitless dispute, which has exercised the pens of some able foreign writers, namely, whether the works of Callot or De la Bella possess the greater merit. For my own part, I see no reason to compare them together; especially if it be true, as I conceive it is, that the excellence of De la Bella consists in the freedom of his point, and the lightness and elegance of his figures; and of Callot, in the clearness and perspicuity of his designs, the arrangement of his groups, and the firmness of his outline.

De la Bella drew very correctly, and with great taste. His works manifest much genius, and vast fertility of invention. The fire and animation, which appears in them, compensates for their slightness; and we may reasonably expect to find them slight, when we are told, that he engraved 1400 plates. The limits of this work will admit but of very few; and first the following, in which he has imitated the style of Callot:

Six views of Livourne, middling sized plates, length-ways.

Several sets of *shipping*, &c. the same.

Add to these,

A *holy family*, the Virgin is represented seated under a tree, and Joseph is reading in a book.

Several *madonas*, &c.

The *reposoir*, a large plate, length-ways: it is very difficult to find a good impression of this print.

The *view of Pont-Neuf* at Paris, a large plate, length-ways. The firſt impreſſions of this plate were taken before the weathercock was added to the ſteeple of St. Germain l'Auxerrois.

St. Proſper, a middling ſized plate, length-ways, ſaid to be a very ſcarce print.

A ſet of five ſmall ovals, in which he has repreſented *Death carrying away perſons of various ages*.

Death mounted on the ſkeleton of a horſe, riding furiouſly into a battle, a ſmall plate length-ways.

Parnaſſus, a middling ſized upright plate, a ſcarce print.

The *rock*, another ſcarce print, the ſame ſize as the foregoing.

A *book of ſtudies*, for drawing.

Several ſets of *animals*.

A ſet of *beggar-men, women*, &c.

A variety of ſets of *hunting, ſhipping, landſcapes, ornaments*, &c.

JAMES BELLANGE.
Flouriſhed,

A French artiſt, who flouriſhed towards the latter part of the laſt century. He learned the principles of drawing from Claude Henriet, a painter of very moderate abilities. I find no account of the parentage of our artiſt: but it appears that he was a native of Chalons, and eſtabliſhed at Nancy. He ſeems to have acquired ſome honorary title, as his plates are often inſcribed *Bellange, eques*.

Baſan ſays of him, that "he was a bad painter, and worſe engraver. In "his etchings, which are from his own compoſition," adds the ſame author, "we find much fire, more caprice than judgment, little correction, and a "very bad taſte in the engraving." If theſe obſervations be true in ſome few inſtances, I think I may confidently aſſert, that they are too harſh upon the whole. I have now before me a ſmall upright plate by this artiſt, etched from a deſign of his own. It repreſents the *Virgin with the infant Jeſus*. The ſtyle of engraving, however ſingular, is by no means deſtitute of merit; his drawing appears to me to be incorrect, rather from affectation, than want of knowledge; the whole figure of the child is well executed; there is, indeed, an awkwardneſs in the turn of the figure of the Virgin; and the character of her head is childiſh, and deſtitute of that dignity, which is requiſite for this holy perſonage. His etchings, in general, are ſlight, but free, and often maſterly. The naked parts of his figures he finiſhed with ſmall dots, made by the graver, to harmonize the roughneſs of the ſtrokes left by the aquafortis. I ſhall only mention the following by this artiſt; becauſe his works are by no means uncommon:

A *holy family*, with St. John and St. Catherine, a large upright plate.

The *reſurrection of Lazarus*, a middling ſized upright plate.

A *dead Chriſt*, ſupported on the knees of the Virgin, a ſmall upright plate.

Chriſt carrying the croſs, a large plate, length-ways, &c.

J. A.

BEL [81] BEN

J. A. BELLANGER.
Flouriſhed,

If I underſtand Baſan, this gentleman was a modern connoiſſeur, who reſided at Paris. He deſigned and etched for his own amuſement. The ſame author ſpecifies two prints by him, namely, the *miracle of the loaves and fiſhes*, and the *ſchool of Athens*, both ſmall plates, length-ways; and informs us, that he did ſeveral others from his own compoſition, in which, adds he, we diſcover great taſte, knowledge, and correction.

DU BELLAY.
Flouriſhed,

An engraver on wood, who flouriſhed about the middle of the laſt century. I have never ſeen any of his performances; Papillon ſpeaks of him in the following manner: " I make mention of Du Bellay, engraver on wood, not for the beauty of his works, but becauſe he had the honour of inſtructing, in this art, the famous Peter le Sueur, the elder. He alſo taught, at the ſame time, John Papillon my grandfather."

JAMES BELLI.
Flouriſhed, 1641.

This artiſt was a native of Chartres, but he appears to have reſided chiefly in Italy. From the ſtyle of his etchings, for they are little more than etchings, I ſuppoſe he was a painter. They are ſlightly executed, but with ſpirit, and often in a maſterly ſtyle. His drawing, however, is not correct, nor are the extremities well marked. We have ſeveral prints by him, from Annibale Carracci and other maſters; and the following perhaps from his own compoſitions:

Jupiter and *Juno*, a middling ſized plate, nearly ſquare.
Hercules and *Omphale*, the ſame.
Venus and *Adonis*, the ſame.
Diana and *Endymion*, the ſame. Theſe laſt are dated 1641.

BENAI.
Flouriſhed,

This is a name, which I have ſeen inſcribed upon ſome ſmall copies of the *labours of Hercules*, from John Sebald Beham. I inſert it, however, with caution; becauſe on one of theſe prints, namely where Hercules is repreſented ſtrangling the lion, I found the letters L. R. upon a ſtone at the bottom, which are ſaid to be the initials uſed by a very ancient engraver, named *Lubert Ruſt*. But according to all appearance, theſe prints are by no means ſufficiently old to be attributed to that artiſt.

J. F. BENARD.
Flouriſhed, 1672.

His chief employment ſeems to have been in the architectal and ornamental

tal line. He engraved many of the plates of ornaments for Berain, which were publifhed at Paris in a large folio volume, towards the end of the laft century.

R. BENARD.
Flourifhed, 1756.

A name I have feen affixed to fome flight French prints, of little merit, by a very modern artift, who engraved in the ftyle of P. Aveline, and they are dated 1756.

JOHN BAPTIST BENASCHI.
Born, 1636. Died, 1690.

This artift was a native of Piedmont, where he was born A. D. 1636. He was a difciple of Pietro del Po. The works of Lanfranchi fo greatly delighted him, that he applied himfelf affiduoufly to imitate them; and fucceeded fo well in his attempt, that his pictures have been miftaken for the performances of that mafter. He is generally fpoken of as a man of great genius; and the freedom and facility, which appear in his pictures, are highly commended. He died at Rome, A. D. 1690, aged 54. For his amufement he etched,

A *holy family*, a middling fized, upright plate, from Dominicus Cerini, who was his intimate friend.

F. BENASECH.
Flourifhed,

A modern engraver as it fhould appear; and, according to Bafan, an Englifhman, by whom we have fome *landfcapes*, after Vernet and other painters.

BENEDETTO, See CASTIGLIONE.

BENOIST.
Flourifhed, 1760.

A modern engraver, by birth a Frenchman; but eftablifhed in London, where he died a very few years fince. He chiefly confined himfelf to fmall plates, which he executed in a neat ftyle, though with little tafte. We have fome *battles* by him, from defigns of his own; and a few *portraits*, and *book plates*, of very little eftimation.

J. BENSHEIMER.
Flourifhed, 1680.

An engraver, whofe employment appears to have been chiefly in the portrait line. A fet of portraits of the *Electors of Saxony*, are by this artift. His ufual mark is I. B. the initials of his name.

GIULIO

GIULIO BENSI.
Born,   Died, 1668.

A painter and artift of great eminence, born at Geneva. In the Abecedario he is fpoken of with great commendation. According to Bafan, he etched feveral plates from his own compofitions. He died, A. D. 1668.

JOHN BERAIN or BERRAIN.
Flourifhed, 1670.

This artift was a native of France, and a defigner, as well as an engraver. Conjointly with Chauveau and Le Moine, he drew and engraved the plates for a large work in folio, entitled *Ornamens du Peinture et de Sculpture, dans le Gallerie d'Apollon du Louvre, et dans le grand Apartement du Roy aux Tuilleries*: in Englifh, " the Ornaments of Painting and Sculpture, which are in the Gallery of Apollo at the Louvre, and the great Apartment of the King at the Tuilleries." The ftyle, in which thefe plates are engraved, is very neat; but ftiff, and without much tafte; and the figures, which occafionally occur, are by no means correct.

BERARDI.
Flourifhed,

A modern Italian artift, whofe chief employment feems to have been engraving portraits. I fhall only mention three, which are from Piazetta; namely, the *portraits of that painter*, of *J. B. Albuzzi*, and of *G. B. Cignazelli*.

JOHN BERBE.
Flourifhed,

An obfcure engraver, but of great merit. His works, which probably were very few, have efcaped the notice of the generality of authors. Of what country he was a native, or where he refided, I cannot fay. His ftyle of engraving is neat, and fomething bordering upon that of Paul Pontius. I have feen by him,

A *holy family*, a middling fized upright plate, arched at top, from Francifco Franca.

A *Virgin* and *Child*, a fmall upright plate, arched at top. In this print, which has no name of the painter, a bird is reprefented, coming from a cage to the infant Chrift. It was publifhed by T. Galle.

It is with caution, that I diftinguifh the works of this artift from thofe of John Baptift Barbe, fpoken of in a former page. The name on the abovementioned prints is evidently *Berbe*; and the ftyle of engraving, though in fome refpects fimilar to that of Barbe, yet, on the whole, appears to me to manifeft a fufficient difference to juftify this diftinction.

NICHOLAS BERCHEM, or BERGHEM.
Born, 1624. Died, 1683.

This excellent artift, a native of Haerlem, was born, A. D. 1624.

BER [84] BER

He received inſtructions in the art of painting from ſeveral very eminent maſters; and it was no ſmall addition to their fame, that Berchem was their ſcholar. The charming pictures of cattle and figures, by this admirable maſter, are juſtly held in the higheſt eſtimation. He has been ſingularly happy, in having many of them finely engraved by John Viſſcher, an artiſt of the firſt rank; of whom an account will be given hereafter. Bercham died, A. D. 1683, aged 59.

We have ſeveral etchings by the hand of this maſter, which are much more finiſhed and determined, than one generally expects to find from the point of the painter. They are executed in a fine, bold, maſterly ſtyle; and the animals, which form the chief part of them, are finely drawn. From the beautiful etchings of this great artiſt, John Viſſcher ſeems to have formed that admirable ſtyle, in which he engraved the copies from his pictures mentioned above. I ſhall notice the following by Berchem:

A *boy ſeated on an aſs, ſpeaking to another boy*, who holds a pair of bagpipes; a middling ſized plate, length-ways.

A *boy playing on a flute, and a girl ſpinning*, with cows and ſheep in the fore-ground, dated 1652; a middling ſized, upright plate, with four others, which complete the ſet.

A *woman waſhing her feet in a brook, and a man behind her leaning on a ſtick*; with various animals, and a ruin, in the back-ground; a ſmall plate, length-ways.

Two cows lying down, and a third ſtanding up, with a fine landſcape background, a ſmall plate, length-ways.

A ſet of four ſmall plates, length-ways, of *animals*; in one of which is repreſented an *aſs ſtanding, and other animals lying down*.

A variety of other ſmall prints of *cows, oxen, ſheep, goats*, and other *animals*, equally beautiful.

The author of the Abecedario has made a ſtrange miſtake, with reſpect to this artiſt, miſled by his mark or cypher, which is compoſed of a B. with a C. upon the ſtroke at the top; he calls him Cornelius Berchem. Florent le Comte has gone ſtill farther, and made two artiſts of this name; one, Nicholas, the celebrated cattle painter; the other, Cornelius, who, ſays he, painted landſcapes; and ſome plates are done from his pictures, marked with his name; but they are, however, etched by John Viſſcher. The latter aſſertion is as groſs an overſight, as the former. See his mark on the plate at the end of the volume. The C. ſtands for *Claus*, the common abbreviation of *Nicholas*, as we ſhall ſee hereafter in ſeveral other inſtances.

PETER BERCHET.
Born, 1659. Died, 1720.

A native of France, who ſtudied, as a painter, under La Foſſe. In the year 1681 he came into England, and worked under Rambour, a French painter of architecture; and afterwards was employed by ſeveral of the Engliſh nobility. The ceiling of the Chapel of Trinity College, Oxford, was painted by him; and the ſtair-caſe, at the houſe of the Duke of Schomberg in London, &c. His paintings are ſpoken of with ſome degree of praiſe. He alſo

amuſed

amufed himfelf with the point. I have feen by him a fpirited etching, from a compofition of his own, reprefenting a figure of *St. Cecilia in the clouds*, playing upon the violin, and furrounded by angels. This plate was a ticket of admittance to a concert at St. Bride's Church, Fleet-Street, on Monday, November 23, 1696.

We have alfo etched by him, from his own defigns, fome *children playing*, &c. but none of them are of any great confequence.

His laft performance, a Bacchanalian picture, to which he is faid to have affixed his name, the day before he died, in the year 1721, he being then 61 years of age.

NICOLAS VANDER BERG or BERGH.
Flourifhed, 1764.

According to Bafan, this artift refided at Antwerp, and etched feveral plates from Rubens; among others, the portrait of *Juftus Lipfius*, a fmall upright plate; a portrait of a *religious perfon*, half length, before a crucifix, the fame fize, &c. He ufually marks his plates N. V. D. Berg.

P. VAN DER BERGE.
Flourifhed,

Apparently a Dutch artift, and probably a painter. He appears, at leaft, to have etched the greater part of his plates from his own defigns. The moft confiderable work, that I have feen by him is, a folio volume of prints, entitled *Theatrum Hifpaniæ*, or views of the towns, palaces, &c. of Spain; publifhed at Amfterdam without date; but, according to all appearance, thefe plates were executed towards the end of the laft century. They are flightly etched, in a clear, determined ftyle, but very ftiff; yet fufficiently finifhed to convey a good idea of the places they reprefent, and of which they appear to be juft copies. The figures which are introduced to enliven the views, are very incorrectly drawn, and as indifferently engraved.

He alfo engraved fome portraits; but thefe are in a ftiff, laboured ftyle, without much tafte: among the reft,

A *Jew Rabbi*, a middling fized upright plate, with a Hebrew infcription, marked " P. V. D. Berge ad vivum del. et fec."

I have alfo feen by him,

The *triumph of Galatea*, from Antony Coypel, a middling fized plate, length-ways, which has much of that dry, taftelefs ftyle, in which P. Gunft engraved.

BERGERS.
Flourifhed,

A modern engraver, by whom we have the portrait of the *prince* and *princefs* of *Pruffia*, &c.

BERGHEM.

BERGHEM. See BERCHEM.

JOHN DE BERGMAN.
Flourished, 1490.

He was, says Papillon, a native of *Olpe*; he engraved one hundred and eighteen prints on wood, for a book, entitled, *Stultifera Navis*, or the Ship of Fools; the first edition of which is supposed to have been printed, 1490; the second is dated 1494. I wish my author had produced his authority for this article; and especially, because he afterwards says, *Stultifera Navis* by Sebastian Brant, after James Locher, with one hundred prints, published 1490, is a very scarce book. These prints are usually attributed to S. Brant, or Brand; but without foundation; for, says M. Heineken, Sebastian Brand was a doctor, not an engraver; and Locher was a poet, not a painter. This mistake arose from Florent le Comte, who misunderstood Marolles, where he cites in his catalogue the book of S. Brand.

JOHN GEORGE BERGMULLER.
Flourished,

A native of Germany, and according to M. Heineken, a painter as well as an engraver; but I have never seen any of his works.

BERGQUIST.
Flourished,

A modern artist, but of no great eminence, who appears to have resided at Stockholm, where at least some of his portraits were published. I shall only notice by him, the portrait of *Andre Geringius*, Pastor de Betna; another, of *Eric Geringius*, at Stockholm.

HIERONYMUS BERLLARMATO.
Flourished, 1536.

This artist, said to have been a native of Italy, is cited by Papillon, who informs us, that he had seen a *geographical chart* of Mercator, engraved on wood, which, continues he, is entitled, *Chorographia Tuscia*, and dedicated to Signior Valerio Orsino, at Rome, A. D. 1536. Its size is three feet and an half in length, and two feet five inches in breadth, French measure, and is cut on four blocks. At the bottom is the dedication, with some Latin verses, and the name of the engraver subscribed, *Hieron. Berllarmato*. It is, adds he, well engraved; but the names of the towns and places occasion some confusion, because the letters are not exactly cut.

SOLOMON BERNARD.
Flourished, 1550 to 1580.

This ingenious artist is commonly called *Le Petit*, or Little Bernard; but

for

for what reason, I cannot discover, unless it be because his engravings are usually very small. He appears to have been a native of France; and his chief residence was at Lyons, where he worked considerably for the bookfellers, not only at that place, but at Tournay and Roville. The engravings I have seen by him are all on wood, designed with spirit, and executed in a very clear, neat style. His works prove him to have been a man of much genius, and fertility of invention. His most esteemed performance is the set of prints for the Bible, which were published at Lyons, at different times.

The mark D. B. is generally attributed to this master; but professor Christ observes, that he sees no reason why the D. should be supposed to belong to him, because his baptismal name was certainly Solomon.

SAMUEL BERNARD.
Born, 1615. Died, 1687.

A native of France, born at Paris, 1615. He was a painter in miniature; and sometimes engraved for his amusement. We have but few prints by him; and those have no great merit to recommend them. His drawing is incorrect, especially in the extremities of his figures. His draperies are stiff and heavy; and a constant want of harmony hurts the general effect of his performances. They are executed neatly enough, with respect to the mechanical part of the engraving, being etched and retouched with the graver, and softened with dots upon the lights.

Bernard died 1687, aged 72.

Among his best prints, the following are usually mentioned.

Attila frighted by a vision, on which he abandons the siege of Rome: a middling sized plate, length-ways, from Raphael.

Astyanax discovered by Ulysses in the tomb of Hector, a large plate, lengthways, from Sebastian Bourdon.

The portrait of *Louis du Garnier,* a small upright plate.

A. BERNARD.
Flourished,

A native, I presume, of France; at least, great part of his works appear to have been done there. He was an engraver in mezzotinto; but his performances have very little to recommend them in any respect.

Basan mentions the following:

A *nativity,* from Rembrandt, a middling sized, upright plate; and a *landscape,* from John Forrest. He also scraped several portraits: among the rest, that of *Tristan de la Baume, Archeveque d'Auch.*

D. BERNARD.
Flourished, 1720.

A name subscribed to several Bible plates, engraved from the designs of Picart, in folio, which were published at Amsterdam, 1720. All these plates are so very indifferent, in every respect, that they are by no means worth the trouble of describing.

JOHN MARTIN BERNIGEROTH.
Flourished, 1746.

A modern artist, who appears to have resided chiefly at Leipsic, in Saxony; and perhaps he was a native of that place. His principal employment appears to have been the engraving of portraits, which he performed in a clear, neat style, bearing some small resemblance to that of Houbracken; but he never nearly equalled that excellent artist.

Some of the *portraits* in a quarto publication, entitled, *Portraits Historiques des Hommes illustres de Dennemark*, dated 1642, are by him: also the portrait of *Tycho Brahe*, dated 1743.

JOHN BENOIT BERNIGEROTH, brother to the above-mentioned artist, was an engraver; and both of them sons of MARTIN BERNIGEROTH, who is cited by M. Heineken as an engraver also.

GIOVANNI LORENZO BERNINI.
Born, 1598. Died, 1680.

The son and scholar of Pietro Bernini, the famous sculptor. He is cited by M. Heineken as an engraver; but I do not recollect to have seen any of his works.

JOHN BERNYNCKEL.
Flourished,

An artist little known; but whose works possess some merit. From his manner of engraving, I should suppose he was a disciple of the Sadelers; for he has imitated their style, and not without success; though he never equalled them in that great requisite of the art, correctness of outline. Among other prints, engraved by him, is a small upright oval plate, representing the *adoration of the shepherds*, from Hans or John Van Achen; to which he signs his name, Joan. Bernynckel.

LUCAS BERTELLI.
Flourished,

An ancient engraver of no great eminence, who appears from the style of his works to have flourished towards the end of the sixteenth century, and was most probably an Italian. He worked entirely with the graver, in a manner much resembling that of Cornelius Cort; but from whom he learned the art of engraving is by no means certain. Nor are his works of sufficient consequence to leave us much to regret upon that head. I have seen by him some small upright plates, representing *several subjects of hunting*, to which he signs *Lucæ Bertelli f.*

A set of plates, in which is shown *the follies of love.*

He also engraved from the pictures of *Michael Angelo Buonerota, Titiano, Corregio,* &c.

Of the same family perhaps with this engraver were HORATIO and FERRANDO BERTELLI, both printsellers, if not engravers; and they also appear

to

to have been cotemporary with him. The former however certainly flourished about 1588; and to the other is attributed the entry of the prince of Savoy into Turin.

CHRISTOFANO BERTELLI.
Flourished,

This artist appears to me to have been of the same family with Lucas Bertelli, mentioned in the preceding article; and, as far as I can judge from the style of the prints engraved by him, lived at or near the same time. He worked entirely with the graver, but in a stiff, mannered style, without much merit; and his drawing is very incorrect. I shall only mention,

A large upright plate, arched at top, representing the *Virgin* and *Child*, with St. Sebastian, St. Helena, and St. Augustine. Joseph is depicted sleeping. It is signed, " per me Chriſtofano Bertelli."

A large upright plate, where the *Virgin* and *Child* are represented appearing to St. Francis and St. Sebastian, from Correggio.

Another plate, of the same size, in which is represented the *Virgin* and *Child*, with St. George, &c. from the same painter, marked as above.

DONATO BERTELLI is also cited by Le Comte, as the engraver of a set of portraits of the *Popes* and *Cardinals*; but these prints I never saw.

J. BERTERHAM.
Flourished, 1696.

An obscure engraver, who adopted the style of Francois de Poilly; but he has by no means succeeded in his imitation. His drawing is exceedingly defective; and the mechanical part of the engraving is executed in a stiff, laboured manner, without effect or harmony. He appears to have resided at Bruſſels; but whether he was a native of that place or not, I cannot take upon me to say. I shall only notice a small upright plate, representing *St. Roch* and other figures, without any painter's name, and signed, " J. Berterham sculp. Brux. 1696."

CHARLES BERTRAM.
Flourished, 1758.

He published in the year 1758 a work, entitled, *Britannicarum Gentium Hiſtoriæ Antiquæ Scriptores tres*, to which he prefixed a *frontiſpiece* etched by himself, from a compoſition of his own. It has no merit, either with respect to the design or the engraving, to recommend it. He has subscribed it, " C. B. inv. et sc. 1758." He also etched a large *map* for the same book.

P. BERTRAND.
Flourished,

A modern engraver of portraits, but of no great eminence. Among others, we have by him the portrait of *Pope Clement the Tenth*, &c.

£. M. BESNART.
Flourished,

An engraver on wood, cited by Papillon, who mentions with great disapprobation some small prints by him, for a mass-book.

AMBROGIO BESOZZI, or BEZUTIUS.
Born, 1648. Died, 1706.

A painter of great eminence, born at Milan 1648. He worked some time under Gioseffo Danedi, called Montalti, and afterwards went to Rome, where he studied from the antiques and the pictures of the greatest masters; and, at last perfected himself in the school of Ciro Ferri. His great excellency consisted in painting architecture, friezes, imitations of bass-relieves, and other decorations. He died at Milan, A. D. 1706, aged 58 years. He etched some few plates, and among them the following:

The *apotheosis* of a princess, the bust of which was engraved by Bonacina, a middling sized upright plate, from Cesare Fiori.

JOHN BETTES.
Born,   Died, 1570.

An artist mentioned by the Hon. Mr. Walpole, as a painter, as well as an engraver. He was brother to Thomas Bettes the painter. Fox in his Ecclesiastical History tells us, that John Bettes performed a *pedigree* and some *vineats* [vignettes] for Hall's Chronicle, and speaks of him, in 1576, as then dead.

PIETRO BETTINI, or BETINI.
Flourished, 1681.

An Italian artist, and, if I mistake not, a painter; but of no great eminence. By him we have some few etchings, which are very slight and incorrect. I shall only mention the following: *Christ appearing to Peter after his resurrection*, from Dominicus Campellus, a small upright plate, arched acutely at the top, marked, "Pietrus Betinus del. et sculp. 1681." The *martyrdom of St. Sebastian*, from the picture of Dominichino, which is in St. Peter's church at the Vatican, a large upright plate, arched at the top.

CAJETANUS BETTOLI.
Flourished,

A name of a modern artist, which I found subscribed to a slight spirited etching of the *death of St. Joseph*, after Franceschini. From the style and freedom of this etching, I should suppose Bettoli was a painter.

F. VAN BEUSEKOM.
Flourished,

The name of an obscure engraver, affixed to the portrait of *Ant. le Brun*, from a picture painted by. A. V. Hulle.

JAMES BEUTLER.
Flourished, 1593.

An engraver, who, according to professor Christ, was a native of Ravensburg. He is ranked in the class of artists, distinguished by the name of little masters, because the plates which he engraved were chiefly very small. His mark is I. B. the initials of his name. Great care must be taken not to confound him with James Binck, John Burgmair, and several other German artists, who flourished nearly at the same time, and used the same mark. The engravings by this master were published about the year 1593.

J. BEXTERHAM.
Flourished,

An engraver of no great eminence, who appears by his works to have flourished about the latter end of the last century, or the beginning of the present. He seems to have been chiefly confined to portraits; and, I believe, worked for the booksellers only. His plates are executed with the graver, without any assistance from the point; however they are not worth specifying particularly. If he was not a native of Brussels, it appears from his works, that he resided there; for he usually signs his name, *J. Bexterham fec. Brux.*

M. BEYLBROUCK.
Flourished, 1713.

I have not been able to procure any account of this artist; but, I believe, he resided in England. I have seen a middling sized upright print by him, representing the *death of Dido*, from Sebastian Bourdon, which is dedicated to the duke of Devonshire by James Grame, the publisher. It is dated 1713. The engraving is executed in a neat, stiff style, without effect, and the figures are very indifferently drawn. From the strong resemblance it bears to the manner of engraving, adopted by Scotin, it seems not improbable, but that the latter might have received instruction from the former.

CLAUDE BEZARD.
Flourished,

An engraver on wood, cited by Papillon, who mentions a large print as executed by him, but has not specified the subject.

P. BIAND.
Flourished,

From the style, in which the etchings signed by this name are executed, they

they appear to be the works of a painter. They are slight and incorrect; but, at the same time, very spirited, and prettily composed. I shall only notice *several Bacchanalian figures*, represented upon a vase, a small plate, length-ways. I have inserted this name here, because it is so perfectly written upon the etching above mentioned, which I found, with two or three others by the same master, without any name, among a large miscellaneous collection of old prints at the British Museum; but I really believe the engraver is the same with Peter Biart; who also wrote his name Biard (of whom the reader will find an account under BIART) the N. being written by mistake for the R. However, I own there is some small difference between the style of the etchings marked as above, and those marked Biard: the latter seem to approach rather nearer to the manner of Tempesta; but this I leave to the judgment of my readers.

SEBASTIAN BIANCHI.
Flourished,

An obscure engraver, whose works have nothing to recommend them, more than their antiquity; they seem to have been performed in the sixteenth century. I shall only mention a small upright plate, representing the *emblems of our Saviour's sufferings*, with angels and seraphs, &c. It is executed entirely with the graver, in a coarse, bad style. The drawing and effect are equally reprehensible. It is signed, *Sebastiano Bianchi Fec.*

PAOLO BIANCHI.
Flourished, 1670.

An engraver of portraits, whose chief employment seems to have been for the booksellers. He worked principally with the graver, in a stiff, tasteless style, sufficiently neat, but without much effect. I shall only notice the following: " *Flavio Chigi Nep. Alex.* 7 *Card.* 1633; in Priorato Hist. Leopold. vol. 2. *Luigi de Benevides Carillio,* 1678;" the same, vol 3, &c. He sometimes puts his initials only to his plates, as P. B. F. and at other times, the name at full length: the letter F. stands for *fecit*.

PETER BIART, or BIARD.
Flourished, 1627.

A sculptor of Paris, who is mentioned by Le Comte as the engraver of twelve plates; but the subjects of these plates are not specified by him. Besides some small etchings, I have seen a middling sized plate, length-ways, representing an emblematical subject; into which the artist has introduced many figures. It is executed in a bold, spirited style, exceedingly like that adopted by Ant. Tempesta; and it is subscribed, " Petrus Biard fecit, 1627." Peter Biart left a son who was also a sculptor, and flourished in the reign of Louis XIII. See PETER BIAND mentioned in a former article, whose name I suspect should have been written Biard.

GEORGE

GEORGE BICKHAM.
Flourished, 1709 to 1767.

A native of England, whose chief employment was engraving of writing, and he is spoken of in this line with great commendation. However, we have several portraits, and some few other subjects by him; but these do no credit to his graver. He retired to Richmond towards the latter part of his life; and in the year 1767, sold part of his plates and stock in trade by auction. I shall only mention the following portraits:

George Shelly, a writing master, drawn by the engraver from the life, and dated 1709. *Sir Isaac Newton*, &c.

GEORGE BICKHAM junior, the son of the above, was also an engraver; but he never excelled his father. To him, among a variety of other things, are attributed his own *portrait* and that of his *father*; both large prints, and very indifferently executed in every respect.

B I E. See BYE.

DE BIEVRE.
Flourished, 1760.

A modern engraver of portraits, by whom, among others, is that of Carolina Matilda, queen of Denmark.

FRANCOIS BIGNON.
Flourished, 1690.

A native of France. He was a painter; but, I believe, of no great eminence. He appears to be better known, at least in England, as an engraver. His chief employment was in the portrait line. The greater part of his works he executed with the graver only; but sometimes he called in the assistance of the point. Several of his portraits are ornamented with borders, containing little historical figures, &c. His style of engraving is sufficiently neat, but stiff, cold and unharmonized; yet by no means destitute of merit. We have by him,

The portraits of the *plenipotentiaries*, presiding at the peace of Munster, on thirty-five quarto plates.

The portraits of the *illustrious personages of France*, from the pictures of S. Vouet, painted in the gallery of the *Palace Royal*. These were engraved conjointly with Zachery Heince, and are dated 1690: large upright plates.

NICOLA BILLY.
Flourished, 1762.

A modern engraver of portraits, and a native, I believe, of Italy. His works are, however, by no means excellent. He appears to me to have chiefly executed his plates with the graver, in a stiff style, without much taste.

JAMES

JAMES BINCK.

Flourished, 1528.

This artist was a native of Cologne in Germany; but the time of his birth is not known. He is ranked in the class of *little masters*, so called, because their performances were generally very small. The strange confusion of marks, among the artists of this period, makes it not only very difficult, but often impossible to attribute to each his due; and perhaps in no names more than those, which have the letter B. for their initial.

I shall therefore give my opinion diffidently upon this head, making every distinction I can, and leave the reader to judge for himself.

It has been said, that Binck resided at Rome, and assisted Marc Antonio Raimondi. It is certain, that he was in Italy, and engraved several plates, from the designs of Raphael; therefore, it is also highly probable, that he perfected himself in engraving, in the school of that great master. But if all those prints belong to him, which have generally been attributed to him, I shall not hesitate to say, that he received his first instructions from Albert Durer, or his pupils. If from any one of the latter, I should suppose it to be Aldegrever, whose style he seems the nearest to have imitated. His manner of engraving is not always the same; though his productions are generally very neat, and possess much merit. The nearer they approach to the imitation of the Italian artist, the better we find them, not only in freedom of execution, but also in the correctness of the drawing. His usual mark is I. B. but another mark, namely, a cypher, composed of an H. a C. and a B. joined together, (which cypher is copied on the plate at the end of the volume) is attributed to him also; and I think with great justice, because that mark appears on a print, which he certainly engraved from a composition of his own, and the style of the engraving as well as the dates agree exactly. He must not, however, be confounded with another artist, who engraved on wood nearly at the same time, and also used the last mark; nor with another more ancient engraver on copper and on wood, who marked his plates with an I. and a B. to which he added a bird. I shall only notice a few of this artist's engravings, distinguishing them by the marks. First, those with the I. B.

An allegorical subject, a small upright print, in which is represented *four women, forging a flaming heart upon an anvil*, from the emblems, says Basan, of Bilibard Pyrckeimel. The letters of his name are intermixed with the date in this manner, " 15 I. B. 29." This is much in the style of Aldegrever.

A very small upright plate, on which is represented *two women and a man marketing together*, where the I. B. is on a tablet without any date.

Several small upright prints, representing the *cardinal virtues*, &c. without date, greatly in the style of John Sebald Beham.

A frieze, where *children are represented filling a tub with grapes*, a small plate, length-ways, with the mark, and date above it, 1520.

Secondly, those marked with the H. C. and B. joined together, which are also attributed to him.

A small upright portrait, inscribed, *Christiernus II. Danorum Rex*, which is also graved in imitation of a wooden cut. It is well executed; and dated 1525.

A small

A small upright plate, representing a *man havited in the German fashion, with a scull hanging at his breast*. This has not only been considered as a portrait by Binck, but it has even been said to be his own portrait; and given as such by Sandrart; yet certainly without the least foundation. It is an exact copy of an engraving of the same size, or nearly so, by Israel Van Meck, which was published, in all probability, long before the birth of Binck.

The *murder of the innocents*, a small upright plate, with the mark, but no date, and in a style of engraving approaching near to the Italian manner.

A *soldier defending himself from Death, who has overthrown him*, a very small upright plate.

St. Anthony. Only part of the figure is represented, a small upright plate. Here the mark is varied; and it is I. C. B. without the cross bar of the H.

To these I beg leave to add the following print: A figure of *Saturn*, standing in an arch, devouring one of his children, a small upright plate. This differs greatly, in the style of engraving, from any of the foregoing; and is much more bold, spirited and correct. It is executed entirely with the graver, as all his works were, in a free style, founded apparently on that of Marc de Ravenna. On a tablet is this inscription, " JACOBUS BINCK Coloniensis fecit, 1530."

BINET.
Flourished,

A modern engraver, in France, of no great eminence, by whom we have some *views*, &c. from Vernet and other masters.

WALTER BINNEMAN.
Flourished.

A very obscure and indifferent engraver of portraits. He was most probably an Englishman. I am led to think so, because I have never seen his name affixed to any but English heads. He flourished apparently in the last century; but his works, which are very few, are scarcely worth noticing. I shall only mention the following:

The portrait of *Chamberlaine*, an arithmetician, with some vile verses in English underneath it, an octavo plate. Another *portrait*, without the name of the person represented, a small upright plate, with four verses underneath it, " *View here his shadow*," &c. subscribed, *Walter Binneman sculp*.

PETER BIORD.
Flourished,

A name I found affixed to a slight etching, in the style of a painter, free, but incorrect, and the extremities poorly drawn. The subject, I believe, is *Cupid and Psyche*; a woman is represented seated in a chariot, holding a Cupid upon her lap; two other Cupids are also represented with them. It is a small upright plate, marked *Pet. Biord fec.* and the letters are reversed upon the impression.

PAUL

PAUL BIRCK.
Flourished,

I have seen four small upright plates, exclusive of a title, by this artist, on which are represented the *four elements* in circles, surrounded with such ornaments, as appear to be patterns for goldsmiths and jewellers to work from; and these ornaments are relieved by a dark ground, in imitation of enamel. The figures, if not quite correctly drawn, are however executed in a very meritorious style. The manner of the engraving, which greatly resembles that of De Brie, is performed entirely with the graver, and is rather stiff, and without effect. But, considering them as ornamental patterns, the effect was not of much consequence. On the title, which makes a fifth plate, is the following inscription, inclosed by an ornamental border: *Quatuor Mundi Elementa, Elegantibas figuris feu Imaginibus Artificiosa expressa.* PAULUS BIRCK. F. On some of the plates he substitutes the letters P. B. F. instead of his name, the F. standing for *fecit*.

BIRCKART.
Flourished,

If this artist was not a native of Prague in Bohemia, it appears by the signatures upon his plates, at least, that he resided there. By him, among many other things, we have some very large plates of *theatrical architecture*, with figures, executed entirely with the graver, in a very stiff, tasteless style. The name is affixed, *Birckart sculp. Prag.* but no date. However, from the manner of the engraving, I should suppose, that he flourished towards the latter part of the last century. Basan writes his name Birckaert, and attributes to him a print representing the *martyrdom of forty Portuguese Jesuits*, after Bourguinon, &c.

PAUL BIRCKENHULT.
Flourished,

We have by this engraver, among other things, a set of small upright plates, representing *ornamental trophies, with figures*, &c. chiefly executed with the graver, in a neat, stiff style. The title to these plates is, *Omnis generis Instrumenta Bellica* ; to which he puts his name, " Paulus Birckenhult sculp. et excud." But, on the plates themselves, he signs the initials only, P. B. F. the F. standing, according to the usual custom, for *fecit*. Judging from the manner of the engraving, I suppose he flourished about the middle of the last century, and was perhaps a printseller, as well as an engraver; at least, we see he published these plates himself.

BARTOLOMEO BISCAINO.
Born, 1632. Died, 1657.

This young artist, whose early death is much to be lamented, was the son of Giovanni Andrea Biscaino, a landscape painter of some eminence. He was born at Genoa, and was instructed in the first principles of painting and
design

design by his father; but afterwards perfected himself under Valerio Caftelli. The early indications, which he gave of a fuperior genius, were fuch, that the greateft expectations were formed of his future excellence. But he died, A. D. 1657, aged only 25 years. He has left behind him fome few etchings, which are executed in a flight bold ftyle, fomething refembling that of Caftiglione; but ftill more finifhed and more determined. His figures are elegant, and finely compofed, and drawn in a very mafterly manner. He has given both beauty and character to the heads; and the other extremities are generally correct, and marked with great fpirit. I fhall notice the following:

Mofes in the ark of bulrufhes, a fmall plate, length-ways.
A nativity with angels, a fmall upright plate.
The *wife men's offering*, the fame fize.
The *circumcifion of Chrift*, the fame.
A *Bacchanalian*, the fame.
Several beautiful *madonas*, and other *devout fubjects*, &c.

JOHN DE BISCHOP, or BISKOP.
Born, 1646. Died, 1686.

An excellent artift born at the Hague, A. D. 1646. He is fpoken of with great commendation as a painter; and his drawings from the great mafters are held in the higheft eftimation by the curious. In thefe he has fucceeded fo happily, as to preferve with the greateft exactnefs the ftyle of the painter, whofe picture he copied. But as an engraver he is moft generally known; and his works are numerous. They are chiefly etchings, harmonized with the graver; and though flight, yet free, fpirited and pleafing. He gives a richnefs to the colour, and a roundnefs to the figures, far beyond what is ufually done with the point, fo little affifted by the graver. His figures, in general, are well drawn; but in a mannered, rather than a correct ftyle. The extremities, indeed, are not always well marked, or his heads equally expreffive or beautiful. It is faid of him, that he owed his excellency to his own genius alone, having never ftudied under any mafter, by whofe inftruction he might have been benefited. He worked chiefly at Amfterdam, where he died, A. D. 1686, aged 40 years. I fhall notice the following prints by this artift:

Chrift and the Samaritan woman, a large upright plate, from Annibale Carracci.
Jofeph diftributing corn to the Egyptians, from Bartholomew Breenberge, a large plate, length-ways, with many figures.
The *Martyrdom of St. Laurence*, its companion, the fame, from the fame.
A large book of *defigns*, from the greateft mafters.
A book of *ftatues*, &c.

It is to be obferved, that the mark ufed by this mafter is a cypher, compofed of a *J.* and an *E.* joined together in the manner reprefented on the plate at the end of the volume. He affected to Latinife his name, fubftituting *Epifcopius* for *Bifchop*, or, as we call it in Englifh, *Bifhop*; and for this reafon has joined the *E.* with the *J.* inftead of the *B.*

BONAVENTURA BISI.
Died, 1662.

We muſt not wonder, if we find an artiſt even in the gloomy retirement of a monaſtery; nay, confidering the leiſure time, which people devoted to a monaſtic life muſt often have, it is rather ſurpriſing that we do not meet with artiſts among them more frequently. For the arts, confidered abſtractedly as an amuſement only, have often been found to poſſeſs charms, ſufficient to repay the labour, which is neceſſary for the attainment of them. But an exalted genius ſeems as if it could not brook the confinement of a ſolitary cell; for at the time, when nearly all the learning of Europe was ſhut up in the boundaries of the monaſtic walls, one would have expected much greater and more frequent exertions of literary genius, from thence, than has appeared. It is the ſame with the artiſt, as with the poet or the orator, if he does not feel the ſubject, which he treats upon, within his own breaſt, he cannot poſſibly reach the feelings of another. Biſi was a man of great abilities, and, according to ſome authors, a monk of the order of St. Francis. He was the diſciple of Lucio Maffari; and his chief excellence lay in copying, in miniature, the pictures of Corregio, Guido, Titian, and other maſters, which he finiſhed with aſtoniſhing beauty and elegance. He died, 1662; but his age is not known. For his amuſement he etched ſome few plates, from Parmegiano, Guido, &c. I ſhall only notice the following, which was probably from his own deſign. A *holy family*, with Elizabeth and St. John, a ſmall upright plate, dated 1631, and marked F. B. B: F. This is the uſual method, in which he marked all his plates. Some read theſe letters, " Franceſco Bonaventura Biſi fecit;" whilſt others, inſtead of the word Franceſco, ſubſtitute that of *Frater*, which is Latin for *Brother*, the common appellation, by which the monks and other eccleſiaſtics addreſs one another; and this laſt is the moſt generally received interpretation.

BIURMAN.
Flouriſhed,

A modern engraver of *portraits*, and chiefly, I believe, for the bookſellers.

J. BLACKMORE.
Flouriſhed, 1771.

A modern Engliſh engraver in mezzotinto, by whom we have ſeveral portraits, after Sir Joſhua Reynolds and other maſters; among the reſt is that of *Samuel Foote* the player, dated 1771. This plate is exceedingly well ſcraped, and a very fine likeneſs of that facetious perſonage

JOHN BLAGRAVE.
Born, Died, 1611.

An excellent mathematician. He was the ſecond ſon of John Blagrave, of Bulmarſh-Court, in the County of Berkſhire. The former part of his education

education he received at Reading, from whence he removed to St. John's College, Oxford. When he quitted the Univerfity, where he did not long refide, he retired to Southcote-Lodge, and devoted his time to ftudy, his genius chiefly leading him to the fcience of mathematics. He alfo reduced his ftudies to practice, and gave to the public the fruit of his labours. He was a man of a benevolent difpofition; and his judicious charities are ftill remembered at Reading with gratitude. One efpecially is too fingular to be omitted in this place. Annually on Good Friday, he appointed the church-wardens of the feveral parifhes in that town, to choofe three maidens of fair character, each of which had lived three years in her place, and to bring them to the town hall, where, before the mayor and aldermen, they caft dice; and fhe, who is fo fortunate as to throw the higheft number, is prefented with a purfe containing ten pounds, and attended by the other two maidens who loft the caft. The year following, the maidens, who loft the caft the year before, come again, with a third added to them, and throw again. But if any one is fo unfortunate, as to loofe three throws, fhe cannot caft a fourth time, but is excluded from the benefit of the charity. Mr. Afhmole, who gives a full account of this cuftom, adds: " It is lucky money; for I never " heard, but that the maid that had the ten pounds fuddenly got a good huf-" band." Mr. Blagrave died at his houfe near Reading, Auguft 9, 1611, and was interred, near his mother, in the church of St. Laurence in that town. His principal works are the following: A Treatife on *the Making and Ufing the Familar Staff*. The *Aftrolabium Uranicum generale*. The Art of *Dialing*, and the *Mathematical Jewel*. This laft is his greateft and moft efteemed performance. It was printed in 1585, at London, with this note in the frontifpiece: " By John Blagrave of Reading, gentleman, and well-willer to the " mathematics, who hath cut all the prints or pictures of the whole with his " own hands." They are wooden cuts and neatly executed. Where he has not put his name at length, it is thus abreviated, " I. BLAG. SCULP."

C. J. BLAKE.
Flourifhed, 1775.

A young lady of diftinction, who for her amufement etched the portrait of her uncle, *Sir Francis Blake Delaval*, in the year 1775.

BLAKEWELL.
Flourifhed,

He was, I believe, a printfeller; at leaft, his name is affixed to feveral mezzotintos, as the publifher. He alfo is faid to have engraved in mezzotinto himfelf; and among others, the portrait of *Henrietta Maria*, the queen of Charles the Firft, is attributed to him.

JAMES BLANCHART, or BLANCHARD.
Born, 1600. Died, 1638.

A painter of fome eminence, born at Paris, A. D. 1600. After being inftructed instructed in the first principles of painting in his own country, he went to Italy, where he acquired such a habit of colouring, that, at his return, he was honoured with the appellation of the French Titian. According to Florent le Comte, he etched several plates from his own compositions.

BLANCI.
Flourished,

A name subscribed to several portraits; among the rest, to that of *Flavius Chigi*, in Gualdo's Hist. Leopold. part 2nd. He worked, I believe, chiefly for the bookfellers.

CHRISTOPHER BLANCUS.
Flourished, 1600.

I know not what country gave birth to this engraver, if he be not a German. It appears from his works, that he resided some time at Rome. He worked with the graver only, and imitated, though but indifferently, the style of Cherubino Alberti; yet, in some plates of his from Spranger, he seems to have followed that of John Muller; with no better success. I shall only notice by him a *holy family*, accompanied by angels, half figures, from Spranger, dated 1595. The portrait of *Michael Angelo Buonarota*, marked, " Christophorus Blancus faciebat, 1612."

JOHN PAUL BLANCUS.
Flourished, 1628.

This artist was probably a relation of Christopher Blancus, mentioned in the former article; but he did not follow his manner of engraving. He seems chiefly, if not entirely, to have applied himself to etching, which he executed very slightly, in a heavy indifferent style. The mechanical part is neither clear nor neat; and the drawing of his figures is by no means to be commended. I have seen by him, among other pieces, an *emblematical print*, from C. Stores, a middling sized plate, length-ways, marked Jo. Paul Blancus incid. and *Christ praying in the garden*, a middling sized upright plate, dated 1628, without any painter's name.

BLEAVIT.
Flourished,

An obscure artist, whose employment seems to have chiefly been engraving of portraits. Among others by him, is that of *Rene des Cartes*, the philosopher.

PETER VAN BLEEK, or BLEECK.
Born, Died, 1764.

Van Bleek was a painter, but, I suppose, of no great eminence; for I find no account of him. He was probably of Dutch extraction; but he resided

resided at London. His father's name was apparently the same as his own; for he generally subjoins the word junior to his signature, which can be of no use, but for the sake of distinction. His engravings are all in mezzotinto; and, though he never rose to any superior excellency in the art, there are some of them, which are clearly scraped, and possess great merit. There was R. Van Bleek, a painter; for we find his *portrait* from a picture of his own, engraved by Peter Van Bleeck, and dated 1735. I shall notice by this artist, the portraits of *Griffin* and *Johnson*, in the characters of Tribulation and Ananias, a middling sized upright plate. The portrait of *Mrs. Cibber*, in the character of Cordelia; and the portrait of *Mrs. Clive*, in the character of Phillida, a middling sized upright plate. It is remarkable, that he signs this plate, " P. Van Bleeck, junior, pinx. et fecit;" and adds the date 1735, because we have the same composition, engraved in mezzotinto by Faber, without any variation in the figures or back ground, and of the same size, reversed, and dated 1734. The portrait of *Rembrandt Gerretsz*, a small upright plate, from a painting by that master.

J. G. BLECKER, or BLEKER.
Flourished, 1638.

He was a painter; but in what degree of estimation his pictures were held, I know not. We have some etchings by him, as well from his own compositions, as from those of other masters: among the rest, a *crucifixion*, with the three Maries and St. John, at the foot of the cross, and two angels in the air, weeping; a middling sized upright plate, after Cornelius Poelembourg. The Lystrians attempting to sacrifice to Paul and Barnabas, a middling sized plate, length-ways, from the same, dated 1638.

CORNELIUS BLECKER, or BLEKER.
Flourished, 1638.

This engraver (who, I should suppose from the style of his etchings, was also a painter) was apparently of the same family, and perhaps a near relation of J. G. Blecker, mentioned in the preceding article; and we find they both flourished at the same time; but the works of this artist are by no means equal to those of the former. They are slight, incorrect etchings, chiefly *landscapes*, into which he has introduced historical subjects: as, the meeting of Abraham's servant with Rebecca, &c. He has worked upon the etching to harmonize it (especially upon the heads of his figures) with the point of the graver, scratching upon the copper, in a style something like that which Worlidge afterwards adopted; but he has by no means succeeded. His landscapes are generally small plates, length-ways. One of the best prints I have seen of this master is a view of an *inn yard*, with a waggon, and a horse standing by it eating; a small plate, length-ways.

SAMUEL BLESSENDORF.
Flourished,

A Swedish artist of some eminence. He flourished, according to Basan,
in

in the laſt century. His chief employment ſeems to have been in the portrait line. His plates are generally ſmall, and very neatly finiſhed. By him we have the portrait of *Charles XII.* of Sweden, a ſmall upright plate. Many other portraits of the illuſtrious perſonages of Sweden, Denmark, &c.

CONSTANTINE BLESSENDORF, brother to the above artiſt, alſo an engraver of portraits.

F. VAN BLEYSWICK.
Flouriſhed, 1746.

This artiſt, like thoſe immediately preceding, was an engraver of portraits. His plates, in general, are ſmall, and neatly finiſhed, but without much taſte. His principal work, I believe, was part of the plates for the collection entitled, *Portraits Hiſtoriques des Hommes illuſtrees de Dannemark*, dated 1746, 4to.

BLOEM. See BLOOM.

A. BLOEM.
Flouriſhed, 1674.

An engraver of no great eminence, a native, I believe, of Germany. Among other things, he engraved the portraits, views, plans, battles, &c. for a book entitled, *Hiſtoria di Leopoldo Ceſare*, in folio, publiſhed at Vienna, A. D. 1674. They are all etched, and retouched with the graver, in a ſlight, heavy ſtyle.

ABRAHAM BLOEMART.
Born, 1567. Died, 1647.

Sandrart informs us, that this excellent artiſt was born at Goricum, A. D. 1567; whilſt Houbraken and others have placed his birth in the year 1564. The firſt author, however, is moſt generally followed. His excellency as a painter is too well known to need a repetition here, even if it were not foreign to the plan of this work to mention him under that character. Some ſlight, maſterly etchings are attributed to him, which are executed in a manner imitating drawings with a pen, from his own compoſitions. He alſo publiſhed ſome ſpirited claro-ſcuros, the outlines of which, contrary to the uſual cuſtom, were not cut on blocks of wood, but etched upon copper. Of this kind are two large prints by him, repreſenting *Moſes* and *Aaron*, both ſitting figures. His name is not always ſubſcribed at full length, either at the bottom of the prints executed by his own hand, or of thoſe where he only made the deſign, and the engraving was performed by other artiſts. It is often thus, *Ab. Bl. in.* or thus, *A. Bl.* or thus, *A. Bloem.* And to a ſmall upright etching of a ſingle figure, repreſenting *Juno*, which belongs to a ſet, it is put thus, *A. Bloem. fe.* the A. being joined together with the B. in a cypher.

Abraham Bloemart reſided chiefly at Utrecht, where he probably died A. D. 1647, aged 80 years. He left four ſons, who were all of them artiſts;

but

but the moſt famous was Cornelius the youngeſt, of whom we ſhall ſpeak in a ſucceeding article.

FREDERIC BLOEMART.
Flouriſhed, 1620.

Was the ſon of Abraham Bloemart, mentioned above. He worked chiefly, if not entirely, from the deſigns of his father, and imitated his ſtyle in his etchings and claro-ſcuros. He appears to have made, conjointly with his father, a large drawing book, conſiſting of figures, animals, landſcapes, &c. He alſo engraved ſome plates entirely with the graver, in a bold, free ſtyle. His neater performances in this laſt ſtyle, though they be not equal to thoſe of Cornelius Bloemart his younger brother, do him no ſmall honour, as an artiſt. To his engravings he frequently ſubſcribed the initials of his name, with thoſe of his father's, in the following manner: *A. Bloem inv. F. B. filius fecit*; and frequently the initials F. B. in Roman letters alone. I ſhall mention, beſides the claro-ſcuros above ſpoken of, the following, all from his father's deſigns:

Several ſets of *landſcapes*, chiefly ſmall plates, length-ways.

The *four elements*, repreſented by ſingle figures, ſmall upright plates.

St. John preaching to the people, a ſmall upright plate.

St. Marcellinus preaching, a large upright plate.

St. Francis praying, with a crucifix before him, and a *landſcape back-ground*, a middling ſized, upright plate.

A ſet of ſmall *landſcapes*, length-ways, *cottage ſcenes, out-houſes*, &c. dated 1620.

HENRY and ADRIAN BLOEMART were both ſons of Abraham Bloemart, and painters. They are alſo mentioned as engravers; but as their works are not ſpecified, I can make no reference to them; for I freely confeſs, I never ſaw any prints to which either of theſe names was affixed.

CORNELIUS BLOEMART.
Born, 1603. Died,

This great artiſt, according to De Piles, was the youngeſt ſon of Abraham Bloemart. The moſt generally received opinion is, that he was born, A. D. 1603; though ſome ſay, 1606. However, all agree, that Utrecht, where his father chiefly reſided, was the place of his birth. The firſt principles of drawing and painting he learned from his father, but his natural inclination for the art of engraving was ſo powerful, that he applied himſelf wholly to the purſuit of it. He firſt ſtudied under Criſpin de Paſs, an engraver much more famous for the neatneſs, than the good taſte of his works. Not ſatisfied with what he learned from this artiſt, he went to Rome, in order to perfect himſelf from the works of the greateſt maſters. And in that city (where the far greater part of his engravings were made) he died at a very advanced age.

The manner of engraving, adopted by this excellent artiſt, appears to me to be not only quite original, but the ſource, from which we may trace that ſtyle, in which the greateſt and beſt French maſters excelled: thoſe I mean, who worked with the graver only. He covered the lights upon his diſtances, and the other parts of his plates, which required tinting, with great care. The lights, whether on the diſtant hills, trees, buildings, or figures, in the engravings prior to his time, had been left quite clear, and by ſo many white ſpots ſcattered in various parts of the ſame deſign, the harmony was deſtroyed, the ſubject confuſed, and the principal figures prevented from relieving with any ſtriking effect. By this judicious improvement, Bloemart gave to his prints a more clear and finiſhed appearance, than all the laboured neatneſs even of Jerom Wierix had been able to produce.

He drew correctly; but from his ſtyle of engraving, which was executed entirely with the graver, the extremities of his figures are heavy; and his heads are not always equally beautiful or expreſſive. With reſpect to the mechanical part of the works, few indeed have excelled him, either in clearneſs or freedom of execution. His great fault, however, is want of variety. The naked parts of his figures, the draperies, and the back-ground, are equally neat, and engraved preciſely in the ſame manner. Hence the effect is flat, and the fleſh, for want of ſufficient diſtinction, appears cold and ſilvery. His works are juſtly held in high eſtimation. They are very numerous, and many of them difficult to be procured. I ſhall only notice the following; the firſt impreſſions of ſome of which are very rare.

The *chaſtity of Joſeph*, a ſmall upright plate, from Blanchart.
The *adoration of the ſhepherds*, a large plate, length-ways, from Raphael.
The *ſame ſubject*, a middling ſized plate, from Pietro de Cortona.
The *holy family* of the *ſpectacles*, ſo called, becauſe Joſeph holds a pair of ſpectacles in his hand, a middling ſized upright plate, from Annibale Carracci.
Another *holy family*, from Parmegiano, a middling ſized, upright plate.
The *Virgin* and *Child*; the child is ſleeping; a middling ſized circular plate, from Guido.
St. Luke painting the Virgin and Child, a middling ſized upright plate, from Raphael.
St. Peter raiſing Tabitha from the dead, a middling ſized print, length-ways, an admirable print, from Guercino. Gerſaint and others, have miſtakingly called this print the *death of the Virgin*.
St. Marguerita, leaning on a pedeſtal, and ſetting her foot upon the dragon, a ſmall upright plate, after Annibale Caracci.
The *four fathers of the church*, from Abraham Bloemart, a large upright plate.
Chriſt appearing to St. Ignatius, the ſame ſize, from the ſame painter.
Meleager preſenting the boar's head to Atalanta, a ſmall upright plate, from Rubens.
Several *prints for a miſſal*, after Ciro Ferri and other maſters.
A ſet of ſmall prints length-ways, of *ruſtics*, &c. from Abraham Bloemart.
A ſet of *heads*, from the ſame.
A variety of other ſubjects, from different painters; many of them equally eſtimable.

JOHN FRANCIS VAN BLOEMEN.
Born, 1656. Died, 1740.

A painter of landſcapes, whoſe works are held in the higheſt eſtimation.

He is called by the Italians HORIZONTI, or ORIZONTI, from the delicate manner in which he painted his diftances. He was born at Antwerp, 1650; but as he refided chiefly in Italy, he is generally confidered as an Italian artift; and in that country he died, A. D. 1740, aged 84. By him we have five fmall etchings, which he probably made for his amufement. They are *perfpective views*, apparently near Rome. Four of them are middling fized upright plates; and there is one fmaller plate, length-ways. Bafan has confounded this artift with Peter Van Bloemen, his brother, who was a painter, and, according to M. Heineken, etched fome plates alfo. I have never, to the beft of my recollection, feen any of them.

BLOKHUYSEN.
Flourifhed,

A name affixed to fome portraits; among the reft, to that of *Profper Alpinus*.

A. DE BLOIS.
Flourifhed, 1720.

An engraver of no great eminence, who flourifhed towards the latter part of the laft century. His employment was chiefly, I believe, in the portrait line. There are, however, other fubjects engraved by him; among the reft, part of the plates for a work entitled, *Figures de la Bible*, in folio, from the defigns of Picart and others, publifhed at Amfterdam, 1720. The portrait of *Antonius a Leeuwenhoek*, prefixed to his works, publifhed in quarto, A.D. 1695, engraved by De Blois, is fufficiently neat; but very ftiff and taftelefs. There was a De Blois, who was an engraver in mezzotinto; among other prints by him is the portrait of *Nell Gwynn*.

MICHAEL LE BLOND.
Born,   Died, 1650.

A Dutch engraver, who refided at Amfterdam. He is one of thofe artifts, who are diftinguifhed by the name of *little mafters*, from the fmallnefs of their works. His chief employment appears to have been ornamental figures and foliage, &c. for goldfmiths, jewellers, and chafers. He worked entirely with the graver, in a very neat ftyle; which, as Bafan juftly obferves, greatly refembles that of Theodore de Bry. Michael le Blond died at Amfterdam, A. D. 1650. His cypher, which is compofed of an M. with a fmaller B. under it, fee copied on the plate at the end of the volume. I fhall only notice a few prints by this artift: namely,

St. Jerom, feated at a defk writing, in a fmall circle hardly as large as a fhilling, with an ornamental border, and his name at length, dated 1610.

Some *dancing figures*, in a fmall oval, furrounded by an ornamental border, marked " M. Blondus, 1612."

VOL. I.   P   Some

Some very small circles, wherein *death is represented with people of various ranks*.

Susanna and the elders, a very small upright oval plate.

JAMES CHRISTOPHER LE BLOND, or BLON.
Born,   Died, 1740.

This artist was born in Flanders; and, according to Basan, he went to Italy, where he studied under Carlo Maratti; but his genius being admirably well adapted for mechanics, and his head continually full of schemes of various sorts, he cannot be supposed to have employed as much time, as was requisite to acquire any great perfection, in the arts. He, however, discovered a method of printing mezzotinto plates in colours, so as, in some faint degree, to imitate the pictures, of which they were copies. In this manner he executed, in England, several large plates, from pictures of the greatest masters; and disposed of the prints by lottery: but those who obtained the prizes, appear not to have held them in any very great estimation. He made known the manner, in which he performed these plates, in a publication entitled, *Coloritto*, or the harmony of colouring in painting, reduced to mechanical practice, under easy precepts and infallible rules. And the book was printed in French and English. Finding this species of engraving did not sufficiently answer his purpose, he set on foot a project for copying the cartoons of Raphael in tapestry, and made drawings from the pictures for that purpose. Houses were built, and looms erected, at the Mulberry Ground at Chelsea; but the expences being too great, or the contributions not equal to the first expectations, the scheme was suddenly defeated, and Le Blond disappeared, to the no small dissatisfaction of those, who were engaged with him. From hence he went to Paris, where, Basan informs us, he was in the year 1737; and in that city he died, 1740, in an hospital. The prints, which he produced, certainly possess some merit, exclusive of their novelty; but, in general, the colours are flat and dirty; the effect is neither striking, nor judiciously managed; and the drawing is frequently very incorrect, especially in the extremities of his figures.

Among his portraits, which are the only prints of his that I shall specify, are the following: *George II. king of England, Louis XV. king of France; Cardinal Fleury, Antony Vandyck*, &c.

JAMES BLONDEAU.
Flourished, 1670.

I believe this engraver was a Frenchman, and perhaps learned the art of engraving from Cornelius Bloemart, whose style he seems chiefly to have followed. It is certain, however, that he lived at that time, and engraved some of the plates from the pictures of Pietro da Cortona, in the palace of Pitti, at Florence. The rest were executed by Bloemart, Spierre, Clouet, and others. Blondeau worked entirely with the graver, in a style, as before observed, much like that of Bloemart; but he by no means equalled that artist, either in the freedom of the mechanical part of the engraving, or the

the correctness of the outline. His prints, in general, are cold and silvery, without much effect; and the extremities of his figures are heavy, and frequently incorrect. I shall only mention by him,

The *martyrdom of St. Laurence*, from Pietro da Cortona, a middling sized upright plate.

The *crucifixion of Christ*, a middling sized upright plate, from Ciro Ferri.

JEAN FRANCOIS BLONDEL.
Flourished, 1740.

An artist of great eminence, a native of France. He published several large folio volumes of Architecture; some of the plates for which he etched himself. Also the description of the entertainments given by the city of Paris, A. D. 1740, at the marriage of Madam Louise Elizabeth of France, with Don Philip, infant and high admiral of Spain. The plans and elevations of the *fire-works, temporary buildings*, &c. are chiefly his own engravings.

ABRAHAM BLOTELING, or BLOOTELING.
Flourished, 1672.

This artist, a native of Amsterdam, designed as well as engraved. Whose scholar he was I cannot discover; from the style of his etchings, which have great merit, he appears to have frequented the school of the Visschers. He came into England about the year 1672, or 1673, at the time the French invaded Holland; but he did not reside here long. He not only etched, but also scraped, several mezzotintos, which were much esteemed. Vertue informs us, that whilst he was in England, he received thirty guineas for an etching of the duke of Norfolk. From hence he returned to Amsterdam, where, in all probability he died.

In the year 1685, he published at Amsterdam the *gems* of Leonardo Augustino, and etched the plates himself. I shall notice also,

Some small plates, length-ways, of *hunting*, &c. "Bloteling fecit," etched in a free, spirited style.

A set of *lions*, from Rubens, small plates, length-ways.

A set of *landscapes*, small plates, length-ways, from J. Van Ruysdael, dated 1670.

The portrait of the *marquis de Mirabel*, a small upright plate, from Vandyck.

The portrait of *admiral Kortenaer*, a large upright plate, from Bartholomew Van der Helst.

The portrait of *D. Hieronymus Van Beverningh*, dated 1680, without the name of the painter. It was probably drawn by Bloteling himself.

The portrait of *prince Rupert*, after Lely, dated 1673.

The portrait of *Anthony earl of Shaftesbury*, who is represented sitting, is said by the Hon. Mr. Walpole to be one of the scarcest prints of this artist.

Among his mezzotintos, I shall mention the following portraits only.

A clear, well-scraped head of the *earl of Derby*; and *Abraham Symonds*, from Lely, small upright plates.

See his cypher, compofed of an A. and a B. joined together (which he frequently ufed, when he did not put his name at length) on the plate at the end of the volume.

ROBERT BLYTH
Born,   Died, 1783.

This engraver, whofe merit was never very confpicuous, died young, A. D. 1783, in London. His moft capital performances are feveral flight etchings, from the beautiful drawings, with pen and ink, of John Mortimer, an artift, whofe works are held in the higheft eftimation. Among Blyth's beft prints may be reckoned, *the foldier's courtfhip*, a middling fized plate, length-ways, and its companion, belonging to a fet of four prints, entitled, *the life and death of a foldier*, and fome circular groups of heads. In thefe laft he was affifted by Mr. Bartolozzi. *Caius Marius, reflecting on the ruins of Carthage*; and *Nebuchadnezzar, recovering his reafon*, its companion: both middling fized upright plates. *Homer reciting his verfes to the Grecians*, a large plate, length-ways, &c.

FRANCIS VAN BOCHOLT
Flourifhed,

A very ancient engraver on copper, and probably a native of Germany. *Matthias Quad* of Kinkelback, an author of the fixteenth century, in his book intitled, *The Excellency of the German Nation*, fpeaks of this artift, and informs us, that he was a fhepherd of the country called Mons, in the Netherlands; and that he was the firft inventor of engraving on copper. " His figures," fays he, " however, though they are hard, appear to be " taken rather from nature than imagination." The opinion, that he was the inventor of engraving on copper is, with the greateft juftice, generally exploded, though indeed fuch an artift is allowed to have exifted, and with great appearance of truth. The prints which are marked with the letters F. V. B. are attributed to him. I cannot agree with the above mentioned author, that his figures have the appearance of being taken from nature: they are, in general, ftiff, laboured copies, from the works of Ifrael Van Mecheln, and Martin Schoon. If, confidering the antiquity of the prints attributed to Bocholt, the probability fhould be urged of their being the originals, rather than the copies, a careful examination of them, and the works of the above-mentioned artifts, will foon clear up the matter, I believe, beyond a doubt. The ftyle, in which Ifrael Van Mecheln engraved, differed confiderably from that adopted by Martin Schoon, in fo much, that, without the leaft diftinguifhing mark, their works may eafily be feparated from each other. Yet the ftyle of both thefe artifts is laborioufly imitated by Bocholt, as continually as he copied from either of them. It feems to me, therefore, highly improbable, that the works of Bocholt fhould be the originals, fince this difference is fo uniformly found in them, whenever they correfpond with thofe of Ifrael Van Mecheln, or Martin Schoon.

But though he generally copied from the above-mentioned artifts, yet there

are

are several engravings by him, apparently from his own designs. I shall mention, FIRST, the following from J. V. Mecheln, in which he has imitated the style of that master.
The *judgment of Solomon*, a middling sized upright plate.
The *annunciation of the Virgin*, the same.
The *Virgin* and *Child*, in an arch, a small upright plate.
SECONDLY, those from Martin Schoon.
St. Anthony, carried into the air by dæmons, a middling sized upright plate. J. V. Mecheln also engraved this subject; but this plate is copied from that of Martin Schoon; and his style of engraving is exactly imitated.
St. James reading, a small upright plate.
St. Michael and the *dragon*, the same.
THIRDLY, those that appear to be from his own designs.
A friar behaving rudely to a young girl, who is defending herself with her distaff, a small plate length-ways.
Sampson strangling the lion, a small upright plate.
Two men quarrelling in a nine-pin ground, a small upright plate.
All these have the mark F. V. B. He also engraved a variety of other subjects, as well copies from the above masters, as from his own designs. I shall only mention one more, namely, *St. George and the dragon*, with the mark, a small upright plate, under which is written, in a very old hand, *Francis Van Bocholt*.

CHARLES VAN BOCKEL.
Flourished,

A name mentioned by M. Heineken, as an engraver; but he has not specified any of his prints. C. V. B. the initials of his name, according to the same author, are frequently subscribed to his engravings. I have never seen any of his works.

G. BOCKMAN.
Flourished, 1743.

A mezzotinto scraper; but of no great merit. He was, however, a painter also; and to a half sheet print of *St. Dunstan*, in which the saint is represented holding his crosier in one hand, and the tongs with which, (according to the lying legends of superstition,) he secured the devil by the nose, in the other; he signs his name, to which he adds, *pinx. et fecit*. It is dated 1740. There are also several portraits of the late *duke of Cumberland*, and the portrait of *Thomas Chubb* the deist, &c. His mark, when he does not sign his name at length, is a cypher composed of a G. and a B. which is copied on the plate at the end of the volume.

JOHN BOCKSBERGER.
Flourished,

The name of a modern engraver, according to professor Christ, whose initials

tials were an H. with a B. joined together in a cypher. He has unfortunately, according to his ufual cuftom, omitted to fpecify the works of this artift. I have never feen any prints by him.

NICOLAS BOCQUET.
Flouriſhed, 1601.

This engraver was, I believe, a native of France. As an artift, however, he cannot be fpoken of with any great commendation. I have feen by him, *Adam* and *Eve*, a middling fized upright plate, from Raphael. It is etched, and finifhed with the graver, in a poor, thin ftyle; and the drawing is incorrect, and totally deftitute of that fimplicity, which is the great characteriftic of the painter.

St. Bruno, kneeling before a crucifix, a large upright plate, from Bon de Boullogne.

PETER BODART
Flouriſhed, 1723.

A modern engraver, who refided fome years fince at Leyden, and probably was a native of that place. His works, however, are little known in England. I have feen by him a fmall folio volume, entitled, *Les Principaux fondementes du Deffein*, which was publifhed at Leyden, 1723. This is a drawing book; and it confifts of a prodigious number of plates, fuch as heads, hands, feet, whole figures, and groups of figures, &c. from the defigns of G. Hoet. They are chiefly etched, and in a very poor, incorrect ftyle. When he does not write his name at full length, he fubftitutes the initials, P. B. or P. B. F. the F. as ufual, ftanding for fecit.

J. F. BODDECKER.
Flouriſhed,

I know not when, or where, this artift (for fo I fuppofe he called himfelf) flourifhed. I have only feen by him fome few mezzotintos, very badly executed, in every refpect. Among the reft, a fmall upright plate, reprefenting a *boy* and a *girl*, half figures, with flowers, from J. de Baen.

JOHN GEORGE BODENEHRS.
Flouriſhed,

A modern engraver of the German fchool. The greater part of his family were artifts. He was chiefly employed in the engraving of *portraits* for the bookfellers. Befides the above-mentioned artift, M. Heineken enumerates the following, without fpecifying their works: GEORGE CONRAD BODENEHRS, MAURICE BODENEHRS, GABRIEL BODENEHRS, JOHN GEORGE BODENEHRS the younger, JOHN GOTTFRIED BODENEHRS, and GABRIEL BODENEHRS the younger; all of them engravers.

MARK BODERECHT.
Flourished, 1739.

A native, I believe, of Germany, and an engraver in mezzotinto, by whom, among other things, we have the portrait of *Joan. Tho. Rauner*, dated 17 39.

CHARLES FRANCOIS BOECE.
Flourished,

A modern artist, mentioned by Bafan, without any reference to his country, or the place of his residence. By him we have several engravings. Among the rest, a *woman holding a pot with coals, and a boy blowing*. The only light in the painting comes from the fire: from a picture of Rubens, in the Dresden gallery. He also engraved several of the plates, from the pictures of different masters, in the cabinet of the count De Bruhl, &c.

HUBERT BOEHM.
Flourished,

A name mentioned by M. Christ, without any reference to his works, or the time in which he lived, excepting that he was a modern artist. I have never seen any of his engravings. According to the above-mentioned author, he used by way of mark, a cypher composed of an H. and a B. joined together, as expressed on the plate at the end of the volume.

GIOVACCHINO BOEKLAER, or BUECKLAER.
Flourished,

This name is cited in the index of engravers, at the end of the Abecedario; and the artist, to whom it is attributed, is said to have been a native of Antwerp, and a scholar of Peter Artsens, from whom he learned the art of engraving. I have never seen any of his works. Perhaps the name being falsely written, makes the only difference between this engraver and an artist called John Bocklein, mentioned by professor Christ, who usually marked his engravings in this manner, I. B. fe.

CORNELIUS BOEL.
Flourished, 1611.

This artist was probably of Antwerp, and of the same family with Peter Boel the painter, who is spoken of in the next article. From the style of his engraving, which is chiefly with the graver, I should suppose he had been instructed in the school of the Sadelers. He worked in a clear, neat style; and his prints are by no means destitute of merit. We have, engraved by him, a set of small oval plates for the *Fables of Otho Vænius*, with Latin, English, and Italian verses, under them, which were published at Antwerp, A.D. 1608. I have also seen by him a middling sized plate, length-ways, representing the *last judgment*, which is signed, " Cornelius Boel fecit," without the name of the painter. It is probably from a composition of his own.

I believe

I believe this artist was in England; for the *frontispiece* to the large folio Bible, published by the royal authority, A. D. 1611, which is ornamented with figures and other decorations, and very neatly engraved, has his name inscribed, *C. Boel fecit in Richmont*, 1611. He also engraved a portrait of *Henry prince of Wales*, in a small oval, surrounded by an ornamental border. But his great work was the *battles of Charles the Fifth*, and *Francis the First*, eight large plates, length-ways, from Antony Tempesta.

PETER BOEL.
Born, 1625. Died, 1680.

An excellent painter of fruit, flowers, and animals, born at Antwerp, A. D. 1625. A disciple of Snyders, whose widow he married. He went into Italy, where his uncle Cornelius de Wael resided; and, in his return through France, was there greatly employed. He died, A. D. 1680, aged 55 years. There are some few slight, but spirited etchings, by this artist, from his own compositions, representing *various animals*, &c.

CORYN or QUIRIN BOEL.
Flourished, 1660.

This engraver was a native of Antwerp, and of the same family with the preceding artist. His works are chiefly etchings, which are executed in a very coarse, heavy, incorrect style. The greater part of them are, I believe, contained in the collection of prints, from the pictures of the greatest masters, known by the name of *Tenier's Gallery*. They do not require to be particularized, as the book itself is very common. I have seen among other things by this engraver, a middling sized plate, length-ways, representing some *Dutch peasants playing at nine-pins*, from Teniers. This artist has, in general, been carelessly confounded with Cornelius Boel, mentioned above, but he never nearly equalled him in point of merit.

L. DE BOER.
Flourished,

An obscure engraver of portraits, by whom, among others, is that of *Quinkhard*, to which he signs his name L. de Boer.

C. F. BOETIUS.
Flourished, 1753.

A modern German artist, who engraved several of the plates from the collection of pictures at Dresden. The work is in two volumes, large folio, entitled, " Recueil d'Estampes, d'apres les plus celebres Tableaux de LA GALLERIE DE DRESDE." The first volume was published 1753, and the second 1757.

MICHAEL

BOG [113] BOI

MICHAEL BOGNER.
Flourished, 1487.

The name of a very old German artist, probably a goldsmith. The print, to which this name is affixed, I found in the collection of Dr. Monro. It is a small plate representing a coat of arms. The bearing is a wheel, and the crest a wheel upon an helmet. The name 𝕸𝖎𝖈𝖍𝖆𝖊𝖑 𝕭𝖔𝖌𝖓𝖊𝖗 is written upon a scroll. It is executed entirely with the graver; and the ornamental part is white upon a black ground. On the space, which divides the ornaments, is the date intermixed with the letters in the following manner:
𝕬. 𝕯. 1487. 𝕵. 𝕬. 𝕮. This curious ancient engraving is three inches high, by one inch one fourth wide.

J. L. BOJAN.
Flourished, 1670.

An ornamental engraver, who seems to have been chiefly employed by J. Berain, in the large works of ornaments, which he published. His prints, which are etched, and finished with the graver, have, however, nothing very striking to recommend them.

H. BOILING.
Flourished,

An engraver in mezzotinto, mentioned by professor Christ, who informs us, that some prints representing *peasants*, &c. were executed by him; and, that he often put the initials of his name only, H. B. I have never seen any thing by this engraver.

MARTIN DES BOIS.
Flourished, 1691.

This artist was, I presume, a native of France. By him we have several *frontispieces*, for books, after Louis Dorigny; and other prints from the paintings of Italian masters, which were published by C. Paten, A. D. 1691. These, however do him little credit.

ELIAS DU BOIS.
Flourished, 1614.

The name of an artist, cited by Florent le Comte, who informs us, that he engraved the portrait of *Monsieur de Sully*; which print is dated 1614.

PETER DE BOIS.
Flourished,

He is mentioned by Florent le Comte as an engraver of funeral processions, monuments, &c. but none of his works are specified.

ROBERT BOISSART.
Flourished,

A name mentioned by Florent le Comte, as an engraver of portraits, and resident in England; but I am not acquainted with his works.

L. BOISSEVIN.
Flourished, 1623.

His chief employment was, I believe, that of a publisher and a printseller. However, it is thought, that he engraved also himself; and to him are attributed the following portraits: *Franc. Barberini,* cardinal; dated 1623. *Charles the First,* and *Oliver Cromwell.*

S. DE LA BOISSIERE.
Flourished, 1682.

This engraver, who, I suppose, was a native of France, is mentioned by Bafan, without any reference to the time or place of his birth. He tells us, that S. Boissiere (for so he writes his name) engraved " *the death of a prince, surrounded by his court,*" a large plate, lengthways. I suspect him to be the same with that artist, who engraved several of the plates for a large work in folio, entitled, *Les Edifices Antiques de Rome,* par Antoine Degodetz, Architecte, à Paris, 1682. To these plates he signs his name, De la Boissiere. They are neatly executed, but in a stiff, laboured style; and may be considered as the productions of patience rather than of genius.

BOISSIEUX.
Flourished,

By this artist we have a confiderable number of landscapes, views, &c. Judging from the free, masterly style, in which they are etched, I should suppose he was a landscape painter, and a man of great abilities. They are very slight, in general; but, at the same time, spirited. Some of them are apparently from his own designs; others are from various masters. I shall only mention a set of ten landscapes, small plates length-ways, with this title : *Suite de dix Paysages,* gravé à l'eau forte, par Boissieux. If I mistake not, this artist was a native of France. The Hon. Mr. Walpole mentions the name of Boisseau, as affixed to a plate for Aaron Hill's History of the Ottoman Empire; this was probably a different engraver, though perhaps of the same family.

L. BOITARD.
Flourished, 1760.

This engraver was a native of France. He frequently worked from his own compositions. His employment was chiefly for the bookfellers. He engraved in a neat though slight style, without taste; and his drawing is, in general, very defective. Small figures he executed best; but even these are
often

often faulty. Among his moſt eſtimable prints, may be reckoned thoſe which he engraved, for *Spence's Polymetis*; and a large plate repreſenting the *Rotunda at Ranelagh*, after Paolo Panini. He alſo engraved ſeveral portraits; among the reſt, that of *J. Brown*, the ſoldier, who diſtinguiſhed himſelf at the battle of Dettingen, *Elizabeth Canning*, &c. Boitard, who reſided chiefly in England, married an Engliſhwoman. He died at London ſome years ſince, leaving a ſon who followed his father's profeſſion, and a daughter.

RENE' BOIVIN, or BOYVIN.
Flouriſhed,

This artiſt was a native of France, born at Anjou; but the year of his birth does not appear. The ſtyle of his engravings, however, in my opinion, ſufficiently teſtifies, that he flouriſhed towards the end of the ſixteenth century. His plates, in general, are executed with the graver only, in a manner much reſembling that of Cornelius Cort; but we have alſo ſome etchings by him. His works, though not held in the higheſt eſtimation, are by no means devoid of merit, eſpecially in the mechanical part of them. He handled the graver with much facility; and if, in good taſte, and correctneſs of drawing, he had equalled the command he had of that inſtrument, he certainly might have been ranked among the firſt maſters. In theſe great eſſentials he is defective, eſpecially in his drawing, which is very incorrect. The extremities of his figures, in particular, are poorly expreſſed. He ſometimes ſigned his plates with his baptiſmal name only, as *Renatus fecit*; but more generally with a cypher, compoſed of an R. and a B. in the manner expreſſed upon the plate, at the end of the volume. He engraved a great variety of prints. I can only mention a few of them.

An emblematical plate, repreſenting *the triumph of virtue*, with the defects of vice, a large print, length-ways, from *Rous. Florent*, marked Renatus fecit.

Suſanna and the elders, a middling ſized plate, length-ways, without any painter's name, marked with his cypher.

The plates for a work, entitled *Livre de la Conqueſte de la Toiſon d'or, per le Prince Jaſon de Teſſalie*; or The Book of the Conqueſt of the Golden Fleece, by the Prince Jaſon of Theſſaly. Theſe hiſtorical compoſitions, which are encloſed in ornamental borders, were deſigned by Leonard Thiri; and they are marked with the cypher of Boivin, whoſe name in the dedication is ſpelt Boyvin.

A ſpirited etching of a cottage yard, in which is introduced the departure of *Hagar and Iſhmael from the houſe of Abraham*, a middling ſized plate, length-ways, marked with his cypher.

Another etching, in which is repreſented *four banditti men robbing the cart of a peaſant*, a ſmall plate, length-ways, marked with the cypher.

MARIE L. A. BOIZOT.
Flouriſhed, 1762.

A modern engraver, a native of France, and pupil to Flipart. He reſided at at Paris, and engraved a variety of *domestic subjects* from Greuze and other masters, also some *portraits*.

HANS or JOHN BOL.
Born, 1534. Died, 1593.

He was a native of Mechlin, where he was born, A. D. 1534. His genius leading him to the arts, he was at first instructed in painting by a master of no great repute, whom he soon left, and going to Heidelberg, employed himself in copying several pictures of the eminent artists. His subjects are chiefly landscapes with animals; but he also sometimes painted history, with no small success. We have by him a set of landscapes, *views in Holland*, slightly etched, but in a style that indicates the hand of the master, they are middling sized plates, length-ways, marked "H. Bol;" the H. and the B. are joined together in the style of a cypher, and they were published by Jerom Cock. A large plate, length-ways, in which is represented an *aquatic diversion in Holland*: a man appears in a boat, catching at a goose, which is fastened to a string over the river, and a prodigious number of spectators are depicted upon the banks on each side.

Some circular prints, representing *historical subjects*. I shall only mention two, namely, *the meeting of Jacob and Esau*; and *the first interview between the servant of Abraham and Rebecca*: both very slight, but spirited etchings; and marked with his name as above.

I have seen also a slight, spirited etching, greatly in the style of those by this artist. It is a small sea view, with ships. Over it is written DEN BRIEL; and at the right hand corner, *C. Bol fecit*. who was probably another artist of the same family.

FERDINAND BOL.
Born, 1611. Died, 1681.

A celebrated painter both of history and portraits. He was born at Dort, A. D. 1611, and educated at Amsterdam. In the school of the celebrated Rembrant Gerretz, he received his instructions as a painter, and imitated the style of his master with no little success, not only in his pictures, but in his engravings. Bol's etchings are bold and free. The lights and shadows in them are broad and powerful, which renders the effect very striking; but they want that lightness of touch, and admirable taste, which those of Rembrant possess in so great a degree. Bol died at Dort, the place of his birth, A. D. 1681, aged 70.

Among his etchings, the following from his own compositions, are generally much esteemed:

Abraham's sacrifice, a middling sized upright plate.

St. Jerom seated in a cavern, holding a crucifix, a small upright plate, arched at the top.

A *philosopher*, a half figure, holding a book, a small upright plate.

NICCOLO

NICCOLO BOLDRINI.
Flourished, 1566.

An engraver on wood, who worked chiefly from Titian, and by some thought to have been the scholar of that great master. The time of his birth and death are equally unknown. I have seen by him a large upright print, cut in wood, which represents *Venus naked*, seated on a bank, holding Cupid, a squirrel appears behind upon the branch of a tree. The figures, back-ground, &c. are executed in a bold, free style, chiefly with a single stroke; but there is some hatching in the deep shadows. It is marked *Titianus inv. Nicolaus Baldrinus Vincentinus inciaebat*, 1566.

IL BOLOGNA. See PRIMATICCIO.

IL BOLOGNESE. See GRIMALDI.

GIOVANNI BATISTA BOLOGNINI.
Born, 1611. Died, 1688.

This artist, a native of Bologna, was born, A. D. 1611. He was instructed in the principles of painting by Guido; and succeeded so well, in his studies, that he became the favourite scholar of that excellent master. He imitated the style of Guido; and his works are held in general esteem. He died, A. D. 1688, aged 77. We have several etchings by him from the compositions of Guido. They are slight, and often spirited, but by no means equal to those, which were produced by Guido's own hand. Among his most esteemed etchings may be reckoned the following:

The *murder of the innocents*, a middling sized upright plate.

St. Peter receiving the keys, nearly the same size as the preceding.

A *crucifixion*, with St. John and the two Maries, standing at the foot of the cross, nearly the same size as the former.

Bacchus and Ariadne, a large print length-ways, engraved on three plates. These are all from Guido.

BOETIUS ADAM A BOLSWERT, or BOLSUERD.
Flourished, 1620.

This artist, an engraver and printseller, established at Antwerp, was the descendant of a family, who resided at the city of Bolswert in Friefeland, from whence he derived his name. He commonly signs the prints engraved by him, with the first of his baptismal names, *Boetius*; but sometimes he has substituted the second, and omitted the first. Hence it is, that the generality of authors, on the subject of engraving, have run into a strange mistake, and made two artists of the same man; one named *Boetius*, the other *Adam*: the latter supposed to have been the father of the former. According to Basan, *Boetius Adam a Bolswert*, " who," says he, " is mis-
" takenly mentioned as an engraver, because we find upon several plates,
" *B. Adams*, or B. A. Bolswert; or certain other marks, nearly resembling
" them

" them, which Boetius sometimes used. All of which in Flemish signify
" Boetius the son of Adam." It is highly probable, that the father's name
might be Adam; but that these signatures are to be interpreted according to
Basan's idea, is not so certain. Both names doubtless did belong to him;
and accordingly, to a set of *twenty landscapes*, engraved by him from Abraham Bloemart, he signs them at length thus, *Boetius Adam Bolsuerd sculp.*
By what master he was instructed in the art of engraving, does not appear.
He worked with the graver only; the free, open style of the Bloemarts
he imitated with great success; and perhaps perfected himself in their school.
When he worked from Rubens, he altered that style; and his plates are
neater, fuller of colour, and more highly finished. I shall mention

FIRST, some of those plates, wherein he has imitated the style of the Bloemarts.

A set of twenty *landscapes*, from Abraham Bloemart, mentioned above;
slight, small plates, length-ways. I have seen them marked, Amsterdam,
with the date 1664, which time perhaps they were republished by a new
proprietor.

The plates for a quarto book, entitled, *the Forest of the Hermits and Hermitesses of Egypt and Palestine*, from the same painter, published at Antwerp,
A. D. 1619.

The *nativity of Christ*, a large upright plate, from the same painter, a
very beautiful plate, dated 1618.

SECONDLY, the following from Rubens in a more finished style:
The *resurrection of Lazarus*, a large upright plate.
The *last supper*, the same, its companion. Basan, speaking of this print,
says, that it proves by its beauty, and the knowledge with which it is engraved,
that Boetius could sometimes equal his brother Scheltius. It is certainly a
very beautiful engraving; but I cannot help thinking, the compliment a
little overstrained; especially if we look at the admirable *crucifixion* from
Vandyck by Scheltius Bolswert, at the same time.

SCHELTIUS A BOLSWERT, or BOLSUERD.
Flourished, 1626.

This admirable artist was the brother of Boetius Adam a Bolswert, mentioned in the preceding article. We have no other account of his family
than what is there given; nor unfortunately any of himself, of the least consequence. The time of his birth and of his death, and the name of the master he studied under, are equally obscure. And though it is not likely, that
the knowledge of these circumstances could add to the fame he has so justly
acquired, yet we naturally wish to know something of the man, whose genius
we admire; and of course every little anecdote concerning him becomes
interesting. Bolswert worked entirely with the graver, and, I believe, never
called in the assistance of the point. His general character as an artist is
well drawn by Basan, in the following words: " We have a large number of
" prints, which are held in great esteem, by this artist, from various mas-
" ters; but especially from Rubens, whose pictures he has copied with all
" possible knowledge, taste and great effect. The freedom, with which
" this

"this excellent artift handled the graver, the picturefque roughnefs of etching, which he could imitate without any other affifting inftrument, and the ability he poffeffed of diftinguifhing the different maffes of colours, have always been admired by the connoiffeurs, and give him a place in the number of thofe celebrated engravers, whofe prints ought to be confidered as models by all hiftorical engravers, who are defirous of rendering their works as ufeful as they are agreeable, and of acquiring a reputation, as lafting as it is juftly merited." He drew excellently, and without any manner of his own; for his prints are the exact tranfcripts of the pictures he engraved from. His beft works, though not always equally neat or finifhed, are always beautiful, and manifeft the hand of the mafter. Sometimes we find his engravings are in a bold, free, open ftyle: as, the *brazen ferpent*, the *marriage of the Virgin*, &c. from Rubens. At other times they are very neat, and fweetly finifhed: as, the *crowning with thorns*, and the *crucifixion*, &c. from Vandyck. Indeed, I have generally obferved, that his boldeft engravings are from Rubens, and his neateft from Vandyck and Jordans.

How greatly Bolfwert varied his manner of engraving appears from fome prints, which, like the greater part of thofe of his brother Boetius, bear great refemblance to the free engravings of the Bloemarts, and to thofe of Frederic Bloemart efpecially; and form a part of the plates for a large folio volume, entitled, *Academie de L'efpee*, by Girard Thibault of Antwerp, where it was publifhed, A. D. 1628; and to thefe he figns his name, " Sheltius," and fometimes " Schelderic Bolfwert," adding the word *Bruxelle*. His name is ufually affixed to his plates in this manner, " S. A. Bolfwert;" but on the plate at the end of the volume may be feen a mark, attributed to him, which he is faid to have ufed, when he was not willing to fign his name.

It is very neceffary to caution the collectors of this mafter's works (thofe efpecially, who are not very converfant with them) that many of them have been copied in a very careful manner, fo as eafily to deceive the unfkilful. Some of thefe copies, as the *marriage of the Virgin*, from Rubens, &c. are by Lauwers. But thofe, which are moft likely to miflead, are by Ragot, a French engraver, employed by Mariette the printfeller, who frequently meeting with the reverfes or counterproofs, from the prints of Bolfwert, gave them to the engraver; and he imitated them with the utmoft precifion. By this means the impreffions from the plate copied come upon the paper the fame way with the original. It is true, his name is ufually affixed at the bottom; but it is often cut off, and then the copy is not eafily diftinguifhed from the original. Among other prints thus imitated by Ragot from Bolfwert, is *Chrift crucified between the two thieves*; where the foldier is reprefented piercing his fide, from Rubens.

Among the variety of eftimable engravings by this great artift, I can only mention the few following:

The *brazen ferpent*, a large plate, length-ways, from Rubens. Thofe impreffions are the moft eftimable, which have only the word *Antuerpiæ* at the right hand corner, without the name of *Giles Hendrix*, which was afterwards inferted above it, and part of the fmall circle over the arms is left white.

Abraham offering his fon Ifaac, a large plate nearly fquare, from Theodore Rombout.

The *education of the Virgin by Saint Anne*, a middling fized upright plate, from Rubens. Thofe impreffions, without the name of Hendrix, are the moft efteemed.

The *marriage of the Virgin*, a middling fized upright plate, from the fame painter. Thofe impreffions are beft, in which the word " Antuerpiæ" is not added to the name of Hendrix.

The *nativity of Chrift*, a middling fized upright plate, from the fame, firft publifhed by Martin Vanden Enden.

The *adoration of the wife men*, a middling fized upright plate, from the fame. The good impreffions of this plate alfo, have the name of Vanden Enden.

The *feaft of Herod*, in which is reprefented the daughter of Herodias, prefenting the head of John the Baptift to her mother, a large plate, lengthways, from the fame.

The *miraculous draught of fifhes*, a large print, length-ways, on three plates, from the fame.

Chrift crowned with thorns, a large upright plate, from Vandyck. An admirable print. With the name of Vanden Enden.

A *crucifixion*, where a figure appears prefenting the fponge to Chrift. St. John and the Virgin are ftanding at the foot of the crofs, and Mary Magdalen is reclining towards it, a large upright plate, from Vandyck; and it is, in my opinion, one of the moft beautiful prints engraved by Bolfwert. In the firft impreffions, which are very fcarce, the left hand of St. John is not feen. In the fecond, the hand appears upon the fhoulder of the Virgin, the name of Vandyck is transfpofed from the left to the right hand corner of the plate; and the dedication, which confifts of two lines, is erafed from the bottom of the plate, probably to make thefe impreffions pafs for the firft. After this, to deceive the purchafers, the hand was again erafed, and the dedication reinferted; but the imitation of the letters is fo poorly executed, that the cheat is eafily difcovered. The firft impreffions are diftinguifhed without much difficulty, as well by their fuperiority in clearnefs and colour, as by the difference alluded to; efpecially from the laft; for the ftrokes, which were re-engraved over the place, where the hand had been, are very poorly executed. And both in the fecond and third impreffions, the fhort ftrokes upon the ground, near the great toe of the figure, who holds the fponge, are croffed with a fecond ftroke, but in the firft they are without any croffing.

A *crucifixion*, where St. Dominicus and St. Catherine of Sienna are reprefented. At the foot of the crofs is a large ftone, on which is feated a fmall cherub, with a lamp before him. On the ftone is an infcription beginning thus: *Ne Patris fui manibus*; a large upright plate from the fame mafter.

A *crucifixion*, where the foldier is piercing the fide of Chrift, St. John and the Virgin are ftanding by the crofs, a large upright plate from Rubens.

A *crucifixion*, with the Virgin and St. John at the foot of the crofs, from James Jordaens, a large upright plate.

A *dead Chrift* on the lap of the Virgin, with St. John and two Angels, a middling fized plate, length-ways.

A *dead Chrift* on the lap of the Virgin, a large upright plate, from A. Deipenbeck.

The *Trinity*, a large upright plate, where Chrift is reprefented dead, a fore-fhortened figure fupported by the Deity, from Rubens.

The *affumption of the Virgin*, a large upright plate, arched at top, from the fame mafter.

The *deftruction of idolatry*, a large print, length-ways, on two plates, from the fame mafter.

The *triumph of the church*, the fame from the fame.

The *infant Jupiter fuckled by the goat Amalthea*, a middling fized plate, length-ways, from Jordaens.

The *infant Jupiter crying, and fhowing a difh to a woman, who is milking the goat; and a fatyr is playing on a tambour*, a middling fized plate, length-ways, from the fame.

The *god Pan playing upon his flute*, the fame from the fame.

Mercury and Argus, a large plate length-ways, from the fame.

The *drunken king*, the fame from the fame.

A *drunken Silenus*, fupported by a fatyr, and another figure, a middling-fized upright plate from Rubens. The impreffions, with the name of " Bolefwert" only, without the addrefs, are the beft.

A *chafe of lions*, a large plate, length-ways, from the fame.

Five large *landfcapes*, length-ways, from the fame.

Twenty fmall *landfcapes*, length-ways, from the fame.

GIOVANNI BATISTA BONACINI.
Flourifhed,

This artift, who was a native of Milan, never arrived at any fuperior degree of excellence. He worked entirely with the graver, in a ftiff, laboured ftyle. He appears by his engravings to have flourifhed towards the beginning of the laft century, and may have been inftructed in the fchool of Cornelius Bloemart. I fhall only notice by him a middling-fized upright plate, reprefenting *the Virgin with the infant Jefus*, and St. Martin kneeling before him, from Pietro de Cortona; and a *holy family*, with St. John, St. Catherine, &c. a middling fized upright plate, from Andrea del Sarto. We have alfo feveral *portraits* by him; but they are by no means commendable.

GIULIO BONASONI.
Flourifhed, 1540.

He was a native of Bologna, and for that caufe is fometimes called *Bolognefe*. He was a painter as well as an engraver, and the fcholar of Marc Antonio Raimondi. He worked from the pictures of Raphael, Giulio Romano, and other great mafters; and occafionally from his own defigns. Excepting one or two fubjects, in which he called in the affiftance of the point (which, however, he never well underftood the ufe of) his plates are executed entirely with the graver, in a manner though much varied from that of his tutor, yet evidently founded upon it. It is neither fo firm, nor fo clear

clear and masterly. His drawing is often heavy, and the extremities of his figures frequently neglected. The folds of his draperies are seldom well expressed, and the back-grounds to his prints, especially his landscapes, are extremely flat and stiff. However, with all these faults (which are not always equally conspicuous) his best prints possess an uncommon share of merit; and, though not equal to those of his master, are deservedly held in no small degree of estimation by the greatest collectors. One thing in particular is remarkable in them, namely, the attempt which he has made, of preserving the masses and a breadth of light and shadow, as well upon the groups of figures as upon the figures separately.

I shall notice the following by him, from his own compositions:

The *loves of the gods*, a set of twenty-one small upright plates.

A *warrior, surrounded by several naked women*, a middling sized plate, length-ways.

Apollo in his chariot with the hours, Time walking on crutches before, and at the bottom a *man and a woman waking from sleep*, a middling sized plate, length-ways, marked "Julio Bonasone inventore."

Venus attended by the Graces, a small upright plate.

The *judgment of Paris*, into which he has introduced a great variety of figures. All the back ground and much of the draperies and some small part of the figures, &c. are etched; but the work with the graver only is by no means well harmonized with the etching, a large plate length-ways.

Clelia and her companions, escaping from the camp of Porsenna, a middling sized plate, length-ways, marked IV. BONASO IMITANDO PINSIT CELAVIT.

I shall add the following only from other masters:

The *animals departing from the ark*, a middling sized plate, from Raphael, dated 1544.

The *infant Jupiter suckled by the goat Amalthea*, the same from the same.

St. Cecilia, from the picture by Raphael, which differs from the print of Marc Antonio in several particulars, a small upright plate.

A *dead Christ upon the lap of the Virgin*, a small upright plate, from Michael Angelo. Beatrici also engraved a print from the same picture, dated 1546.

The *last judgment*, a large upright plate, arched at the top, from the same master, with this inscription, *Julius Bonasonius Bonon. è propriá Michaelis Angeli pictura, quæ est in Vaticano, nigro Capillo excepit, in aesque incidit.*

The *entry of the wooden horse into Troy*, inscribed *BOL inventor*, 1545.

Moses striking the rock, a middling sized plate, length-ways, from Parmigiano.

Some portraits, particularly those of *Raphael* and *Michael Angelo*. When he did not inscribe his name at length, he often substituted the initials, as "I. B." sometimes thus, " I. Bo." or thus, " Julio B. F."

BONAVENTURA. See BISI.

DOMENICO MARIA BONAVERA.
Flourished, 1700.

This engraver, who appears to have been a native of Bologna, flourished
according

according to Bafan, at the beginning of the prefent century. All the prints, which indeed are but few, that I have feen by him, are flight, incorrect etchings, by no means very eftimable. A mark faid to have been adopted by him, may be feen upon the plate at the end of the volume. I fhall only notice, the *baptifm of our Saviour*, from Albano, mentioned by Bafan; and the *martyrdom of a female faint*, a large upright plate, from Domenico Maria Canuti.

NATALIS BONIFACE.
Flourifhed, 1590.

An engraver of great merit, who flourifhed in Italy towards the conclufion of the fixteenth century. His works are chiefly etchings, which he performed in a flight, free ftyle; and where fmall figures were required, he executed them with great fpirit. His chief work was the plates for the large folio volume compofed by D. Fontana, architect to Pope Sixtus V. concerning the removal of the Vatican obelifks. To thefe plates he figns his name, " Natalis Bonifacius Sibenicenfis fecit." This book was publifhed at Rome, 1590, and contains the portrait of *Fontani*, furrounded by an ornamental border, which, I believe, was performed by Boniface; but the portrait itfelf, which is executed entirely with the graver, I fufpect was the work of another artift.

FLORIANUS DE BONIS.
Flourifhed,

The name of an obfcure engraver of little merit, affixed to a middling fized plate, from Guercino, reprefenting *a dead Chrift, fupported by St. John, with the Virgin ftanding by him*. It is all executed with the graver, in a black heavy ftyle.

ROBERT BONNART.
Flourifhed, 1680.

This engraver, with NICHOLAS BONNART his brother, who were both of them natives of France, engraved, among other things, feveral of the plates from the defigns of Vander Meulen, for the large edition of his works. They chiefly confift of *views, landfcapes* with *figures*, &c. and are executed in a very heavy, coarfe ftyle. JOHN BONNART, perhaps another brother, engraved with them a variety of figures *a-la-mode*, with grotefque portraits of the actors in the Italian comedy, &c. which have very little to recommend them. Nicholas and John Bonnart fometimes figned their plates with the initials only of their names: as, " N. B. fecit," and " I. B. F. or fecit."

JOHN BONNART the younger, who was probably fon of John Bonnart mentioned above, appears to have been a painter. There is a plate by him in Perault's *Cabinet des Beaux Artes*, publifhed at Paris, 1690. It is a ceiling ornamented with figures, which he has etched in a free, mafterly ftyle, and retouched with the graver. He figns his name " Joan. Bonnart " junior del, et fculp."

E. BONNCIONNE.
Flourished,

A name I found affixed to a very small plate, length-ways, from F. Boel, representing *Diana, seated in a chariot drawn by dragons, and a Cupid behind her*. It is a slight, dark etching, incorrectly drawn, and possesses little merit to recommend it.

BONNEAU.
Flourished, 1741.

A very indifferent engraver, probably a Frenchman, who resided in London, and engraved for the booksellers. Among other things by him, are the heads of the *American Bucaniers*, prefixed to their history, which was published at London, A. D. 1741.

FRANCOIS BONNEMER.
Flourished,

A native of France, who flourished in the last century, and engraved several prints from Le Brun and other masters; among the rest, the *Deity appearing to Moses in the burning bush*.

L. BONNET.
Flourished,

A modern French engraver, who resided some time in Russia, by whom we have several prints, executed in a very particular manner, so as to represent *drawings in crayons*; in performing which, two, and sometimes more, plates are necessary for the same print. This mode of engraving, however, notwithstanding its novelty, was not long encouraged. He engraved from Boucher and other masters.

FR. BONNONIENSIS.
Flourished,

I have seen this name affixed to some slight, spirited etchings, in a bold, masterly style, from Paolo Veronese. In the Abecedario, the prints marked *B. S. fecit* are attributed to this artist; but apparently without the least foundation.

J. BONSER.
Flourished, 1642.

An obscure engraver, who, if he was not a native of Leyden, at least resided there. He worked chiefly for the booksellers. I have seen some few frontispieces by him, with figures and ornaments, &c. he worked entirely with the graver, in a very stiff, bad style. His prints are by no means worth particularising. One of them is dated 1642.

BOOMS, or BOON. See VINCKENBOOMS.

DANIEL BOON.
Born, Died, 1698.

A native of Holland, and a painter in the grotefque ftyle. He refided fome time in England; and Mr. Walpole informs us, that he etched feveral things, but has not fpecified what they are. There is a portrait of *Fred. Guillieme* of *Pruffia*, marked Boon, who was apparently another artift, though perhaps of the fame family.

HENRY VANDER BORCHT.
Born, 1583. Died, 1660.

He was, according to the moft generally received opinion, born at Bruffels, A. D. 1583, and the youngeft fon of a painter of the fame name, who afterwards refided at Frankendal. The earl of Arundel, finding this young artift at Frankfort, where he fought an afylum from the wars, which difturbed his native country, fent him into Italy to Mr. Petty, who was then collecting for his lordfhip; and that nobleman retained him in his fervice as long as he lived. After the death of his patron, Vander Borcht was employed by the prince of Wales (afterwards Charles the Second) and lived in efteem at London feveral years, till he returned to Antwerp, where he died, A. D. 1660, aged 77. He chiefly excelled in painting fruit and flowers. We have fome few etchings by him; among the reft, the *Virgin and child*, a fmall upright print, from Parmigiano; which plate was engraved at London, and dated 1637. A *dead Chrift, fupported by Jofeph of Arimathea*, a fmall upright plate, from the fame mafter. *Apollo and Cupid*, a fmall upright oval, from Perin del Vago. The mark, attributed to him by profeffor Chrift, may be feen upon the plate at the end of the volume.

PETER VANDER BORCHT.
Flourifhed, 1622.

It is highly probable, that this artift was of the fame family with the preceding, and perhaps a near relation. He was a painter of landfcapes, and acquired fome reputation in that line. He appears alfo to have applied himfelf very affiduoufly to etching; and we have a great number of prints by his hand. Among the reft, a fet of prints from *Ovid's metamorphofes*, confifting of one hundred and feventy-eight fmall plates, length-ways. Alfo a fet of prints from the *old and new teftament*, middling fized plates, length-ways. Thefe may be properly called hiftorical landfcapes. They are etched in a rough, carelefs ftyle; and the figures, which are chiefly fmall, are very incorrectly drawn. The extremities are heavy, and the heads by no means expreffive. His works, in general, manifeft a great fertility of invention, but little judgment, either in the choice of the attitude of his figures, or the diftribution of his groups, to form a pleafing or a ftriking effect. His ufual mark, when he does not fign his name at length, is P. B. F. The F. ftanding for fecit.

Great

Great care must be taken not to confound him with several other engravers, who used the same mark.

JAMES A BORCHT.
Flourished, 1628.

This artist, whose works are by no means destitute of merit, engraved several of the plates for the large folio volume, entitled, Academie de L'Espee, by Girard Thibault, which was published at Antwerp, 1628. They are executed entirely with the graver, in a style greatly resembling that of James de Gheyn.

BORDE.
Flourished, 1725.

An obscure engraver of little merit. He worked entirely with the graver, in a style sufficiently neat, but destitute of taste. Among other things, we have by him, the *crown of precious stones*, which the queen of France wore at her marriage, A. D. 1725, with the *medal* struck upon that occasion.

MATTHEW BOREKENS.
Flourished, 1644.

He resided chiefly at Antwerp, and worked entirely with the graver, in a laboured style, something resembling that of Pontius. His drawing is incorrect; and his works (the principal part of which are the copies he made from Bolswert, and other eminent engravers, for Vanden Enden) have no great share of merit to recommend them. I shall only notice, the *good shepherd*, a small upright plate, from Diepenbeck. The *Virgin, standing upon a globe, treading upon a serpent*, a middling sized upright plate, from Rubens, dated 1644. We have also some few portraits by him.

J. F. BORDINO.
Flourished, 1604.

An engraver who executed the plates to a volume in quarto, entitled, *Series et Gesta Pontificum*, published 1604.

ORAZIO or HORAZIO BORGIANI.
Born, 1630. Died, 1681.

He was born at Rome, and instructed in the art of painting by his brother Giulio Borgiani, called Scalzo; and he made such a progress in his studies, that his works were held in no small estimation in Spain, where he resided some time. On his return to Italy, the ill treatment and villainy of a cotemporary painter broke his heart, and he died, A. D. 1681, aged 51 years. His etchings are in a bold, free manner; and more finished than usual, when considered as the works of a painter. His drawing is not correct; but the style is masterly, and the effect agreeable. His most finished etching, I believe,

believe, is a small square plate, in which is represented a *dead Christ*; the figure vastly foreshortened, and behind appear the two Maries and St. John, who is kissing one of the hands of our Saviour, from a composition of his own, dated 1615. Add to this, *St. Christopher*, a gigantic figure, carrying the infant Christ, a small plate, nearly the same size with the former; a very spirited etching, but not so well finished as the preceding. The *bible histories*, which were painted by Raphael, in the Vatican, commonly called *Raphael's bible*; small plates, length-ways, dated 1615. These are very slight, and seem to be the hasty productions of his point. His mark was an H. and a B. joined together in the manner of a cypher; to which he usually affixed the date. See it copied on the plate at the end of the volume.

CHRISTOPHANO BORTENO.
Flourished,

Florent le Comte adds " *De Remini*" to his name, and cites him as chiefly to have excelled in engraving of cavalcades, processions, &c. though he has not specified any of his prints.

CORNELIUS BOS. See Bus.

JEROM BOS. See Bosche.

ANTHONY BOS.
Flourished, 1648.

Who, according to Baldanucci, engraved the plates for the geometrical works of Defargue, published A. D. 1648.

MARIE RENARD DU BOS.
Flourished,

A modern French artist, and the scholar of Dupuis, by whom we have several plates from Rosalba, Basseporte, &c.

CLAUDE DU BOSC.
Flourished, 1714.

This artist was a native of France, but came over into England, at the instigation of Nicholas Dorigny, to assist him in engraving the *cartoons* of Raphael; but some difference happening between them, he quitted Dorigny, and undertook to engrave the *cartoons* for the printsellers. He also engraved the *duke of Marlborough's battles*, for which he received four score pounds per plate; and the work was finished in two years. At first he had no help, except what he received from Du Guernier; but he sent to Paris for Beauvais and Baron, who assisted him in the completion of those plates, which was done, A. D. 1717. He afterwards commenced printseller, and published in numbers, by a weekly subscription, the translation of Picart's
religious

religious ceremonies. In the profecution of this work, he was affifted by Gravelot and Scotin, who came over into England for that purpofe. Du Bofc was an engraver of no great merit. His ftyle of engraving is coarfe and heavy; and the drawing of the naked parts of the figure in his plates is exceedingly defective. However, he engraved from feveral great mafters. Among the reft of his plates is the *continence of Scipio*, from a picture of Nicholas Poufin, which was in the Houghton collection. Some of the plates of the *Turkifh habits*, &c. publifhed at Paris, 1714, by M. de Ferriol, are engraved by him.

ELIAS BOSCH.
Flourifhed,

The name of an obfcure engraver, whofe works, however, are by no means deftitute of merit. He worked with the graver only, in a very neat ftyle. I have feen, among other things by him, a fmall upright oval plate, reprefenting a *holy family*, with angels attending upon the infant Jefus, from John ab Ach.

JEROM BOSCHE.
Born,   Died, 1500.

He was a very ancient painter, a native of Bois le Duc in Germany, and probably a difciple of Martin Schoon. He feems to me to have been the firft artift, who attempted to engrave in the grotefque ftyle; and from him Peter Brueghel borrowed much of the whimfical drollery, which abounds in his pictures. As a painter, Bofche, who is alfo called Bos, is more generally known; and his works have been held in no fmall eftimation. His engravings are in the fame ftiff ftyle, which fo ftrongly characterifes the works of the early German mafters. They prove, however, that he poffeffed a great fertility of invention, though perhaps but little judgment. I fhall only mention two plates by him: in one is reprefented *St. Chriftopher*, carrying the infant Jefus crofs the water, and bending under his load. To the left is a hermit, coming from his cell with a lanthorn. The whole compofition is furrounded with fmall grotefque figures of all fhapes, in the moft ridiculous attitudes. This print is thirteen inches and a quarter wide, by feven inches three quarters high. The fecond is the *laft judgment*. Chrift appears in the air feated on a rain bow, and on each fide of him are two angels founding trumpets, with this infcription on labels, *Hic eft dies quem fecit*; *Surgite mortui, venite ad judicium.* At the bottom are fmall figures of men and devils of all fhapes intermixed. To both thefe prints he figns his name at length, BOSCHE. At other times, he abbreviates it, and writes only BOS. and adds to it a knife; as on a fmall upright plate, reprefenting *John baptifing Chrift*. Le Comte and others attribute to this artift the plates, marked with the Gothic A. only; but, I believe without foundation. All the prints, which I have feen with the Gothic A. only, are fmaller and neater, and engraved in a very different ftyle from thofe by Bofche. They were doubtlefs led into this miftake from the A. and the mark unknown to me at the bottom
of

of it, which Bofche frequently added, when he put his name at length. See the name and marks copied on the plate, at the end of the volume.

ANDREA BOSCOLI.
Flourifhed,

He was a native of Florence, and according to Marolles and Florent le Comte, engraved nineteen plates; but the fubjects are not fpecified by either of thefe authors.

ROBERT BOSSART.
Flourifhed, 1595.

He was, I believe, a native of Germany; and, it is highly probable, learned the firft principles of the art of engraving in the fchool of Henry Goltzius; his ftyle, in many refpects, bears much refemblance to that adopted by Saenredam, and other difciples of that mafter. But from the want of fufficient knowledge in drawing, his engravings are ftiff fervile copies of the defigns he imitated, without tafte, and very incorrect, efpecially the heads and the other extremities of his figures. The lights, however, are left broad and clear, particularly upon the draperies; but they are fo fcattered and confufed, that they entirely deftroy the harmony of the effect. Among other prints by this artift, is a fet of middling fized plates, length-ways, in which the different nations of Europe are reprefented by emblematical figures, furrounded with fuch things as each country was famous for, or fuch as had been invented in it. In the plate which reprefents Germany, befides the *cannon*, the *printing prefs*, and other inventions attributed to that nation, is a *copper plate*, with *two gravers* and the common mark of Albert Durer engraved upon it; which compliment, I fuppofe, he pays to that great artift, as the improver of the art of engraving. He certainly could never be fo ignorant as to fuppofe, that he was the inventor of it. I fhall only add the portrait of *Bart. Sprenger*, dated 1595.

ABRAHAM BOSSE.
Flourifhed, 1630.

A French artift, born at Tours, in the beginning of the laft century. He executed great part of his works from his own defigns. I know not from whom he learned the firft principles of the art of engraving; but he manifeftly imitated the coarfer manner of Callot, and with no fmall fuccefs. The figures, with which he ufually embellifhed his plates, are drawn in a fpirited ftyle, and etched with great freedom. He afterwards retouched the etching with the graver, in a bold, expeditious manner. The effect, however, of his plates is clear and pleafing, but his lights are ufually too much fcattered. It is generally remarked, that he fucceeded beft in fmall fubjects, where fo great a correctnefs of outline was not required. We have by him a treatife on *the art of drawing*, the beft edition of which, according to Bafan, is with the additions and corrections of M. Cochin; the *fchool of the painter*, and of the *sculptor*, and the workshop of a *copper-plate printer*, three middling sized plates, length-ways, from his own designs; the *school master and mistress*, the same, from the same; the ceremonies of the *contract of marriage* between the king of Poland and the princess Louisa de Gonzague, the same; a set of small upright plates from *Ovid*, *Metastasio*, &c. the *five senses*, on five small plates; the *works of mercy*; the *prodigal son*; *La Pucelle, ou France délivrée*, containing on many small upright plates, the *history of the Maid of Orleans*, from the designs of Vignon; a variety of other plates, frontispieces, &c. from his own designs, and those of La Hire, Paul Farinati, &c.

JAMES BOSSIUS.
Flourished, 1562.

A native of Flanders, but apparently he learned the art of engraving in Italy; perhaps from some of the scholars of Marc Antonio. His style is neat and stiff; the drawing of his figures not very correct, especially in the extremities, which are generally heavy, and not well marked. However, his works are by no means devoid of merit. Among other things by this engraver, is the *statue of Pyrrhus king of Molossus*, from the antique marble, a middling sized upright plate, arched at the top. It is subscribed " Jacobus Bossius Belgia incid. 1562."

LE BOSSU.
Flourished,

This engraver, whose works are of no great value, imitated the style of Francis de Poilly, in a very coarse, and indifferent manner. His drawing is also equally defective. I shall only mention by him, the *resurrection of Lazarus*, a large plate, length-ways, from Hyacinth Brande, which appears to have been engraved at Rome.

JOHN BOTH.
Born, 1610. Died, 1650.

A very celebrated landscape painter, born at Utrecht, A. D. 1610. He was first the disciple of Abraham Bloemart; but afterwards went to Italy, in order to perfect himself from the works of the Italian masters; and he resided at Rome several years. His excellence as a painter is so generally known, that any eulogium in this place is unnecessary. He is said to have been drowned in a canal at Venice, into which he fell by accident, returning home late one night, A. D. 1650, being only forty years of age. We have by his hand a set of ten *landscapes*, middling sized plates, length-ways, which are etched in a slight, free, masterly style. The *figures and cattle*, which are very spirited and fine, are attributed to his brother Andrew, and not without some appearance of truth.

ANDREW

ANDREW BOTH.
Flourished, 1640.

He was brother to John Both, the artist mentioned in the preceding article, and was also a disciple of Abraham Bloemart. He went with his brother to Italy. But his genius led him rather to the study of figures than of landscape; and he imitated the style of Bamboccio with great success, so that joining his talents with those of his brother, they produced a great number of pleasing pictures, to their mutual profit. After the unfortunate death of his brother, he returned to his native country, where he settled, but did not long survive him. Andrew Both etched some few plates in a free, masterly style, something resembling that of Ostade; namely, six small upright plates of *Dutch merry makings*, &c. to which he affixes his name " A. Both, inv. et fecit." *St. Anthony praying with a scull before him*, a small upright plate; and *St. Francis with a crucifix before him*, its companion. The name " A. Both," is reversed on both these prints; the A. and the B. are joined together in a sort of a cypher. See the plate of monograms at the end of the volume.

SAMUEL BOTSCHILD.
Flourished,

According to Basan, this is the name of a modern artist, born at Sangerhausen in Saxony, who etched several subjects of his own composition.

SANDRO or ALESSANDRO BOTTICELLI.
Born, 1437. Died, 1515.

He was born at Florence, A. D. 1437, and learned the rudiments of painting under Filippo Lippi. He executed several pictures for pope Sixtus IV. and others for the city of Florence; for these he received large sums of money, all of which he expended, and died at last, A. D. 1515, in great distress, aged 78. He was not only a painter, but a man of letters. Baldini according to the general report communicated to him the secret of engraving, then newly discovered by Finiguerra their townsman. I shall say the less of this artist here, because I have spoken so largely of him in the preceding essay, to which the reader is referred. The famous edition of Dante's Poem of *Hell*, printed at Florence by *Nicholo Lorenzo della Magna*, A. D. 1481, and to which, according to some authors, Botticelli undertook to write notes, was evidently intended to have been ornamented with prints, one for each canto; and these prints (as many of them as were finished) were designed, if not engraved, by Botticelli. It is remarkable, that the two first plates only were printed upon the leaves of the book, and for want of a blank space at the head of the first canto the plate belonging to it is placed at the bottom of the page. Blank spaces are left for all the rest; that as many of them as were finished might be pasted on. Mr. Wilbraham possesses the finest copy of this book extant, in any private library; and the number of prints in it amount to nineteen. The two first, as usual, are printed on the

leaves;

leaves; and the other seventeen, which follow regularly, are pasted on the blank spaces. And these apparently were all that Botticelli ever executed. About the year 1460, it is said, that he engraved a set of plates, representing the *Prophets and Sibyls*; I have already spoken of them in the Essay. Basan, on what authority I know not, tells us, that he marked these plates with a *monogram*, composed of an A. and a B. joined together: this mark, however, I never saw.

MARTIN BOUCHE.
Flourished, 1680.

This artist seems to have been chiefly employed for the booksellers; and portraits, I believe, constituted the greater part of his works. He worked almost entirely with the graver; and his style is neat but stiff. His portraits, however, are not destitute of merit. Among the rest is that of *John Fenwick*, a jesuit, who was executed at Tyburn, A. D. 1679, a small upright plate. He also engraved the portraits of several other *jesuits*, who suffered in England at the same time. They are in general represented with a knife sticking in the breast, emblematical, I suppose of their sufferings. To that of *Thomas Harcott* he signs his name "Martin Bouche sc. Antwerpiæ;" from whence I conclude he resided at Antwerp; of which place, it is probable, he was a native. When he does not sign his name at full length, he substitutes the initials, according to professor Christ in this manner, M. B.

P. P. BOUCHE.
Flourished, 1693.

He was probably a relation of the artist above mentioned; and perhaps resided in England. This name, however, is found affixed to some of the plates of *ornaments for iron work*, published by J. Tijou in London, A. D. 1693.

JOHN BOUCHER.
Flourished,

A native of France, born at Bourges. He was a painter, and, according to Florent le Comte, etched five plates; but the subjects are not specified.

FRANCIS BOUCHER.
Born, 1706. Died, 1770.

A modern French painter, whose works were held in high estimation. He was a man of great fertility of invention; but in my opinion he was defective in correctness, and grandeur of design. We have some few slight etchings by him, as well from his own compositions, as from those of other masters.

BOUCHARDON.
Flourished,

He was son to Bouchardon, the sculptor at Paris; and engraved, from the

the drawings of his father, a set of *female academy figures*, in a slight, feeble style; and signs his name, "Bouchardon junior sculp."

R. BOUD.
Flourished,

An engraver of portraits of no great eminence. He worked chiefly, I suppose, for the booksellers. Among other portraits by him, I have seen that of *Henry Goltzius the painter*. It is all graved in a stiff, unpleasing style; and the drawing is particularly defective in the figure of *Fame*, which he has represented flying over the head of the artist with a laurel crown.

BOUGEY.
Flourished,

A name prefixed to a small copy of the *battle of Constantine*, from Raphael, executed in a style greatly resembling that of Theodore de Brye.

JOHN BOULANGER.
Flourished, 1657.

This engraver, who flourished towards the end of the last century, was, I believe, a native of France. His first manner of engraving, appears to have been copied, in some degree, from that of Francis de Poilly; but soon after he adopted one of his own, which, though not original, he however greatly improved: He finished the faces, hands and all the naked parts of his figures very neatly with dots, instead of strokes, or strokes and dots. The effect is singular enough, and by no means unpleasing; only, in some few instances he has opposed the coarse graving of his draperies, and back-ground, so violently to the neater work of the flesh, that the outline of the latter is thereby rendered hard, and the general appearance of it flat and chalky. This style of engraving has been carried to its greatest perfection in the present day, particularly in England. He did not draw the naked parts of his figures correctly, or with fine taste. His draperies are apt to be heavy, and the folds not well marked. However, his best prints possess much merit, and are deservedly held in great esteem. I shall mention the following:

A *holy family*, a middling sized plate, from Fran. Corlebet.

Virgin and Child, from Simon Vouet, half figure, a small upright plate, dated 1657.

The *pompous cavalcade* upon the day the French king, Louis XIV. came of age; a large print, length-ways, from Chaveau. In these three prints the flesh is finished with strokes in his finest manner, and in those which follow with dots only.

The *Virgin with the infant Christ*. The child is holding some pinks; hence the print is called the *Virgin of the Pinks*: a middling sized upright plate, from Raphael.

The *Virgin de Passau*, a middling sized upright plate, from Salario.

Christ carrying his cross, a middling sized upright plate, from Nicolas Mignard.

A dead

A dead Chrift, fupported by Jofeph of Arimathea, a large upright plate. Alfo a variety of portraits: among the reft, that of *Charles the Second* of England. He alfo engraved from Leonardo de Vinci, Guido, Champagne, Stella, Coypell, and other great mafters; and feveral from his own defigns. In figning his name to his plates, he frequently joins the J. to a fmall b. in fuch a manner, as greatly to refemble an H. Hence thofe, who are not better informed, read it *Houlanger*; it has been often fo inferted in printfellers catalogues.

MATTHEW BOULANGER.
Flourifhed,

An obfcure engraver of portraits, probably a relation of the laft mentioned artift. Among other things, I have feen by him the portrait of *Raymundus Vievffens*, Med. Doc. a fmall oval plate. It is all graved in a ftiff, heavy ftyle, and very poorly drawn.

BON DE BOULLOGNE.
Born, 1649. Died, 1717.

A painter of no fmall eminence, born at Paris, A. D. 1649. From his father, Louis de Boullogne he learned the firft principles of painting; but went to Rome, in order to perfect himfelf from the works of the beft mafters. He abode in Italy five years. He excelled in hiftory and portrait. His talents for copying the pictures of the great Italian painters, were fo very extraordinary, that he frequently deceived the greateft judges. He died at Paris, A. D. 1717, aged 68. We have three etchings by him: the firft a fpecies of *almanack*; the fecond, *St. John in the defert*, a large upright plate; the third, *St. Bruno feated in a landfcape*, its companion: all from his own compofitions.

LOUIS DE BOULLOGNE.
Born, 1654. Died, 1734.

This artift, who was born at Paris, was the younger brother of the preceding, and, like him, learned from his father the firft principles of painting; and afterwards went to Rome to complete his ftudies. His works, on his return, were fo much efteemed, that Louis XIV. honoured him with the order of St. Michael; and after the death of Antony Coypell, appointed him his principal painter. He chiefly excelled in hiftorical and allegorical fubjects. He died at Paris, 1734, aged 80 years. By him we have a few flight etchings. They are fpirited and free, though by no means correctly drawn, or equal in effect to what might have been expected from his hand. Among them, are the following:

The *fcourging of St. Andrew*, from Paolo Veronefe, a middling fized plate, length-ways

The *martyrdom of St. Peter*, a middling fized upright plate, from a compofition of his own.

The *martyrdom of St. Paul*, its companion, the fame.

E. DE BOULONOIS.
Flourished,

He is said to have been a printseller and designer, as well as an engraver. He flourished apparently about the middle of the sixteenth century; and his chief, if not entire employment was engraving of portraits, which he executed in a neat, dry style, without much taste, and entirely with the graver. I shall notice the following portraits only:

Christiophorus Plantinus Turonensis, an octavo plate, apparently for a book.
Georgius Buchananus, the same, " Esme de Boulonois fecit."
Lady Jane Grey, the same.
Hans or John Holbein the painter.   *Anthony More*, the painter, &c.

SEBASTIAN BOURDON.
Born, 1616.   Died, 1671.

He was born at Montpellier, A. D. 1616; and the first rudiments of painting were taught him by his father, who was a painter on glass. He afterwards studied at Paris, under an artist of very little note. At eighteen he went to Italy, to perfect himself in the knowledge of drawing, and other requisites of the art. The great esteem his works are generally held in, sufficiently prove, how profitably he applied himself to his studies. His chief faults, are want of force in the colouring, and correctness in the outline, but these are greatly overbalanced by the beauties of his composition, and the lively fertility of his imagination. His etchings (which are numerous) are executed in a bold, masterly style; and much more finished, than those we generally meet with, from the point of the painter. They convey a very clear idea of his manner of painting. The lights are broad, the draperies are set with great taste, and the folds well marked. Sometimes perhaps they are a little too dark and hard upon the lights. The heads of his figures are very expressive; and though his drawing upon the naked parts is often censurable for its incorrectness, yet he knew how to give a pleasing turn to them which renders them constantly agreeable. The back-grounds to his plates are always finely conceived, and executed in a grand style, which gives a consequence frequently to the whole composition. The etchings by this celebrated master are justly held in the highest estimation, by the generality of collectors; yet as they are by no means uncommon, I shall content myself with mentioning only a few of them, all from his own compositions.

The *seven acts of mercy*, seven large plates, length-ways.

The *flight into Egypt, and the return from thence*, six small plates, length-ways.

Several other subjects of the *Virgin and Child*; in one of which, a small plate length-ways, is seen a woman washing linen : thence it is distinguished by the name of the washer-woman.

The *return of the ark*, a middling sized plate, length-ways, said to be very scarce.

The *baptism of the Eunuch*, a small upright plate.

Twelve large landscapes, which are very spirited and fine prints.

PETER

PETER BOURDON.
Flourished, 1703.

I have seen a small book of *ornaments with figures, for goldsmiths and jewellers*, very neatly executed, and entirely with the graver. The plates are marked, " Peter Bourdon inv. et fecit :" this book was published at Paris, A. D. 1703.

DU BOURG.
Flourished,

He engraved in Holland, according to Basan, several pretty *vignettes*, and other *small compositions*; many of them from his own designs, in the style of Bernard Picart.

J. BOURQUET.
Flourished, 1723.

A goldsmith, resident at Paris, who engraved, in a very neat style, a set of small *plates of ornaments for goldsmiths and jewellers*, which he published A. D. 1723.

BOURGUIGNON or BORGOGNONE. See CORTESI.

FRANCIS BOURLIER.
Flourished,

A native of France, who, according to Basan, was a painter, and flourished in the last century. He etched several plates; among others, *Moses saved from the water by Pharoah's daughter*, a large plate, length-ways, from Francis Perrier. He also engraved from Giulio Romano, and a variety of other masters.

FRANCIS BOUT.
Flourished,

Basan, on what authority I know not, calls this painter Peter Bout. He was a native of Flanders, and flourished about the beginning of the present century. His chief employment was painting figures for the landscapes of Bodewyns, with which artist he worked conjointly. There are, however, some slight etchings by his hand, from his own compositions; namely, the *bride conducted to the church*, a middling sized plate, length-ways; and a *country market*, its companion; four small plates, length-ways, representing a *great number of figures skating*.

FREDERIC BOUTATS.
Flourished, 1555.

He was, I believe, chiefly a publisher; as such, I have seen his name to a print,

print, reprefenting the *Virgin and Child*, with St. John, dated 1555; which was perhaps engraved by himfelf. There is alfo a fmall plate, lengthways, reprefenting, *gentlemen and ladies playing at cards*. It is executed with the graver, in a neat, ftiff ftyle, but not entirely deftitute of merit; and fubfcribed " F. Bouttats fecit;" it appears to be older than the works of FREDERIC BOUTTATS, who flourifhed towards the middle of the laft century. His fole employment, I believe, was engraving book plates, and portraits, of the laft we have a great number by him. They are in general, neatly performed with the graver only, in a taftelefs incorrect ftyle. Among them are feveral of the portraits of the *painters, and other artifts*, publifhed at Antwerp (where the engraver refided at that time) by John Meyffens, A. D. 1649: the beft of which appears to me to be that of Henry Hondius.

GASPAR BOUTTATS.
Flourifhed, 1621.

He refided, I believe, at Antwerp, and was probably of the fame family with the preceding artift. His works are chiefly, if not entirely, (light etchings, and they have no great merit to recommend them. I fhall only notice the plates, which compofe a large folio volume, etched by him from the defigns of John Peters, confifting of views of *Jerufalem, and the furrounding country*; of *Antioch, of Mecca, and other parts of Afia*. They are executed in a heavy, dark ftyle, without effect; and the figures, introduced, are very flight and incorrect. Bafan fays, he alfo etched feveral plates from Wouvermans; but thofe I never faw.

PHILIBERT BOUTTATS.
Flourifhed, 1649.

If not a native of Antwerp, it is evident, that he refided there, and, without doubt, was of the fame family with the artifts, mentioned in the preceding articles. His engravings appear to be chiefly copies for books, and confifted principally of portraits, which are far lefs valuable than numerous. Several of the plates for the folio collection of the *heads of the painters*, publifhed at Antwerp, 1649, are by him. To the portrait of *Le Brun*, which feems to be one of his beft prints, he fubfcribes his name, " Phi. " Bouttats junior fecit Antwerpiæ." The word junior may perhaps imply, that there was another artift of the fame name and family, otherwife the diftinction will appear to be unneceffary. To the portrait of *John. III. king of Poland*, he writes both his names at length, Philibert Bouttats, without the word junior; but the ftyle of engraving feems to be the fame with thofe above-mentioned.

PETER BALTHAZER BOUTTATS.
Flourifhed, 1707.

Some bad engravings by this artift, fays Bafan, were publifhed at Antorff,

BOU [138] BOY

A. D. 1707. According to profeffor Chrift, he fometimes omitted his name, and figned the initials to his plates in this manner, P. B. B. F. the F. as ufual, ftanding for fecit.

BOUSONNET. See STELLA.

DANIEL BOUTEMYE.
Flourifhed,
He is cited by Florent le Comte, as excelling particularly in engraving of *Vafes*. I have never feen any of his works.

A. BOUYS.
Flourifhed, 1720.
He was a painter, and the difciple of Francis de Troy. He alfo engraved feveral portraits in mezzotinto; but he never attained to any great degree of perfection in that art. Among the reft of his prints are the following: The portrait of *J. Bap. Maffilon*, from a picture of his own; that of *M. de Bofe*, the fame; and that of *Marais* a famous mufician, the fame. He alfo engraved feveral plates after the pictures of De Troy, &c.

E. BOWEN.
Flourifhed,
This engraver refided, I believe, in England. His works, however, are fo very indifferent, that they do not merit a particular defcription. He feems chiefly to have been confined to the loweft clafs of engraving, as *ornaments for fhop bills*, &c.

SAMUEL BOYCE.
Born, Died, 1775.
He was author of feveral poetical pieces; and to him is attributed the portrait of *Edward Ruffel, earl of Orford*.

JOHN BAPTIST BOYER, MARQUIS D'AIGUILLES.
Flourifhed, 1700.
This celebrated nobleman was counfellor and procurator general to the parliament of Aix in Provence. Being exceedingly fond of the arts, he collected in Italy, during a voyage which he made thither, a great number of pictures, fculptures, drawings, prints, &c. and he was himfelf at once a connoiffeur, defigner, painter and engraver. He caufed to be publifhed two folio volumes of prints, engraved from his own pictures, chiefly by Sebaftian Barras and James Coelmans. In the firft edition of this work there were fix prints, engraved by himfelf, and a feventh from a picture of his own painting, they are as follow:
The *marriage of St. Catherine*, from Andrea del Sarto.

Two

Two figures of *Christ when young*, on one plate.
A *landscape*, from Brecourt; another *landscape*, its companion, from the same.
These four plates are engraved with strokes.
St. John, from Manfredi.
A *small bust of a man*.
These two plates are engraved in mezzotinto.
The seventh, by Coelmans, is the portrait of *Honore Moulin* playing upon the lute. All these plates being lost, the impressions are now become very rare.
In the second edition there are three others by himself.
The frontispiece engraved by Coelmans, is after a design made by the marquis, dated 1698. Those engraved by him are as follows:
The portrait of the *mistress of Paolo Veronese*. A *Magdalen*, from J. F. Romanelli. The *adoration of the Magi*, from a composition of his own.

GIOVANNA BATISTA BRACELLI.
Born, Died, 1607.

This artist was a painter, and a native of Genoa. He engraved, in a slight, stiff style, the plates of *architecture* for a work, published at Rome by Jacomo Barozzio, an architect of the last century. He signs his name, *Joan. Baptista Bracellus Flo. incidebat Romæ.*

NICOLUS BRAED.
Flourished,

The name of an obscure engraver of very little merit, which I found affixed to a small upright print, representing *Christ before Pilate*, after Tintoretto. It was published by J. Maetham, whose style of engraving it slightly resembles

C. DE BRAEN.
Flourished,

An obscure engraver of portraits, by whom, among others, we have that of *Peter Poiret*, from Verkolye. The word *junior* is added to the name of this engraver, to distinguish it probably from some person of the same family, who might be an artist also.

FRANCIS BRAGGE.
Flourished,

The name of an obscure English engraver, mentioned by the Hon. Mr. Walpole, on the authority of Mr. Thoresby. I have never seen any of his works.

AMBROSIUS BRAM.
Flourished,

A name affixed as the engraver of a large print, length-ways, entitled,

Benedictione del Pontifice nela Piaza de Santo Pietro. There is a great number of figures introduced in this composition, which are executed in a flight, incorrect, heavy style, bearing some resemblance to that usually adopted by Tempesta. It is marked, "AMBROSIUS BRAM. F." from a painting, as it appears, of Claud. Duchetti. I by no means pretend to say, that this is not the abreviation of the name Brambini, which artist is spoken of a little lower.

BRAMANTE.

Born, 1444. Died, 1517.

This great artist was born at Castel du Sante, in the dutchy of Urbino, A. D. 1444. His genius for the arts discovered itself in the very early part of his life; but as his parents were by no means in affluent circumstances, his progress in them for want of proper assistance might be in some measure retarded. It is likely that he went to Milan, about the year 1470, when he was 26 years of age. He certainly spent much time in that city, where he saw the works of Leonard de Vinci; From Milan he went to Rome. Vasari speaks of him with the highest commendation, and informs us that he was a poet, a painter, a musician, and, above all, a most skilful architect. Though he is not mentioned as an engraver, yet the knowledge and practice of this art may be added to his other accomplishments. Dr. Monro has in his collection a very curious print, which is two feet three inches and an half high, by one foot eight inches wide; representing a perspective *view of the inside of a magnificent church or temple.* The mechanical part of the engraving is executed exactly in the style, adopted by Andrea Mantegna; that is, with the strokes running from one corner of the plate to the other, without any crossing. On a column near the altar is written, in large capitals, BRAMANTIS FECIT IN MLO; which Dr. Monro conceives should be read, *Bramantis fecit in Milano.* As he resided a considerable time at Milan, where he determined to follow architecture, he might there have learned the art of engraving, for we certainly know that it was practised at Florence, as early, at least, as the year 1464. Bramante died A. D. 1517, aged 73.

AMBROSIUS BRAMBINI.

Flourished,

He engraved, says professor Christ, some plates from the designs of Dominicus Fontana, concerning the elevation of the obelisks at Rome. See the mark attributed to him on the plate at the end of the volume.

SEBASTIAN BRANDT.

Flourished,

A man of letters, who flourished in the fifteenth century, and on whom the doctors degree was conferred. Le Comte and others, mistaking the words of Abbé Marolles, have called him an engraver, and attributed to him the wooden cuts after Locher, for the book, entitled, *Stultifera Navis,* or the Ship

Ship of Fools. But this mistake has been already considered under the name *Bergman*, to which the reader is referred.

R. BRANT.
Flourished,

The name of a designer and engraver, affixed to a middling size upright plate, representing the *Virgin and Child*, with Joseph and an angel. It is etched in a dark slight style, something resembling that adopted by Castiglione, but very incorrectly drawn.

G. BRASNI.
Flourished, 1768.

A modern designer, who resided some time in London, where he made a bad mezzotinto of the *present king of Denmark*, whilst he was in England.

BRAUWER. See BROUWER.

JACOB DE BRAY.
Flourished, 1664.

By this artist, who was a painter born at Haerlem, I have seen a small portrait, very spiritedly cut in wood, of *Salomon de Bray*, his father: It is marked with his name, and dated 1664.

J. B. BREBES.
Flourished, 1682.

This artist was, I believe, a native of France; at least, he appears to have resided at Paris, where he engraved some of the plates for the large folio work, entitled *Les Edifices Antiques de Rome*, drawn by Antoine Desgodetz, which was published 1682. They are all graved in a very neat style, without much taste. He also engraved from Sebastian Bourdon, and other masters; but his historical prints are by no means excellent.

PETER BREBIETTE.
Flourished, 1625.

This artist was a native of France, born at Mante upon the Seine. He was a painter of some degree of eminence; and, as an engraver, he is also very well known. We have many slight, spirited etchings by him, which prove him to have been a man of genius, and great fertility of invention. His compositions are frequently very agreeable, and abound, in general, with figures, which, though not correctly drawn, are well grouped, and executed in a masterly manner. Among others are the following:

The *martyrdom of St. George*, a small upright plate from Paolo Veronese.
Paradise, a large print, length-ways, on two plates, from Old Palma.

A holy

A *holy family*, with St. John, whose foot is upon the cradle, from Raphael, a small upright plate.

The *Virgin kneeling by the side of the infant Christ*, attended by two angels, a middling sized upright plate, from a design of his own.

Two small plates, length-ways, one representing the *battle of the Lapithæ*; the other the *death of the children of Niobe*, from his own designs; the latter is dated 1625.

A variety of friezes, which possess great merit, and other compositions of the same kind, from his own designs. He also engraved many other plates from the paintings, &c. of the great masters. The letters P. B. included in a heart, surmounted with a sort of figure resembling a 4, are attributed to him by the author of the Abecedario. But, I think, the matter rather doubtful. See the mark copied on the plate at the end of the volume.

CHRISTOPHER BRECHTEL.
Flourished,

This engraver, and another named JOACHIM BRECHTEL, are cited by professor Christ; but he has not specified any of their works. The former, however, he tells us, was an engraver on copper, and marked his plates C. B. The latter used the letters I. B. These initials were used by so many masters, several of them living nearly at the same time, and working much in the same style, that it is a total impossibility to separate them with any certainty, so as to attribute to each those prints only, which belong to them.

G. V. BREEN.
Flourished,

An artist, who has escaped the notice of the generality of authors on the subject of engraving. He worked entirely with the graver; and very probably received his first instructions from James de Gheyn, whose style he seems, at least, to have adopted, and though he never equalled that artist, either in the correctness of his drawing, or the execution of the mechanical part of the engraving, yet his prints are not devoid of merit. I shall notice the following plates, only:

A woman with a basket of eggs, marketing with a man, who has a basket of fowls; a bridge and other buildings are in the back ground; a middling sized plate, length-ways, from Claus Clock. *A man and woman walking, with a figure of envy pulling the cloaths from the back of a lady*; the same, from the same. *A man seated, to whom another is showing a slipper*; *two men are disputing at a distance*; *one of whom is drawing his sword*; *and near them is represented a lady, purchasing some cloth*, a small plate, length-ways, from Karl Van Manderen. A set of small long prints, representing *sea-ports with shipping* from C. Nicolai. The G. the V. and the B. are joined together in a sort of cypher, in the manner represented in the plate at the end of the volume.

BARTHOLOMEW BREENBERG.
Born, 1620. Died, 1660.

This excellent painter is best known by the name of Bartolomeo, an appellation

pellation bestowed upon him, for distinction sake, by the society of Flemish painters at Rome, called *Bentvogels*. He was born at Utrecht; but in the early part of his life went to Rome. His studies in the art of painting were attended with such success, that his pictures were held in the highest estimation. He greatly excelled in landscapes, and these he enriched with historical subjects. The figures and animals, which he introduced, were very spirited, and drawn in a masterly manner; especially when they were not larger than the size, in which he usually painted them. He died 1660, aged 40 years. We have, etched by him, a set of twenty-four *views, and landscapes, ornamented with ruins*, &c. from his own designs. His mark when he did not sign his name, according to professor Christ, was " B. B. F." the F. as usual, standing for fecit.

ANGELICA BREGEON.
Flourished,

This lady, who, according to Basan, was the wife of Tillard, a modern French artist, was herself an engraver. We have by her hand *a youth learning the art of drawing*; a small upright plate, from Carlo Vanloo.

D. V. BREMDEN.
Flourished,

An artist of no very great eminence, who worked entirely with the graver, in a style sufficiently neat, but stiffly executed. The drawing also of the figures is very incorrect. We have by him a small plate, lengthways, representing *ladies and gentlemen at an entertainment*, from S. de Vliger. He also engraved from A. Vanden Venne. When he did not sign his name at length, he substituted the cypher, which is copied on the plate at the end of the volume.

V. BRENNER.
Flourished, 1708.

An engraver of *portraits*, who flourished at the beginning of the present century; but his works by no means merit a separate list.

FREDERIC BRENTEL.
Flourished, 1608.

Professor Christ reads this name Brendel; but the artist himself signs it Brentel, to the pompous parade at the funeral of *Charles III. duke of Lorrain*, which is well designed by him, and etched in a slight style, but with great spirit. The procession consists of a great many plates, these, bound up together with the description, make a large folio volume. They were published at Nancy, A. D. 1608. This engraver frequently substitutes the letters F. B. when he does not sign his name at length. In Florent le Comte, by a typographical

typographical error, the name is Breutel; but it is evidently meant for the same artist.

HANS or JOHN BRESANG.
Flourished, 1619.

Bresang was a native of Germany. He is ranked in the class of little masters, because the prints which he executed, in general, were small. He chiefly engraved on wood; but there are some copper-plates also, which have his cypher, and from the date appear to belong to him. Among other prints attributed to him, are the *twelve apostles, with Christ and St. Paul,* dated 1619; and a set of small historical plates, taken from the *New Testament.* See his mark or cypher, composed of an H. a G. and a B. on the plate at the end of the volume. Great care must be taken not to confound this engraver with another, superior to him, called Hans Baldung, who used the same mark and flourished a century before him.

COMTE DE BRETEUIL.
Flourished, 1752.

This gentleman, according to Basan, was a great lover of the arts, who for his amusement etched several small plates, from Berchem, and other masters.

CHARLES BRETHERTON.
Born, Died, 1783.

He was the son of James Bretherton of Bond Street, (well known to the public for his etchings, after the designs of Mr. Bunbury.) The chief of this young artist's performances in the engraving line were *views, landscapes,* and *portraits.* He also designed several subjects, which prove him to have been a man of genius; particularly *Kate of Aberdeen,* a half sheet circle, engraved by Tompkins. He died in a decline, July, A. D. 1783.

ANDRE BRETSCHNEIDER.
Flourished, 1610.

An artist cited by professor Christ, who, he tells us, resided at Leipsick, where he worked from 1600 to 1620. See the mark, attributed to this engraver, at the end of the volume.

PETER BREUGHEL.
Born, 1510. Died, 1570.

This artist is usually called *old Breugbel,* to distinguish him from his son, who was also a painter of considerable eminence. He was born at Breda, and learned the first principles of painting from Peter Cock; after which he went to Italy, to improve himself from the study of the works of the greatest masters.

ters. He excelled chiefly in landscapes, and droll subjects, resembling those of Jerom Bosche. He also, for his amusement, is said to have engraved some few plates of landscapes and grotesque subjects, which according to professor Christ, he marked with the initials of his name, P. B.

PETER BREUGHEL the younger, was the son of the above-mentioned artist, and named Hellish Breughel, from the horrible subjects he delighted to represent. He engraved also, according to M. Heineken; but his works are not specified. He died 1642.

JOHN BREUGHEL, brother to the preceding artist, distinguished by the name of Velvet Breughel, was a painter of greater eminence than either his father or his brother. He particularly excelled in flowers, fruit, and landscapes, with small figures. He died, according to the best accounts, 1625, aged 52. To him is attributed some small plates of *landscapes*, &c. &c.

BRICART.
Flourished,

A modern engraver, who resided, I believe, in France. He is mentioned, however, by Basan, by whom we are informed, that he engraved several prints, from Joan. Baptista Santerre and others; the subjects of which he has not specified.

PAUL BRILL.
Born, 1554. Died, 1626.

This great artist was born at Antwerp, A. D. 1554. His excellence, as a landscape painter, is so generally known, that it needs no repetition here. He died at Rome, A. D. 1626, aged 70 years. He etched several *landscapes* in a very spirited, masterly style, of which four large ones are found in the set, published by Nieulant, his disciple.

MATTHEW BRILL, the elder brother of the above-mentioned artist, was an eminent painter of landscape, and history; and, according to M. Heineken, he also engraved.

BRILLON.
Flourished,

A modern French engraver, by whom, according to Basan, we have several prints, from Watteau and other masters.

J. BRIOT.
Flourished, 1632.

An artist of very moderate abilities, who worked entirely with the graver, imitating the style of Jerom Wierix. He succeeded tolerably well with respect to the neatness of the mechanical part of his engravings; but in drawing, harmony, and effect, he was greatly deficient. His productions are stiff and tasteless, without the least mark of genius. He appears chiefly to have worked

worked from his own defigns, which, however do him no great honour. I fhall only notice,

The *feven theological and cardinal virtues*, on feven fmall folio plates.

A fet of prints for *Ovid's Metamorphofis*, fmall plates length-ways.

The *fybils*, a fet of fmall circular plates.

A variety of *frontifpieces*, and other *ornaments* for books, &c.

N. BRIOT is alfo mentioned as an engraver, by profeffor Chrift, and other authors; and to him is attributed a fet of *dreffes*, &c. from the defigns of Saint Igny.

BRIRIETTE.
Flourifhed,

The name of an obfcure artift, which I found affixed to fome flight fpirited etchings. To his name he adds the words, *inv. et fecit*; from whence we may conclude, that he engraved thefe plates from his own defigns.

BRISSART.
Flourifhed,

The name of an artift affixed to a large whole fheet print, reprefenting a bird's eye view of the *royal palace of Vincennes*, which is very flightly etched by him, from a drawing of his own. It is fufficiently neat, but totally devoid of effect. He alfo engraved feveral plates, from the drawings of J. B. Santerre.

GIOVANNA MARIAE BRIXIENSIS, or DA BRESCIA.
Flourifhed, 1562.

This fingular artift, a native of Brefcia in Italy, was an ecclefiaftic of the order of the Carmelites. He painted, at the beginning of the prefent century, the hiftory of *Elifha* and *Elijah*, for the monaftery to which he belonged. For his amufement, he alfo took up the graver; and we have feveral prints by his hand, which evidently prove him to have been a man of ability, though he never reached to any fuperior degree of perfection. His ufual ftyle of engraving bears fome refemblance to that of Marc Antonio, fufficiently neat, and croffed with hatchings upon the fhadows; but there are fome few of his plates, in which he has followed the manner of Andrea Mantegna; and the ftrokes, which form the fhadows, are laid from one corner of the plate to the other, without any hatching, or crofs ftrokes, thefe are commonly among the artifts diftinguifhed by the name of *fecond ftrokes*.

Florent le Comte, and others, who have followed him, have fallen into a ftrange miftake, and attributed to this artift thofe prints which are marked with a monogram, compofed of an I. a B. an A. and an M. which certainly belonged to John Baptifta of Mantua, of the fame family as George Ghifli. See the account of this artift under Ghifli.

I fhall only mention the following prints by this artift: A *miracle of St. Gregory*, where a boy is reftored to life. It is thirteen inches high by nine wide; and the name is affixed in this manner: OPUS. FRS. IO. MARIAE BRIXIENSIS

XIENSIS. OR. CARMELITARUM. MCCCCCII. The mechanical part of the engraving of this print is executed in a fort of mixed ftyle, between that of Marc Antonio, and of Andrea Mantegna; but it is by no means equal to either. The drawing is defective, efpecially in the extremities of the figures, which are heavy, and not well marked. A large upright plate, reprefenting the *Virgin, feated upon the clouds*, with St. John Baptift, St. Jerom, and three ecclefiaftics of the order of the Carmelites, at the bottom, dated alfo 1502.

GIOVANNA ANTONIO BRIXIENSIS, or DA BRESCIA.
Flourifhed, 1509.

An artift of the fame family with the preceding. He was apparently a difciple of the fchool of Mantegna; for the ftyle of engraving of that artift he almoft conftantly adopted; and the mechanical part of the execution of his plates is ftill more neat and regular. But the advantage he may be faid to have gained hereby over Mantegna, is abundantly over-balanced by the defectivenefs of his outlines, and the heavinefs of the extremities of his figures, which are ufually very poorly drawn. I fhall notice by him,

The *fcourging of Chrift*, a large upright plate; with the name, Io. ANTON. BRIXIAN. on a tablet, dated 1503. The fecond impreffions are marked 1509.

Hercules ftrangling a lion, marked D. HERC. IN. VICTO, and with his name.

A middling fized upright plate, *Hercules and Antæus*, the fame.

A *white horfe*, like that by Albert Durer; the back-ground only varied in the latter. In this he has intermixed fome hatching: it is marked with his name, and dated 1505, a fmall upright plate.

St. Peter, a fmall upright plate. In this he approaches nearer to the ftyle of engraving adopted by Marc Antonio: it is marked Jo. AN.

FRANCESCO BRIZIO, or BRICCIO.
Born, 1574. Died, 1623.

This artift excelled in painting architecture, and landfcapes. He was born at Bologna, A. D. 1574, and received his firft inftructions in the art of painting from Pafferotti; but completed his ftudies under Ludovico Carracci. It is faid, that he frequently affifted Agoftino Caracci in the plates, which he engraved. Perhaps he might; at leaft, it is certain, that he generally worked with the graver only in the fame ftyle; and in the mechanical part of the execution fometimes equalled him; but in correctnefs of outline, beauty, or expreffion, never. We have alfo fome few etchings by him. Among the prints by this artift I fhall mention the following:

A *holy family*, from Corregio, a large upright plate, arched at the top.

St. Roch, from Parmigiano, a middling fized upright plate.

The *flight into Egypt*, a fmall upright plate from Ludovico Caracci.

Chrift and the woman of Samaria, a middling fized plate, length-ways, from Agoftino Carracci, engraved, A. D. 1610. At the fame time, Guido etched the *charity of St. Roch*, from Annibale Caracci.

CRISPIN

CRISPIN VANDEN BROECK.
Flourished, 1590.

He was a native of Antwerp, and a painter of some eminence in the historical line. We have a considerable number of prints, engraved from his designs, which prove him to have been a man of genius, and great fertility of invention. His usual mark was a cypher, composed of a C. a V. and a B. joined together, which is copied on the plate at the end of the volume. He also is said to have engraved; and among other things attributed to him, is the *circumcision of Christ*, a middling sized circular print, in chiaro-scuro. The outline is etched in a bold, free manner, on copper; and the block of wood, which produces the lighter tints, is so contrived as to imitate the hatchings of white chalk upon the lights. It is marked with his cypher.

BARBARA VANDEN BROECK.
Flourished, 1600.

She was daughter to the above artist. It is highly probable, that she learned to draw of her father: but from whom she received instructions in the art of engraving is very uncertain; perhaps in the school of the Colaerts, who engraved many plates from her father's designs. However, the progress she made was such, as does no small credit to her abilities. I shall mention, in the first place, a middling sized upright plate, representing the *last judgment*, into which is introduced a great variety of figures. She has executed this plate entirely with the graver, and copied the style of Martin Rota with great success. The figures, in general, are well drawn; the heads expressive; and the other extremities marked with great judgment. It wants effect, from the lights being too equally powerful, and too much scattered; but this was an error, that almost all the engravers, and many of the painters of that age, were very apt to run into. It is marked at the bottom, " Crispin Vanden " Broeck inv. et Barbara filia Crispine sculpsit." I shall notice also a *holy family*, with St. John and several angels. This is marked with her father's cypher, as described above; and to it is added, " B. filia sculp." It is a small upright plate, dated A. D. 1600. Another *holy family*, with St. John kneeling, and angels attendant upon them, the same, and marked as above. This plate was published by Hondius, A. D. 1621.

J. VAN BROEDELET.
Flourished, 1700.

A Dutch artist, who flourished at the begining of the present century, by whom we have several mezzotintos. Among the rest, *Cephalus and Procris*, from Gerard Hoet, a middling sized upright plate, companion to *Venus and Adonis*, engraved in mezzotinto by Verkolie, from the same master.

BRO   [149]   BRO

C. DE BROEN.
Flourished,

An artist of no great merit, whose chief employment was engraving of portraits for the bookfellers, &c. To some plates the name is signed, " C. de Broen, jun." as to the portrait of *Piere Poicet*, from N. Verkolie.

JOHN VAN BRONKHORST.
Born, 1603.

This artist was born at Utrecht, and, after having studied under several masters, entered the school of Cornelius Poelemburg, whose style of painting he imitated with great success. He painted both history and landscapes; and his pictures, which are very highly finished, are held in great estimation. He amused himself with the point; and some *landscapes* from Poelemburg, together with other subjects from his own compositions, are attributed to him. His mark, according to the generality of authors, was a cypher, composed of a *J.* a *G.* and a *B.* But the use of the second letter, if the cypher really belonged to him, I know not. See the mark copied on the plate at the end of the volume.

JOHN VAN BROOKS.
Flourished, 1742.

He was a native, as I have heard, of Ireland. He engraved in mezzotinto. His works, however, do him no great credit as an artist, either with respect of the drawing, or the execution. His prints are chiefly portraits; but there is a large historical mezzotinto by him, representing the *battle of the Boyne*, after Wyke. Among his portraits, are the following: *Hugh Boulter, archbishop of Armagh, and primate of Ireland*, from F. Bindon, a large whole length. *William Aldrich, lord mayor of Dublin*, a half sheet print, dated 1742, &c.

R. BROOKSHAW.
Flourished, 1770.

A very modern engraver in mezzotinto, who resided in London, and executed several portraits; among the rest, that of *Mr. Bergeret*, after Cotes, *Lady Erskine, General Paoli*, &c.

BROON.
Flourished,

A name mentioned by Mr. Evelyn in his *Sculptura*, as an engraver. I do not recollect to have seen any of his works: perhaps it is the same artist as C. de Broen, mentioned above.

HANS

HANS or JOHN BROSAMER.
Flourished, 1545.

A native of Fulda in Germany. He is one of those artists, who on account of the smallness of their engravings, are ranked in the class of *little masters*. It is impossible, at this distance of time, to ascertain the school, in which he learned the principles of the art of design and engraving. His style sometimes bears a resemblance to that of Aldegrever; but, in general, he has finished his draperies and back-ground with small dots between the strokes. His drawing of the naked figure is very deficient. In the mechanical part of his plates he by no means equalled, either that celebrated artist, or John Sebald Beham, his cotemporary. His usual cypher is composed of an H. and a B. joined together in the manner represented on the plate at the end of the volume. I shall only mention the following by him.

The *Philistines coming upon Sampson, after Dalilah had shorn the locks of hair from his head*; a very small plate, length-ways. It is dated 1545, and has the cypher between the two first and the two latter figures of the date; and to it is added his name at full length, *Johannes Brosamer Fuldæ Degens Faciebat*.

Solomon with his wives, adoring the idol, a small upright plate, dated 1545, and marked with the cypher.

The *rape of Helen*, a very small long frieze, dated 1540, marked with the cypher.

Marcus Curtius leaping into the gulph, a small circular plate, marked the same.

Biblia Veteris Testamenti Artificiosis picturis effigiata, Franckfort 1552, a set of small wooden cuts, copied chiefly from the excellent work of the same kind, executed by Hans Holbein, and published at Leyden 1547, with some additions; but by no means equal to the original in spirit, or neatness of execution.

M. V. BROUCK.
Flourished, 1621.

By this artist, who appears to have been a painter, we have a small plate, length-ways, representing *Mercury and Argus*, with the cow in the background. It is a slight etching, very poorly drawn, and destitute of effect. In retouching it with the graver, he has attempted to imitate something of the style of Cornelius Visscher, but without success. It is dated 1621.

ADRIAN BROUWER, or BROWER.
Born, 1608. Died, 1640.

According to the generality of authors, this artist was a native of Oudenarde; though some have affirmed, that he was born at Haerlem, A. D, 1608. He was the disciple of Francis Hals, and proved an excellent artist. The subjects of his pictures were always taken from low life, and represent *Boors fighting, tavern scenes*, and *drunken quarrels*. But these he executed with so much spirit, and transparency of colouring, that his pictures are held in the highest estimation. His levity of temper prevented his continuing with Rubens, who had procured his release from prison at Antwerp, where he had been

BRO [151] BRU

been confined as a fpy. And his debauched manner of living put an end to his days, at the age of 32. By him we have fome few etchings of fuch fubjects, as his pictures ufually reprefented. He frequently figned them with the initials of his name only, thus: H. B. the name Adrian being frequently written with an H.

J. BROUWER.
Flourifhed,

An engraver of portraits of no great eminence. He worked entirely with the graver, and imitated the ftyle of Cornelius Vifcher; but without fuccefs. Among other things by him, is a large portrait of the *emperor Leopold*, from W. Vaillant.

ALEXANDER BROWN.
Flourifhed, 1669.

According to the Hon. Mr. Walpole, we have fome mezzotintos by this artift, who alfo wrote a treatife on the art of painting, drawing, limning, and etching. This treatife is illuftrated with 31 copper-plates in folio, and was firft publifhed at London, A. D. 1669. Thefe plates, Mr. Walpole fuppofes, were engraved by his own hand. This matter however appears to me in a very doubtful light; for he is profeffedly writing a treatife on etching, in the part which may be faid to refer to them, and fpeaks very little concerning the ufe of the graver; now all the plates for this work are executed with the graver entirely, except perhaps the bare outline, which has fometimes the appearance of etching; and they are copied from the book of defigns publifhed by Abraham Bloemart, well known by the name of *Bloemart's Drawing-book*.

There was a modern printfeller of the fame name with the above artift, who publifhed a great variety of mezzotintos; fome of them probably executed by himfelf.

J. BROWN.
Flourifhed, 1676.

He was probably a native of England; and engraved perhaps only for his amufement. According to Ames, we have by him the portrait of *Richard Collins, fupervifor of excife* at Briftol. This plate was engraved at Tedbury.

ROGER BRUGES.
Flourifhed, 1611.

An artift of little note, who affifted Aaron Rathburne in engraving a map of London and Weftminfter; for which they obtained a patent, A. D. 1611.

JOHN VANDER BRUGGEN.
Flourifhed,

This artift, according to M. Heineken, was a native of Flanders, and refided, as it feems, at Bruffels. He is faid to have flourifhed towards the
end

end of the last century. By him we have a large number of mezzotintos; which, however, though not entirely destitute of merit, are such as do him no great honor as an artist. See the mark, which he frequently used, when he did not chuse to sign his name at length, on the plate at the end of the volume. I shall only mention the following prints by him: Several *droll subjects*, from Teniers: among the rest the *tooth-drawer*, an upright half sheet print. The *gold weigher*, copied from Rembrandt Gerretz. The portrait of *Vandyck*, a small upright plate, arched at the top, from a picture painted by that artist. His own *portrait*, a half sheet oval plate from Largilliere. He also engraved from Adrian Brouwer, Ostade, and other masters.

D. P. BRUGGHE.
Flourished,

A very obscure artist, who, etched some few plates, in a style greatly resembling that of Romain la Hooghe, into which he usually introduced a great number of figures; and these he executed very prettily. The other parts of his compositions are stiff and tasteless; and a want of effect generally prevades the whole.

ABRAHAM DE BRUIN.
Flourished, 1570.

This artist was a native of Flanders, and resided at Antwerp. He may be reckoned among the class of artists, distinguished by the appellation of *little masters*, for his engravings, in general, are very small. He worked entirely with the graver, in a neat, stiff style. His drawing is by no means correct; and the extremities of his figures are usually very defective. His prints are evidently rather the productions of labour and assiduity, than of genius. The lights in them are scattered and unharmonized, which destroy the effect, and give them a cold, silvery appearance. But inattention to the chiaro-scuro was rather the fault of the age, than of the artist. His best prints, according to my judgment, are small *friezes*, length-ways, representing the *various modes of hunting, hawking*, &c. Add to these,

A *figure on horseback*, a small upright plate from Sebald Beham. His cypher is here made in a singular manner; the A. and the B. are joined together, and the D. is under the A. it is dated 1566.

A small upright plate, representing *three men conversing together*; one of which has a basket of eggs, copied from Albert Durer. In this the D. is joined to the A. and the B. is under the A. all the letters as well as the date, which is 1567, are reversed.

The *habits of the different nations of Europe, Asia and America*, published in quarto, A.D. 1581.

Pyramus and Thisbe, a small plate, length-ways, from Francis Floris.

The *seven planets*, very small upright plates, dated 1569.

The *five senses*, &c. small plates length-ways, the same.

The *resurrection of Lazarus*, a small upright plate, from a painter whose mark is a C. a V. and a B. joined together: perhaps Crispin Vanden Broech, who

who muſt, however, have been a young man at that time; for it is dated 1571. See all the marks uſed by Abraham de Bruin, copied on the plate at the end of the volume.

NICHOLAS DE BRUIN.
Flouriſhed,

This artiſt was the ſon of Abraham de Bruin mentioned in the foregoing article, and by him we have a great number of prints. He did not follow the example of his father, either in his ſtyle of engraving, or the ſize of the prints which he executed. He imitated Lucas Jacobs of Leyden, whoſe works he appears diligently to have ſtudied; and, engraved large plates. His prints evidently prove, that he had more fertility of invention, than taſte, and he wanted judgment to ſelect ſuch forms only as were beautiful or ſtriking. His compoſitions, which uſually abound with figures, are deſtitute of effect. The lights are too much diffuſed, and the breadth of ſhadow by no means ſufficiently ſtrong to relieve the principal objects from thoſe at a diſtance; by which defect, the harmony is deſtroyed, and the whole appears confuſed and unfiniſhed. He worked entirely with the graver, in a very neat, but laboured ſtyle, copied, as before obſerved, from Lucas Jacobs of Leyden. His drawing is carefully attended to; but it is rather mannered, than correct. The heads of his figures are frequently very expreſſive; and amidſt all the diſadvantages which the artiſt labours under, much ſterling merit is very conſpicuous in his works. As I can only mention a few from the vaſt variety of plates engraved by this maſter: I ſhall confine myſelf to thoſe which are moſt generally eſteemed.

Boys playing, a ſet of ſmall plates, length-ways. In one of them is repreſented two children ſlain by lions: theſe plates are dated 1594.

The *paſſion of our Saviour*, repreſented in a ſet of large plates, lengthways, from his own compoſitions, dated 1612.

Adam and Eve in Paradiſe, the ſame, dated 1600.

Solomon and the queen of Sheba, the ſame.

Solomon adoring the idol, the ſame, dated 1602.

Reſurrection of the dry bones, the ſame.

The *golden age*, from Abraham Bloemart, a large plate, length-ways. This is generally conſidered as his fineſt print: it was admirably copied, in a ſmall circle, by Theodore de Brye.

A ſet of large *landſcapes*, length-ways, from Egidius Coninxlogenſis, J. Savery, D. Vinckboons, &c.

He uſually ſigned his name at length; when he neglected that, he ſubſtituted the initials in this manner, N. de B. and ſeldom omitted the date.

CHARLES LE BRUN.
Born, 1619.   Died, 1690.

This celebrated French artiſt was a native of Paris. He was born, A. D. 1619, and died in that city 1690, aged 71. The *battles of Alexander*, among other eſtimable performances, painted by his hand, are ſufficient teſtimonies of his superior merit; and the excellent engravings from them, by Girard Audran, have contributed not a little to render that merit more generally conspicuous. As a painter, I need not speak of him here; but for his amusement he etched several plates in a dark bold style; and though they are but slightly executed, the hand of the master appears very evidently in them. Among the rest,

The *four times of the day*, small upright plates, from his own designs.
An *infant kneeling upon a cross*, the same.

GABRIEL LE BRUN.
Flourished, 1660.

He was brother to Charles le Brun, mentioned above, and was also a painter; but he never arrived at any great degree of excellency. By him we have also several engravings; among the rest, the *twelve apostles*, from his brother. He also engraved from Tintoret, Augostino Carracci, L. Testelin, and other masters.

F. BRUN.
Flourished,

Perhaps of the same family with the two preceding artists. His name I have found, however, affixed to some portraits, executed entirely with the graver, in a neat style; but very stiff and tasteless. Among the rest are the following:

The *king and queen of Bohemia*, a middling sized upright plate.
Leopold, archduke of Austria, in a small oval.
Frederic Henry, prince of Orange, a large upright plate.

ORAZIO BRUNI.
Flourished,

He was a native of Sienna, and judging from the style in which he engraved, I should conclude, that he flourished towards the middle of the last century. He worked chiefly with the graver, and seems to have aimed at copying the style of Francis de Poilly; but he has by no means happily succeeded. He worked chiefly from Andrea de Ancona, Rutilio Mannini, and other masters; but we have also some few prints by him, which appear to have been executed from his own designs.

ISAAC BRUNN.
Flourished, 1615.

This obscure artist appears to have been a native of Strasburgh in Alsace. By him we have a neat, laboured engraving of the *church at Strasburgh*, to which he signs his name Isaac Brunn Argentiensis, χαλκογραφους, A. D. 1615.

D. BRUNN.

D. BRUNN.
Flourished, 1628.

Apparently this engraver was of the same family with the preceding artist; for he resided at the same place. He worked entirely with the graver, in a neat style, something resembling that of Paul Pontius; but he by no means nearly equalled that great artist. Besides his drawing is exceedingly defective. Among other prints by him, is a *Bacchanal*, from Rubens, a small plate, length-ways. Also a *Bacchanal with boys*, from Vandyck, marked " D. Brunn Arg^{is}. sculp." and dated 1628.

A. F. BRUNN.
Flourished,

A name I found affixed to a small upright plate, neatly engraved, but in a stiff, tastelefs style. It represents *Christ standing on a mountain*, accompanied by an angel, and a female figure representing the church; and Satan, with his accomplices, appear below. It is marked " A. F. Brunn fecit," without any date, or painter's name: hence we may conclude, it is from a design of his own.

FRANCIS BRUNNER.
Flourished, 1620.

This artist was an engraver, and, according to professor Christ, worked under *Aubry*. He engraved, among other things, the figures of the *Sylloge de Luckius*, about the year 1620.

JOHN THEODORE DE BRYE.
Born,   Died, 1598.

This excellent artist was a native of Liege; but he resided chiefly at Franckfort, where he carried on a confiderable commerce in prints. It does not appear, when he was born, nor to what master he owed his instructions in the art of designing and engraving. The works of Sebald Beham were certainly of great service to him. He copied many of the plates engraved by that artist, and seems to me to have principally formed his taste from them. He worked almost entirely with the graver, and seldom called in the affistance of the point. He acquired a neat, free style of engraving, excellently well adapted to small subjects, in which many figures were to be represented; as, *funeral parades, proceffions*, and the like, which he executed in a charming manner. He also drew very correctly. His heads, in general, are spirited and expreffive, and the other extremities of his figures well marked. His back-grounds, though frequently very flight, are touched with a masterly hand. He died, as his sons inform us, in the third part of Boiffard's collection of *portraits*, March 27, 1598; the two first parts of which collection were engraved by himself, affifted by his sons, who afterwards continued it. See his mark on the plate at the end of the volume.

His great works were the following: The plates for the first four volumes of Boiffard's *Roman Antiquities*; the two laſt volumes of which work was completed by his two fons.

The plates for the illuſtration of the defcription of *the Manners and Cuſtoms of the Virginians*, in " *the brief true Report of the new found land of Virginia, publiſhed by Thomas Hariot, fervant to Sir Walter Raleigh, and employed by him in the difcovery*." This work was printed at Franckfort by J. Wechelius, A. D. 1590. The plates were executed at De Brye's own expence from drawings made by J. White, who was ſent thither for that purpofe. Theſe plates were copied by Picart for his *Religious Ceremonies of all Nations*.

The plates to the Latin narrative of the *Cruelties of the Spaniards in America*, publiſhed 1598.

About the ſame year, namely, 1598, appeared De Brye's great work, entitled, *Defcriptio Indiae Orientalis et Occidentalis*, in nineteen parts, contained in five large folio volumes.

Among his detached prints, the following are greatly eſteemed:

The *little village fair*; and its companion, the *fountain of youth*; two ſmall plates, length-ways, from Sebald Beham.

A *Bacchanalian proceſſion*, a ſmall plate, length-ways, from Julio Romano.

The *Venetian ball*, a ſmall circular plate, from Theodore Bernard.

The *golden age*, a ſmall circular plate, copied from the print engraved by Nicholas de Bruin, from a defign of Abraham Bloemart.

The *proceſſion for the funeral of Sir Philip Sidney*, engraved at London. This is a long roll, " *contrived and invented by Thomas Lant, gent. fervant of that honourable knight, and graven in copper by Derick or Theodore de Brie, in the city of London*, 1578." It contains about thirty-four plates; and prefixed is the portrait of Mr. Lant, aged 32. This has uſually been confidered as the firſt Engliſh work by De Brye. John Fenn, eſq. of Eaſt Dereham in the county of Norfolk, is poſſeſſed of a very ſingular curiofity, which, as it is thought to be *unique*, certainly merits a very particular defcription. I have little doubt, but that it was executed by De Brye; and if ſo, it is certainly one of his beſt works. That gentleman has obligingly favoured me with the following account of it.

A Defcription of a Roll reprefenting the Proceſſion of the Knights of the Garter in 1576, 18*th of Elizabeth*.

The proceſſion is repreſented as moving along a portico, quite open on the ſide next the obferver, but ſupported by thirty-three pillars of the Ionic order on the ſide from him, in the following order:

The verger alone bearing his ſilver rod.
The twelve alms knights, two and two in their proper habits.
Their governor alone.
Four purſuivants, two and two,
Six heralds, two and two,
Two kings of arms, a-breaſt, } in black gowns, over which are their tabords with the fovereign's arms.
The twenty-four knights companions, two and two,
The emperor alone, - - } all in the full habit of the order.

Garter

BRY   [157]   BRY

Garter king of arms, with his sceptre,
The regifter, with his book,
The ufher of the black rod, with his rod, } a-breaft, with their mantles, &c.

The prelate,
The chancellor, } a-breaft with their mantles, &c.

Two gentlemen ufhers, a-breaft.
A nobleman (not of the order) carrying the fword of ftate, alone.
The fovereign in the full habit of the order, alone.
Amounting in the whole to fixty.
Over each knight companion of the order, are his arms within the garter, and in a compartment below, his name, titles, &c. are written in French. The laft ftall was vacant, and there is only a fancy portrait, given without name or arms. There are fixty portraits in the proceffion, each of them between four and five inches in height; under the arches of the portico, is a delightful view of a hilly country, (too hilly for an Englifh profpect) interfperfed with caftles, churches, houfes, rivers, woods, men, animals, &c. and an exact view of Windfor Caftle, as it appeared in that reign. The roll is fixteen feet three inches long, and one foot deep, and was engraved on twelve plates.

Who was the original poffeffor of this curious roll, I know not, but in the beginning of this century, it belonged to Peter le Neve, Efq. norroy; from him it came to Mr. Thomas Martin of Palgrove; after his deceafe it was the property of Mr. Worch, and from him, in 1773, it came into my poffeffion.

The date under the dedication, written by Dawes, is altered with a pen from 1576 to 1578, but the proceffion was in 1576, as two of the knights reprefented, were dead before 1578, though, perhaps the engraving was not finifhed before the latter year.

Hollar, to his plate of the proceffion copied in fmall from this engraving, in Afhmole's order of the garter, fays, the original was defigned by Marc Garrerd, who could be then only fifteen years old, being born in 1561, and I believe did not come into England till after the time this was done.

Mr. Walpole fays, Garrerd drew a proceffion of the queen, knights of the garter, &c. in 1584, from whence Afhmole took his plate for the Hiftory of the Order of the Garter. It certainly could not be this, which was not only drawn, but engraved before 1578, and from the dedication, I have no doubt, but that the drawings of this were executed by Thomas Daws, Rougecroix. It is a proof print, as the titles, names, dedication, &c. are written, and not quite finifhed; fo that the engraver had not added his name. The queftion is, what became of the plates? for I never heard of another proof having been feen by any one.

The following is a lift of the knights, companions, and officers, reprefented by their portraits in the proceffion.

Charles Howard, E. of Effingham,   Void,
Henry Stanley, E. of Derby,   Henry Herbert, E. of Pembroke,
                                                      William

William Cecil, Lord Burleigh,
Henry Haftings, E. of Huntingdon,
Sir Henry Sydney, Knt.
Henry Carey, Lord Hunfdon,
George Talbot, E. of Shrewfbury,
Anthony Browne, Vifcount Montague,
Edward Clinton, E. of Lincoln,
Henry Fitz Allen, E. of Arundel,
Emanuel, D. of Savoy,
Philip II. King of Spain,
Arthur, Lord Grey of Wilton,
Walter d'Evereux, E. of Effex,
William Somerfet, E. of Worcefter,
Francis Ruffel. E. of Bedford,
Ambrofe Dudley. E. of Warwick,
Robert Dudley, E. of Leicefter,
Thomas Ratcliffe, E. of Suffex,
F. Montmorency, D. of Montmorency,
Adolphus, D. of Slefwick, Holftein, &c.
And Henry III. King of France,
Maximilian II. Emperor.
Sir Gilbert Dethick, Garter. William Day, Dean of Windfor, Regifter.
Ufher of the Black Rod.
Robert Horne, Bifhop of Winchefter, Prelate. Sir Thomas Smith, Chancellor.
Two Gentlemen Ufhers.
A Nobleman with the fword.
Queen Elizabeth.

He alfo engraved a great number of portraits, proceffions, and a variety of other fubjects, as well from his own compofitions, as thofe of other mafters.

JOHN THEODORE DE BRYE.
Flourifhed, 1620.

He was the fon of the preceding artift. After the death of his father, affifted by his brother, he completed the plates for Boiffard's *Roman Antiquities*, two volumes of which were left unfinifhed. They alfo added feveral parts to the collection of portraits of illuftrious perfons, which their father had begun.

JOHN ISRAEL DE BRYE.
Flourifhed, 1620.

The younger fon of John Theodore de Brye the elder, and brother to the above-mentioned artift, whom he affifted in the completion of the works, which their father had left unfinifhed. They both of them imitated the ftyle of their father; but in a ftiff, taftelefs manner. They never nearly equalled him in merit.

HENRY BRYER.
Died,

He was pupil to the late Mr. Ryland, with whom he afterwards entered into partnerfhip; and they opened a print-fhop in Cornhill. When that partnerfhip was diffolved, he went into bufinefs for himfelf; but he did not engrave many plates. By him, among others, are the two following:
Bacchus and Ariadne, a middling fized upright plate; and *Mars difcovered with Venus by Vulcan*, a large plate, length-ways. For this laft he obtained a premium from the fociety for the encouragement of arts and fciences. His
widow

widow lives at prefent in Poland-Street, where fhe ftill continues to publifh prints from the pictures of Angelica Kauffman, &c.

L. B U B E.
Flourifhed,

An engraver on wood, by whom we have a fmall upright print of a *holy family* in chiaro-fcuro. It is engraved on three blocks; the firft for the outline and dark fhadows; the fecond for the light fhadows; and the third for the demy-tint. Though it is executed in a very flight manner, it is, however, very fpirited, and manifefts the hand of the mafter. It is from a compofition of Abraham Bloemart.

SAMUEL BUCK.
Died, 1779.

This ingenious artift, affifted by his brother NATHANIEL BUCK, drew and engraved a large number of plates of various fizes. They confift of views of churches, monafteries, abbies, caftles, and other ruins. Alfo views of the principal cities and towns in England and Wales; and, among them, a very large one of the cities of *London* and *Weftminfter*. They are all executed much in the fame ftyle. The back-grounds are flightly etched, and the buildings finifhed with the graver, in a ftiff manner. Their drawings, efpecially thofe of the ruins, &c. appear to have been too haftily made; for which reafon, on examining the prints with the objects they reprefent, they are frequently found to be very inaccurate. However, in many inftances, they are the only views we have of the places reprefented; and in fome, the only views we can have, as feveral of the ruins engraved by them, have fince that time been totally deftroyed. Samuel Buck died at his apartments in the Temple, in the month of Auguft. A. D. 1779. The prints by thefe artifts, which amount in the whole to 500, are too well known to need a feparate lift. The two brothers were employed upwards of 32 years in this undertaking.

CARLO BUFFAGNOTI.
Flourifhed,

A native of Bologna. By him we have feveral plates of *architecture*, into which he has ufually introduced fome figures. They are very flightly etched, and the figures are incorrect. To fome circular plates his name is figned; to which he adds, *inv. et fecit*. Thefe, therefore, were manifeftly engraved from his own defigns.

A. VAN BUISEN or BUYSEN.
Flourifhed, 1710.

An indifferent engraver, who was, I think, a native of Holland. He worked entirely with the graver in a ftiff ftyle, very like that adopted by Gribelin; but he did not equal that artift. Buifen, I believe, engraved for the bookfellers only. We have by him a print of *David playing on the harp*, an octavo plate for the edition of Cowley's poems, printed, A. D. 1700. He alfo did fome of the folio plates for the work entitled *Figures de la Bible*, from Picart and others, publifhed at Amfterdam, 1720.

W. BUITWECH.
Flourifhed,

According to profeffor Chrift, he engraved fome plates, reprefenting the various habits of different nations, which he figned W. B. and W. BW.

BUGEY.
Flourifhed,

An obfcure engraver of portraits, who probably worked only for the bookfellers. By him we have the portrait of *marfhal de Broglio* on horfeback, from M. Loir.

MICHAEL BUMEL, or BIMEL.
Flourifhed,

A very indifferent engraver, by whofe hands we have fome *fmall figures of faints*, and *fubjects of devotion* ; executed neatly enough with the graver ; but without the leaft tafte or correctnefs.

C. BUNO.
Flourifhed, 1650.

This artift, according to profeffor Chrift, flourifhed about 1650; when he engraved fome plates, which he marked with the initials of his name C. B. But the fubjects of thefe engravings are not fpecified.

FLORIANO DEL BUONS.
Flourifhed,

A name I found affixed to the portrait of *Guido*, a fmall oval plate, all graved in a poor, feeble, ftiff ftyle, and without effect. It appears by the word *fecit*, which he had added to his name. that he engraved it from a defign of his own.

FRANCIS BURANI.
Flourifhed,

He was, according to Bafan, a painter, a native of Reggio, and flourifhed in the laft century. He etched a plate from a compofition of his own, in the ftyle of Spagnoletto, reprefenting *Bacchus feated upon a tub*, accompanied by three fatyrs, a middling fized print, length-ways.

THOMAS

THOMAS BURFORD.
Flourished, 1750.

He was an engraver in mezzotinto, and not destitute of merit. We have some few landscapes, and other subjects by him; but, I believe, he chiefly confined himself to portraits; some of which he also drew himself from the life; as that of the *Rev. Roger Pickering*, F. R. S. poster size, half figure, which is dated 1747. Add to this, Mr. *Warburton*, from Philip; Mr. *Charles Churchill*, from J. H. Schlanck, dated 1765. He resided in London, where, I believe, he died a few years since.

H. BURGH.
Flourished,

An engraver of no great eminence, who resided, I believe, in London, and worked for the booksellers. Among other prints by him, are the two following: The *Irish dwarf*, from B. Smith, a small upright plate. The portrait of *Thomas Bradbury*, minister of the gospel, a small oval print, which is signed " H. Burgh del. et sculp." These are both slight, and indifferent etchings.

MICHAEL BURGHERS.
Flourished, 1670.

This engraver, who was probably a native of the United Netherlands, came into England soon after Utrecht was taken by Louis XIV. and settled at Oxford. From the multiplicity of his works, he appears to have been employed, not only by that university, but by most of the chief booksellers. His plates are executed entirely with the graver, in a stiff, laboured style, without genius, or knowledge of the art of design. His drawing, when he attempted to represent the naked figure, is exceedingly defective. He has, however, painfully preserved many ancient reliques, the originals of which are now lost. And though we cannot admire the taste, with which they are executed, yet they become estimable, because they still continue to us an idea of those monuments of antiquity, which time had otherwise obliterated for ever. At the bottom of several of his plates he adds to his name, *Academiæ Oxon. calcographus*. Among other things for the university, he engraved the *almanacks*; and the first that appeared with his name, was for the year 1676.

Speaking as an artist, I should say, that his best prints are some few frontispieces which he copied from Mellan, and imitated in them the style of engraving adopted by that master very successfully. Of this sort is the octavo frontispiece to the first edition of *Creech's Translation of the Satires of Horace*, where a woman is represented taking a satyr's mask from the face of the poet.

But his most estimable works are the *antiquities, ancient pavements, views of churches, ruined abbies, and other curiosities*, which were chiefly executed for that indefatigable antiquary, Thomas Hearne. He also engraved a great

BUR [162] BUR

variety of portraits; among the beft of thefe may be reckoned that of *Sir Thomas Bodley*, with the heads of the other benefactors to the library, at the corners of the plate; this engraving was placed as a frontifpiece to the catalogue of the manufcripts, contained in the Bodleian library. The portrait of *Anthony Wood*, a fmall plate in mezzotinto, is by Burghers, and I believe the only one he ever executed in that manner of engraving. See the mark which he ufed, when he did not fign his name at length, on the plate at the end of the volume.

LE CHEVALIER BURGHESE.
Flourifhed,

A name cited by Florent le Comte, as an engraver of *thefes* and *emblematical fubjects*; but he has not fpecified any of his works.

HANS or JOHN BURGKMAIR.
Flourifhed, 1518.

A native of Germany, and according to the general account, a fcholar of Albert Durer. He worked chiefly, if not entirely, on wood; and his prints poffefs much of that fire and fpirit, which we difcover in thofe of his mafter. Some of his engravings are dated as early as 1510; for this reafon, profeffor Chrift attributes to him, and with great appearance of reafon, fome fmall, fpirited wooden cuts which were made for the ancient edition of the works of Geyler de Keiferberg, marked I. B. and dated 1510. He fometimes ufed the two letters in this manner: H. B. feparate from each other; and at other times, both joined together; again, an H. and a B. joined together, with a C. upon the crofs bar of the H. the fame cypher, which James Binck afterwards ufed, is attributed to him, when the date is from 1510 to 1518. Of this fort is a fmall upright wood cut, reprefenting the *three fates, with Cupid at the bottom plucking a flower*. It is dated 1513. Florent le Comte informs us, that, about the year 1518, he engraved a fet of thirty-fix prints, the *emperors or kings*. I never faw the fet complete; but I have frequently met with odd prints belonging to it. They are on wood, in chiaro-fcuro; on two blocks, one for the outline and principal fhadows, and the other for the half tints. The figures are reprefented on horfeback. One I have before me has his name, " H. Burgkmair;" and it is dated 1518: the others have the initials of his name, H. B. only.

St. Sebaftian ftanding in an arch, a fmall upright print, with his name, and dated 1512.

BURNFORD.
Flourifhed,

One of thofe book plate makers whofe labours have adorned the publications of the former century. I have before me a frontifpiece to the *Practife of Piety*, or fome other book of devotion in twelves; it is executed entirely with the graver, but in a ftyle that does no honour to the artift or credit to the tafte of his employer.

2   COR-

CORNELIUS BUS, or BOSC, or VANDEN BOSCH.
Flourished, 1543.

He was a native of Bois le Duc in Flanders, and established at Antwerp, where, exclusive of his profession as an engraver, he carried on a considerable commerce in prints. His manner of engraving sometimes resembles that of Marc de Ravenna; at other times that of Æneas Vico. He never arrived at any superior degree of excellence. He worked entirely with the graver, in a stiff, dry style, without taste. His drawing is by no means correct; neither are the heads, and other extremities of his figures, sufficiently attended to; and from the lights being diffused, and the feebleness of the masses of shadow, his engravings are usually destitute of effect. He generally marked his plates with the initials of his name, C. B. and the date in the manner represented at the end of the volume. The following prints may be reckoned among his best:

The *taking down from the cross*, a large upright plate, dated 1545, without any painter's name.

The *entombing of Christ*, the same, from Franciscus Floris, and marked " Cornelius Bus fecit, A. D. 1554."

Christ preaching to the Jews, a middling sized upright plate, nearly square, with the initials, and no date. On a pedestal is written, *Beati que audiunt verbum Dei, et Custodiunt*.

Moses breaking the tables of the law, a middling sized plate, length-ways, from Raphael, dated 1550.

Moses presenting the law to the people, the same, from the same, dated 1551.

Battle of the giants, with his mark: no painter's name.

Triumph of Bacchus, a large print, length-ways, engraved on three plates, from Julio Romano, dated 1543.

Venus and Cupid coming to Vulcan, who is working, with the three Cyclops, at the forge; a middling sized plate, length-ways, dated 1546, with the mark. Both the mark and the date are reversed on this print, being engraved the right way upon the plate.

He also engraved from Michael Angelo and other masters.

B U S C.
Flourished,

According to Basan, this gentleman was inspector of the galleries of the duke of Brunswick; and for his amusement, engraved a set of twenty-eight small plates, after Rembrandt, and twenty heads, &c.

JOHN BUSH.
Flourished,

He engraved some few portraits; but never arrived at any superior pitch of excellency. Among others by him, is a small print of *Gaven*, a Jesuit.

LOUIS BUSINCK.
Flourished,

This artist, according to Basan, flourished during the last century; and by him we have several prints in chiaro-scuro, performed in a very spirited and masterly manner, from George L'Allemand. I shall only mention the following: A middling sized print representing a *holy family*. It is executed on three blocks of wood; the first for the outline, the second for the deep shadows, and the third for the demy tint.

Æneas saving his father from the destruction of Troy, a middling sized upright print, the same, with the painter's name.

Moses, a single figure seated, the same.

JOHN BUSSE.
Flourished, 1528.

He may be ranked in the class of little masters, and was apparently a disciple of Aldegrever; at least, he copied the works of that artist. He usually signed his prints with the initials of his name, I. B. and added the date. Among others by this engraver, are the *seven planets*, very small upright plates, marked I. B. 1528. On a small plate length-ways, representing a *man and woman dancing*, with two men playing on musical instruments, the name is signed at length, " *John Busse*." If any one should object against the name, and suppose that it does not belong to the engraver, bringing, for instance, several of the small dancing figures by John Sebald Beham, which seem to be a species of portraits, and have the names written over them, as *Martinus Winterton, Nicolas Cristman*, &c. adding, that, like Beham, the present artist has also represented the portrait of John Busse. I shall observe, that the prints of this sort by Beham have constantly *his* mark upon them, as well as the names of the dancing figures; this seems to be an invariable rule established among the ancient engravers: and sometimes they added it, even when they signed their name at length. Now this is the only print by this master, (for it is evidently by the same hand as the planets mentioned above) without his mark; which, I think, he would hardly have omitted on this occasion; especially as the initials of the name were the same as his own. Besides, if the dancing figure of the man be a portrait, why should not those who are playing on the music be portraits also? yet their names are not expressed. In this manner, the name *Bussemaker* is affixed to a small print of *Jupiter and Leda*, copied from Henry Aldegrever, by Martin Pohem. But then that artist has added his monogram, composed of a P. and an M. joined together, to prevent the purchaser from attributing by mistake the engraving to Bussemaker, who was probably only the publisher.

MARTIN VAN BUYTEN.
Flourished, 1588.

An engraver of no great note, who resided at Rome, and worked, I believe, chiefly for the booksellers. By him, among other things, we have the frontispiece to a book, entitled, *Lanotomia delle Cancellares che corsive et altre maniere*

maniere di Lodovico Curione, in folio. It is executed entirely with the graver, in a neat, dry ftyle, without effect.

JAMES DE BYE.
Flouriſhed, 1600.

This artift, if he was not a native of Antwerp, certainly refided there, and carried on a confiderable commerce in prints and books. He very probably learned the art of engraving in the fchool of the Collaerts, whofe ftyle he feems to have imitated, and with great fuccefs. He drew correctly, and executed his plates entirely with the graver, in a neat, clear, determined manner. The heads of his figures are very accurately finiſhed, and the other extremities well marked. The effect indeed of his prints is not powerful, but confufed, from the lights being too much fcattered; and a certain ftiffnefs or formality appears in the management of the ftrokes, which is unpleafing to the eye of the artift. His prints, however, may rank with thofe of the beft early Flemiſh mafters. He, with his cotemporary, John Baptifta Barbe, affifted the Collaerts in engraving the *life, paſſion, and refurrection of Chriſt*, which confifted of fifty middling fized plates, length-ways, from Martin de Vos. No. 18, repreſenting *Peter's wife's mother healed of her fever by our Saviour*, and No. 30, the *refurrection of Lazarus*, both in that work, are, I think, fine fpecimens of our artift's abilities. He alfo affifted Philip and Theodore Galle, in the *life of the Virgin*, engraved alfo from the defigns of Martin de Vos. The portraits of the defcendants of the *Maifon de Croy*, which are contained in a folio volume, are by him, and marked in the manner expreffed on the plate of monograms, at the end of the volume. Likewife the portraits of the *kings, queens, and dauphins of France*, for the large edition of the hiftory by Mezeray, &c.

MARC DE BYE.
Flouriſhed, 1664.

By this artift, who probably might be of the fame family with the preceding, we have fome very neat, fpirited etchings of *animals*, &c. from Marc Gerard and Paul Potter. They are fmall plates, length-ways, dated 1664.

NICHOLAS DE BYE.
Flouriſhed,

He might perhaps be related to the forementioned artift. We have by him fome portraits, and other fubjects; though I believe, the former chiefly employed his graver. Among them, is that of *Charles IX.* king of France.

CORNELIUS BUZZI.
Flouriſhed,

The name of an engraver mentioned by Florent le Comte, as chiefly excellent in the architectal line. He has not, however, fpecified any of his works.

C.

ADRIAN VANDER CABEL.
Born, 1631. Died, 1695.

This juftly celebrated artift was born at Ryfwick, near the Hague, A. D. 1631. He was the difciple of John Van Goyen, and chiefly excelled in painting landfcapes, fea-ports and cattle; all of which he conftantly ftudied from nature, with great accuracy; and his pictures are defervedly held in the higheft eftimation. He died, A. D. 1695, aged 64. By his hand we have fome few etchings, in a flight, free ftyle. Among others,

A large upright *landfcape*, in which is a figure of *St. Antony*. It is remarkable, that the figure is engraved in the ftyle of Mellan, with fingle ftrokes, without any crofs hatching, perhaps inferted by another mafter.

Another large upright *landfcape*, with *St. Jerom*, its companion.

Two large *landfcapes*, length-ways.

Thirty fmall *landfcapes*, the fame.

Six fmall upright *landfcapes*.

VINCENZIO CACCIANEMICI.
Flourifhed, 1540.

This gentleman was a native of Bologna, and of a noble family. He is faid to have ftudied under Francefco Mazzoli, who is more commonly known by the name of Parmigiano; and the engravings marked with the letters V. C. are attributed to him. Among others, thus marked, are the two following: *Diana returning from hunting*, with fome oxen in the background, a middling fized plate, length-ways. A *landfcape* in which a Nymph appears with dogs, oxen and other animals reprefented in the back-ground, apparently companion to the former. They are both neatly executed, entirely with the graver, and in a ftyle, greatly refembling that of Æneas Vico, the difciple of Marc Antonio.

CAESIUS. See CESIO.

G. V. CAFFEELS.
Flourifhed,

The name of an engraver of no great note, affixed to the portrait of *Lodowick Muggleton*, the fchifmatic.

CAGLIARDI.

CAGLIARDI. See Gagliardi.

PAOLO CAGLIARDI, called VERONESE.
Born, 1530. Died, 1588.

This admirable hiftorical painter was born at Verona, A. D. 1530, and was the difciple of Antonio Badile, his uncle. The works of this artift, and his fuperior merit, are too generally known to need any repetition here. For his amufement he etched fome few plates, which though flight, hafty productions, evidently fhow the hand of the mafter. Among them are the following:

The *adoration of the Magi*, a large upright plate, nearly fquare, marked " Paolo Veronefe fec."

Two *faints fleeping*, a fmall upright plate, without a mark.

There are alfo fome etchings, marked P. C. and PA. CAL. attributed to him.

D. CAGNONI.
Flourifhed,

A name affixed to a portrait of *Victor Armid. III.* king of Sardinia.

CAILUS. See Caylus Count De.

HENRY DE CAISSER.
Flourifhed,

An artift, who was chiefly excellent, according to Florent le Compte, in engraving *funeral proceffions, monuments,* &c. but that author has not fpecified any of his works.

JOHN CALCAR.
Born, 1499. Died, 1546.

He was a painter of no fmall eminence, born at Calcar, a city of Cleves. He was the difciple of Titian, and copied the ftyle of that excellent mafter fo exactly, as to deceive Henry Goltzius. He died at Naples, A. D. 1546, aged 47. It is faid, that he engraved fome few prints; but I have not feen any of them.

POLIDORO CALDARA, called DA CARAVAGGIO.
Born, 1492. Died, 1543.

This celebrated artift was one of the difciples of Raphael, and affifted him in the paintings, which he executed in the Vatican. He was born at Caravaggio in the duchy of Milan; but refided chiefly at Rome; where, befides the works above-mentioned, he painted a great number of pictures, which are held in the higheft eftimation. He was murdered in the 51ft year of his age,

age, by his own valet, who had difcovered, that his mafter had a large fum of money in his poffeffion. According to Florent le Comte, he etched fome plates from his own compofitions, but this author has neglected to fpecify the fubjects.

CALLIARI, See PAOLO CAGLIARDI.

JAMES CALLOT.
Born, 1593. Died, 1635.

This juftly celebrated artift, who was of a noble family, was born at Nancy in Lorraine, A. D. 1593. His paffion for the arts was fo ftrong, that contrary to the inclination of his parents, he refolved to purfue them. Accordingly, at the age of twelve, he determined to go to Italy, in order to improve himfelf; and fecretly departed from his father's houfe. But having no money, he joined himfelf to a travelling company of Bohemians; and being arrived at Florence, an officer of the great duke placed him with Remigio Canta Gallina; under whofe infpection he copied the works of the great mafters, in order to acquire facility in the art of defign, and a proper tafte. When he left Gallini, he purfued his journey to Rome, where he was met by fome merchants from Nancy, who knew him, and took him with them back to his family. Here, however, he did not long remain; for in order to complete his darling ftudies, he made a fecond elopement; but was difcovered by his elder brother at Turin; and was a fecond time brought back to Nancy. His father now finding, that it was impoffible to prevent his following his inclination for the arts, confented, at laft, to his folicitations, and permitted him to fet out for Italy the third time, in the fuite of a gentleman, whom the duke of Lorraine fent to the pope. Being arrived at Rome, he applied himfelf affiduoufly to drawing, under Giulio Parigii. After which, defirous of acquiring a facility in handling the graver, he entered the fchool of Philip Thomaffin; but that artift having a pretty wife, who expreffed more kindnefs for Callot, than he approved of, a difagreement between them took place; and the latter having greatly improved himfelf, went to Florence; where he was particularly noticed and employed by the great duke, Cofmus II. At this city it was, that he firft began to etch; and he executed feveral fmall fubjects with great fuccefs.

Upon the death of the duke his patron, Callot returned to his own country, and fettled at Nancy, where he married a gentlewoman of diftinction, A. D. 1625, being then 32 years of age. His reputation increafed daily, and he was fent for by the infanta Elizabeth-Clara-Eugenia to Bruffels, at the time the marquis de Spinola was befieging the town of Breda, to draw and engrave the taking of that town; which he accordingly performed. In the year 1628, he went to Paris; where he engraved for Louis XIII. feveral other great fieges; among the reft, that of Rochelle, and the ifland de Re; after which he returned to Nancy.

He was a great favourite with the duke of Lorraine, who not only frequently honoured him with his vifits, but even condefcended to learn to draw under his inftructions. The troubles arifing afterwards in

Lorraine,

Lorraine, which concluded with the fiege and taking of Nancy, by the king of France, occafioned his forming the refolution of returning to Florence with his wife; but he was prevented from putting it in practice by death, March 28, 1635, being then forty-two years of age.

The following curious anecdote is related of him. After the reduction of the town of Nancy, in the year 1631, Louis XIII. fent for him to draw and engrave that fiege, as he had done thofe of Rochelle and Ré; but he intreated his majefty to difpenfe with his complying with this command; becaufe he did not think it confiftent with the refpect he bore to his prince, and love to his country, to reprefent any thing that fhould appear to their difgrace. A courtefan belonging to the king's fuite, furprifed at the refufal of the artift, and not feeling the delicacy of his fentiments, replied, in a menacing tone of voice, " you fhall be made to obey." To which he boldly anfwered, " I will fooner difable my right hand, than be conftrained " to do any thing contrary to my honour." The king was pleafed with the greatnefs of foul, which appeared in this noble reply, and offered him a penfion of three thoufand livres, if he would attach himfelf to his fervice. Callot thankfully refufed the advantageous offer, preferring the love of his country to the amaffing of a fortune.

The fertility of invention, and the vaft variety, which are found in the works of this excellent artift, are very aftonifhing. One could hardly have fuppofed it poffible, to combine fo great a number of figures together as he has done, and vary the attitudes, without forced contraft, fo that all of them, whether fingle figures or groups may be eafily diftinguifhed from each other, even in the maffes of fhadow; efpecially when we confider, that they are often minute to admiration. He generally (in his large prints efpecially) raifed the point of fight to a confiderable height in his compofitions, to afford a greater fpace for the figures, and confequently a greater fcope for his invention. In that charming print, called the *punifhments*, the number of figures he has introduced is wonderful; all of them difpofed in different groups, with the greateft judgment; and the actions of the fmalleft of them, in the diftance feem confpicuous, though the largeft figure, in the fore-ground, fcarcely exceeds three quarters of an inch. The fame may be faid of the *fair*; and indeed of many others nearly equal to them in beauty. Where fo great a number of figures is introduced into one print, it cannot be fuppofed, that there fhould be any great general effect, to ftrike the eye at firft fight. On the contrary, in cafting it curforily over the *fair*, the *punifhments*, or the *temptation of St. Anthony*, one would be at a lofs to declare the fubject, the whole appears confufed and without harmony: But the trouble of a careful examination is well repaid by the richnefs, the beauty, the tafte, and the judgment we difcover in the difpofition of the figures, the management of the groups, and the variety and propriety of the attitude, which fteal as it were, upon the mind.

He engraved in feveral ftyles; the firft of which was in imitation of his tutor Canta Gallina. After which he worked entirely with the graver; but without fuccefs. Of this fort are the *acts of the apoftles*, fmall plates from Ludovicus Civolius. His next ftyle was a mixture of the point and the graver, with coarse, broad hatchings in the shadows: as, the *card-players*, the miracle of *St. Mansuetus restoring to life the son of king Leucorus*, who had fallen into a river, in reaching for his tennis ball. The *Virgin seated at a table, with Joseph giving drink to the child Jesus*. But his best manner is that, which appears to have been executed with the most freedom; by which we may say, as it were, he has expressed with a single stroke, variety of character, and correctness of design.

He was, according to report, the first who used hard varnish in etching; which certainly is greatly superior to that which was before adopted. The works of this master amount to 1500 prints. Of these but few can possibly be mentioned in the following list.

The *murder of the innocents*, a small oval plate, engraved at Florence. Callot engraved the same subject at Nancy, with some difference in the figures on the back-ground. The former is the most rare: a fine impression of it is very difficult to be found.

The *marriage of Cana in Galilee*, from Paolo Veronese, a middling sized plate length-ways.

The *passion of Christ*, on twelve very small upright plates: first impressions very scarce.

St. John in the island of Palma, a small plate, nearly square.

The *temptation of St. Anthony*, a middling sized plate, length-ways. He also engraved the same subject larger; which, though not the best, is notwithstanding the scarcest print. There is a considerable difference in the treatment of the subject in the two prints.

The *punishments*, wherein is seen the execution of several criminals. The marks of the best impressions of this plate are, a small square tower which appears above the houses, towards the left, and a very small image of the Virgin placed in an angle of the wall, near the middle of the print.

The *miseries of war*, eighteen small plates, length-ways. There is another set on the same subject, consisting of seven plates, less than the former.

The *great fair of Florence*, so called, because it was engraved at Florence. As several parts of this plate were not equally bitten by the aqua-fortis, it is difficult to meet with a fine impression. Callot, on his return to Nancy, re-engraved this plate, without any alteration. The copy, however, is by no means equal to the original. The first is distinguished from the second by the words, *in Firenza*, which appear below at the right hand corner of the plate. The second has these words in the same place, *Fe Florientis, & excudit Nancei*. There is also a large copy of this print, reversed, published by Savery; but the difference is easily distinguished between it and the true print.

The *little fair*, otherwise called the *players at bowls*; where also some peasants are represented dancing. This is one of the scarcest of Callot's prints; and it is very difficult to meet with a fine impression of it; for the distances, and other parts of the plates, failed in the biting it with the aqua-fortis.

The *tilting, or the new street at Nancy*, a middling sized plate, length-ways.

The *Garden of Nancy*, where young men are playing with a baloon, the same.

View

View of the Port Neuf, a small plate, length-ways.
View of the Louvre, the same.
Four landscapes, small plates, length-ways.

ANDREA CAMASSEI.
Born,   Died, 1695.

A painter of Bevagna. He is cited in the list of Engravers at the end of the Abecedario; but none of his works are specified. I do not recollect having seen any engravings by this artist.

GIOSEFFE CAMERATA.
Flourished, 1740.

A modern engraver, a native of Venice, who flourished 1740. He was the disciple of G. Lazzarini. His works are not held in any great estimation. The principal part of them were for the collection of engravings, from the pictures in the Dresden gallery. I shall only notice the following:

The assumption of the Virgin, a large upright plate, from Annibale Carracci.

St. Roch relieving the people afflicted with the plague, a large plate, length-ways, from Camillio Procaccini.

The *charity of St. Roch*, a large plate, length-ways, from Annibale Carracci; the same subject as Guido made an etching of.

DOMENICO CAMPAGNOLA.
Flourished, 1517.

This artist, a native of Vienna, was one of the disciples of Titian; and his reputation as a painter is by no means inconsiderable. He is said to have chiefly excelled in landscapes. He engraved on wood a variety of subjects, as well from his own designs, as those of his master. They are executed in a bold, spirited style; but very slight. The drawing of the naked figure, when it is introduced, is not correct, nor are sufficient pains taken to determine the extremities. He frequently marked his plates in this manner, DO. CAP. without writing it at length: to which also he usually added the date. I shall only mention the following:

A *holy family, with St. John and St. Jerom*, a large plate, length-ways, without the painter's name, which I take to be Titian: it is dated 1517.

Two circular prints, in one of which is represented the *beheading of a woman before a king*, dated 1518.

Basan appears to me to have been very much mistaken, when he says of this artist, that "*he etched some plates from his own compositions.*" He has run into the same error, with respect to the following engraver.

GIULIO CAMPAGNOLA.
Flourished, 1516.

According to the author of the Abecedario, this artist was the brother of Domenico;

Domenico; and Florent le Comte affures us, that he worked from 1507 to 1517. He engraved entirely with the graver, in two manners very different from each other. The following plates are by this artift:

A fmall upright print, reprefenting *Ganymede upon the back of the eagle*. In this he has imitated the ftyle of Marc Antonio, and with fome fuccefs, refpecting the mechanical part of the engraving; but the drawing of the figure is by no means fo mafterly, or equally correct. This is marked, " Julius Campagnola Antenoreus fec."

A middling fized upright print reprefenting a *fingle figure* ftanding, holding a cup and looking upwards. In this plate he has entirely varied his former manner. The back ground is executed with round dots, made apparently with a dry point. The figure is outlined with a ftroke deeply engraved, and finifhed with dots, in a manner greatly refembling thofe prints, which Demarteau engraved at Paris, in imitation of red chalk. The hair and beard are expreffed by ftrokes. It is a very extraordinary print, and proves the antiquity of that mode of engraving, which has been erroneoufly confidered as a modern invention; but its merit confifts chiefly in its fingularity; for the drawing of the figure is ftiff and incorrect; and there is nothing in the general effect to recommend it.

PIETRO CAMPANA.
Flourifhed, 1755.

A modern Italian engraver, by whom among other things, we have *St. Peter delivered from the prifon by an angel*, from Matthias Preti, for the collection of prints, engraved from the pictures in the Drefden gallery.

C. D. CAMPIGLIA.
Flourifhed,

An engraver of no great note, whofe chief employment appears to have been in the portrait line. Among other portraits engraved by him, are thofe of *Julius Romano* the difciple of Raphael, and *James Jordans* the fcholar of Rubens.

L'ABBE TERSAN DE CAMPION.
Flourifhed,

A modern connoiffeur, who, together with his brother, engraved feveral *landfcapes*, and other fubjects, from Monet, and other mafters. I have feen a fmall head in an oval, neatly executed, entirely with the graver, but in a ftiff ftyle, without much tafte: it is marked " Campion fculp." without any painter's name or date.

ANTONIO CANAL.
Born,   Died, 1768.

A modern Venetian artift who excelled in painting *views*, fome of which he engraved. He was uncle to the famous IL CANALETTO. That juftly efteemed artift was his pupil, and painted alfo greatly in the fame ftyle.

ſtyle. According to M. Heineken, Canaletto is called by the Germans COMTE BELLOTTI: He alſo etched ſeveral large views of the town of *Dreſden.*

JOSEPH CANALE.
Flouriſhed, 1755.

A modern Italian artiſt, who, among other things, etched the *incredulity of St. Thomas the Apoſtle,* a middling ſized plate, length-ways, from Matthias Preti, for the collection of prints engraved from the pictures in the Dreſden gallery. This plate was finiſhed by Jean Beauverlet.

P. C. CANOT.
Flouriſhed, 1760.

This artiſt, who was a native of France, reſided the greater part of his life in London, where he engraved a great variety of plates, chiefly *views, landſcapes,* &c. from Vangoyen, Claude Gellee Lorrain, Pilement, &c. Some of them have much merit; but his moſt excellent prints appear to me to be *ſea views,* with ſeveral *naval engagements,* large plates from Paton.

REMEGIO CANTAGELLINA.
Born,   Died, 1620.

A native of Florence. He was a painter and deſigner, of the ſchool of the Carraccii; and his drawings with the pen are very eſtimable. He alſo engraved *landſcapes, triumphal entries, opera ſcenes, feſtival decorations,* &c. as well from his own deſigns, as from thoſe of Giulio Parigi, from whom he learned the art of engraving. Among the reſt, is a ſet of plates by him, called *Palazzo della Fame.* They are very ſlightly engraved, in a dark, heavy manner, and repreſent *triumphal chariots, veſſels, and a variety of other pompous decorations.* They were publiſhed 1608. It is no ſmall addition to the fame of this artiſt, that Callot and De la Bella were his diſciples. He had two brothers, namely, ANTONIO and GIOUANNA FRANCESCO, who, according to M. Heineken, alſo engraved, but he has not ſpecified their works.

SIMON CANTARINI, called IL PESARESE.
Born, 1610. Died, 1648.

This excellent young artiſt was born at Peſaro, a city in the dutchy of Urbino in Italy, A. D. 1610. The firſt principles of deſign and painting he learned from Gio. Giocamo Pandolfi. After which he entered the ſchool of Guido, where the rapid progreſs he made was ſuch, that the greateſt expectations were formed of his future excellence. He died at Venice, A. D. 1648, aged 38 years. Florent le Comte, who gives us a liſt of this maſter's etchings, ſays he was a native of *Oropeza*; and that the name of Pezaroro (for ſo he writes the *cognomen*) was given him, " *parce que ſes pieces furent ſi*
" *recherchés,*

"*recherches, que lon les payoit au poids de l'or,*" because his pictures were so much sought after, that they were bought for their weight in gold. To this he gravely adds, and with more justice, " the great painters of his time were ex- " ceedingly jealous of him, because there was no doubt, but that he would " have surpassed them, had he lived to attain to their age; but he died very " young." His being a native of Pasaro, which, according to the most authentic accounts, he was, is most probably the reason of his being called *Il Pesarese*, and not the great price of his pictures, though certainly he was an artist of very extraordinary talents. We have a considerable number of etchings by his hand, which are very spirited and masterly. In them he has so nearly imitated the style of Guido (from whom we may reasonably conclude he learned the art of etching), that his prints are frequently mistaken for those of that great artist. Yet, on close examination it must be owned, that those of Canterini are inferior in the marking of the naked parts of the figures, and especially the extremities. Among the rest of his etchings, which amount to about thirty, are the following:

St. Sebastian tied to a tree, with an angel bringing the crown and palm, a large upright plate, from Guido.

Christ carrying his cross, a small plate, length-ways.

The *Demoniac cured by St. Benoit*, a middling sized plate, length-ways, from Lodovico Carracci.

Mars and Venus, a middling sized upright plate, from Paolo Veronese.

Adam giving the apple to Eve, a small plate nearly square, from his own composition.

Mercury and Argus, a middling sized plate, length-ways, the same.

The *rape of Europa*, the same.

Several prints of the *Virgin, holy family*, and other *subjects of devotion*, &c.

DOMINICO MARIA CANUTI.
Born, 1623. Died, 1671.

This extraordinary artist, by the force of his own natural genius, without the assistance of a master, acquired such a knowledge of design and colouring, that Guido beheld his works with astonishment, and highly commended the taste and judgment, which were manifested in them He was born at Bologna, A. D. 1623, and died, A. D. 1678, aged 55. We have some etchings by his hand, in which he has followed the manner of Guido, though in a style which is sometimes neater and more finished; but in the excellency of the drawing, and the spirit of the outline, he has not equalled that artist. Among others by him are the following:

The *Virgin seated in the clouds, with Christ standing by her*, a small upright plate, from his own compositions, marked D. M. C. F. The initials of his name, and the F. as usual standing for fecit.

St. Roch, a small upright plate, the same.

St. Francis praying, a small upright plate, from Guido. This last is marked " Doms. Ma. Canuti fec."

BERNARDINO

BERNARDINO CAPITELLI.
Flouriſhed, 1633.

This artiſt was a native of Sienna in Italy, and the diſciple of Rutilio Maneti. As a painter, I believe he never made any very confiderable figure; nor can any great praiſe be attributed to him, confidered as an engraver. We have feveral prints by him, which are etched, and retouched more or lefs with the graver, as he thought the effect required. They are all executed in a dark, coarſe, heavy ſtyle; and the drawing of the figure is by no means correct or maſterly. Among his principal engravings are the following:

The *life of St. Bernard of Sienna*, twelve ſmall plates, length-ways, including the title, on which he figns his name, " Bernardinus Capitellius Senenfis." When he omits to fign his name at length, he uſually fubſtitutes the initials in this manner: B. C. F. the F. as ufual, ſtanding for fecit.

A *Repofo, where the Virgin holds a diſh with water, and the infant Chriſt is drinking*, a ſmall upright plate, from Rutilio Maneti.

Ceres drinking at the cottage of the old woman, a middling ſized upright plate, from Elſheimer, dated 1633. Count Goudt alfo engraved the fame ſubject; but in a much fuperior manner.

The *Aldobrandine marriage*, from an antique painting, a ſmall plate, length-ways. He alfo engraved fome *portraits*, and a variety of other *ſubjects*, from Correggio, Aleſſandro Cafolano, and other maſters.

ALESSANDRO CAPRIOLO.
Flouriſhed, 1600.

This engraver appears to have been chiefly employed by the bookfellers; and we have a great number of portraits by his hand. He worked entirely with the graver, in a ſtiff, mannered ſtyle. His prints are, however, very ſlight, and without any pleafing effect to recommend them. Among the engravings by this artiſt, are the portraits for a work, entitled, *Ritratti di cento Capitani illuſtri*.

GIOVANNI GIACOMO DEL CARAGLIO, or CARALIUS.
Flouriſhed, 1526.

This artiſt was a native of Verona, and moſt probably inſtructed in the art of engraving by the celebrated Marc Antonio Raimondi, whoſe manner he imitated with great fuccefs. And though he never equalled the beſt prints of that great maſter, either in correctnefs of outline, or neatnefs of execution, he may without doubt, be confidered, as one of the beſt of his difciples. He poſſeſſed great knowledge in drawing the human figure, and paid no little attention to the extremities, which he marked with judgment. His heads efpecially, are in general, very characteriſtic and expreſſive. His draperies however are not equally well drawn. The folds, which are too much broken, are not fufficiently varied, or properly determined; and the management of the chiaro-fcuro is very defective. But this was rather the fault of the age, than of the artiſt. Vafari informs us, that he was alſo ſkilful.

in engraving gems and precious stones; for which he was advantageously employed by the king of Poland. Professor Christ seems desirous of attributing to this artist the prints marked I. C. dated 1526; only, says he, " I am not " certain, that this engraver had begun to work at so early a date." He then adds, " the figures, or the statues of the *heathen deities*, which appeared " under his name, are not by him: I find these ancient plates come originally " from James Binck." But here he is certainly mistaken. Those by Caralius are dated 1526; and the copies by Binck 1530; which is four years posterior to the first publication of them. These are small upright plates; and the figures are represented standing in the niches. They are from Rossi.

Caraglio engraved for Rossi, a painter of Milan, among other plates, according to Vasari, an *anatomical figure holding a skull in its hand*. Afterwards he worked from the paintings of Perino del Vaga, Parmiggiano, and other great masters. I shall notice by him the following only:

The *loves of the gods*, on twenty small upright plates, from Perino del Vaga.

The *annunciation of the Virgin Mary*, a large upright plate from Titian.

The *marriage of the Virgin*, the same, from Parmiggiano.

Christ preaching to the multitude, a small plate, length-ways, from Lambert Lombard. On the first impression of this plate, the name of Caraglius, or Karolus, as it is written, is wanting.

LUDOVICO CARDI, called CIVOLI.
Born, 1559. Died, 1613.

This celebrated master, who possessed all the requisites of a great painter, first studied under Alessandro Allori, and afterwards under Andrea del Sarto, and Correggio. He first grounded himself perfectly in the art of design, as well from the antique statues, as the works of Michael Angelo, Buonaroti, and other masters, eminent for their taste and correctness of drawing. When he had succeeded in this, he applied his studies to colouring; and the works of his pencil are generally held in the highest estimation. He died at Rome, A. D. 1613, aged 54.

This great artist also engraved a few plates in a slight, neat style, which, however, evinces the hand of the master. Among others is a small plate, length-ways, representing *Mary Magdalen, washing the feet of Christ*, at the table of Simon the Pharisee. The heads of the figures, and there are many of them in print, are remarkably beautiful; those especially of our Saviour and Mary Magdalen. This print is marked, c. L. CIV. F. the c. and the L. being joined together, in form of a cypher, in the manner represented on the plate at the end of the volume.

LUCA CARLEVARIIS.
Born, 1665. Died,

This painter was born at Udino in Italy; but he appears to have generally resided at Venice. He was chiefly excellent in painting *landscapes*, and *sea views with shipping*. He also engraved a set of *views of Venice*, consisting fifting of one hundred large plates, length-ways. They are flight, but bold, fpirited etchings; and give us a clear idea of the places they are intended to reprefent. Thefe were publifhed at Venice, May 27, 1703.

SALVADOR CARMONA.
Flourifhed, 1760.

A native of Spain. He was pupil to Charles Dupuis; but afterwards fettled at Madrid. Among other prints by this artift are,

The *refurrection of Chrift*, a large upright plate, from Vanloo; and the *adoration of the fhepherds*, a large plate, length-ways, from Pierre. Among the portraits which he executed, is that of *Mr. M. Colin de Vermont*, a middling fized upright plate. This portrait, together with that of *Boucher* the painter, he engraved for his reception into the Royal Academy of Arts at Paris.

CAROLUS REX.
Flourifhed, 1735.

It is no fmall honour to the art of engraving, when confidered as an amufement only, that it has had charms fufficient to engage the attention of a king. The works of genius, and the ftudies of the learned, lay a juft claim to the patronage of the great; and furely the condefcending to employ a leifure hour in the improvement of any ufeful art or fcience, cannot reflect difhonour even upon royalty itfelf.

The king of Naples and the two Sicilies, has very carefully preferved from deftruction a prodigious number of valuable reliques of antiquity, difcovered at Herculaneum, and other neighbouring places, which were overwhelmed by the irruption of Vefuvius; and he has caufed them to be drawn, engraved, and publifhed. They are contained in five large folio volumes. He may therefore be called the patron of the arts; yet not as the patron of the arts only, but as an artift, this royal perfonage claims a place in this work. The following plate is engraved by him:

The *Virgin and Child*, in a fmall circle. The Virgin, which is only a half figure, leans her head upon her right hand; and the infant Chrift is upon her lap, holding a crofs in his right hand. It appears to be executed entirely with the graver, except upon the lights, which are foftened with round dots, apparently made with the dry point. Under it is written, MARIA, VIRGO *felicitates*, and marked, *C. R. V. S. Meffanæ*, 1735. The *C. R.* and *V. S.* are joined together, cypher-ways, in the manner expreffed on the plate at the end of the volume; and the initials are thus explained at the bottom: *Carolus Rex utriufque Siciliae*. This print is in the collection of Dr. Monro.

CAROT.
Flourifhed, 1585.

By this artift, who refided at Rome, I have feen a fmall upright print, reprefenting *St. Francis holding a crofs*. From the broad, fpirited ftyle, in which it is etched, I fhould fuppofe he was a painter; and it appears from the word *fecit*, which he has added to his name, without attributing the design to any body else, that it was his own.

UGO or HUGO DA CARPI.
Flourished, 1500.

He was a native of Italy, and a painter of no very considerable talents; though a man of ingenuity. The following anecdote is recorded of him, that he painted a picture with the ends of his fingers, without using a pencil; which picture was preserved at the altar of the church of St. Regard at Rome, and Michael Angelo Buonarota, being greatly importuned to give his opinion concerning it, replied simply, that it would have been better, had he used his pencil. His engravings on wood, however, have secured to him that fame, which, perhaps, his paintings might not have done. I shall not, in this place, enter into an examination of the claim, which has been given him, of being the first engraver on wood. That he was not, will hereafter be abundantly proved, in the essay on that subject, prefixed to the second volume of this work. His claim to the invention of that species of engraving on wood, distinguished by the name of chiaro-scuro, in imitation of drawing, will appear to be better founded. This is performed by using more blocks than one; and Ugo da Carpi usually had three; the first for the outline and dark shadows; the second for the lighter shadows; and the third for the half tint. The prints by this artist, though very slight, are usually very spirited, and in a masterly style. They preserve, at least, a bold striking resemblance of the sketches of the great painters, from whose designs they are taken. His first work of this kind appears from Vasori to have been,

A *Sibyl reading in a book, with an infant holding a flambeau to light her*, from Raphael. We have also by him

The *burning of Troy, with Æneas saving his father Anchises*, a large upright print, from the same.

A *descent from the cross*, from the same, a middling sized upright print.

David cutting off the head of Goliah, a middling sized plate, length-ways, from the same.

A *Magician*, seated on the ground, with a book open before him; and in the back-ground to the right appears a bird, with all its feathers plucked off, a large upright print, from Parmigiano. The same subject was also engraved on copper by one of the disciples of M. Antonio. Basan calls it, *Diogenes seated at the entrance of his tub*.

These are all I can mention; but he engraved a great number more, from masters above-mentioned, and from others also.

GIULIO CARPIONE.
Born, 1611. Died, 1674.

This artist, a native of Venice, was a painter of great eminence. He chiefly excelled in painting *Bacchanals, processions, and triumphs*, which he executed in a superior style. His pictures are generally small, and consist of a great variety of figures, which are finely composed with much grace,

grace, and great excellency of colouring : fo that his paintings were greatly fought after, and have always borne a good price. He alfo etched feveral plates, which though flight, are performed in a very mafterly manner, and bear fome refemblance to thofe of Guido. The drawing of the naked parts of the figures indeed is not fo correct, nor are the extremities fo well marked. I fhall notice by him, from his own compofition,

Two fmall plates, length-ways, reprefenting *Bacchanalian fubjects, with boys playing*, &c.

Love blinding temperance, a fmall plate, length-ways.

Chrift in the garden of olives, a middling fized upright plate.

A *holy family, with angels, and the Deity reprefented above*, a fmall upright plate.

A *repofo: the Virgin is reading and Jofeph is ftanding by her*, a fmall upright plate.

R. CARR.
Flourifhed, 1668.

This engraver, who was certainly an Englifhman, imitated the ftyle of Hollar, but with no great fuccefs. We have etched by him a map of England dated 1668.

LODOVICO CARRACCI.
Born, 1555. Died, 1619.

The family of the Carracci have immortalized their names, not only by the extraordinary merit of their performances, but by the fchool of defign, which they eftablifhed at Bologna, in order to encourage the drawing of the human figure from nature. And they not only fucceeded themfelves wonderfully in this branch of the art, but alfo brought up feveral very excellent fcholars; and the very fame thofe fcholars have acquired, reflects no fmall degree of honour upon their tutors. The firft artift of this well known family was Lodovico Carracci, who was born at Bologna, A. D. 1555, and firft ftudied under Profpero Fontana; but he perfected himfelf by an affiduous examination of the works of the greateft mafters. And he fucceeded fo well in colouring efpecially, that his pictures are juftly held in the higheft eftimation.

By this celebrated artift we have a few fmall engravings, from his own compofitions. He firft etched his defign, and afterwards finifhed it with the graver. His etchings are flight and free; and the extremities of the figures are marked in a mafterly manner. I fhall notice the following by his hand:

A *holy family*, a middling fized plate, length-ways, wherein Jofeph is reprefented, leaning his head upon his hand.

The *Virgin, half figure, feated, holding the infant Jefus, furrounded with angels*, a fmall upright plate.

The *Virgin giving the breaft to the infant Chrift*, the fame.

The *Virgin feated, holding a book in her hand; the infant Chrift and St. John are feen at the corner*, the fame.

He often marked his plates with the initials of his name, as L. C. or I. O. C.

AGOSTINO CARRACCI.
Born, 1558. Died, 1602.

He was the second artift of this extraordinary family, firft coufin to the preceding painter, and brother to Annibale Carracci. Their father's name was Antonio, and he was a taylor by occupation; but being willing to make a better provifion for his children, he gave them a good education. Agoftino, in particular, was bred a fcholar; but his violent inclination for the arts foon manifefting itfelf. Antonio placed him with a goldfmith; where, it is highly probable, he acquired fome knowledge in the art of engraving. This bufinefs, however, not fuiting his temper, he at laft refolved to follow painting; and firft placed himfelf under Fontana. Afterwards he became the difciple of Pafferotti; but he completed his ftudies with his coufin Louis Carracci. With all his excellence as a painter, he could not give up the defire he had formed in his mind of improving himfelf in the art of engraving; a tafte for which he had difcovered, fo early as the age of fourteen. Accordingly he applied to Cornelius Cort, one of the moft celebrated artifts of that time; and imitated his manner fo exactly, with refpect to the mechanical part of it, that were it not for the great fuperiority, which appears in the drawing of the prints of Carracci, it would be difficult to diftinguifh them from each other. A ftriking inftance of the truth of this affertion, may be feen in the *holy family with St. Jerom*, from Correggio, which was engraved by both artifts.

Agoftino Carracci worked entirely with the graver, in a bold, free ftyle: and his drawing of the naked parts of the figure is admirable. The heads are remarkably fine, and the extremities are marked in a moft accurate and mafterly manner. His draperies are frequently ftiff, and croffed with a fquare fecond ftroke, which gives them an unpleafing effect. But perhaps his greateft defect is the prevalent fault of that age, namely, the little attention paid to the chiaro-fcuro. The lights are too much fcattered, and left untinted, as well upon the diftances, as upon the front and principal objects; which not only deftroys the harmony of the effect, but gives a flight, unfinifhed appearance even to the neateft engraving. Bafan fpeaks of him in thefe words: " This " excellent artift, equally verfed in the fciences and the fine arts, treated his en-
" gravings in fo perfect a ftyle, that one knows not which to admire moft, " the correctnefs of his drawing, or the beauty of the performance. All young " artifts ought carefully to obferve, with what facility and perfection he " expreffed the extremities of his figures, and with what art he executed even " landfcape with the graver."

Agoftino Carracci died 1602, aged 44.

The following are the principal engravings by this great artift:

The *adoration of the Magi*, a very large upright print, arched at the top, engraved on feven plates, from Baldaffare Peruzzi.

A *holy family, with St. Jerom, and Mary Magdalen kiffing the foot of the*

the infant Chriſt, a large upright plate from Correggio, dated 1586. Cornelius Cort alſo engraved a print from this picture, which bears the ſame date.

The *Virgin ſeated upon a flight of ſteps, holding the infant Chriſt. St. John is ſtanding by them, and Joſeph appears behind. Towards the left is St. Michael treading on the devil, holding a pair of ſcales, in which are two ſmall figures*, a large upright plate, from Lorenzino da Bologna.

A *holy family, repreſented on a ſort of pedeſtal, with St. Anthony and St. Catherine below*, a large upright plate from Paolo Veroneſe, dated 1583.

The *marriage of St. Catherine*, a large upright plate, from the ſame.

An *ecce homo*, half figures, a middling ſized upright plate, after Correggio, dated 1587.

The *crucifixion*, a large print, length-ways, on three plates, after Tintoretto.

A *dead Chriſt in the tomb, with an angel holding one of his hands*, a middling ſized upright plate, from Paolo Veroneſe. The ſame ſubject was alſo engraved by Gaſper Duchange, for the Crozat collection.

Chriſt appearing to St. Anthony, and conſoling him during his temptation, a large upright plate from Tintoretto.

The *Virgin appearing to St. Jerom*, the ſame, from the ſame. Dated 1588.

The *martyrdom of St. Juſtina*, a large upright print on two plates, from Paolo Veroneſe.

The *extaſy of St. Francis*, a ſmall upright plate, copied from the beautiful etching of Franciſco Vanni. This is dated 1595.

Æneas ſaving his father from the deſtruction of Troy, a large plate, length-ways, from Frederico Baroccio.

Mercury and the Graces, a ſmall plate, length-ways, from Tintoretto.

Wiſdom accompanied by Peace and Abundance, driving away the God of War, the ſame from the ſame.

The two following are from his own compoſitions :

St. Francis receiving the ſtigmatics ; in the front of the print is a ſcull ; a large upright plate.

The *cord or girdle of St. Francis*, thus called becauſe St. Francis is repreſented in the clouds, diſtributing pieces of his cord to the popes, cardinals, biſhops, and kings, who appear below; a very large upright plate, dated 1586.

He marked his plates A. C. or AVG. F. or Agos. C. or Ag. C. or Ag. Bononiæ. But when the collector is acquainted with his manner, he cannot eaſily be miſtaken in his prints.

ANNIBALE CARRACCI.
Born, 1560. Died, 1609.

He was the ſecond ſon of Antonio Carracci, and brother to Agoſtino, mentioned in the preceding article. He was born at Bologna, and applied himſelf wholly to painting. That the works of genius and merit do not always meet with their juſt reward, we have a ſtriking inſtance in the hiſtory of this great artiſt. Poſſeſſed of ſuperior abilities, which he cultivated with great ſtudy and application, he arrived at ſo high a pitch of excellence, that

few

few have furpaffed him in any of the great requifites of the art of painting; and none I believe, in correctnefs of drawing the human figure. To his correctnefs he joined an admirable tafte. His pictures are held in the higheft eftimation, and juftly ranked among the productions of the firft mafters; but his labours were by no means recompenced as they deferved; and he died of chagrin, to the lafting difgrace of cardinal Farnefe. That opulent ecclefiaftic employed Carracci, for a very fmall ftipend, to ornament his palace with paintings; which he performed with unremitting affiduity, juftly expecting at the end of eight, or, as fome fay, ten years, the time employed in the execution of the work, to receive a bountiful reward for his labour; but to his great aftonifhment, was prefented with five hundred crowns. This paltry fum for fo noble a performance was rather an affront, than a reward. And it lay fo heavy upon the mind of the artift, that it is faid to have thrown him into a confumption, which haftened by his own intemperance, put an end to his life, at Naples, where he had retired for his health, A. D. 1609, he being then only 49 years of age.

This great work of Carracci, which has been engraved feveral times, is well known by the name of the *Farnefian Gallery*. We have fome few etchings which are retouched with the graver, by the hand of this artift. And though the point appears to have been taken up for amufement only, yet the hand of the mafter is vifible in his productions; one of the beft of which, in my opinion, as well in point of finifhing, as in fpirit and character, is

The *crowning of Chrift with thorns*, a fmall upright plate, dated 1606. This as well as all the following, is from his own compofition, and has been copied feveral times.

A *dead Chrift on the lap of the Virgin*, who is accompanied by St. John and Mary Magdalen, a fmall plate, length-ways, called the *Chrift du Caprarole*, dated 1597.

The *adoration of the fhepherds*, a fmall plate, length-ways, called the *little crib or manger*; part of which a fhepherd is leaning againft, in the middle of the print. This has been copied feveral times, the fame fize.

The *adoration of the Magi*, a fmall upright plate.

Chrift and the woman of Samaria, a middling-fized plate, length-ways.

A *holy family, where Jofeph is feated, leaning againft a column, holding a book*, a fmall plate, length-ways.

The *Virgin holding the infant Chrift, and giving drink to St. John*. This print is diftinguifhed by the name of the *Virgin of the porringer*, a fmall plate, length-ways.

The *defcent of the Holy Ghoft*, a fmall upright plate nearly fquare. This is marked with a fingular cypher, compofed of an A. a C. and a B. for *Annibale Carracci, Bolognefe*. See this cypher copied on the plate at the end of the volume.

Sufanna and the elders, a middling fized plate, nearly fquare.

Jupiter and Antiope, a fmall plate, length-ways, dated 1592.

Silenus with two fatyrs, a fmall circular plate, about eight inches and a half diameter; the border of which is ornamented with vine branches, and bunches of grapes. This is commonly called the *difh of Annibale Carracci*; and

and is said to have been engraved upon the bottom of a salver, belonging to cardinal Farnese.

He often uses the letters A. C. when he does not sign his name at length. However, his works are easily distinguished from those of his brother Agostino, who I believe never etched.

FRANCESCO CARRACCI, called FRANCESCHINO.
Born, 1594. Died, 1622.

This imprudent young man, possessed of superior talents for the art of painting, might with proper application, have acquired perhaps a reputation, equal, if not superior to any of the Carracci's. He was nephew to the two foregoing artists, and instructed in the art of design by Lodovico Carracci. In a short time he attained to a prodigious knowledge of the human figure, which he drew so correctly, as to astonish his tutor. But neglecting the dictates of genius and of reason, he gave way to vice and debauchery, which soon brought his life to a miserable end. He died in an hospital at Rome, A. D. 1662, aged only 28 years. He etched some few prints, from the compositions of his uncle, Annibale Carracci. Among them are the following :

The *Virgin with the infant Jesus, seated upon a cloud*, a small upright plate.

Semiramis, and three other *famous women of antiquity*, four small upright plates.

He sometimes marked his plates with an F. and a C. joined together, in the fashion of a cypher, in the manner expressed on the plate at the end of the volume.

LAURENCE CARS.
Flourished, 1760.

A modern French engraver of great merit, who resided at Paris. By him we have a considerable number of prints, from Le Moine, and other masters. Among the rest,

The portrait of *Louis XV. king of France, surrounded with emblematical figures*, a large upright oval plate, from Le Moine.

Hercules and Omphale, a middling sized upright plate, from the same.

Perseus and Andromeda, the same from the same.

Time and Truth, the same, from the same.

Nymphs bathing, the same from the same.

CARTARUS. See KARTARIUS.

W. CARTER.
Flourished, 1660.

This ingenious artist was the disciple of Winceslaus Hollar, and imitated his style of etching with great success. Apparently, he assisted his master in the execution of his large works; and this might probably be the reason, that his name so seldom appears. And indeed I do not ever recollect

lect to have seen it, at full length, affixed to any plate; but he substituted the initials W. C. Among other things by this engraver, are the ornamental vignettes and letters, at the top of the pages, at the begining of each book in *Ogilby's Tranſlation of Homer*.

STEPHEN CARTERON.
Flouriſhed, 1615.

By this artiſt, who appears to have worked from his own deſigns, we have ſeveral prints, which he has marked S. C. or S. C. F. with the date 1615, underneath it. The F. as uſual, ſtands for fecit. He alſo engraved ſome ornaments for goldſmiths and jewellers, &c.

THOMAS CARTWRIGHT.
Flouriſhed, 1571.

He was an architect and builder, and by him it is ſaid, was engraved a plan of the *Royal Exchange* of London.

WILLIAM CARTWRIGHT.
Flouriſhed,

A name affixed to the portrait of *Thomas Cranmer, archbiſhop of Canterbury*, a half ſheet print, after Holbein.

J. CARWITHAM.
Flouriſhed, 1730.

This engraver was I believe a native of England. We have a conſiderable number of book-plates and other prints by him, ſome of them executed with the graver only, but the greater part etched and retouched with the graver in a ſtyle reſembling that of Bernard Picart. I ſhall only notice by him the *ſtatue of the Laocoon*, a middling ſized upright plate from the antique, dated 1741. An *emblematical frontiſpiece* in twelves, from B. Picart, dated 1723.

NICHOLAS DE LA CASA.
Flouriſhed,

An engraver of great merit, who appears to have been a native of Lorraine in Italy, and from the ſtyle of his engraving, to have flouriſhed towards the end of the ſixteenth century. We have by him the portrait of *Baccio Bandanelli*, a ſmall upright plate, executed entirely with the graver, in a ſtyle greatly reſembling that of Agoſtino de Muſis, whoſe ſcholar perhaps he may have been. But his beſt print is the portrait of the *Emperor Charles V*. in an oval, ſurrounded by an ornamental border, with ſeveral figures, copied from a print of the ſame ſize, engraved both on wood and copper by Æneas Vico, from a deſign of his own. It is a large upright plate, ſigned N. D. LA CASA, LOTARINGUS. F. without any mention of the name of Vico, or any date.

ANDREA

ANDREA CASALI.
Flourished, 1740.

A modern Italian artist, who resided some time in London, and was employed to paint the transparent pictures, which were exhibited at the magnificent fire-works in the Green Park, A. D. 1749. He also painted a great variety of *historical pictures*, for the nobility, &c. of England. By him we have several etchings from his own compositions: Among others,

The *princess Gunhilda, or innocence triumphant*, a middling sized, upright plate.

Lucretia comforted by her friends, a middling sized upright plate.

Simon Francis Ravenet has engraved both these subjects, from the pictures of Casali, for Mr. Boydell's collection.

ABRAHAM CASEMBROT.
Flourished,

By him we have several etchings, representing *sea-ports, with gallies and other shipping*; some *views* also, embellished with *prospects of the city of Messina*. He signs his name, *Abraham Casembrot, Belgicus*.

GIOVANNI FRANCESCO CASSIONE.
Flourished, 1678.

By this artist are performed several of the portraits, cut on wood, for the book, entitled, *Felsina Pittrice*, by C. C. Malvasia, in quarto, published 1678. Among those by this artist is the portrait of Malvasia himself.

PETER CASTEELS.
Flourished, 1726.

This artist painted birds, in a style greatly resembling that of Barlow, whose scholar, I am inclined to believe he was. He resided in London, A. D. 1726, where he engraved a set of different birds, consisting of a considerable number of plates, from his own paintings. They are slightly etched, but have much merit.

BERNARD CASTELLI.
Born, 1557. Died, 1629.

This painter was a native of Genoa, and a disciple of Andrea Semini. He engraved in a style something resembling that of Cornelius Bus. Among other works by this artist, is a set of prints for Tasso's Poems. His mark was a B. with a C. upon the top of it, in the manner of a cypher. See it copied on the plate at the end of the volume.

CASTELLUS GALLUS. See CHATEAU.

GIOVANNI BENEDETTO CASTIGLIONE.
Born, 1616. Died, 1670.

This juftly celebrated artift was born at Genoa. His firft mafter was Gio. Battifta Paggi. Afterwards he ftudied under Andrea Ferrari; and laftly perfected himfelf from the inftructions of Anthony Vandyck, who at that time refided at Genoa. He painted *portraits, hiftorical pieces, landfcapes, and caftles.* In the latter of which he is faid chiefly to have excelled; as alfo in *fairs, markets,* and all kinds of *rural fcenes.* He died at Mantua, A. D. 1670, aged 54.

His etchings, of which we have a great number, are fpirited, free, and full of tafte. The effect is, in general, powerful and pleafing. And many of them have a more harmonized and finifhed appearance, than is ufual from the point, fo little affifted by the graver. His drawing of the naked figure, though by no means correct, is notwithftanding managed in a ftyle that indicates the hand of the mafter. Among his moft eftimable plates, may be reckoned the following, all from his own compofitions:

The *animals coming to the ark,* a middling fized plate, length-ways.
Laban fearching for his gods in the tent of Jacob, the fame.
The *angel appearing to Jofeph in a dream,* a fmall plate, length-ways.
The *nativity of our bleffed Saviour,* a middling fized plate, length-ways.
The *flight into Egypt,* a fmall upright plate.
The *refurrection of Lazarus,* a fmall plate, length-ways, dated 1645.
Diogenes with his lanthorn, a fmall plate, length-ways.
A *magician with feveral animals,* the fame.
The *little melancholy,* a fmall upright plate.
A *ruin with a vafe, and two men ; one of them is reprefented pointing to a tomb,* a fmall plate, length-ways.
Two *rural fubjects, with fauns and fatyrs,* fmall plates, length-ways.
A *fet of heads,* on fixteen fmall upright plates.
Another *fet of heads,* on fix plates, the fame.

The initials of his two baptifmal names he frequently formed into a kind of a cypher, in the manner expreffed on the plates at the end of the volume.

J. B. CATENARO.
Flourifhed,

This artift was a painter, of whom I find no fatisfactory account. He refided, however, both at Madrid and at London, as appears from the portrait of *L. Jordani* by him, which is thus infcribed: " J. B. Catenaro pinx. " Madridi, et Londini fculp." It is a flight, fpirited etching, by no means devoid of merit. We have alfo by this artift, a *woman feated in a landfcape, with five children,* a fmall upright plate, from a compofition of his own. *Apollo furrounded by Cupids,* the fame.

L. J. CATHELIN.
Flourifhed, 1760.

A modern French engraver, by whom we have feveral neat *views,* from Vernet and other mafters.

JOHN

JOHN CATINI.
Flourished, 1760.
A modern engraver, who resided at Venice; by whom we have a set of fourteen large *heads*, from Piazzetta.

THOMAS CATLETT.
Flourished,
An obscure English engraver, whose name I found affixed to a *coat of arms*, surrounded with ornaments. We have also several book plates by this artist equally indifferent.

GIOVANNI BATTISTA CAVALERIIS.
Flourished, 1570.
This artist, who, I believe, was a native of Brescia in Italy, flourished from 1559 to 1688; as we find by the date of his engravings, which were very multifarious, and, according to Abbé Marolles, amounted to three hundred and seventy-seven or upwards. His manner of engraving sometimes resembles that of Æneas Vico, one of the disciples of Marc Antonio. His prints have, in my opinion, very little to recommend them. They are usually executed entirely with the graver, in a dry tastelefs style, without effect; the lights being scattered, and unharmonized; and his drawing is exceedingly defective; particularly in the extremities of his figures. Sometimes he etched his plates, and retouched them with the graver. A great part of his engravings are no other than copies from those of different masters.

I shall only mention the following prints by this artist:

Beati Apollinaris Martyris, primi Ravanatum Episcopi, Res Gestæ, Romæ 1586; or the *Life and Miracles of Apollinaris, first Bishop of Ravenna*, in folio, consisting of many plates, which are coarsely etched and retouched with the graver.

Ruins of Rome, from Joan. Ant. Dossius, on thirty-three plates, dated 1579.
The *Frontispiece and heads to the Lives of the Popes*, dated 1588.
Ecclesiæ Anglicanæ Trophæa, in folio, from Nicolaum Circiniaum.
The *murder of the innocents*, a large plate, length-ways, from Raphael.
The *miracle of the feeding of five thousand*, on two plates, a large print, length-ways, from the same.
The *battle of Constantine*, from the same.
The *descent from the cross*, from Daniello de Volterra, a middling sized, upright plate.
The *resurrection of Christ*, a very large upright plate from Livio Agresti da Forli.
He also engraved from Michael Angelo, Polidoro, and other great masters.

F. MORELLON LE CAVE.
Flourished, 1730.
He was the disciple of Bernard Picart, and resided in England; where he was

was principally employed in engraving portraits for the bookfellers. He worked chiefly with the graver; but never attained to any great degree of merit, among other things by him is the head of *Dr. Pocock*, before T. Wells's edition of his works.

CORNELIUS VAN CAUKERKEN.
Flourifhed, 1657.

He was a printfeller, and eftablifhed at Antwerp, where he engraved feveral plates from Rubens and other mafters. He worked entirely with the graver, in a heavy, laboured ftyle, without much tafte. He ufually croffed his fecond ftrokes fquarely upon the firft, which mode of engraving requires more exquifite handling of the graver, than Caukerken poffeffed, to render the effect agreeable. His lights are generally too much covered; and his drawing is in particular very defective. However, fome of his beft prints are by no means devoid of merit. Among which may be reckoned the following:

The *martyrdom of St. Lievinus*, a large upright plate, from Rubens. The beft impreffions of this plate are before the name of Gafp. de Hollander was put at the bottom: it is dated 1657.

The *Roman charity*, a large plate, length-ways, from the fame painter. The firft impreffions are without the name of Corn. de Hollander. This appears to me to be one of his beft prints. Capt. Baillie has a proof print, in which the outlines of the naked parts of the figures are corrected by Rubens, with red chalk.

A *dead Chrift lying upon the ground, with his head repofed on the knees of the Virgin*, from Annibale Carracci, a middling fized plate, length-ways.

A *dead Chrift fupported by the Virgin and St. John*, a large upright plate, from Vandyck.

L. CAUQUIN.
Flourifhed,

He engraved part of the plates for a fmall book of *ornaments* for goldfmiths and jewellers, from the defigns of Gilles Legare, which were publifhed at Paris.

H. CAUSE.
Flourifhed, 1690.

A name affixed to the portrait of *Ferdinand D'Adda*, cardinal, dated 1690. I. CAUSE, another indifferent artift, apparently of the fame family. He engraved the head of *Joan. Baptifta Tavernier*, for Hondius's collection of portraits.

LE COMTE DE CAYLUS.
Flourifhed, 1730.

This nobleman, who was a great lover of the arts, has diftinguifhed himfelf, not only as an able connoifieur, but as an artift. He copied the flight
mafterly

masterly sketches of the most eminent painters with great precision, in a manner that proves his taste and judgment. His engravings are chiefly performed with the point; for he seems to have made little use of the graver. The number of plates which he executed, sufficiently testify, that his application to the arts must have employed a large share of his time. We have by him,

A set of upwards of two hundred plates, engraved from the *drawings of the great masters*, in the cabinet of the king of France.

A *collection of heads*, from the drawings of Rubens and Vandyck, in the cabinet of M. Crozat.

A set of *grotesque characters of heads*, from Leonardo da Vinci, published 1730.

A set of *antique gems*, from drawings by Boucherdon.

This artist rarely signed his name at length; but usually the initials are substituted in this manner: " M. le C. de C. sculp."

NICHOLAS CAZA. See CASA.

THOMAS CECIL.
Flourished, 1630.

Mr. Evelyn, speaking of the English engravers, says of Cecil, that he engraved heads from the life, and was little inferior, for the excellence of his "burin" or graver, and happy design, to any of the greatest Italian, French, or Flemish artists. A little may, and perhaps ought to be allowed to a writer, if in some instances of comparative merit, he should appear to be biassed in favour of his friend or countrymen; but when his zeal for the honour of either carries him beyond the reasonable bounds of discretion, his decision must appear too partial to claim any credit; and he, without doubt, weakens rather than strengthens, the cause he undertakes to defend. In the present instance, Mr. Evelyn, after having spoken of the most celebrated engravers of the age in which he lived, and of Nanteuil, in particular, whose extraordinary genius for drawing and engraving portraits from the life, has so justly immortalized his name, must be said to have decided too hastily at least; when he added, that in " excellency of the burin," Cecil was little inferior to him, or any of those masters he had mentioned before. The art of engraving was certainly at this period very low in England; whilst, on the continent, it flourished in its meridian splendour.

Cecil worked entirely with the graver, in a stiff, tasteless style. His plates, in general, are very neatly executed; the best of which are his portraits, and some of them are by no means devoid of merit. I shall only mention a few prints by this artist, all of which appear to be from his own designs.

Thomas Curle, bishop of Winton, a small upright plate.
Thomas Kedermister of Langley, the same, dated 1628.
John Weaver, prefixed to his Funeral Monuments, in folio, dated 1631.
The *frontispiece* to Ambrose Parry's Works, published in London, 1634, in folio.

The frontispiece to a book entitled, *Devout Contemplations*, a large folio, published in London, A. D. 1629.

The figures which he has introduced occasionally into his frontispieces, some of which are nearly naked, sufficiently prove, that he did not well understand the drawing of the human figure; for the outline is not only incorrect and heavy, but the extremities, in general, are very badly marked.

The scarcest print by this engraver is the portrait of *Sir John Burgh*, who was killed at the Isle of Rhee; and the reason assigned for it is, that the plate was afterwards altered a little, and the inscription erased, and the name of Gustavus Adolphus inserted in place of it.

JOAN. BAPTISTA CENCENSIS. See PASQUILINI.

DU CERCEAU.
Flourished,

By this engraver, who according to all appearance, never reached any very great degree of excellence, we have a set of *ornaments à la mode*, middling sized prints, length-ways, executed entirely with the graver, in a neat, tasteless style. They were published by Nicholas Visscher, and are marked, " inventé et gravé par Du Cerceau."

MICHAEL ANGELO CERQUOZZI, called DI BATTAGLIA.
Born, 1600. Died, 1660.

This artist was born at Rome, A. D. 1600, and was called Di Battaglia, because his genius chiefly led him to paint *battles, marches and skirmishes*. He also painted *fruit and flowers* with great success; and his pictures were held in very high estimation. He died A. D. 1660, aged 60 years. He etched, says Basan, several prints, which are more estimable for their scarcity than their beauty.

CARLO CESIO.
Flourished, 1660.

This artist is said to have been a disciple of Pietro da Cortona; but he is much better known by his engravings, than his paintings. His plates are chiefly etched, and harmonized with the graver, in a free, masterly manner. He drew correctly; and the extremities of his figures are in general finely marked; though slight, and in the broad, bold style of a painter. Cesio engraved a great variety of prints, from the greatest painters that flourished in the age in which he lived. The following may be considered as his greatest works.

The *Farnesian gallery*, from Annibale Carracci.
The *Pamphilian gallery*, from Pietro Berettini da Cortona, consisting of fifteen plates, including the title.

GASPER

GASPER DU CHANGE.
Flourished, 1707.

This artist was a native of France, and flourished at the commencement of the present century. In the year 1707, he was received as a member of the Royal Academy of Arts at Paris. His manner of engraving seems greatly to resemble that of *John Audran; but in general, it is neater; and the etching is not so predominant; his drawing is by no means so correct as Audran's; neither are his heads, and other extremities, marked in so masterly a style. The prints of Duchange, however, though mannered, and often rather laboured, have much to recommend them to the notice of the connoisseur, especially to such as are pleased with an agreeable management of the graver. He engraved several portraits; and, among them, that of *Charles de la Fosse*, for his reception into the Royal Academy 1707; and that of *F. Giradon*, for the same purpose. I shall also notice the following prints by this master:

Jupiter and Leda, a large plate, length-ways, from Correggio.
Jupiter and Diana, the same, from the same.
Jupiter and Io, a middling sized, upright plate, from the same.
Sornique retouched these plates, and added draperies.

Our Saviour in the tomb, supported by the Virgin; and an angel holding his right hand, from Paolo Veronese.

Peace confirmed in Heaven, and some other subjects, for the collection of prints engraved from the Luxembourg gallery, painted by Rubens.

Mary Magdalen washing the feet of Christ, a large plate, length-ways, from Jouvenet. The *merchandizers driven from the temple*, the same, from the same.

John Audran engraved the other two companions, namely, the *miraculous draught of fishes*, and *the resurrection of Lazarus*.

Tobit restoring sight to his father, from Antony Coypel, a middling sized plate, length-ways; and, in my opinion, one of his best.

He also engraved from Le Seur, Noel Coypel, and other masters.

JOHN CHANTRY.
Flourished, 1660.

He worked chiefly for the booksellers, and performed his plates entirely with the graver, in a stiff, dry style, which has nothing to recommend it. Among the portraits engraved by him are the following: *Edward Leigh*, *Esq.* M. A. of Magdalen Hall, Oxford; *Thomas Whitaker*, physician to Charles II. *Gething*, a writing master, &c. He also engraved some *ornamental frontispieces* for books, with figures, very indifferently performed.

NICHOLAS CHAPREON.
Flourished, 1649.

This artist, a native of France, born at Chateaudun, was the disciple of Simon Vouet, he never made any considerable progress in the art of painting; which perhaps induced him to take up the point. He resided a long time at Rome; we have engraved by him,

The *bible histories* painted in the Vatican by Raphael, commonly known by the name of *Raphael's Bible*. This collection chiefly consists of fifty-two plates, which are chiefly estimable as being (upon the whole) the best copies of that noble work; but however, the sweet simplicity of style, and correctness of drawing, so manifest in the works of that celebrated painter, are totally lost in the affected manner of the engraver. The heads are very indifferent, in general, and the other extremities very poorly marked. He frequently signs his plates with the initials of his name only, thus: N. C. F. the F. as usual standing for fecit; they are dated 1649.

One of his best single prints appears to me to be a small upright etching, representing *satyrs*, with *women and children*, a bold, and spirited etching.

P. F. CHARPENTIER.
Flourished,

A modern French engraver, by whom we have several prints, from Berghem, Vanloo, Boucher, &c.

LE CHARPENTIER, perhaps of the same family, another modern engraver, by whom we have some *sea views and landscapes*, from Vernet, Patel, &c.

LOUIS DE CHASTILLON.
Flourished, 1682.

This artist, who was a native of France, flourished towards the conclusion of the last century, and the beginning of the present. I do not find whose disciple he was; but he evidently attempted to imitate the free style of Girard Audran; and though he falls far short of equalling that great master, especially in taste and correctness of drawing; yet many of his prints possess great merit. Among the best of them may be reckoned the following:

The *seven sacraments*, large plates, length-ways, from the pictures painted by Poussin for the chevalier Pozzo; and something different from those of the Palais Royal, engraved by Pesne.

The *Fates spinning the thread of destiny for Mary de Medicis*, a middling sized upright plate, from Rubens, for the collection of prints from the Luxembourg gallery.

The *fountain of Apollo in the garden at Versailles*, a large plate, length-ways.

Part of the plates for *Les Edifices Antiques de Rome*, published at Paris, A. D. 1682, by Antoine Desgodetz, architect.

C. CHASTILLON, or CHATILLON, is mentioned by Florent le Comte, as the engraver of *views of towns and palaces, &c. in France*.

WILLIAM CHATEAU, or CASTELLUS.
Born, 1633. Died, 1683.

This artist was born at Orleans, A. D. 1633; and the strong desire he had of pursuing the arts engaged him, early in life, to go to Lyons, in order to

visit

visit Italy, as soon as occasion offered. After having worked there some time, he determined to go to Rome; where, on his arrival, hearing of the reputation, which Frederic Greuter had acquired as an engraver, he courted his acquaintance, and became his disciple. Under that artist he completed his studies, and was employed to engrave the portraits of the *popes*; in which work he succeeded so well, that he had a quantity of other plates given to him, by which, in a short time, he established his character as an artist. He then travelled from Rome to Florence, Parma, Genoa, and other places, in order to contemplate the works of the greatest masters; and afterwards returned to Lyons, where he remained some time with the Marquis de Sonozin. From thence he went to Paris, where he resided under the patronage of M. Colbert, till his death, which was occasioned by a violent fit of the cholic, A. D. 1683, he being then 50 years of age.

Chateau worked chiefly with the graver; but in some instances he has etched his back-grounds, especially when they were landscapes. It appears evidently, that he had a great command of that instrument. There is much clearness in his style of engraving; but from the square manner in which his first and second strokes intersect each other, the effect is rendered unpleasing, and his plates have a cold, silvery appearance. The style of his drawing is stiff and laboured; the outline is not always correct; and the extremities of his figures, in particular, are heavy, and poorly marked. In short, his prints seem to be the laboured productions of patience and assiduity, rather than the works of genius, assisted by good taste.

He frequently latinized his name, especially when it was subscribed to those plates he executed at Rome; and then it is put thus: *Guilielmus Castellus, Gallus*.

Among his best prints may be reckoned the following:

The *assumption of the Virgin*, a middling-sized, upright plate, from Annibale Carracci, for the collection of prints, engraved from the pictures in the king of France's cabinet.

The *martyrdom of St. Stephen*, the same, from the same master, and for the same collection.

The *Israelites gathering manna in the desert*, the same, from Nicholas Poussin, for the same collection.

Christ restoring sight to the two blind men of Jericho, the same, from the same, and for the same collection.

The *preservation of the young Pyrrhus*, a large plate, length-ways. This is a bad copy of that admirable picture, which Gerard Audran etched in so masterly a manner.

St. Paul caught up into Heaven, a middling sized upright plate, from the same painter: This was also engraved by Pesne.

The *death of Germanicus*, a large plate, length-ways, from the same painter, and for the same collection.

Paul restored to sight by Ananias, a middling sized upright plate, from Pietro de Cortona: Charles Allet also engraved this subject.

Rinaldo and Armida, from Le Seur, a large plate length-ways.

He also engraved from Raphael, Correggio, Ciro Ferri, Carlo Maratti, and other great masters.

J. B.

J. B. CHATELAIN.
Flourished, 1744.

Had this man been possessed of prudence and assiduity, equal to his great abilities, what might not have been expected at his hand? He would not work, but when necessity compelled him. With a piece of tobacco taken from his mouth, he could make an admirable drawing of a landscape. It was in drawing and engraving landscapes that he chiefly excelled; and the freedom of touch, and spirit, with which he performed them on paper and copper, has justly stamped a value upon them. From this artist, Vivares, so deservedly celebrated for his copies from Claude Audran, and other excellent prints, learned the first rudiments of engraving. The following curious anecdotes concerning Chatelain, were communicated to me by Mr. Grosse, who heard them from Mr. Rossiere, a great collector of prints.

Chatelain was so great an epicure, that if by accident he earned a guinea, he would immediately go to a tavern, and lay, at least, half of it out on a dinner.

He lived some time in a large old house, at or near Chelsea, said to have belonged to Oliver Cromwell, which he took in consequence of having dreamed he should find a treasure there. He was so prepossessed by this idea, that he used to spend whole days, lying upon his face, listening if by the shaking, occasioned by the carriages passing to and fro, he could hear the chinking of money. Sometimes he would work in pulling up the floors, searching behind the wainscot, and removing walls, in quest of this hidden treasure, till he so blistered and bruised his hand, that he could not work for a considerable time.

He etched a variety of *landscapes*; some from his own designs; but the greater part from Gasper Dughet, called Poussin, and other masters. Among them is a middling sized plate, length-ways, from Rembrandt, published by Pond, 1744.

I. B. CHATELAIN, a name I have seen affixed to a print, intitled, "*Le Cuisiniere Italienne*," engraved greatly in the style of Beauverlet. This probably is a more modern artist, and a native of France.

CHATILLON. See CHASTILLON.

CHAUFOURIER.
Flourished,

A very indifferent modern French engraver, who apparently flourished at the beginning of the present century. He worked for the booksellers; and I have seen some bad plates for a book of gardening, which were engraved by him.

FRANCOIS CHAUVEAU.
Born,   Died, 1676.

This artist was a native of France, born at Paris. He was instructed in the art of design by Laurent la Hire, and applied himself to the graver; which instrument he soon quitted for the point; and the prints he produced with it soon convinced him, that it was better suited to his taste, and the celerity of execution, which the fecundity of his genius seemed to require. That he was a man possessed of a lively imagination, and great fertility of invention, is evident from the prodigious number of compositions, which we have by his hand. He seems to have sketched his thoughts upon paper, as fast as they entered his mind, and taken little or no pains to correct or expunge any part of them afterwards. Hence it is, that his works are frequently faulty, and unequal to each other. " If," says Basan, " we find not in his prints a " beautiful style of engraving, we see, at least, with pleasure, the fire, effect, " truth, variety, and ingenious turns of his compositions." I have made the following observation concerning the engravings of this artist: His small plates, which I think are his best, are executed in a style, much resembling that of Le Clerc; which was evidently founded upon that of Callot. In his large prints, he approaches near to that coarse, dark style, which was adopted by La Hire, his tutor. He died at Paris, A. D. 1676. His works consist of upwards of three thousand plates; among which the sets of prints for the following books are from his own compositions. The *Bible History*. The *History of Greece*. The *Metamorphosis of Benserade*. The *Jerusalem of Tasso*. The *Fables of la Fontaine*. *Alaric, or Rome conquered*, and several romances, &c. Among the prints engraved by him from other masters, are the following:

Christ with the disciples at Emaus, a middling sized plate, length-ways, from Titian. Masson engraved the same subject; and his beautiful print is known by the name of the *table cloth*.

A *concert*, a middling sized plate, nearly square, from Dominichino.

The *life of St. Bruno*, from Le Sueur, engraved conjointly with Le Clerc.

Apollo and Daphne, from Nicholas Poussin, a middling sized plate, dated 1667.

A *Virgin and Child, with St. John and little angels*, finely etched, and finished with much taste. It is marked, " F. Chauveau pinx et fecit," a small plate, length ways.

Meleagre presenting the head of the boar to Atalanta, a small upright plate from Laurent la Hire.

He also engraved from Le Brun and other masters.

See the cypher he frequently substituted for his name, copied on the plate at the end of the volume.

QUENTIN PETER CHEDEL.
Flourished,

A modern engraver, who, according to Basan, died some few years since. He etched his plates with great spirit, and retouched them with the graver, in a ſtyle ſomething reſembling that of John Viſſcher; and his works prove him to have been a man of ability. By him we have ſome ſmall plates length-ways, repreſenting *banditti and troops of ſoldiers ſkirmiſhing, with landſcape back-ground*, from Vander Meulen. Alſo,

Aurora, a ſmall landſcape, length-ways, from David Teniers.

The *well*, a ſmall upright plate, from Boucher.

The *hermitage*, from Pierre, its companion.

PETER CHENU.
Flouriſhed, 1760.

A modern engraver, who reſided at Paris, and engraved in a ſlight ſtyle a large number of prints from various maſters. Among others, the *ſailor's amuſement*, a ſmall plate length-ways. from D. Teniers.

The *Flemiſh baker*, from Oſtade, a ſmall upright plate.

FRANCOIS CHEREAU.
Flouriſhed, 1730.

This engraver appears to be a native of France. We have a large number of prints by him, which prove what great command he had of the graver; for his prints are executed entirely with that inſtrument, in a manner ſo nearly reſembling that of the Drevets, that I have little doubt but that he was brought up in their ſchool. The mechanical part of his engraving is exceedingly neat and well executed; and his drawing is correct. Yet from a ſameneſs of the ſtyle in the engraving of his fleſh, his draperies and background, his prints have a cold, heavy, laboured appearance; and the lights being too much covered, prevents that brilliancy of effect, which might be expected from an artiſt of equal abilities. His prints, however, poſſeſs great merit, though they cannot be ſaid to deſerve a place among thoſe of the firſt claſs of artiſts. I ſhall only mention the following by his hand:

St. John in the deſart, a ſmall upright plate from Raphael, for the Crozat collection.

The *crucifixion of Chriſt*, a large upright plate from Guido, publiſhed by Drevet.

The portrait of *Eliza Sophia Cheron*, from a picture painted by herſelf, a middling ſized, upright plate.

The portrait of *cardinal de Polignac*, from Rigaud, the ſame.

He alſo engraved a variety of other ſubjects, portraits in particular, from different maſters.

JAMES CHEREAU.
Flouriſhed, 1730.

This artiſt uſually diſtinguiſhes himſelf from his brother Francois Chereau, mentioned in the foregoing article, by adding the word *le june*, or *the younger*, to his name. He reſided at Paris, and like his brother, worked entirely with the graver, and in a manner greatly reſembling his. The prints by by this artift are very neat, and highly finifhed; but cold and filvery in their effect. They want that animation fo effentially neceffary to render an engraving particularly interefting, and which Girard Audran was mafter of in fo fuperior a degree. This it is, that makes the flight fcratchy etching of the painter fo much more eftimable, than the cold, laboured efforts of patience unaffifted by the warmth of imagination, and the impulfe of genius. Chereau's portraits poffefs great merit; and his beft prints are very defervedly held in high eftimation. Among them are the following:

A *holy family*, from Raphael, a middling fized upright plate, for the Crozat collection.

The *Virgin and Child, with St. John*, the fame, from the fame mafter, and for the fame collection.

The *transfiguration*, from the fame mafter, a large upright plate, arched at the top.

David, a half figure, with the head of Goliah, a middling fized upright plate, from Dominico Feti.

Vertumnus and Pomona, a middling fized upright plate, from Francois Marot.

The portrait of the *bifhop of Montpelier*, a middling fized upright plate, from Raoux.

The portrait of the *bifhop of Senez*, the fame from the fame.

He alfo engraved a variety of other plates from different mafters.

Chereau came over into England, being invited hither by Du Bofc; and, among other things, engraved the profile portrait of *George the Firft*; but the extravagant price he demanded for his works, was the occafion of his meeting with but little encouragement; upon which he foon returned to Paris.

ELIZABETH SOPHIE CHERON LE HAY.
Born, 1648. Died, 1711.

This lady, whofe name is juftly celebrated by the biographers of the artifts was the daughter of Henry Cheron, a painter in enamel, and by her father firft inftructed in the art of defign and painting. She made a rapid progrefs; and the productions of her pencil were greatly admired, efpecially her portraits, which fhe executed in a pleafing ftyle. She alfo painted hiftory with great fuccefs. She died, A. D. 1711, aged 63. She was prefented to the Royal Academy of Arts at Paris by Le Brun, A. D. 1676, and honourably received as a member. For her amufement fhe alfo engraved; and we have a fet of cornelians from her own defigns, of which three are etched by herfelf, namely, *Bacchus and Ariadne, Mars and Venus*, and *night fcattering her poppies*. The reft were engraved by Urfaline and Jane de la Croix her nieces, J. Audran, C. Simoneau, and others.

She alfo engraved a *defcent from the crofs*, which is etched, and retouched with the graver, in a very mafterly manner, from a medal in wax, coloured by Zumbo, a Sicilian.

Alfo a *drawing book*, confifting of thirty-fix prints in folio.

LOUIS CHERON.
Born, 1660. Died, 1713.

This artist was brother to the lady mentioned in the preceding article, and born at Paris, A. D. 1660. After being instructed in the first principles of the art of painting in his own country, he went to Italy, where he remained, supported by the bounty of his sister, eighteen years. He composed with facility, and drew correctly, but not gracefully. The troubles, which arose in his native country on account of religion, obliged him, who was a Calvinist, to quit it, and seek a refuge in England, where he was employed by the duke of Montague, and died in London, A. D. 1713, aged 53. He engraved with great taste the following prints:

St. Peter healing the lame man at the gates of the temple, a middling sized plate length-ways, from his own composition.

The *death of Ananias and Saphira*, the same.

St. Philip baptising the Eunuch, the same.

CHERPIGNON.
Flourished,

An engraver of merit, by whom, among other things, we have *a holy family*, wherein is represented the Virgin seated, the infant Christ asleep in her lap, and Joseph is leaning on a large stone behind her. It is etched in a bold, free style, and retouched with the graver, in such a manner, as proves the artist had great command of that instrument. The lights are broad and well, but too much scattered: it is engraved from a composition of Laurent de la Hire.

CHERUBIN ALBERT. See ALBERTI.

G. CHEVILET.
Flourished,

A very indifferent modern engraver, by whom we have several large plates of *foreign views, ruins*, &c. from Innocente Bellavite and other masters. He etched in a neat scratchy style, and retouched his plates with the graver, without producing the least pleasing effect. The figures which are occasionally introduced, he has executed in a manner that does him no kind of credit.

FABRIZZIO CHIARI.
Born, 1621. Died, 1695.

This painter was born at Rome, A. D. 1621, and acquired a considerable reputation in his profession. He died 1695, aged 74 years. By his hand we have several etchings from Poussin. They are executed in a slight scratchy manner, by no means correctly drawn; yet, however, they manifest the hand of the master. Among others are the following:

CHI [199] CIA

Mars and Venus in a landscape, a small plate, length-ways, marked FABRITUS. CLARUS SCULP. 1635.

Venus and Adonis a middling sized plate, length-ways, marked NICOLAUS PUSSINUS IN F. without the name of Fabrizzio. This etching has been usually attributed to Poussin himself; but it is undoubtedly the work of Fabrizzio.

Venus with Mercury and several children, the same.

CHISBOUT.
Flourished,

This engraver appears to have resided at Paris, and worked for Drevet; at least, his name as the publisher, is affixed to a coarse, incorrect etching, representing *Dutch boors playing at cards*, marked " Chisbout fecit," a small plate, length-ways.

PETER PHILIP CHOFFARD.
Flourished, 1760.

This artist was a native of France, and resided at Paris. He was a designer, as well as an engraver. By him we have a variety of small book prints, and some views, as well from his own designs, as from those of other masters.

CHRISTOPHER CHRIEG.
Flourished, 1572.

" Christoph^s. Chrieg^r. All^s. inci. is the signature," says Papillon, " of an
" engraver, affixed to a large print, representing the *sea-fight* at Lepanto.
" It is a magnificent engraving on wood, containing more than three hun-
" dred vessels and gallies. The combatants, which are exceedingly nume-
" rous, are distributed with the greatest judgment. The dreadful confusion
" of the vessels with gallies on fire, or sinking to the bottom, cannot be re-
" presented in a superior style. It is cut on two blocks of wood, in the form
" of an oval, about two feet long, by sixteen inches in height. Upon the
" two upper corners of the oval are represented, the arrangement of the
" Christian army; and that of the Turks; and below, three Christian ge-
" nerals dividing the spoil; and the destruction of the Turkish fleet. This
" fine print was published at Venice, A. D. 1572, by Cæsare Vecelli, a rela-
" tion of the famous Titian, who, I believe, made the design, it being
" quite his taste."

LUCAS CIAMBERLANO.
Flourished, 1609.

This artist appears to have been a native of Urbino, and flourished towards the beginning of the last century. He worked entirely with the graver in a slight neat style, but there is not always that freedom in the turn of his
strokes,

strokes, which is requisite to render them perfectly agreeable to the eye. He drew the naked parts of the human figure with some degree of correctness. His heads indeed, and other extremities, are not always equally well executed. The lights upon the figures especially, are kept broad and clear. The general effect, however, is much hurt, by their being too much scattered, and equally powerful. Among other plates, engraved by this artist, are the following:

Christ appearing to Mary Magdalen in the garden, a middling sized upright plate, from Frederico Baroccio, to which his name is affixed in this manner: " Lucas Ciamberlanus Urbinas, I. V. Doct^r, del. et sculp." It is dated 1609.

St. Jerom dead, lying upon a stone, a middling sized upright plate, from Raphael.

The *twelve apostles*, small upright plates, from the same.

He also engraved from Polydoro, Palma, Cherubin Alberti, Annibale Carracci, Dominichino, and other great masters. He sometimes used the initials of his name only, thus: L. C. or L. C. sculp.

FRANCOIS CICHE.
Flourished,

This artist seems to have resided in Italy, and to have worked chiefly for the booksellers. I have seen by him some slight architectal etchings, finished with the graver, with little figures occasionally introduced. The manner, however, in which those plates are executed, does him no credit as an engraver.

CIROFER. See CIRO FERRI.

CIVITELLA. See CÆSAR ROBERTUS.

WILLIAM CLARKE.
Flourished,

An engraver of little merit, who flourished towards the end of the last century, by whom we have some portraits; among the rest, that of *George duke of Albemarle*, from Barlow; and *John Shower*, from a picture of his own. This last is engraved in mezzotinto.

THOMAS CLARKE.
Flourished, 1635.

An engraver, probably of the same family with the foregoing; his works possess no kind of merit, except that of neatness, to recommend them. We have by him several *frontispieces*, one especially for a book of devotion, printed at London, 1635.

JOHN

JOHN CLARKE.
Flourished, 1690.

This engraver was, I believe, a Scotsman; at least, he resided at Edinburgh, where he engraved the portrait of *William prince of Orange*, and the *princess Mary*, in the form of a medallion, dated 1690. We have several other portraits by him. I shall only mention, *Matthew Hall*, and *Andrew Marvell*, an octavo plate. He worked chiefly, if not entirely, with the graver, in a style which does him very little credit as an artist.

JOHN CLARKE.
Flourished,

Another engraver of the same name with the preceding, who, according to the Hon. Mr. Walpole, lived in Gray's Inn. By him we have the portrait of *Rubens*, a quarto sized plate, Also a print representing *Hercules and Deianira*, which prove him to have been a very indifferent artist.

CLARUS. See CHIARI.

D. CLASENS.
Flourished,

The name of an ancient engraver of no great merit, affixed to a coarse, incorrect etching, representing the *Virgin Mary holding the infant Christ, accompanied by St. John and an angel*, a small upright plate from Procaccini: it is without date, and marked, *D. Clasens F. et de*.

MARC CLASERI.
Flourished,

According to Papillon, this artist flourished in the sixteenth century, he was a native of Venice, and engraved several prints on wood; among which are enumerated the *four seasons*, and the *four ages of the world*, middling sized prints, length-ways.

VICTORIUS CLASSICUS.
Flourished,

Florent le Comte informs us, that this artist was a sculptor and an architect; and adds, that he also engraved some prints, from the paintings of Tintoretto; but the subjects of these prints are not specified.

CLEEMAN.
Flourished,

To this artist professor Christ, attributes the engravings on wood, marked with a knife and a trefoil; but the reason he gives for this conclusion, does not appear to me to be entirely decisive.

FRANCISCO DE CLEIN, or KLEYN.
Born, Died, 1658.

This artift was born at Roftock, in Germany, where, it appears, he learned the firft rudiments of painting; after which he went to Italy, where he refided four years. He chiefly excelled in hiftorical and grotefque fubjects, and is greatly commended for the fertility of his invention. In the reign of James the Firft, he came into England, and was employed by that monarch to make defigns for tapeftry, &c. He alfo etched feveral plates, in a ftyle much refembling that of Hollar, to which he fometimes put the initials of his name F. C. or F. K. but in general he figned it at length. I fhall only notice the following plates by him :

The *feven liberal arts*, with an ornamental frontifpiece, fmall fquare plates, marked " F. Clein fecit, 1645." And the *five fenfes, with grotefque ornaments*.

JOHN LE CLERC.
Born, 1587. Died, 1633.

He was born at Nancy in Lorrain, A. D. 1587; but ftudied in Italy, and imitated the manner of his mafter, Carlo Saraccino, called Venetiano, fo perfectly, that his pictures have frequently been taken for the productions of that artift's pencil. He died 1633, aged 46. He is called the Chevalier, becaufe he was knighted at Venice. Le Clerc etched feveral plates from the compofition of Venetiano; among others, the *death of the Virgin*, a middling fized upright plate. The invention of this fubject has been falfely attributed to Guido. This print, though flight, is performed in a fpirited and mafterly ftyle, and dated 1619.

Papillon mentions JOHN LE CLERC, who, he informs us, was of the fame family with the above mentioned artift, born at Paris, and an eminent engraver on wood. He cites feveral things, as performed by this artift; among the reft, a book of the *proportions of the human figure*, publifhed with the royal privilege, A. D. 1593.

SEBASTIAN LE CLERC.
Born, 1637. Died, 1714.

This artift was a native of France, born at Metz in Lorrain, and probably of the fame family with John le Clerc, mentioned in the preceding article. His genius for the arts difplayed itfelf in very early life; and from his father he learned the firft principles of drawing. Being defirous of habituating himfelf to the ufe of the graver, he executed feveral prints with that inftrument, but foon quitted it for one better fuited to his tafte, namely, the point, with which he could not only copy his defign with greater facility, but alfo more fpeedily; judging from the productions of this artift with the graver only, it feems reafonable to conclude, that he would never have eftablifhed by it a reputation, equal to that which he did by the point. His firft print is faid to be *the head of our Saviour*, which bears the date 1655, confequently was executed at the age of 18. Going to Paris, he was countenanced by Le Brun,

Brun, who advised him to devote the whole of his time to the study of engraving. Some time afterwards he was introduced to the minister, M. Colbert, and obtained an apartment in the Gobelins, and a pension of 1800 livres assigned to him, on condition that he worked for the king, who also honoured him with the title of his engraver; and by pope Clement XI. he was created a knight of Rome.

In the year 1672, he was appointed to engrave the *mausoleum*, erected by the Royal Academy of Arts, in the church of L'Oratoire at Paris under the direction of Le Brun; and for it received from the Academy a pension of 300 livres. The following year he married Charlotte Jeaune, the daughter of Vanden Kerchove, the king's dyer at the Gobelins; and by her he had eighteen children.

As his family increased, Le Clerc gave up the pension, settled upon him by the king, conceiving that he could work to greater advantage upon his own account. The multitude of plates, which he executed, and chiefly from his own designs, are said to have exceeded 3000; and some of them are very large, consisting of a prodigious variety of figures.

He died at Paris, A. D. 1714, aged 77 years; and was buried in the church of St. Hippolite, belonging to the parish, in which he resided. " This excellent artist," says Basan, " who designed with equal facility histori-
" cal subjects, landscapes, and animals, possessed a lively and brilliant imagi-
" nation, which was regulated by sound judgment. His compositions are full
" of knowledge and variety; and his drawing is very correct. His manner
" of engraving is neat, and the touches of his point easy and graceful. In a
" word, all the requisites are found in his works, which ought to render them
" worthy the admiration of connoisseurs." And this high compliment is not, in my opinion, greatly overstrained; though I think him inferior to Callot, whose style of engraving he frequently imitated, and appears to the greatest advantage, as he approaches the nearer to it.

The following are among his most estimable prints:

The *passion of our Saviour*, on thirty-six small plates, length-ways, from his own compositions. The best impressions are without the borders.

The *miracle of the feeding five thousand*, a middling sized plate, length-ways. In the first impressions, which are very rare, a town appears in the back-ground; in place of which a mountain is substituted in the common ones.

The *elevation of the large stones, used in building the front of the Louvre*, a large plate, length-ways. The first impressions are without the date, 1677, which was afterwards added.

The *academy of the sciences*, a middling sized plate, length-ways. The first impressions are before the skeleton of the stag and tortoise were added. The second impressions are before the shadow was enlarged at the bottom, towards the right hand side of the print. Both these impressions are very scarce. The first is rarely met with. This print was copied for Chambers's Dictionary.

The *monument of the king of Sweden*, a large upright plate.

The *monument of the chancellor Seguier*, the same. The latter is the most estimable,

estimable, because it procured the reception of the artist into the Royal Academy of Arts

The *triumphal arch of the port St. Antoine*, a large plate length-ways.

The *may of the Gobelins*, a middling sized plate, length-ways. The first impression is before the woman was introduced, who covers the wheel of the coach.

The *four conquests*, large plates, length-ways, representing the *taking of Tournay*, the *taking of Dovay*, the *defeat of the comte de Marsin*, and the *Switzerland alliance*.

The *battles of Alexander*, from Le Brun, six small long plates, including the title, which represents the picture gallery at the Gobelins. The first impressions of the *tent of Darius*, which plate makes part of this set, is distinguished by the shoulder of the woman, who is seated in the front, being without the shadow, which was afterwards added; for which reason they are called the prints with the *naked shoulder*.

The *entry of Alexander into Babylon*, a middling sized plate, length-ways. In the first impressions, the face of Alexander is seen in profile; in the second, it is a three quarter face, and therefore called the *print with the head turned*.

Also a vast number of beautiful *vignettes, title pages*, &c. &c.

HENRY VAN CLEVE or CLEFF.
Born, Died, 1589.

He is also called *Clivensis*. Generally, however, his name is not written at length, but a singular monogram, composed of an H. a V. and a C. is substituted in its stead. See this monogram copied on the plate at the end of the volume. The place of this artist's birth does not appear; but he resided at Antwerp; and was a painter of no small degree of eminence, especially in landscape; some few of which he also engraved himself. These are marked with his monogram, and the word *fecit* is added to it.

MARTIN VAN CLEVE or CLEFF.
Flourished,

According to professor Christ, this master adopted a very singular rebus, by way of a mark. It was a monkey seated, with the letters V. C. upon its belly. A monkey, it seems, in Flanders is called by the name of *Martin*. The initials are then easily decyphered. The prints also marked, M. C. are attributed to this master.

G. CLOCHE.
Flourished, 1616.

According to Abbé Marolles, this engraver flourished about the beginning of the last century, and by him we have engraved a view of the *town of Renes*.

CLAUSE or NICHOLAS CLOCK.
Flourished, 1589.

This name is affixed to a large print, length-ways, representing the *judgment*

ment of Midas, from Karl Van Mandere. It is executed entirely with the graver, in a coarse, flight style, somewhat resembling that of Cornelius Cort; but by no means equal to the works of that master; particularly with respect to the drawing, which is very defective in this print, especially in the extremities of the figures. It is dated 1589.

CORN. CLOCK is also mentioned in the list of engravers, by Evelyn; but none of his works are specified. I am not acquainted with them.

JOHN CLOPPER.
Flourished,

An obscure engraver of no great merit, who worked, I suppose, for the booksellers. To a very indifferent portrait of *Elias Benoist, an ecclesiastic*, executed entirely with the graver, he has affixed his name, " Joannes Clopper sculp."

PETER CLOUET or CLOWET.
Flourished,

This artist was a native of Antwerp, where he learned the first principles of the art of engraving. From thence he went to Italy to complete his studies, and worked at Rome, under Spierre and Bloemart. He afterwards returned to Antwerp, where he died, aged 62 years. He worked entirely with the graver, in a clear firm manner, something resembling that of Paul Pontius. His prints are usually deficient in harmony; and though full of colour, and boldly engraved, from too equal a distribution of the shadows, and the lights being too much scattered, they lose a great part of their effect. He neither drew with taste, nor correctly. The extremities of his figures are generally very defective. However, his prints, those especially which he engraved from Rubens, are held in no small estimation.

Among his best prints the following are usually reckoned:

The *death of St. Anthony*, a large upright plate, from Rubens.

The *descent from the cross*, the same from the same.

A *conversation, where several lovers are represented in a garden*, a large plate, length-ways, from the same.

A *landscape*, with a cottage; and the snow is represented falling, a large plate, length-ways, from the same, belonging to a set of six: the other five were engraved by S. Bolswert.

A *holy family*, a middling sized upright plate, from Vandyck.

The *battle of Joshua against the Amalekites*, a large print, on two plates, from William Courtois.

He also engraved from several other masters.

ALBERT CLOUET or CLOWET.
Flourished, 1672.

He was nephew to the preceding artist, and went to Italy to improve himself in his studies under C. Bloemart. He resided some time at Rome, where he engraved several of the portraits for the Lives of the Painters by Bellori. His principal employment seems to have been in the portrait line.

We

We have, however, some other subjects by him; among the rest, part of the set of prints, engraved from the pictures of Pietro Berretino da Cortona, in the palace of the duke of Tuscany; and in these he has imitated, with tolerable success, the neat manner of Cornelius Bloemart. Speaking of his portraits, many of them are attempted in the style of Mellan. At other times they are more like those of F. de Poilly; and sometimes bear a resemblance to those of Nanteuil; but they by no means equal, either in drawing, effect, or mechanical execution, the works of these great masters. He has succeeded, I think, the least in imitation of Mellan. Among a variety of other plates by him, are several of those, which were engraved for a work, entitled, *Effigies Cardinal. nunc viventium*, published at Rome by J. Rosie.

HERMAN COBLENT.
Flourished, 1576.

This artist was probably instructed by the Collaerts in the art of engraving, and their neat manner he seems, I think, in general, to have imitated, in the mechanical part of it especially, with no small success. But his drawing is by no means equally commendable: the outline is often incorrect, and the extremities of his figures are very heavy, and badly marked. His monogram is composed of an H. a C. and an F. joined together in the same manner as expressed upon the plate at the end of the volume. Among other engravings by this artist are the following:

The *four Evangelists*, very small upright plates.
Lucretia standing in an arch, the same.
The *Heathen deities*, single figures, in arches, the same. On some of these plates, that of *Vulcan* in particular, the monogram is reversed.

A *man seated at a table, with a quantity of provision, part of which is flying away as at his command; behind, a woman appears eating an egg*, with several other figures, a middling sized plate, length-ways.

PIETRO PAOLO COCCETTI.
Flourished, 1725.

Some indifferent plates of *architecture*, engraved by this artist, were published, A. D. 1725, in quarto.

ANTHONY COCHET or COGET.
Flourished,

An engraver, who flourished in the last century. According to Basan, he worked with the graver only; and by him we have *Time crowning Industry, and punishing Idleness*, a middling sized upright plate, from Rubens. He also engraved from other masters; and several portraits; among them that of *David Beck*, the painter, &c.

NICHOLAS COCHIN.
Flourished, 1660.

This artist was born at Troys in Champagne; and was probably the disciple

ciple of Callot, whose style of engraving he has frequently imitated very successfully. He designed also; and a large part of his works, which are exceedingly multifarious, are from his own compositions. His small figures have great merit; but when he attempted to execute large ones, he failed considerably. I shall only mention the following by him:

Part of the plates for a large folio volume of *plans and views of the camps, towns, battles, &c. appertaining to the conquests of the French army under Louis XIV.* published by Beaulieu, 1645, &c.

Part of the plates for the *entry of Louis XIV. and his queen into Paris.* The whole consisted of 22, which were published at Paris, 1622.

A *procession, with the flags, trumpets, &c. taken at the battle of Rocroy,* a large narrow plate from a design of his own.

The *life and passion of Christ,* small plates.

The *history of Judith,* the same, on ten plates.

The *passage through the red sea,* a middling sized plate, length-ways, from his own design.

Moses receiving the tables of the law, the same.

The *adoration of the shepherds,* the same.

The *conversion of St. Paul,* the same.

He also engraved from Rembrant, Callot, Del la Bella, Chauveau, &c.

He often omitted his name; and then he usually substitutes the initials, " N. C. fecit."

NOEL or NATALES R. COCHIN.
Flourished, 1691.

He was probably of the same family with the preceding artist, and engraved somewhat in the same style; but not with equal success. We have a great number of coarse dark etchings by this artist; among the rest, *St. Anthony restoring a foot to a boy,* which had been cut off, a middling sized upright plate. A *holy family,* from Titian, and several of the plates for the volume of prints, from select pictures, with a dissertation upon them by Carolina Catherina Patin, daughter of the celebrated physician Charles Patin. The title runs thus : *Tabellæ selectæ ac explicatæ à Carola Catherina Patina, Parisina Academica.* Batavii 1691. The same work was also published at Venice, with an Italian translation of the discourses, the same year. The prints, however, do no kind of honour to the artist who engraved them.

CHARLES NICHOLAS COCHIN.
Flourished, 1750.

By this ingenious artist, we have several good prints in the modern French style. They are very slight, in general; and the drawing of the naked parts of the human figure is rather mannered than correct. Yet his prints possess a certain spirited touch, which renders them agreeable to the eye. Among others by his hand are the following:

The *meeting of Jacob and Esau,* a middling sized upright plate, from Le Moine.

Jacob and Laban, the same, its companion, from Restout.

Alexander

Alexander and Roxana, two plates, from the studies of Raphael, for the Crozat collection.

He also engraved from a variety of other masters.

MARIE MAGDALENE HORTHEMELS, the wife of Nicholas Cochin, engraved also; and his son CHARLES NICHOLAS COCHIN, a very ingenious designer and engraver, is living at present, and a member of the Royal Academy of Arts at Paris.

MICHAEL COCK. See COXIE.

JEROM COCK.
Flourished, 1550.

This industrious man is better known as a printseller and publisher, than as an engraver. However, we have a sufficient number of prints, which are the productions of his own point; and the chief among them are *ruins and ancient remains, in and about Rome,* and a set of *landscapes* after old Brughel. He was born at Antwerp, where he resided and carried on a great commerce in prints. According to Florent le Comte, he engraved in that city the *seven liberal arts.* His etchings are very slight, executed in a poor scratchy style, and without effect; his name is frequently reversed upon the plate; he signs them " H. Cock fecit," and usually adds the date, as 1550, 1551, &c.

He also engraved from Michael Coxie, Martin Hemskirk, and other masters.

JOHN CLAUSE DE COCK.
Flourished,

By this artist, who appears to have been a painter, we have a slight etching in a free masterly style. It represents the *martyrdom of a saint,* whose hands are first cut off. His name is affixed, *Joan. Claus. de Cock fecit.*

COCK.
Flourished, 1559.

He was a Dutchman, and, according to Virtue's Catalogue published by the Hon. Mr. Walpole, engraved an oval portrait of the *queen of Scots,* from a genuine picture; but, adds he, it is not certain, that he was in England. This print is dated 1559: he might be a relation of the above artist.

THOMAS COCKSON.
Flourished, 1630.

This artist, apparently an Englishman, engraved a great variety of portraits, entirely with the graver, in a neat, stiff style, which seem to prove, that he had much more industry than genius. He sometimes used a mark, composed of a T. and a C. joined together, in the manner as expressed upon the plate

plate at the end of the volume. Among the prints executed by him are the following:
King James the First sitting in parliament, a whole sheet print.
King Charles the First sitting in parliament, the same.
Princess Elizabeth, daughter to James the First.
Charles earl of Nottingham, on horseback.
Francis White, &c.

PETER COECK.
Born, Died, 1550.

This artist was born at Aloft in Flanders, and became a painter of some eminence, as well as an architect. To perfect himself in his studies, he went to Italy. Prior to his return to Flanders he made a voyage to Turkey, where he drew whatever he found remarkable concerning the manners and customs of the Turks. These he cut on seven wooden blocks, divided into as many compartments, which being joined together make a very large long print, resembling a frieze. On a tablet, belonging to the first block, is written in bad French, *les moeurs et fachom de faire de Turcz, avecq les Regions y appertenantes, ont est au vif contrefaicetz par Pierre Coeck d'Aloft, luy estant en Turque, l an de Jesu Christ MDXXXIII. le quel aussy de sa main propre a pourtraict ces Figures duysantes a l'impression dy'celles.* That is, the manner and customs of the Turks, with the countries belonging to them, were drawn from nature by Peter Coeck of Aloft, when he was in Turkey, the year of Jesus Christ 1533; who also with his own hand executed these prints according to the drawings he had made. And upon a tablet in the last block is this inscription: *Marie ver Hulst, vesue du dict Pierre d'Aloft, trespasse en l'an MDL. a faict imprimer les dict Figures, soubz grace et privilege d'l'imperialle majeste en l'an MCCCCCLIII.* In English: Mary Verhulst widow of the said Peter d'Aloft, who died in the year 1550, caused these figures to be printed under the grace and privilege of his imperial majesty 1553, This large print contains a vast number of figures, all executed with great care, but not much taste. The work is, however, very curious; and doubtless at that time was very estimable.

JAMES COELMANS.
Born, 1670. Died,

This artist was born at Antwerp about the year 1670, and was the disciple of Cornelius Vermulen. M. de Boyer, comte d'Aguilles, and counsellor of the parliament at Aix in Provence, employed this artist, conjointly with Sebastian Barras, to engrave his collection of pictures by the great masters. The set of engravings was finished, A. D. 1709, but did not appear till 1744, This is Coelmans' largest and best work. He executed his plates chiefly with the graver, in a dark, heavy style. His lights are usually sudden and unharmonized, and his drawing, with respect to the naked parts of the human figure, is particularly defective. I think *the murder of the innocents*, from Claude Spierre, and the *fall of the giants*, with *Victory crowning David*, from Nicholas Poussin, may be reckoned among his best prints for the above mentioned collection.

VOL. I. E e LAU-

LAUVERS COENRADT.
Flourished,

This artist engraved part of the portraits for the collection of cardinals, published by Rossi; but these plates do him no great credit.

C O G E T. See COCHET.

S. COIGNARD.
Flourished, 1702.

The name of an obscure and indifferent engraver, affixed to the following prints: the portrait of *Sir Christopher Wren*, in octavo; *John Dryden the poet*, a bad copy of the print from Kneller by Edelink. The latter is dated 1702.

STEPHEN COLBENSCHLAG, or COLBENIUS.
Flourished,

This artist, who flourished at the commencement of the last century, was a native of Germany; but he resided at Rome, where he engraved several plates from Dominichino and other masters. The mark attributed to him is composed of three letters joined together, namely, an E. a C. and an L. The first is the initial of his baptismal name, when written in the French style *Etienne*. I shall only notice,

A *descent from the cross*, a middling sized upright plate, from Annibale Carracci.

The *adoration of the shepherds*, from Dominichino, a middling sized upright plate.

HUMPHRY COLE.
Flourished, 1572.

This artist was born in the north of England, and is supposed to have been brother to Peter Cole the painter, mentioned by Meres, in his *Wit's Commonwealth*, A. D. 1572. He belonged to the mint in the Tower; and the Hon. Mr. Walpole supposes him to be one of the engravers, employed by archbishop Parker; for he engraved a large *map and frontispiece*, in which is represented a portrait of *Queen Elizabeth*, and the earl of Leicester as Joshua, and lord Burleigh as David, accompanying her. Both of them for the folio edition of the bible, known by the name of Parker's Bible. It was published, A. D. 1572.

J. COLE.
Flourished, 1720.

A very indifferent engraver, employed principally by the booksellers, and upon works of the commonest kind. One of the best prints that I recollect to have feen by him, is a view of the *Royal George*, a large plate, length-ways, from T. Bafton. It is executed entirely with the graver, and chiefly with a fingle ftroke: what little hatching is introduced is croffed fquarely upon the firft ftroke. It is highly probable, that the following engravers were of the fame family, namely,

B. COLE, by whom, among other things, is the portrait of Mrs. *Behn*; and N. P. COLE, who engraved the portrait of *James Puckle*, &c.

FRANCOIS COLIGNON.
Flourifhed, 1646.

Apparently a Frenchman by birth; but he was eftablifhed at Rome, where he carried on a confiderable commerce in prints. His great excellency lay in *views of buildings, gardens*, &c. with fmall figures, which he executed in a free, fpirited ftyle, and at times he refembles Callot, De la Bella, and Ifrael Silveftre; from all of which mafters he engraved. He did many of the plates for the collection of all the principal cities and towns in Europe; alfo fome of thofe for the great collection of plans and views publifhed under the direction of M. de Beaulieu. He alfo engraved many plates from compofitions of his own.

ADRIAN COLLAERT.
Flourifhed, 1550.

An artift of great merit, born at Antwerp. After having learned in his own country the firft principles of engraving, he went to Italy, where he refided fome time to perfect himfelf in drawing. He worked entirely with the graver, in a firm, neat ftyle, but rather ftiff and dry. The vaft number of plates executed by his hand, fufficiently evince the facility with which he engraved; and though exceedingly neat, yet they are feldom highly finifhed. His maffes of lights are rarely well managed, or fkilfully blended; and from their being too much fcattered, and equally powerful on all parts, they impoverifh, and in fome inftances, entirely deftroy the effect. To make up for thefe deficiencies, which was rather the fault of the time than of the artift, he drew admirably. The heads of his figures are, frequently, beautiful and characteriftic, and the other extremities very correctly marked. I fhall only notice the following prints by his hand:

The *Ifraelitifh women finging the pfalm of praife for the deftruction of the Egyptian hoft in the Red Sea*, a middling fized plate length-ways, from J. Straden.

St. Martin dividing his cloak between two beggars, a middling fized upright plate, from the fame mafter.

Great part of the plates for a fet of prints, reprefenting the *life and paffion of Chrift*, which confifts of 50, from Martin de Vos.

A *fet of hermiteffes*, engraved conjointly with his fon John Collaert.

The *twelve months*, in circles, from Hans, or John Bol.

The *twelve months*, from Joffe Momper; thefe Callot copied. He alfo engraved from a variety of other mafters, and fometimes ufed the marks which are copied on the plate at the end of the volume, compofed of an A. and a C.

HANS or JOHN COLLAERT.
Flourifhed, 1600.

This excellent artift was fon to the foregoing. He drew and engraved exactly in the ftyle of his father; and was, in every refpect, equal to him in merit. He muft have been very old when he died; for his prints are dated from 1555 to 1622. He affifted his father in all his great works, and engraved befides a prodigious number of plates of various fubjects. I fhall only notice the following:

Mofes ftriking the rock, a large print, length-ways, from Lambert Lombard. A great number of fmall figures are introduced into this print; and they are admirably well executed: the heads are fine, and the drawing very correct. This I confider as one of his beft prints. It was publifhed by Jerom Cock, 1555, and is marked " Hans Collaert fec."

Time and Truth, a fmall upright plate, from J. Straden: this is very neatly engraved.

The prints for the *Miffal of Moretius*, from the defigns of Rubens.

Part of the plates for the *Life of Chrift*, from Martin de Vos, mentioned above in the lift of his father's works.

A fet of twenty middling fized plates, length-ways, entitled, NOVA REPERTA, from the defigns of J. Straden. They reprefent in a fort of emblematical manner, the *modern inventions: as, printing, the ufe of guns, the compafs*, &c.

He alfo engraved a great number of *hiftorical fubjects*, as well facred as prophane, *titles to books*, &c. from Martin Hemfkirk, Joffe Momper, Henry Goltzius, and other mafters. He fometimes marked his plates with the initials of his name only: as, H. C. F. the F. as ufual ftanding for fecit.

CHARLES COLLAERT appears to have been of the fame family with the preceding artift, and publifhed many of the plates, engraved by the father and fon; but I do not recollect that he engraved himfelf.

Mr. Evelyn, upon what authority I know not, mentions the name of Collaert without any diftinction detween the father, fon, or relation; and fays he " *graved fome things rarely in fteel."*

COLLET.
Flourifhed, 1770.

He engraved part of a fet of plates of *ornaments for goldfmiths and jewellers*, from the defigns of Gilles Legare, which were publifhed at Paris. They are very neatly executed with the graver.

JOHN COLLET.
Flourifhed, 1760.

He was a painter of ludicrous fubjects. His works are well known. He was

was a very ingenious, sensible man; but extremely shy. He etched two plates; one representing *antiquarians smelling to the chamber-pot of queen Boadicea*; and the other a *monkey pointing to a very dark picture of Moses striking the rock*, in ridicule of the admirers of Rembrandt Gerretz, whose works were then much in fashion. This has since his death been attributed to Hogarth, partly owing to the head of a connoisseur in a tye wig, which was etched by Dawes, a pupil of that master. A little before Mr. Collet's death he retired to Chelsea, having by the decease of a relation inherited a comfortable annuity. Mr. Grosse obligingly favoured me with this account of Mr. Collet and his etchings.

RICHARD COLLINS.
Flourished, 1676.

A very indifferent engraver, who resided at Antwerp, towards the conclusion of the last century, by whom we have *Esther before king Ahasuerus*, a large plate, length-ways, from Rubens: Panneels also copied the same picture. Several *portraits* in a neat, laboured style; and some *antique statues*, from the drawings of Sandrart, &c. To the portrait of *Anna Adelbildis uxor principis de la Tour et Taffis*, he signs his name, *Richard Collins, chalcographus Regis*, and adds, *advivum del. et sculp. Bruxella* 1682. Mr. Walpole mentions Richard Collins jun. a name affixed to a print, engraved for the *life of Francis Peck the antiquary*.

JOHN COLLINS.
Flourished, 1682.

What countryman this engraver was I cannot discover; but I think it appears, that he resided in England. By him we have some very indifferent copies from the grotesque figures, published by the Bonnarts in France, called *Signior Scaramouch and his company of comedians*. They are middling sized upright plates, a single figure on each. We have also some portraits by him, equally indifferent. Among them, the head of *Keay Nabe Naia wi-praia*, principal ambassador from the *Sultan Abdulcahar, king of Surosoan*, printed from N. Yates, dated 1682. Add to these the *funeral procession of George duke of Albemarle*. There are also some etchings by him.

M. COLM.
Flourished,

A name affixed to a small head of *queen Elizabeth* in an oval, engraved for the Genealogy of the Kings of England from the Conquest, quarto.

COSMIO COLOMBINI.
Flourished, 1754.

A modern Italian artist, who engraved some of the plates for the *Museo Fiorentino*, &c.

A, D. COLONIA.
Flourished,

This name is affixed to a slight incorrect etching, which has nothing to recommend it, representing *Apollo with the Muses*; a small upright plate.

MICHAEL COLYN.
Flourished,

This artist, who is said to have been a native of Antwerp, engraved the *Change at Amsterdam*, &c.

JOVAN COMIN.
Flourished,

This name is affixed to some plates of *antique statues*, executed entirely with the graver, in a very stiff, tasteless style. The originals, from whence these prints were taken, are in the Guistinian gallery.

CAMMILLO CONGIO.
Flourished,

This engraver flourished the beginning of the last century; and by him we have a great variety of engravings from Tempesta, Andrea D'Ancona, Bernard Castelli, Gasper Celio, and other masters. His plates are usually marked with two C's, the top of one joined to the bottom of the other, in the manner expressed upon the plate at the end of the volume; or in this manner: C. C. F. the F. standing for fecit.

CORNELIUS CONINCK.
Flourished,

An artist of great merit, by him we have the portrait of *Adrianus Tetrodius* of Haerlem, a small upright plate from Grebber, executed with the graver in a neat pleasing style, well drawn, and the effect is clear and good.

SOLOMON CONINCK, or KONNINCK.
Born, 1609. Died,

This artist was a native of Amsterdam. He first studied under Francois Fernando, and afterwards became the disciple of Nicholas Moyaert. He excelled in historical painting, and we have by him several etchings from his own compositions, in imitation of the style of Rembrandt.

ABRAHAM CONRAD.
Flourished,

This engraver, according to Basan, was a native of Holland, and flourished towards the end of the last century. He was chiefly employed in engraving portraits, which he performed with great success; and sometimes

from

from his own designs. His works prove him to have been a man of great ability. I shall only mention the portrait of *Jacob. Friglandus*, in which he has finely imitated the style of Lucas Vosterman, and that of *Godefroid Hotton*. A half figure, from H. Merman. In finishing the face he has scratched the copper with the point of the graver, in a manner bearing some slight resemblance to that adopted by Worlidge.

GIOVANNI BATISTA CONSTANTINI.
Flourished, 1619.

From the appearance of this artist's works, I should suppose he was a painter, for he etched in a slight, free style, something resembling that of Guido, but not so correct or masterly. I have seen by him, a small *Bacchanal* surrounded with a grape vine in the fashion of a border, a circular plate, from Guido. It is dated 1619, and the name by mistake is written *Costantino*; to it he adds the word *Roma*, probably he resided in that city.

PETER COOL.
Flourished,

This name is affixed to a middling sized upright print, representing *Christ carrying his cross, with St. Veronica, and several other figures*, from Martin de Vos. It is executed with the graver in a stiff, coarse style; and the drawing is exceedingly defective.

PETER COMBES.
Flourished,

An engraver in mezzotinto, by whom we have a small whole length portrait of *Master Charles More, son to the bishop of Ely*. This print possesses a very small share of merit.

RICHARD COOPER.
Flourished, 1730.

This artist, who was a painter, resided at Edinburgh. He engraved the portrait of *William Carstares*, and of *Andrea Allan* the painter, after W. Robinson.

RICHARD COOPER.
Flourished, 1762.

This artist resided at London, and engraved portraits. Among others, are the *five children of Charles the First, with the great dog*, from Vandyck; also the portrait of *Taylor, the oculist*.

EDWARD COOPER, the printseller, is also thought to have engraved; but I do not recollect his name, as an engraver, to any of the plates published by him.

R. COR-

C. CORBUTT.
Flourished, 1760.

A modern mezzotinto scraper, who resided at London. By him we have several portraits from different masters; among the rest, that of *Anne Bastard*, of Kitely in Devonshire.

R. CORDIER.
Flourished, 1647.

This engraver, a native of Abbeville in Picardy is mentioned by Florent le Comte, who attributes to him the engraving of a *writing book*, for Petre, the writing-master at Paris; and another for Louis Barbedor. He also engraved a map of the *port of Brest*. I suppose he was little more than a writing engraver; but I never saw any of his performances.

FRANCESCO CORDUBA.
Flourished,

This artist, who adds *Eques*, or Knight to his name, imitated the style of Callot. We have engraved by him from drawings of his own, a set of middling sized upright plates of the *fountains which are in the gardens at Rome*; and he has introduced many little figures. These plates are slightly etched, and with some spirit. He signs his name *Eques Franc. Corduba del et sculp.*

CHRISTOFANO CORIOLANO.
Flourished,

This artist, according to M. Heineken, was a native of Nuremberg, and an engraver on wood; but none of his works are specified.

BARTOLOMEO CORIOLANO.
Flourished, 1637.

This artist was the son of Christopher Coriolanus, mentioned in the preceding article, and was also an engraver on wood. He was born at Bologna in Italy, as appears from the inscription at the bottom of his prints. It seems that he was honoured with a title; for he adds the word *Eques*, or Knight, to his name; and according to Papillon, he pretended to have been a descendant from Caius Martius Coriolanus, the great Roman general. He learned the art of design in the famous academy of Bologna, founded by the Carraccii; and he applied his studies to engraving on wood in chiaro-scuro. In general, he used no more than two blocks of wood; on the first he cut not only the outline, but the darker shadows, in imitation of the hatchings with a pen; and the second block served for the demy tint: and with these two blocks so judiciously managed he produced a pleasing effect. We see by the bold spirited works of this master, that he drew admirably well. His heads are finely characterised; and the other extremities of his figures are
marked

marked in a masterly style. I can only mention the following prints by this artist:

St. Jerom, a half figure, a small upright print from Guido. This print is engraved on three blocks of wood; the first for the outline and dark shadows; the second for the middle shadows; and the last for the lightest tints. It is inscribed, " Barthol. Coriolanus Eques sculpsit, Bonon. 1637."

The *fall of the giants*, a large upright print, on four separate sheets, which paste together.

Two female figures from Guido, marked, Romæ 1627.

TERESIA MARIA CORIOLANO, the daughter of this artist, painted and engraved also for her amusement.

GIOVANNA BATISTA CORIOLANO.
Flourished, 1639.

This artist was brother to Bartholomew Coriolanus, mentioned in the preceding article. He was born at Bologna, and, after being instructed in the first principles of design, became the disciple of Valisco, a painter of some eminence. As a painter, I believe, he never acquired any great degree of reputation. He engraved a variety of prints both on wood and copper; but the former, in my opinion, are greatly superior to the latter.

I shall mention the following only by this artist: Some heads cut on wood, in a bold, free, spirited style; among the rest, the portrait of *Fortunius Licetus Genevensis*, dated 1689. *Christ crowned with thorns*, a middling sized upright copper plate, from Ludovico Carracci, a slight, bold etching. He also engraved from Guercino, and other great masters.

JOACHIM THEODORVS CORIOLANVS, the name latinised of an artist, perhaps of the same family with the preceding. According to Papillon, he engraved on wood, and flourished in the year 1600; and marked his prints with these initials, I. T. C. F. B. for " Joachim Theodorus Coriolanus fecit Basileæ;" but that author has not specified any of his works.

JOHN BAPTIST CORNEILLE.
Born, 1636. Died, 1695.

This artist was born at Paris, A. D. 1636, and instructed in the principles of painting by his father, Michael Corneille, under whom he attained to a considerable degree of perfection. He also etched several very spirited plates, and finished them with the graver, in a style far superior to what one usually meets with from the hand of the painter. Among others, is a figure of *Mercury flying in the air*, from a composition of his own. This print is in the *Cabinet des Beaux Artes*, published at Paris, 1690, by Perault. Corneille died A. D. 1695, aged 59.

MICHAEL CORNEILLE.
Born, 1642. Died, 1708.

This great artist, whose works do not appear to me to be so well known or esteemed, as they justly deserve, was a painter, brother to John Baptist Corneille;

neille, mentioned in the preceding article, and his father's pupil. He went to Italy to complete his studies, and perfect himself in the art of design. He understood the management of light and shadow, so as to produce a powerful and pleasing effect; and though he chiefly excelled in history, he also succeeded greatly in landscape. I shall confine my observations to his etchings only; and beg the indulgence of criticising a little upon the four following ones. They are middling sized plates, length-ways, and represent, 1. The *Deity appearing to Abraham*. 2. *Abraham journeying with Lot.* 3. *Abraham overcoming the army of the confederate kings.* 4. *Abraham setting out with his son Isaac to sacrifice him.* They are etched in a fine, bold, free, style; the compositions are full of grandeur; the heads are peculiarly characteristic; the extremities, like those of Raphael, are finely drawn, and the draperies disposed with the greatest taste. One may see how closely he has studied the celebrated Italian painters, and admire the good use he has made of those studies. The figure of Abraham, in the last, has much of the style of Polidoro Carravagio in it; and all the naked figures, in the third, are drawn in the manner of the Carraccii. He died at Paris, A. D. 1708, aged 66. I shall mention besides, by this artist,

A *holy family, with Elizabeth and St. John in a landscape*, a small plate, length-ways, from Raphael.

St. Andrew kneeling before the cross, a beautiful small upright plate, from a composition of his own.

St. Francis interceding with Christ for the redemption of mankind, a middling sized upright plate, from the same.

Notre Dame des Anges called *la Portioncule*, a middling sized upright plate.

LAMBERT CORNELIS.
Flourished,

This engraver worked, I believe, chiefly for the booksellers; and his employment seems to have been principally in the portrait line. We have by him, among others, the portrait of *Tycho Brahe*, the astronomer.

CORNHERT. See CUERENHERT.

CORNISH.
Flourished,

An obscure engraver, by whom, among other things, we have the portrait of *Dr. Charles Rose*, a slight etching in quarto.

VINCENT CORONELLI.
Born,   Died, 1718.

This artist was a native of Venice, where he engraved some *maps*, which are dated 1697.

P. CORO-

P. CORONELLI.

Flouriſhed, 1716.

This artiſt, who probably was of the ſame family with the preceding, engraved the plates for a work, entitled, *Roma Antica Moderna del P. Coronelli coſmografo Publico ad uſo de ſuoi Argonauti in Venezia,* 1716. They are poor, ſlight, indifferent etchings, conſiſting of *views of buildings,* &c. ſmall plates, length-ways.

CORREGIO. See ALLEGRI.

JEROM CORRIDORI.

Flouriſhed,

A native of Modena, and reſided at Rome, where he publiſhed many fine prints. He is ſpoken of with great commendation in the Abecedario. And it ſeems, that his great talents loſt him his life; for being puſhed into the Tyber by ſome envious perſon, he was unfortunately drowned. He is mentioned as an engraver; but I do not recollect to have ſeen any of his works.

NICOLO CORSI.

Flouriſhed, 1503.

He was a native of Genoa, and a painter of ſome eminence. To him is attributed the engraving of a portrait of *Franceſco Mazzuola,* called Parmigiano.

M. ANTONIO CORSI, is the name of a modern engraver, who flouriſhed 1760, and executed ſome of the plates for the Muſeo Fiorentino.

CORNELIUS CORT.

Born, 1536. Died, 1578.

This juſtly celebrated artiſt was born at Hoorn in Holland, A. D. 1536. After having learned the firſt principles of drawing and engraving, (perhaps from Cuerenhert) he went to Italy to complete his ſtudies, and viſited all the places, famous for the works of the great maſters. At Venice he was courteouſly received by Titian; and engraved ſeveral plates from the pictures of that admirable painter. He at laſt ſettled at Rome, where he died 1578, aged 42.

This artiſt worked entirely with the graver, in a bold, open, ſlight ſtyle. His back-grounds eſpecially, if they be landſcapes, are executed with much taſte and freedom, and evidently ſhow the great command he had of that inſtrument. But there is a dryneſs and ſtiffneſs, in general, about his figures, particularly thoſe that are covered with drapery, which frequently, joined with a want of harmony, produces an unpleaſing effect. His drawing is uſually correct and maſterly; ſometimes, indeed, the outlines are hard and the extremities marked in a negligent, ſlovenly manner. But in his beſt prints, theſe faults are by no means conſpicuous. Baſan ſays of him, that he was " the beſt engraver with the *burin* or graver only, that Holland ever pro- " duced.

"duced. We find in his prints," adds he, "correctness of drawing, and an ex-
"quisite taste." This compliment perhaps, by some connoisseurs, may be
thought to be a little overstrained; but that he was an artist of great merit,
must be allowed by all, who are acquainted with his works, though he was
not always equally happy in the execution of them. Bafan with great justice,
praises the taste and lightness of touch, with which he engraved landscapes,
and that without the assistance of the point. It is no small honour to this
artist, that Agostino Carracci was his scholar, and imitated his style of engraving, rather than that of any other master. I shall mention by him the
few following prints only, his engravings being very numerous (151 according to Abbé Marolles) and by no means uncommon.

Paradise, a large upright plate, from Titiano, dated 1566.

St. Jerom, a small upright plate, from the same master, dated the same.

The *discovery of the incontinency of Califta*, a large upright plate, from the
same, dated the same.

Prometheus chained to the rock: this figure is finely drawn; a middling
sized upright plate, from the same master, and dated the same.

The *seven penitents*. These are seven large landscapes, with small figures
of the Saints, Mary Magdalen, St. Anthony, &c. Six of them are upright
plates, and the seventh, length-ways, from Jerom Mutian, dated from 1575
to 1573.

A *holy family, with St. Jerom standing in front, and Mary Magdalen kissing
the feet of the infant Christ*, a large upright plate from Corregio. Agostino engraved the same subject; and both are dated 1586. They are not
easily distinguished from each other.

The *adoration of the shepherds*, from Polydore, a large plate, length-ways.

A *holy family*, with St. John holding a bird, a middling sized upright
plate from Frederico Baroccio, a very fine print, dated 1577.

The *adoration of the shepherds*, a middling sized upright plate, from M. R.
Senensis, dated 1568.

A *saint reading, holding a lily, represented in a landscape*, a middling sized
upright plate, from Bartolomeo Spranger. The back ground to this plate
is remarkably fine. It is dated 1573.

The *transfiguration*, from Raphael, a large upright plate. In this print the
artist has greatly failed; the character and expression of the heads, so admirable in the picture, are quite lost in the engraving.

The *last supper*, a large upright plate, from Tadeo Zuccaro.

The *last supper*, the same, from Livio de Forli, called Livio Agresti, dated
1578.

Christ praying in the garden, a middling sized upright plate, without the
name of the painter or the engraver. This print is distinguished by a small
instrument at the bottom of the plate, near the feet of one of the disciples,
which is usually taken for a lamp; and for this cause the engraving has been attributed to an old master, who flourished 1509, and used a
mark something resembling it. See this mark copied on the plate at the end
of the volume. He also engraved from Michael Angelo, Andrea del Sarto,
M. Heemskerck, Franc. Floris, James Stradan, Marcello Venusti, and other
masters.

masters. Those from Heemskerck appear to have been his first works, and executed before he left Holland. They are *bible subjects*, and very indifferently executed.

GIACOMO CORTERI, called BOURGUIGNON.
Born, 1621. Died, 1676.

This admirable and well known artist was born at St. Hippolito, in Franche Compte. His great excellence consisted in painting *historical subjects, and battles*, particularly in the last. He had occupied a post in the army himself; and from being an eye witness of several actions, he composed those subjects with great fire and spirit. In Italy, where he went whilst young, he formed an acquaintance with Guido and Albano, and profited not a little from their instructions. He was exceedingly expeditious in the execution of his pictures; and it is said, that he never found it necessary to make a sketch of the subject he meant to paint before-hand; but drew it at once upon the canvas, and proceeded to the finishing of it. He entered into religious orders, and became a jesuit. He died at Rome, A. D. 1676, aged 55 years. By this artist we have some small etchings of *battles*, very slight, but prodigiously free and masterly. The masses of light and shadow are finely preserved in them, so as to produce a powerful and striking effect. He was not equally successful in drawing of the naked parts of the human figure, wherever we find them represented by him they are incorrect.

GUGLIELMO CORTERI.
Born, Died, 1679.

This artist, who was brother to the preceding master, was scholar to Pietro da Cortona. He is spoken of also, as a painter, with commendation. He died at Rome, A. D. 1679, two years after his brother. We have but one engraving by him, which represents *Tobias burying the dead*, from a design of his own.

JOHN AUGUSTUS CORVINUS.
Flourished,

A modern German engraver of views, buildings, &c. which he executed in a style sufficiently neat, but stiff and without taste. Among other things by him, are a set of ornaments for *ceilings*, from the designs of Carlo Maria Pozzi, in large folio. He engraved most of the plates for the work, entitled, *Representatio Belli ob successionem in Regno Hispanico*, &c. a large folio volume, published at Augsburg. And great part of the plates for a work, containing *views of churches*, &c. at Vienna, which was also published at Augsburg by John Andrea Peeffel, 1724, are by him.

LOUIS COSSIN.
Flourished, 1690.

This engraver appears to have been a native of France. He resided at
Paris.

Paris, and called himself engraver to the king. He worked entirely with the graver in a poor, tastelefs style. In drawing and effect he is alfo exceedingly deficient. Among other things by him, is a figure reprefenting *Sculpture*, in the *cabinet des Beaux Artes*, publifhed at Paris, A. D. 1690. He alfo engraved fome few portraits, which are however of but little value.

LAURENCE JOHNSON COSTER.
Born, Died, 1441.

I fhall by no means enter into the long and unfatisfactory difpute concerning this artift, or whether fuch an artift really exifted or not. The Dutch have laid claim to the invention of engraving on wood, and the ftill nobler art of printing, which appears immediately to have followed. And according to them, the following trivial accident gave birth to both. Cofter one day walking in a wood, near the city of Haerlem, where he was born, amufed himfelf with cutting letters upon the bark of a tree, which for fancy fake being impreffed upon paper, he printed one or two lines, as a fpecimen, for his children. He then proceeded to cut letters in wood, and joined them together with thread; and by degrees produced a book, entitled, *Speculum Salvationis*, which he ornamented with vignettes, cut in wood. There are alfo fome rude portraits attributed to this doubtful artift; but as every one may not poffefs Baron Heineken's *Idea Generale d'une Collection d'Eftampes*, wherein a full account is given of this man, and the works attributed to him, (which, indeed, the author looks upon as entirely fabulous) I will tranfcribe his lift.

A fmall *buft of a man*, with a cap, near two inches high, by one inch wide, marked Laurence Jaffoen, fuppofed to be the portait of Cofter.

A *buft of an old man in profile*, two inches high, by one inch and three quarters wide, marked at bottom, Halckart Seil da Harleim.

Another *buft*, the face turned to the left, marked Jn Dabin b har.

Another *buft*, a three quarter face, marked on the back-ground towards the left with an L. and below Hugo Jacob' foe b Lid.

Another, marked Jan ban Hemfen Scilder b Harlem.

Another, marked Alb Ovatis Scilder Harlem.

Another, of which the mark is not plain, but appears to be, *J. v. Mercken*.

In the royal library at St. James's is a *Virgin, with the inftruments of Chrift's fufferings*, attributed alfo to Cofter.

I fhall have occafion to fpeak of this man again, in the Effay on the rife and progrefs of engraving on wood, which will be given in the fecond volume.

D. COSTER.
Flourifhed,

The name of an obfcure engraver, affixed to the portrait of *Franc. Hals* the painter, from Vandyck.

JACOPO

JACOPO COTTA.
Flourished,

This name is affixed to an etching which I have before me, very badly executed, and exceedingly defective in the drawing. The subject, I believe, is the *meeting of Isaac and Rebecca*. Two men are unloading a horse in the front: it is a middling sized plate, length-ways, from Storer.

PETER COTTART.
Flourished,

This artist was an architect, and flourished in the seventeenth century. By him we have some rough etchings of *vases and ornaments*, See the monogram, with which he usually marked his engravings, on the plate at the end of the volume.

J. DE COURBES.
Flourished,

An artist of no great merit, chiefly employed for the bookfellers. By his hand, among others, we have the portrait of *Sir Philip Sidney*, a small octavo oval plate. *Mary countess of Pembroke*, a small octavo. As he does not cite the name of the painter, and adds the letter F. for fecit to his name, it is probable, that he engraved them from designs of his own.

COUCHET. See COGET.

ANNE PHILBERT COULET.
Flourished, 1760.

This lady is mentioned by Basan, as residing at Paris. By her hand we have several very pretty landscapes, well etched and retouched with the graver, in a style that does her honour: among the rest,

The *fair afternoon*, a landscape, ornamented with figures, from Vernet, a middling sized plate, length-ways.

The *happy passage*, and its companion, the *departure of the boat*, two sea views, the same from the same.

The *Florentine fishermen*, and the *Neapolitan fishermen*, companions, middling sized upright plates, from the same.

COURTOIS. See CORTESI.

P. F. COURTOIS.
Flourished, 1750.

A young engraver, and native of France; but he never reached any great excellence. We have several prints by him after *S. Aubin*, and other masters.

J. COUSE.

J. COUSE.
Flourished, 1750.

This artist was, I presume, a native of England, though his works are but little known. He engraved a neat half sheet view, length-ways, of *Berkley castle*, from a drawing by the countess of Berkley, and some other plates, which prove him to have been no indifferent artist.

ELIZABETH COUSINET.
Flourished, 1760.

This lady was the wife of Lempreur, an engraver of great merit, honoured with the title of engraver to the king, and member of the Royal Academy of Arts at Paris. By Madame Cousinet, we have several prints, that do her no discredit. Among others,

The *pyramid of Sextus*, and its companion, the *columns of Campo-Vacino*, two middling sized plates, length-ways, ornamented with figures, from J. Paolo Panini. The *departure of Jacob*, a small upright plate, from Boucher, &c.

H. COUSSIN.
Flourished, 1760.

A modern engraver, who resided at Aix in Provence, where he etched several plates from Puget, Rembrant and other masters.

JOHN COUSSIN, a painter and designer of some eminence, and native of France, is said by Papillon to have engraved on wood; but the matter is very uncertain, though it be allowed, that many of his designs are cut on wood by the artists in that line then living.

JOHN COUVAY.
Flourished,

This artist was a native of France, and flourished towards the conclusion of the last century. He worked chiefly, if not entirely, with the graver, in a coarse bold style, founded apparently on that of Vilemena. His works are flight and heavy. They manifest a great command of hand; but little judgment in softening the shadows, harmonizing the lights, or keeping the distances back, in order to relieve the front and principal figures. His drawing of the naked parts of the human figure is often incorrect, and the extremities are usually heavy, and badly marked. Among his most esteemed prints are the following.

A *saint tempted by the flesh, has recourse to the crucifix*, half figures, a small upright plate, from Guercino: a night-piece, and the candle is overturned upon the table.

The *martyrdom of St. Bartholomew*, a middling sized upright plate from Nicholas Poussin. Mitellus engraved the same subject, under the name of the *martyrdom of St. Erasmus*.

A set

C O X [225] C O Y

A fet of fmall upright plates, entitled *Les Tableaux de la Penitence*, from the defigns of T. Chauveau.

Mary queen of Scotland, a half figure, feated, and the execution feen through the window. He alfo engraved from Raphael, Annibale Carracci, Guido, Bourdon, Le Sueur, and other mafters.

MICHAEL COXIS.
Born, 1497. Died, 1592.

This artift was born at Mechlin, and learned the firft principles of painting in his own country; going to Rome, he became the fcholar of Raphael, and acquired to himfelf a tolerable fhare of reputation. Many of the old engravers worked from his defigns. There are a fet of fixty-eight prints, reprefenting the *hiftory of the Arabs*, dated 1567, which are marked with a curious monogram, compofed of a C. an M. an L. and an F. placed above the M. in the manner reprefented on the plate at the end of the volume. The defigns for thefe plates are generally attributed to Coxis; and it is thought that he alfo engraved them. Michael Coxis died, A. D. 1592, aged 95 years.

NOEL COYPEL.
Born, 1628. Died, 1707.

This artift was born in Lower Normandy; but difcovering an early inclination for the arts, he ftudied under a painter of no great reputation at Orleans, named Poncet; from thence he went to Paris, to perfect himfelf in drawing and painting, and became the difciple of Charles Errard. His pictures manifeft a fertility of invention, fome grace in the compofitions, and a tolerable good tone of colouring. He drew the human figure with a great degree of correctnefs, but in a mannered ftyle; and the extremities are not always fufficiently determined. He died at Paris, where he refided, A. D. 1707, aged 79 years. By him we have a *holy family*, which he etched with alterations, three times on three feparate plates.

ANTHONY COYPEL.
Born, 1661. Died, 1722.

This artift was the fon and fcholar of the preceding. He was born at Paris 1661; and his father being nominated director of the academy eftablifhed by the king of France at Rome, he accompanied him thither, and employed his time in ftudying the works of Raphael, Michael Angelo, and Annibale Carracci, with great affiduity. The improvement he made during his refidence in Italy, was fo great, that at his return to Paris, his merit was generally acknowledged, and he was ranked among the firft clafs of hiftorical painters. He died 1722, aged 61 years. We have feveral excellent etchings by his hand, very highly finifhed, efpecially when confidered as the works of a painter. The figures in them are correctly drawn, and in a mafterly ftyle. The character and expreffion of the heads are admirable, and the general effect

effect finely harmonized. I shall mention the following only from his own compositions.

An *ecce homo*, a small upright plate.
Judith, the same.
Saint Cecilia, the same.
The *head of Democritus*, the same.
Two portraits of *Le Voisin*, one large and the other small.
Bacchus and Ariadne, a large plate, length-ways. This was finished with the graver by Gerard Audran; and is a most admirable print.
Galatea, the same, finished by Charles Simonneau.

NOEL NICHOLAS COYPEL.
Born, 1692. Died, 1735.

He was brother to Anthony Coypel, and born at Paris. He learned the first principles of painting from his father, and perfected his studies without going to Italy. He was also a much esteemed historical painter, and died at Paris 1735, aged 43 years. We have some pretty etchings by him; but not equal to those by his brother. They are as follow, from his own compositions:

Saint Therese with many angels, a small oval plate.
The *triumph of Amphitrite*, a small plate length-ways.
A woman sleeping under a canopy, surprised by a satyr, the same.
A woman caressing a pigeon, the same.

CHARLES COYPEL.
Born, 1694. Died, 1752.

He was the son of Anthony Coypel, and born at Paris. He was the pupil of his father; and his works are spoken of with great commendation. He also possessed great taste for the Belles Lettres; and distinguished himself by several estimable writings, which manifested at once his delicacy and good taste. He was made first painter to the king of France, and died A. D. 1752, aged 58 years. According to Basan, he also etched several plates from his own compositions.

FRANCESCO COZZA.
Born, Died, 1664.

A native of Palermo in Sicily, where he received his first instructions in the art of painting. Going afterwards to Rome, he became the scholar of Dominichino; and the progress he made under the instructions of that master was such, as did honour to both. He excelled in historical subjects, and painted much in fresco. He died, A. D. 1664. We have some few etchings by him; among others,

St. Peter's contrition, which, though slightly executed, is well drawn and shows the hand of the master: it is a small upright plate, marked, " Fra. Cozza inc. ex." And the *Roman charity*, a small plate, length-ways, half figures only.

CRACHE.

CRACHE.
Flourished,

According to Papillon, this is the name of an engraver on wood. That writer mentions some *cavalcades* as executed by him.

CRALINGE.
Flourished,

An obscure engraver, by whom we have the portrait of *Menno Simonis*, a whole length.

LUCA CRANACH, or KRANACH.
Born, 1470. Died, 1553.

This artist was a painter of portraits, history, and poetical subjects, born at Cranach in Westphalia. Under whom he studied does not appear; but the reputation he acquired was such, as recommended him to the favour of the elector of Saxony, and he was many years employed in painting for that prince. He died, A. D. 1553, aged 83. I shall speak of him only as an engraver; and therefore the following observations are founded upon his prints alone. He possessed far more fertility of invention than judgment; and being led away by the liveliness of his imagination, did not pay sufficient attention to the choice of what was beautiful, but contented himself with the first forms that offered, and followed the stiff, Gothic taste, which prevailed in his country at that time, without any attempt to improve it. His manner of drawing is rather dry and tasteless, than absolutely incorrect; and the heads which he has given to his figures, have both character and expression, though they are not marked with precision, or in a pleasing style; the hands and feet indeed are frequently very defective; and a total ignorance of the distribution of light and shadow destroys the general effect, and renders it confused and unpleasing. Mr. Pilkington, looking on the dark side only of the performances of this artist, seems to wonder, that he should have any modern admirers. But let any unprejudiced person examine carefully the *Life of Christ* by this artist, which consists of fourteen middling sized upright prints, and I humbly conceive the many beauties of composition, character and expression, he will discover in those engravings, will amply repay the labour, and convince the examiner, that Cranach, with all his faults, was a man of great ability. Lucas Cranach left a son of the same name, a painter of portraits; but it does not appear that he ever engraved. He sometimes marked his plates with the initials of his name, thus, L. C. or L. V. C. or the L. and the C. joined together cypher ways; but more frequently with a dragon, holding a ring in its mouth, with or without the arms of Saxony, to denote his being painter to the elector, the dragon being the crest to the arms; and sometimes with the arms, crest, and the initial letters also. See the marks copied on the plate at the end of the volume. I shall only mention the following few prints, from the numerous engravings by this artist; and, FIRST, those on wood.

Adam and Eve in Paradise, a large upright plate.

Christ and the twelve apostles, middling sized upright prints.

The *same*, small uprights.
The *paſſion of Chriſt*, smaller than that above-mentioned, fourteen prints.
The *martyrdom of St. John*.
A *man in armour dying, and three naked women ſtanding by him*, dated 1506.
Chriſt and the woman of Samaria, a middling ſized upright print.
The *baptiſm of Chriſt*, a large print length-ways, the Deity appears above, and a kneeling figure is seen on each ſide.
A *large hunting-piece*, length-ways, on two blocks.
A *large tournament*, length-ways.
Several other *tournaments, proceſſions, portraits*, &c.

SECONDLY, a claro-ſcuro, said to be the only one executed by this artiſt, namely, *S. Chriſtopher carrying the infant Chriſt over the river*. It is executed on two blocks, the firſt for the outline and dark ſhadows, and the ſecond for the demy tints and lights.

THIRDLY, thoſe on copper; but I ſhall only mention the following, they being greatly inferior, in every reſpect, to his prints on wood:
A *naked woman lying down, with a child aſleep before her; and a naked man appears in the back ground*, a middling ſized upright plate, dated 1509. I take this ſubject to be Adam and Eve after their fall,

CARY CREED.
Flouriſhed, 1730.

He etched a ſet of plates from the *ſtatues and buſts* at Wilton Houſe. They are ſlight, but yet poſſeſs great merit. I have not been able to meet with any ſatisfactory account of this artiſt; but I ſuppoſe, that he was a native of England.

RIDOLFO CREIN.
Flouriſhed,

This artiſt is cited in the liſt of engravers, at the end of the Abecedario; and the word *Tirugino* is added to his name. His works are not mentioned, nor have I seen any of them.

ANTONIO CREMONIENSIS.
Flouriſhed,

By this artiſt we have a ſlight ſpirited engraving on wood, repreſenting *Mutius Scævola burning his hand, in the preſence of Porſenna*. It is a very ſmall upright print, nearly ſquare, and executed on a ſingle block, without any croſs hatching.

L. CREPY.
Flouriſhed,

A very indifferent engraver, who apparently flouriſhed at the beginning of the preſent century. Among other things by him, are the following: a ſmall and bad copy of *Alexander entering the tent of Darius*, from Le Brun, or rather from the print, engraved after the picture of Le Brun, by Girard Edelink. The portrait of *A. Wateau, the painter*, a ſmall upright plate. To both

both thefe prints he figns his name, " L. Crepy filius fculp." Probably his father was alfo an engraver, and he puts the word *filius* for diftinction fake.

GIUSEPPE MARIA CRESPI.
Born, 1665. Died, 1747.

This eminent painter was born at Bologna; and after having fuccefsfully ftudied under feveral eftimable mafters, entered into the fervice of the great duke of Tufcany, to whom his merit had been made known. The pictures, which he executed for that prince, gave much fatisfaction to him; and they contributed, in no fmall degree, to raife the reputation of Crefpi with the public. He received great prefents from the duke, and was honoured with his protection, and the title of his painter. The harmony and force of the colouring, the elegance of the compofitions, and the correctnefs of defign, which appears in his works, are fpoken of by thofe acquainted with them with great commendation. He died at Bologna, A. D. 1747, aged 82 years.

He etched feveral plates, among the reft,

The *adventures of Bertholde and Bertholdino*, a fet of fmall upright plates, from his own compofitions.

The *refurrection of our Saviour*, a middling fized upright plate, the fame.

CRESPY.
Flourifhed,

A very indifferent engraver, who, according to Bafan, died towards the beginning of the prefent century. He engraved among other things, a *defcent from the crofs*, a large upright plate, from Carlo Cignani.

PAUL CREUTZBERGER.
Flourifhed,

According to profeffor Chrift and Papillon, this is the name of an engraver on wood, who marked his prints with a P. and a C. joined together in form of a cypher. See this mark copied on the plate at the end of the volume. I am not acquainted with his works, nor are any of them fpecified by the above author.

S. JOHN CRISOSTOMUS.
Flourifhed,

A name affixed to a fmall plate length-ways, well executed, and in the ftyle of Aldegrever, reprefenting a *back figure of a woman lying down*, and the back-ground is a landfcape. It is indeed very doubtful whether this name was intended for that of the engraver or not.

BARTHOLOMEO CRIVELARI.
Flourifhed,

A modern Venetian artift; but of no great eminence. By him, among other things, we have a fmall upright plate, reprefenting a *faint carried up to Heaven*, from M. Bartoloni.

TEODORO DALLA CROCE. Se CRUYS.

URSULA DE LA CROIX.
Flourished, 1700.
This ingenious lady, with JANE DE LA CROIX, her sister, etched several of the plates of *gems*, which were drawn by Elizabeth Sophia Cheron, their aunt. They are neatly executed in a free, spirited style.

HUBERT DE CROOCK.
Flourished,
The name of a very ancient engraver on wood. It is affixed at full length, with the monogram also, composed of an H. a D. and a G. at the bottom of a large folio print, representing the *Trinity*. Christ as dead is lying upon the lap of the Deity, and the Holy Spirit appears in the air above. It is very neatly cut, but stiff to a great degree. Albert Durer engraved the same subject; but the print by him is so much superior in freedom and expression to this, which has all the servility of a copy, that one does not hesitate to pronounce it so, though in point of antiquity it appears coeval, at least, with that of Albert. This print is in the collection of Dr. Monro. See the monogram, used by this engraver, upon the plate at the end of the volume. The baptismal name on the print is written 𝕳𝖚𝖇𝖗𝖊𝖈𝖍𝖙, which I suppose, is the same as Hubert.

MARTIN GOTTFRIED CROPHIUS
Flourished,
An engraver of no great merit, by whom, among other things, we have an *emblematical* subject, from John Daniel Herz, a middling sized upright plate.

THOMAS CROSS.
Flourished, 1648.
A laborious artist possessed of no great share of taste or genius. He worked chiefly, if not entirely with the graver, in a stiff, unpleasing style. he confined himself to portraits, and frontispieces for books. These according to the custom of the time, were generally engraved from drawings of his own; and which as far as one can judge from the engravings, were equally indifferent. We have by him the *frontispiece* to an octavo book, published at London 1648, entitled, a *Voyage through Rome*; also, among others, the following portraits: *Richard Brownlowe*, in quarto; *James Burroughs*, A gospel minister, in quarto, dated 1648; *John Richardson*, bishop of Armagh, 1654, &c.

CRUCHE.
Flourished, 1550.
The name of an engraver on wood, who flourished in France towards the middle

middle of the sixteenth century, where he performed several works. " I have," says Papillon, " by him a *plan of the city of Paris*, which," continues he, " I believe, was engraved for an ancient edition of the *Geographie of Belle Forrest*."

LOUIS CRUGER. See Krug.

THEODORE CRUGER.
Flourished, 1617.

This artist was a German by birth; but he resided chiefly in Italy, and imitated the style of Francesco Vilemena. His mode of engraving was in a bold style, with the graver only, and it shews that he had great command of that instrument; but he did not possess much taste or judgment to direct him in the prosecution of his studies. The outlines of his figures are hard and incorrect, the heads badly drawn, and the other extremities entirely neglected. He does not appear to have had, even a distant idea of harmonizing the lights with the shadows: hence his prints are totally destitute of effect. His chief work was,

The *life of St. John the Baptist*, from Andrea del Sarto, on twelve middling sized upright plates, with the portrait of the painter. Some of these prints are dated 1617.

The *last supper*, a large plate, length-ways, from the same.

We have some portraits by him, from Gabriel Wayer, dated 1614: to these his name is signed, " Ditrich Cruger."

He also engraved from Andrea D'Ancona, Lanfranchi, and other masters. See his cypher composed of a T. and a C. joined together, on the plate at the end of the volume.

MATTHIAS CRUGER.
Flourished, 1617.

He was brother to the preceding artist; and flourished about the same time. He engraved some plates from the chevalier Borghese, Guido, and other masters; and some also from his own compositions. See his manner of marking his prints on the plate, at the end of the volume.

L. CRUYL.
Flourished, 1667.

This artist resided at Rome, where he drew a considerable number of views, which he occasionally enriched with cattle and figures, in a very spirited, pleasing style. The chief of these were engraved by Julius Testa; but we have some fine etchings of his own: namely,

Several *views of the Pantheon at Rome*, and other ruins; small plates, length-ways.

Several *architectal views*, with ruins, &c. small plates, length-ways, marked, L. Cruyl inv. et fec. Rome, 1667.

THEODORE VER CRUYS, or DELLA CROCE.

Flourished,

This engraver was a native of Holland, according to the author of the Abecedario; but he refided chiefly in Italy, and, among other things, engraved part of the plates from the pictures in the *Florentine gallery*; fome large *views of shipping*, on two plates each, from Salvator Rofa, &c. Alfo feveral *portraits* from various mafters. The prints by this artift do not difcover any extraordinary marks of genius. They are etched and retouched with the graver. I fuppofe he flourifhed towards the commencement of the prefent century.

DIRICK, or THEODORE VAN CUERENHERT.

Born, 1522. Died, 1590.

This extraordinary man was a native of Amfterdam. It appears, that early in life he travelled into Spain and Portugal; but the motives of his journey are not afcertained. He was a man of fcience, and, according to report, a good poet. The fifter arts, at firft he confidered as an amufement only; but, in the end, he was, it feems, obliged to have recourfe to engraving alone for his fupport. And though the different ftudies, in which he employed his time, prevented his attachment to this profeffion being fo clofe as it ought to have been, yet, at leaft, the marks of genius are difcoverable in his works. They are flight, and haftily executed with the graver alone; but in an open, carelefs ftyle; fo as greatly to refemble defigns made with a pen. His drawing is by no means correct; yet it is certain, that he knew more than his hurry would let him exprefs; but the extremities of his figures he has, in general, negligently paffed over. It is true, the compofitions he worked from were fuch, as could not well recommend themfelves: yet a little more pains would, at leaft, have fecured more credit to himfelf.

He was eftablifhed at Haerlem; and there purfuing his favourite ftudies in literature, he learned Latin, and was made fecretary to that town, from whence he was fent feveral times as ambaffador to the prince of Orange, to whom he addreffed a famous manifefto, which that prince publifhed, A. D 1566.

Had he ftopped here, it had been well; but directing his thoughts into a different channel, he undertook an argument as dangerous as it was abfurd. He maintained, that all religious communications were corrupted, and that, without a fupernatural miffion, accompanied with miracles, no perfon had a right to adminifter in any religious office; and he pronounced that man to be unworthy the name of a Chriftian, who would enter any place of public worfhip. This he not only advanced in words, but ftrove to fhew the fincerity of his belief by practice; and for that reafon, would not communicate with either proteftant or papift. His works were publifhed in three volumes, folio, A. D. 1630. And though he was feveral times imprifoned, and, at laft, fentenced to banifhment, yet he does not appear to have altered his fentiments. He died at Dergoude, A. D. 1590, aged 68 years. It is no fmall addition to the honour of this fingular man, that he was the inftructor of that juftly celebrated artift, Henry Goltzius.

Cuerenhert

Cuerenhert worked conjointly with the Galles, and other artifts, from the defigns of Martin Hemfkerck. The fubjects are from the Old and New Teftament, and confift chiefly of middling fized plates, length-ways. He alfo engraved feveral fubjects from Franc. Floris. His mark, which he frequently fubftituted for his name, compofed of a D. a V. and a C. is copied on the plate at the end of the volume.

HANS or JOHN CULENBACK, or CULMBACK.
Flourifhed, 1517.

This artift is faid to have been a difciple of Albert Durer; and engraved both on wood and copper. He marked his plates, H. V. C. or I. C. and ufually put the date. Among the few prints we have by this artift, is the following: a *foldier armed converfing with a country woman*, dated 1517, and marked H. V. C.

WILLIAM CUNYNGHAM, M. D.
Flourifhed, 1559.

He was a phyfician, who refided at the city of Norwich in Norfolk, and was alfo an author, as well as an engraver. He publifhed a book, entitled, *A Cofmographical Glafs*, in which are many *prints*, with a *large map of Norwich*, engraved by his own hand. It was printed in folio, A. D. 1559, and dedicated to lord Dudley, afterwards earl of Leicefter.

DOMINECO CUNEGO.
Flourifhed, 1760.

This engraver, who appears to have been a native of Italy, refided, I believe, in England, and engraved fome of the plates for Mr. *Boydell's collection*. He never exceeded mediocrity. I have feen by him a fmall print upright arched at the top, reprefenting *St. Gaetano furrounded with angels*, from Solimene. It is executed entirely with the graver, in a clear, neat ftyle, but without much tafte, and marked " Dom^{cus}. Cunego del et fculp. Verone."

C. CUNGI.
Flourifhed,

The name of an obfcure and indifferent engraver, affixed to a fmall octavo *frontifpiece*, confifting of three emblematical figures. It is executed in a manner fufficiently neat, but without the leaft degree of tafte or correctnefs.

CAMILLIUS CUNGIUS.
Flourifhed, 1642.

A name affixed to a portrait of *Taffo the poet*. This artift alfo engraved fome of the *ceilings and antiquities* for the defcription of the Barbarinean Palace, publifhed at Rome, A. D. 1642.

CURE.
Flourished,

The name of an engraver, spoken of by Ames, in his catalogue of English heads; but I am not acquainted with his works.

DENIS CUREMBERG.
Flourished,

The name of an artist, who according to Florent le Comte, engraved some plates from the designs of Michael Angelo Buonaroti.

FRANCESCO CURTI.
Flourished, 1670.

This artist was a native of Bologna, and flourished towards the conclusion of the last century. He worked chiefly with the graver, for we rarely find, that he called in the assistance of the point. His manner is founded upon that of Cherubin Albert; and his execution, in general, is neater; but in correctness of outline, character or taste, he by no means equalled that great artist. In drawing especially Curti is very defective: the extremities of his figures are heavy, and badly marked. By him we have, among others, the following: The *Virgin teaching the infant Christ to read*, from Guercino, a small upright plate, half figures only. The *marriage of St. Catherine*, a very small upright plate, from Denis Calvaert. *Venus coming to the forge of Vulcan*,, the same, from Carracci. A *drawing book*, from the designs of Guercino. *Hercules and the Hydra*, a small plate, length-ways, from the same. A *boy sleeping*, from Guido, a small upright oval: this plate is etched, and retouched with the graver.

BERNADINO CURTI, or CURTIS.
Flourished, 1645.

This artist, probably a relation of Francesco Curti, mentioned in the preceding article, was also a native of Italy. He worked occasionally with the graver only, and at times with the point and graver; but his productions are by no means estimable; the principal part of which consists of portraits. Among his other subjects, is a middling sized plate, length-ways, representing an *emblematical subject*, from Luc Ferrar. See the mark which this artist substitutes for his name; on the plate at the end of the volume.

DOMENICO CUSTOS, or CUSTODIS.
Flourished, 1600.

He was born at Augsburg in Germany, and learned, as it should seem, the principles of engraving from Peter Custos, his father, who followed that profession. He worked entirely with the graver, in a very neat style; but there is a stiffness, and want of taste in his prints, which gives them a laboured, rather than a pleasing appearance. His drawing is not correct, and the outlines of his figures are hard and dry. The lights are left too equally uncovered, so that the harmony of the effect is entirely destroyed. Florent le Comte informs us, that " *Dominique Custodis,* who he falsely says was a native of Antwerp, *a grave des portrait dans le gout de Van Dyck,* engraved portraits in the taste of Vandyck. But, I profess, I do not understand his meaning; nor can I conceive the least resemblance, in any respect, between the stiff portraits of Custos, and those so highly and so justly esteemed of Vandyck, which generally speaking, are slight etchings.

The greatest work by Custos is, I believe, the *effigies of the German emperors.* These are large whole length figures in folio, and they were published A. D 1601. Besides which we have by him,
The portraits of the *Fuggera family.*
The portraits of *heroes and great men.*
Several *female saints,* half lengths, from Frantz Aspruck.
He also engraved from Joseph Hentz, M. Kayer, Rottenhamer, and other masters. His mark is composed of a D. joined to a C. and an A. and an F. also joined together; the A. standing for Augsburg, the name of which in Latin is Augusta; and an F. for fecit. See these marks on the plate at the end of the volume,

DAVID CUSTOS, or CUSTODIS.
Flourished,

This artist was probably nearly related to the preceding; but he seems chiefly to have applied himself to landscapes and small figures, which he etched in a coarse, rough style; they are, however, by no means devoid of merit, which would have been more conspicuous, had his judgment led him to make in general, a better choice of nature, we have by him, and I believe, from his own designs,

A set of small *landscapes,* length-ways; *Views in the low countries.*
Abrisder Landschafft, a large map.
A small *landscape,* length-ways, in the front of which he has introduced some boors, playing at nine-pins : this is one of his best prints.

RAPHAEL CUSTOS, or CUSTODIS.
Flourished,

This artist was established at Antwerp, about the commencement of this century, and there are some few engravings by his hand.

D.

ABRAHAM DA.
Flourifhed,

This artift appears to have been a defigner, as well as an engraver. We have by him the *laft fupper*, a fmall plate, length-ways, neatly executed with the graver, in the ftyle of De Brye. This print is by no means devoid of merit: it is marked " Abraham Da fecit."

DADO.
Flourifhed,

I much doubt the exiftence of fuch an artift. The prints marked with a die are attributed to him, which in my opinion, belong rather to Bartolomeo Beham; and my reafons for thinking fo are given in the account of that artift.

M. DAIGREMONT.
Flourifhed, 1670.

This artift, who was by no means a man of fuperior talents, refided at Paris, and affifted J. Berain in the *books of ornaments*, which he publifhed in that city. He alfo engraved feveral plates in the large folio collection of *views of Verfailles*.

CORNELIUS VAN DALEN.
Flourifhed, 1640.

This artift is called the younger, becaufe he generally adds the word *junior* to his name. For what reafon this diftinction was made I know not. It does not appear, that his father was an engraver, though perhaps of the fame baptifmal name. He was a native of Holland; but under what mafter he learned the art of engraving is uncertain. It is difficult to form a proper judgment of his merit; for fometimes his prints refemble thofe of Cornelius Vifcher, of Lucas Vorfterman, of P. Pontius, of Bolfwert, and other mafters. A fet of antique ftatues, engraved by him, are in a bold, free ftyle, as if founded upon that of Goltzius; others again feem imitations of that of Francis Poilly. In all thefe different manners he has fucceeded; and they plainly manifeft the great command he had with his graver; for he worked with that inftrument only. He engraved a great variety of portraits, fome of which are very valuable, and form the beft, as well as the larger part of his works.

works. He did not succeed so well in drawing the naked parts of the human figure; his outlines are heavy, and frequently incorrect, and the extremities, the feet especially, are seldom well marked.

I shall only mention the following by this master:

The *four fathers of the church*, a middling sized upright plate, from Rubens. This print bears great resemblance to the style of P. Pontius.

The *Graces embellishing a statue of Nature*, a large upright print, on two plates, from the same. In the execution of this print, he seems to have had an eye to the neater works of S. Bolswert.

A *shepherd crowning a shepherdess*, a small plate, length-ways, from J. Casteleyn. Here he has followed the style of Cornelius Visscher; but more particularly so in many of his portraits.

The *Virgin presenting the breast to the infant Christ*, a middling sized upright plate, from Flinck.

Venus and Love, the same from the same.

Among his portraits I shall mention the following:

Bocace and *Aretin*, two middling sized upright plates, for the collection of prints, entitled the Cabinet de Reynst. These have been attributed to C. Visscher.

Charles II. in armour, a half sheet print, much esteemed.

James II. when duke of York, from Simon Luttichuys, the same.

Henry duke of Gloucester, the same, from the same.

Andreas Rivetus and *Fred. Spanheim*, from Van Negre, dated 1644. These two last portraits are engraved in the style of Lucas Vorsterman.

A. DALLE.
Flourished, 1686.

The name of an obscure and very indifferent engraver. I found it affixed to a species of triumphal processions, on a great number of plates, entitled, *Givochi Festivi e militari*, published at Venice 1686. They are coarse, slight, incorrect etchings, and have nothing but the singularity of the design to recommend them. The initials A. D. are joined together in a sort of a cypher; but the family name is written at length, *A. Dalle via sculp*.

GILLES LE DAME.
Flourished,

This engraver is mentioned by Florent le Comte, who informs us, that he imitated the style of Melan; but with no great success. His best works were *subjects of devotion* and *madonas*.

LUCAS DAMMAZE. See JACOBS.

CORNELIUS DANCKERS.
Flourished,

This artist was a printseller, established at Antwerp. He flourished towards the

the commencement of the laft century, and engraved a variety of fmall plates, which are by no means deftitute of merit; among others, we have by him an etching of *Meleager, who is prefenting the boar's head to Atalanta,* from R. Picou, a fmall upright plate; alfo a fet of prints reprefenting the *ruins of Rome;* and a fet of prints reprefenting the *paſſion of Chriſt,* &c.

DANCKER DANCKERS.
Flouriſhed, 1660.

He was fon to Cornelius Danckers, mentioned in the preceding article, and refided alfo at Antwerp, where it is probable he was born. He not only etched, but frequently worked with the graver alfo, and we have a great number of prints by his hand; particularly landfcapes, from Berghem, in which he attempted to imitate the ſtyle of that maſter; but by croffing his firſt ſtrokes with a fquare fecond, the effect is rendered heavy and unpleafing. The figures and cattle are fometimes prodigioufly incorrect; and the fpirit of Berghem is often much loft in the imitation. His beſt work, in my opinion, is a fet of large *landfcapes,* lengthways, from Wouvermans. Thefe are bold, free etchings, in a maſterly ſtyle. I ſhall mention

A fet of *landfcapes,* middling fized plates, length-ways, from Berghem.

Another fet of *landfcapes* length-ways, fmaller, from the fame maſter.

He alfo engraved from Peter Nolpe, Titian, Gerrard Seghers, P. de Jode the younger, &c.

JOHN DANCKERS.
Flouriſhed, 1660.

This artift, it is highly probable, was of the fame family with the preceding. He refided at Amſterdam, where he died; but he was not, I believe, born there; for his brother Henry, of whom we ſhall fpeak in the next article, declares himſelf to be a native of the Hague. He was an hiſtorical painter of no great eminence. By him we have a flight, incorrect etching reprefenting *Venus lying upon a couch,* from Titian, figned " Joh. Danckers fculp. aquâ forti, 1657."

HENRY DANCKERS.
Flouriſhed, 1670.

He was brother to John Danckers, mentioned in the preceding article, and inſtructed in the art of engraving; but the perfuafion of his brother John, joined perhaps with his own natural inclination, occafioned him to quit that profeffion, and take up the pallet and pencils. He excelled in landfcape, and went into Italy to perfect his ſtudies, where he remained fome time. From thence he came into England, and was patronized by Charles II. who employed him to draw *views of the royal palaces,* and the *fea ports of England and Wales.* Thefe drawings are dated 1678 and 1679. He alfo made feveral defigns for Hollar to engrave. At the time of the difcovery of the popiſh plot, being himfelf a Roman catholic, he left England, and returned to Amſterdam, where he died foon after. We have engraved by him the following portrait:

Charles

DAN [239] DAR

Charles the Second, a middling fized upright plate, from Adrian Hannerman. He has figned his name, " Hen. Danckers Haga Batavus fculp."

JUSTUS DANCKERS is alfo mentioned by M. Heineken as an engraver, but I am not acquainted with his works.

LEON DANET. See D'AVON.

JOHN DANET. See DUVET.

DANGERS.
Flourifhed, 1700.

He was the difciple of G. Chateau, by whom he was inftructed in the firft principles of engraving; but from a diflike to the profeffion, or the more powerful motives of religion, he foon quitted it and embraced an ecclefiaftic life. I am not acquainted with the works of this artift.

P. DANNOOT.
Flourifhed,

This engraver flourifhed towards the conclufion of the laft century. He engraved a *head of Chrift* from P. P. Rubens, a fmall upright plate; alfo the portrait of *Pere Maftrille*.

DANZEL.
Flourifhed,

A modern French engraver, who was probably a pupil of Daulle's; at leaft, he imitated the manner of engraving, adopted by that artift. By him we have the *two children of Rubens in their infancy* from a picture painted by Rubens, a middling fized upright plate. This picture was alfo engraved by Daulle.

PHILIP DAQUIN.
Flourifhed,

The name of an engraver, mentioned by Florent le Comte; but none of his works are fpecified. I am not acquainted with them.

PETER DARET.
Flourifhed, 1641.

This artift was a native of France, born at Paris, where he learned the firft principles of the art of engraving; and afterwards he went to Italy to complete his ftudies, where he worked a confiderable time. At his return he eftablifhed himfelf at Paris, and died at a very advanced age. He was not only a defigner and an engraver, but an author. For Florent le
Comte

Comte informs us, that he compofed a Life of Raphael, the celebrated painter, which he caufed to be printed, A. D. 1650. His works are chiefly performed with the graver, without any other affiftance; and though fome of them are not devoid of merit, yet they have not a fufficient fhare to place them in any high degree of eftimation. The mechanical part of his engraving is cold and filvery, the effect flat and unharmonized, and the drawing of the naked parts of his figures is frequently incorrect and heavy, efpecially upon the extremities. His works are very confiderable, and amount to upwards of 296 prints. I fhall only mention the following.

The *meeting of Elizabeth and the Virgin Mary*, a middling fized plate, length-ways, from M. Corneille.

A *holy family, with an angel prefenting fruit to the infant Jefus*, a middling fized upright plate, from Simon Vouet.

A *Madona giving fuck to the infant Chrift*, the fame, from Annibale Carracci.

St. John feated in the defert, holding a lamb upon his lap. The fame, from Guido.

St. Peter delivered from prifon, a large upright plate, from Dominichino. Mariette alfo engraved a plate from the fame picture.

Upwards of 100 fmall plates for a work, entitled, *La Doctrine des Mœurs*, by Mr. Le Roy de Gomberville, from the defigns of Otho Vænius, printed at Paris 1646.

A variety of other fubjects from his own defigns, many portraits, &c.

He alfo engraved from Polydoro, Vandyck, Champagne, Stella, La Hyre, Le Sueur, Le Brun, &c. See the mark, attributed to this mafter, on the plate at the end of the volume.

D A R G E N V I L L E. See Dezalier.

JAMES DASSONVILLE.
Flourifhed,

This artift, who appears to have been a native of France, etched feveral plates in the ftyle of Oftade, which, though not equal to the engravings by that mafter in fpirit or effect, are notwithftanding poffeffed of very great merit. He has fucceeded beft in the heads of his figures; the other extremities are often much neglected.

LOUISA DE MONTIGNI DAULCEUR.
Flourifhed,

This lady, the wife of M. Daulceur, etched feveral plates from the defigns of Boucher, Pierre, Cochin, &c.

JOHN DAULLE.
Born, Died, 1763.

This artift, I have been informed, was born at Abbeville in Picardy. He refided resided at Paris, where he died 1763. He worked entirely with the graver; and his performances sufficiently manifest the great command he had of that instrument. His strokes are laid with much freedom, yet without any affectation. They are very clear, and produce a pleasing, harmonized effect. Had his knowledge in drawing been equal to his management of the mechanical part of his engravings they would have ranked with the first performances the world ever produced. But in this great requisite, he was exceedingly defective. His portraits, which are the least exceptionable part of his works, are justly held in the highest estimation. The following by him are ranked among his best prints.

The *Quos Ego*, or *Neptune calming the tempest*, as described in the first book of Virgil's Æneid, a large plate, length-ways, from Rubens.

Mary Magdalen in the desert, reading a book, a middling sized plate, length-ways, from Corregio, for the collection of prints from the Dresden gallery.

Diogenes with his lanthorn, a small upright plate, from Joseph Ribera, called Spagnoletto, for the same volume.

The *triumph of Venus*, a middling sized upright oval, from Boucher.

The *two children of Rubens*, from a picture painted by that master, a small upright plate.

The portrait of *Peter Mignard*, and of the *countess of Feuquieres*, his daughter, two middling sized upright plates, from P. Mignard.

Gendron, the famous oculist, a middling sized upright plate, after Rigaud.

Maupertuis, the same, from Tourniere.

John Mariette, the engraver and printseller, the same, from Pesne.

Mademoiselle Pelissier, the same, from Drouais.

He also engraved a variety of other prints, from several masters.

LEON DAVEN.
Flourished, 1547.

This eminent engraver, who used the mark L. D. is by some called Louis Danet. He was apparently a native of France. The principal part of his works are engraved from the pictures of Francesco Primaticcio of Bologna, and especially those executed by that artist in the royal palace at Fontainbleau. His plates are chiefly etched in a very coarse, yet spirited manner, singular enough, but not without merit. The lights are kept broad and clear; but the masses of shadow are too equally powerful to produce any striking effect. His outlines are made by dark strokes in a stiff, tasteless manner, which render them hard and disgusting. The heads, with the other extremities and the naked parts of the figures, are incorrectly drawn. I shall only mention a few prints by this artist, as his works are not very uncommon, all from Primaticcio.

Jupiter and Europa, a middling sized plate, nearly square.

A *sacrifice to Priapus*, the same.

Cupid blinded, and mounted upon an ass; and two satyrs, with a man walking before them, blowing a trumpet.

Diana repofing after the chafe, a middling fized plate, length-ways.
The *death of Meleager*, a fmall upright oval plate.
A *man playing upon a harp, with fome figures dancing*, a large plate, length-ways.

Thefe are all marked with the initials L. D. for the name of the engraver; and befides, we often read upon them, " Bologna invent;" and " A. Fontana Bleo. Bol." which is the word Bologna abbreviated put inftead of the painter's name, he being a native of Bologna. The other words evidently mean Fontainbleau, where the pictures were preferved.

CHARLES DAVID.
Flourifhed, 1640.

He was a native of France, and refided at Paris. From whom he learned the art of engraving does not appear. His ftyle of mechanical execution feems to have been founded on an examination of the works of feveral artifts, rather than a direct imitation of any one in particular. He worked entirely with the graver, in a clear neat manner; but with great freedom of hand, he often rendered the effect of his prints lefs pleafing, than it would otherwife have been, by crofling his fecond ftrokes too fquarely upon the firft. He certainly drew the human figure with a confiderable degree of correctnefs; but he was apt to overcharge his outline, and mark the appearance of the mufcles too powerfully. The extremities efpecially are, in general, rather heavy and defective. His lights, a fault ufual with the engravers of that age, are too much fcattered, and too equally powerful. His beft prints are defervedly held in great eftimation. I fhall mention the following only:

The *labours of Hercules*, twelve middling fized plates, length-ways, from Franc. Floris

The *cries of Rome*, middling fized upright plates, copied from Villamena fo exactly, that they would eafily deceive one, if feen feparate from the originals. He has alfo added the mark of that artift.

The *Virgin and Child furrounded by angels*, a fmall upright plate, from Champagne.

A *man with a fnail upon his finger, accompanied by a goat, with a crown of fnails upon his head. A difh full of fnails is feen upon a table*; a fmall upright plate from Callot. This print is very rare.

A fet of *landfcapes*, from Paul and Matthew Brill.

He alfo engraved from Camillio Procaccini, Tempefta, Albert Durer, Simon Vouet, Vignion, Brebiette, &c. and he frequently fubftituted the initials of his name, when he did not write it at full length, C. D. F. the F. ftanding as ufual for *fecit*.

JEROM DAVID.
Flourifhed, 1640.

He was brother to the preceding artift; and alfo engraved a great number of prints, portraits efpecially, in a ftyle fomething refembling that of his brother,

brother, but not with equal freedom and correctness. I shall mention by this artist the following prints only:

The *heads of the philosophers*, on 36 plates from designs of his own. These are executed with the graver, in a coarse, dark style.

Christ carrying the cross, a large plate, length-ways, from Hercul. Ferrariers, dated 1630. The naked parts and extremities of the figures are very defective.

An *Ecce homo*, a small upright plate, from Guercino.

The *Virgin of the rosary*, a small upright plate, from Guido, dated 1633.

The *Virgin and Child*, a small circular plate, from the same master.

The *assumption of the Virgin*, from Camillio Procaccini.

Among his portraits are the following:

Charles the First on horseback, a large half sheet print.

Henrietta Maria, queen to Charles the First, also on horseback.

He usually signed his prints " H. David," the H. and D. being joined together cypher-ways; and some times the H. and the D. in a cypher alone, in the manner represented on the plate of monograms, at the end of the volume. The H. stands for *Hieronymus*, which in Latin signifies Jerom. The author of the Series of Engravers, published at Cambridge, not attending to this circumstance, has made two artists, the one H. David, the other Jerom David; whereas, in fact, they are both one and the same person.

LOUIS DAVID.
Flourished, 1667.

This engraver, according to professor Christ, resided at Venice; and the prints, marked L. D. published at that place, about the year 1667, belong to him. I shall only mention by this artist, the *descent from the cross*, a small upright plate, engraved in a neat style, resembling that of Lucas van Leyden; but the drawing is exceedingly defective. This print is marked with the L. and D. joined together, in the manner represented on the plate at the end of the volume.

CLAUDE DAVID.
Flourished,

This artist was a native of Burgundy, and is mentioned as an engraver by Vertue, who informs us, that he published a print from a model of the *fountain*, *ornamented with the statues of queen Anne, the duke of Marlborough on horseback, and several river gods*, which was proposed to have been erected at the Conduit in Cheapside. Under the print is written, *Opus Equitis Claudii David comitatus Burgundiæ*.

JEROM DAVIDLO.
Flourished,

This artist is mentioned by professor Christ as an engraver; and those prints are attributed to him, which are marked with an H. a D. reversed,

and

and an F. See this mark copied on the plate at the end of the volume. I own, it appears to me more like H. C. F. and may perhaps ftand for Hans, or John Collaert fecit. I have feen a fmall upright print, reprefenting a *man in armour*, *holding a flag*, which is all graved in imitation of Albert Durer, but very indifferently executed. It is marked H. D. the H. and D. being joined together, and dated 1517. Perhaps this may be by the above mafter.

EDWARD LE DAVIS.
Flourifhed,

Le Davis was of Welch extraction, and fhowing fome inclination for the arts, he was put as an apprentice to Loggan the engraver, with whom it appears, however, he did not ftay long; for being maltreated by his miftrefs, who obliged him to wear a livery, and follow her as a fervant, he ran away, and went to France, where he became a dealer in pictures; by which occupation he acquired an eafy fortune. At his return, he drew and engraved feveral portraits, and fome other fubjects. They have, however, very little merit to recommend them in any refpect. I fhall only mention the following:

Charles the Second feated: the face was afterward taken out, and king William the Third fubftituted in its place.

Catherine, queen of England, a large whole length, from John Baptift Carpers.

James, duke of York.

The dutchefs of Portfmouth, from Lely.

An *ecce homo*, from Carracci, faid to be very fcarce.

A *man laughing, holding a fool's cap*, only part of the figure feen; marked " Edward le Davis Londini fculp."

We have alfo by him, fome loofe etchings from Algardi, very indifferently executed.

DAWES.
Flourifhed, 1760.

He was a pupil of Hogarth's, and painted humorous fubjects. He alfo etched a few plates; among them, *Kidgell with a pair of tongs taking paper from a jakes*; the *reformers of manners throwing down the bafkets of fome induftrious fruit women, in the fore-ground is reprefented an old foldier in the ftocks*. This artift died a few years fince. Mr. Groffe obligingly favoured me with this account of him.

THOMAS DAWKS.
Flourifhed, 1679.

I have feen a large engraving, with a printed defcription, of the murder of *Sir Edmond Bury Godfrey*, very badly executed in every refpect; and, at the bottom, this infcription, " Printed for Thomas Dawks, the defigner of thefe " Emblems, 1679;" and he very probably was the engraver alfo.

C. DECKER.

C. DECKER.
Flourished,

This artist, who, according to professor Christ, resided at Nuremberg, was a designer as well as an engraver. Indeed he seems chiefly to have worked from his own compositions. I should suspect, that he was the disciple of Roman de Hooghe, whose style of designing and engraving he seems to have closely copied. The figures, of which he usually introduces many into his compositions, are by no means devoid of merit. They frequently manifest a tolerable degree of taste, and knowledge of design; but his manner of engraving, or rather etching, is coarse, and hard, with dark outlines on the lights, are also greatly scattered, without the least attention paid to the chiaro-scuro; by which means the effect is harsh, confused, and disgusting. Allowance made for these faults, Decker will appear to be a man of genius.

By him we have the large folio plates (into which he has introduced a vast multitude of small figures) for *Athanasii Kercheri Turris Babel*.

A great variety of *book plates*, and *small subjects*, &c.

He usually marked his plates with his name; when he did not, he substituted the initials, C. D. sometimes separate, and sometimes joined together, in the manner expressed on the plate at the end of the volume.

PAUL DECKER.
Flourished, 1740.

A modern engraver, probably of the same family with the preceding artist; and also established at Nuremberg. By him we have some engravings; but I am not acquainted with them.

I. DE DECKER, a name affixed to a small copy of the *treaty of Munster*, originally engraved by Suyderhoef, from Terburg. He has attempted to copy the style of Suyderhoef; but with no great success.

J. C. DEHNE.
Flourished, 1723.

By this engraver, who resided at Brandenburg in Germany, we have upwards of 200 plates of *masquerade figures*, representing, in the most ridiculous manner, the gods, goddesses, demi-gods, heroes, heroines, &c. of antiquity, in folio. They are executed with the graver, in a style, that does no sort of credit to the artist. He also engraved several plates of portraits for the work entitled *Jcones Bibliopolarum et Typographorum*, in folio, published at Nuremberg.

DE LAUNAY. See LAUNAY.

FRANCIS DELARAM.
Flourished, 1620.

This artist was cotempory with Elstracke and the Passes. Whose disciple he was does not appear; but he engraved in the stiff, formal manner, which prevailed too generally at that time, exceedingly neat, but devoid of all taste

D E L. [246] D E L

or expreffion. He affected much to crofs his firft ftrokes fquarely with the fecond. He drew very indifferently; his outlines are hard and incorrect; and his draperies are heavy and the folds badly expreffed. His portraits are the beft part of his works; but even thofe are rather valuable for their fcarcity, than for their merit. I fhall only mention the following prints by him from his own defigns:

Nero Cæfar, or *monarchie depraved*, London, 1627. A frontifpiece.
The frontifpiece to the *Seven Golden Candlefticks*, 1624.
The frontifpiece for *Wyther's Preparation to the Pfalter*, ornamented with emblematical figures. This I confider as one of his beft prints. It is dated 1619.

Add the following portraits, namely:
James the Firft, as large as nature, an upright whole fheet print.
Queen Mary, a fmall upright print.
Queen Elizabeth, the fame.
Hen. Percy, earl of Northumberland, dated 1619.
Frances, duchefs of Richmond and Lenox.
Sir Thomas Grefham, &c.

A. DELFOS.
Flourifhed, 1760.

A modern engraver, who refided in Holland, where he engraved a *landfcape* and a *fea port*, two large plates, length-ways, from Berchem; alfo feveral prints from D. Teniers, &c.

WILLIAM JAMES DELFT, or VAN DELPHUS.
Flourifhed, 1640.

This excellent engraver, a native of Holland, was born at Delft foon after the commencement of the laft century. He drew and painted portraits with great tafte, and in a ftyle that acquired him confiderable reputation; but as an engraver of portraits, he is more generally known; and in that light only I fhall confider him. He worked entirely with the graver; and handled that inftrument with the greateft facility. He drew correctly, and his beft prints are very finely finifhed. Confidering the great number of plates, which were completed by the graver of this artift, it is not reafonable to fuppofe they fhould be all alike, or equal in merit. Accordingly I fhall diftinguifh two manners, in which he engraved, and produced many excellent plates in both: Firft, a bold, powerful, open ftyle, productive of a fine effect; and as a fpecimen of it, I would refer the reader to the portrait of *Hugo Grotius*, dated 1652. Secondly, a neat and much more finifhed manner, as we find in the admirable portrait of *Michael Miravelt*, a near relation to the engraver, from a picture of Vandyck. He ufually figned his name at length; when he omitted to do fo, he fubftituted the letters G. V. D. or a cypher compofed of a G. and a D, which is copied on the plate at the end of the volume.

Delft engraved feveral Englifh portraits; but it does not by any means appear, that he was ever in England. He ftyles himfelf the king's engraver. I fhall mention the following portraits only by this artift:

Charles the Firft of England, a middling fized upright print.

Henriette

DEL   [247]   DEN

Henriette Maria, queen to Charles the First, the fame.
George Villars, duke of Buckingham, a large half fheet after Miravelt.
Elizabeth, queen of Bohemia, a large upright plate.
Three *princes of Orange,* namely, *William, Maurice,* and *Frederic Henry,* large heads, upright plates.
Hans des Ries, an upright oval, from M. Miravelt.
Jacobus Triglandus, profeffor in the academy of Leyden, dated 1636, a. fmall upright plate.
Abraham van der Meer, the fame.
John Olden Barnevelt, the fame.
He alfo engraved a number of portraits from Michael and John Miravelt, Ant. Vanden Venne, David Mytins, Henry Merman, C. Vandervoort, Peter Moreels, R. van Voert, and other mafters.

DELLA BELLA. See BELLA.

CATERIN DELLIO.
Flourifhed, 1611.

This artift worked entirely with the graver, and adopted a neat ftyle, fomething refembling that of Agoftino Veneziano. He engraved the figures for a large folio volume of Anatomy, publifhed at Venice, A. D. 1611. The drawing of thefe figures is by no means incorrect, and the anatomical markings are well expreffed.

DELPHIN. See DOLFIN.

JOHN ADAM DELSENBACH.
Flourifhed, 1721.

A modern engraver, who apparently refided at Vienna, where he engraved part of the plates for the *Hiftory of Architecture,* with *views of the moft famous buildings in the world,* defigned by John Henhard Fifchers, a large folio volume, publifhed at Vienna, 1721; alfo part of the plates for the work entitled, *Views of the Principal Buildings in the City and Suburbs of Vienna,* in folio. They are neatly engraved, but in a very ftiff ftyle. We may add to thefe by him, feveral portraits for the work entitled *Icones Bibliopolarum et Typographorum,* publifhed at Nuremberg.

JOHN DEMER.
Flourifhed, 1621.

This name is given by Florent le Comte, as of an engraver; and we have by him, according to the fame author, a print of a *little infant walking.*

FRANCESCO DENANTO.
Flourifhed,

By this artift we have a very large upright print, cut on wood, in a very flight but fpirited ftyle. It reprefents *Chrift healing the lame man ;* and the engraver has introduced many figures, which are executed with great tafte.
The

The heads are well characterifed, and very expreffive. Part of the background is performed in a very fingular manner : fmall round holes, clofe to each other, were punched into the block of wood, which in the impreffion, make a multitude of white fpots ; and the effect of them is by no means unpleafant. On a ftone at the bottom is the following infcription, *Francifcus Denanto de Sabaudia f.*

DENISOT.
Flourifhed,

A name mentioned, as an engraver, by Mr. Evelyn, without the leaft reference to any of his works. I am not acquainted with them.

MICHAEL DENTISLER.
Flourifhed,

This name is mentioned by Florent le Comte, as an engraver of embroideries, and other ornamental works.

DEODATE.
Flourifhed,

A name affixed to a portrait of *Sir Theodore Mayerne*, phyfician to James the Firft and Charles the Firft. The Hon. Mr. Walpole adds, that an Italian, called Deodate, was phyfician to Prince Henry, and perhaps the engraver of this print.

DE ROY. See Roy.

N. DERSON.
Flourifhed, 1625.

By this artift we have an engraving of the fumptuous front of the *church of Notre Dame de Reims*. It is a very laborious performance, neatly etched, and finifhed with the graver. The figures which he has introduced are very fpirited ; and the ftyle, in which they are executed, refembles that of Callot. This print does honour to the engraver, who figns his name, *N. Derfon, Reim. fe. fculp.* It is dated 1625.

NICHOLAS DERUSE.
Flourifhed,

Florent le Comte mentions this artift, as chiefly excelling in engraving ornaments and foliage, for goldfmiths and jewellers, &c.

CLAUDE DERVET.
Flourifhed,

This artift was a painter, born at Nancy in Lorrain, and flourifhed in the
laft

last century. He was the disciple of Claude Henriet. Being a native of the same city with Callot, an acquaintance was formed between these two artists, and they lived in friendship with each other. Dervet etched several plates in a style greatly resembling that of Callot.

DES BOIS. See BOIS.

DES CHAMPS. See CHAMPS.

DES GODETZ. See GODETZ.

DES MARTEAU. See MARTEAU.

DES PLACES. See PLACES.

DES PERINI. See PERINI.

DES ROCHERS. See ROCHERS.

DEUTECUM. See DUETECUM.

NICHOLAS MANUEL DEUTSCH.
Flourished, 1518.

This ancient artist was a native of Berne in Switzerland; and is spoken of as a celebrated painter in his time. He cut on wood several of his own designs, in a bold, free, but slight style; and the naked parts of his figures are sometimes incorrect. He marked his prints with an N. an M. and a D. joined together, and a dagger underneath the letters, in the manner represented on the plate of monograms at the end of the volume. I shall only mention the two following prints by this master:

A figure of a *woman standing*, a middling sized upright print. He has added, VON BERNN to the initials of his name, and the dagger.

Several *women figures in a composition*, a middling sized print, length-ways. To the initials of the name and the dagger is added the date, 1518. This is one of his neatest, and I think best engravings.

RODOLPHE MANUEL DEUTSCH.
Flourished, 1548.

There are some prints marked with an R. an H. an M. and a D. joined together in a cypher, in the manner expressed upon the plate at the end of the volume, attributed by professor Christ to this artist, who flourished about the year 1548, and was an engraver on wood. The prints executed by him are cut in a bold, spirited manner, which prove him to have been an artist of considerable merit. The same author supposes him to have worked

worked conjointly with Hans or John Holbein; and this conjecture arises from the initials H. H. being often found upon the prints, marked with the cypher above-mentioned. Most of the engravings by this artist were published, A. D. 1548. Among other things by him, I have seen some *animals*, small prints length-ways. Also, *three figures conversing, with a landscape back-ground*, a small square plate. See the mark of this engraver copied upon the plate at the end of the volume.

DE WAEL. See WAEL.

DE WIT. See WIT.

ANTOINE JOSEPH DEZALIER DARGENVILLE.
Flourished, 1740.

A modern connoisseur, and a man of letters. By him we have an Abridgment of the Lives of the Painters. He etched several *small subjects*, and *landscapes*, from his own compositions.

GIOSEFFO DIAMENTINI.
Flourished, 1710.

A modern Italian painter, who resided at Venice. He flourished at the commencement of the present century, and etched several subjects from his own compositions, which, according to Basan, show more indications of genius, and fertility of invention, than correctness of drawing. I have seen so few of the works by this artist, that I cannot form a decisive judgment, but from the few I have seen, I think much more favourably of him than that author seems to do with respect to his knowledge of drawing. The following engravings are by him:

Four *emblematical subjects*, small upright plates.

Two *emblematical subjects*, large square plates.

Two other *emblematical subjects*, one a large hexagon plate; the other an oval.

These, in my opinion, are etched in a free, masterly style, with a fine point; the designs are spirited; the actions of the figures are often very graceful, and the heads and other extremities of them drawn in a superior style. They are marked, *Eques Diamantinus in. f.* Hence it appears, that he was honoured with a title.

H. F. DIAMER.
Flourished,

An artist of merit, who etched a set of prints for a *Dutch bible*, in octavo, in the style of Le Clerc. He also engraved some few portraits; among the rest, that of *Aubert Miræus*, from Anthony Vandyck.

J. DICK-

J. DICKSON.
Flourished, 1660.

This artist, it seems, resided at Oxford, where he engraved among other things, according to the Hon. Mr. Walpole, the head of *Edward Parry, episcopi Laonensis*, dated 1660. I have never seen this print, but in another account of it I find the name written *Ed. Parry, bishop of Killalse*.

ABRAHAM DIEPENBECK.
Born, 1607. Died, 1675.

This well known artist, was at first a painter on glass; and though he excelled his cotempories in that art, yet disgusted by a variety of accidents, he quitted it, and turned his thoughts to painting in oil. He had studied in Italy, and now became the scholar of Peter Paul Rubens; and under the direction of that master, made great improvement.

Diepenbeck was a man of genius. He possessed great fertility of invention, and no small knowledge of drawing; and it is observed, that had he taken time to correct his first ideas, he would doubtless have produced such works, as might have ranked him among the first artists; but being greatly employed in making drawings for prints, and books of prints, he hurried his compositions, without attending to the propriety of his choice. He died 1678, aged 68.

He is said to have engraved several *devotional subjects* with great success.

ADRIAN VAN DIEST.
Born, 1655. Died, 1704.

This artist was born at the Hague, A. D. 1655. He resided chiefly in England, and painted landscapes with great success. He studied much from nature, in the western parts of the kingdom; and had he met with encouragement equal to his genius, he would probably have arrived at a very superior degree of excellence. But being often obliged to paint pictures at low prices, he hurried them over, without bestowing sufficient study upon them: and this is the reason why his works are so very unequal. He died, A. D. 1704, aged 49.

We have etched by this master, in a very slight, but masterly style, several sets of small *landscapes*, some of them upright, and some of them lengthways.

F. A. DIETEL.
Flourished,

This artist, assisted by another, who signs his name CHR. DIETEL, and was very probably his brother, engraved conjointly a set of *fountains and theatrical scenes at Rome*; though it appears from the signature at the bottom of the plate, that they resided at Vienna.

CHRISTIAN WILLIAM ERNEST DIETRICH, or DIETRICY.
Born, 1712. Died,

A modern artist, who was born at Weimar, and resided chiefly at Dresden, where he was profeſſor of the Academy of Arts. He was a painter of very extenſive abilities, and ſucceeded both in hiſtory and landſcape. We have by him a great number of ſmall ſubjects, to the amount of 150 or more, which he engraved from his own compoſitions, in the ſtyle, ſays Baſan, of Oſtade, of Laireſſe, and of Salvator Roſa. Sixty of theſe etchings are exceedingly rare. I ſhall only mention the following print by this maſter: A *ſatyr entertained by a peaſant and his family.* This is a very neat etching, finely drawn, and executed in a maſterly manner: it is dated 1739.

VANDER DIETTERLIN.
Flouriſhed,

The name of an engraver, mentioned by Florent le Comte, by whom we have, according to that author, ſome *embroideries,* and other *ornamental works.*

J. C. DIETZSCH.
Flouriſhed,

He etched ſeveral ſets of ſmall *landſcapes,* length-ways, in imitation of the ſtyle of Waterloo; they are executed in a more determined manner, but by no means equal in ſimplicity, or reſemblance of nature, to thoſe of that maſter. They poſſeſs, however, a very conſiderable ſhare of merit.

J. DIEU DE SAINT JOHN.
Flouriſhed,

This artiſt is mentioned by Florent le Comte, as one of the firſt engravers of *figures a la mode,* or the different modes and dreſſes in faſhion. His prints are hardly worth enumerating.

F. DIODATE.
Flouriſhed,

A name affixed to the portrait of *Iſbrandus de Diemerbroeck,* profeſſor of anatomy. This print, however, does no great credit to the engraver. I ſuſpect this artiſt to be the ſame with him before mentioned, under the name of Deodate.

D. DIRICKSEN.
Flouriſhed,

This artiſt reſided at Hamburgh, and ſeems to have been chiefly employed by the bookſellers. He engraved portraits in a neat pleaſing ſtyle, greatly reſembling that of the Paſſes. Among other prints, by him is that of *Hadrianus a Minſicht,* a ſmall upright oval plate, with an ornamental border, and ſome Latin verſes underneath the head.

JOHN DITMER.
Flouriſhed, 1574.

By this engraver we have, among other things, a middling ſized upright plate,

plate, nearly square, reprefenting a *figure of Chrift*, feated in the clouds, with the fymbolical animals, reprefenting the Evangelifts, and angels bearing the crofs, crown of thorns, &c. It is executed in a ftyle greatly refembling that of Cornelius Cort; but coarfer, and by no means fo well drawn, as the works of that mafter generally are.

J. DIXON.
Flourifhed, 1770.

A modern engraver of mezzotinto, by whom we have feveral portraits from Sir Jofhua Reynolds, and other mafters; among them, that of *Anabella Bunbury*, with the emblems of Juno, dated 1771.

WILLIAM DOBSON.
Born, 1611. Died, 1647.

Amidft all the difadvantages of life, the genius of this artift made its appearance; and his inclination led him to portrait painting. Vandyck, found him working in a garret, and was fo pleafed with his performances, that he took him under his patronage, and introduced him to Charles the Firft, who honoured him with the flattering appellation of the Englifh Tintoret. At the deceafe of Vandyck, Dobfon was appointed ferjeant painter to the king, and groom of the privy chamber. No man ever had a fairer opportunity than this artift, of acquiring an eafy fortune; but leading a diffolute life, he ruined his conftitution, and fpent all his fubftance. He was imprifoned for debt, and died in London, in which city he was born, foon after his releafe, A. D. 1647, aged 37 years only.

By this artift, it is faid, we have his own portrait, a fmall half fheet print, very rudely etched, and in a ftyle greatly inferior to what one would have expected from him; efpecially, as he had the fpirited etchings of his tutor Vandyck for examples. Bafan, I apprehend, never faw this engraving, otherwife he would hardly have faid it was *digne de Van-Dyck*, or worthy of Vandyck. This portrait, though attributed to Dobfon, was, I believe, certainly etched by Mr. Evelyn; accordingly I have referred to it in the account of that artift; and there given my reafons for fuppofing fo.

DODD.
Flourifhed, 1760.

The name of an Englifh artift, affixed to the portraits of *Leveridge* the actor, and of *Buckhorfe*, the noted boxer.

ANTHONY VANDER DOES.
Flourifhed, 1649.

I fuppofe this engraver was of the fame family with the Vander Does, who were painters, and natives of Amfterdam. His chief employment feems to have been in the portrait line; and if he was not a difciple of Paul Pontius, at leaft he imitated his ftyle. And though he never equalled that mafter, yet his beft engravings are by no means devoid of merit.

J fhall only mention the following prints from the works of this artift:

Part of the plates belonging to a work, entitled, *Portraits des Hommes illuftres dans 17 Siecle*, publifhed at Amfterdam. Some of them are dated 1649.

Ferdinand, Cardinal-Infant of Spain, and Governor of the Low Countries, on horfeback. In the back-ground is the reprefentation of the battle of Nortlingen, in which this prince, affifted by the king of Hungary, obtained a victory over the Swedifh army, A. D. 1634; a middling fized upright plate, from Diepenbeck. By fome connoiffeurs this compofition is attributed to Rubens.

A *Magdalen*, half figure, a fmall upright plate, from Vandyck.

A *Madona and child*, a fmall upright plate, from Erafmus Quillinus.

A *holy family* with an angel warming the linen for the child, a fmall upright plate, from the fame mafter. One can hardly be perfuaded, that a man, in his fober fenfes, would have employed the angel in fo ludicrous a manner; but it is not uncommon, in the compofitions of the Dutch and Flemifh mafters to meet with thefe *ferious burlefques*, if I may be allowed the term. We fhall not, however, wonder at fuch fmall abfurdities in painting, if we give credit to the following anecdote of a Dutch tragic writer, who, according to M. du Bos, in his Reflections upon Poetry and Painting, has reprefented Scipio, the great Roman general, fitting in his tent, and very gravely fmoaking a pipe of tobacco, with a pot of ale by his fide; whilft he is meditating upon the event of the battle of Zama, which he was to fight with Hannibal, the enfuing morning, and on which the fate of Carthage depended.

JACOB VANDER DOES.
Born, 1623. Died, 1673.

This artift was a native of Amfterdam, and a difciple of Nicholas Moyert. He went to Italy to improve himfelf in the art of painting, and refided there fome time. He excelled in landfcapes and cattle, and imitated the ftyle of Bambochio. Being a man of a melancholy turn of mind, and crofs temper, he incurred the hatred or contempt of all his acquaintance. Karel du Jarden, at laft, became his only companion; whofe friendfhip for him was fuch, that he put up with his croffnefs, rather than forfake him. This unfortunate man died at Amfterdam, A. D. 1673, aged 50 years.

We have feveral fmall *landfcapes* etched by this artift from compofitions of his own, which are ornamented with animals. They are in a flight, free, mafterly ftyle.

This mafter is frequently confounded with his fon, who was alfo named JACOB VANDER DOES. He was a hiftorical painter, and never engraved.

SIMON VANDER DOES.
Born, 1653. Died, 1717.

This artift was the fon and pupil of Jacob Vander Does, mentioned in the preceding

preceding article. He imitated his father's manner, and acquired a considerable share of reputation. He was in England, where he abode but one year; perhaps he did not meet with sufficient encouragement. On his return to Holland, he settled at the Hague, where, though he was in a very advantageous way of business, his circumstances were constantly low, from the extravagancies of his wife. He died, A. D. 1717, aged 64 years. We have etched by this artist a few small *landscapes*, with *animals*, from his own compositions.

J. DOESBURGH.
Flourished,

A very indifferent engraver, who worked chiefly, if not entirely, for the booksellers. He executed several plates of the old *Roman customs*, in a slight, poor style, etched and finished with the graver. Also *Van Trump, the Dutch admiral, engaging with the English fleet*, a small plate, length-ways.

JOHN A DOETECHUM, or DOETECOM.
Flourished,

This artist, with BAPTISTA A DOETECHUM, who, I suppose, was his brother, executed conjointly a work of considerable magnitude, in which are represented the *various habits and manners of the Indians*. Both these artists worked with the graver only, in a stiff, open style, without effect; and the drawing of the naked parts of the human figure is very indifferent on the plates of both. These engravers are often confounded with the Duetecums; and perhaps they were of the same family, the name being spelt with with an O. instead of the E. However, their styles of engraving are manifestly very different. These artists worked entirely with the graver, and the Duetecums usually etched their plates in a slight manner. But of this matter I speak very diffidently. See DUETECUM.

BARTHOLOMEW DOLENDO.
Flourished, 1590.

This engraver, who was a native of Germany, flourished at the conclusion of the sixteenth century. He worked entirely with the graver in an open, slight style. He was probably one of the scholars of Henry Goltzius. Gerard Douw learned the first principles of drawing from this artist, who might probably have more judgment than execution in that art; for the outlines, and markings of the naked parts of the figures, upon his plates, are by no means correct. See the cypher composed of a B. and a D. which he frequently used, when he did not put his name at length, on the plate at the end of the volume. The following prints are by this master:

A *Dutch merry-making*, a middling sized plate length-ways, probably from a design of his own.

Adam

Adam and Eve receiving the forbidden fruit, a middling sized upright plate, from Carl van Mander.

A *holy family*, a small plate, length-ways, from Michael Coexy.

St. John preaching in the desert, a middling sized plate, length-ways, without the painters name

Pyramus and Thisbe, a middling sized upright plate, from Crispen Vander Borcht.

He also copied some of the plates of Lucas Jacobs of Leyden, and engraved several others from Spranger and other masters.

ZACHARY DOLENDO.
Flourished, 1581.

This artist was probably of the same family with the preceding, if not his brother, he imitated his style of engraving; but was greatly his superior in taste and correctness of drawing. We have some portraits by this master, which are equal in neatness to any by Jerom Wierix. He often used a cypher, composed of a Z. and a D. joined together, in the manner expressed upon the plate at the end of the volume. I shall mention the following prints by this engraver, which will sufficiently prove his great merit.

Adam and Eve embracing each other, whilst Eve receives the apple from the serpent, a small upright print, from Spranger.

Andromeda naked, chained to a rock, a well drawn figure; the head and other extremities are marked in a fine style; a very small upright, perhaps from a design of his own.

The *continence of Scipio*, a small circular plate, from A. Bloemart.

A *set of the Pagan gods and goddesses*, copied small from the prints of Henry Goltzius.

St. Martin dividing his cloak between two beggars, a small upright plate, from Spranger.

I shall only take notice of the following portrait, which I think a very fine one by this artist, namely,

William, prince of Orange, a half figure in armour, a small upright plate, without any painter's name: It is dated 1581.

OLIVER DOLFIN, or DOFIN.
Born,   Died, 1693.

This artist was, I believe, a native of France; but he resided at Bologna, where he etched a great number of plates, from the Carraccii, and other great masters. He died about the year 1693.

WILLIAM DOLLE.
Flourished, 1630.

This artist worked chiefly, if not entirely with the graver, in a very poor, stiff style; and his employment was in the portrait line for the booksellers. His plates, in general, appear to be engraved from designs of his own, which, as far as we can judge from the prints, were equally indifferent. However, antiquity or scarcity frequently stamps a value upon things, totally

destitute

deflitute of merit in themselves. By him we have the following portraits, among many others:
Sir Henry Wootton, a small upright print.
Mark Franke, master of Pembroke Hall, Cambridge; a small half sheet print.
George Villars, duke of Buckingham, the same.
Robert, earl of Essex, &c.

JOHN DOLIVAR.
Flourished, 1680.

This artist was a native of France, and a designer as well as an engraver. His works are usually, says Basan, placed with those of Chauveau and Le Pautre, but in fertility of genius he never equalled either of those masters. Some of the plates for *Berain's Ornaments* are by him; and one of the *Ceilings in the Cabinet des Beaux Artes*, published at Paris by Perault, 1690.

DOMINICO FIORENTINO. See BARBIERE.

CÆSAR DOMINICUS.
Flourished, 1614.

This name is affixed to a set of *ornaments*, neatly engraved from the invention of Lud. Scal. They are middling sized upright plates, and usually marked, " Cæs. Dom. inc. 1614."

JOHN DONALDSON.
Flourished,

A modern artist by whom we have several small upright etchings of *beggars*, from Rembrant, by no means badly executed.

W. DONNE.
Flourished,

An obscure engraver, by whom, among other things, we have a small plate, length-ways, from Elsheimer, representing *Venus and Cupid* in a landscape, with several other distant figures. This is a slight scratchy etching, badly drawn, and without effect.

S. DONNET.
Flourished,

An obscure engraver, who apparently worked for the booksellers only. He executed his plates with the graver, in a heavy, stiff style, without taste or correctness. Among other things by him, is a small print, length-ways, representing a *man seated reading a book*, which is upon a table before him.

DORS.
Flourished,

The name of an engraver, mentioned by Evelyn, without any reference to his

his works. Perhaps his name should have been written Durr, of whom an account will be found below.

P. VAN DOORT.
Flourished,

This artist, a man of no great merit, worked entirely with the graver, in a style resembling that of Cornelius Cort; but without taste or correctness of design. The heads and other extremities of his figures are peculiarly reprehensible. We have by him a small upright *holy family*, where Elizabeth is giving an apple to the infant Christ, and St. John is seated near them, from Bernard Passarus.

DORBAY.
Flourished, 1690.

This artist appears to have been a native of France. Among other things engraved by him, are some of the *plans and views of the royal palaces in France*; and they are executed in a very neat pleasing style. He adds to his name, del. et sculp.

MICHAEL DORIGNY.
Born, 1617. Died, 1665.

This artist was born at St. Quentin in France; and discovering an early inclination for the arts, he was placed as a disciple under Simon Vouet, a painter, at that time in great repute, and whose daughter he married. Dorigny copied the manner of his master; and was himself a painter of some note; but he is much better known as an engraver. He performed his plates chiefly with the point, in a bold, powerful style; the lights are broad and massy, especially upon the figures. But the marking of the folds of the draperies, and the shadows upon the outlines of the flesh, are frequently so extravagantly dark, that they form a harsh, disagreeable effect, and sometimes destroy the harmony of the engraving entirely. He certainly understood the human figure; and in some few instances, we find it correctly drawn. But, in general, from the *manner* which he had contracted in copying the style of Vouet, rather than the simple forms of nature, his outlines are affected, and the extremities of his figures too much neglected.

He was made professor of the Royal Academy of Painting at Paris, where he died, A. D. 1665, aged 48. According to Abbe Marolles, his works consist of 105 prints. I shall only mention the following:

The *adoration of the Magi*, a very large print, length-ways, on four plates, in the manner of a frieze, from a picture painted by Simon Vouet, dated 1638.

The *nativity of Christ*, a large upright plate, from the same master.

Venus at her toilet, a middling sized plate, length-ways, from the same.

Venus, Hope, and Love, plucking the feathers from the wings of Time, the same, from the same.

Mercury and the graces, the same from the same.

The *rape of Europa*, the same.

Some slight *Bacchanalian subjects*, from his own compositions. He also engraved from Le Sueur, Sarasin and other masters.

LOUIS

LOUIS DORIGNY.
Born, 1654. Died, 1742.

This artift was fon to Michael Dorigny, mentioned in the former article. After having learned the firft principles of defign from his father, he became the pupil of Le Brun; and when he had finifhed his ftudies under that mafter, he went to Italy, where he took up his refidence. He is greatly commended for the fertility of his invention, the grandeur of his compofition, and the harmony of his colouring. He is alfo faid to have drawn the human figure very correctly. He died, A. D. 1742, aged 88 years. By the hand of this artift we have feveral etchings; among others, the following:

A fet of thirty-two fmall upright plates, comprehending the title, from his own compofitions; which were engraved for an Italian edition of the *Penfées Chretiennes*, by Pere Bouhours.

Five *emblems of Horace*, fmall plates nearly fquare, the fame.

The *landing of the Saracens at Port D'Oftie*, a middling fized plate, lengthways, from Raphael.

SIR NICHOLAS DORIGNY, KNIGHT.
Born, 1657. Died, 1746.

This artift was the fon of Michael Dorigny, and brother to Louis, mentioned in the preceding article. He was born at Paris; and his father dying whilft he was young, he was brought up to the law. But at the age of 30 he quitted that profeffion, and ftudied drawing for a year very affiduoufly. Intending to engage in the arts, he went to his brother, who refided at Rome, in order to learn the principles of painting. After fome practice in that art, being advifed by him, he took up the point; and, in the courfe of feveral years, produced a number of different etchings. He ftrove to imitate the ftyle of Girard Audran; and after ten years purfuit, finding he could by no means fucceed in his attempt, fo well as he expected, he refumed the pencil. But being of a very eafy difpofition, he was foon perfuaded to lay it down again; and having received fome inftructions, with refpect to the handling of the graver with more freedom, to harmonize the roughnefs of the etching, he began again to engrave; and the feven planets from Raphael, it feems, were his firft productions. Some time after, he finifhed the transfiguration, from the fame mafter. His reputation was now increafed; and he was invited into England, in order to engrave the cartoons, then at Hampton-Court. He arrived June 1711, but did not begin to work upon them till the year following, the intermediate time being fpent in raifing a fund for the payment. At firft it was propofed, that they fhould be done at the queen's expence, in order to be given away, as prefents to the nobility, foreign princes, minifters, &c. and the lord treafurer Oxford exerted himfelf greatly in the caufe of the artift. But he demanding the fum of four or five thoufand pounds, the plan was rendered abortive. He had, however, an apartment affigned him in Hampton Court, with requifite perquifites. The work, at laft, was undertaken by fubfcription, at four guineas each fet. Dorigny fent for Dupuis and Dubofc from Paris to affift him; but from some difference, which happened between them they both left him, about two years and a half after their arrival, before the work was half completed. April 1, A. D. 1719, he prefented to king George the Firſt two complete ſets; and a ſet a piece to the prince and princeſs. The king give him a purſe with a hundred guineas; and the prince, a gold medal. The duke of Devonſhire, who had aſſiſted him with the loan of 400l. remitted the intereſt of it for four years; and in the year following, 1720, procured him the honour of knighthood from the king.

During his reſidence in England, he painted ſome few portraits; but with no great ſucceſs. His eyes failing him, he returned to Paris, where, A. D. 1725, he was made a member of the Royal Academy of Painting, and died 1746, aged 89.

If the great excellence of an engraver conſiſts in diveſting himſelf of all manner of his own, and tranſcribing faithfully on copper the ſtyle of the maſter, whoſe picture he copies; and if he ought to be conſidered as faulty, in proportion as he recedes from this rule, Dorigny will fall under very heavy condemnation. He drew in an incorrect affected manner. The naked parts of his figures are often falſely marked; and the extremities in particular are defective. His draperies are coarſe, the folds ſtiff and hard, executed without being properly harmonized, or well formed. And a *manner* of his own pervades all his prints; for the ſtyle of the painter is conſtantly loſt in that of the engraver. But he ſeems never to have failed more, than when he worked from the paintings of Raphael. The ſweet ſimplicity, and chaſtneſs of outline, which are the great characteriſtics of that admirable artiſt, required much more judgment and attention, than Dorigny poſſeſſed, to expreſs them properly. But, with all theſe faults, the prints of Dorigny are the beſt copies we have from ſeveral of the pictures of Raphael, and other great maſters. Baſan ſpeaks of him in the following manner; and a little partiality to a countryman may be well excuſed: " We have many excellent prints by his hand, in which one juſtly " admires the good taſte of his drawing, and the intelligent and picturesque " manner, which he acquired by the judicious reflections he made upon the " works of the great maſters, during the reſidence of 22 years in Italy." We have by him, among others, the following prints:

St. Peter curing the lame man at the gate of the temple, a large upright plate, from Civoli. This I take to be one of his firſt engravings. It is a dark, heavy print, executed exactly in the ſtyle of M. Dorigny his father.

The *transfiguration*, from Raphael, a large upright plate.

The *deſcent from the croſs*, the ſame, from Daniello da Volterra. This and the following, I conſider, in my own opinion, as the beſt prints by this maſter.

The *martyrdom of St. Sebaſtian*, a large upright plate, arched at the top, from Dominichino.

The *Trinity*, the ſame from Guido.

The *hiſtory of Cupid and Pſyche*, from the pictures painted by Raphael in the Vatican.

The *cartoons*, ſeven very large plates, length-ways, from the pictures of Raphael, which were then at Hampton Court, but at preſent at the Queen's Houſe in St. James's Park.

He

He also engraved from Annibale Carracci, Lanfranche, Louis Dorigny, and a variety of other masters.

MICHAEL DOISIER.
Flourished, 1710.

This artist, if not a native of Paris, resided there about the commencement of the present century. He worked with the graver in a very neat style, something resembling that of Drevet. The naked parts of his figures are not well drawn; the extremities in particular, are very faulty. Among other prints by him are the following:

Mary Magdalen washing the feet of Christ in the house of Simon the Pharisee, a large plate, length-ways, from Nicolas Colembel. The companion, *the woman taken in adultery*, from the same master, was engraved by Claude Duflos.

The *two blind men of Jericho cured*, a large upright plate, from the same.

Christ driving the merchandizers out of the Temple, the same, from the same.

The *marriage of the Virgin*, the same from Jouvenet. This appears to me to be one of his best prints.

The portrait of *J. B. Colbert, marquis de Torcy*, a large upright plate.

DOUET.
Flourished,

This artist, according to Papillon, engraved on wood a small upright print, from Andrea Del Sarto, representing the *Virgin with the infant Jesus*.

W. DOUGHTY.
Flourished, 1760.

This modern artist was, I believe, a native of England, and a painter. He etched some few portraits; among others the two following: *Thomas Beckwith*, the antiquary of York; *Thomas Gay*, the poet.

LE DOYEN.
Flourished, 1666.

An indifferent artist, who resided at Paris, and was perhaps a native of that place. He worked entirely with the graver, in a stiff, tasteless style; and his employment appears to have been chiefly for the booksellers. I have seen some *ornamental frontispieces* by him; and he engraved the plates for a work in quarto, entitled, *Figures des different Habits des Chanoines reguliers en ce Siecle*, &c. Paris 1666; or, the Figures of the different Habits of the regular Canons of this Century.

JOHN

JOHN DRAPENTIERE.
Flouriſhed, 1691.

A very indifferent engraver of *portraits* and *frontiſpieces*. He reſided in London; but that he was a native of England, does not appear. He worked with the graver, in a ſtyle ſufficiently neat, but without taſte. His drawing of the human figure is below criticiſm. Among his portraits are the following: *Daniel Burgeſs*, dated 1691. *Jacob Dyer*, *Mr. Perkins*, &c. Add to thoſe, a ſmall ſatyrical print in an oval, repreſenting a *lady ſhaving a gentleman*, half figures, with this inſcription, *Le beau ſervice*.

DREBBER.
Flouriſhed, 1590.

This engraver is ſaid to have worked from the deſigns of Goltzius. I am not acquainted with his works; nor are they ſpecified by the authors who mention him.

DRUEFKEN.
Flouriſhed,

The prints cut in wood, and marked with a cluſter of grapes, are by Mr. Evelyn attributed to this artiſt; one in particular, which repreſents the *king of the Boors in Hungary, eaten alive by the rebels, whom he ſeduced*. See this mark on the plate at the end of the volume.

PETER DREVET, the ELDER.
Flouriſhed, 1700.

This excellent artiſt was a native of France. Under what maſter he learned the firſt principles of engraving, is uncertain. Apparently it might be Girard Edelink. However, the progreſs he made in that art was ſuch, as raiſed his reputation above any of his cotempories. The command, which he had of the graver, was very great. His prints are firm, yet highly finiſhed. He drew well, and copied faithfully the ſtyle of the maſters from whom he worked. He confined himſelf to portraits; and the ſoftneſs and beauty, which appears in them, have ſtamped a conſiderable value upon the firſt impreſſions. I ſhall only mention the following, which are reckoned among his moſt eſteemed prints:

Louis XII. a whole length figure, ſtanding, a large upright plate, from Hiacinthe Rigaud.

Louis XV. upon his throne, companion to the former, after the ſame painter.

The *prince of Conde*, the ſame, from the ſame.

The *comte de Thouloufe*, a middling ſized upright plate. This portrait was twice engraved. In the one, the hand has a glove on; in the other, the glove is taken away.

Cardinal de Fleury, the ſame, from the ſame.

Marechal de Villars, a large upright plate. The beſt impreſſions of this plate,

plate, are before the change was made in the infcription, which is eafily diftinguifhed.

PETER DREVET, the YOUNGER.
Born, 1697. Died, 1739.

This artift, the fon of Peter Drevet, mentioned in the preceding article, was born at Paris, A. D. 1697. He was inftructed in the art of engraving by his father, whofe ftyle he adopted, and furpaffed his tutor in clearnefs and delicacy of finifhing. He did not confine himfelf to portraits: we have feveral hiftorical prints by him, which in point of neatnefs and exquifite workmanfhip, are fcarcely to be equalled. His drawing, though he fcrupuloufly copied his original, appears in general rather heavy; and the figures, from being entirely executed with the graver, without fufficient variation of the ftyle, have fometimes a cold and filvery effect. His moft efteemed and beft hiftorical print is very valuable; but the firft impreffions of it are rarely to be met with: it is,

The *prefentation of Chrift in the temple*, a very large plate, length-ways, from Louis de Bologna. The following are alfo by him.

Adam and Eve in their ftate of difobedience, a large upright plate, from Ant. Coypel.

The *meeting of Abraham's fervant with Rebecca at the well*, the fame, from the fame.

Abraham, with his fon Ifaac on the altar, the fame, from the fame, dated 1707.

Among his portraits the two following are juftly held in the higheft eftimation.

M. Boffuet, bifhop of Meaux, a whole length figure, ftanding, a middling fized upright plate, from Rigaud: a moft admirable print.

Samuel Bernard, a whole length figure, fitting in a chair, a large upright plate. The firft impreffions are, before the words *Confeiller d'Etat* were inferted upon the plate. This print is finifhed in a very wonderful manner. I fhall add the following excellent portraits only:

Cardinal Dubois, a middling fized upright plate from the fame.

L'Abbé Pucelle, counfellor of the parliament, the fame, from the fame.

Louis XV. when young, conducted by Minerva to the temple of Glory, a middling fized upright plate, from Coypell.

CLAUDE DREVET.
Flourifhed, 1740.

He was firft coufin to Peter Drevet, mentioned in the preceding article, and was living at Paris, at the time Bafan publifhed his Dictionary of Engravers. He chiefly confined himfelf to portraits, and worked with great fuccefs. The following portraits are by him:

The *cardinal d'Auverge, fitting in a chair*, a middling fized upright plate, after Rigaud.

M. de

M. de Vintimille, *archbishop of Paris*, the same, after the same master.
M. le comte de Zinzindorff, the same, from the same.

MARTIN DROESHOUT.
Flourished,

One of the indifferent engravers of the last century. He resided in England, and was employed by the booksellers. His portraits, which are the best part of his works, have nothing but their scarcity to recommend them. He engraved the head of *Shakspeare*, *John Fox the martyrologist*, *John Hewson, bishop of Durham*, &c. Also several of the plates for Haywood's *Hierarchy of Angels*; and the *death of Dido* for Stapylton's Virgil, octavo, &c.

JOHN DROESHOUT.
Flourished, 1635.

Probably a relation of Martin Droeshout, mentioned in the preceding article. Like him he worked for the booksellers, with the graver only, in a style that does him but little credit as an artist. We have by this engraver the portrait of *Richard Elton*, a head, the figure in armour, marked " John " Droeshout, Lond. f." Also, the portrait of *Joan. Danesy*, affixed to his *Paralipyomena*, published in quarto, A. D. 1639. Several *frontispieces*, and other *book plates*.

DU BOIS. See Bois.

DU BOSC. See Bosc.

DU CHANGE. See CHANGE.

GASPER DUCHE.
Flourished,

He resided at Rome, and probably was a painter. I have seen a *landscape* etched by him, in a free, slight style; but without effect. It is marked, *Gaspero Duche in. sculp. Romæ*.

P. DUCHESNE.
Flourished, 1700.

An engraver on wood of no great eminence, mentioned by Papillon. His chief employment seems to have been in the ornamental line.

JOAN LE DUCQ.
Born, 1636. Died,

He was born at the Hague, and became a disciple of Paul Potter, the celebrated painter of animals, whose manner he imitated with great success. In the year 1671, he was appointed director of the Academy at the Hague. By him we have several etchings; among others, a *set of dogs*, on eight plates very neatly executed, and with great spirit.

THOMAS

DUD [265] DUG

THOMAS DUDLEY.
Flourished, 1678.

He was a native of England, and one of the pupils of the famous Hollar, whose manner of engraving he imitated. But though he never equalled his master in the lightness of his point, or freedom of execution, his etchings are not without merit. His most considerable work was a set of cuts for the *Life of Æsop*, prefixed to the last edition of his fables, published by Barlow. He also etched the portrait of *bishop Russel*, which is subscribed, " Thomas " Dudley, Anglus fecit, 1679." He frequently adds to his name, *quondam condiscipulus W. Hollar*; and sometimes he signed his plates with the initials of his name, T. D. only.

JOHN A DUETECUM.
Flourished, 1559.

By this engraver, conjointly with LVCAS A DUETECUM, who was probably his brother. We have several large whole sheet prints in folio, representing the magnificent and pompous funeral of the *emperor Charles V.* they are slight coarse etchings; but the figures are designed with spirit; and some of the heads are executed in a masterly manner. By John a Duetecum also is engraved an ornamental frontispiece for a book of *Perspective*, by John Tridmanus Trisius, in folio, which print is chiefly, if not entirely, executed with the graver, in a style which does no credit to the artist. The *Doetecums*, mentioned as engravers in a preceding article, were probably of the same family; but the absurd custom of spelling names so many ways, is frequently the cause of much confusion. If this be true, John a Duetecum, and Doetecum, will be the same person; and the other two, Baptista and Lucas, his brothers.

CLAUDE DUFLOS. See FLos.

GASPAR DUGHET.
Born, 1600. Died, 1663.

This admirable artist is better known by the name of Gaspar Pousin; which latter name was given him, because he was the scholar of Nicholas Pousin, who married his sister. According to the general report, Gaspar was a native of France; but some authors tell us, that he was born at Rome. However, his great excellence in landscape painting is too well known, to need any repetition here. His brother in law, Nicholas Pousin, frequently painted the figures for him; which he himself was not so well able to execute. We have several slight, but spirited etchings of *landscapes* by this artist; among the rest, a set of four small round plates; and another set of small plates, length-ways.

JOHN DUGHET.
Flourished, 1640.

He was the brother of Gasper Dughet, mentioned in the preceding article, and

and as nearly related to the famous Nicholas Poufin, under whofe inftructions one might have expected he would have made great progrefs. Whether he ever attained to any degree of perfection in the art of painting, I cannot tell; but with all the advantages he had on his fide, he never fhone as an engraver. Among other etchings, from the pictures of his brother in law Poufin, are the following:

The *feven facraments*, from the pictures painted by that artift for the Commandeur del Pozzo, which differ much from thofe in the royal collection in France: Large prints, on two plates each. Chatillon copied thefe plates upon a fmaller fcale.

The *judgment of Solomon*, a large plate length-ways, from the fame mafter.
Mount Parnaffus, the fame, from the fame.
The *birth of Bacchus*, the fame.

D U G Y.
Flourifhed, 1760.

By this modern artift, who is apparently a native of France, we have fome flight prints, from F. Boucher and other mafters.

D U H A M E L. See HAMEL.

D U J A R D I N. See JARDIN.

D U N K E R T O N.
Flourifhed, 1770.

A modern artift, who refided in London, by whofe hand we have feveral portraits in mezzotinto; among others, *Mifs Hornick*, from Sir Jofhua Reynolds; *John Elliot*, from Dance; and *Mifs Bamfyeld*, from W. Peters. He alfo engraved from other mafters.

D U P I N. See PIN.

J O H N D U N S T A L L.
Flourifhed, 1660.

He was a drawing mafter, and lived in the Strand, London. He alfo engraved feveral plates, which he etched, and retouched with the graver in imitation of the ftyle of Hollar. His performances, however, do him no great honour. The following prints are by his hand: A fet of prints reprefenting *birds, beafts, flowers, fruit, flies and worms*. On the title he writes, "invented, etched, and graven, by John Dunftal, 1662." He likewife engraved fome *frontifpieces* for books, and feveral *portraits*; among the laft are the following: *king William and queen Mary*; *Samuel Clarke*, the martyrologift; *Jacobus Ufferius*, &c.

D U P O N T. See PONT.

D U P U I S.

DU PUIS. See Puis.

J. DURANT.
Flourished,

He was an engraver, employed chiefly, if not entirely, by the bookfellers. It was greatly the fashion, in the last century, to ornament books with cuts; and little attention it seems was paid to the manner in which they were designed or engraved. Of course, I should suppose, very small prices were given; so that the artist had no inducement to study for improvement; since, in the first instance, he had sufficient employment; and, in the second, little hope of having his price advanced, in proportion to his merit. And this, I believe, was the cause that so many indifferent artists flourished at that time. Durant possessed no great merit to recommend his works to the notice of the collectors; but worse engravers than he may be found among his cotemporaries. We have by him a variety of book plates and some portraits; among the last, is that of *queen Mary*, from Kneller, a middling sized upright oval plate.

DURELLO.
Flourished, 1674.

This artist was, I believe a German. It is certain he resided at Vienna, where he engraved some of the portraits for the large work entitled, *Historia di Lepoldo Cesare*, published in that city, 1674.

ALBERT DURER.
Born, 1471. Died, 1528.

The powerful efforts of genius, however they may be retarded by compulsion, or interested pursuits, or depressed by the hand of poverty, can seldom be totally extinguished in the mind. Like the latent flame, they are still expanding; and generally, at one time or other, manifest themselves; and sometimes indeed more powerfully, in proportion to the resistance they meet with. Genius is often found surrounded with all the disadvantages and discouraging circumstances of life, and too frequently unable to support the man who is guided by her influence. This, however, was not the case with Albert Durer; for though born in poverty, he followed the dictates of his genius, and obtained in the end, what he certainly deserved, a comfortable subsistance. From his father, who was a goldsmith at Nuremberg, he learned the first principles of engraving; but afterwards he studied under Michael Wolgemuth, who not only engraved on wood and copper but is said to have practised etching with great success, and was an artist of no mean abilities. It was Albert's desire to have placed himself with Martin Schoen, whose reputation was, at that time, very confiderable; but he was prevented by the death of that master. He studied however from his prints; many of which he copied, as well as some of those of Israel van Mecheln. But he seems evidently to have preferred the first, and upon them he formed, that style of engraving, which he ever after practised. His first print, or, at least,

least, the first that is dated, is marked with the year 1497; at which time he must have been 26 years of age. And, if we may believe Sandrart, he did not begin to paint till some time after; 1504 being the earliest date that writer had ever seen upon any of his pictures.

To free himself from the noise and impertinence of his wife, who was a very great shrew, he travelled into the Low Countries, where he contracted an acquaintance with his cotemporary, Lucas Jacobs of Leyden; and a strict friendship continued between these excellent artists till the death of Albert Durer. Being persuaded to return to Nuremberg, on promise of his wife's amendment, he complied with the request of his friends; but he soon felt the ill effects of his goodnature; and, though a man of most excellent temper, she broke his heart by her ill treatment. He died at Nuremberg, the place of his birth, A. D. 1528, aged 57 years.

He was honoured with a seat among the magistrates of the city of Nuremberg; and the emperor Maximilian gave him an armorial bearing.

The following story is related by Vasari, and others after him, that on seeing some of his woodcuts, copied by Marc Antonio at Venice, he set out for that city, and complained to the senate of the damage he sustained. But the only redress he could obtain was, that Marc Antonio should not in future counterfeit the mark of Albert Durer. The truth of this relation indeed is not greatly depended upon.

Albert Durer was a man of universal genius. He understood the arts in all their various branches; and wrote Treatises on Anatomy, Perspective, Geometry, and Architecture both civil and military. As a painter, Vasari says of him: "If this exact and admirable artist, whose genius was so extensive, had been "born at Tuscany, rather than Germany, so that he might have had an op- "portunity of studying the beautiful pieces which are at Rome, as the rest of "us have done, he would have been the best painter in Italy, as now he is to "be reckoned the most excellent and most celebrated genius of the Fle- "mish school:" which character he undoubtedly deserved in every respect. But in order to conceive an idea, equal to the merit of this great master, it is requisite, that without prejudice we should examine many of his works; and we shall then find, that he possessed astonishing fertility of invention. His conceptions were excellent; he composed his figures with great propriety; he varied the characters and expressions of the heads in a judicious manner; and the hand of the master is evident in all his works. He engraved on copper, and on wood. The first, a few etchings excepted, are executed with the graver only, in so neat and excellent a style, that for facility of execution, and command of that instrument, he has never been excelled. His etchings are coarse, but spirited; however, they do not equal the rest of his works. His engravings on wood are in a slight, bold style, resembling the masterly sketches he made with the pen. He certainly understood the human figure, and often drew it very correctly; but his outlines are by no means beautiful and flowing, or his choice of forms the most pleasing. But these defects are owing to the prevailing taste of the country where he resided, and his want of those advantages, which Vasari has justly mentioned. The works of Albert Durer are very numerous, and many of them exceedingly valuable.

valuable. I can only mention fome few under the following heads.

FIRST, thofe on copper, executed entirely with the graver.

Three naked women, with a globe above their heads, and an appearance of Hell in the back-ground, a fmall upright plate. On the globe is the date 1497, with thefe letters, 𝔇. 𝔊. 𝔥. which mean in German 𝔇. 𝔊𝔬𝔱𝔱. 𝔥𝔦𝔩𝔣, *O! God help,* or *affift us.* This plate was copied by Albert Durer, from Ifrael van Mecheln. Originally the letters on the globe were 𝔊. 𝔅. 𝔄. 𝔊𝔬𝔱𝔱 𝔅𝔢𝔥𝔲𝔱𝔢 𝔄𝔩𝔩𝔢, *God keep all.* There are feveral other copies of this print with variations.

A *holy family,* where Jofeph is leaning on a ftone, and three figures behind him; one of them with a high crowned hat on, dated 1506. Captain Baillie has a copy of this print, with fome flight variation, which he fuppofes, and with great reafon, was executed by Rembrant.

Adam and Eve in Paradife, and the ferpent entwined round the tree, a fmall upright plate, dated 1504. Jerom Wierix, A. D. 1566, at the age of 16, made a very furprifing copy of this plate. I have myfelf one of the original pictures (for Albert Durer repeated this fubject feveral times) which was certainly painted prior to the engraving of the print; for in the print there is a moufe, playing directly before a cat, which bears fome analogy to the harmony that exifted in Paradife. But in my picture, there are two frogs, inftead of the moufe. The former was doubtlefs an improvement too material to have been omitted, had the picture been pofterior to the print.

A nativity, called the *fmall nativity,* where Jofeph is feen filling a vafe with water at a well, a very fmall upright plate, dated 1504.

A *holy family, with a monkey in the fore-ground,* called the Virgin with the Monkey, a fmall upright plate.

The *prodigal fon,* a middling fized upright plate. Thofe impreffions, before the date 1513 was added to the plate, are the moft eftimable.

St. Hubert kneeling before the crucifix, which appears upon the head of the ftag, a middling fized upright plate.

St. Jerom in the defert, kneeling before a crucifix, and holding a ftone in his hand, the fame.

St. Jerom, feated in a room, writing at a defk, the fame, dated 1514. There is a copy of this print by Jerom Wierix.

Melancholy, a fmall upright plate. This has been copied the fame fize, and the fame way, the date 1514 being added.

Pandora's box, as it is falfely called. It reprefents a winged woman, ftanding on a globe, holding a fort of cup in her hand, a middling fized upright plate.

A man armed on horfeback followed by a fpectre, and accompanied by Death on horfeback. This print is called Death's Horfe; the fame. The beft impreffions are before the date, 1513, was added to the plate. There is a clofe copy of this print, dated 1564.

The *death's head,* fo called becaufe a fcull is reprefented on a coat of arms, furmounted with an helmet; a fatyr, with a young woman liftening to him, are ftanding by it, a fmall upright plate.

A *coat of arms,* reprefenting a lion rampant, with a cock, the fame.

The

The *life and paffion of Chrift*, a fet of very neat fmall upright plates.
The *twelve apoftles*, the fame.
He alfo engraved, among a variety of other fubjects, feveral excellent portraits.

SECONDLY, among his etchings on copper are the following:
Chrift feated, leaning his head upon his left hand, and a figure lying down in the front, and pointing towards him, a fmall upright plate.
Mofes receiving the tables of the law, a very fmall upright plate, dated 1524.
The *cannon*, fo called becaufe a cannon is feen in the fore-ground, a fmall plate, length-ways, dated 1518. From the rough appearance of this print, it has been thought by fome, though I believe without foundation, that it was etched on a plate of iron. This was copied fmaller, the fame way, by Jerom Hopfer.

THIRDLY, his wooden cuts, among which are the following:
A fet of fifteen folio prints, the fubjects of which are taken from the *Apocalypfe*.
The *life and paffion of Chrift*, on thirty fix fmall upright prints. Thefe are the engravings, the copying of which, according to Vafari, occafioned the difpute between Albert Durer and Marc Antonio. Certainly the latter did copy them the fame fize on copper. It is equally certain, that he did not put the mark of Albert Durer, but his own.
The *life of the Virgin Mary*, on twenty fmall folio prints; feventeen of thefe were alfo copied by Marc Antonio, and with the mark of Albert Durer, except upon the laft plate, to which he has put his own.
Two large prints, confifting of feveral blocks, reprefenting the *triumphs of the emperor Maximilian*.

P. DURET.
Flourifhed, 1760.

A modern engraver, who refided at Paris, by whom we have feveral landfcapes, from Ruyfdael, Wouvermans, Venet, &c.

JOHN DURR.
Flourifhed, 1625.

The name of a very indifferent artift, who was chiefly employed in engraving portraits, and book plates. He worked entirely with the graver, in a very flight poor ftyle, without tafte or correctnefs. Among other portraits by him, is that of *H. I. Erneft*, with his family; and of *J. Zimmer*, dated 1625.

CORNELIUS DUSART.
Born, 1665. Died, 1704.

He was born at Harlem, and became the pupil of Adrian van Oftade. He imitated the ftyle of his mafter with no fmall fuccefs; and his fubjects were alfo taken from low life. We have feveral etchings by him, and fome few mezzotintos;

DUV [271] DYC

mezzotintos; and indeed some of his etchings are helped in the shadow with a mezzotinto tool. Among others by him, are the following:

An *old man playing on the violin, while a Dutch peasant is regaling*. Marked " Corn, Dusart pinx. et fecit 1685."

A *Dutch peasant reading a paper, and holding a bottle in his right hand*, a small upright print.

These two are mezzotintos; the following are etchings.

Dutch boors making merry at a fair, a small plate, length-ways, dated 1685.

A *man with a hurdy gurdy, playing at the door of a cottage*, the same.

The *shoemaker, and its companion*, the *village doctor*, two middling sized upright plates.

The *inside of a Dutch cottage with boors drinking, and a man playing upon the violin*, dated 1685; with verses underneath beginning thus: *Rusticus ex animo*, &c.

DUVAL. See VAL.

JOHN DUVET.
Flourished,

This artist flourished at the commencement of the sixteenth century. The Gothic style of his engraving has given occasion to many to suppose, he was more ancient than he really was. In some few instances, his name is found subscribed at length upon the plates; but, in general, he substituted the initials I. D. either separate or joined together. He is called, says Professor Christ, the *master of the Unicorn*; because it is likely, that he engraved several *allegorical subjects*, concerning the triumph of that animal.

SIR ANTHONY VAN DYCK.
Born, 1599. Died, 1641.

This admirable painter was born at Antwerp. His genius led him to the study of the arts, he became the disciple of P. P. Rubens; and by the rapid progress that he made, not only acquired a lasting reputation to himself, but was an honour to his master. He succeeded both in historical and portrait painting; but especially in the latter; and his pictures are justly held in the highest estimation. During his residence in England, he was honoured with the order of knighthood by Charles the First, A. D. 1632; and he died in London, A. D. 1641, aged 42, and was buried in the cathedral church of St. Paul. For his amusement he took up the point; and the etchings which he produced are executed in a free, and masterly style; those especially, which are more highly finished, cannot be sufficiently admired.

I shall only mention the following:

The *ecce homo*, a small upright plate, half figures, an excellent print from a composition of his own.

The portrait of *Lucas Vorsterman*, a small upright plate, the same. Add to these,

Paul Pontius, the same,

Joss de Momper, the same.
Peter Sneyders, the same.
Titian with his mistress, who is leaning upon a box, containing a scull, half figures, a small upright plate, from a picture painted by Titian himself.

DANIEL VANDEN DYCK.
Flourished,

This artist was a painter, who resided at Venice, during the last century, by his hand we have some few etchings, as the *deification of Æneas*. This is very slight, but spirited. The masses of light and shadow are broad and well preserved; and the naked parts of the figures correctly drawn; excepting only, that the extremities are rather heavy. Also a spirited *basso relievo*, resembling a Bacchanal, a middling sized plate, length-ways, both from his own compositions.

E.

ECHARDTS.
Flourished,

The name of an obscure and indifferent engraver, affixed to a portrait of *Conyers Middleton*.

EDWARD ECGMAN, or ECKMAN.
Flourished, 1621.

This artist, who appears to have been a native of France, was a most excellent engraver on wood. He copied many of Callot's prints, and even imitated the free style of that master with great success. The distant parts of his engravings are very neatly executed; and the perfect forms of the smallest figures exceedingly well preserved. Among other things by him, is the representation of the *fire-work upon the river del'Arne* from Callot, which Papillon, who certainly was a good judge in this instance, calls an admirable print; adding, that it is impossible to find a more delicate engraving on wood.

Ecgman engraved also from Louis Busink, Abraham Bosse, &c. The number of his prints is said to be 105.

GEORGE DAVID ECKSTEIN.
Flourished, 1721.

A very indifferent engraver, who was apparently a native of Germany, by him we have part of the portraits for a work entitled *Icones Bibliopolarum et Typographorum*, published at Nuremberg, 1721.

GIRARD EDELINCK.
Born,   Died, 1707.

This admirable artist was a native of Antwerp, where, probably, he learned the first principles of engraving. About the year 1665 he went to Paris, where he resided. His great merit procured him the favour and protection of Louis XIV. who appointed him an apartment in the Gobelins, and honoured him with the title of *Chevalier*. He was also a member of the Royal Academy of Painting and Sculpture at Paris; and he died in that city, A. D. 1707, at a very advanced age.

He worked entirely with the graver, and, I believe, never called in the point to his assistance. The freedom and delicacy, with which he executed his plates, cannot be too much admired. He neglected no part of his engravings, but finished them with great care, and perhaps too close an attention to neatnefs prevented his making more variety between the dark parts of the fore-ground and the diftances. He fucceeded particularly in the heads of his figures, which are often uncommonly fine. He certainly underftood the human figure; yet he did not draw it with that great tafte and correctnefs, which is fo remarkable in the prints of Girard Audran; neither are his hands and feet marked in that mafterly manner, or with equal truth. And if we compare that excellent engraving by him, reprefenting the Tent of Darius, from Le Brun, which he has finifhed in fo beautiful a manner, with the battles of Alexander by Audran, from the fame mafter, we fhall readily agree, I believe, that the animation, correctnefs, and tafte which we find in the latter, amply compenfates for the want of that clearnefs and neatnefs, which appears in the execution of the former. Among the moft eftimable prints by this great artift, may be reckoned the following.

A *battle between four horfemen, with three figures flain upon the ground*, a large plate length-ways, from Leonardo de Vinci. By miftake the name is written at the bottom, " De la Finfe pinxit."

A *holy family, with Elizabeth, St. John, and two angels, one of which is fcattering flowers*, a middling fized upright plate, from the famous picture of Raphael, in the king of France's collection. The firft impreffions are before the arms of M. Colbert were added at the bottom of the plate; the fecond are with the arms; and in the third the arms are taken out; but the place where they had been inferted is very perceptible. Giacomo Frey has made a very exact copy of this plate, of the fame fize as the original.

The *crucifixion of Chrift, who is furrounded with angels*, a large upright print on two plates, from Le Brun.

Mary Magdalen bewailing her fins, and trampling upon the riches of the world, a middling fized upright plate, from the fame painter. The firft impreffions are without the narrow border which furrounds the print.

St. Louis praying, a large upright plate, from the fame.

St. Charles Borromeus, its companion, the fame.

Mofes with the tables of the law, a half figure, engraved conjointly with Nanteuil, a large upright plate, from P. Champagne.

Alexander entering into the tent of Darius, a large print length-ways, on two plates, from Le Brun. This engraving belongs to the three battles, and triumphal entry of Alexander into Babylon, by Girard Audran, and compleats the fet. The firft impreffions have the name of *Goyton* the printer at the bottom.

Alexander entering into the tent of Darius, a large print, length-ways, on two plates, from Peter Mignard. This plate was finifhed by P. Drevet.

He alfo engraved feveral admirable portraits; among the reft the following:

Philip Champagne, the painter, from a picture painted by Champagne himfelf, a middling fized upright plate.

M. d'Hozier, the genealogift, from Rigaud, the fame.

Martin Vanden Bogaert, the fculptor, the fame from the fame.

Madam Helyot, the fame.

M. Arnauld

E D E   [275]   E E C

M. Arnauld d'Andilli, a small upright plate, from Champagne.
Nathaniel Dilgerus, a small oval.
M. le Brun, the painter, from a picture painted by Le Brun himself.
He also engraved from Corregio, Pietro de Cortona, Guido, Rubens, Jouvenet, Ant. Coypel, &c.

JOHN EDELINCK.
Flourished, 1679.

He was brother to Girard Edelinck, mentioned in the preceding article, whose style of engraving he closely imitated; but he never equalled him either in drawing or the execution of the mechanical part of his plates. Several of the *statues in the garden at Versailles* are by him. They do him great credit, though the effect is cold, and the extremities rather heavy. But his best performance is, I think, the *deluge*, a large plate length-ways, dated 1681, from Alexander Turchi, called Veronese. This engraving so nearly equals the best works of Girard Edelinck, that it is generally believed he assisted John considerably in the execution of it. This plate was engraved from the collection of prints, for the pictures in the collection of the king of France.

NICHOLAS EDELINCK.
Flourished, 1760.

He was the son of Girard Edelinck, mentioned above. He imitated the style of his father; and though the plates he produced do him no discredit, they are by no means equal to what one might have expected, from the son of so capital an artist. He resided at Paris, A. D. 1760; but according to Basan, had been in Italy, and engraved at Venice a *Madona and Child*, half figures, a middling sized upright plate arched at top, from Corregio. *Vertumnus and Pomona*, the same, from J. Ranc. Several portraits for the Crozat collection; and other subjects from various masters.

J. EDELING.
Flourished,

This engraver was a native of Holland. The principal part of his employment was in the portrait line, and chiefly, I believe, for the booksellers. Among other portraits by him are the following: *J. Deimerbroeck*, a small half sheet print, and *Timon van Geiffel*.

GERBRANT VANDEN EECKHOUT.
Born, 1621. Died, 1674.

A celebrated painter of portraits and history, born at Amsterdam. He was the disciple of Rembrant, and imitated the style of that master so nearly, that his pictures have frequently been mistaken for the productions of Rembrant's pencil. We have by him an etching of *Cornelius Tromp*, a half sheet print.

GEORGE CHRISTOPHER EIMMART.
Flourished, 1680.

This engraver was a native of Ratisbon, and flourished towards the conclusion of the last century. He etched some small plates, in a free, masterly style, of *ruinated buildings, vases* with figures also upon them, which though not perfectly correct in the outline, have nevertheless great merit. He also engraved several of the plates for Sandrart's *Academia Pictoriæ*.

FRANCOIS EISEN.
Flourished, 1750.

This artist was a native of Brussels, but established at Paris, where, among other things, he etched a small upright plate from Rubens, representing *Christ giving the keys to Peter*.

CHARLES EISEN, son to Francois, was a celebrated designer of *vignettes and book-plates*, of all kinds; several of which he etched himself, in a free, spirited style: perhaps he may be still living.

WILLIAM ELDER.
Flourished, 1680.

This was one of those industrious engravers, whose labours were bestowed on the ornamenting of books with frontispieces, portraits and other ordinary decorations. Indeed many of the publications of the last century deserved no better embellishments; It is by no means uncommon to find some commendatory scraps of poetry annexed to them, which are often as totally devoid of merit, as the prints themselves are of taste. Engraving, among the greater number of these book-plate makers, seems to have been merely mechanical; and their stiff, formal productions, convey to us the idea of their having been executed by a machine, rather than the hand of an artist, directed by the least taste or genius.

William Elder was a Scotsman by birth; but he resided, I believe, chiefly in London. Among the portraits by this artist, which were chiefly, if not entirely, with the graver, are the following: *Ben. Johnson, the poet*, half sheet. *Theodore de Mayerne*, a small oval. This is by far his best print. *His own portrait*, with a fur cap; and the same with a wig, &c.

OTTOMAR ELLIGER.
Born, 1666. Died, 1732.

This artist, the son of Ottomar Elliger, a famous flower painter of Berlin, was born at Hamburgh. He learned the principles of painting from Gerard de Lairesse, and succeeded in history. His place of residence was almost entirely at Amsterdam, where he died, A. D. 1732, aged 66. He engraved several plates from compositions of his own; a great part of which were for the *History of the Bible*, in two volumes, folio, published by Mochir. The first volume appeared, A. D. 1700, and the second, A. D. 1702.

WILLIAM ELLIOT.
Born, Died, 1766.

This ingenious artist was an Englishman, and resided at London. He excelled in landscapes, which he engraved with much taste. The freedom of his point, in particular, was admired; and great expectations were justly formed in his favour; but he died in the prime of life, at his house in Church-street, Soho, A. D. 1766. He was a man of an amiable and benevolent disposition, and greatly beloved by all who knew him. His best engravings are from the pictures of the three Smiths, landscape-painters, who resided at Chichester, and frequently worked conjointly. Among these is a large *landscape,* length-ways, in which a city appears at a great distance; also a *landscape* from Gasper. Poussin, in which a boat is seen in the front with fishermen in it, a middling sized plate, length-ways. He also engraved the portrait of *Helena Formans,* the second wife of Rubens, from a picture painted by that master.

ADAM ELSHEIMER.
Born, 1574. Died, 1620.

This great artist was born at Franckfort upon the Maine, and learned the first principles of drawing and painting from Philip Uffenback, a man of no great note. He afterwards completed his studies in Italy, where he settled. He excelled in *landscapes* with small figures, *moonlight scenes,* and *subjects illuminated by fire or torch light.* His pictures are finished in a most admirable manner. They were never large; yet the time bestowed upon them was such that the prices he received though considerably great, were inadequate to the labour, and insufficient for the support of himself and family. He was thrown into prison for debt; and notwithstanding the time of his confinement was very short, it had such an effect upon his spirits, that it broke his heart. He died, A. D. 1620, aged 46. We have some small etchings by him from his own compositions.

RENOLD, or REGINALD ELSTRACKE.
Flourished, 1620.

A very laborious engraver, who flourished soon after the beginning of the last century, and worked chiefly for the booksellers. His best engravings are portraits; but these are very stiff and destitute of taste, though neatly executed, entirely with the graver; and I believe, usually from his own designs. Among his portraits are the following: *Sir Philip Sidney,* said to have been engraved soon after his death. *Mary, queen of Scots,* one of his best prints. BAZIΛIΩLOGIA, *or the true and lively effigies of all our English kings, from the conquest to the present time,* dated 1618. He sometimes substituted the initials of his name, R. E. when he did not choose to write it at length.

EMPEREUR,

EMPEREUR. See LEMPEREUR.

PHILIP ENDLICH.
Flourished,

A Dutch engraver. He worked chiefly in the portrait line, and for the bookfellers. Among other plates by him are the following portraits, *J. G. E. Alſtein, Peter Holleboek*, and *John Philip, governor of the iſle of St. Martin*.

ENFANT. See LENFANT.

JOSIAS ENGLISH.
Born,   Died, 1718.

This perſon, of whom I find no ſatisfactory account, reſided at Mortlake, in Surry, where he died 1718. He etched a print from Titian, repreſenting *Chriſt with the two diſciples at Emmaus*: probably a copy only from the engraving of Maſſon, well known by the name of the *table cloth*. He imitated the ſtyle of Hollar, but with no great ſucceſs; we have alſo by him a ſet of ſmall upright prints, repreſenting the gods and demy-gods, dated 1654. See his cypher, compoſed of an *I*, an *E*, and an *F*, upon the plate at the end of the volume.

CHRISTIAN ENGELBRECHT.
Flourished, 1721.

This engraver, with his brother MARTIN ENGELBRECHT, were eſtabliſhed at Augſburg, where they carried on a conſiderable commerce in prints. The former engraved ſome *ornamental works* for jewellers and goldſmiths, conjointly with J. A. PFEFFEL, from A. Morriſon; alſo ſome views for the *Hiſtory of Architecture*, publiſhed by John Hernhard, in folio, 1721; and the latter part of a ſet of prints for *Ovid's Metamorphoſes*, ſmall plates, length-ways.

The latter engraved from Rugendas and other maſters, alſo part of the plates for the work entitled, *Repræſentatio Belliob ſucceſſionem in Regno Hiſpanico*, in folio, are by him.

Both of them worked chiefly with the graver; but their prints are not very highly eſteemed.

There was a very ancient engraver named ENGLEBRECHT, mentioned by Sandrart, and to whom, falſely, ſome authors have attributed the engravings marked with a Gothic E, which I take to be an E and S joined together; I have ſpoken of theſe old prints, in the fifth chapter of the Eſſay at the beginning of the volume.

EPISCOPIUS. See BISCHOP.

APICIE. See LEPICIE.

I. ERRAR.
Flourished,

This artiſt engraved ſeveral *landſcapes*, from Anthony Waterloo, and is ſaid to have marked his prints with the initials, I. E. F. the F. as uſual, ſtanding for fecit.

E R T [279] E V E

FRANCOIS ERTINGER.
Flourished, 1680.

He was, according to some authors, a native of Antwerp; however, he resided chiefly, I believe, at Paris, where he engraved a great variety of plates, which are not very excellent, though possessed of some merit. Amongst his best, I think may be reckoned the following:

Several *large views of towns and landscapes with figures*, from Vandermeulen. He sometimes, in his landscapes, imitated the style of Callot, but not with great success.

The *marriage at Cana* in *Galilee*, a large plate, length-ways, from Raymond Le Fage.

The *history of Achilles* from Rubens, a set of eight middling sized plates; some upright, and some length-ways, the same that were afterwards engraved by Baron.

Twelve prints, from the *Metamorphoses of Ovid*, after the miniatures of de Werner.

The history of the *Comtes de Thoulouse*, ten large plates, length-ways, from Le Fage.

A *Bacchanalian*, a large plate, length-ways, from Nicholas Poussin, dated 1685.

He also engraved a great variety of other subjects, from different masters.

ESPAGNOLETTO. See RIBERA.

GEORIG ETLINGER.
Flourished,

An ancient engraver in wood, a native, I believe, of Germany, by whom we have among others a middling sized upright print, representing *Bishop Blaize*, the portrait is inclosed in an ornamental border, embellished with the symbols of the Gospel; it is cut in a very spirited manner, and marked " Georig Etlinger Zu Bamberg, f."

JOHN EVELYN.
Born, 1620. Died, 1705.

This ingenious gentleman was a great lover of the arts. As a man of science he undoubtedly claims a distinguished place in the learned world. He was the first in England, who undertook to write upon the subject of engraving; and though his List of the principal Artists is very defective, yet he has preserved the remembrance of several curious circumstances, which might otherwise have been entirely lost. He has treated his subject, more like a man of letters, than an artist. However, it plainly proves, that he had the undertaking much at heart; and it is much to be wished, that he had entered more fully upon it. There are attributed to him the following etchings, namely,

Five small prints of *his journey from Rome to Naples*, after drawings of his own.

The portrait of *William Dobson, the painter*, after a picture painted by Dobson himself, a middling sized upright oval plate, with this inscription,

Vere

Vere Effigies Guilielmi Dobſon armiger et pictor Regiæ Majeſtatis Anglice; and this mark upon the margin, *in aqua forti per J. E.* The letters J. E. are frequently cut off; for they are quite at the edge of the plate: and for this reaſon it has falſely been attributed to Dobſon himſelf; a plain proof of the abſurdity of the cuſtom of cutting prints cloſe to the edges, by which means an inſcription or date of conſequence is often irrecoverably loſt.

ALBERT VAN EVERDINGEN.
Born, 1621. Died, 1675.

This artiſt was born at Alkmaer in Holland, and learned the firſt principles of painting from Roland Savery. After which he was a diſciple of Peter Molyn; and he profited ſo much by their inſtructions, and his own ſtudies, that he became a moſt admirable landſcape painter. He died, A. D. 1675, aged 54. We have a great number of ſlight, ſpirited etchings, in a very maſterly ſtyle, by this artiſt, which he uſually marked with theſe initials, A. V. E. Among others are the following:

A ſet of 100 ſmall *landſcapes*, length-ways.

A ſet of 56 very ſmall plates, length-ways. The ſubjects are taken from a German book, entitled, the *Tricks, or Deceits of the Fox*.

EXSHAW.
Flouriſhed, 1760.

A modern artiſt, who was a native of Holland. We have a variety of engravings by his hand; among the reſt, a *young girl carrying a baſket of cherries*, accompanied by two little boys, each having a gun; a middling ſized upright plate from Rubens. The *ſhip in which the apoſtles are croſſing the water, beaten by the tempeſt*, a large upright plate, from Rembrant, and executed in imitation of the ſtyle of engraving adopted by that maſter.

REMOLDUS, or ROMBAUT EYNHOUEDTS.
Flouriſhed, 1660.

This engraver reſided at Antwerp; but I am not certain, whether he was born in that town, or not. His plates are chiefly etched, and in a very ſlight, dark ſtyle. If he was not a painter himſelf, I ſuſpect that he learned to engrave from a painter. His drawing, though not correct, in general, is often very ſpirited, and his maſſes of light and ſhadow well preſerved. Among other plates by this artiſt are the following:

The *adoration of the Magi*, a very ſmall upright plate, from Rubens.

The *tomb of Rubens*, the ſame, from the ſame.

Cambyſes king of Perſia, having ordered an evil judge to be flead alive, cauſed his ſkin to be put upon the ſeat of juſtice, and placed the ſon of the culprit upon it, making him judge in his father's ſtead; a ſmall ſquare plate, from the ſame.

Pope Gregory ſurrounded with emblematical figures, a middling ſized upright plate, from the ſame.

The *aſſumption of the Virgin*, a large upright plate, from Cornelius Schut.

GIOVANNA

F.

GIOVANNA FABBRI.
Flourished,

A modern Italian artist, who, I believe, resided at Bologna, where he engraved a *nativity, with attendant angels, and other figures,* from Franc. Francia, a middling sized upright plate. It is executed entirely with the graver, in a neat, stiff style.

PETER FABER.
Flourished, 1621.

This artist resided at Lyons in France, and worked chiefly for the booksellers, in a neat tastelefs style, with the graver only. His name is affixed to an *ornamental frontispiece,* belonging to the second volume of the work, entitled, *Operis Moralis,* &c. by T. Sanchez in folio, published at Lyons, 1621. A portrait of *Henry IV. of France,* &c.

GABRIEL FABER.
Flourished, 1633.

According to Florent le Comte, he was procureur of the order of St. Francis; and in the year 1633, engraved a *genealogical tree of the order of that Saint.*

JOHN FABER, the ELDER.
Born,   Died, 1721.

He was born in Holland, where he learned the art of mezzotinto scraping. He also drew portraits from the life, on vellum, with a pen. What time he came into England does not appear; but he resided here a considerable time, and lived in Fountain Court in the Strand, London. He died at Bristol in the month of May, A. D. 1721. We have by him a considerable number of portraits; many of which he also drew himself from nature; but they do no great honour to his taste; neither do they manifest any superior skill in the execution. His greatest and most esteemed work was the

Portraits of the *founders of the colleges at Oxford,* half sheet prints.
Also, the *heads of the philosophers,* from Rubens, the same are by him.
And the portrait of Dr. *John Wallis,* the celebrated *mathematician,* after Kneller, the same; this is one of his best prints.

JOHN FABER, the YOUNGER.
Flourished, 1730.

He was son to John Faber, mentioned in the preceding article. He was born in Holland, and brought into England, whilst yet an infant, being only three years old. His father first instructed him in the rudiments of design; but he improved himself in Vanderbank's Academy. He resided at London; and in the year 1735, lived at the Golden Head in Bloomsbury-Square, where I believe he died of the gout, A. D. 1756. Like his father, he chiefly confined himself to the engraving of portraits in mezzotinto; and he excelled him in every requisite of the art. The following are his chief and most esteemed works:

The portraits of the *Kit Cat Club*, half sheet prints, from Lely.
The *beauties of Hampton Court*, the same, from the same.
Charles II. sitting in his robes of state, a whole sheet print, from the same.
The *taking of Namur*, a large half sheet print, very fine, from Wyck.
The *children of Frederick prince of Wales*, after Dupan, a sheet print.

D. FABRICIO.
Flourished,

This artist, according to Florent le Comte, engraved a print from a design of Abraham Bloemart, which, if I understand him, should be a single figure. The name is affixed in this manner, D. *Fabricio della Corvia fecit*.

FABRIZIO. See CLARUS.

RAYMOND LA FAGE.
Born, 1648. Died, 1690.

He was a native of France, born at Thoulouse, according to some authors; or, at Lille, according to others. The first opinion is most generally followed. It is said of him, that he never had any master, but following the dictates of his own genius, he applied himself to drawing; and his works sufficiently testify the surprising progress he made in that art. His drawings are compositions of his own, chiefly outlines, and flight sketches, made with a pen; but executed in a most masterly style. The actions of his figures are spirited, bold, graceful, or elegant, as the subject required. His groups of figures are finely contrasted. And frequently, without the assistance of shadow, he has contrived to detach them from each other, in such a manner, that the subject is by no means confused, or the effect disagreeable. Certainly no man ever possessed greater fertility of invention, or facility of execution; and though he has sometimes borrowed whole figures from the works of other masters, and ingrafted them in his own, yet he so well adopted those of his own invention to the style and action of those he borrowed, that the plagiarism seems rather to do him honour, than tend to his discredit. He resided some time in Italy; and when he showed his designs at Rome, they astonished every one who beheld them. Going one day to visit Carlo Maratti, he found that artist at work. Maratti, pleased

to

to see him, received him very affectionately, and rising up from his place, offered to put his pallet and pencils into his hand; but he refused, declaring that he did not understand the management of the pencil. " I am very " happy," replied Maratti, " to find that is the case, for had you known how " to paint, as well as you do how to draw, I should have been the first to aban- " don the art, because you could have filled my place so much better." He led a loose, depraved life, which his repeated debaucheries put an end to, A. D. 1690; he being only at the age of 42. The following prints, among others are engraved by the hand of this artist:

The *fall of the angels*, a large upright plate.
The *brazen serpent*, a large upright plate.
A *Bacchanalian*, a large plate, length-ways.
Several *friezes*, &c.

WILLIAM FAITHORNE, the ELDER.
Born, Died, 1691.

This celebrated artist, a native of London, was the disciple of Peak the painter, and worked with him three or four years. At the breaking out of the civil war, Peak espoused the cause of his sovereign, and Faithorne, who accompanied his master, was taken prisoner by the rebels at Baring-house, from whence he was sent to London, and confined in Aldersgate. In this uncomfortable situation, he exercised his graver; and a small head of the first *Villars duke of Buckingham*, in the style of Melan, is reckoned among his performances at that time. The solicitations of his friends in his favour at last prevailed; and he was released from prison, with permission to retire to the continent. The story of his banishment for refusing to take the oath to Oliver Cromwell, and studying several years under Champagne, is by no means sufficiently authenticated, not to admit of a doubt. However, in France he found protection and encouragement from Abbé de Marolles; and at this time it was, that he formed an acquaintance with Nanteuil, from whose instructions he derived very considerable advantages. About the year 1650, he returned to England, and soon after married the sister of captain Cround. By her he had two sons, Henry, who was a bookseller, and William an engraver in mezzotinto.

Faithorne opened a shop near Temple-Bar, where he sold, not only his own engravings, but those of other English artists, and imported a considerable number of prints from Holland, France and Italy. About the year 1680, he retired from his shop, and resided in Printing-House Yard; but he still continued to work for the booksellers, especially Royston, Martin, and Peake the younger, his former master's brother. He painted portraits from the life in crayons; which art he learned of Nanteuil, during his abode in France. He also painted in miniature; and his performances in both these styles were much esteemed.

He seems to have been well paid for his works. Mr. Ashmole is said to have given him seven pounds for the engraving of his portrait; which, if the plate was not a large one, or very highly finished, could not at that time have been a bad price. But unfortunately for him, his son William, not acting with the difcretion he ought, involved himfelf in trouble fo deeply, as to affect his father's fpirits to a very great degree; this vexation joined to a lingering confumption, with which he was afflicted, put an end to his life, A. D. 1691. He was buried by the fide of his wife, in the church of St. Ann, Black-Friars, the 13th of May the fame year.

He publifhed a Treatife upon the Art of Engraving, A. D. 1662, which he dedicated to his mafter Sir Robert Peake.

Portraits conftitute the greater part of this artift's performances. He worked almoft entirely with the graver, in a free, clear ftyle. In the early part of his life, he feems to have followed the Dutch and Flemifh manner of engraving; but at his return from France, he had confiderably improved it. Some of his beft portraits are admirable prints, and finifhed in a free, delicate ftyle, with much force of colour. It is certain, he did not draw the human figure correctly, or with good tafte; having chiefly confined his ftudies to the drawing and engraving of portraits, his hiftorical plates, which indeed are chiefly neat, laboured copies from prints, do by no means convey to us a proper idea of the abilities of this great mafter. From his inattention to the art of defign, may proceed the difference between the works of this artift, when he copied the pictures of other mafters, and when he engraved from drawings of his own. The former have, by repeated obfervations, been thought to be the beft. I can mention only two or three of his hiftorical prints, and a few of his excellent portraits, which are exceedingly numerous, and many of them very valuable.

A *holy family* from S. Vouet, a middling fized plate, length-ways, in the ftyle of Couvey.

A *dead Chrift*, from Vandyck, a fmall upright plate.

The *laft fupper*, without any painter's name, in folio.

Chrift praying in the garden, the fame.

The *fcourging of Chrift*, from Diepenbeck. Under this is written, "Fai-" thorne fculp. Antwerp. 1657."

The *marriage of Cana in Galilee*, an etching, the fame. Thefe four laft plates are, among others, engraved by this artift for *Taylor's Life of Chrift*, publifhed 1653.

Lady Pafton, from Vandyck.

Thomas Mace, a fmall half fheet print.

William Sanderfon, the fame, from Sourt, dated 1658.

Thomas Stanley, the fame, from Lely.

William Harvey. The face of this portrait is finifhed with little dots.

Henry Lawes. This portrait appears to have been firft roughly etched.

In fome few inftances, Faithorne omitted his name, and ufed a cypher compofed of two F's. in the manner reprefented on the plate at the end of the volume.

WILLIAM FAITHORNE, the YOUNGER.
Flourifhed, 1680.

He was fon to William Faithorne, mentioned in the preceding article; and from whom, without doubt, he learned the firft principles of defign. He did not, however, follow his father's mode of engraving, but fcraped portraits in mezzotinto; by which employment, had he been induftrious, he might have acquired

acquired a comfortable fubfiftance; but neglecting his bufinefs, he fell into diftrefs, and involved his father in fo much trouble, that his death was thought to be haftened by it. This unfortunate young man, who never reached any fuperior degree of excellence, died about the age of thirty, and was buried in St. Martin's church-yard. I fhall only mention the following portraits by him:

Mary princefs of Orange, a middling fized upright plate, from A. Hannaman.

Sir William Reade, oculift to queen Mary.

The *duke of Schomberg,* from M. Dahll.

DOMENICO FALCINI.
Flourifhed,

This artift engraved on wood, from the defigns of Raphael and other mafters. He ufed three feparate blocks for one print. On the firft he cut the outline; on the fecond, the dark fhadows; and on the third, the fainter tints, bordering upon the lights. See the mark, attributed to this mafter, copied on the plate at the end of the volume.

JEREMIAH FALCK.
Flourifhed, 1660.

According to the generality of authors, this artift was a native of Poland; but he has written upon fome of his plates, *van Stockholmia,* or of Stockholm, which feems plainly to indicate, that he was a Swede; unlefs it fhould be fuppofed, that he refided in Sweden, and ufed the fignature for that reafon only.

This engraver certainly poffeffed a very confiderable fhare of merit in general. He worked entirely with the graver, in a bold, free ftyle. His plates are fometimes rather defective in harmony; his drawing is in common tolerably correct, the extremities excepted, which are often heavy. Among others by this artift, are the following prints:

St. John preaching in the wildernefs, from A. Bloemart, a large plate, length-ways, dated 1661.

The *virgin feated with the infant Chrift, prefenting fome flowers to a lamb, which St. John holds in his arms,* a middling fized upright plate.

The *four evangelifts,* half figures, fmall upright oval prints, probably from his own defigns; for the fet I have before me has no painter's name affixed.

A *lady with three men, one of whom holds fome mufical notes,* half figures, a large plate length-ways, from Guercino. This plate was firft etched, and then finifhed with the graver: it is not equal to fuch of his works, as are executed with the graver only.

A confiderable number of portraits of *Polifh and Swedifh noblemen.*

The *queen of Sweden,* a fmall upright plate, from David Beck.

Adrian Spigelius, for the folio edition of his works, publifhed at Amfterdam, 1645.

Axelio Oxenftierna, a middling fized upright oval print. This portrait is marked " I. F. V. Stockholmiæ, fecit et excud. 1652." He frequently ufed the initials of his name only.

FREDERIC

FREDERIC VAN FALCKENBOURG.
Flourished,

To this artist are attributed certain prints, marked F. V. F. They are loose, scratchy etchings of *portraits, genealogical stems,* &c. Francesco Vanni, and Francesco Villamena, both used this mark; but their works are easily distinguished; the former by the beauty of his etching; and the latter by his plates being executed with the graver only.

LUCAS VAN FALCKENBOURG, perhaps of the same family as the foregoing artist, according to professor Christ, was an engraver; and those prints are attributed to him, which are marked in this manner, L. V. F.

ANGOLO FALCO.
Flourished,

I have no account of this artist. I found the name affixed to a middling sized plate, length-ways, representing a *landscape,* designed by himself, and rudely etched, in a very tasteless style. He has introduced the story of *Apollo and Daphne,* from Ovid; but the figures are exceedingly bad.

GIOVANNA BATISTA FALDA.
Flourished, 1660.

This excellent artist, according to the generality of authors, was a native of Italy, born at Milan. Whose disciple he was, does not appear; but he executed his plates in a clear, neat style, bearing no small resemblance to that of Israel Silvestre. He drew and engraved a prodigious number of views of palaces, gardens, &c. which he enriched with small figures, exceedingly well designed, and etched with great taste, The works of this artist are deservedly held in very high estimation. Among them are the following:

Several sets of views of *churches, palaces, gardens, and fountains at Rome,* small plates, length-ways.

A very large view, length-ways, of *St. Peter's at Rome.*

GIOVANNA ANTONIO FALDONI.
Flourished,

A modern Italian artist, who affected greatly to imitate the style of Melan, and frequently succeeded very happily. He was a man of ability; and some of his works possess great merit. By this engraver, among others are the following prints:

A *holy family with St. John,* a small plate, length-ways, from Sebastian Ricci.

The *portrait of Sebastian Ricci,* a small upright plate, from Rosalba.

Part of the *designs of Parmigiano,* for the collection in two volumes, folio, published by Zanetti. He sometimes signed his plates with the initials of his name only.

JOHN

FAL   [287]   FAR

JOHN FALLER.
Flourished,
The name of an artist, mentioned by Florent le Comte, as an engraver of *ornaments, grotesque figures*, &c. I am not acquainted with his works.

CESARE FANTETTI.
Flourished,
An Italian artist who flourished about the conclusion of the last century. He drew and etched in the style of a painter. His outlines are not always correct, or the extremities of his figures well marked. He worked conjointly with Pietro Aquila, in engraving the paintings in the Vatican by Raphael, known by the name of *Raphael's Bible*. The first thirty six prints, and the fortieth, of this collection, which consists of fifty-five, are etched by Fantetti; the rest by Pietro Aquila. I cannot help thinking, that the plates executed by the former, are neater, more determined, better drawn, and superior to those by the latter. Fantetti engraved besides,

Several *friezes and antique bass reliefs*. Also,
The *death of St. Ann*, a middling sized upright plate, from Andrea Sacchi. Jacomo Frey engraved a plate also from the same picture.
Several other subjects, from different Italian masters.

FANTUZZI. See FONTUZZI.

BENOIT FARIAT.
Flourished, 1700.
This engraver was born at Lyons. He became the pupil of William Chateau, and followed the style of his master with great success. His works discover more command of the graver, and laborious neatness, than refined taste, or correct drawing. They are, in general, like those of his master, heavy, cold and silvery. The heads, and other extremities of his figures, are by no means well expressed. This artist, however, is not without his admirers. After he left Chateau, he went to Italy, and resided chiefly at Rome, where, I believe, he died. The following plates are ranked among his best works:

The *marriage, or, as some think, the crowning of St. Catherine*, a large upright plate, from Agostino Carracci.
The *marriage of Joseph and the Virgin*, from Carlo Maratti, the same.
The *temptation of St. Anthony*, a small upright plate from Annibale Carracci.
The *death of St. Jerom*, a large upright plate, from Dominichino. This picture was also engraved by Jacomo Frey, Cæsar Testa, and others.
A *holy family*, from Pietro de Cortona.
Some few *portraits*, and a variety of other subjects, from Guido, Albano, Ciro Ferri, Solimene, &c.

PAOLO FARINATO.
Born, 1522. Died, 1604.

This artist was a native of Italy, and born at Verona. He learned the first principles of painting from Antonio Badiale; after which he became the disciple of Nicolo Golfino. His genius led him to historical subjects, and in this line he acquired a very confiderable reputation. He also etched several plates from his own compositions, in a free, slight style, which manifest, however, the hand of the master. His plates are frequently marked with his name at length, and sometimes with the initials, P. F. or P. V. F. the V. standing for Verona, to signify that he was a native of that city. The following etchings are by this master.

St. John, a small upright plate, marked " Paulo Farinato f."
St. Jerom kneeling and leaning upon a bank, the same, marked, P. F.
Mary Magdalen seated, with a book and crucifix before her, a small plate length-ways, marked " Paul Farinat. f."
Several angels bearing the cross, a small upright plate, marked P. F.

ORAZIO, or HORATIUS FARINATO.
Flourished, 1550.

This artist was son and pupil of Paolo Farinato, mentioned in the preceding article. He imitated his father's style of painting, and from the superior abilities, which he discovered early in life, promised fairly to have equalled the greatest masters; but he died very young. He etched several plates from his father's designs; and though they are easily distinguished from the etchings by the father, yet they have constantly been confounded with them. The following etchings, among others, are the productions of his point:

The *destruction of Pharoah's host in the Red Sea,* a large plate, length-ways, marked, HO. F. F. Paulus Fa. V. I.
A *holy family with St. John,* a small upright plate, &c.

CHARLES FAUCCI.
Flourished, 1760.

This engraver was a native of Italy; but he resided some time in London, where he worked for Mr. Boydel. His prints are held in no very high estimation. The following, among others, were done by him.

The *birth of the Virgin,* from Pietro de Cortona, a middling-sized upright plate.
The *adoration of the shepherds,* the same, from the same.
The *coronation of the Virgin,* from Rubens, a middling sized upright plate. Pontius engraved a print from the same picture.

Also several other plates, for the collection of prints engraved from the pictures in the gallery of the marquis Gerini, which he executed at Florence before his arrival in England.

A *Bacchanalian* subject, a middling sized upright plate, from Rubens, published by Mr. Boydel, May 11, 1763.

He also engraved several *portraits,* &c.

R. FAU-

R. FAUCCI, probably a relation of Charles Faucci, mentioned above. He engraved some of the portraits which appeared in *Allegrini's Hom. illuſt. &c.* published 1764.

J. DE FAVENNES.
Flouriſhed, 1760.

A modern engraver, who, I believe, was a native of France, and reſided at Paris. By him, according to Baſan, we have a print, entitled the *Pleaſures of the Summer*, from Watteau.

T. M. FAULTE.
Flouriſhed,

The name of an obſcure engraver, who apparently worked for the bookſellers. It is affixed to the portrait of *Joan. Paſſirus*. If we may judge of his merit by this performance, he never roſe above mediocrity: it is a ſmall upright oval print.

NICHOLAS DE LA FAYE.
Flouriſhed,

He was a native of France, and reſided at Arles in Provence. If I underſtand Le Comte rightly, he painted patterns for embroidery and needlework. The ſame author adds, that he etched ſix prints; but he has not ſpecified the ſubjects: they were probably ornamental.

FAYRAM.
Flouriſhed, 1740.

I believe this artiſt was a landſcape painter. We have by him ſome ſlight coarſe etchings of *views about Chelſea and Batterſea*, alſo the *hermitage in Kew gardens*.

CLAUD LE FEBURE, or LE FEVRE.
Born, 1633. Died, 1675.

This artiſt, a native of France, was born at Fontainbleau. He principally excelled in painting portraits; but he ſucceeded alſo in flowers and hiſtorical ſubjects. He reſided at London, where he met with encouragement, and died, A. D. 1675, aged 42. He etched ſome few plates; among others, *his own portrait*, a ſmall upright print; that of his *mother*, the ſame, and that of *Boudan*, the copper-plate printer, a middling ſized upright plate, &c.

VALENTINE LE FEBURE, or LE FEVRE.
Flouriſhed, 1680.

This artiſt was a native of Bruſſels, and a painter; for he is ſpoken of as ſuch; but he is much more generally known as an engraver;

we have a variety of prints which were executed by him, during his long residence at Venice, from the works of Titian and Paolo Veronese these collected together, form a large folio volume. They are flight etchings, feeble in effect. The lights are broken and scattered, without any broad masses of shadow, or depth of colour. The drawing of the naked parts of the figures is not incorrect, but executed in a mannered style, that is by no means agreeable. We find much spirit and freedom in several parts of these etchings; and some of the back-grounds discover a masterly hand. They are the more valuable, as they are the best transcript of the designs of those great painters.

The engravings by Le Febure, from the painters above-mentioned, were published at Venice, 1680, with this title: *Opera selectiora, quae Titianus Vecellius Cadubriensis, et Paulus Calliari Veronensis inventârunt & pinxerunt; quaeque Valentinus le Febre Bruxellansis delineavit et sculpsit.* A second edition was published in 1682; and a third, with the plates retouched, A. D. 1749.

This artist is said to have resided some little time in London, and for this cause several persons, says Basan, have confounded him with another, named Roland Le Febure, a portrait painter, who died in London, A. D. 1677; and was distinguished by the name of Lefevre of Venice.

SIMON FELICE.
Flourished, 1665.

A very ingenious artist, who worked conjointly with Giovan. Batista Falda, in a set of prints, entitled, *Le giardini de Roma*, or the *gardens of Rome*, middling sized plates, length-ways. They are exceedingly neat, ornamented with spirited little figures, and nearly, if not entirely equal to those executed by Falda.

DE FEN.
Flourished,

I insert this name with caution, because I am by no means positive, that I read it properly. The letter which I take for an F. may perhaps be an E. but it certainly bears the greatest resemblance to the former. It is affixed to a large upright, spirited wood cut, representing the *Temptation of St. Anthony*. This print possesses great merit. There is much grandeur in the figure of the saint; and the head is finely characterised. Two naked women are standing before him; and at the bottom, on a small tablet, the name is written. There is also a figure engraved by Schaeuflen the younger, which is marked with this artist's name also, who was probably the inventor. See the manner in which the name is written on the plate at the end of the volume.

TOBIE FENDT.
Flourished,

The name of an engraver, who, according to professor Christ, resided at Breslaw, and marked his prints in this manner: T. F. The professor has not, however, specified any of his works.

LOUIS

LOUIS FERDINAND.
Flourished, 1640.

This artist was a painter of portraits, and flourished near the middle of the last century. He was the son of Ferdinand Elle, the first instructor of Nicholas Poussin. He also engraved a confiderable number of plates; among which are some *portraits* from Vandyck, and *friezes with boys*, from Louis Teftelin, Louis de Boullogne, &c.

GIOVANNISA TISSTA FERDINANDI, a name affixed to some *jewellers ornaments*, executed in a neat dark style, with the graver only.

J. FERDINAND.
Flourished, 1644.

This artist was probably of the same family with Louis Ferdinand, mentioned in the preceding article. They were cotemporary, and etched in a similar style. By Ferdinand we have a drawing-book, in folio, with this title: *Le Livre Original de la Portraiture, pour L'Jeuneffe, tire de Bologne et autres bon Peintres a Paris*, 1644. Though the figures in this book are not correctly marked, or in a masterly manner, yet the lights and shadows are well disposed in masses, and they may certainly be of use to young beginners. He sometimes omitted his name, and substituted one of the initial letters, as F. F. the second F. standing for fecit; and sometimes he affixes the single F. without any other letter.

A *lady's head*, a small upright plate, from Vandyck.

The portrait of *Nicholas Pousin*, from a painter, whose initials are V. E.

FRANCESCO FERDINAND, is a name affixed to a small upright etching, emblematical of *gluttony and debauchery oppofed to virtue*; it is executed in a coarse flight style.

FRANCIS PAUL FERG.
Born, 1689. Died, 1740.

This artist was born at Vienna, where he learned the first principles of painting, and became very celebrated for his landscapes, which he enriched with ruins, cattle, and figures. He resided at London, where he might have lived in a very comfortable manner; but an imprudent marriage greatly depressed his circumstances. Mr. Grose favoured me with the following anecdote concerning him: Ferg was always poor, not from any excesses in his manner of living, but merely from indolence. His pictures were much sought after by the Virtuosi; and if he took earnest to paint one, he would not let the person have it, by whom it was bespoken, but carried it immediately after it was finished to the pawn-broker, from whose hand he rarely redeemed it. He died, as it is said, for want of common necessaries, A. D. 1740, aged 51, and was buried by subscription.

He etched eight plates, seven of them very small upright prints, and one larger length-ways, representing *landscapes with ruins, fountains, and figures drawing water*; to which set he gives this title, *Capricci fatti per F. V. F.*

FERNAZERUS. See FOURNIER.

MARTINO FERRABOSCO.
Flourished, 1620.

An artist of no great note, who engraved the architectal plates for the work entitled, *Architettura della Basilica di S. Pietro in Vaticano*, published at Rome, A. D. 1620. They are executed entirely with the graver, in a stiff, slight style.

CIRO FERRI.
Born, 1634. Died, 1689.

This excellent historical painter was born at Rome, and became the disciple of Pietro da Cortona, in whose school he finished his studies. The great reputation this artist acquired did honour to his industry, and procured him the favour and protection of the Duke of Tuscany, who entrusted him to finish the works, begun by his master, in the palace of that Prince. He died, A. D. 1689, aged 54. He is said to have etched several plates from his own compositions: he is called by the French Cirofer.

JEROM FERRONI.
Flourished, 1700.

This artist was a native of Italy, who etched several plates in the slight, spirited style of a painter, with great taste. Among others by him are the following:

The *chastity of Joseph*, a middling sized upright plate, from Carlo Maratti.
Jael killing Sisera, the same, from the same.
Judith cutting off the head of Holophernes, the same, from the same.

DOMINICO FERRUCCIO.
Flourished, 1670.

The works of this artist have very little merit to recommend them. His labours appear to have been confined to the service of the booksellers; and his mode of working, which was with the graver only, might sufficiently answer their purpose. We have by him a number of *naked figures fencing*, (perhaps from his own designs, for the compositions of these prints are as indifferently executed as the engraving itself) for a book, entitled, *La Scherma illustrata composta da Giuseppe Morsicato Palermitano*, dated 1670.

M. DE LA FERTE.
Flourished, 1760.

A modern connoisseur, who, for his amusement, etched several little *landscapes*, from Boucher and other masters.

DE FERTH.
Flourished, 1760.

A modern engraver, a native of France, by whom we have several prints, after Vanden Bosch, Fontaine, and other masters.

STEPHEN

STEPHEN FESSARD.
Flourished, 1760.

This artist who resided at Paris, was a native of France. He engraved a great variety of neat plates; but he succeeded best in small subjects, though some of his larger engravings are by no means devoid of merit. The following, among others, are by him:

A *Flemish festival*, a large plate, length-ways, from Rubens.
The *birth of Venus*, the same, from De Troy.
The *triumph of Galatea*, from Boucherdon, the same.
Jupiter and Antiope, a middling sized plate length-ways, from Carlo Vanloo.
Also several *portraits*, and a variety of *small plates for books*, &c.

SIGISMOND FEYERABEND.
Flourished, 1587.

The celebrated family of the Feyerabends, well known in the literary world, were established at Franckfort upon the Mayne, towards the conclusion of the sixteenth century, where they printed and published a prodigious number of books, and books of prints. They employed most of the designers and engravers on wood. It is generally believed, and not without good reason, that they engraved themselves a considerable part of those prints, with which they embellished their publications, Sigismond, who is the most conspicuous amongst them, marked the prints, which he executed; with the letters S. F. under which he usually represented a small knife, to denote that he was the engraver.

The following initials so frequently found upon the little wooden cuts, published at this time by Sigismond, are also attributed to engravers of the same family, though the baptismal names of these artists are not certainly known: I. F. and S. H. F. the F. is usually joined to the H. and M. F. the M. and the F. are also joined together: and V. F.

ODOARDO FIALATTI.
Born, 1573. Died, 1638.

He was born at Bologna, and learned the first principles of design from Cremonino; but he finished his studies in the school of Tintoretto. He painted historical subjects; and his works are spoken of with the warmest commendation. He etched a great number of plates, as well from his own composition, as from those of other masters. His etchings are executed in a slight, masterly style. He drew correctly, composed his figures with much taste, and frequently selected very graceful actions. If he had no other testimony left of his merit, than the prints he has engraved, they would abundantly prove him to have been a man of great ability. I shall take notice of the following by this artist:

The *pastimes of love*, a set of 20 small upright prints, from his own designs: the title is *Scherzi d'Amore*.

Venus

Venus and Cupid; *Diana at the chace*; the *god Pan*; and a *man holding a vase*; four small plates, length-ways, from *Le Pordenon*.

The *marriage of Cana in Galilee*, a middling sized plate, length-ways, from Tintoretto.

St. Sebastian, a small upright plate, from the same master.

A *book, with studies for drawing*, in folio, published at Venice, A. D. 1608. See the mark usually adopted by this master, composed of an O. and an F. on the plate at the end of the volume.

BARTOLEMEO FIALETTI.
Flourished,

This artist, of whom I find no account, engraved, according to Florent le Comte, the *ceremony of the Agnus Dei*, which prints I have never seen.

STEPHEN FIQUET.
Flourished, 1760.

A modern French engraver of portraits. This artist knew how to unite neatness, and high finishing in the greatest degree, with excellent drawing. His portraits are very astonishing exertions of the art; and so prodigiously delicate, that the strokes and dots upon the faces cannot be seen distinctly, without a magnifying glass. I shall only mention the following:

La Fontaine.
T. Corneille.
Descartz, &c, All of them very small upright plates.

PAOLO FIDANZA.
Flourished, 1760.

This artist was a native of Italy, and resided chiefly at Rome, where he engraved the *Mount Parnassus*, and the *miracle of the fire extinguished at the intercession of the pope*, two large plates, from the pictures of Raphael, in the Vatican. *A descent from the cross*, a small upright plate, from Annibale Carracci, &c.

MARC FIDUCIUS.
Flourished,

An artist cited by Florent le Comte, who informs us, that he excelled in engraving *processions and cavalcades*; but he has not specified any of his works.

JOHN DE FILHET.
Flourished,

Florent le Comte calls him Jean de Filhet de la Curee, chevalier de la Promenade de Zutphen, and tells us, that he engraved on copper, from his own design, an *image of human life*.

TEODORO FILIPI.
Flourished,

This artist (who perhaps was of the same family with Camillo Filipi, an Italian painter of some eminence) etched several small plates of single figures, in a very spirited manner, and with great taste. He signs his name " Teodor. " Filipi de ligno Nap. f."

GILBERT FILLEUL.
Flourished,

An artist of no great eminence, who flourished in the last century, and engraved several plates from Le Brun and other masters.

PETER FILLEUL.
Flourished,

He was son to Gilbert Filleul, mentioned in the preceding article. By him we have the *carriers*, a middling sized plate, length-ways, from Wouvermans, and several of the prints for the fables of *La Fontaine*.

JOHN FILLIAN.
Flourished, 1676.

This artist, an Englishman, was the disciple of the elder Faithorne, and because there are but few plates engraved by him, it is very reasonably conjectured, that he died young. Those we have, out of the portrait line, do him no credit. He imitated, in his heads, the style of his master; and probably, had he lived to have improved himself by more extensive study and practice, he might have claimed a much higher rank, than can at present be allowed him. We have by him, the portrait of *Faithorne*, his master, copied from a print engraved by himself; that of *Thomas Cromwell*, and a head of *Paracelsus*. Among his other works is the frontispiece to *Heylen's Cosmography* in folio.

MASO, or TOMASO FINIGUERRA.
Flourished, 1460.

To this ingenious artist, a goldsmith and enameller of Florence, the Italians attribute the invention of engraving on copper; and, according to Vasari, we owe it to the following accident. Having one day engraved upon a piece of plate the objects he meant to represent, and intending to fill up the strokes with a black enamel, in order to try the effect of it, previously to the putting on of the enamel, he cast some melted sulphur upon it; and, on taking it off, perceived, that the dirt collected at the bottom of the strokes adhered to the sulphur, and gave an impression of the object. Struck with this observation, he tried several other schemes, and at last succeeded, by filling the strokes with black paint, and laying damp paper upon the plate, over which he contrived to pass a roller.

He communicated this discovery to Baccio Baldini, from whom it passed to Sandro Boticelli, and in the end, to Antonio Pollajolo, Andrea Mantegna, and the rest of the Italian artists. The justness of this claim to the invention of the art of engraving, has been already considered in the Essay at the beginning of this volume. It is very true, we can speak with no certainty, with respect to the works of Finiguerra. Some may be inclined to think that the *seven planets*, described in the foregoing Essay, one of which, with the callender, are exactly copied, are by him. These must have been engraved as early as the year 1464; but I cannot conceive that they are sufficiently well done, either with respect to the drawing or the execution. I should rather attribute to him the plate of the artist, of which an exact copy is also given in the Essay; and the F. which appears upon the stone near his hands, may be thought to strengthen the conjecture.

J. FINLAYSON.
Flourished, 1770.

This artist, who, I suppose, was a native of England, resided chiefly in London, where he engraved a considerable number of portraits from various masters. Among others by him, are *Signiora Zamperini*, a half sheet print from Hone; *Shooter, Beard, and Dunstal, in Love in a Village*, a large plate, length-ways, from Zofany.

DOMENICO FIORENTINO. See BARBIERE.

PETER FIRENS.
Flourished, 1640.

This engraver resided at Paris, where, perhaps, he was born. He was one of those artists, who endeavour by labour and assiduity to compensate for the want of genius. Having no taste of his own, he copied servilely whatever was placed before him; and was as utterly incapable of mending the faults, as of expressing the beauties of the original. We have some *portraits* by him, among others, that of *Henry the Fourth of France*, a large upright plate. It appears also by the word *excudit*, which he has added to his name, that he was a publisher, as well as an engraver. His best work, I think, is the *hermits*, which he copied from the Sadelers. He also engraved from Simon Vouet, Claude Vignon, &c.

JOHN FISCHER.
Born, 1580. Died, 1643.

He is mentioned by Sandrart as an engraver on wood; and the prints to the *Bible*, printed at Strasbourg, A. D. 1606, which are marked with the initials I. F. are attributed to him.

EDWARD FISCHER.
Flourished, 1760.

This artist is falsely named *Etienne*, or Stephen Fischer, by Basan. He resided

FIS [297] FLE

refided at London. By his hand we have feveral eftimable mezzotintos from Sir Jofhua Reynolds and other mafters; among them,
Lord Ligonier on horfeback, a large upright plate.
Two *young ladies*, one in the habit of a fultanefs holding a bird, the fame, from the fame : the fine impreffions of this plate are not common.
Elizabeth Keppel, the fame, from the fame.
Lady Sarah Banbury, companions to the laft, from the fame.

A. FISCHER.
Flourifhed, 1760.

A modern artift, mentioned by Bafan, who, he informs us, engraved a print called the *carriers*, from Wouvermans. Filleul alfo engraved from the fame picture.

ALBERT FLAMEN.
Flourifhed,

This artift, a native, I believe of Flanders, flourifhed towards the conclufion of the fixteenth century. He was a painter of fome eftimation, and excelled in landfcapes, birds, fifhes, &c. but he is more generally known as an engraver, from the number of very excellent etchings we have by his hand, which, though flight, are exceedingly fine and mafterly. I fhall mention the following:

A fet of *views*, length-ways, ornamented with fmall figures, executed in a pretty ftyle: one efpecially ftrikes me as excellent, which reprefents an *encampment at the end of the Fauxbourg St. Victor, by the fide of the Horfe-walk*.

A fet of twelve plates, reprefenting *fifh of all forts, with landfcape backgrounds, and fea-ports*, &c.

See his mark, compofed of an A. and a B. joined together, which he fometimes ufed, when he did not fign his name at length, on the plate at the end of the volume.

A. C. FLEISCHMANN.
Flourifhed, 1626.

A very indifferent artift, who engraved feveral of the heads for a work, intitled, *Icones Bibliopolarum et Typographorum*, publifhed at Nuremberg and Altdorf, 1626.

T. F. FLEISHBERGER.
Flourifhed, 1660.

This engraver, who worked for the bookfellers, was apparently a German, and refided at Nuremberg. He executed his plates with the graver only, in a ftiff, heavy ftyle, without tafte or correctnefs of outline. By him I have feen an ornamental frontifpiece, with figures, for *Gregorii Horfti opera Medica*, printed at Nuremberg, A. D. 1660, in folio. To this work is alfo prefixed the portrait of *Horftius*, a three quartered figure in folio.

HENRY FLETCHER.
Flourifhed, 1729.

An artift, who refided, I believe, at London, where he engraved feveral portraits

portraits for the bookfellers, and a print of *Bathfheba*, with her female attendants, at the bath, from Sebaftian Conca: a print, however, that does him no great credit as an artift.

A. FLETCHER.
Flourifhed,

An engraver fays Bafan, of this century, by whom we have feveral views of *Rome*, from Canaletti.

PETER FLEUNER.
Flourifhed, 1549.

An ancient engraver on wood, by whom we have a very fpirited print, executed in a bold, free ftyle. It is an emblematical fubject, and apparently reprefents the *proceffion of Gluttony*. On a ftone at the bottom his name is figned at length, with the date, 1549.

NICHOLAS WILLIAM DE LA FLEUR.
Flourifhed, 1639.

This artift was a native of Lorrain, but he refided chiefly at Rome, where he engraved a *book of flowers*, confifting of twelve fmall plates, with a title, on which is reprefented his portrait furrounded with flowers.

JOHN CHARLES FLIPART.
Flourifhed, 1720.

He was a native of France, and refided at Paris, where he engraved the *Virgin and Child*, from Raphael, a fmall upright plate, for the Crozat collection. *Chrift praying in the garden*, the fame, from the fame painter, and for the fame collection. Thefe are neatly finifhed with the graver; but they want effect, and correctnefs of outline.

JOHN JAMES FLIPART.
Flourifhed, 1760.

Of the fame family with the preceding artift. He refided at Paris, where he engraved a large number of plates; among the reft, *a holy family* from Julio Romano, a middling fized upright plate, for the Drefden Collection. *Venus and Æneas*, the fame, from Natoire. A *tempeft*, from Vernet, a large plate, length-ways. The *fick man furrounded by his children*, the fame, from Greufe, &c.

PETER FLODING.
Flourifhed, 1760.

A Swedifh engraver, by whom we have an allegorical fubject, reprefenting the *king of Sweden, as the protector of religion, the laws, the arts, and the fciences*, a large upright plate in an oval, from Cochin. He alfo engraved from Boucher and other mafters.

ISAAC

ISAAC FLORE.
Flourished,

An engraver, according to Florent le Comte, of *ornamental plates* for goldsmiths and jewellers, &c.

JOHN FLORIMUS.
Flourished,

According to Florent le Comte, this artist was an engraver of portraits. I have seen by him a frontispiece to a collection of *antique heads*. It consists of several figures; and is executed entirely with the graver, in a neat, dry style.

FRANCIS FLORIS.
Born, 1520. Died, 1570.

This artist was a native of Antwerp, and followed the profession of a statuary, till he was twenty years of age; when preferring painting, he entered the school of Lambert Lombard, whose manner he imitated very perfectly. He afterwards went to Italy, and completed his studies from the works of the most eminent masters. The great progress he made in historical painting, at his return procured him much employment; and his countrymen complimented him with the flattering appellation of *the Flemish Raphael*. He got much money, and might have rendered his acquaintance more worthy of the attention of the great, had he not debased himself by frequent drunkenness. He died 1570, aged 50. We have some few etchings by him, which, though slight, are very bold and spirited; and the extremities are marked with a masterly hand. Among the rest is a middling sized plate, length-ways, representing *Victory standing by a figure, surrounded with warriors in chains:* It is dated 1552.

A. DE FLOS.
Flourished, 1760.

A modern engraver, who, according to Basan, resided in Holland. By him we have a *landscape*, and a *view of a sea-port*, both large plates lengthways, from Bergham. He also engraved from Teniers and other masters.

CLAUDE DU FLOS.
Flourished, 1710.

This ingenious artist was a native of France. I know not under what master he studied; but the works of Poilly and Edelinck seem to have been the sources from which he formed his taste. He worked chiefly with the graver, and occasionally with the point. He had great command of the former instrument; and his prints are neat and well finished, but rather cold and silvery. He understood the human figure very well, though the extremities are very often rather heavy. Basan, who published his Dictionary of engravers, 1567, mentions him, as having been dead about four years. We have engraved by this artist,

Christ with the two disciples at Emmaus, a large plate, length-ways, for the Crozat collection.

The *woman taken in adultery*, the same, from Nicholas Colombel. Part of this plate is etched, and it makes a companion to the *anointing of the feet of Christ by Mary Magdalen*, engraved by Nicholas Dossier.

The *entombing of Christ*, a middling sized plate, length-ways, from Pietro Perrugino, for the Crozat collection.

St. Michael and the Devil, a middling sized upright plate, from Raphael, for the same collection.

Love stung by a bee, a large upright oval print, from Anthony Coypel, companion to *Zephyrus and Flora*, engraved by Picart.

St. Cecilia, a middling sized upright plate, from P. Mignard. This plate is engraved in a very singular taste: the drapery and back-ground are executed in a bold, free manner; and the flesh of the saint, and a naked cherub, who stands before her, is finished in a neat style, with dots only. The drawing is good, and the effect is by no means unpleasing.

PAUL FLYNT.
Flourished,

According to M. Heineken, he was an engraver; and he sometimes named himself Paul de Nuremberg. His works are not specified.

F O.
Flourished, 1551.

This artist, a Swifs by nation, says Papillon, was an excellent engraver in wood, and contemporary with the famous Holbein. He ornamented with prints the books, which Conrad Gesner, the physician of Zurick in Switzerland, wrote in Latin, upon animals of all kinds. He also engraved the *coins and medals of the Roman emperors*, published by Gesner, in folio, 1559; and several other works of consequence. Papillon, who certainly was a good judge, with respect to the execution of these prints, speaks very highly of them, and assures us, that Fo was an artist of great ability.

MARCELLO FOGELINO.
Flourished,

An old Italian master (who was probably of the school of Marc Antonio) by whom, according to M. Heineken, we have some prints, marked with his name; but the subjects are not specified.

SIMON FOKKE.
Flourished, 1744.

A modern engraver, who resided at Amsterdam. A great part of his employment

ployment was for the bookfellers. Small portraits and vignettes he performed neatly and tolerably well; but when he went out of that line, and undertook large hiftorical plates, he failed very confiderably. We have by this artift part of the portraits for a work in quarto, entitled, *Portraits Hiftoriques des Hommes illuftrees de Denmark*, publifhed 1746. The *prodigal fon*, from Spagnoletto, a middling fized upright plate. *Jacob keeping the fheep of Laban*, the fame from the fame, for the collection of prints from the Drefden gallery. A variety of Vignettes and other fubjects, as well from his own compofitions, as from thofe of other mafters, as Picart, Trooft, De Beyer, &c.

JACOB FOLKMA.
Flourifhed, 1746.

This artift, who, as Bafan informs us, was a native of Holland, engraved fmall portraits and vignettes for books, in which he fucceeded tolerably well. We have alfo fome few hiftorical fubjects by him; but they are not equal to his other works. Several of the portraits of the *illuftrious men of Denmark*, publifhed 1746, are by him. He alfo engraved a variety of other *portraits, book-plates*, &c. and the *martyrdom of St. Peter and St. Paul*, a large upright plate, arched at the top, from Nicholo dell'Abbate, for the Drefden collection.

FONBONE.
Flourifhed, 1715.

This artift, a man of no very fuperior abilities, was a native of France. He engraved, among a variety of other fubjects, part of the plates for the large folio publication of the *views of Verfailles*, &c.

GIACOMO BATISTA FONTANA.
Flourifhed, 1573.

This artift, a native of Verona, defigned as well as engraved. We have feveral prints by his hand. They are flight etchings, by no means correctly drawn; yet in the execution we fee fome appearance of the hand of the mafter. I fhall mention the following:

Several fubjects from *Virgil's Æneid*, middling fized plates, length-ways, from his own compofitions.

The *battle of Cadora, between the imperial troops and the Venetians*, a middling fized plate, length-ways, from Titian.

The *martyrdom of a Saint in a foreft*, a middling fized upright plate. Martin Rota and Le Febre both engraved from this picture. Papillon, miftaking Marolles and Le Comte, fays, that this fubject was engraved by this artift on wood; when nothing can be more contrary to truth.

GIULIO FONTANA, who, according to Le Comte, was of Verona, and probably, if that be true, of the fame family with the preceding artift. He is alfo faid to have engraved feveral plates.

D O M I-

DOMINICO MARIA FONTANA.
Born, 1673. Died,

This artift was born at Parma, and learned the art of drawing in the fchool of Bologna. He engraved a great number of prints, which, according to profeffor Chrift, he marked with the initials D. F. This matter is at leaft doubtful. Le Comte and others have confounded this artift with Domenico Fontana, the famous architect.

VERONICA FONTANA, daughter to the above artift, learned the art of defign from her father and Elizabeth Sirani. She engraved very neatly fmall portraits in wood.

CÆSAR FONTANA.
Flourifhed,

This artift is mentioned by Florent le Comte as an engraver, who excelled in the execution of *funeral proceffions, cavalcades*, &c.

GERARDO FONTANA is inferted in the lift of engravers, at the end of the Abecedario; but his works are not fpecified.

E. FONTAIN.
Flourifhed, 1681.

An obfcure and indifferent engraver on wood, a native, as it fhould feem, of France, by whom, among other fmall fubjects, we have the *figure of Chrift, ftanding upon a pillar*, under which is written, *Sauveur du Monde aves pities de nous*: In Englifh, "Saviour of the world, have mercy upon us." It is marked *E. Fontaine fculpfit*, anno 1681.

M. D. FONTANIEU.
Flourifhed, 1760.

This gentleman, a lover of the arts, was a native of France, and for his amufement made feveral fmall etchings of animals, &c.

FRANCESCO FONTEBASSO.
Flourifhed,

He was born at Venice, about the beginning of the prefent century; and after having learned the firft principles of painting at Rome, he perfected himfelf in colouring under Sebaftian Ricci, he etched

A fet of feven *whimfical fubjects* from his own compofitions, middling fized plates, length-ways.

The *Virgin appearing to St. Gregory, who is offering up his prayers for the delivery of fouls from Purgatory*, a middling fized upright plate, from Sebaftian Ricci. He alfo etched feveral other fubjects, from the fame mafter.

LE COMTE DE FORBIN.
Flourished, 1760.

By this gentleman, who, according to Bafan, was a lover of the arts, we have feveral fmall etchings; but the fubjects are not fpecified.

M. FORD.
Flourished, 1760.

A modern engraver in mezzotinto, by whom we have feveral portraits; among others, that of the *earl of Harrington*; alfo of *Henry Singleton, Chief Juftice of the common pleas in Ireland*, half fheet prints.

LE FORE.
Flourished,

The name of an obfcure engraver, affixed to the following portraits: *Henry de Mauffes*, and *Nicolaus de Netz. Epifc. Aurelianenfis*, &c.

FORNACERYS. See FOURNIER.

J. P. FORNAVERT.
Flourished,

This artift worked, I believe, chiefly, if not entirely, for the bookfellers. He executed his plates with the graver only, in a ftiff, formal ftyle, very neatly, but without any tafte; and the outlines of his figures are exceedingly incorrect. I have before me a fmall folio frontifpiece to a book of devotion: it reprefents *Mofes and Aaron, with the four Evangelifts*.

DAVID ANTONIO FOSSATO.
Flourished,

A modern Italian artift. He flourished, according to Bafan, towards the beginning of this century. By him we have a fet of *landfcapes*, from Marco Ricci.

DE LA FOSSE.
Flourished, 1760.

A modern French engraver of no great note, who refided at Paris, where he engraved feveral portraits after Carmontel; among the reft,

The *Calas family*, a middling fized plate, length-ways.

A variety of fmall book-plates, as part of thofe for the laft edition of *Fontaine's Fables*, and for *Ovid's Metamorphofes*, &c.

MOSES FOUVARD.
Flourished, 1690.

He was a native of France, and one of the artifts employed by Beaulieu to engrave the plates for the *sieges, towns, conquests, combats, and other military expeditions,* during the reign of Louis XIII. and XIV.

JAMES FOUQUIERES.
Born, 1580. Died, 1659.

This artist was born at Antwerp, and received his chief instructions in the art of painting from Velvet Brughel. He applied himself to the study of landscapes, and went to Italy to improve himself in colouring; and succeeded so happily, that his works are said to be nearly equal to those of Titian. He resided much in France; and being honoured by the king with the title of chevalier, he was so puffed up with pride and vanity, that he was called, by way of ridicule, Baron de Fouquieres. He is said to have thought it beneath him to work, but in a full dress with a bag and sword. He died at Paris in very low circumstances, A. D. 1659. We have etched by him several small *landscapes,* from his own designs.

N. DU FOUR.
Flourished, 1760.

A modern French engraver, by whom, among other things, we have several small *views,* after Veirotter, &c.

PETER FOURDRINIERE.
Flourished, 1740.

He was, if I mistake not, a native of France; but he resided at London, where he died a few years since. He was one of those industrious men, whose labours were chiefly confined to the embellishment of books, plays, and pamphlets. It was a happy circumstance for the artists of this class, that the taste of their employers was not more refined, otherwise they would, without doubt, have considered the engravings as a disgrace, rather than an ornament, to any creditable publication. The best works of Fourdriniere are his large *architectal plates,* which are often very neatly and carefully executed; but without the least taste. Some of these may be found in a large folio volume, entitled the *Villas of the Ancients,* illustrated by Robert Castel, and printed in London, 1728. He also engraved part of the plates of the *plans and elevations, &c. of Haughton Hall,* in Norfolk, published by J. Ware, A. D. 1735.

ISAYE FOURNIER.
Flourished,

This artist, who is also called Fornaceriis, was painter to king Henry IV. of France. Florent le Comte informs us, that he engraved several plates; but has not specified the subjects, probably portraits. To the head of *Camillus B.* (Paulus V.) the name " Fornageris" is affixed; perhaps a corruption of the name Fornaceriis, which was given to him.

FOURNIER.
Flourished,

A much more modern artist than the foregoing; but a man of no great note. His works are chiefly executed with the graver, in a cold, flight style, and very poorly drawn. Part of the plates for a set of prints, entitled, *Les Tableaux de la Penitence*, a small folio volume, are by him.

JACOB DE FORNAZERIS.
Flourished, 1615.

This artist, who, I believe, was a native of France, and resided at Lyons, appears to have worked chiefly for the booksellers; but in a style far superior to the generality of engravers of that class. We have a variety of frontispieces by him, which he usually ornamented with small historical figures, designed in a pretty manner, and with a tolerable degree of correctness. He executed his plates entirely with the graver, very neatly, but in a formal, stiff style, excepting which fault, his prints, generally speaking, possess great merit. Among many others, the following frontispieces are by him:

To the *Commentaries of I. Fernandus*, in folio, published at Lyons, 1622.
To the *Tabula Chronographica*, Lugduni, 1616, in folio.
To the *Praxis Fori Pœnitentialis*, Lugduni, 1616, the same.
To the *Biblia Sacra* in quarto, Lugduni, 1606.
To the *Biblia Sacra* in folio, 1609.

J. FOUTIN.
Flourished, 1619.

By this artist, who was probably a goldsmith, we have a set of engravings, by no means well executed, representing *ornamental foliage, with grotesque heads, figures*, &c. He signs his name, *J. Foutin, a Chasteaudun*; and they are dated 1619.

HONORE FRAGONARD.
Flourished, 1760.

A modern artist, and native of France. According to Basan, he was a painter. For his improvement he went to Italy, where he engraved several prints from the pictures of the great masters. On his return to Paris (where he resided at the time Basan wrote his Dictionary) he etched several plates from his own compositions; but the subjects are not specified.

D. FRANCESCHINI.
Flourished, 1725.

A modern Italian artist, by whom we have a slight and indifferent etching of *L'Anfiteatro Flavio*, or the Ampitheatre of Flavius, in folio, dated 1725.

VICENZIO FRANCESCHINI.
Flourished, 1748.

A modern Italian artist, and probably of the same family with D. Franceschini, mentioned in the former article. He engraved part of the plates of portraits for the *Museo Fiorentino*, published 1748. He sometimes substituted the initials of his name only, in this manner, V. F.

FRANCESCO MARIA FRANCIA. See Raibolini.

ADAM of FRANCKFORT. See Elsheimer.

HANS, or JOHN FRANCK.
Flourished, 1666.

This artist resided at Nuremberg, and was probably a native of that place. We have many prints, which were engraved by him, principally portraits, in which line he appears to have been greatly employed. Several of those in *Priorata Hist. Leop.* are by him. He also engraved part of a set of the fountains, which are in and about Rome, conjointly with Sufan Sandrart, A. Zelt, and J. Meyer.

BAPTISTA FRANCKALS.
Flourished,

An artist, whose excellence, according to Le Comte, consisted in engraving *tournaments, theatrical scenes, and magnificent decorations*.

BAPTISTA FRANCO.
Born, 1498. Died, 1561.

This celebrated artist was born at Venice, where he learned the first principles of design. He afterwards went to Rome, and particularly attached himself to the study of the works of Michael Angelo Buonaroti. The improvement he made in the art of drawing the human figure was such, as acquired him a very considerable share of reputation. The correctness of his outlines, and the scientific manner in which he marked the appearance of the muscles, is highly commended; but his colouring by no means equalled the other merits, which as an artist he possessed: his pictures are said to be hard and dark, and without harmony. The sensibility of this imperfection was perhaps the cause, that he applied himself so much to designing and engraving. From whom he learned the practice of these arts is uncertain: some have said in the school of Marc Antonio Raimondi; and indeed there is no small resemblance between the mechanical part of the execution of the plates of Baptista Franco, and of those of Julio Bonosona, who was, without doubt, the scholar of that excellent master. Franco worked chiefly, if not entirely, with the graver; yet many of his prints have the appearance of etchings. They are very freely performed, in a slight, but agreeable style.

The lights upon the single figures are broad and massy; but in his larger compositions they are too much scattered; and there is a great want of depth of shadow, to relieve the objects represented as close to the eye, from those which should recede from it. His compositions in general, however, are well conceived. His figures are often grand, and constantly well varied and contrasted with no small degree of taste. The heads perhaps are sometimes rather too small; but they are well drawn and finely characterised, and the other extremities are marked in a masterly manner.

He died 1561, aged 63. He usually marked his plates in this manner, B. F. V. F. that is *Baptista Francus Venetus fecit*.

I shall mention the following only by this master:

Abraham's sacrifice, a middling-sized plate, length-ways, from a composition of his own.

Abraham meeting Melchizedek, the same. To this plate he signs his name at length, BAPTISTA FRANCO FECIT.

Moses striking the rock, the same.

Adoration of the shepherds; in the clouds are six angels seated, a middling sized upright plate, the same.

Christ disputing with the learned men in the temple, a middling sized plate, length-ways, the same.

The *disciples putting the body of Christ into the tomb*, a small plate length-ways, the same.

The *donation made to the church by the emperor Constantine*, a large plate, length-ways, from Raphael.

A *Bacchanalian subject*, a large plate length-ways, from Julio Romano.

The *deluge*, a middling-sized plate, length-ways, from Polydore.

The *cyclops at their forge*, a large plate length-ways, from his own composition, &c.

GIACOMO FRANCO.
Flourished, 1590.

This artist was born at Venice, and was probably of the same family with Baptista Franco, mentioned in the preceding article. He adopted a bold free style of engraving, much resembling that of Agostino Carracci, with whom he was contemporary. He drew well, and marked the heads and other extremities of his figures in a very masterly manner. Among other valuable prints by the hand of this estimable artist are the following:

Part of the plates for an edition, in quarto, of *Tasso's Jerusalem Delivered*. The rest were executed by Agostino Carracci. They are from the designs of Bernard Castelli, and were published at Genoa, 1590.

Habiti delle donne Venetiane, published 1626.

A collection of *portraits* of the great men, dated 1596.

A *crucifixion*, a small plate lenthways, marked " Giacomo Francha. f."

He also engraved from Baptista Franco and other masters.

J. C. FRANCOIS.
Flourished, 1760.

A modern French artist, who resided at Paris, where he engraved several plates,

plates, from Boucher, Parocel, Pierre and other masters, in a manner representing *drawings made in crayons*, which is performed by two or more copperplates, according to the number of tints required. He also engraved with strokes, several small portraits; among others that of *comte de St. Florentin*.

J. DE FRANSSIERES.
Flourished, 1714.

A modern engraver of no great merit, by whom, among other things, we have some plates of Turkish habits. The whole set was published at Paris, A. D. 1714, by M. de Ferriol; the rest were engraved by Huressard and Basan.

FREMONT.
Flourished,

A name inscribed upon some portraits, which signifies them to have been drawn from persons confined in the Fleet Prison, London, about the year 1730. Among others, *as non common Groves*, a quarto print, is signed *Fremont*.

GEORGE FRENTZEL.
Flourished, 1600.

This engraver was a native of Germany, born at Ingolstadt. He was, according to professor Christ, a very famous artist in his time. The prints which he engraved are marked with a G. and an F. joined together, in the manner expressed upon the plate at the end of the volume.

CHARLES DU FRESNE.
Flourished, 1680.

This gentleman, a native of France, was a great lover of the arts, and a man of letters. For his amusement he engraved several prints; and among others, according to Basan,

The *interview between S. Nil, and the emperor Otho III.* a large plate, length-ways, from Dominichino.

AGNES FREY.
Flourished, 1510.

She was the wife of Albert Durer, and, according to the report of several authors, engraved also, using a mark or cypher something resembling two A's. joined together, in the manner expressed upon the plate at the end of the volume. The wife of Albert Durer, according to the history which is given of her, had not patience enough, one would think, to become an engraver. And, with respect to the mark itself, it is exceedingly uncertain to whom it might properly belong; unless it should, as some have supposed, denote Philip Adlar Patricius, of whom we have spoken before. This point however must be left to the determination of the curious; but I cannot conceive

ceive that there is the least good foundation for attributing it to Agnes Frey, admitting she really was the wife of Albert Durer, and did also engrave.

JOHN JAMES FREY.
Flourished, 1730.

This admirable engraver was a native of Switzerland. Possessed of great genius, with every requisite to form the artist, he pursued his studies succefsfully; and having the good fortune of being placed in the school of Carlo Maratti, and working under his immediate inspection, with Robert van Audenarde his fellow disciple, it is no wonder he made such hasty strides towards perfection; especially as his rival was also a man of great ability. Frey drew with much taste, and carefully attended to the effect and harmony of his engravings. To produce which, he very judiciously executed the flesh in a more soft and delicate style than his draperies; and kept his distances properly covered, in order to relieve and bring forward the principal objects of the composition. He etched with great spirit and freedom, and worked over the etching with the graver with great firmness and facility. In short, his best prints are justly held in the highest estimation, as being admirable transcripts of the pictures he copied. If we may venture to blame him at all, it will be for the sameness of style, which appears in all his prints, though they are engraved from a great variety of masters. He was established at Rome, where he died some years since. Among his most esteemed works, the following may be numbered:

A *holy family*, a middling-sized upright plate, copied exactly from that which Gerard Edelink engraved after Raphael.

Aurora with the Hours dancing before the chariot of the Sun, a large plate, length-ways, from Guido. Audenaerd, Pascalini, and others, also engraved from this picture.

Bacchus consoling Ariadne, after the departure of Theseus, companion to the former, from the same.

The *communion of St. Jerom*, a large upright plate, from Dominichino. Cæsar Testa, and Farjat, also engraved from this picture.

The *adoration of the shepherds*, a large upright plate, from Sebastian Conca.

A *saint kneeling, and an angel showing him a picture of the Virgin and Child*, with this inscription: *In conspectu Angelorum psalmam tibi*, a middling sized upright plate, from Carlo Maratti.

The *Virgin giving the scapular to St. Simon Stock*, a large upright plate, arched at the top, from Sebastian Conca.

St. Francis de Paul, restoring sight to a child, a large upright plate from Bonaventura Lamberti.

An *emblematical subject*, where some ecclesiastics are represented as ascending into the clouds, a large upright plate, from Andrea Sacchi.

St. Charles Borromee causing a procession to be made, to obtain from Heaven the cessation of the plague, a large upright plate from Pietro de Cortona.

A *repose, where Joseph is presenting cherries to the infant Christ*, a middling sized upright plate, from Carlo Maratti.

St. Andrew kneeling before the cross, previous to his martyrdom, a middling sized plate, length-ways, from the same.

The

The *four cardinal virtues*, namely, *Fortitude, Prudence, Temperance*, and *Justice*, commonly called the four angels, from Dominichino, four large upright plates.

He also engraved from Guercino, Baleſtra, Pietro Bianchi, and other maſters.

GIOVANNI GIROLAMO FREZZA.
Flouriſhed, 1700.

This artiſt, a native of Italy, was an engraver of ſome note, and reſided at Rome. He etched his plates very carefully, and finiſhed them much with the graver, in a neat ſtyle; but without any force of colouring, or boldneſs of execution. His drawing, though not very incorrect, is nevertheleſs heavy; and the extremities of his figures in general, are poorly marked. We have by his hand,

The firſt and ſecond plates for the Crozat collection, one repreſenting *Venus*, the other *Pallas*, from antique paintings.

The *Veroſpian gallery*, conſiſting of ſeventeen folio plates, including the title; theſe were publiſhed at Rome, 1704.

The *twelve months*, middling ſized plates, length-ways, from Carlo Maratti. I. B. de Poilly engraved the ſame ſubjects.

The *judgment of Paris*, a middling ſized plate, length-ways, from the ſame.

He alſo engraved from Dominichino, Rubens, and other maſters.

JAMES ANDRE FRIEDRICH.
Flouriſhed, 1760.

A modern engraver, and native of Germany, by whoſe hand we have ſeveral prints; among others, ſeveral *huſſars and other ſoldiers on horſeback*, after Rugendas.

LOUIS FRIG.
Flouriſhed,

An ancient engraver on wood, by whom we have the *plan of the town of Zuric*, in the coſmography of Munſter. His mark, according to profeſſor Chriſt, was an L. and an F. joined together, in the manner repreſented upon the plate at the end of the volume.

FRIQUET DE VAUROSE.
Flouriſhed,

This artiſt was a painter, the diſciple of Sebaſtian Bourdon. He engraved ſeveral prints after the deſigns of his maſter.

JOHN VREDEMAN FRISIUS.
Flouriſhed, 1563.

By this engraver, who was, I believe, a native of Holland, we have a book of monuments, &c. entitled *Cænotaphiorum, tumulorum, & Mortuorum Monumentorum*, published 1563, by Jerom Cock: they are etched, and retouched with the graver in a coarse, heavy style.

JOHN EILLART FRISIUS.
Flourished,

This engraver was probably of the same family with the foregoing. His labours seem to have been chiefly confined to the booksellers. He engraved several portraits; and among the rest that of a *prince of Nassau*.

SIMON FRISIUS.
Flourished, 1640.

This artist was a native of Holland, and very probably related to the engravers mentioned in the two preceding articles; but he was greatly superior to either. Simon Frisius was a man of no mean talents; he handled the point with great taste and facility; his etchings, though usually very slight, are nevertheless free, broad, and masterly. The small figures, which he frequently inserted into his views and landscapes, are executed in a very agreeable manner. The following are his chief works:

A set of *heads*, small upright plates, representing *female saints, the sibyls,* &c. He adds the word *fecit*, to his name; hence it is probable, that he engraved them from his own designs.

A large collection of *views*, small plates, length-ways, from Matthew Bril, entitled *Topographia Variorum Regionum*, date 1651.

Several *portraits* after Henry Hondius.

A set of *birds and butterflies*, twelve small prints, length-ways, from Marc Gerard, dated 1610.

He also engraved from A. Bloemart and other masters.

Sometimes he omitted to sign his name at length, and substituted the initials, S. F.

CHRISTIAN FRITZSCH.
Flourished,

A native of Hamburg. He was an engraver of portraits, and worked probably for the booksellers only. This name is affixed to the following portraits: *John duke of Marlborough*, a small octavo print. *Benedictus XIV. Pont. Max.*

CHRISTIAN FRITZSCH, son to the above artist, was also an engraver.

JOHN FROSNE.
Flourished, 1654.

This engraver was a native of France, and resided, I believe, at Paris. He was a man of moderate abilities as an artist. His best works are in the portrait line. He seems to have imitated the style of Nanteuil; and, in some few

few inftances, not without a tolerable fhare of fuccefs. He engraved, among other things, part of the large *ornamental plates* in folio, for the Collection of Views, &c. by S. de Beaulieu; alfo the following portraits: *Louis de Lorraine, duc de Joyeufe*; *Henry D'Orleans, duc De Longueville*; *Nicholas Potier*; *M. Dreux D'Aubray*, &c.

FROYEN.
Flourifhed,

A very obfcure and indifferent engraver. His name is affixed to a fmall print, reprefenting the *head of our Saviour*, executed entirely with the graver.

PHILIP FRUYTIERS.
Flourifhed,

This artift was a native of Antwerp. He was firft inftructed in oil painting: but he afterwards preferred water colours, and excelled greatly in miniature. His works are chiefly *portraits* and *converfations*, which he executed in a very mafterly ftyle. Rubens was fo pleafed with his performances, that he, with his family, fat to him; and the picture which he produced on this occafion, was confidered as his mafter-piece. According to Bafan, he etched feveral plates; but the fubjects are not fpecified.

THOMAS FRYE.
Flourifhed, 1740.

This ingenious artift was a portrait painter of fome eminence. He refided in London, where he drew and engraved in mezzotinto, a fet of heads as large as life. Among them are the following: *His prefent majefty*; *the queen*; *his own portrait*; the celebrated *Mifs Pond*, &c. large upright plates.

ADAM FUCHS.
Flourifhed, 1543.

An ancient German engraver, who worked both on copper and on wood. To him are attributed thofe prints, dated 1543, or about that time, which are marked with an A. and an F. joined together in a kind of cypher, as reprefented on the plate at the end of the volume. I have feen a fmall upright etching, reprefenting the *flight into Egypt*, with this mark; but it apparently belongs to another mafter: for Fuchs, I believe, worked entirely with the graver, when he engraved on copper.

SEBASTIAN FURCK, or FULCARUS.
Flourifhed, 1720.

This engraver appears, fays profeffor Chrift, to have been born at Goflar in Germany, as the name of that town is inferted upon feveral of his prints. He went to Italy, and worked at Rome, as early as 1612, if it can be proved, that Furck and Fulcarus were one and the fame artift, which not only the mark,

mark, but the style of engraving, seems to prove sufficiently. From 1620 to 1630, he is said to have resided at Franckfort upon the Maine, and other neighbouring places. I do not recollect, that any of his engravings appeared after the year 1650; at which time a genealogical work, entitled *Arboretum Principis Augusti*, was printed at Wolfenbuttel. This artist possessed great merit, and worked with the graver chiefly. However we have some few etchings by his hand. See the marks he frequently substituted upon his plates, when he omitted to sign his name at length. The following prints are by him:

The portraits of the *Columna family*, and a variety of other portraits, apparently most of them for books.

An ornamental frontispiece for the works of *Gul. Fabricius*, a very spirited etching, and dated 1646; to this he signs his name *S. Furck, f.*

The *last judgment*, from Michael Angelo Buonarota, a very small upright plate. On the tomb-stone, at the left hand corner, is the cypher in capitals; and underneath it is written, *Sebastian Fulcarus reinciditque*, which was not added till after he had retouched the plate.

St. Sebastian, a half figure, a middling sized plate, length-ways.

He also engraved from Titian, and several other masters.

JOHN FULLER.
Born,   Died, 1676.

He was born in England, but resided much in France, where he studied under Perrier. He professed historical painting; but never arrived at any great degree of perfection. His drawing is, however, much commended for its correctness; and he is said to have understood the anatomical markings of the figure exceedingly well. His pictures are held in no great estimation. We have etched by him a set of prints, from his own designs, for the *Moral Emblems of Cæsar Ripa*, in quarto. They are very slight, incorrect performances, every way unworthy of the hand of an artist.

PETER FURNIUS.
Flourished, 1570.

This artist was an excellent designer, and probably a painter. He was contemporary with the Sadelers and the Galles, who worked considerably from his designs. If we may judge by his style of engraving, it is probable he learned that art from his connection with them. He resided at Antwerp; but whether he was actually a native of that city or not, I cannot discover. His compositions have generally much merit in them; though sometimes they have an air of affectation, from the violent contrast of his figures, and an attempt at the grand style, in which Michael Angelo alone succeeded so happily. He drew the human figure correctly; the heads have much character, and the other extremities are well marked. But from a want of proper knowledge in the distribution of the light and shadow, the effect of his compositions is confused and feeble. The following are executed by him in a slight style, entirely with the graver.

The *escape of Celia*, with several other subjects, taken from the Roman History, marked " P. Furnius, fecit," small plates, length-ways.

The *martyrdom of St. Felicia*, a middling sized plate, length-ways, " P. Furnius inventor et fec."

The *parable of the good Samaritan*, on six small plates, length-ways.

He also engraved a variety of other subjects, as well from sacred as prophane history. See the marks, which he frequently used himself, and which are often on prints composed by him, but engraved by other artists.

JOHN FYTT.
Flourished, 1640.

This admirable artist was born at Antwerp, about the year 1625. The subjects which employed his pencil were all forts of animals, fruits, flowers, and landscapes. He excelled greatly in these branches of the art; and his pictures are held in very high estimation. We have by him some very spirited, bold etchings, executed in a hasty manner. They are small plates, length-ways, representing *dogs and other animals*, marked Io. Fyt. and dated 1640.

G.

BALDASSARE GABBUGGIANI.
Flourished, 1750.

ONE of those modern Italian artists, who were employed to engrave the plates for the *Museo Fiorentino*, which was published at Florence in ten folio volumes.

BARTOLOMEO GAGLIARDI.
Born, 1555. Died, 1620.

This artist was born at Genoa. He was a painter of reputation, and by his hand we have several plates, both etched, and finished with the graver; among others is a large *emblematical print*, length-ways, executed in a style greatly resembling that of Cherubino Alberti, but not equal to the works of that master.

GAGNIERES. See GANIERES.

ROBERT GAILLARD.
Flourished, 1760.

A modern French engraver, who resided at Paris, by whom we have, among others, the following plates:

Jupiter and Califta, a middling sized plate, length-ways, from Boucher.
Bacchants sleeping, a middling sized upright plate, from the same.
The portrait of the *queen of Sweden*, a middling sized upright plate, from Lantinville.

PETER JOSEPH GAILLARD DE LONJUMEAU.
Flourished, 1750.

This gentleman, a modern connoisseur and lover of the arts, took up the point for his amusement; and we have several small etchings by his hand of the *antiquities of Aix*. His portrait was engraved by Balechou, from a picture of J. B. Van Loo.

GIOVANNA BATISTA GALESTRUCCI.
Flourished, 1657.

This artist was born at Florence, from whence he went to Rome, where he he refided. He is fpoken of as a painter, but is much better known as an engraver. We have feveral etchings by him, in a neat, correct, mafterly ftyle, greatly refembling that of Salvator Rofa. The chief of them are as follows:

Several fets of *friezes and bafs reliefs*, from Polodoro Caravaggio.

A fet of *antique gems*, with explanations, by Leonardo Agoftino, in four volumes, quarto.

John Baptift beheaded in prifon, from Batifta Ricci, &c.

PHILIP GALLE.
Born, 1537. Died, 1612.

The family of the Galles make a very confpicuous figure in the hiftory of engraving. By Philip Galle, conjointly with the Sadelers, the Wierixes, and the Collaerts, we have a prodigious number of fmall hiftorical prints, both facred and prophane, but efpecially the former. The great object with thefe artifts appears to have been, that of putting forth fets of prints as haftily as poffible; therefore no pains were taken by them to improve the manner of engraving, which prevailed at that period. Hence we fee the fame ftiff, formal ftyle is difcoverable in all of them, without any attempt to add tafte and freedom to correctnefs. Thefe hafty and numerous publications, however they might enrich the artifts, evidently retarded the progrefs of the art: for, in any other point of view, it is not reafonable to fuppofe, that it fhould have remained ftationary, as it were, fo long, in the hands of fo many men of great abilities.

Philip Galle, if not a native of Antwerp, refided there, and carried on a very confiderable commerce in prints. He was, as before obferved, a man capable of improving the art; for he drew correctly, and handled the graver with fufficient facility. His engravings are, in general, flight; and from the lights being too much difperfed, the harmony and force of effect are much weakened, and too often entirely deftroyed. We have by him,

Several fets of prints from the *Old and New Teftament*, after Martin Hemfkerck, Martin de Vos, Abraham Blockland, the elder Brughel, and other mafters; chiefly fmall middling fized plates, length-ways.

The *triumph of Death, Fame, and Honour*, a fet of middling fized plates, length-ways, from Martin Hemfkerck.

Divinarum nuptiorum conventa et acta, a fet of twenty-eight fmall plates, length-ways, dated 1580.

A fet of prints, entitled, *Medicia Familia Geftarum*, from John Straden, publifhed 1583.

The *feven wonders of the world*; to which he has added the *ruins of the ampitheatre of Vefpafian at Rome*, for the eighth, from Martin Hemfkerck, eight fmall plates, length-ways.

A *book of defigns for drawing*, in fmall folio.

The *Trinity*, a very large upright plate, with many figures, from Martin de Vos, dated 1574. This, I conceive to be one of his beft prints.

See his cypher, compofed of a P. and a G. joined together, on the plate at the end of the volume.

THEODORE GALLE.
Flourished, 1580.

He was the eldeſt ſ⸺ ⸺o Galle, mentioned in the preceding article; and having learned from his father the firſt principles of the art of engraving, he went to Italy in order to improve himſelf, and reſided ſome time at Rome, where he ſtudied from the antique, and engraved from the works of ſeveral great maſters. He, however, ſtill continued too cloſely to imitate his father; and though his works were neater, and more finiſhed, in general, yet the ſame ſtiffneſs, and defects in the diſtribution of the light and ſhadow, appear in them. They are well drawn, and executed with the graver only. At his return to Antwerp, he commenced printſeller; and we find he was a very conſiderable publiſher. The following prints are by his hand:

The *life of St. Norbeti*, a ſet of ſmall upright plates, publiſhed at Antwerp.
The *life of Joſeph and the Virgin*, a ſet of twenty-eight ſmall upright plates.

CORNELIUS GALLE, the ELDER.
Flourished, 1600.

He was the younger ſon of Philip Galle, and brother to Theodore Galle, mentioned in the preceding articles. He learned the art of engraving from his father, and imitated his ſtyle; till, following his brother's example, he went to Rome, where he reſided a conſiderable time, and there acquired that freedom, taſte, and correctneſs of drawing, which are found in his beſt works, and render them far more eſtimable, than thoſe of his father or his brother; though, like them, he worked entirely with the graver. He ſettled at Antwerp, upon his return from Italy, where he carried on a conſiderable commerce in prints. Among many others, the following engravings are by his hand:

The *life of John the Baptiſt*, a ſet of middling ſized plates, length-ways, from J. Straden.

The *life of the Virgin Mary*, the ſame, from the ſame maſter.

Part of the plates for the *Life of Chriſt*, after Martin de Vos, publiſhed by Collaert.

Theſe prints are in the ſtiff, formal ſtyle of his father, and were probably engraved at Antwerp, previouſly to his going to Rome.

Adam and Eve, a middling ſized upright plate, from J. B. Paggi.

Judith cutting off the head of Holophernes, a large upright plate, from Rubens.

The *Virgin Mary ſtanding in an arch, which is ornamented with flowers by ſeveral little cherubs*, a large upright plate, from the ſame maſter.

The *Virgin holding the infant Chriſt, to whom St. Bernard of Sienna offers a book, with a branch of laurel*, a ſmall upright plate, from Franceſco Vanni.

The *flight into Egypt*, a large upright plate, arched at the top, from J. B. Paggi.

A *crucifixion*, from Franceſco Vanni, a middling ſized upright plate.

St. Peter baptiſing St. Priſcia, a ſmall upright plate, from Civoli.

The *four fathers of the church*, a middling ſized plate, length-ways, from Rubens.

Rubens. The first impressions of this plate are before the work was enlarged, which is distinguished by two black strokes, one on each side.

Seneca in the bath, a middling sized upright plate, from the same.

Venus bound, and Minerva chastising Cu̧ ̧ ̧ ̧ ̧ upright plate, from Agostino Carracci.

Venus kissing Cupid, a small upright plate: Venus is a half figure only, from J. B. Paggi.

A *naked woman grinding colours*, a small upright plate, from Rubens. The first impressions are without the French verses, which were afterwards inserted at the bottom of the plate.

A *repast*, with figures playing on Music, &c. a middling sized plate, length-ways, without any painter's name.

Several excellent portraits: among them, that of *Rubens*, brother to P. Paul Rubens, by whom the picture was painted; also *Artus Walfort*, a small upright plate, from Vandyck. *Charles I. of England* from N. V. Horst, in quarto. *Henrietta Maria, queen to Charles I.* the same, from the same. He also engraved a variety of other subjects from different masters.

CORNELIUS GALLE, the YOUNGER.
Flourished, 1640.

He was the son of Cornelius Galle, mentioned in the preceding article. He learned the principles of drawing and engraving from his father, whose style he imitated; and though he certainly never equalled the best works of that artist, yet he produced several plates, which have much sterling merit, and prove him to have been a man of genius. He worked entirely with the graver; and some of his portraits, which, I think, superior to the rest of his performances, are very clear, and executed with great freedom. His outlines are the most defective; for he did not understand the human figure. But whether this arose from his inattention to drawing, or the not having an opportunity of studying in Italy, as his relations had done, I leave to the determination of the experienced collector. We have by him,

A *nativity, with the angel appearing to the shepherds*, a small upright plate, from D. Teniers.

Venus suckling the loves, a small upright plate, from Rubens.

The *descent from the cross*, a middling sized upright plate, from Diepenbeck.

The *hospitality of Bachus and Philemon towards Jupiter and Mercury*, a middling sized plate, length-ways, from John van Hoeck.

The portrait of the *emperor Ferdinand III.* from Vandyck.

The portrait of *Mary of Austrich*, his consort, the same.

The portrait of *Henriette of Lorraine*, the same.

The portrait of *John Meissens*, the painter, the same.

SEBALD GALLENDORFER.
Flourished, 1494.

A very ancient engraver on wood, and apparently a native of Nuremberg.

He

He was employed by Sebald Schreyer, in the year 1494, to ornament with prints a little book, written by Peter Danhaver, entitled, *Archetypus triumphantis Romæ*.

CLAUDE GALLIMARD.
Flourished, 1780.

A modern engraver, who resided at Rome. By him we have several plates from Sebastian Bourdon, I. F. de Troy, Subleyras, and other masters. His engravings are flight and sufficiently neat; but they possess no superior degree of merit.

BERNARD GALLO.
Flourished, 1559.

In the Abecedario we are told, that this artist flourished about the middle of the sixteenth century, when he engraved a set of historical prints from the Old Testament; another set of prints from the New Testament; and also a third set for the Metamorphoses of Ovid, printed at Lyons, A. D. 1559. He usually marked his engravings with the initials B. G.

JOHN GALSTOT.
Flourished,

This artist is mentioned at the end of the Abecedario, as an engraver. He marked his plates, J. Gal. Nardois, F. The F. as usual, stands for *fecit*. Dr. Monro has in his collection a *small landscape*, executed with some spirit, in which is badly represented Tobit, with the angel. The figures are below all criticism. It is marked Galtoth, N. F. However, they are apparently both the same artist, the name by mistake being differently spelt.

JAMES GAMMON.
Flourished, 1660.

A very indifferent engraver, who resided, I believe, in London, about the year 1660, where he engraved a variety of portraits, in a stiff, tasteless style. Among them are the following: *Richard Cromwell*, a small upright plate, in an oval. Sir *Toby Matthews*, the same. *Catherine* of *Braganza*, the same. *Mascall the painter*, the same. As there is no painter's name affixed to these plates, we may suppose they were drawn by the engraver himself; and the miserable style of the attitudes, will, I think, sufficiently justify the opinion.

V. GAMPERLIN or GEMBERLIN.
Flourished, 1510.

A very ancient engraver on wood, who resided chiefly at Strasburg in Alsace, where he executed a set of twenty-two prints, for the *Life of our Saviour*, which was printed in that city by John Knobbouch, A. D. 1507.

These

These engravings are eight inches and a half high, by six inches wide. They are very neatly cut; but in a stiff style exceedingly incorrect, and tastelefs; yet some few good figures may be pointed out. According to the ancient custom, the principal personages and places are distinguished by their names, which are written over their heads: as, *Lazarus, Mary Magdalen, Bethany,* &c. It is singular enough, that in the print, which represents *Christ riding to Jerusalem,* the crowd are meeting him as he is passing a bridge; and one of them is spreading his garment. But he, and the rest of the figures behind him, are nearly as small again as those on the other side of the river, notwithstanding they are equally near to the eye of the spectator. But this master had not the most distant idea of perspective. His prints are marked with the initals V. G. The letters are formed in the old Gothic style, and separate from each other. We must be careful not to confound the works of this artist, with those of another engraver on wood, who used the same letters, but joined together in the style of a cypher, apparently not so ancient, but far superior. See an account of his works, under the article Goar. The same letters were also used by an engraver on copper, who flourished about the year 1574.

GANDENSIS. See AUDEN-AERD.

GANIERE.
Flourished, 1650.

He was apparently a native of France, and resided at Paris. He engraved a variety of subjects; but portraits constitute the greater part of his works. He executed his plates entirely with the graver, in a stiff, tastelefs style. The following prints are by him: a *boy sleeping, with a skull lying near him,* a small plate, length-ways, dated 1640.

Louis XIII. of France, a small head in an oval, surrounded with ornaments, for a book printed at Paris, 1640.

Flavio Chigi Card. a small upright plate.

M. de la Melleraye, a middling size upright plate, dated 1679.

He also engraved from Valentin, Blanchard, and other artists.

STEPHEN GANTREL.
Flourished,

He was a native of France, and exclusive of his profession as an engraver, traded considerably in prints. By him we have, among others, the following plates:

The *rod of Moses as a serpent, devouring the rods of the magicians,* from Nicholas Poufin, a large plate, length-ways.

The *Israelites passing the Red Sea,* the same, from the same master.

A *descent from the cross,* a middling sized plate, length-ways, from the same.

St. Francis Xavier restoring an Indian to life, a middling sized upright plate, from the same.

THOMAS

THOMAS GARDNER.
Flourished, 1735.

He was, I believe, a native of England, and worked for the bookfellers. By him we have a fet of prints for the *Common Prayer*, paraphrafed by James Harris, A. D. 1735.

NOEL GARNER.
Flourished, 1560.

A very indifferent engraver, both upon wood and upon copper. He is fuppofed to have been the firft that introduced the latter manner of engraving into France; but there is much obfcurity in this matter. His works, it is true, are very rude, and badly executed; but this is, by no means, a fufficient proof of their antiquity. I have before me a very fmall plate, length-ways, reprefenting *feveral naked men fighting*, in which he feems to have made a feeble attempt at copying the ftyle of Sebald Beham, his cotemporary. On a fmall tablet, at the bottom, the name is thus written, NOEL G. At other times, it appears, that he figns the three firft letters of his baptifmal name only, and adds a Gothic character, refembling the figure 8, fuppofing it to be open on the top. He engraved befides feveral *grotefque ornaments*, and a fet of 48 figures, reprefenting the *arts, fciences, trades*, &c.

Le Comte mentions two other Garners: one, fays he, ufes the letter A. for the initial of his baptifmal name; and the other the letter V. for the fame purpofe: I doubt not but he means by the firft Antoine Garnier, mentioned in the following article, and by the latter V. Gamperlin; and I am more inclined to think fo, as he attributes the *life and paffion of Chrift* to the Garner, who ufes the V. and Gamperlin's mark was V. G. which he has affixed to the *life of Chrift* executed by him.

ANTOINE GARNIER.
Flourished,

This artift, who was a native of France, flourifhed about the commencement of the laft century. He etched his plates in a dark, bold ftyle, and finifhed them with the graver. They are however by no means finely executed. The heads, and other extremities of his figures, are fometimes rather heavy, and his outlines hard and incorrect; yet, in general, they are by no means deftitute of merit. He engraved twelve plates from the pictures of Primaticcio, which are in the chapel belonging to the palace de Fleury at Fontainbleau. *Charity*, a middling fized plate, length-ways, from Blanchard. He alfo engraved from Poufin, Michael Angelo Caravaggio, and other mafters. See his mark upon the plate at the end of the volume.

HENRY GASCAR.
Flourished, 1660.

He was a native of France, but fent for into England, to paint the portrait of the duchefs of Portfmouth, his countrywoman. He met with great encouragement here, notwithstanding Sir Peter Lely was living, and he himself a most miserable artist. What he wanted in grace and elegance, he endeavoured to supply by rich embroidery, fine clothes, laced drapery, and tawdry trimmings, which may, and do too frequently, deceive the eye of the ignorant. It is said, that he amassed upwards of ten thousand pounds in this kingdom, in a short time; with which he retired to the continent; and, if report be true, imposed as grossly afterwards upon the Spanish nobility, as he had done upon the English. We have a few vile mezzotintos by him, which he engraved from his own pictures, among the rest, the *duchess of Portsmouth*, and some other portraits.

GASPER. See AVIBUS.

OLIVIERO GATTI.
Flourished, 1626.

This painter was born at Parma. He studied in the academy at Bologna, and was received as a member of it A. D. 1626; and in that city he resided the greatest part of his life. Apparently, he learned the art of engraving from Agostino Carracci; for he certainly imitated his style; and though he by no means equalled that great artist, his prints have a considerable share of merit. He drew the human figure very correctly; but the extremities are sometimes heavy, and not marked in that masterly style, so conspicuous in the admirable engravings of Carracci. The following prints, among others, are by him:

St. Francis Xavier kneeling on the sea shore, and taking up a crucifix which was floating in the water, a middling sized upright plate, from a composition of his own.

An *emblematical subject*, from Lodovico Carracci, representing an armorial bearing, supported by two river Gods, with a figure completely armed, standing alone, surrounded by Jupiter, Hercules, Neptune, Apollo, and Minerva, a middling sized plate, length-ways.

The *Deity forming the world*; *the creation of Adam*; *Abraham's sacrifice*; and *Judith with the head of Holophernes*, four small upright ovals, from H. Pordenone.

A *drawing book*, from Guercino, &c.

GAUDE. See GOUDT.

GIOVANNA BATISTA GAULLI.
Born, 1639. Died, 1709.

This artist, who was also named Le Bacici, was a native of Genoa. He studied at Rome, and painted a great number of portraits, though he chiefly excelled in historical subjects, to which his genius more naturally inclined. He coloured with great force, and is particularly commended for the judgment with which he foreshortened his figures. He died at Rome, A. D.

A. D. 1709, aged 70. The portrait of *Cardinal Cælio Piccolomini*, is said to be engraved by him.

LEONARD GAULTIER.
Flourished, 1620.

This artist is generally considered as a native of France; but professor Christ, without assigning his reason, supposes him to have been a German. He imitated the style of the Wierixes; and his works are executed with the utmost precision, with the graver only. But while we admire the excessive neatness, which is discovered in them, we cannot help lamenting the want of taste, freedom, and correctness of design, by which they are equally characterized. He excelled chiefly in small figures and portraits. Of the latter we have a considerable number by his hand. According to Abbé Marolles, the number of prints, engraved by this master, amount to 800, and chiefly from his own designs. I can only mention the following: A number of small plates, the subjects taken from the *Old and New Testament*.

Many very small upright plates, forming sets, of the *Prophets*, *Apostles*, and *Evangelists*.

The *Psyche of Apuleius*, a set of thirty very small plates, length-ways.

The *last judgment*, copied from the print, which Martin Rota engraved from Michael Angelo.

The portrait of *Henry the Fourth of France*, a small upright plate.

The portrait of *Stephen Paschius*, a middling sized upright oval print.

The portrait of *Alexander Bouchart*, from D. Dumonster, a large upright oval print, and he also engraved from Daniel Rubel, John Caron, &c. See his cypher, composed of an L. and a G. on the plate at the end of the volume.

J. GAULTIER.
Flourished,

This artist was perhaps of the same family with the preceding, whose manner of engraving he imitated. Among other things by him, is part of a set of small upright plates of *emblematical subjects*, which are by no means destitute of merit.

PETER GAULTIER.
Flourished, 1730.

This artist was a painter of the present century, and he also engraved several plates from different masters. He resided at Naples, where, I believe, he died some years since. The following are by him:

The *visitation of the Virgin*, a middling sized plate, length-ways, from Solimena.

St. Michael overthrowing the Devil, a small upright plate, from the same.

The *defeat of Darius*, a middling sized plate, length-ways, from the same.

The *battle of the Centaurs*, the same, from the same.

The *four quarters of the world*, small oval plates, from the same.

G. GAUW.
Flourished,

This name is affixed, as the engraver, to a very fingular print, reprefenting a head of the fabulous deity, Mercury, a large upright plate, from J. Matham. It is engraved in a bold, open ftyle, fo as to imitate precifely a drawing with a pen.

R. GAYWOOD.
Flourifhed, 1660.

Gaywood was a native of England, and the difciple of Hollar, whofe manner of engraving, or rather of etching, he imitated. But he fell greatly fhort of the merit of his tutor. He had neither that tafte nor judgment, which was fo confpicuous in the works of the latter. His outlines are hard and incorrect, and the etchings are heavy and laboured. We have a great variety of portraits by Gaywood; and as fpecimens of them may eafily be acquired, I fhall pafs them over. His beft print, I think, is a couchant *Venus, with a man playing upon an organ,* a middling fized plate, length-ways, from Titian. The original picture was in the collection of Charles the Firft, from whence it came into the poffeffion of lord Cholmondeley.

A fet of *lions,* fmall plates, length-ways, from Rubens.

A *book of birds,* middling fized plates, lengthways, from Barlow, &c.

CORNELIUS VAN GEEST.
Flourifhed,

The name of an artift, affixed to a portrait of *Gilbert Burnet, bifhop of Salifbury,* a half fheet print.

G. D. GEIIN.
Flourifhed,

An obfcure engraver, who imitated, in fome faint degree, the ftyle of Paul Pontius; but he had neither fufficient tafte nor judgment to harmonize the effect, and render it agreeable to the eye. By this artift, among other book plates, we have the portrait of *Carolus Aleafpinæus,* in octavo.

WILLIAM GELDORP.
Flourifhed,

He was, according to Le Comte, an engraver of portraits, and refided in England. I am neither acquainted with his works, nor can I find any further account of the artift.

SIGISMOND GELENIUS.
Flourifhed, 1576.

To this artift profeffor Chrift attributes fome ancient engravings on wood, marked with a G. having an S. within its circle, and furmounted with a

fort

sort of double crofs, as reprefented on the plate at the end of the volume. Among others diftinguifhed by this mafter, are twelve fmall upright prints, reprefenting the *labours of Hercules*. They are very neatly executed in a fingular manner, with fine ftrokes, accurately cut, and chiefly fingle, without any crofs ftrokes or hatching. The lights are too much covered, and the fhadows are not fufficiently ftrong to produce any ftriking effect. Yet there is much fpirit in them; and the drawing of the naked parts of the human figure, though not quite correct, is well managed, upon the whole; and the heads have fome degree of merit. The other extremities are heavy, and badly marked. This artift was apparently a native of Germany, and flourifhed, according to profeffor Chrift, about the year 1576.

CLAUDE GELEE, called CLAUDE LORRAINE.
Born, 1600. Died, 1682.

It is rarely the cafe, that a man of fine natural abilities can help manifefting them at times, however they may be obfcured by indolence, or loft in purfuits of an improper tendency. Yet, in fome few inftances, nature has concealed her favours for a time, fo that, like a diamond in the rough, their value has been unobferved even by the poffeffor himfelf. Thus it was with Claude; born in obfcurity, he ferved his time to a paftry-cook; and no diftant appearance of thofe great talents, which fhone fo confpicuoufly afterwards, was obferved in the early part of his life. Nay, at fchool he could learn nothing; and it was with difficulty he could be taught a few rules, relative to perfpective, and the mixing up of his colours. His tutor was Taffi, a fcholar of Paul Bril. Claude's genius difplayed itfelf by flow degrees. He ftudied nature for every thing; and treafured up in his mind whatever he obferved either beautiful or ftriking in her. And the admirable works, which afterwards he produced, fufficiently certify how well he remembered what he had remarked, and the excellent ufe to which he could apply thofe ftudies. The works of Claude are too generally known to need any eulogium here. The enormous prices which they fetch, when ever they come to fale, prove the great eftimation in which they are held.

This great artift, for his own amufement, etched a fet of 28 middling fized *landfcapes*, length-ways, from his own compofitions. They are prodigioufly flight, but very fpirited, and abundantly teftify the hand of the mafter. The fubjects are precifely the fame with thofe, which ufually employed his pencil, and confift of *views, rivers, fea-ports*, &c. enriched with *figures and cattle*.

JOHN GELLE.
Flourifhed, 1628.

This artift was apparently a native of Cologne, in Germany. He engraved part of the plates for a work, entitled *Academie de l'Efpie, per Girard Thibault*, a large folio volume, publifhed at Antwerp, 1628. They are
executed

executed with the graver only, in a stiff, tasteless style. By the same artist is a portrait of *Frederic II. Emp.* surrounded by a border of medals, a middling sized upright plate, dated 1619, and signed " Joan. Gelle fec. et ex."

JACINTO GEMIGNANO, or GEMINIANI.
Born, 1611. Died, 1680.

This artist was born at Pistoia. He went to Rome, and became the disciple of Pietro da Cortona. He studied with great application, and excelled in historical painting. He resided a considerable time in Rome, where he acquired great reputation. Afterwards he returned to Pistoia, where he died, A. D. 1680, aged 70. By him we have, among others, a set of twelve slight etchings, executed with great spirit. They represent *children at play*, and are small plates, length-ways, from his own compositions.

THOMAS GEMINUS, or GEMINIE.
Flourished, 1545.

Geminus was a printer; but, it seems, he took up the graver, in order to ornament his publications with cuts. Virtue, who certainly was a good judge, speaks of his engravings as exceedingly bad. He dwelt in Black-Fryers, London, where he published a prognostication, relating to the weather, phenomena of the Heavens, &c. decorated with a number of cuts, probably by his own hand. It was we find, " Imprinted by Thomas Gemine." In the year 1545, he published a book, with this title, *Thomæ Gemini Lysiensis compendiosa totius anatomes delineatio, æra exarato*, in folio; and the plates, according to Ames, were the first printed with a rolling-press in England. But the truth of this assertion is doubtful, at least. The book just mentioned was a new edition of *Vesalus's Anatomy*, first published at Padua, A. D. 1542, with large wooden cuts. These Geminus imitated on copper; and it was dedicated to Henry the Eighth. He also published a translation of the same work, by Nicholas Udal, A. D. 1552, which he dedicated to Edward the Sixth. The cuts in a book, relative to Midwifry, are also attributed to him. He published a second edition of his Anatomy, A. D. 1559, which was dedicated to queen Elizabeth.

ABRAHAM GENOELS.
Born, 1640. Died,

This artist was born at Antwerp. He learned the first principles of landscape painting in his native country, under Jacques Bakkerel. In order to improve himself, he went to France, where he was employed by de Seve and Le Brun; and the latter procured for him a royal pension, and apartments in the Gobelins. He also studied in Italy, and returned to Antwerp with the reputation of an excellent artist. He died there at a very advanced age. We have by him many bold free etchings of *landscapes*, executed in a masterly style, and ornamented with spirited figures and cattle. A considerable number of them are from his own compositions; and they are of various sizes;

sizes; the large ones are particularly excellent. Also a set of six *landscapes*, middling sized plates, length-ways, from Vander Meulen. Six small *landscapes*, length-ways, from the same.

See his cypher, composed of an A. and a G. which he frequently put upon his plates, when he omitted his name, on the plate at the end of the volume.

B. GENTOT.
Flourished, 1693.

An artist of no considerable note. He engraved some of the plates of *ornaments for iron works*, which were published, in a large folio volume, by Tijou in London, A. D. 1693.

ANDREW GENTSCH.
Flourished, 1616.

An artist who may rank among the *little masters*, so distinguished because of the diminutiveness of their works. He resided at Augsburg, where he engraved on copper several plates of *grotesque ornaments*, which are dated 1616. This artist used the same mark as Aldegrever; but his works are easily distinguished, not only by the date, but by the great inferiority there is between them, and those by Aldegrever.

GIOVANNA GIORGIO.
Flourished, 1650.

This engraver, according to the signatures upon his engravings, appears to have been a native of Padua, where he chiefly resided. His works, which are performed with the graver only, in a coarse, incorrect style, do him no credit. I suppose the booksellers were his principal employers. I have seen by him a *frontispiece with figures* to a book of Anatomy, in quarto, by Joan Veslingi, dated 1647, to which he signs " Joan. Georgius Patavii." The plates for a a collection of antique lamps, a large folio volume, entitled, *De Lucernis Antiquorum reconditis*, Patavii, 1653.

The *bath of the Anabaptists*, a ludicrous subject, from Raphael, &c.

GERARDIU.
Flourished, 1680.

This artist worked entirely with the graver, in a very neat style, but without much taste or correctness of outline. The extremities of his figures are particularly defective. By him we have some of the plates, which belong to a collection of engravings, from the pictures of Pietro Berretino, which are in the palace of the Duke of Tuscany, &c.

ANTONIO GERARDI is mentioned by Florent Le Comte, as an engraver of *funeral pomps, monuments*, and *tombs*. He and Gerardiu were probably the same artist; the last letter in the name being dropped by accident.

B. GERCO.

B. GERCO.
Flourished,

A name affixed to fome fmall landfcapes, length-ways, in which the engraver has attempted to imitate the flight etchings of Waterloo. He has fcratched upon the etchings with the point of the graver; and the barb was not afterwards properly fcraped away. The effect is by no means pleafing.

REMBRANDT GERRETSZ.
Born, 1606. Died, 1674.

This admirable artift is better known by the name of Rembrandt Van Ryn. He was born at a village near Leyden, and by fome connoiffeurs is faid to have been a miller's fon. Others again deny this ftory; which feems to have had its only foundation from his often reforting to a wind-mill; a print of which he alfo etched.

Rembrandt's genius manifefted itfelf at a very early period of his life. He refided three years with Jacques van Zwanburg; and at the expiration of that time, he became the fcholar of Peter Laftman. I only need obferve, that he excelled principally in hiftorical painting, and in portraits. His colouring is excellent; and the lightnefs of his pencil cannot fufficiently be commended. He copied nature exactly, even perhaps to a fault; but then it was, becaufe he did not always choofe her in her fineft forms. His greateft deficiency lay in drawing of the human figure, which was ufually very incorrect, when he reprefented it naked. But to compenfate for this neglect he added to his works fuch breadths of light and fhadow, that the effect of them is rendered furprifingly powerful; and they prove, that no man ever furpaffed him in the knowledge of the *chiaro-fcuro*.

His prints, which are partly etchings and partly engravings, performed with the point of the graver in a fingular manner, have all that freedom of touch, fpirit, and greatnefs of effect, difcoverable in his paintings, fuppofing them to be affifted by the variety of colours. Confidering the great quantity of etchings which he made, we cannot fuppofe they fhould be all equally well executed, or equal in value. However, (according to the common courfe of things, on which an imaginary value may be raifed by accidental caufes) it is not always his beft prints, which produce the greateft prices; but thofe, which are the fcarceft. Thus, we frequently fee a print of great intrinfic worth in itfelf, if confidered as a beautiful fpecimen of the abilities of an artift, thrown afide for no other fault, than that of being too eafily obtained; whilft another, which perhaps is rather a difgrace, than an honour to him, is purchafed at an extravagant price, and anxioufly preferved, becaufe it is unique. It is merely owing to this caprice, that fo many trifling alterations in the prints of Rembrandt, rather than a proper examination of their real merit, increafe or diminifh the worth of the fame print. I myfelf, commiffioned by an eminent collector, gave fix and forty guineas for the great Coppenol, with the white back-ground, that is, before it was finifhed; when, the fame evening, at the fame fale, I bought a moft beautiful impreffion of the fame print finifhed, diftinguifhed by having a black background

ground, &c. which had an addrefs to Rembrandt at the bottom, written by Coppenol himfelf (for he was a writing-mafter of Amfterdam, and this print is his portrait), for fourteen guineas and a half. In the fecond inftance, I exceeded my commiffion by the half guinea; in the firft, I did not reach it by nearly twice ten guineas. It cannot be reafonably fuppofed, that fuch a difference could exift between two good impreffions of the fame plate; and, fpeaking as an artift, I fhould certainly have taken the laft in preference to the firft.

This great mafter died at Amfterdam, the city where he chiefly refided, 1674, aged 68. Upwards of 340 prints are acknowledged to have been engraved by him; the catalogue of which was publifhed at Paris by Gerfaint, and has been fince reprinted, with confiderable additions, and tranflated into Englifh. I fhall only mention the few following:

Jofeph relating his dream, a fmall upright plate. The fcarceft impreffions of this plate are thofe, in which part of the curtains of the bed, and the head of the figure, ftanding at the feet of the bed, with a turban, are without the fhadows, which was afterwards added.

The *triumph of Mordecai*, a middling fized plate, length-ways.

The *prefentation of Chrift in the Temple*, the fame.

The *tribute money*, a very fmall print, length-ways; a firft impreffion of this print is very rare.

Chrift and the woman of Samaria, a fmall upright print. The firft impreffions of this plate, which are very rare, have not the name of Rembrandt, or date; they have other marks to diftinguifh them from the fecond impreffions, which will be eafily obferved.

The *refurrection of Lazarus*, a middling fized upright plate, arched at the top. The firft impreffions, which are very fcarce, are diftinguifhed by the figure running away affrighted, with his head uncovered; in the fecond, he has a fpecies of turban.

Chrift healing the fick and the lame, commonly known by the name of the *Hundred Guilder Print*, a middling fized plate, length-ways. Captain Bailie purchafed this plate in Holland; and has fince retouched it in an admirable manner.

The *good Samaritan*, a fmall upright plate. The firft impreffions of this plate are thofe where the tail of the horfe is white, and the wall on the fteps unfhaded. In the fecond, the tail of the horfe is darkened; but the wall is ftill white. In the third, the wall is alfo darkened, and the name and date added.

The *ecce homo*, and its companion, the *defcent from the crofs*, two large upright plates. Thefe are the largeft prints engraved by Rembrandt.

The *gold weigher*, or the portrait of *Vtenbogaerd*, a middling fized upright plate. This has been admirably copied by captain Bailie.

The *three trees*, a landfcape, diftinguifhed by this name, becaufe it has three trees in the fore-ground, a fmall plate, length-ways. A fine impreffion of this is very fcarce.

A *landfcape*, with a windmill in the foreground, a fmall plate, length-ways. Some have faid that this is a view of the mill where the father of Rembrandt lived; and therefore it is called Rembrandt's Mill.

The *great Coppenol*, or the portrait of *Coppenol the writing-master of Amsterdam*, a middling sized upright plate. The impressions with the back-ground unfinished are very rare; those with the black back-ground are also scarce.

The *burgomaster John Six*. This celebrated portrait is very rare. It sold at Mr. Grosse's sale, some years since, for five and thirty guineas. It is said there is an impression of this plate, without the name of the burgomaster and of Rembrandt.

S. GESNER.
Flourished, 1730.

This celebrated author is better known to the learned world by his poem on the Death of Abel, and other performances, than as an engraver. However, Basan assures us, that he has etched several landscapes from compositions of his own.

WILLIAM DE GEYN.
Flourished,

The name of an engraver, who, according to professor Christ, marked his plates with the initials of his name in this manner; G. d. G. Fec. But that author has not specified any of his works. Perhaps he was one of the same family with Jaques de Gheyn, of whom I shall speak in the following article.

JAQUES DE GHEYN, the Elder.
Flourished, 1590.

This artist is generally considered as a native of Holland, but Le Comte says, he was born at Antwerp. He is spoken of as a painter; but as a designer and engraver he is most generally known. He was contemporary with John Muller, and, like him, the disciple of Henry Goltzius. He imitated the manner of his master, and worked with the graver only, in a bold, free style, which manifests the great command he had of that instrument. He drew correctly, and frequently with much taste; but all his works want effect, from the lights being scattered, and too equally powerful; neither are the masses of shadow sufficiently broad, or well harmonized. But this was a fault common to all the artists of his time. Jaques de Gheyn engraved a considerable number of plates from different masters, and some from designs of his own; many of them are justly held in high estimation. I shall mention the following only:

The *life and passion of Christ*, on fourteen small upright plates, exclusive of the title, from Carl van Mander.

The *confusion of tongues at the building of Babel*, a large plate, length-ways, from the same.

Daniel in the lion's den, a middling sized plate, length-ways, from Theodore Bernard.

The *annunciation of the Virgin*, a small upright plate, from A. Bloemart.

Christ feeding the five thousand, a middling sized oval plate, length-ways, from the same, dated 1595.

The *crucifixion of Christ*, a middling sized upright plate, from C. Vander Broeck.

The *four Evangelists*, from Henry Goltzius, four small circular plates.

Neptune surrounded by Tritons and naked women, a middling sized circular plate, from Guil. Telrho, published by H. Goltzius, 1587.

The *feast of the gods*, a middling sized plate, length-ways, from C. V. Broeck, dated 1589.

A small *landscape*, length-ways, from Brughel. This is a free spirited etching, dated 1598.

He also engraved several other *landscapes*, and a variety of excellent *portraits*; among which may be reckoned that of *Tycho Brahe*, the philosopher. See the mark composed of an I. a D. and a G. frequently used by this artist, on the plate at the end of the volume.

JAQUES DE GHEYN, the YOUNGER.
Flourished,

He was, I believe, of the same family with the preceding artist; but whether his son or grandson is not certain. I am inclined to think, the latter; because he worked conjointly with Coryn Boel, who does not appear to have engraved prior to the year 1650. I should suppose, that he was a disciple of Tempesta; for he imitated his manner of etching with no small success; I do not know that he executed any plates with the graver only, in which style his predecessor chiefly excelled. We have by him part of the plates for *Le Vie de l'Empereur Charles* V. from A. Tempesta. The rest are executed by Coryn Boel. It consists of a set of middling sized prints, length-ways. He marks his plates J. de Gheyn, jun. fecit.

PIETRO LEONE GHEZZI.
Born, 1674. Died, 1755.

He is also called Chevalier Ghezzi, because he was knighted by Francis the First Duke of Parma. He was a native of Rome, and instructed in the art of painting by his father Giuseppe Ghezzi. He excelled chiefly in history; but he also painted portraits with very great success. His works are spoken of with the highest commendation. He etched some few plates, in a free, neat style, from his own, and from his father's compositions. Among the last, is a fine plate, representing the *Virgin and Child*, half figures, marked *Petrus Leo Ghezzius, del et sculp. Romæ,* 1700.

MARC ANTONIO GHIARINI.
Born, 1652. Died,

This artist was a native of Bologna. He is said to have etched and published some etchings of the *Aqueducts and Fountains at Rome*.

GIOVANNI BATTISTA GHISI, called MANTUANO.
Flourished, 1538.

He was the first of the famous family of the Ghisi, noticed as an artist. They are usually distinguished by the word *Mantuanus*, which was added to their names, because they were natives of Mantua. The present artist is said by some authors to have been the father, and by others, the uncle of those that follow. I own, there is some obscurity, with respect to him, unless he be the same with Joan. Batista Britano of Mantua, from whom George Ghisi engraved several plates. According to Vasari, he was the scholar of Giulio Romano, and was a painter, a sculptor, an architect, and an engraver. But in the last light only, he will come under our consideration. It is impossible to say with certainty, from whom he learned the art of engraving. His manner, I think, bears some resemblance to that adopted by Marc Antonio Raimondi, in his celebrated print of Neptune rebuking the winds, from Raphael, where he has finished the light with small dots, intermingled with the strokes, in a very pleasing manner. Giov. Bat. Ghisi, certainly understood the human figure, and drew it correctly; but in a hard mannered style. The lights being scattered and too equally powerful, in his engravings, give them an unharmonized appearance, and destroy the effect. We have by him,

A large *naval combat*, length-ways, from a composition of his own, dated 1538.

The *Virgin giving the breast to the infant Christ*, a small upright plate, from the same, dated 1539.

David cutting off the head of Goliah, a large plate, length-ways, from Giulio Romano, dated 1540.

A *river god*, a small plate, length-ways, from Luca Pens, dated 1538.

See the mark, composed of several letters, which this artist usually affixed to his prints, upon the plate at the end of the volume.

GIORGIO GHISI, called MANTUANO.
Flourished, 1560.

He was a native of Mantua, and the nephew, or as some say, the son of Giovan. Bat. Ghisi, mentioned in the preceding article; and probably learned the art of engraving from him; for the style, which he adopted, greatly resembles that of his relation, though considerably improved, and rendered much more agreeable in the effect.

It is evident from the works of Giorgio Ghisi, that he studied with much attention the extremities of the human figure. He expressed the knitting of the joints, and the turn of the limbs, with great accuracy. The knees, in particular, he frequently drew in an admirable manner. There is, indeed, a great sameness of style in the drawing and marking of the figures, which appears too generally in his works. It seems as if he studied from one model only; and by that means acquired a certain manner or habit of his own, which he constantly adopted, without considering the style and character of the masters he engraved from, which differed of course prodigiously from one another.

And

And this may be the reason, why he has succeeded less happily from Michael Angelo Buonarota, than from any other painter. The outlines of the figures copied from this master are hard, and sometimes incorrect; and the swellings of the muscles too powerfully expressed upon the light parts, with harsh shadows. By which means the lights are divided, the masses confused, and the roundness of the objects destroyed. These faults are perhaps no where more conspicuous, than in the *last judgment*, engraved from the famous picture by that great master. In this print the extremities of the figures, the feet especially, are all of them treated in the same affected style; and the marking of the abdominal muscles, as well as those of the back, are, in general, very heavy and unpleasing. These defects, however, which are not always predominant, are more than sufficiently overbalanced by the beauties, which we find in the works of this admirable artist: and his productions are deservedly held in the highest estimation by the curious collectors. Indifferent impressions of his prints are by no means rare; but such as are fine, clear, and well preserved, appear but seldom; and yet, without seeing many of these, it is impossible to form an idea adequate to his merit. The following are among his most valuable prints:

The *last judgment*, an upright print arched, ten large plates, from Michael Angelo Buonarota.

The *prophets and sibyls*, six large upright plates, from the pictures by the same master, painted in the chapel at the Vatican.

The *school of Athens*, a large print, length-ways, arched, on two plates, from the picture of Raphael in the Vatican. Florent le Comte says, this is falsely called the school of Athens, for, according to him, it represents St. Paul preaching in the Areopagus at Athens.

The *dispute of the sacrament*, its companion, from the same.

A large *emblematical print*, representing an aged man, standing and looking upon a shipwrecked vessel, whilst a nymph appears on the opposite side as coming towards him. In the back-ground are represented several strange and fantastic appearances. This print is usually called *Raphael's dream*. Basan, upon what authority I know not, says, that Raphael had no hand in it; and that the master by whom it was invented is unknown. I can only say, the words *Raphaelis Urbinatus inventum* are affixed to it; and certainly the style of composition, and the design of the figures, justify the inscription: it is dated 1561.

An *allegorical print*, representing the birth of a prince of the house of Gonzague, a middling sized plate, length-ways, from Giulio Romano, dated 1568.

Cephalus and Procris, a large plate, length-ways, from the same.

The *judgment of Paris*, a large plate, length-ways, from J. Bap. Britano Mantuanus.

The *tombs, with skeletons and emaciated figures*, a large plate, length-ways, from the same. This print is also called the *resurrection of the dry bones*; and is a fine specimen of the artist's great ability: it is dated 1554.

Venus and Adonis, from Theodore Ghisi, a small upright plate.

A *young huntsman carrying a nymph upon his shoulders*, the same, from Luca Pennis.

An *allegorical fubject*, *reprefenting a judge upon his throne with affes ears*, and feveral other figures, a middling fized plate, length-ways, from the fame mafter.

The *adoration of the fhepherds*, a large upright print on two plates, from the elder Bronzin.

The *laft fupper*, a large plate, length-ways, from Lambert Lombard.

The *meeting of the Virgin with Elizabeth*, a large plate, length-ways, from a compofition of his own.

Chrift upon the crofs furrounded by angels, a fmall upright plate, the fame.

See the mark, which he ufually affixed to his prints, upon the plate at the end of the volume.

DIANA GHISI, called MANTUANO.
Flourifhed, 1580.

This ingenious lady was fifter to George Ghifi, and a native of Mantua. She probably learned to draw and engrave from her brother, whofe ftyle fhe clofely imitated, and with great fuccefs. We have feveral excellent prints by her hand; among others,

The *woman taken in adultery*, a large plate, length-ways, from Giulio Romano.

The *Virgin feated in the clouds, with St. Michael ftanding on the demon, and an angel introducing the young Tobit*; in a bold, free ftyle, and varied from her ufual manner, apparently from the fame painter.

The *birth of Adonis*, a middling fized plate, length ways, from the fame.

The *feaft of the gods at the nuptials of Cupid and Pfyche*, a large print, length-ways, on three plates, from the fame.

The *meeting of the Virgin with Elizabeth*, a large upright plate, from G. Vafari. It is marked *Diana Mantouana Romæ incidebat*, 1588.

She frequently marked her plates with the word DIANA only; but never ufed any particular cypher.

ADAM GHISI, called MANTUANO.
Flourifhed, 1560.

Another engraver of the fame family, who was born alfo at Mantua, and by fome faid to have been brother to the two preceding artifts. He certainly worked greatly in the fame ftyle. He drew correctly; and his prints, though not equal to thofe of George Ghifi, poffefs, however, great merit. His chief work was a fet of *figures*, from the Angles, painted by Michael Angelo in the chapel of the Vatican, fmall upright plates. He alfo engraved from Raphael, Giulio Romano, Polydore, &c. See his mark, compofed of an A. and an S. on the plate at the end of the volume.

GIULIO GIAMPICOLI.
Flourifhed,

A modern Italian artift, who flourifhed in the prefent century, and refided

at

at Venice. By him we have several landscapes after Marc Ricci and other masters.

P. GIFFART.
Flourished, 1700.

By this engraver, a native of France, who never reached any superior degree of excellence, we have some few portraits; among the rest, that of *Franc. Daubigny, marquise de Maintenon*. Also a set of *medals*, from the French king's cabinet; and a *book of ornaments*, neatly executed, from the designs of J. Berain.

GEORGE GIFFORD.
Flourished, 1640.

This engraver appears to have been a native of England. By him we have several portraits very poorly executed. He was one of those artists, whose labours were exerted for the booksellers. The following small portraits are by him: *Hugh Latimer bishop of Worcester; Edward Marmion, John Bate*, &c.

M. GILLIG.
Flourished,

A name affixed to a portrait of *Gerard de Vries*, philosopher of Utrecht.

CLAUD GILLOT.
Born, 1673. Died, 1722.

He was born at Langrees in Champagne, and was the disciple of John Baptist Corneille. He appears to have applied himself much more assiduously to the art of design, than to painting. His works manifest great fertility of invention; but little judgment, and less correctness. His drawings are much esteemed. We have a very considerable number of etchings by him, from his own compositions, executed in a very free, spirited style, and well finished. His genius was best suited to comic and satirical subjects. He died, A. D. 1722, aged 49. It is no small addition to the honour of this master, that Watteau, a painter of great eminence in France, was his pupil. Almost all the plates for an edition of the *Fables of La Motte-Houdart*, are engraved by him.

R. GABRIELLO GIOLTO.
Flourished, 1552.

This artist, according to Abbé Marolles, was a native of Ferrara in Italy, and resided at Venice; where, in the year 1552, he engraved on wood the *figures de l'Alemanna*, which were excellently well executed.

LUCA GIORDANO.
Born, 1629. Died, 1705.

This celebrated artift was born at Naples, and firft ftudied under Giufeppe de Ribera, called Spagnoletto; after which, he entered the fchool of Pietro da Cortona; but he completed his ftudies from the works of the greateft mafters, particularly thofe of the Venetian fchool. He excelled in hiftorical painting; yet he painted fome few portraits with great fuccefs. He refided a confiderable time in Spain, where he had the honour of knighthood conferred upon him by the king of Spain. He was a man of great genius, and his pictures are defervedly held in the higheft eftimation. We have by him fome flight mafterly etchings, from his own defigns. The heads, and other extremities of the figures, in thefe compofitions, are very finely expreffed. I fhall mention the following:

The *priefts of Baal flain, when Elijah called for fire from Heaven to confume the facrifice*, a large plate, length-ways.

Chrift difputing with the doctors in the temple, the fame.

The *woman taken in adultery*, the fame.

St. Ann received by the Virgin into Heaven, a fmall upright plate.

GIACOPO MARIA GIOVANNINI.
Flourifhed, 1696.

This artift was born at Bologna, and learned the firft principles of drawing from Giufeppe Rolli. He afterwards ftudied from the works of the greateft mafters, and etched a vaft number of plates, from the drawings he made after them. They are, in general, very neatly executed, and carefully finifhed; but they are flat and feeble, without fufficient depth of fhadow, or breadth of light, to conftitute a powerful or pleafing effect. The outlines of his figures are often incorrect, and the extremities very poorly marked. Among his beft works may be reckoned the following.

A fet of twelve prints, from the pictures of *Correggio*, painted in the Cupola of St. John's church at Parma.

A fet of twenty large folio plates, from the pictures painted by Ludovico Carracci and others, in the cloifter of St. Michael in Bofco at Bologna, publifhed at Venice, 1696.

The *communion of the apoftles*, a large upright plate, from Marc Antonio Francefchini, &c.

MELCHIOR GIRARDINI.
Flourifhed,

An Italian artift, who flourifhed about the middle of the laft century. He is fpoken of as a painter of fome eminence, who for his amufement etched feveral plates from Pietro da Cortona, Guido, and other mafters. He ufually marked his plates, " Mel. Gir. fec."

G L A [337] G L O

HANS, or JOHN HENRY GLASER.
Flourished,
An artist, mentioned by professor Chrift, without the least reference to his works, only that he marked them with a double H. followed by a G. and sometimes the first syllable of the name Glas.

JOHN GLAUBER, called POLIDORE.
Born, 1646. Died, 1726.
This celebrated landscape painter was born at Utrecht in Holland. He was the disciple of Nicholas Berchem, under whose instructions he made a very rapid progress. But, in order to complete his studies, he set out for Italy; and in his route he was detained some time at Lyons by Vander Cabel. He afterwards visited Rome and Venice; and returning to his native country, settled at Amsterdam. He contracted a firm friendship with Gerard Lairesse, who usually ornamented his landscape with figures. Glauber's paintings are held in very great estimation, those especially, which have the figures by Lairesse. He died at Amsterdam, A. D. 1726, aged 80.
His etchings are executed in a slight style, without any strength of shadow to relieve the fore-ground, or produce a powerful effect. The following are by him.
Several *landscapes with cattle*, &c. from Berchem.
A set of *views*, middling sized plates, length-ways, from his own compositions.
A set of *views*, middling sized upright plates, the same.

ALBERT GLOCKENTON.
Flourished, 1510.
An ancient German artist; who if he did not learn the art of engraving from Martin Schoen, certainly not only imitated the manner of that master, but copied a great number of his prints. Indeed, I believe these copies constituted the greater part of the works of Glockenton. He executed his plates with the graver entirely, in a neat, servile style; and by no means improved the drawing, however defective it might be in the originals. Glockenton possessed little or no taste; and, as an artist, seems to have had very few ideas of his own. He marked his plates with the initials A. G. formed in a rude, Gothic character; and sometimes he added the date 1510. I have seen by him the following engravings:
Christ carrying his cross, a large plate, length-ways, from Martin Schoen.
The *wife and foolish Virgins*, ten small upright plates, from the same. I say from Martin Schoen rather than from Israel van Mecheln, who also engraved the same figures (and as some think, prior to those of Martin Schoen) because Glockenton has copied the style of Schoen's engraving, and not that of J. van Mecheln.
The *death of the Virgin*, a middling sized upright plate, copied from M. Schoen.

The *paſſion of Chriſt*, ten ſmall upright plates, from the ſame.

Papillon declares, that he engraved alſo on wood, in a coarſe ſtyle; but his authority is hardly ſufficient to eſtabliſh the fact. I have not ſeen this engraver's mark to any wooden cuts; and Papillon may confound Van Goar with this artiſt,

G. GLOVER.
Flouriſhed, 1637.

This engraver was, I believe, a native of England. His labours were confined to the bookſellers. We have a ſuficient number of portraits, drawn and engraved by him, which, though poſſeſſed of no ſuperior excellence in themſelves, have been thought valuable, as conveying ſome faint reſemblances, at leaſt, of many illuſtrious perſonages, who flouriſhed in his time. And indeed his portraits are by far the beſt part of his works. If he be not one of the beſt, he is certainly far from being one of the worſt of our early Engliſh artiſts. He worked entirely with the graver, in a bold, open ſtyle, without much taſte. His ſhadows are not properly harmonized with the lights, which gives his engravings a dark, heavy appearance. When he departed from the portrait line, and attempted fancy figures, he failed prodigiouſly. Of this ſort are ſome of his *frontiſpieces*, and the *cardinal virtues*, half figures, a ſet of ſmall upright plates, apparently from his own deſigns. I ſhall mention the following portraits only:

John Lilburne, a ſmall upright plate.
Lewis Roberts, a quarto print, dated 1637.
Sir Thomas Urquhart, a ſmall whole-length quarto, ſaid to be very ſcarce.
Sir Edward Dering, from C. Johnſon, in quarto, dated 1640.
John Fox the martyrologiſt, a middling ſized upright plate, &c.

J. G. GLUME.
Flouriſhed, 1760.

According to Baſan, this artiſt is a native of Germany, and a painter. For his amuſement, it ſeems, he etched ſeveral ſmall plates from his own compoſitions, portraits and other ſubjects.

VAN GOAR.
Flouriſhed, 1516.

An ancient engraver on wood, and an artiſt of no ſmall merit. He was apparently a native of Germany. By him we have ſome very ſpirited prints, executed in a bold, maſterly manner. It is to be lamented, that the labours of a man of genius, like Van Goar, ſhould have been confined to the trifling decorations of *books, and ornamental frontiſpieces.* But, at the ſame time, it is no ſmall honour to him, on the other hand, that notwithſtanding this manifeſt diſadvantage, he has proved the goodneſs of his taſte, and the fertility of his genius by ſuch ſubjects, as can have no conſequence in themſelves.

The engravings of this master are easily distinguished, being marked with a V. and a G. joined together cypher-ways, in the manner expressed on the plate at the end of the volume.

J. GODDARD.
Flourished, 1651.

It is remarkable, that this engraver is said to be known by a single print only, which is the portrait of *Martin Billingsley*, a writing master, in an oval border, dated 1651, with a motto of four English verses. I find, however, that he engraved several other plates; though it is true, his labours were confined to the bookfellers. He worked entirely with the graver in a stiff, incorrect style, which has but little merit to recommend it. I shall notice only a single *figure of a woman standing*; a small upright plate, under which is written *Vetura*; another, its companion. A *frontispiece* to a book, a small upright plate, &c.

ANTOINE DES GODETZ.
Flourished, 1682.

A celebrated artist, and native of France, who published a large folio volume of engravings, entitled, *Les Edifices Antiques de Rome*, or the Ancient Edifices of Rome; he etched the *frontispiece* himself; and all the plates are engraved from designs made by him.

R. B. GODFREY.
Flourished, 1760.

This artist was, I believe, a native of England. He engraved a variety of *views, and plates of antiquities*, &c. and in these he chiefly excelled. We have also some portraits by him.

THOMAS GOEL.
Flourished,

A name mentioned by Florent le Comte as an engraver of *English portraits*. The author, according to his usual custom, has neglected to specify any of this artist's works. I own they are perfectly unknown to me. I rather suspect some mistake in the orthography of the name.

J. GOERCE.
Flourished,

This artist was a native of Holland. He worked chiefly, if not entirely, from his own designs. We have some *frontispieces* and other *book-plates*, done by him, he then residing at Amsterdam.

HENRY GOERTING.
Flourished,

This artist, according to M. Heineken, engraved some small prints on tin. I suppose he means *blocked tin*; but he has not specified the subjects.

GOTTFRIED BERNARD GOEZ.
Flourished,

This artist, and his son FRANCIS REGIS GOEZ, are mentioned by M. Heineken as painters and engravers, belonging to the German school. I am not acquainted with their works.

JOHN GOLDAR.
Flourished, 1760.

A modern English engraver, who resided at London, where he engraved a variety of *humorous subjects*, from Collet and other masters. His works are by no means held in any high estimation.

JOHN GOLE.
Flourished, 1690.

This artist was a native of Holland, and resided at Amsterdam. He worked with the graver in strokes, and in mezzotinto. We have a vast number of prints by him; but none of them are very estimable. Those, however, appear to me to be best, which he executed with the graver. His mezzotintos are very indifferently performed. He engraved a variety of *humorous subjects* from Ostade, Brouwer, Teniers, Schalken, and other Dutch masters; but I prefer his portraits. I shall only mention the following from his own designs; as it should seem from the word *fecit*, which he annexed to nis name.

Frederick, king of Poland, a middling sized upright mezzotinto.

Balthazar Becker, the same.

Charles XI. king of Sweden, a middling sized upright plate, engraved in strokes, dated 1685.

The *duchess de la Valliere*, the same.

HUBERT GOLTZIUS.
Born, 1526. Died, 1583.

This artist was born Venloo, in the United Netherlands; but was educated at Wirtemburg, where his parents resided. He learned the first principles of painting from Lambert Lombard; and afterwards travelled through Germany, France, and Italy. As he was a man of science, and a great lover of antiquity, during these journeys he collected a considerable quantity of materials upon that subject, which he afterwards published, in several large volumes, consisting of *inscriptions, medals*, and other *ancient reliques*. Part of the plates for this work he engraved himself. He died at Bruges, A. D. 1583.

1583, aged 57. He was twice married; and the abominable croſsneſs and ill temper of his ſecond wife (ill ſuited as a companion to a ſtudious man) is ſaid to have ſhortened his days. His paintings are ſpoken of with commendation; and are very rare; but as a man of letters, I believe his character is moſt generally known. He is alſo ſaid to have engraved on wood in *chiaroſcuro*, and marked his prints with the initials H. G. but theſe engravings appear to me to belong rather to Henry Goltzius.

HENRY GOLTZIUS.
Born, 1558. Died, 1617.

This extraordinary artiſt was born at Mulbrach, near Venloo. He was the ſon of John Goltzius, a painter on glaſs. From his father he learned the firſt principles of deſign; and afterwards he became the ſcholar of Jaques Leonherd. But it was chiefly owing to the ſtrength of his own natural genius, and the ſtudious application he made to the arts, that he owed the great character he ſo juſtly obtained. He was taught the art of engraving by Theodore Cuerenhert; and ſucceeded very wonderfully in it, notwithſtanding the diſadvantage of a lame hand, which was occaſioned by his falling into the fire whilſt young. He was firſt employed by his maſter, and afterwards he worked for Philip Galle. Domeſtic troubles and ill health occaſioned him to travel. He went through Germany into Italy, and paſſed under a feigned name, that his ſtudies might not be interrupted. He viſited Bologna, Florence, Naples, and Venice, conſtantly applying himſelf to drawing, from the antique ſtatues, and the works of the great maſters. At Rome he reſided the longeſt; and there he produced ſeveral excellent engravings, from Polidoro Raphael, and other eminent painters. On his return to his native country, he eſtabliſhed himſelf at Haerlem, where he engraved many of the drawings, which he had made during his abode in Italy.

He married a widow lady, but it does not appear that he had any children by her. Her ſon, James Maetham, the fruit of her former marriage, was inſtructed by his father-in-law in the art of engraving; and he arrived to a very ſuperior degree of excellence. Goltzius died at Haerlem, A. D. 1617, aged fifty-nine. He is ſaid to have been forty years old before he began to paint; yet his pictures are ſpoken of with the greateſt commendation; but as he did not produce any great number of them, they are, of courſe, but rarely to be met with.

This celebrated artiſt poſſeſſed great anatomical knowledge. He was perfect maſter of the human figure, and drew the extremities admirably. But endeavouring, with Spranger and others, to correct the ſtiff taſteleſs manner of the little maſters, his countrymen, he frequently run into the other extreme, and twiſted his figures into ſuch affected poſitions, that they appear diſpleaſing to the eye. And that pure drawing, of which he was ſo much maſter, is loſt in a bombaſtical ſtyle, if I may be allowed the expreſſion, into which he fell, by attempting to imitate that grand guſto, ſo conſpicuous in the works of Michael Angelo Buonarota.

His compoſitions were often wild and extravagant; and they appear to be rather the effect of ſtudy, than of nature, which requires more ſimplicity and truth. They manifeſt however his great knowledge in the art of deſign;

sign; and prove him to have been a man of superior abilities. But as an engraver, he deserves the highest commendation. No man ever surpassed, and few have equalled him, in the command of the graver, and freedom of execution. He copied the style of Albert Durer, Lucas of Leyden, and other old masters, with astonishing exactness. Sometimes his engravings are neat in the extreme; at other times they are performed in a bold, open manner, without the least restraint. And it is hard to say, in which of the two the mechanical part of the engraving is most excellent; the latter, without doubt, is superior in taste and freedom, exclusively. Small portraits he drew and engraved in a very masterly manner; in these he united neatness, taste, and excellent drawing. He also engraved several of his own designs on wood, in that manner which is distinguished by the appellation of *chiaro-scuro*. It is performed with three blocks; one for the outline, which he cut in a free, spirited manner; the second for the darker shadows; and the third for the lighter tint. In this species of engraving he has succeeded very happily; and the prints, which he has produced, are truly excellent.

I shall mention the following engravings only by this great artist:

Some of the plates for the *life of Christ*, published by Philip Galle. These are middling sized plates, length-ways, from A. Blockland.

Penitence and Impiety, a large upright emblematical print, from a design of his own.

Tarquin and Lucretia, a small plate, length-ways, the same.

These are in the stiff style, which distinguished the German and Flemish engravers of this æra.

The *life of Christ*, on twelve small upright plates, from designs of his own. Great care must be taken not to purchase a set of stiff copies, which were afterwards made. In these plates Goltzius has professedly imitated the style of Lucas Van Leyden.

Six large upright plates, known by the name of his *master-pieces*. These, it is said, he engraved to convince the public, that he was perfectly capable of imitating the styles of Albert Durer, Lucas Van Leyden, and other masters, whose works were then held in higher estimation than his own. For he had adopted a new manner, which he justly thought superior; for which reason he pursued it; and not, as had been ignorantly imagined, because he could not imitate their works. It is reported, that with one of them, the *circumcision*, which he smoked, to give it the more plausible air of antiquity, he actually deceived some of the most capital connoisseurs of the day; by one of whom it was bought for an original engraving of Albert Durer. The subjects of these plates are as follow:

The *annunciation of the Virgin*.
The *meeting of the Virgin with Elizabeth*, called the *Visitation*.
The *nativity of Christ*.
The *circumcision of Christ*.
The *adoration of the wise men*.
The *holy family*.

A *dead Christ upon the lap of the Virgin*, a small upright print, beautifully finished in the style of Albert Durer.

A *dead Christ in the tomb, with the four Evangelists standing by him*, a middling

middling fized plate, length-ways, from A. Blockland, dated 1583: a fingular print, but very finely drawn.

St. Jerom feated, a middling fized upright plate, from J. Palma, dated 1596. I think this is one of the fineft prints by this great mafter. The drawing is admirable, and the engraving is executed with the utmoft freedom.

Hercules, a fingle figure ftanding in the front, holding his club; in the back ground are reprefented his labours: a large upright plate, from his own defign. This figure is greatly overcharged with markings; the parts are too much divided; and from want of maffes, it has no effect.

The *judgment of Midas*, a large plate, length-ways, the fame.

The *Nine Mufes*, fmall upright plates, the fame.

The *Five Senfes*, the fame.

The *affembly of the Gods*, a large print, length-ways, on three plates, from Spranger.

The *Venetian Ball*, a large plate, length-ways, from Theodore Bernard.

The antique ftatues of the *Apollo Belvidere*, the *Hercules Farnefe*, and the *Hercules Commodus*, middling fized, upright plates.

A fet of fifty-two middling fized plates, length-ways, for *Ovid's Metamorphofes*, from his own defigns. Alfo the *gods and goddeffes of antiquity, and the heroes of antient Rome*.

The *boy and dog*, a middling fized upright plate, from a defign of his own, an admirable print. This is, with great reafon, fuppofed to be a portrait; but that it was intended for Goltzius himfelf, when young, is by no means probable.

His own portrait, a large upright plate.

Henry IV. of France, a middling fized upright plate.

Cuerenbert the engraver, a large upright plate.

Joan Zurenus, a very fmall upright plate.

Joan Bollius, the fame.

The *Necromancer*, a middling fized upright oval print, in *chiaro-fcuro*.

Night in her chariot, the fame.

Pomona and other goddeffes, the fame.

Jupiter, Neptune, and other gods, the fame.

See the mark, compofed of an H. and a G. joined together, which this mafter frequently ufed, when he did not fign his name at length.

JULIUS GOLTZIUS.

Flourifhed, 1580.

This artift was probably of the fame family with Henry Goltzius, mentioned in the preceding article, and apparently inftructed in the fchool of the Galles, whofe ftyle of engraving he feems chiefly to have imitated. His figures are by no means correctly drawn, or executed with the leaft tafte. He engraved upon copper only.

A great part, if not all, of the figures in a book, entitled, *Habitus Variorum Orbis Gentium*, by Joan Jacq. Boiffard, a fmall folio, 1581.

The *good and bad Shepherd*, a fet of middling fized prints, lengthways, from Martin de Vos.

Christ appearing to Mary Magdalen, a middling sized upright plate, from Fred. Sucaris.

JAQUES and CONRAD GOLTZIUS are both of them mentioned by Florent le Comte, as engravers. He informs us, that they worked after the defigns of Henry Goltzius; but he has not fpecified the fubjects, which are executed by them.

ABRAHAM GOOSE.
Flourifhed, 1627.

One of the map engravers, employed by the induftrious John Speed, for his folio edition of maps, publifhed 1627. Thefe performances require no comment. *Europe, Afia, Africa, America, Hungary, Perfia,* &c. are by him.

HENRY GOUDT.
Flourifhed, 1610.

This extraordinary artift was born of a noble family at Utrecht. He is ufually called Count Goudt, and was a knight of the Palatinate. Being paffionately fond of the arts, particularly painting and engraving, and defirous of engaging in them, he applied himfelf diligently to drawing, and made a great proficiency therein. He went to Rome, to examine the works of the great mafters in that city; and there contracted an intimacy with Adam Elfheimer, a painter of confiderable reputation; and endeavoured to imitate his ftyle. He purchafed feveral pictures of that artift, feven of which he alfo engraved.

On his return to his native country, a young woman who was in love with him, and defirous of fixing his affections upon her, gave him in his drink a love philtre; which however terminated in a very melancholy manner, by depriving him totally of his fenfes; and in the dreadful ftate of idiotifm, he dragged on a miferable life. It is remarkable, that though loft to every other fubject, when painting was fpoken of, he would difcourfe upon it in a very rational manner.

He worked with the graver only, in a very neat ftyle, and produced a moft powerful effect, not by ftrengthening the ftrokes, according to the ufual method, but by croffing them with additional ftrokes, equally neat, and that five or fix times, one over another, in the deep fhadows. Confidering the precifion with which he executed his engravings, the freedom of handling the graver, which may be difcovered in them, is very aftonifhing. The weeds, and other parts of the fore ground, in that admirable print of the *Ceres,* are very finely expreffed. The heads of the figures are correctly drawn, and the other extremities are managed in a judicious manner. The following are the feven prints by him, from Elfheimer, mentioned above:

Ceres drinking from a pitcher. An old woman appears holding a candle at the door of the cottage, and a boy naked, ftanding by her, is laughing, and pointing at the goddefs; for which contempt he was metamorphofed by her into a frog, a middling fized upright print. The powerful and ftriking effect of this engraving cannot be properly defcribed. The very deep fhadows are

perhaps

perhaps rather too fudden upon the ftrong lights, in fome few inftances; but in the fine impreffions this is by no means fo confpicuous, as in thofe after the plate had been retouched. This print was well copied by Hollar; who, with the point only, has given us all the effect, though not the neatnefs, of the original. It is diftinguifhed alfo by the name of the *forcery*.

The *flight into Egypt*, a large landfcape, length-ways: a *night fcene*, in which the moon and ftars are introduced with great fuccefs.

The *angel with Tobit, who is drawing a fifh by his fide*, a fmall plate, length-ways, The back-ground is a landfcape; the weeds in the fore-ground, and the branches of the trees in front, as well as the foliage and weeds hanging from them, are beautifully expreffed. He fails moft in thofe parts, where the graver alone is by no means adequate to the undertaking; namely, the diftant woods, and affemblage of trees, which gradate one from another, and require that freedom of determination, which the point only can give: when executed with the graver, they always appear flat and heavy.

The *angel with Tobit, croffing a ftream of water*. Tobit holds the fifh under his arm. The back-ground is a *landfcape*. This is a fmall print, length-ways, confiderably lefs than the preceding. Hollar copied this print with much fuccefs.

Baucis and Philemon entertaining Jupiter and Mercury, a fmall plate nearly fquare.

A landfcape, called the *Aurora, reprefenting the dawn of day*, a fmall print, length-ways. The effect is very beautiful.

The *beheading of St. John in prifon*, a very fmall upright oval print, which is by far the fcarceft.

JOSEPH GOUPY.
Flourifhed, 1760.

This painter refided in London, where he died fome few years fince. He was a man of genius, and etched feveral very fpirited plates, fome few of them from compofitions of his own. He adopted the ftyle of Salvator Rofa, and particularly excelled in landfcapes, which he executed with great tafte, and in a very mafterly manner. The following are by him:

Mutius Scævola burning his hand, in the prefence of Porfenna, a middling fized plate, length-ways.

Diana hunting with her nymphs, the fame, from Rubens.

Zeuxis painting a woman who is nearly naked, the fame, from Solimene.

A fet of eight *landfcapes*, from Salvator Rofa.

Variety of other fubjects, from different mafters.

GOURAND. See GOYRAND.

GOURMONT.
Flourifhed,

The name of an obfcure French engraver, affixed to the portrait of *Charles duke*

duke of Bourbon, &c. His works were chiefly, I believe, confined to the decorations of books.

GOUSBLOOM.
Flourished,

An obscure engraver of no great merit, whose name is affixed to the portrait of *Leonard Vander Goes*, &c.

G. VANDER GOUWEN.
Flourished, 1716.

An engraver of no great note, who was apparently a native of Holland, and resided at Amsterdam. By him we have some bad prints for the Bible, published at that city, A. D. 1720, from the designs of Picart and others. He also engraved several *ornamental frontispieces*, with figures, and other works of the same trifling kind, for the booksellers. The name of GOUWT is also affixed to one or two plates, in the same work, which is meant perhaps for *Gouwen*, but mis-spelt. The exact similitude, between the style of engraving on both those plates, seems greatly to favour this conjecture.

JOHN JOSEPH VAN GOYEN.
Born, 1596. Died, 1656.

This excellent artist was a native of Leyden. He was the disciple of William Gerretz, and afterwards studied under Esaius Vander Velde. He excelled in painting landscapes, cattle, and sea-pieces; and his pictures are held in the highest estimation. The works of this great master are too well known, to render any comment upon them necessary in this place. He resided chiefly at the Hague, where he died, A. D. 1656, aged 60. He etched some few spirited *landscapes* from his own compositions.

CLAUDE GOYRAND.
Flourished,

This artist was a native of France; but he resided at Rome, where he engraved a small *head with an ornamental border*, to which he signs his name, "Cl. Goyrand Gall. sculpsit Romæ." This is all graved in a neat, tasteless style. He does not appear by any means, to have handled the graver with facility; but we have a variety of neat, spirited etchings by him, which consist of landscapes, views of ruins, gardens, and a variety of other subjects. He engraved from Stella, Quesnel, Mauparche, Callot, &c.

J. GOZANDURUS.
Flourished,

A name, mentioned by Florent le Comte as an engraver of *ornaments and grotesque figures*. None of his works are specified; neither am I acquainted with them.

FRANCESCO

FRANCESCO DE GRADO.
Flourished, 1690.

An Italian artist, who, according to his own signature, was a native of Naples, where he appears to have chiefly resided. He was a very indifferent engraver, and worked, I believe, entirely for the booksellers; and executed his plates with the graver only, in a stiff, tasteless style. By him we have the portraits of illustrious personages, published at Naples, A. D. 1693. He also did part of the plates for *Bellori's Lives of the Painters, Sculptors*, &c.

JOHN ANDRE GRAF.
Flourished, 1576.

A German painter, who is also said to have engraved; but this point, in my opinion, is by no means clearly proved. The prints marked with an A. and a G. joined together, in the manner expressed on the plate at the end of the volume, are attributed to him.

CAMILLIO GRAFFICO.
Flourished, 1588.

This artist was a native of Friuli in Italy. He engraved several devotional subjects; and worked entirely with the graver, in a style greatly resembling that of Cornelius Cort; but his engravings are by no means equally well executed, or so correctly drawn. We have by him, a *holy family*, wherein the Virgin is represented giving the breast to the infant Christ, a large upright plate, from Bernardinus Passarii. He was an ingenious man, and invented certain fountains of brass, which would cast water upwards into the air; and brought them to very great perfection. It is said, they would continue playing four and twenty hours, being supplied from the midst, by a very curious contrivance. They were bought by several of the nobility to adorn their palaces; and Graffico amassed a considerable sum of money by means of this invention.

GRAFTON,
Flourished,

An English engraver, says Basan, by whom we have several mezzotinto prints. He has not, however, specified any of them; nor can I meet with any account of such an engraver. I am inclined to think, Balan has made some mistake in the name.

CONRAD GRAHL.
Flourished, 1620.

This artist was a native of Leipsic. According to professor Christ, the mark composed of a C. and a G. as expressed upon the plate at the end of the volume, is attributed to him.

LE GRAND.
Flourished, 1750.

An engraver of no great note. His best prints are *vignettes*, and *small subjects*, which he engraved from the designs of Gravelot, Eisen, and other masters. Several of the plates for the new edition of *Ovid's Metamorphoses*, lately published at Paris, are by him. He also engraved some large plates of *ruins*, &c. sufficiently neat, but without any great taste.

JACQUES GRANDHOMME, or GRANTHOMME.
Flourished, 1600.

This artist was a native of Heidelberg. According to professor Christ, he was pupil to Theodore de Bry; which seems very probable; for his style of engraving greatly resembles that of De Bry. His best works are in the portrait line. His plates are executed with the graver only; they are sufficiently neat; but stiff and laboured; and do not discover any marks of a superior genius; though some of them are by no means entirely destitute of merit.

He generally used a cypher, composed of an I. and a G. joined together, or else an I. with a G. an H. and a T. interwoven with each other. See both these marks, expressed upon the plate at the end of the volume. Professor Christ has, by a strange mistake, confounded Grandhomme, with John Van Vliet, the disciple of Rembrandt.

I shall notice the following prints by this master:

The portraits of the *theological doctors and reformers of the church*, or the *heresiarch*, as they are styled, from a painter whose initials are J. M. F.

The *infant dauphin of France strangling a serpent*, a small whole-length, dated 1601.

Henry Smetius, a small upright oval, to which he adds the word *fecit*, which seems to imply, that it was also drawn by him.

The *death of Adonis*, a very small upright plate, apparently from his own design.

Venus and Adonis, its companion, the same.

The *murder of the innocents*, a small upright print.

The *apostles*, twelve small upright plates, from his own designs.

The *rape of Helen*, a small plate, length-ways, copied from the print which Marc Antonio engraved after Raphael, &c.

D. DES GRANGES.
Flourished, 1634.

An engraver of no note, who apparently resided in London. His name is affixed to some very indifferent *frontispieces*, *books* and *plates*; among others, the ornamental title for the second edition of a small octavo publication, entitled, *Bethel, or a Form for Families*, dated 1634, is by him.

HENRY GRAVELOT.
Born,   Died, 1773.

This ingenius artift was a native of France; but he refided much in London, about the year 1720. He was a man poffeffed of great fertility of invention, and compofed with much judgment, fmall fubjects for vignettes, and other book ornaments. He drew alfo admirably *ancient buildings, tombs, and profpects*; and he was employed in all thefe branches by the artifts in London. He had been, it feems, in Canada, as fecretary to the governor of that province. But the climate difagreeing with him, he returned to Paris, from whence he came into England, invited by Claude du Bofc. He etched a great variety of plates for books; among others, feveral for Sir Thomas Hanmer's edition of *Shakefpere*, in quarto; fome of which he defigned himfelf; but the greater part of them were compofed by Hayman. Alfo the cuts to *Theobald's Shakefpere*, in octavo, from his own defigns. The large print of *Kirkftall Abbey*, is a fine fpecimen of his abilities, as an engraver. He returned to Paris, where he died, A. D. 1773, aged 74.

GRAY.
Flourifhed,

He was apparently a native of England, and certainly refided at London, where he engraved a fet of *views*, middling fized plates, length-ways, in a flight, coarfe ftyle, without any tafte. The work bears this title: *Thirty different Draughts of Guinea*, by William Smith, furveyor to the Royal African Company of England, fold by C. Clark, engraver and printfeller, Gray's-Inn. The frontifpiece is by far the beft print. It reprefents an *elephant*; and is very freely etched, in a ftyle greatly refembling that of Hollar; but it is evidently not executed by Gray.

PETER GREBBER.
Flourifhed, 1600.

He learned the firft principles of painting from his father, Francis Peter Grebber; after which he became the difciple of Henry Goltzius. He excelled in painting hiftory and portraits; and his tafte is highly commended. For his amufement, he engraved, our *Saviour and the woman of Samaria*, a fmall upright plate, from a compofition of his own.

JEROM GREFF.
Flourifhed,

This artift was born at Franckfort; and, according to fome authors, he learned the art of painting and engraving from Albert Durer. The prints we have by him are wooden cuts, copied from Albert Durer, with furprifing exactnefs. Hence perhaps arofe the idea of his being the pupil of that mafter. We have by him,

The *Apocalypfe of St. John*, in folio, from Albert Durer, the fame fize as the originals, and admirably well executed. See his monogram, composed of an I. an M. and an F. on the plate at the end of the volume.

J. GREEN.
Flourished, 1758.

This young artist was a native of Owen in Shropshire. He was pupil to Basire, the map engraver. He succeeded best in landscapes; and apparently, had he been under a more able tutor, might have made a considerable progress in the arts. He was employed by the University of Oxford, to engrave their Almanacks. We have also by him a variety of *views*, and the plates for *Borlase's Antiquities of Cornwall*, together with some few *portraits*.

CARLO GREGORI.
Flourished, 1748.

A modern Italian engraver. Part of the plates in the *Museo Fiorentino* are by him, and several of those in the collection from the cabinet of the marquis Gerini; also the *antique statues* in the gallery at Florence, with a great number of portraits.

CARLO BARTOLOMEO GREGORI, and FERDINANDO GREGORI were, I believe, the sons of Carlo Gregori, and assisted him in the above-mentioned works.

M. GREISCHER, or GRYSCHER.
Flourished,

This engraver was a native of Germany. By him we have several prints from various masters; among others, the *Virgin seated in a landscape, holding the infant Christ*, and St. John is represented standing by her, from Frederic Baroccio.

JOSEPH GREUT.
Flourished,

This artist apparently flourished about the end of the last century, and seems chiefly to have been confined to portraits, which he executed in a neat style, entirely with the graver. They are, by no means, devoid of merit. I shall mention only the portrait of *Hieronymus Bartholomaeus*, a small upright plate.

MATTHEW GREUTER.
Flourished, 1585.

Strange confusion has been made, respecting the time of this artist's birth. In the Abecedario, it is said to have been in the year 1566. But Basan and other authors give us the same year for the birth of his son. I am inclined to agree with the latter account; for the engravings of Matthew Greuter are, several of them, dated as early as 1582; at which time he could be only 16 years old, And though it is not impossible, but that

he

he might engrave at that early age, yet it is not likely, that he should have worked in such perfection, or have performed so many plates, as we find by him about that time. The generality of authors are however agreed, that he was a native of Germany; though in the Abecedario, he is said to have been born at Strasburgh, in Alsace. He is supposed to have learned the art of engraving in his own country; after which he went to Italy for improvement, where he executed a variety of plates. The time of his death is uncertain, unless we agree with the Abecedario; in which it is said to have been, A. D. 1638, at the age of 72. It is highly probable, that he was living between the years 1620 and 1630; for he engraved, according to Le Comte, a *cavalcade*, in conjunction with Lucas Vorsterman, whose principal works were executed during that period.

With respect to Matthew Greuter, he was a man of genius; and, though he never rose to any very high degree of eminence, many of his engravings possess great merit. His drawing is, by no means, correct, especially with respect to the extremities of his figures, which are in general heavy, and not well marked. He sometimes executed his plates with the graver only, in a very neat style; and sometimes he etched, and finished them with the graver, in a slighter manner; when he did not sign his name at length, he substituted the initials thus: M. G. F. the F. as usual standing for *fecit*; and generally he added the date.

Venus naked standing on a globe, with a variety of *figures, emblematical of virtue and vice*, very neatly finished, and entirely with the graver, marked. *M. Greuter inv. et fecit*, 1587, a middling sized plate, length-ways.

Mary Magdalen seated in a landscape, holding a book, leaning her right hand upon a skull. M. G. F. 1584, from S. Gaetano.

A set of small plates of *insects*, etched in a style, bearing some resemblance to that of Gaywood.

The *magnificent cavalcade of the emperor Charles V.* engraved by him, conjointly with Lucas Vorsterman, a large print, length-ways, on several plates.

The *burning of Troy*, a middling sized plate, length-ways, mentioned by Basan, with the painter's name.

He also engraved several portraits; among them, is that of *pope Sixtus V.* with his coinage, as an ornamental border. Also *Innocent X.* the same; others with their *monuments*, and small *ornamental figures*, all middling sized upright plates.

JOHN FREDERIC GREUTER,
Flourished, 1620.

Basan, as before observed, has given the year assigned by the author of the Abecedario for the birth of M. Greuter the father, to the son; who, says he, was born at Franckfort, A. D. 1566. Yet this assertion is also attended with much difficulty. I have seen engravings by J. F. Greuter, as late as 1644; at which time he must have been 78 years of age. Yet it is generally allowed, that he died at the age of 72: I rather suspect, there was another artist of the same family, whose name was Frederic; for I have remarked, that the prints, with the latter dates, though something resembling those which precede them, are not so well executed, and have Frederic Greuter only, without

the

the firſt baptiſmal name, John. But this I muſt leave to better judgment. John Frederic Greuter certainly reſided at Rome, where he engraved a variety of plates. He worked with the graver only, in a neat, clear ſtyle; but without much taſte. His drawing is often incorrect, and the extremities of his figures are very poorly expreſſed.

I ſhall mention the following only by this artiſt:

The *Virgin and Child, with St. Francis kneeling*, a middling ſized upright plate, arched at the top, from a deſign of his own, dated 1623.

An *emblematical ſubject*, repreſenting the growth of Chriſtianity, a large plate, length-ways, from Romanelli.

The *death of St. Cecilia*, a ſmall plate, nearly ſquare, from Dominichino.

The *forge of Vulcan*, a large plate, length-ways, from Lanfranchi.

A *battle*, from Anthony Tempeſta, a large plate, length-ways.

The portrait of a *cardinal*, who is ſeated, with three boys, portraits alſo; a ſmall upright plate.

He alſo engraved ſeveral other *portraits*, and a variety of other ſubjects, from different maſters, as, Guido, Vouet, Stella, Andrea d'Ancone, &c.

See the mark attributed to him, on the plate at the end of the volume.

K. GREUTER is ſubſcribed to a print, repreſenting *Hercules in the garden of the Heſperides*, from Pietro da Cortona. I ſuſpect the K. was ſubſtituted by miſtake for the F. I do not by any means believe it to be the work of another artiſt, with the ſame family name.

JOSEPH GREUTER is mentioned by Florent le Comte as an engraver; but I am not acquainted with his works.

SIMON GRIBELIN.
Born, 1661. Died, 1733.

This artiſt was born at Paris, where he learned the art of engraving. Coming into England, he worked for the bookſellers, and was near twenty years, before any particular notice was taken of his engraving. The *tent of Darius*, which he copied from Girard Edelinck's print after Le Brun, was the firſt plate, that raiſed his reputation to the public view. He afterwards engraved the *cartoons*, and engaged in other conſiderable undertakings. But as he was one of thoſe painful, plodding artiſts, who are obliged to ſubſtitute laborious formality, and mechanical preciſion, in the place of taſte, much pleaſure cannot be expected, from the examination of his works, by the connoiſſeur, or profit by the artiſt. They are executed entirely with the graver, in a cold, neat ſtyle. His drawing is incorrect; the heads of his figures want expreſſion, in general; and the other extremities are by no means well marked.

He caught cold, by going to ſee the king in the houſe of lords, and died in conſequence of it, three days after, aged 72. He left a ſon and a daughter. The following engravings are by him:

The *cartoons*, ſeven ſmall plates, length-ways, from the pictures of Raphael, then at Hampton court, but now at the Queen's palace. Theſe, I think,

think, are his best prints. Upon the title is engraved the portrait of *queen Anne*, and the representation of the room in which the pictures hung.

Six *historical plates*, from the pictures in the royal collection at Kensington, painted by Tintoret and other masters.

The *ceiling at Whitehall*, after Rubens.

He also engraved several portraits, and a great variety of other subjects, from different masters.

GRIBELIN.
Flourished, 1733.

He was son to Simon Gribelin, mentioned in the preceding article. He was also an engraver, and followed his father's style. He went to Turkey, in the retinue of the earl of Kildare, to draw *views of the country*; but he returned in two years.

JOHN GRIFFIER.
Born, 1645. Died, 1718.

This celebrated painter of landscapes, cattle, and ruins, was born at Amsterdam, and became the disciple of Roland Roghman. He resided a considerable time in England, where he met with great encouragement from the duke of Beaufort, and other noblemen. His pictures are held in the highest estimation. By him we have several plates of birds and other animals, etched, in a very superior style, from Barlow. They manifest great freedom of the point, and an excellent taste. The animals are finely drawn, with much spirit; and the effect is very clear and pleasing.

JACQUES GRIGNON.
Flourished,

Florent le Comte calls him John Grignon. He was a native of France, and flourished towards the end of the last century. His best works, I think, are his portraits, which he executed entirely with the graver; and some of them do him great credit. That of *Francis Maria Rhima, an ecclesiastic*, a small upright oval plate, is executed in a very clear, good style. His historical plates, and subjects with figures, are by no means equally meritorious. They are dark and heavy, without effect, and, in general, very incorrectly drawn. He engraved some few of the plates for a work entitled *Les Tableaux de la Penitence*, in small folio size, from the designs of Chauveau.

GIOVANNA FRANCESCO GRIMALDI, called BOLOGNESE.
Born, 1606. Died, 1680.

This celebrated artist was born at Bologna, and became the disciple of Annibale Carracci; from whose school he went to Rome, where he was encouraged by the patronage of Pope Innocent X. He painted history with great success; but he more particularly excelled in landscapes. He also etched a considerable

considerable number of the latter, from his own defigns. They are finely executed with great freedom, tafte and fpirit. The compofitions are grand, and the effect of them is produced in a very mafterly manner.

ALESSANDRO GRIMALDI.
Flourifhed, 1670.

He was the fon and difciple of Giovanna Francefco Grimaldi, mentioned in the foregoing article. He imitated the ftyle of his father; but never equalled him in merit: yet his works are held in no fmall degree of eftimation. By him we have fome few engravings; and among them, the *brazen ferpent*, from a compofition of his own, which, though flight, is a fpirited, free etching, in the ftyle of a painter.

JOHN GROENSVELT, or GROENVELT.
Flourifhed,

He etched, fays Bafan, feveral *views and landfcapes* after Berghem, Van Gogen, and other mafters. The name J. GROENVELT I have feen affixed to feveral portraits; among others, to that of an *anonymous lady*, from Vandyck, exceedingly neatly engraved; but in a ftiff, taftelefs ftyle. The face is almoft entirely finifhed with fmall dots.

GERARD GRONINGUS.
Flourifhed,

By this artift I have feen a fet of ten middling fized emblematical plates, length-ways, reprefenting the *life of man from ten to a hundred years*. They are etched in a flight, dark manner. The drawing of the figures is incorrect, and the outlines are hard and heavy; yet, notwithftanding all thefe faults, there is fomething mafterly in their appearance; and fome of the compofitions are by no means devoid of merit. They are marked " Ger. Gronigius invent. " faciebat." Each plate has a Latin and French defcription in verfe underneath it.

MADEMOISELLE GROSNIER.
Flourifhed, 1760.

This ingenious lady, a native of France, applied herfelf to the arts; and by her, according to Bafan, we have feveral plates, after different mafters.

HANS, or JOHN BALDUNUS, or BAUDOIN GRUN.
Flourifhed, 1511.

To this doubtful mafter profeffor Chrift attributes thofe engravings, marked with an H. a C. and a B. joined together cypher-ways, which are ufually put upon a fmall tablet with the date below, and a fmall branch of a tree at the top; but he feems to build his conjectures upon a very flender foundation.

tion. Grun in German, is equivalent to the word Green in English; he therefore supposes, it may have been the design of the engraver to express his name by the small branch. I have not a doubt of his being the same artist with Hans or John Baldung, whose cypher at least was the same, and to which name the reader is referred.

MATTHEW GRUNWALD.
Born, Died, 1510.

Professor Christ ascribes to this artist, who, he informs us, was a native of Aschafenbourgh, some of those prints, which are marked with a cypher, composed of an M. and a G. in the manner represented on the plate at the end of the volume. The works of this master are not specified; but he is said to have imitated Albert Durer.

HANS, or JOHN GRUNWALD.
Flourished,

Probably of the same family with the preceding artist. His cypher is composed of an H. and a G. joined together several ways, but especially with the G. upon the cross bar of the H. in the manner represented on the plate at the end of the volume. By him we have the *Virgin and Child*, a small upright print, incorrectly copied from Albert Durer. A *woman and a satyr, with another woman striking at her, and a man warding off the blow*, a middling sized upright plate, copied the reverse way from Albert Durer; but not correctly.

We have also some wooden cuts by this artist; among others, a small *landscape*, length-ways, with a rock, and a view of the sea.

DERICK, or THEODORE GRYP.
Flourished, 1620.

By this engraver, a native, I presume, of Holland, we have the *map of Tartary*, for John Speed's Geography. The artist has introduced some small figures, boldly engraved, in a style much resembling that of Claude du Bosc: but they are very incorrectly drawn, and otherwise possess but little merit.

GIACOMO GUAVANA.
Flourished, 1720.

This artist was a painter, born at Venice, where he resided. According to Basan, he etched several large *fabulous subjects*, from compositions of his own; but the particular stories are not specified.

MICHAEL VANDER GUCHT.
Born, 1660. Died, 1725.

This artist was a native of Antwerp, and a scholar of one of the Bouttats.

It is uncertain at what time he came into England. Here, however, he met with encouragement, and refided in London. He was greatly afflicted with the gout, which diforder put an end to his life, October 16, 1725. He died at his houfe in Bloomfbury, and was buried at St. Giles's. His chief employment was to engrave anatomical figures; but we have many other fubjects by him; as, a very large print, length-ways, of the *royal navy*, from Bafton. He alfo engraved feveral portraits; among others, that of *Mr. Savage*. The ingenious and induftrious Mr. Virtue was a difciple of this artift. He left two fons, Gerard and John.

JOHN VANDER GUCHT.
Born, 1697. Died,

He was one of the fons of the above-mentioned mafter; and learned the art of engraving from his father; but he received inftructions in drawing from Lewis Cheron, and completed his ftudies at the academy, where he defigned from nature. He was employed by Chefeld to draw and engrave the plates for his *Octology*, a work which does much honour to the artift. He is faid to have had a great fhare in the engraving of the *Cupola of St. Paul's*. There are fix academy figures by him, from the drawings of Cheron, which fhew, that he had more knowledge in the art of defign than power of execution with his graver. A prodigious number of book plates were engraved both by this artift and by his father, but they are foreign from my purpofe.

GERARD VANDER GUCHT, the other fon of Michael Vander Gucht, alfo engraved for the bookfellers; but he did no work of any material confequence.

JAQUES GUCKEISEN.
Flourifhed, 1599.

This engraver refided at Cologne, about the conclufion of the fixteenth century, where he engraved feveral plates; but the fubjects are not fpecified. His mark, compofed of an I. and a G. may be feen upon the plate of monograms, at the end of the volume.

GUELORD.
Flourifhed,

A native of France, who flourifhed at the commencement of the prefent century. He engraved, according to Bafan, feveral prints from Oudry, P. Van Bloemen, &c.

N. GUERARD.
Flourifhed, 1700.

He was a native of France, and an artift of no great note. We have by him fome of the plates for a work of *plans and views*, entitled *Les Edifices Antiques de Rome*, publifhed at Paris, by Antoine Defgodetz, 1682, in folio; the frontifpiece to a *book of ornaments*, publifhed by Peter Bourdon, at Paris, 1703; and a fmall plate, length-ways, reprefenting *foldiers marching*, from

his

his own defign. In this, as well as in feveral of his other works, he has attempted to imitate the ftyle of James Callot; but he falls far fhort of that inimitable mafter.

GUERCINO. See BARBIERI.

RENE GUERNIER.
Flourifhed,

The name of an engraver, cited by Florent le Comte, who informs us, that he excelled in *ornaments and grotefque figures*. I am not acquainted with his works.

LEWIS DU GUERNIER,
Born, 1677. Died, 1716.

He was a native of France, and the difciple of Chatillon at Paris. He came into England A. D. 1708; and it is faid, that he improved confiderably in his drawing by frequenting the Academy, which at that time was fupported by the private contributions of the artifts only. He was chofen director of it; in which poft he continued till his death, which was occafioned by the fmall pox, in September 1716, he being only 39 years of age. Guernier was a man of fome genius; but whether through indolence, or want of time, he neglected the improvement of the mechanical part of his engraving, I cannot tell; certain it is, that he never acquired any tolerable maftery of the point or the graver. His works are coarfe and heavy; and that merit, which is really to be found in them, is hid, as it were, by the rough garb, with which they are cloathed. His labours were chiefly confined to the bookfellers; and it is poffible they might procure him much more profit, than credit. He was concerned in the engraving of the *battles of the duke of Marlborough*, conjointly with Du Bofc. He alfo engraved a middling fized print, length-ways, reprefenting *Lot and his two daughters*, from Michael Angelo Caravagio, at the defire of lord Hallifax; but the engraving does him no great honour.

WILLIAM GUEROULT.
Flourifhed, 1564.

I have feen an octavo volume, containing a fet of fmall neat wood cuts, entitled, *Figures de la Bible*, or Subjects from the Bible, *illuftrees de Huictains Francois*, illuftrated by verfes of eight lines in French, by William Gueroult; who dedicated it to Catherine de Medicis, queen of France, A. D. 1564.

JOHN GUERRA.
Born, 1534. Died, 1612.

He was a man of fcience, born at Modena. His genius led him to the ftudy of mechanics; and he etched fome fingular machines of his own invention. He died 1612, aged 78.

LEWIS L. GUERRE.
Born, 1663. Died, 1721.

An engraver of no great note. He was, I believe, a native of France, and died A. D. 1721, aged 58. I am not acquainted with his works.

FRAN-

FRANCESCO DE LA GUERRIERE.
Flourished, 1650.

A French artist, whom Le Comte distinguished by the title of "painter to the king." According to this author, he drew and etched the *grotesque friezes*, painted by Raphael Urbin in the Vatican, which he dedicated to Edward Jabach. Basan writes this name GUERTIERE.

GUIDO. See RENI.

ASCANIUS DON GUIDO.
Flourished, 1567.

This name I found affixed to a print, engraved from the *last judgment* of Michael Angelo, rather smaller than that of Martin Rota; which it nearly equals in merit. It is executed entirely with the graver, in a very skilful manner. The date, 1567, proves it to have been done two years prior to Martin Rota's, whose style of engraving it much resembles. The name of the artist is written in this manner, *Ascanis. Don. Guido faciebat*.

RAFFAELLO GUIDI.
Flourished, 1598.

This artist was a native of Tuscany; and judging from the style of his engraving, I should suppose he had been educated in the school of Cornelius Cort, or Agostino Carracci. He worked entirely with the graver, which instrument he handled with much facility. He drew correctly, and with great taste; and the extremities of his figures are well expressed. Though he cannot be said to equal Carracci, yet his prints manifest the hand of the master, and prove him to have been a man of very superior talents. I shall only notice the following by him:

A *reposo*, where *Joseph is holding some cherries*, the child points to his mouth, a small upright plate, from Francisco Vanni.

The *entombing of Christ*, a middling sized upright plate, arched on the top, from Frederico Barroccio, dated 1598.

The *crucifixion of Christ*, a middling sized upright plate, from Christopher Swartz.

MICHAEL ANGELO GUIDI, son to the above artist, was also an engraver, and imitated the style of his father; but his works are by no means worthy of a particular recital.

V. GUIGOU.
Flourished, 1676.

This engraver was a native of France; but of no great note. We have by him some *bird's-eye views of palaces, and other edifices*, in France, executed in a very slight, stiff style. He also engraved a variety of portraits for books; which though sufficiently neat, are totally devoid of taste and effect.

SIMON GUILAIN.
Born, 1581. Died, 1658.

This artist was a native of France. He excelled in sculpture; and, for his amusement, etched a variety of plates, in a slight, but masterly style. He died at Paris, A. D. 1658, aged seventy-seven. The following are by him:

The *life of Saint Diego*, a set, consisting of twenty small plates, from the designs of Annibale Carracci.

The *cries of Bologna*, a set of eighty small upright plates, from the same. In this work he was assisted by Alessandro Algorgi.

GUILLEMART.
Flourished,

The name of an obscure engraver, probably a native of France, affixed to the portrait of *Setani, Abbé de S. Genevieve*.

HANS or JOHN GULDENMUNDT.
Flourished,

The name of a very old engraver on wood, a native, I believe, of Germany. It is affixed at full length, together with his cypher, composed of an H. and a B. joined together, in the manner expressed upon the plate at the end of the volume, to a middling sized upright print, representing two soldiers standing; the one holding an halbert, and the other a flag. Over the first is written 𝕳𝖊𝖕𝖙 𝕻𝖎𝖑𝖔𝖍𝖆𝖗𝖙𝖊𝖗, &c. and over the second, 𝕱𝖊𝖓𝖙𝖗𝖎𝖈𝖍; and the name, with the cypher, appears at the bottom. It is executed in a bold, spirited style, and the figures are very correctly represented in the dress of the time. The heads are exceedingly well expressed; and perhaps they were designed for portraits.

PETER VAN GUNST.
Flourished, 1713.

This artist was a native of Holland. He possessed infinitely more patience, than genius or good taste. His style of engraving, which was with the graver only, seems evidently formed upon the works of the Drevets. His first and second strokes are equally neat and powerful; which gives them a cold, silvery effect. The folds of his draperies, though not ill drawn, are marked too harshly, especially upon the outlines of the lighter parts of them. His flesh is often extremely neat, and finished with small dots; but the lights are too much covered, which makes them appear heavy and fatigued. His drawing is also exceedingly defective. His portraits are by far the best, as well as the largest part of his works; but they are, in great measure, liable to the same objection as his figures and historical subjects. We have by him, the *loves of the gods*, nine middling sized upright plates, from Titian. Smith engraved the same plates in mezzotinto.

A set

A set of ten portraits, of *Charles the First, his Queen, and the English nobility of both sexes,* whole length figures from Vandyck. This, I believe, is his greatest work. Houbracken, father to the famous engraver of that name, came over into England, A. D. 1713, to make the drawings for him to engrave from; for each of which he received 160 guilders. The persons, who employed him, were Mr. Cock, Mr. Comyns, and Mr. Swining, formerly a director of the theatre.

The portrait of *M. Chevreau,* a small upright plate, from John Petitot. This is the only print engraved after that master, who was a famous enamel painter.

JOHN GUTTENBERG.
Flourished, 1440.

To this artist many of the German authors have attributed the invention of the useful and noble art of printing. Others have argued as strenuously, for his being the first engraver on wood. His pretensions to both are however greatly disputed. The first is out of my province to meddle with; and the second, I believe, will be disproved hereafter, in the Essay on the Origin of Wood Cuts, which will precede the second volume of this work.

GENNERO GUTTIERER, or GUTTIEREZ.
Flourished, 1760.

The name of a modern engraver, whose works are, by no means, devoid of merit. I have seen by him a large upright plate, representing the *Virgin and Child in the clouds upon a globe,* from Carlo Marratti. It is executed in a neat style, resembling that of Giacomo Frey; but not nearly equal to the engravings of that great master. Several of the plates for the Museo Fiorentino are by this artist.

TABLE I.

The Explanation of the Initial Letters used by the Engravers contained in this Volume.

The first letter, when there are two initials, if the second be not an S. or an F. is usually the baptismal name; the second letter must therefore be referred to, and often the third, when there are three or more letters. The first letters are placed as nearly alphabetical under each general second letter, as the nature of the arrangement would admit of.

A.

A. SUPPOSED mark of Abraham de Bruin.
A. *with an helmet.* Anshelme. See the second table.
A. F. AVG. F. Agostino or Augustino fecit; that is, Agostino Carracci.
F. A. Frants Aspruck.
G. A. Giovanna Aguechia.
G. A. F. Girard Audran fecit.
G. A. P. F.
GAS. F. } Gasper ab Avibus Pativinus fecit.
I. A. John Ammon.
I. A. F. John Almeloven fecit.
I. A. V.
Zurich, 1566. } Jost or Jodicus Ammon Van Zurich.
N. V. A. Nicholas Van Aelst.
P. A. Supposed mark of Peter Aubry.
R.V.A.Gandensis
Gandensis. } Robert Van Audenaerd of Ghent.

B.

B. *upon a dye.* Bartolomeo Beham. See the second table.
B. F. J. Baeck fecit; also *Vittorio Baldini* fecit.
A. Bl.
A. Bloem. } Abraham Bloemart fecit.
A. Bloem. fec.
Ag. *Bononiæ.* Agostino Carracci.
B. B. Bartolomeo Biscanio.
B. B. F. Bartolomeo Beham fecit; also Bartholomew Breenberg fecit.
B. S. Fr. Bononiensis sculpsit.
C. B. inv. et sc.
1758. } Charles Bertram invenit et sulpsit; also Christopher Brechtel; also C. Buno; also Cornelius Bus.
C. Bl.
Corn. Blo. } Cornelius Bloemart.
C. V. B. Charles Van Bockel.
D. B. Supposed mark of Solomon Bernard.
F. B. Francis Barlow; also Frederic Bloemart.
F. B. B. F. Frater Bonaventura Bisi fecit.

A a a   F. B. V.

[362]

F. B. V._ }
F. B. V. F. } Frederico Baroccio Urbinas fecit.
F. V. B. Francis Van Bocholt.
H. B. H. Borling; alfo Hadrian or Adrian Brouwer.
J. B. { James Belli; alfo J. Benfheimer; alfo James Beutler; alfo James Binck;
  alfo John Burgkmair; alfo Julius Bonafona.
J. B. Joachim Brechtel.
I. B.
J. Bo. } Julio Bonafona fecit.
Julio B. F.
I. B. F.
J. B. fe. } John Baeck fecit.
I. B.
I. B. fe. John Bochlein.
I. B. I. Blag. fculp. John Blagrave fculpfit.
Io. An. } Johannis Antonius Brixienfis.
Io. Anton. Brixian.
I. C. B. James Binck.
L. B. fc. Laurentius Beger fculpfit.
M. B. Martin Bouche; alfo Michael Burghers.
N. B.
N. B. L. F. } Nicolaus Beatricius Lotheringus fecit. See the fecond table.
N. B. fe. Nicholas Bonnart fecit.
N. de B. Nicholas de Bruin.
N. V. D. Berg. Nicholas Vander Berge.
P. B. Peter Bodart, alfo Peter Brughel.
  { Pietro Sante Bartoli fecit; alfo Paulo Bianchi; alfo Paul Berck; alfo Paul
P. B. F. { Birckenhult; alfo John. Paul Blancus; alfo Peter Bodart; alfo Peter Vander
  { Borcht.
P. B. B. F. Peter Balthazer Bouttats fecit.
Petr. St. Bartf. fc. } Pietro Sante Bartoli Perugino fecit, or fculpfit.
Romæ.
P. V. D. Berge. Peter Vander Berge.
W. B. John William Baur; alfo W. Buitwech.
W. B. W. W. Buitwech.

C.

A. C. F. Annibale Carracci fecit. See the fecond table.
A C.
Ag. C. } Agoftino Carracci; he alfo ufed thefe marks, A. F. AVG. F. and A.
Agof. C. Bononiæ.
B. C. F. Bernard Capitelli, fecit.
B. C. Eques. Bartolomeo Coriolanus Knight.
C. C. F. Camillo Congio fecit.
Do. CAP. Domenico Campagnola.
D. C. F. Domenico or David Cuftodis fecit.
D. M. C. F. Domenico Maria Canuti fecit.
F. C. { Franchefco Carracci fecit; alfo Francois Clein, or Klein, who fometimes
  { ufed the initials F. K.
H. C. Hadrian or Adrian Collaert.
H. C. F. Hieronymus or Jerom Cock fecit; alfo Hans or John Collaert.
H. V. C. } Hans or John Van Culenback; the laft mark I. C. is alfo attributed to
I. C. Giacomo or Jacopo Caraglio.
I. T. C. F. B. Joachim Theodorus Coriolanus fecit Bafileæ.
L. C.
Lo. C. } Lodovico Carracci.
L. C.
L. C. fculp. } Lucas Ciamberlanus.
L. C.
L. V. C. } Luca Cranach. See the fecond table.
L. C. CIV. F. Lodovico Cardi Civoli fecit. See the fecond table.
M. C. Martin Cleve.

1 M. le

M. le C. de C. sculp. Monsieur le Comte de Caylus, sculpsit.
N. C.
N. C. f. } Nicholas Cochin fecit. See the second table.
N. C. F.   Nicholas Chaperon fecit.
P. C.
PA. CAL. } Paolo Cagliardi, called Paolo Veronese.
R. C. F.   Raphael Custos fecit.
S. C.
1615. } Stephen Carteron fecit.
S. C. F.
V. C.   Vincenzio Caccianemici.
W. C.   William Carter.

D.

A. V. D.   Anthony Vander Does.
C. D.   C. Decker. See the second table.
C. D. F.   Charles David fecit.
Cæf. Dom. inc. } Cæsar Dominicus incidit.
1614.
G. V. D.   Gulielmus Van Delphius, or William Van Delft.
L. D.   Louis Daven.
L. D. fec.   Louis David, fecit.
T. D.   Thomas Dudley.

E.

A. V. E.   Albert Van Everdingen.
C. E.   *George* Charles Eimmart.
J. E.   John Evelyn.
I. E. F.   J. Errar fecit.

F.

F. { Perhaps Finguerra. See the description of plate IV. in the sixth chapter of the Essay on the Art of Engraving at the beginning of this work. A single F. is also one of the marks of John Ferdinand.
A. F. Fec.   Antonio Faldoni fecit.
B. F. V. F.   Baptista Francus Venetus fecit.
D. F.   Dominico *Maria* Fontana.
F. F.   J. Ferdinand fecit.
F. V. F.   Frederic Van Falckenbourg, also Francis Van Ferg.
HO. F. F. { Horatius Farinatus fecit; to the etchings by this artist, the following initials are also usually added, Pa. Fo. V. I. that is, Paolo Farinato of Verona inventor, who was his father.
I. F.   John Fisher; also the supposed mark of one of the family of the Feyerabands.
I. F. V. S.   Jereminh Falck, Van or *of* Stockholm.
I. B. F.   Jacobus Baptista Fontana.
L. V. F.   Lucas Van Falckenbourg.
M. F.   The supposed mark of one of the family of the Feyerabands.
P. F.
P. V. F. } Paolo Farinato, or Paolo Veronefe fecit.
S. F.   Sigismond Feyeraband.
S. F. fc.   Simon Frisius sculpsit.
S. H. F.   The supposed mark of one of the family of the Feyerabands.
T. F.   Tobie Fendt.
V. F. { Vicenzio Francefchino; also the supposed mark of one of the family of the Feyerabands.

G.

G. R. B. F.
G. R. F. } Guidus Rheni Bononienfis faciebat.

A a a 2 .   G. M. F.

G. M. F.	George Ghisi of Mantua fecit. See the second table.
A. G.	{ Albert Glockenthon. See the second table. Also the suppofed mark of one of the family of the Garners.
B. G.	Bernard Gallo.
DIANA	
DIANA INCI-	} Diana Ghisi of Mantua.
DEBAT.	
G. de G. fec.	Gulielmus, or William de Geyn fecit.
H. G.	Hubert Goltzius; alfo Henry Goltzius. See the second table.
M. G.	M. Greifcher.
M. G. F.	Matthew Greuter fecit. See the second table.
Mel. Giri. Fec.	Melchior Giridana fecit.
Noel. G.	Noel Garner. See the second table.
S. G. 1547.	} Simon Guilian fecit.
S. G. F.	
V. G.	V. Gamperlin. Alfo the suppofed mark of one of the Garner family.

TABLE II.

The Explanation of the Monograms, Cyphers, &c. contained in the two Plates annexed.

PLATE VIII.

A.

No.
1. *H. Abbe.*
2. *Leonard Abents.*
3. *P. Adam* invenit et fecit.
4. *Philip Adler.* This mark is also attributed to Agnes Frey.
5. *Cherubino Alberti.* Two marks.
6. *Henry Aldegrever.* With or without a tablet.
7. *Aleffandro Algardi.*
8. *Albert Altdorfer.* Andrea Andreani ufed the fame mark, adding the words, " in Mantoua," and frequently a date.
9. *Joft* or *Jodicus Amman* or *Ammon.* Six marks.
10. *Andrea Andreani.* Three marks; the firft refembles that of Albert Altdorfer.
11. *Aufhelme* fecit.
12. *Silvius Antonianus.*
13. *John Walther Van Affen.*
14. *Robert Van Audenaerd.*
15. *Gafper ab Avibus*

B.

16. *Francis de Babylone.*
17. *Aleffandro Badiale.*
18. *Johannffen Baldung.* Two marks, both of which were ufed by feveral other mafters. See No. 36, 37, 40, 46, 56, 62.
19. *Nicolo Beatrici.* Three marks; the firft of which was alfo ufed by Natalis Boniface.
20. *Hans* or *John Sebald Beham.* With or without a tablet.
21. *Bartolomeo Beham.* Two marks.
22. *Dominico del Ba. biere.* This mark was alfo ufed by Domenica Maria Bonavera.
23. *John William Baur.* The fame mark was ufed by W. Buitwech.
24. *Matthias Beitler.*
25. *Stefano de la Bella.* Two marks.
26. *Claus* or *Nicholas Berchem* or *Berghem.* Three marks.
27. *John George Bergmuller.*
28. *Solomon Bernard,* called Le Petit or Little Bernard.
29. *James Binck.* This mark was alfo adopted by Hans or John Burgkmair.
30. *John de Bifchop* or *Epifcopius* fecit.
31. *Cornelius Blecker.*
32. *Abraham Bloemart.* With or without a date.
33. *Michael Blond.*

34 *George*

34 *George Bockman.*
35 *Abraham Bloteling.*
36 *Hans or John Bockſberger.* This mark was uſed by ſeveral other maſters. See 18, 37, 40, 46, 56, 62.
37 *Hubert Bochm.* See in the preceding number the different maſters by whom this mark was uſed.
38 *H. Boiling.* This mark was alſo uſed by Horazio Borgiani.
39 *Rene Boivin.* Theodore de Bry uſed the ſame mark.
40 *Hans or John Bol.*
41 *Boetius Adams a Bolſwert.* Two marks.
42 *Scheltius a Bolſwert.* Three marks.
43 *Domenico Maria Bonavara.* The ſame mark was uſed by Domenica del Barbiere and Bartolomeo Dolendo.
44 *Natalis Boniface* fecit. The ſame mark was alſo uſed by Nicolo Beatrici.
45 *Henry Vander Borcht.*
46 *Horazio Borgiani.* Two marks, both of which were uſed by other maſters. See No. 18, 36, 37, 38, 40, 56, 62.
47 *Jerom Boſche.* Three marks.
48 *Andrew Both.* The ſame mark was uſed by Andre Bretſchneider.
49 *Ambroſtus Brambini.*
50 *Peter Brebiette.*
51 *D. V. Bremden.*
52 *Hans or John Breſang.* Two marks, the firſt of which was uſed by Johannſſen Baldung.
53 *Andre Bretſchneider.* This mark was alſo uſed by Andrew Both.
54 *Criſpin Vanden Broeck.* Three marks.
55 *John Van Bronkhorſt.*
56 *Hans or John Broſamer.* This mark was uſed by ſeveral other maſters. See No. 18, 36, 37, 40, 46, 56.
57 *Abraham de Bruin.* Three marks, the firſt of which is alſo attributed to Silvius Antonianus.
58 *Nicholas de Bruin.* Two marks.
59 *Theodore de Brye.* Rene Bovin uſed the ſame mark.
60 *W. Buitweech.* John William Baur uſed the ſame mark.
61 *Michael Burghers.*
62 *Hans or John Burgkmair.* Two marks. Several other maſters uſed the ſame marks. See No. 18, 29, 36, 37, 40, 46, 56.
63 *Cornelius Bus.* Four marks.

PLATE IX.

C

64 *James Callot.* The ſame mark, with the date 1545, is attributed to Jerom Cock.
65 *Lodovico Cordi,* called *Civoli.* Two marks; the firſt of which was alſo uſed by Lucas Ciamberlanus.
66 *Carolus Rex Utriuſque Sicilae, Charles, King of the Two Sicilies.*
67 *Annibale Carracci.*
68 *Franceſco Carracci.* The ſame mark was uſed by Francis Cheaveau.
69 *Bernard Caſtelli.*
70 *Giovanni Benedetto Caſtiglioui.* Two marks.
    Francois Cheveau. See No. 68.
    Lucas Ciamberlano. See No. 65.
71 *Cleeman.*
72 *Franceſco de Clein.*
73 *Henry Van Cleve.*
74 *Martin Van Cleve.*
75 *Herman Coblent* fecit. *Hadrian* and *Hans or John Collaert,* both of them uſed this mark alſo.
76 *Nicholas Cochin.*
77 *Jerom Cock.* James Callot uſed the ſame mark, but without the date.

78 *Peter*

78 *Peter Cock or Cocck.*
79 *Thomas Cockson.*
80 *Etiene or Steven Colbenschlag.*
81 *Adrian or Hadrian Collaert.* Four marks. See also No. 75.
   Hans or John Collaert. See No. 75.
82 *Camillo Congio.*
83 *Cornelius Cort, Van Hoorn.* Two marks.
84 *Peter Cottart*
85 *Michael Coxis.*
86 *Luca Cranach.* Four Marks.
87 *Theodore Cruzer.* Two Marks.
88 *Matthias Cruger.*
89 *Dirick or Theodore Van Cuerenhert.* Two marks.
90 *Bernardino Curti.*
91 *Domenico Custos Augusta* fecit.

D.

92 *Peter Daret.*
93 *Jerom David.* Three marks.
94 *Louis David.*
95 *Hieronymus or Jerom Davidloo.* Two marks.
96 *C. Decker.* Two marks.
97 *Gulielmus Jacobus Delphins, or William James Delft.*
98 *Nicholas Manuel Deutsch.*
99 *Rodolphe Manuel Deutsch.*
100 *Wendel or Vander Dietterlin.*
101 *Bartholomew Dolendo.*
102 *Zachary Dolendo.*
103 *A. Drebber.*
104 *Albert Durer.* Five marks.
105 *John Duvet.* Two marks.

E.

106 Three marks attributed to *Engelbrecht.*

F.

107 *William Faithorne.* Two marks.
108 *Domenico Falvini.* Two marks.
109 Two marks attributed to artists of the family of the *Fryerabands.*
110 *Odardo Fialetti* fecit.
111 *Albert Flamen.*
112 *Francis Floris.*
113 *Antonio Fontuzzi.* This artist, a native of Italy, flourished towards the middle of the sixteenth century. He etched a considerable number of plates in a coarse style, not a little resembling that of Tempesta ; but the outlines of his figures are by no means correctly drawn. He worked chiefly from Primaticcio, and his prints are usually dated from 1540 to 1550. We have also some few etchings by him from his own designs.

⁎⁎ *This article was omitted by mistake in the body of the work, where it should have been inserted. It is referred to, however, in the Errata.*

114 *George Frenzel.* Francis Clein used this mark also, but without date or inscription beneath it.
   Agnes Frey. See No. 4, plate 8.
115 *Louis Frig.*
116 *Adam Fuchs.*
117 *Sebastian Furck.* Two marks.
118 *Peter Furnius.* Two marks.

G.

119 *Giovanni Batista Galestruzzi.*
120 *Philip Galle.* Two Marks.

[368]

121 *V. Gamperlin.*
122 *Noel Garner.*
123 *Antoine Garner.*
124 *Leonard Gaulter.*
125 *Sigismond Gelenius.*
126 *Jacinto Gemignano.*
127 *Abraham Genoels.*
128 *James de Gheyn.*
129 *John Baptista Ghisi,* of Mantua, also without the tablet.
130 *George Ghisi,* of Mantua, fecit. Two Marks.
131 *Adam Ghisi,* of Mantua, sculpsit.
132 *Hans or John Henry Glaser.*
133 *Albert Glockenthon.* Three marks.
134 *Van Goar.* Three marks.
135 *Henry Goltzius.* Hans or John Guldenmundt used the same cypher.
136 *John Andre Graf.*
    Conrad Grabl. See the first mark No. 142.
137 *Jaques Grandhomme* fecit.
138 *Jerom Greff.*
139 *M. Greischer.*
140 *G. Greuter.* Two Marks.
141 *John Frederic Greuter,* incid.
142 *Matthew Greuter.*
143 *Bartholomew Groen.*
144 *Bartholomew Groennig.*
145 *C. P. Gerard Groningus.*
146 *Hans or John Grunwald.*
147 *Matthew Grunwald* of Aschaffenbourg.
148 *James Guckeisen.*
    Hans or John Guldenmundt. See No. 135.
149 *Guido Rheni.*

END OF THE FIRST VOLUME.

www.ingramcontent.com/pod-product-compliance
Lightning Source LLC
Chambersburg PA
CBHW030546300426
44111CB00009B/873